Financial Planning & Wealth Management

An International Perspective

Louis Cheng
Leung Tak Yan
Wong Yiu Hing

Mc Graw Hill

Singapore • Boston • Burr Ridge, IL • Dubuque, IA • Madison, WI • New York
San Francisco • St. Louis • Bangkok • Kuala Lumpur • Lisbon • London • Madrid
Mexico City • Milan • Montreal • New Delhi • Seoul • Sydney • Taipei • Toronto

Financial Planning and Wealth Management
An International Perspective

McGraw Hill Education

The certification marks, CERTIFIED FINANCIAL PLANNER™, CFP® and **CFP**®
are owned by Certified Financial Planner Board of Standards, Inc. (CFP Board)
and are awarded to individuals who successfully complete CFP Board's initial and
ongoing certification requirements.

CFP^CM, CERTIFIED FINANCIAL PLANNER^CM and **CFP** are certification marks
owned outside the U.S. by Financial Planning Standards Board Ltd. (FPSB). The
Institute of Financial Planners of Hong Kong is the marks licensing authority for the
CFP marks in Hong Kong and Macau, through agreement with FPSB.

When ordering this title, use ISBN 978-007-124984-3 or MHID 007-124984-2

Printed in Singapore

In memory of my sister, Yuen-Ling Wong

Y. H. Wong

Contents in Brief

Contents

About the Authors

Louis Cheng is Associate Professor of Finance at the School of Accounting and Finance, and the track coordinator of the MBA (Financial Services) program at Hong Kong Polytechnic University. He is a member of the Examination Board and was an executive committee member of The Institute of Financial Planners of Hong Kong (IFPHK) from 2000 to 2005. He also serves as a member of the ISO/TC 222 Committee on global financial planning. He has been a CFP^{CM} certificant since 2001.

Dr. Cheng graduated with a DBA in Finance from Louisiana Tech University in 1989. Before joining Hong Kong Polytechnic University, Dr. Cheng was Associate Professor of Finance at Murray State University in Kentucky. He served as a visiting scholar at Hong Kong Baptist University in 1995–96 and at Southern Illinois University, Carbondale in the Spring of 1997. In the summer of 2003, he served as the HSBC Fellow of Asian Financial Markets at the University of Exeter, UK.

Dr. Cheng's main teaching interests are financial planning, corporate finance, investments, and risk management. He is the co-author of two editions of *Corporate Risk Management*, a co-editor of two editions of *Personal Financial Planning: Theory and Practice,* and the author of *Fundamentals of Financial Planning* (McGraw-Hill, 2006). He has had over 65 articles published in top finance research journals including the *Journal of Finance*. He is ranked among the top ten finance professors in the Asia Pacific in terms of research by articles in the *Pacific Basin Finance Journal* in 2001 and 2005.

Dr. Cheng served as a project consultant for financial companies including Hong Kong Exchange on ELI analysis, Charles Schwab (US) on risk profiling, and Tai Fook Securities on the Leveraged Foreign Exchange Trading Ordinance. He also serves as an internal valuation consultant for firms in their M&A and IPO process He is a frequent speaker on topics related to financial planning, wealth management, and risk management for companies and non-profit organizations including AIA, Prudential, MassMutual, Manulife, New York Life, Shanghai Commercial Bank, Bank of China (PRC), China Merchants Bank, Bank of Communications, Pudong Development Bank, ShenZhen Development Bank, Huaxia Bank, Guangdong Development Bank, Industrial Bank, Oracle, Chinese Banks' Association, Hong Kong Police Force, Asian Federation of Credit Unions, and IFPHK.

Leung Tak Yan is Assistant Professor at the Department of Accountancy, City University of Hong Kong. Dr. Leung obtained her Bachelor of Commerce (Honors) from the University of Melbourne, her Master of Philosophy from Baptist University of Hong Kong, and her Doctor of Philosophy from Hong Kong Polytechnic

University. She is a Certified Public Accountant and a member of the Australian Society of Certified Practising Accountants (ASCPA). Before joining the academic field, Dr. Leung worked in commercial firms, nonprofit-making organizations (Community Chest), and the public sector (Hong Kong SAR Government). Dr. Leung's main teaching interests are financial accounting, ethics in accountancy, auditing, and taxation.

Wong Yiu Hing (PhD, MBA, BSocSc) is Associate Professor of Marketing at the Hong Kong Polytechnic University. Prior to joining the university, he worked as regional manager and general manager for several multinationals in the Asia-Pacific region, including Continental (USA) Corp., Swire Pacific Group in Hong Kong, and Amcor Group (Australia) for more than 12 years. In 1989 his export department received a Certificate of Commendation in the Large Exporter category awarded by the Australian government.

Dr. Wong's journal article, "The Effectiveness of Environmental Claims for Services Advertising" (joint paper with Chan, R. and Leung, T.), was given a Highly Commended Award by Emerald LiteratiNetwork in 2007. Another article, "Insider Selling to China: *Guanxi*, Trust, and Adaptation," was given a Citation of Excellence (highest quality rating) by Anbar Intelligence in 1998.

Dr. Wong's research interests are customer relationship management, ubiquitous marketing, and financial planning and well-being. He is the co-author of *Guanxi: Relationship Marketing in a Chinese Context* published by Taylor & Francis. He has had over 70 articles published in journals and conference proceedings including *Industrial Marketing Management, International Business Review,* and *European Journal of Marketing.*

Dr. Wong served as a PhD external examiner at the University of New South Wales and Monash University and as an examiner for the Certified Professional Marketer examination at the Hong Kong Institute of Marketing. He also serves as a subject specialist in the Hong Kong Council for Academic and Vocational Accreditation and as adviser to the journal *Young Consumers* and the Family and Juvenile Service Association. He is a speaker and training consultant in areas such as relationship marketing, key account management, and sales management for organizations including Prudential Assurance, Hang Seng Bank, Degussa, Manulife, Chevaller, and Glorious Sun.

Preface

Financial planning and wealth management services are young professions in Asia. Financial planning began in the 1960s in the United States but evolved rapidly into a reputable industry in the next four decades. As for wealth management, it has been a proprietary service for the very rich, mostly in North America and Europe. In Southeast Asia, particularly in Hong Kong, the concept of personal financial planning services came much later. During the late 1990s, large financial institutions in Asia gradually recognized the fact that some of their clients had become more sophisticated, demanding more comprehensive personal financial services. At the same time, as substantial wealth accumulated in Asia, especially in Mainland China, wealth management became a viable business in the region.

When the idea of forming a local CFP granting organization was being explored by Don Bills and Roy Charlesley, the representatives of the Certified Financial Planner Board of Standards (CFP Board) who visited Hong Kong in 1999, senior executives of international financial institutions in Hong Kong quickly realized that this was the perfect time to support an internationally recognized financial planning qualification in Hong Kong so that their staff can receive the necessary professional training and the proper international recognition for engaging in comprehensive financial services. The Asian development of CFP certification continues as Noel Maye took office as the CEO of the Financial Planning Standards Board (FPSB) in January 2003. Since then, Mainland China and Indonesia has joined the CFP family and recently Thailand expressed strong interest in gaining the FPSB full member status. We believe that financial planning and wealth management will continue to grow strongly in the Asian region.

Traditionally, comprehensive financial planning services were proprietary services provided to high net-worth clients. Nowadays, traditional commercial banks and international private banks in Hong Kong are paying more attention to the needs of the mass affluent market. Consequently, a more value-added financial planning and wealth management service is needed for a wider clientele and to support a variety of new financial products launched by the financial institutions.

The road ahead for the financial planning profession is still tough. The major challenge is the fact that Asian clients are not ready to pay a fee for a comprehensive financial plan. Thus, most financial services companies depend on income generated from selling financial products to support their employees and contracted professionals to provide advisory services for clients. In other words, the ability to provide sufficient income to support the financial advisory services for clients largely depends on the commission and rebate from their product suppliers. Such a phenomenon of commission-driven services makes it difficult for some independent financial planning firms to grow in Asia. For the same reason, large financial institutions will also have a tendency to emphasize product selling more when providing recommendations to financial planning clients. This challenge of insufficient fee-based services is expected to last for a long while.

Eventually, as more qualified financial planning professionals such as CFP certificants practice in Asia, the consumers will eventually recognize that paying a fee for independent financial advice is acceptable. When more fee-based practitioners provide their services in the region, the coexistence of fee-based and commission-based financial advisory services will push the quality of service in the Asia region to a higher level. Consumers will then have more choices in selecting the type of advice to fulfill their needs.

There are two main purposes of this book. First, we try to provide up-to-date and detailed documentation on what financial planning and wealth management mean and how they are being implemented in theory and practice. Second, we try to provide insights on the future development of these professions and some new theoretical concepts that are not popular now but are critical to enhance the financial planning and wealth management services for clients in the long run. We are hopeful that this book will contribute to the knowledge base for students and practitioners in personal financial services during this period of evolution. As far as we know, this book is the first attempt in Asia combining financial planning and wealth management in a textbook format. We do believe that this book is instrumental for the continuous growth of the financial planning and wealth management professions in the Asian region.

Louis T. W. Cheng, Yan Tak Leung, and Y. H. Wong

Acknowledgments

Writing a textbook is a much bigger task than we could have imagined. Tremendous help has been given to us by colleagues, professional friends, and assistants. Before we thank these individuals, we want to thank the institutions that have helped us in providing critical information in writing this book.

We are grateful to Ameriprise Financial Services, Inc., for their generosity, openness, and hospitality during Louis Cheng's four-day visit at the headquarters and field offices in Minneapolis in the summer of 2004. Bill Moran, Vice President of Financial Planning Operations, and Jeff Lauber, Vice President of International Financial Advice, have been instrumental and helpful in arranging for the visit to collect the necessary information from Ameriprise.

We also want to thank Tim Kochis and Kacy Gott of Kochis Fitz Tracy Fitzhugh & Gott Incorporated, a leading wealth management firm in California, for the interviews and providing compensation data and market segmentation strategies in financial planning. We would like to thank David and Deena Diesslin for the valuable opportunity to visit the firm and interview the staff at the Fort Worth, USA office for two full days in June 2006. The visit allowed us to produce an interview script on successful wealth management practice reported in the concluding chapter.

We are grateful to Harold Evenksy, principal of Evensky, Brown, Katz and Levitt in Coral Gables for his sharing with us on managing client's expectations during his visit to Hong Kong. Harold's comments have helped us to understand the importance of this concept in the financial planning process.

We want to thank Kyra Morris, Morris Financial Concepts, and Elissa Buie, Financial Planning Group, for allowing us to develop a planner-client matching model (based on the material of their financial planning workshop in Hong Kong in 2003) in Chapter 7. We are indebted to Christina Hui, who allowed us to share her story on the change of clientele using Rolls-Royce and BMW as an example. We also want to express our sincere gratitude to Guy Cumbie (FPA Chair 2002), Elaine Bedel (CFP Board Chair, 2002) Robert Barry (FPA President 2002), and Elizabeth W. Jetton, (FPA Chair, 2005, and Principal of Financial Vision Advisors) in providing their valuable views on the six-step financial planning process. Their views are either incorporated in the text or reported as an interview in the "Financial Planning in Practice" section in various chapters. We are also indebted to Dr. Wai Lee, Managing Director at Lehman's New York office for his interview on asset allocation strategies.

A lot of information concerning the CFP® certification comes from the Certified Financial Planner Board of Standards, Inc. (CFP Board) and the Financial Planning Standard Board (FPSB) websites. In addition, information on financial planning professionals is obtained from the Financial Planning Association (FPA).

We want to thank these organizations in allowing us to use their materials. We also want to thank Laura Garrison, International Relations Director of FPA, in providing statistical data from the FPA survey. Thanks are also due to Jin Tian, the CEO of Morningstar Asia, for providing us the mutual funds rating materials in Chapter 14. In Chapter 8 where computer input screens for data collections are shown, we are indebted to Joseph K. S. Chan for his generosity in providing the materials.

We want to thank Monica Law and Anthony So in providing some written material for Chapter 3; and the materials for communication techniques and relationship positioning in Chapter 7. We are grateful to Castor Wai Sun Pang for providing the materials and graphs related to technical analysis in Chapter 12. We also want to thank Jackie Tam for writing an in-depth discussion on managing client expectations in financial planning in Chapter 15. There are also many other individuals who helped in various capacities: they include To Chan, Peri Leung, and Phoebe Ng.

PART I

Fundamental Concepts of Financial Planning and Wealth Management

chapter 1

An Overview of the Financial Planning and Wealth Management Professions

Learning Objectives

After studying this chapter you should be able to:

1 Define personal financial planning, wealth management, and total life planning.
2 Understand the services and compensation of a financial planner and wealth manager.
3 Understand the required knowledge and skills of a financial planner and a wealth manager.
4 Know the history and evolution of financial planning in different countries.
5 Grasp the future development of financial planning.
6 Describe the value of and requirements for the CFP® qualification.
7 Recognize the consumer demand for financial planning in Hong Kong and China.

Personal financial planning services are only a recent phenomenon in Southeast Asia. In the United States, the term *financial planning* is normally regarded as a personal financial service including the delivery of a comprehensive financial plan and the implementation of related services and products necessary to achieve the financial goals agreed in the plan. More recently, owing to the demand for a "one-stop service," wealth management services offered by private banks and high-end wealth management firms have also embraced the concept of comprehensive financial planning. Owing to the relatively young age of the financial planning discipline and the fact that different countries are at different stages of development of the financial planning profession, professionals and even academics in this area are still trying to reach a consensus on the terminologies and boundaries of financial planning through dialog and exploration in practice.

1.1   What is Personal Financial Planning?

personal financial planning A comprehensive process which evaluates all aspects of a client's financial needs in an integrated six-step approach in order to achieve the client's financial goals.

Definition

While personal financial planning will be discussed in detail in Chapter 2, here we will give a brief definition.

Personal financial planning is a comprehensive process which evaluates all aspects of a client's financial needs including consumption, taxation, insurance, investment, retirement, and estate planning in an integrated six-step approach in order to achieve the client's financial goals. The six steps include (1) establishing client-planner relationships; (2) gathering client data and determining goals; (3)

analyzing the client's financial status; (4) developing and presenting the financial plan; (5) implementing the plan; and (6) monitoring the financial plan.

In practice, carrying out financial planning services in a comprehensive manner can be subject to interpretation and practical limitations. In fact, there are two different and distinct features in understanding the term *comprehensive financial planning* or *one-stop-shop financial planning*. The first dimension of comprehensiveness deals with the scope, and the second dimension deals with the depth, of the services. For the first dimension, we refer to the ability of providing the six-step advisory services in all functional areas of financial planning such as investment planning, insurance planning, retirement planning, and so forth. The second dimension refers to the ability of providing all services and products needed by the clients from client engagement to product implementation. The first feature requires the planners and their firms to provide expertise in advisory services in all areas using a well-defined process. However, the second feature requires that the financial planning firms actually manufacture or act as an intermediary to the necessary financial products related to insurance, savings, investment, and retirement planning so that clients can implement all the recommended planning strategies with the required products. Currently, not many firms can provide such a comprehensive menu of services and products. Ameriprise Financial[1] is a good example of a one-stop-shop financial planning firm in meeting the definition of comprehensiveness in both dimensions.

Personal financial planning mainly involves achieving the overall financial objectives of individuals. **Wealth management** is a closely related concept to personal financial planning and is defined as *the practice of comprehensive financial planning with an emphasis on conducting and implementing investment management for clients*. However, recently, there has also been an increasing emphasis on estate planning implementation for wealth management clients. So the term *wealth management* is used when the financial planning service involves large investment portfolios and estate planning, usually for high net-worth (HNW) clients. Owing to the similarity of financial planning and wealth management, professionals engaging in these businesses normally use these two terms interchangeably.

There is no clear differentiation between the services of wealth management and financial planning provided by the industry. To differentiate between financial planning and wealth management, wealth management is often used to label the financial planning services for HNW clients. Financial planning professionals and firms choose the term as they see fit for their market. In fact, two different firms providing similar services may each use a different term. In theory, wealth management implies an emphasis on investment management. However, owing to the evolution of financial planning services, more and more financial planning firms focusing on relatively wealthier clients have also developed a strong expertise in investment management and estate planning, making the differentiation between the two services less obvious.

wealth management
The practice of comprehensive financial planning with an emphasis on investment management, usually involving large investment portfolios and estate planning.

---

[1] Ameriprise Financial Services, Inc. was formerly known as American Express Financial Advisors, Inc. (AEFA), until it became a spin-off from American Express in October 2005.

One may argue that commercial banks and private banks have a stronger presence in wealth management early on while independent financial advisors (IFAs), in general, are credited for their contribution in developing the financial planning industry. However, while such a historical development may describe the picture in the United States, the financial planning and wealth management industries have taken different paths of development in Europe and Asia.

For instance, owing to the rapid economic growth in Asia, personal wealth has accumulated at an alarming speed. Consequently, personal financial services such as financial planning and wealth management have become popular. However, as credible IFAs are scarce and large financial institutions dominate all areas of financial services in Asia, the development of wealth management and financial planning is driven by large international corporations. Personal financial services contribute about 35% of profits of US banks in Asia, with an annual growth rate of 12–15% during the early 2000s.

These days, owing to the popularity of adopting a healthy lifestyle among more sophisticated consumers, top financial planners and wealth managers are going beyond the financial aspects and paying attention to their clients' physical and psychological needs. This development has given rise to the interdisciplinary concept of total life planning (TLP).

total life planning
Financial planning that aims to achieve an optimal balance in the physical, psychological, and financial well-being of clients.

Total life planning (TLP) aims to achieve an optimal balance in physical, psychological, and financial well-being in life when conducting financial planning for clients.

Knowing that most sophisticated clients demanding comprehensive financial planning want to achieve a balance between their physical and psychological health while pursuing financial wealth, successful financial planners should equip themselves with a basic understanding of how to accommodate their clients' desires to pursue a balanced lifestyle. Of course, not all clients want their planners to know details about their physical and psychological conditions, let alone give them advice on a balanced lifestyle. We are not suggesting that a planner should insist on accessing private information in this area in order to conduct financial planning. However, financial planners should possess some training and ability in evaluating their clients' physical and psychological wellness so that these important factors can be considered during the financial planning process.

Services Provided by a Financial Planner

In order to conduct successful wealth management, an individual has to learn all the financial planning concepts. Consequently, for convenience and simplicity, we will use the term *financial planner* to represent both the financial planner and the wealth manager throughout this book. Having said that, we do not imply that a wealth manager has superior skills as compared with a financial planner. After all, in many professions, training and education begin with general knowledge. Afterwards, individuals may choose to stay as a generalist or receive additional training in a specific field and operate as a specialist. For example, all medical schools start their education programs with a broad curriculum covering all areas of medicine. Any student who passes this program qualifies as a general practitioner. If the medical professional decides to go for a special field such as cardiology or surgery, then additional training and internship must be obtained.

It is the same in the field of financial planning. However, because financial planning is a relatively young profession compared with the medical profession, not all specialized fields in financial planning receive a different title formally. In financial planning, students must learn all areas of financial planning including insurance, investment, tax, retirement, employee benefits, estate planning, and comprehensive financial planning process. Comparatively, a financial planner is a generalist to begin with. However, because many planners cannot survive financially by providing fee-based advisory services only, they need to generate additional income through wealth management and/or commission from selling products. Thus, it is very common for financial planners to develop a specialty with the proper license to enable them to engage in selling products related to insurance, retirement, investment, estate planning, and tax planning. However, a tax specialist or an investment advisor in personal financial planning may not necessarily call himself a specialist only. In fact, it is very common for such a professional to call himself a financial planner specializing in taxation or investment. Such a dual-track or multi-track practice is essential and natural for the personal financial planning industry.

Services Provided by a Wealth Manager

Unlike financial planners, who may choose to specialize in any of the areas of financial planning including insurance, investment, tax, retirement, employee benefits, and estate planning, while providing comprehensive financial planning services, wealth managers have to focus on investment management (and estate planning). While most financial planners cannot survive financially by providing fee-based advisory services only, wealth managers are normally employed by large financial institutions or high-end boutique wealth management firms. Due to the large size of the assets under management (AUM), it is possible that the management fee alone is sufficient to support a team of wealth management professionals whose compensation is in the form of a fixed salary and a bonus based on AUM. In the US, the titles of financial planners and wealth managers are used interchangeably.

However, the services provided by wealth managers are different from those provided by financial planners. What then are the services that wealth managers provide for their individual clients? There are both old and new perspectives. The traditional view of wealth management services includes financial asset management and portfolio management with a particular emphasis on investment management rather than other financial needs. A rather new perspective on wealth management services sees wealth managers providing additional services on consumption planning, tax planning, insurance and estate planning as well as offering goal-oriented investment advice to clients to satisfy both their intermediate and long-term needs.

A Survey of Financial Planning Specialties in the United States

Table 1.1 Panel A exhibits the statistics as at 2003 of the members of the US Financial Planning Association specializing in the different areas of financial planning service. From 2001 to 2003 there was no great change in the percentage of members in each specialty area. Retirement planning, investment/asset management, and comprehensive financial planning were still the three most popular specialty areas. In Panel B, according to the survey statistics on the services provided by CERTIFIED FINANCIAL PLANNER™ (**CFP**®) certificants[2] of the Certified Financial Planner Board of Standards, Inc. (CFP Board) (1999), investment planning and advice was the most frequent specialty (90%), with pension/retirement planning ranking second (87%), and comprehensive planning and estate planning ranking third (73%). Although the ranking for these four specialty areas are different in the two surveys, the results of these two surveys of different periods indicate that retirement, investment, comprehensive planning, and estate planning are the four most popular areas of specialization in the financial planning services.

CFP® mark In financial planning, the CFP® mark represents the highest professional qualification that a financial planner can achieve.

Table 1.1 Statistics of financial planning practitioner specialties

Panel A: Types of services provided by financial planners in the United States, 2001–2003

Service area	2001		2002		2003	
	Number	% of total	Number	% of total	Number	% of total
Comprehensive financial planning	16,886	10.45%	17,646	10.43%	14,300	10.40%
Investment/asset management	16,961	10.49%	17,698	10.46%	14,338	10.43%
Tax preparation	5,218	3.23%	5,295	3.13%	4,258	3.10%
Insurance	14,735	9.12%	15,246	9.01%	12,497	9.09%
Charity giving	10,420	6.45%	10,783	6.38%	8,798	6.40%
Fund education	14,044	8.69%	15,001	8.87%	12,239	8.90%
Estate planning	16,746	10.36%	17,272	10.21%	13,958	10.15%
Retirement planning	18,672	11.55%	19,371	11.45%	15,679	11.41%
Banking/trust management	3,140	1.94%	3,496	2.07%	2,807	2.04%
Cash management/budgeting	8,888	5.50%	9,571	5.66%	7,860	5.72%
Stock/bond brokerage	9,814	6.07%	10,267	6.07%	8,397	6.11%
Employee benefits	11,876	7.35%	12,411	7.34%	10,104	7.35%
Closely held business	11,716	7.25%	12,119	7.17%	9,901	7.20%
Other	2,530	1.57%	2,946	1.74%	2,320	1.69%

---

[2] The marks CERTIFIED FINANCIAL PLANNER™, CFP®, and **CFP**® certification marks (collectively the marks) are owned by Certified Financial Planner Board of Standards, Inc. and are awarded to individuals who successfully complete CFP Board's initial and ongoing certification requirements.

Table 1.1 (continued)

Panel B: Types of services provided by CFP® certificants (1999)

Service Area	1999
Investment planning/advice	90%
Pension/retirement planning	87%
Comprehensive planning	73%
Estate planning	73%
Portfolio management	67%
Income tax planning	60%
Insurance planning	59%
Education planning	55%
Elder/Long-term care planning	46%
Closely held business planning	37%
Financial planning employee education	31%
Income tax preparation	25%
Divorce planning	19%

Source: First Annual CFP® Practitioner Survey 1999, Certified Financial Planner Board of Standards, Inc. All rights reserved. Used with permission.

Obviously, countries like the United States and Australia have a longer history in financial planning. Financial planning appears to be a young concept in Hong Kong, Mainland China, and India. There are two major characteristics we can observe in the financial planning industry of a country in order to identify the level of sophistication and the maturity of its financial planning profession.

First, in a young and less mature financial planning market, clients are generally older. The required services for an older clientele normally focus on investment management, retirement planning, and estate planning. The percentage of younger clients is much higher in a younger market. The services needed for such a market include consumption planning, insurance protection, and short- and medium-term investment planning.

Second, in a more mature financial planning market, consumers are generally better educated in terms of financial planning. Consequently, they are more receptive to paying a fee for getting comprehensive financial advisory services. This willingness of consumers to pay for financial planning advisory services allows independent financial planning firms and fee-based financial planners to exist and to compete against product manufacturers and commission-based financial services professionals. The coexistence of fee-based and commission-based financial planners is a critical element in cultivating comprehensive financial planning services. In a less mature market, commission-based financial planners would dominate the industry.

How Is a Financial Planner Compensated?

Earlier we learnt that there are two distinct features in comprehensive financial planning. The first dimension of comprehensiveness deals with the ability of providing the six-step advisory services in all functional areas of financial planning. The second dimension refers to the ability to provide all services and products needed by the clients from client engagement to product implementation. How financial planners receive their remuneration depends mainly on which type of services they provide. In the old days, when consumers were not willing to pay for advisory services, financial planners had to depend on selling products on commission to make a living while providing financial planning and advisory services free to secure clients. In the past 20 years, fee-based financial planning advisory services have gradually become acceptable among consumers in the United States. However, in Europe, fee-based financial planning is less common. In Asia, fee-based planning is almost nonexistent.

There are some good reasons why fee-based and commission-based income should coexist in the financial planning industry. However, for any economy that is not very mature in personal financial planning services, fee-based services in general are less popular, due to the resistance of the consumers. It will take decades for a society to understand that paying a fee for financial planning advisory services is acceptable. In the meantime, for most less developed economies, a commission-based or transaction-based income will constitute most of the financial planner's compensation for a long while.

Table 1.2 shows the statistics of financial planners' compensation in the United States. The statistics show that most of the financial planners in the United States (approximately 55%) are compensated via a combination of fees and commissions. If we compare the popularity of fee-based and commission-based planning, it appears that fee-based planning (approximately 25%) is a more common form of compensation than commission-based planning (approximately 15%). Top financial planners in the United States claim that fees and commissions from asset management generate the most revenue.

The actual amount of fees for financial planning advisory services varies a great deal. For a firm or planner targeting the middle-income or mass-affluent group (an acceptable definition will be clients with a minimum investable asset

Table 1.2 Comparison of fee-based and commission-based income

	2001		2002		2003	
	Number	**%**	**Number**	**%**	**Number**	**%**
Fee only	5,058	25.32%	5,342	25.77%	4,434	25.44%
Fee and commission	10,833	54.22%	11,396	54.98%	9,658	55.42%
Commission only	3,212	16.08%	3,021	14.57%	2,469	14.17%
Other	875	4.38%	970	4.68%	866	4.97%
Total	19,978		20,729		17,427	

Source: Financial Planning Association. All rights reserved. Used with permission.

mass-affluent client
Client belonging to
the middle-income
group with a minimum
investable asset size of
US$80,000–120,000
for the North American
markets.

**high net-worth
clients** Client with
investable assets
exceeding US$1 million.

size of US$80,000–120,000 for the North American markets), the hourly fee to conduct financial planning can be as little as US$100 per hour. In general, most firms will charge a flat fee to conduct a plan, depending on the complexity of the situation of the clients. For instance, it is possible that a middle-income client can receive a simple, fairly comprehensive financial plan for US$800–1,000. A **mass-affluent client** may have to pay a few thousand dollars for a more complicated, more comprehensive plan. Firms dealing with high-income clients or **high net-worth clients** (e.g., investable assets exceeding US$1 million) and really high-end firms focusing on wealthy clients (e.g., a minimum asset size of US$2–3 million) can charge a fee of around US$10,000 or more.

On top of a financial planning fee, which is normally higher for the first time and somewhat lower for subsequent years, a financial planner can also charge transaction fees and management fees for implementing investment advice. For firms that emphasize wealth management, investment management fees can constitute a substantial portion of their total income.

In terms of annual compensation, including both salary and commission components, a brand new financial planner employee (e.g., a junior planner) with no substantial working experience may expect a package of around US$30,000–50,000. With 5–10 years of successful experience in financial planning (e.g., as a planning associate or a regular planner), the annual compensation can easily jump to around US$80,000–100,000. The annual income of financial planners who own their own businesses can easily exceed US$150,000. Many successful financial planners have switched to an emphasis on lifestyle activities instead of money-making. They may spend a substantial amount of their time on professional activities, social services, and other lifestyle activities. Even so, their annual income can still be maintained at a level of US$200,000–400,000. For most of these senior planners providing comprehensive financial planning and wealth management services, a CFP® designation is extremely common, indicating that the CFP® qualification is a valuable asset for a person who wants to become a successful financial planner.

There are some good reasons why fee-based planning is better, from the client's perspective: since financial planners can recommend any product and any service without worrying about product quotas given by their own firms and how much commission they will receive from a particular client, they can conduct more independent research in product selection and recommend the best available products to clients regardless of who the manufacturers are.

From the perspective of the financial planners and financial planning firms, a fee-based income provides the benefit of income diversification, which can be very important when the securities markets are in a down cycle. Portfolio management fees and transaction fees are highly correlated with securities market swings. If a financial planning firm receives most of its revenue through transaction and management fees, when the equity market is in a slump for a long time, the revenue can drop so significantly that the financial health of the company can be under serious threat. However, the business generated from fee-based advisory services tends to be more stable and therefore provides a strong cushion for firms when transaction-based income is low.

How Is a Wealth Manager Compensated?[3]

The remuneration of a wealth manager depends mainly on the types of firms that engage him. The actual amount of fees for wealth management advisory services varies a great deal. A wealth management firm that provides a simple financial plan for middle-income clients can charge US$ 800–1,000. For a complicated situation for mass-affluent clients, a plan can cost a few thousand dollars.

For affluent clients, a top financial planner/wealth manager may charge US$10,000–20,000 per plan, plus an annual maintenance fee for the plan up to a few thousand dollars. On top of that, the financial planner or the wealth manager can also charge a transaction fee and a management fee for implementing investment advice and managing the portfolio. In general, the annual management fee for an investment portfolio is around 1% of AUM, with a decreasing fee structure when the asset size under management increases.

Most wealth managers start their career as junior financial planners or para-planners. Their annual compensation includes both salary and commission components. A brand new financial planner employee (e.g., a junior planner) with no substantial working experience may expect a package of US$30,000–50,000. For a financial planner with five to ten years of successful experience in financial planning, the annual compensation can easily jump to US$80,000–100,000. The annual income of a senior financial planner with a successful business is US$200,000–400,000. For a wealth manager at prestigious private banks, the remuneration is extremely high. Detailed survey data, however, is not available to the public. Nevertheless, some surveys on customer relationship managers do exist. Napier Scott Executive Search Limited (London) conducted an annual survey, a "private banking salary survey", which covered hundreds of private bankers from 24 banks. Based on the April 2004 survey shown in Table 1.3, a junior customer relationship manager (CRM) working in a second-tier private bank has an average annual salary of US$76,000 in the US and US$92,500 in the UK. As for senior CRMs employed by second-tier banks, their average annual salaries in the US and UK are US$107,000 and US$138,800, respectively. Of course, at the first-tier private banks, the salaries are even higher. The annual salaries of junior CRMs at first-tier banks can reach US$92,500 in the US and

Table 1.3 Private banking salary survey 2004 by Napier Scott Executive Search Limited (London)

(The exchange rate is based on quotes in April 2004)

	First-tier private bank		Second-tier private bank	
	Junior CRM	**Senior CRM**	**Junior CRM**	**Senior CRM**
United States	US$92,500	US$148,000	US$76,000	US$107,000
United Kingdom	US$129,500	US$175,000	US$92,500	US$138,800

[3] Our source of data about remuneration and compensation is from an article titled "Your career in financial planning" by the Financial Planning Association (US) and other independent financial advisors.

US$129,500 in the UK. If you are a senior CRM at a first-tier bank, your annual salary can be as high as US$148,000 in the US and US$175,000 in the UK.

In addition, managers at US first-tier private banks can receive bonuses of up to 35% of the revenue generated by the assets they brought in. UK managers can enjoy bonuses of up to 2–3% of the value of financial assets they brought in.

It is believed that the annual remuneration of a top wealth manager can exceed US$400,000.

Knowledge and Skills of a Financial Planner and a Wealth Manager

All-Round Knowledge

all-round knowledge
Knowledge in all aspects of the client's needs: financial, psychological, and physical well-being; various financial analyses; and macroeconomic and microeconomic conditions.

As financial planners need to devise comprehensive and integrated financial planning services for their clients, they need to have **all-round knowledge** of the financial, psychological, and physical well-being of clients, of various financial analyses (e.g., cash flow analysis, financial statement analysis, and actuarial analysis), and of macroeconomic and microeconomic conditions. If financial planners do not have comprehensive knowledge in these different areas, they will not be able to cope with the high diversity of the client base, the great variety of the financial objectives of the clients, and the continuous change in economic conditions.

To maintain a superior position to others, financial planners should have an ongoing commitment to continuously accumulate, supplement, and update their knowledge, experience, and skills. In view of such a need, the financial planning professional organizations impose an ongoing certification requirement on CFP® certificants to participate in a continuous professional development program. In addition, regular seminars and workshops are conducted for their members from time to time to serve this purpose of maintaining and upgrading the competent performance of financial planners.

Excellent Communication Skills

Financial planning is a profession which operates through personal selling. Therefore, besides possessing adequate knowledge of financial planning, financial planners must also have excellent communication and interpersonal skills. Basic communication skills are required to inform the consumer public about financial planning services. However, basic communication skills are not sufficient to convince the consumer public to rely on financial planners to provide financial planning services for them: Financial planners need better communication skills to be able to provide multipurpose financial services.

Once the client-planner relationship is developed, financial planners need to work hard to comprehend the financial status, needs, and goals of their clients and to explain clearly how they can help achieve the financial objectives with their recommendations. In addition, constant and regular contact between financial planners and their clients is essential to demonstrate the willingness of financial planners to follow up on their services and to cultivate long-term relationships.

Communication and interpersonal skills can be enhanced by learning from experience and through peer interaction.

Ethical Practice

Public acceptance and trust are essential for all professions, including the financial planning profession. How then does the financial planner build up public acceptance and trust? The only way is to provide the best services in the best interests of the consumer public. The next question is, how does the financial planner measure the quality of his or her services? Because a financial planner of good standing is able to attract clients and hence business, service quality can be measured by the number of products bought and the amount of capital entrusted. Therefore, a good reputation is the most valuable intangible asset of a financial planner. How does the financial planner develop and maintain a good relationship with clients? One way is by conforming to an ethical financial planning practice.

In conclusion, the key to successful financial planning is a combination of three major ingredients. They are (1) strong interpersonal skills; (2) strong financial planning knowledge; and (3) professional and ethical behavior. Combining these three ingredients, we will be able to produce a strong reputation for the financial planning practice, leading to a trusting relationship with clients and finally a successful financial planning business. Figure 1.1 illustrates the three major ingredients of successful financial planning. In fact, the **four "E" requirements** of the CFP® mark aims at preparing financial planners to obtain these three ingredients through education, examination, experience, and ethics. As the CFP® mark is a widely recognized international qualification, obtaining this mark will certainly enhance the consumer confidence in the planners and the profession as well.

four "E" requirements The requirements for CFP® certification: education, examination, experience, and ethics.

Finally, in order to be successful in the wealth management profession, the CFA® qualification should also be considered. Figure 1.2 shows the successful model for a wealth manager. Depending on the career stage of the wealth manager, there exists a logical path to achieve these qualifications. If the individual is already a financial planner but wants to focus on wealth management services for high net-worth clients, then he should study for the CFP® qualification first before considering the CFA® mark. However, if the individual is in the investment industry and is thinking of switching to the private banking business, then he should consider obtaining the CFA® designation before he goes after the CFP® mark. Figure 1.3 describes some facts about the two professional qualifications.

Positioning Financial Planning in the General Financial Services Industry

Common Misconceptions and the Steps Forward

While many people think that financial planning is very similar to investment planning or insurance planning, this perception is only partially correct. While

Figure 1.1 Ingredients of successful financial planning

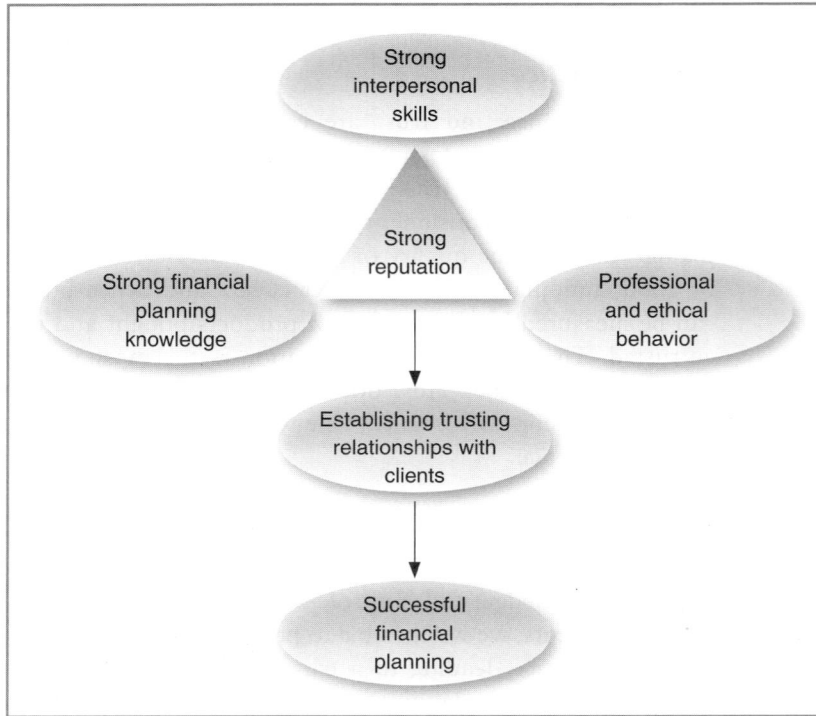

Figure 1.2 The Value of the CFP® and CFA® qualifications

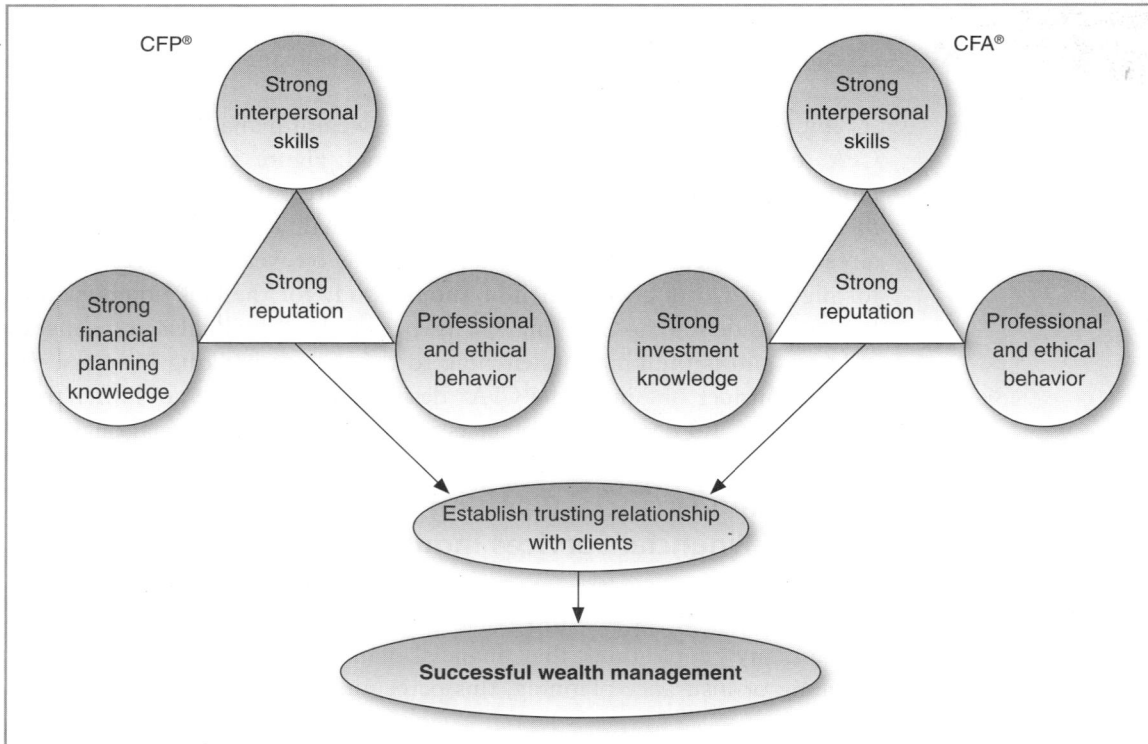

Figure 1.3 An overview of the CFP® and CFA® qualifications

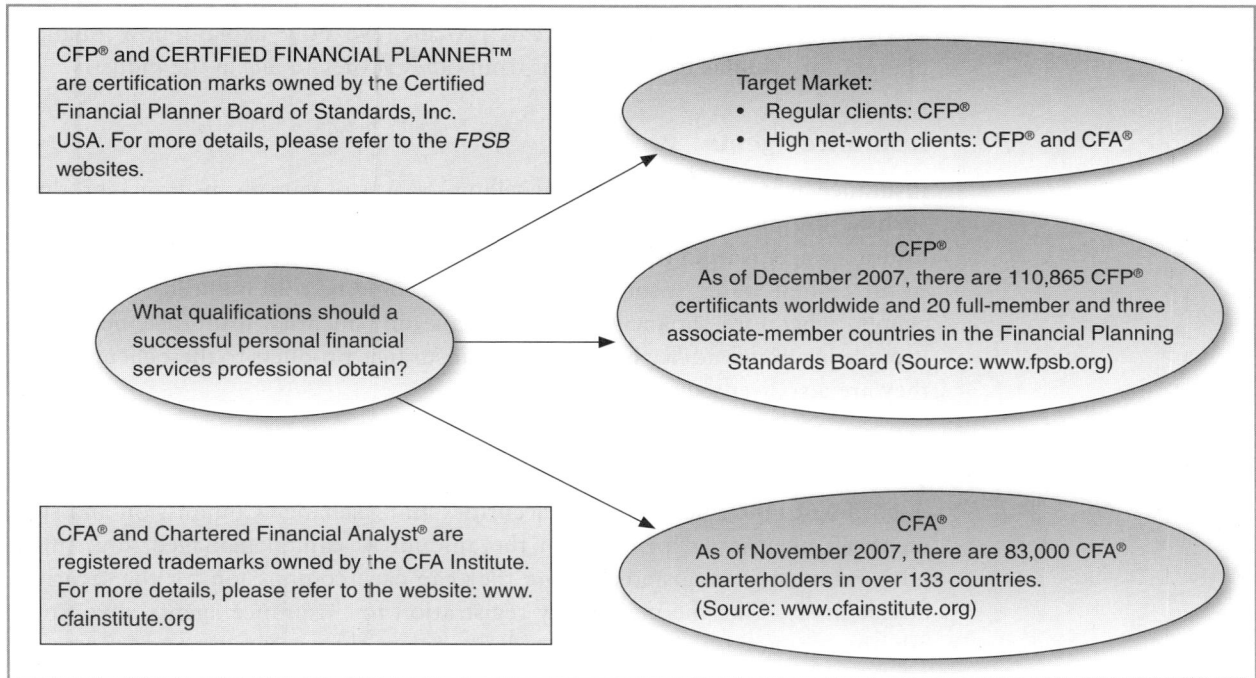

CFP® and CERTIFIED FINANCIAL PLANNER™ are certification marks owned by the Certified Financial Planner Board of Standards, Inc. USA. For more details, please refer to the *FPSB* websites.

What qualifications should a successful personal financial services professional obtain?

Target Market:
- Regular clients: CFP®
- High net-worth clients: CFP® and CFA®

CFP®
As of December 2007, there are 110,865 CFP® certificants worldwide and 20 full-member and three associate-member countries in the Financial Planning Standards Board (Source: www.fpsb.org)

CFA® and Chartered Financial Analyst® are registered trademarks owned by the CFA Institute. For more details, please refer to the website: www. cfainstitute.org

CFA®
As of November 2007, there are 83,000 CFA® charterholders in over 133 countries. (Source: www.cfainstitute.org)

there is no doubt that insurance companies, brokerage houses, and commercial banks are major driving forces behind the promotion of financial planning, they are not necessarily the only financial planning service firms that are interested in the financial planning business. In the United States, traditional financial planning firms are small companies which may be independent of or affiliated with a certified public accounting firm. Most of the top financial planners in the United States come from small firms. In the past decade, large corporations such as Ameriprise Financial, Charles Schwab, and Merrill Lynch began to recruit professional financial planners and aggressively expanded their businesses in financial planning.

In most Asian countries large corporations, not small professional firms, are pushing for a professional financial planning standard. Owing to the limitation of product types of these corporations, the consumer public can have the misconception that financial planners are no more than a high-end sales manager for these financial service companies and their products. Under these circumstances, the perception of a truly independent financial planner is not strong enough to give the financial planning profession the recognition and image it needs. That is why the promotion of the CFP® mark and the development of a professional and ethical code for financial planners are so important to provide the confidence and the recognition that financial planners deserve.

In the 1960s and 1970s, financial planners were perceived as little more than insurance agents and estate planners. In the 1980s, financial planners were more well known as tax planners. In the 1990s, financial planners became more known as asset managers. Through these 40 years, financial planners have provided financial services in all these areas, and more. As there is a common misunderstanding about certain industry-specific or product-specific financial services that financial planners can provide, we now explain how financial planners are similar to or different from other professionals in the industry.

Insurance agents

Insurance agents provide personal selling services of various insurance products such as life insurance, health insurance, and property insurance. Professional insurance agents usually hold the Chartered Life Underwriter (CLU) designation. In the United States, insurance products can only be sold by licensed insurance agents. Therefore, financial planners can only identify insurance needs and provide insurance advice but cannot sell insurance products to their clients unless they are also licensed insurance agents.

Investment advisors and stockbrokers

According to the rules of the US Securities and Exchange Commission and state securities agencies, depending on the amount of capital managed, investment advisors must get registered before they can earn commission for the securities advice made. Like the mandatory registration for insurance agents, investment advisors cannot sell securities products unless they are registered investment advisors. Therefore, if financial planners do not have a securities license, they can only identify securities investment needs and provide securities investment advice. If financial planners are not registered investment advisors, they can perform securities transactions on shares, bonds, and mutual funds through licensed securities representatives called stockbrokers. In the United States, registered brokerage firms are members of the National Association of Securities Dealers (NASD) and registered stockbrokers are individuals who have passed the NASD-administered securities examinations.

Accountants

Traditionally, in most countries, accounting and tax affairs are administered by certified public accountants (CPAs) or similar accounting professionals recognized by local governments. Accountants and tax consultants are professional experts in preparing financial statements and managing tax matters for their clients. If financial planners do not hold a degree in accounting or a CPA license, financial planners may not always be as good as professional accountants and tax consultants in providing tax planning advice.

Estate planning professionals

Professional estate planning advice can be sought from estate planners who hold the accredited estate planner (AEP) designation. However, attorneys, accountants, and trust bankers are also experts in estate taxes and estate planning matters such as preparing legal documents or wills and setting up trusts.

Insurance agents, investment advisors, stockbrokers, accountants, and estate planners are professionals with expertise and skills in their respective specialized areas. Financial planners may not always provide opinions and advice as professionally as insurance agents can on insurance affairs; as investment advisors and stockbrokers can on securities trading; as accountants can on tax issues; and as estate planners can on estate planning matters. However, these various experts can only provide services in the one specialized area of their professions; financial planners have expertise covering more than one area.

Financial planners, who possess a more comprehensive knowledge of budgeting and savings, taxes, investments, insurance, and retirement planning, can give their clients a "big picture" view of their financial situation and make the most appropriate recommendations for their clients. We are not saying that financial planners are superior to all the other professionals. We would just like to stress that financial planners have a broader scope of knowledge to provide multipurpose services for clients. In cases where the financial planners are not professionally competent, they may seek the counsel of these qualified individuals and/or refer clients to such parties. In the best interests of the clients, financial planners have to work closely with these various professionals throughout the whole financial planning process. The close connection between financial planners and these professionals are widely recognized.[4]

Furthermore, the close relationship between financial planners and other professionals can be due to the fact that there is a trend for other professionals to sit for the CFP® certification examination. Table 1.4 reports the licenses and designations statistics of the Financial Planning Association in the United States.

Table 1.4 Licenses and designations statistics

	2001	2002	2003
All insurance licenses	17,490	18,012	15,015
All securities licenses	20,057	20,718	20,107
CFP™	16,767	17,319	17,640
Chartered Financial Consultant	2,298	2,638	2,364
Chartered Life Underwriter	2,839	2,945	2,527
Certified Public Accountant	3,146	3,295	2,654
PFS	1,185	1,095	825
Chartered Financial Analyst	367	421	345
EA	340	349	341
Barrister	872	948	745

---

[4] A mapping of financial planning areas with different categories of specialists (e.g., investment advisor, stockbroker, insurance agent, attorney, trust administrator, estate planner, tax consultant) can be found at http://www.transitionfinancial.com/fo/fee_only_financial.html

The statistics show that many financial planners are also registered investment advisors, licensed insurance agents, chartered financial consultants, chartered life underwriters, chartered financial analysts, attorneys, and certified public accountants. According to the First Annual CFP® Practitioner Survey (1999) of the CFP Board, 91% of CFP® practitioners hold at least one license. There are 74% of the CFP® practitioners holding a license for trading securities. 73% and 16% of the CFP® practitioners are licensed insurance agents and certified public accountants, respectively. Therefore, the CFP® certificants can buy and sell securities in the markets, sell insurance products, and provide sophisticated tax-planning techniques for their clients. With adequate education, suitable qualifications, sufficient experience, and ethical practice, financial planners are able to provide all-round financial planning services for their clients.

Different financial institutions use different job titles to represent the responsibilities of financial planners. Table 1.5 shows examples of financial planning-related job titles of large financial institutions in the United States.

1.2   The Evolution of Financial Planning Services

In the 1960s[5]

The financial planning profession is a broad industry including professionals from many disciplines. The beginning of financial planning services can be traced

Table 1.5 Examples of financial planning-related job titles as of December 2004

Job title related to financial planning	Financial institution
Financial advisor	Merrill Lynch/Ameriprise Financial
Financial consultant	AXA, MassMutual
Financial planner	Lincoln Financial Group
Financial planning advisor	AIG
Financial planning analyst	Bank One
Financial planning associate	USAA
Financial planning educator	The Vanguard Group
Financial planning presenter	The Vanguard Group
Financial services representative	New England Financial Services
High net-worth advisor	Smith Barney
Personal financial advisor	JP MorganChase
Private client advisor	Deloitte
Retirement planning specialist	AXA
Wealth management advisor	RSM McGladrey, Inc.
Wealth strategies analyst	Bank of America

Sources: Data retrieved from various websites of firms listed in the table in August 2004.

---

[5] You can read more about the history of the financial planning profession at www.fphistoryproject.org

back to 1969 in the United States. Thirty-five years ago, financial planning was not yet a profession. Several life insurance agents, who were able to provide additional services on wealth transfer in addition to life insurance products. They became estate planning professionals. With these dual roles of insurance and estate planning practitioners, they were being recognized as financial planners. In other words, the essence of the financial planning profession is the ability to provide a variety of personal financial services.

December 12, 1969 was the day which marked the transition of the financial planning movement to a recognized profession. On that day, Mr. L. Dunton, and six other financial services professionals conducted a meeting at a hotel near Chicago's O'Hare International Airport to explore the possibility of forming a nonprofit professional organization for those providing financial planning services. As a result, the International Association for Financial Counseling was formed, which became the first organization related to personal financial services.

In the 1970s

In 1970, the first organization for financial planners called the International Association for Financial Planners (later changed to International Association for Financial Planning (IAFP)) was set up with the aim of bringing together financial services practitioners with different specializations within the financial services industry. IAFP tried to get financial planning recognized as a profession. However, the earliest financial planners were often perceived by the public as insurance agents who also provided investment services and conducted securities and mutual fund transactions.

To enhance the professional value and technical knowledge of financial planning practitioners, IAFP established the College for Financial Planning and brought about the CERTIFIED FINANCIAL PLANNER™ (CFP®) designation in 1971. Two years later, 36 of the 42 graduates of the College for Financial Planning with CFP® licenses founded a brand new "alumni group-based" organization, the Institute of Certified Financial Planners (ICFP), particularly for the holders of the CFP® designation. Since its introduction in 1972, the CFP® certification has become the forefront of the financial planning profession and a widely recognized financial planning credential among the public. From then on, there were two professional organizations for financial planners in the United States. In 2000, IAFP and ICFP merged to form the Financial Planning Association (FPA), the only professional organization for financial planning practitioners in the US.

In the 1980s

In July 1985, when the Certified Financial Planner Board of Standards, Inc. (CFP Board), a professional regulatory organization and formerly the International Board of Standards and Practices for Certified Financial Planners (IBCFP), was jointly established by the College for Financial Planning and the Institute of Certified Financial Planners (ICFP), the management of the CFP® designation was passed to the CFP Board. Since the establishment of the CFP Board, the College for Financial Planning could focus more on the financial planning training and education responsibilities as an educational institution while the CFP Board could take up the certification responsibilities for maintaining, scrutinizing, and upgrading professional standards.

In the early stages, the financial planning discipline did not have its own unique principles and operational applications. The financial planning service was very similar to a financial consultancy service. During the 1980s, the concept of personal financial planning began to become more widely known by the public with the partial assistance of the US Internal Revenue (Tax) Code. There was a substantial change in the US tax code in the mid-1980s. Financial planners provided a number of tax deduction strategies for their clients to reduce their tax liability. With the provision of tax planning services for clients, financial planners were perceived as "tax-shelter peddlers" in times of high income tax regime.

As the need for financial planning services grew and as standards become higher, the requirement for professional financial planners became stricter. The financial planning service started to become a distinct discipline from 1985 onwards when the CFP Board was established in the United States. The CFP Board imposed a set of standards and code of conduct for professional financial planners in the financial planning industry to comply with. Later, in 1986 and in 1987, two more financial planner associations were set up in the United Kingdom and Japan, respectively. The financial planning profession has developed rapidly in the past three decades, with CFP® certificants practicing personal financial planning in all 50 states in the United States and throughout the world.

The financial planner associations in different countries have developed their own standards and codes of conduct. In order to increase public confidence in financial planners and to protect public interest, there was a need to impose a universal standard for global financial planners.

In the 1990s

In the early 1990s, financial planners involved themselves actively in the securities market by buying and selling mutual funds and so took on the role of asset managers. As financial planners took on different roles through the years, the financial planning discipline gradually gained public acceptance. An increasing number of the consumer public were willing to know more about financial planning and pay for financial planning services per se, in some circumstances without even enjoying associated services related to insurance, tax planning, and asset management.

As the profession gained wider recognition, The International CFP Council, an international assembly of financial planning bodies from different countries, was established in 1990. The major task of the Council was to enforce a worldwide professional standard and ethical code of conduct for all financial planners (individuals as well as professional bodies) with the aim of promoting professionalism, competence, and ethical practice among service providers.

The Council members agree on and endorse the CFP® certification process established by the CFP Board as the best means to demonstrate the competence and ethical practice of financial planners. Based on the principal worldwide standard, each Council member can apply to have its own standard modified as long as the CFP® certification procedures are followed. The Council members strive to publicize the CFP® certification mark as the worldwide recognized standard of excellence for financial planning services.

From the mid-1990s onwards, personal financial planning began to be perceived as a distinct profession with its own unique and widely recognized principles and operational applications.

2000 and Beyond

In 2004, the Financial Planning Standards Board (FPSB) was formed to manage the international marks originally owned by the CFP Board. As at December 2007 there are FPSB members with full-member status from 20 countries and regions. These countries include the following:

- Australia (Financial Planning Association of Australia, Ltd.)
- Austria (Oesterreichischer Verband Financial Planners)
- Brazil (Instituto Brasiliero de Certificação de Professionais Financeiros)
- Canada (Financial Planners Standards Council)
- China (Financial Planning Standards Council of China)
- Chinese Taipei (Financial Planning Association of Taiwan)
- France (Association Française des Conseils en Gestion de Patrimoine Certifiés)
- Germany (Financial Planning Standards Board Deutschland)
- Hong Kong (Institute of Financial Planners of Hong Kong, Ltd.)
- India (Financial Planning Standards Board India)
- Indonesia (Financial Planning Standards Board Indonesia)
- Japan (Japan Association for Financial Planners)
- Malaysia (Financial Planning Association of Malaysia)
- New Zealand (Institute of Financial Advisers)
- Singapore (Financial Planning Association of Singapore)
- South Africa (Financial Planning Institute of South Africa)
- South Korea (Financial Planning Standards Board Korea)
- Switzerland (Swiss Financial Planners Organization)
- The United Kingdom (Institute of Financial Planning, Ltd.)
- The United States (Certified Financial Planner Board of Standards, Inc.)

These 20 financial planning organizations are authorized to award the CFP® certification mark. Table 1.6 shows some examples and numbers of CFP® certificants for selected affiliated associations of the financial planning profession in eight countries.

In addition, there are three associate Financial Planning Standards Board (FPSB) members from Ireland (Financial Planning Standards Board Ireland), Thailand (Thai Financial Planners Association) and the Netherlands (Stichting Register Masters in Financial Planning).

As of December 2007, FPSB has 54,354 CFP® certificants globally. As the financial markets in different regions become more globalized, there is a need for internalized asset management and financial planning services. It is the responsibility of FPSB to set up a series of international standards and to promote

Table 1.6 Examples of international financial planning organizations

Country	Name of association	Abbreviation	Establishment date	Number of CFP® certificants
Australia	Financial Planning Association of Australia, Ltd.	FPA	1992	5,524
Canada	Financial Planners Standards Council	FPSC	1995	17,102
Hong Kong	Institute of Financial Planners of Hong Kong, Ltd.	IFPHK	2000	2,776
Malaysia	Financial Planning Association of Malaysia	FPAM	1999	2,588
Japan	Japan Association for Financial Planners	JAFP	1987	15,012
Singapore	Financial Planning Association of Singapore	FPAS	1998	537
The United Kingdom	Institute of Financial Planning, Ltd.	IFP	1986	760
The United States	Certified Financial Planner Board of Standards, Inc.	CFP Board	1985	56,511

continuous professional development for the CFP® mark worldwide, so as to protect public interest and to enhance public confidence.

In addition, since 2001, the International Organization for Standardization (ISO) has been working on international-wise standards for financial planning. The framework for international-wise standards is largely based on the practice standards used in the US. According to the ISO Technical Committee TC/222, financial planners interested in the ISO qualification are required to fulfill requirements in financial planning process, ethics (including professional behavior), competence (both initial competence and continuing competence), and experience. There are in total 30 countries and regions registered in the ISO Technical Committee TC/222. Active participants include Australia, Austria, Canada, France, Germany, Hong Kong, Japan, South Korea, the United Kingdom, and the United States. The ISO standard on financial planning has been completed, and several European countries are considering promoting this standard.

1.3   Looking Ahead

Current Status of Financial Planning Industries and Consumer Demand

Is the average consumer able to perform financial planning himself? After all, each of us knows our own financial needs. Educated individuals can manage their monthly income and daily expenses. They know how to save, spend, and invest. In addition, they can get assistance from personal finance software packages and self-help books. But is an individual's own financial planning techniques well planned and effective? We believe that consumers can design their own financial plans but their financial plans would be better if they were accomplished with the help of professionals with expertise in investment, financial analysis, accounting, tax planning, and insurance. Even if consumers are financial professionals themselves, they may lack the time to come up with a good plan. Consequently, even financial professionals may need the help of financial planners.

Global Development of Financial Planning

As of December 2007, there are 110,865 CFP® certificants worldwide: 54,354 from the recently formed FPSB, and 56,511 from the CFP Board.

Large corporations such as Ameriprise Financial, Charles Schwab, and Merrill Lynch have aggressively expanded their business in financial planning. Ameriprise Financial recently had plans to establish operations in Asia. Charles Schwab and Morningstar (a mutual fund financial data service provider) recently launched their online financial planning software. Merrill Lynch is converting most of its securities brokers into financial planners.

The Financial Services Skills Council licensed by the UK Government and the Chartered Insurance Institute (CII) in the United Kingdom have expressed interest in studying the possibility of adopting at least partially the ISO standard on financial planning (the ISO TC/222 standard on Global Financial Planning was completed in 2005). According to the Society of Financial Advisors (SOFA, a branch of the CII), the number of examinees for their two Financial Planning Certificates (AFPC and FPC) has greatly increased during the past few years.

The Japanese government has added the financial planning profession to the 133 occupation certifications through the Financial Services Act. The Japan Association for Financial Planners (JAFP) announced that, as of February 2008, there are 160,905 individual members, of which 15,372 are CFP® certificants and 104 are corporate members.

The Financial Planning Association of Australia (FPA) represents about 12,000 financial planning professional individuals and businesses in Australia, of which 90,000 members are practising financial planners. In addition, there are over 5,500 CFP® professionals serving a variety of industries.

The Taiwanese government has established the regulation concerning the Financial Holding Company (FHC) Act in 2001 to provide a legal framework to allow integration among banks, insurance companies, and securities firms to form a comprehensive financial services provider for individuals. The key founders of the Financial Planners Association of Taiwan (FPAT) include a former Minister of Finance. FPAT obtained associate member status in April 2003, and full CFP® certification in January 2005. As of December 2007, there are 514 CFP® certificants, of which 25 obtained certification in China, Hong Kong, and Taiwan.

Various institutions in China including Bank of China, Citibank, and Ping An Insurance have recently introduced or expanded their personal financial services in order to better serve their high net-worth clients. Financial supermarkets are becoming more popular in China to meet the growing demand for personal financial planning services.

What Lies Ahead

Conceptually, one can assert that personal financial planning has been around since the invention of money. With the development of modern finance and retail banking services, formal financial planning has become an important aspect for the average working-class individual or a family who wants financial freedom. The establishment of the CFP Board in 1985, and its takeover of the CFP® mark ownership from the College of Financial Planning in Denver signify a new era for professionals who provide personal financial planning services for clients. The merger of the former Institute of Certified Financial Planners (ICFP) and the International Association for Financial Planning (IAFP) to form the Financial Planning Association (FPA) in Atlanta in 2000 further united financial planning professionals into a single membership body to promote the well-being of the industry.

In the past two decades, the gradual professional and global recognition of the CFP® mark as the highest qualification and standard in financial planning has helped to speed up the formation of a single knowledge base for financial planning. In April 2001, the International Standard Organization (ISO) in Geneva called a meeting in Atlanta to establish a global committee for drafting an ISO standard for personal financial planning (ISO Technical Committee TC/222). The timing for forming such a global committee is ideal as it brings forth an opportunity for the regions or countries which are in need of a national financial planning standard to draft an international standard that is acceptable and applicable in their own country. The ISO standard was completed in 2005 and is now publicly available through the ISO website.

While North America has always led the way in financial planning development, Europe and Asia are catching up though in Asia, financial planning as a profession is only a recent phenomenon. The rapid development of financial planning in Asia, particularly in Hong Kong, Singapore, Malaysia, and Taiwan, is due to the effort and financial support from large financial institutions.

Obviously, the type of firms, large or small, initially dominating the industry has a strong implication on how the profession evolves and matures in the society. If large firms provide most of the support in establishing the financial planning workforce, it will take a relatively shorter period of time to build the industry as large firms have the financial sources, human resources, and necessary political clout to establish the professional image and retail network needed to penetrate the consumer public. While the industry can be built quickly this way, it may result in a slower process in cultivating independent and comprehensive financial planning services. The reason is that large firms have their limitations on selling financial products and providing services that they do not have, preventing their financial planners from recommending products needed by clients. In addition, it may also be more difficult to nurture the practice of fee-based financial planning. Very often, large institutions do not have a pressing need to push for fee-based planning as they have the economies of scale and other monetary gains such as product commission and asset management fees to absorb the added cost of providing the financial planning services. They may even regard financial planning costs as marketing expenses. On the other hand, if small boutique financial planning firms initially dominate the industry, then the only way they can survive is to explore fee-based planning, as many of them are not reputable or big enough to attract clients with a decent size of financial wealth, depriving them of the opportunity to earn fees by managing financial assets.

Challenges of the Financial Planning and Wealth Management Professions

Issues in Financial Planning

Looking at the future of the financial planning profession from a global perspective, we see several major challenges. First, while fee-based financial planning continues its popularity in North America, it will have a slow start in Asia. It is extremely important for Asian countries to educate their consumers and professionals to accept and practice fee-based planning. Compared with commission-based payment, fee-based payment is a more reasonable and fair arrangement. Fee-based services help minimize conflicting interests between the financial planners and the clients, and diversify the risk of overdependence of revenue on asset management. As asset management fees fluctuate and highly correlate with the boom and bust of stock markets, a prolonged bearish stock market can bankrupt many financial planning firms that depend on management fees and trading commissions. Fee-based services can bring in income generated from both large and small clients, creating an income diversification effect for financial planning firms in terms of a bigger client base, and hopefully a lower concentration ratio for income generated from certain clients.

Second, more independent financial planning professionals practicing comprehensive advisory services are needed to provide better services for consumers. The formation of financial planning professional bodies and the promotion of professional qualifications such as the CFP® mark or the ISO standard are critical to the success of independent financial planners who are growing in number. Judging from the development of the accounting profession, the recognition of the CPA qualifications among consumers allows small auditing firms to survive side by side with the Big Four (Deloitte Touche Tohmatsu, Ernst & Young, KPMG and PricewaterhouseCoopers). With a stronger reputation and wider acceptance of the CFP® mark, global consumers may be willing to accept that smaller firms hiring CFP® licensed financial planners can provide quality, ethical, and trustworthy practice. Then smaller independent financial planning firms may have more room to grow, even in Europe and Asia.

Lastly, there is an ongoing change in the type of clients to be served. In the early days of financial planning development, financial planners were usually perceived as insurance agents or estate planners, and the clients consisted mostly of the retired or the nearly retired. As the financial planning profession gradually gains public acceptance, there is an increasing number of young clients seeking information on financial planning and advice from financial planners. A younger client base means financial planners have to serve these clients for a longer time. Therefore, it is extremely important for financial planners to develop good interpersonal skills and maintain a long-term business relationship with their clients.

Issues in Wealth Management

As mentioned earlier, wealth management is a concept synonymous with financial planning. Established by large European (Swiss) private banks and the US commercial banks, wealth management is often used to label the financial planning services for high net-worth clients. Recently, there has been a trend for private banks and high-end wealth management services to lower their hurdles in order to absorb less wealthy clients. By enriching the list of financial products and services provided, wealth managers are able to provide more comprehensive wealth management services targeted at clients who are relatively less wealthy than those being served by the private banking division. It seems that the movement of a more affordable comprehensive wealth management services for mass-affluent and even middle-income clients has begun. The following key factors account for a successful expansion of wealth management services in this direction:

1. The right business model.
2. The right compensation system and wealth management professional with the appropriate skills required for the target market.
3. The scalability of financial planning/wealth management services.
4. Appropriate information technology.

Ameriprise Financial has successfully integrated these four elements in providing financial planning services for middle-income clients at affordable fees. Thus, international firms which are strong in wealth management may be able to use a similar four-factor formula to penetrate the middle-income market with affordable wealth management services.

As with financial planning, Asia and some countries in Europe are developing their wealth management professionals at their own pace. With the increasing popularity of the CFP® and the CFA® marks, the supply of qualified wealth management professionals will increase globally, and the demand for such professionals will certainly increase as the wealth management business is expanding quickly, particularly in China where personal wealth accumulates at a fast speed.

Based on Merrill Lynch's definition, the term *affluent* applies to individuals or households that earn US$100,000 or more per year. High net-worth individuals (HNWIs) are those who have US$1 million of financial assets (excluding first home). Ultra-HNWIs are individuals who own more than US$30 million in assets. The affluent group is the group below the HNWIs. According to the Merrill Lynch Capgemini World Wealth Report 2007, North America has maintained its lead as the wealthiest region in the world with an estimated HNWI wealth of US$11.3 trillion in 2006. Europe ranked second with an estimated HNWI wealth of US$10.1 trillion while the Asia-Pacific was in third place with an estimated HNWI wealth of US$8.4 trillion.

The Merrill Lynch Capgemini World Wealth Report examined the behavior of the HNWI. There is a tendency for the HNWIs to demand institution-like services in the areas of portfolio risk management, strategic asset allocation, and objective investment advice. As these HNWIs become more knowledgeable, they demand more tailor-made and comprehensive financial solutions to their needs. In fact, the HNWIs seek more CFO-style services (CFO: chief financial controller) from their wealth managers, for example tax-sensitive solutions, legal advice, accounting service, general financial planning services, and investment management.

Another interesting observation from the Merrill Lynch Capgemini World Wealth Report concerns individuals in the lower wealth band: they have become more interested in comprehensive financial planning services such as the kind of services offered to HNWIs traditionally. In other words, the financial planning services are now being pushed down to serve the less affluent and retail customer segment. The recent marketing efforts of large Swiss private banks which provide services to less affluent clients are a clear indication of such a phenomenon.

The Merrill Lynch Capgemini World Wealth Report explored the needs and problems of mid-tier millionaires (HNWIs with between US\$5 million and US\$30 million). While the mid-tier millionaires have an increasing complexity in their financial services needs, they are overwhelmed by the task of managing the numerous financial planners and wealth managers who serve them. Unfortunately, the mid-tier group may not be able to afford the one-stop solution provided by the "family office". Thus, the mid-tier millionaires are caught in the middle. In our opinion, the cost of running a family office can be less expensive in Asia, making it a possible solution for mid-tier millionaires.

The picture is rosy, but not necessarily without challenges. There is a need for an increase in the scope and depth of the services provided without significantly increasing the servicing costs. Since a greater variety of services are to be offered, wealth managers may have to improve productivity and efficiency by creating a consistent process and a structured investment methodology that allow continuous financial planning and wealth management services. In order to gain market advantage, there is a need to develop quality service delivery and to expand access to in-house or third-party specialists.

In addition, the development of localized information technology and financial planning wealth management software with content aggregation capability, the culture of focusing on short-term investment gain rather than a long-term diversified investment portfolio with an appropriate risk level, and the formation of a solid wealth management profession with strong technical expertise, communication skills and professional ethics are all critical to the success of wealth management. In time, these hurdles will be gradually resolved, and wealth management will become a basic and necessary financial service embraced by our society.

Information Technology in Financial Planning[6]

Although financial planning operates through personal selling, like all businesses, it needs information technology to deliver its services and products more efficiently. As Friedman (2003) suggests, the use of technology improves service to clients and profitability for the firms. For industries that deal with large

---

[6] Previously published as "Computerizing Financial Planning," Cheng, L., Chan, T., and Lam, C., *HK Financial Planner*, no. 1 (September 2002): 12–13. *HK Financial Planner* permits the authors to retain their own copyright when the article is published.

amounts of personal and financial data, computers can reduce the time spent on routine data entry, paperwork, and technical analysis. Thus, financial planners can focus on establishing relationships with clients. Information technology also helps to reduce human resources on central administrative activities and increase efficiency in customer relationship management.

While there are numerous software programs performing asset allocation, cash flow budgets, tax analysis, retirement plan projections, transaction information, and client reports, these programs serve and operate their functions separately without having linkages with other software. What financial planners desire, as McCarthy (1998) points out, is a seamless data exchange.

What is needed now is therefore a comprehensive program which allows electronic sharing of data among the various programs. The latest information technology on financial planning aims to unify the various platforms and software that clients and financial planners use in performing comprehensive financial planning. Hence, a financial planner will be able to conduct all the necessary financial planning activities by using one Web-based or PC-based platform, while a client can check details on account balances and transaction records using the same platform. Also, the firm can use the same system to manage clients' data, monitor their financial planners' operating and administrative activities, and evaluate the performance of the financial planners.

Financial Planning Software

Traditionally, financial planning software developers have focused on the market for professional financial advisors and financial planning firms. The recent rapid development of World Wide Web and personal computer technology, however, has enabled individual consumers to access financial planning software under a controlled environment provided by financial planning professionals. With the growing sophistication of clients and their demand for content aggregation (i.e., clients using Web-based software to access financial information at a single Web location regardless of the source of the information), financial planning software has become increasingly popular among individual investors and consumers. Various articles on the development of financial planning software have been written, e.g., Starita (2001) and Punishill (2002).

Generally, there are two categories of financial planning software: advisor-oriented and client-oriented:

Advisor-oriented software   Advisor-oriented software is designed for professional advisors as an analytical and database management tool to facilitate the development of financial plans and to maintain a positive client relationship. During the client interview and data collection process, the financial planner can use this software to handle the data input process and provide analysis for clients more efficiently. In addition to analyzing clients' information, some software packages can also help the financial planner to manage clients' data by providing certain data-export functions or avenues to aggregate data from the various financial planners at a corporate level if the same platform is employed within the company. Software that provides comprehensive financial planning support for professional advisors includes NaviPlan by EISI, ESPlanner, and Financeware.com.

Client-oriented software   Client-oriented software focuses on the needs of the individual consumer or investor, and is related more to personal finance than real comprehensive financial planning. Consumers are generally not as "sophisticated" as professional financial planners, and seek tools and software only to help manage their day-to-day accounting and/or investment decisions. Popular software in this category includes Quicken by Intuit and Microsoft Money. Compared to advisor-oriented software, client-oriented software has a smaller market.

Owing to the contrasting goals and requirements of the target customers, the two software markets have coexisted for a considerable period. There has been a growing demand for comprehensive financial planning software from young, well-educated, professional clients who are frequent users of Web-based tools, and are thus considerably more knowledgeable about financial planning software than the older generation.

Nowadays, information is readily and easily available on the Internet. Investors, traders, clients, and the general pubic are going online to invest, to conduct securities trading, and to transfer funds. Financial institutions are pressured to offer various user-friendly Internet-based financial services to their clients. With the increased popularity of Web-based financial services exerting a significant impact on the financial planning industry, the financial planning needs of wealthy clients have changed. The well-educated and wealthy clients are eager to take an active role in participating in the financial planning process with the help of the professional financial planner. This group of clients prefer the financial planner to be the co-pilot (as opposed to being the main driver) and navigate and provide advice on the best financial planning strategies while they, the clients, control the whole process of the strategy formulation.

Consequently, in order to meet the needs of this new breed of clients, a new generation of financial planning software has emerged. It utilizes Web technology and allows clients to fully participate in the financial planning process. Through the use of personal computers, clients can freely access the websites of the financial planning companies as well as interact with their financial planners. Such a Web-based application would serve the needs of both the new clientele and the financial planning companies that would like to "co-pilot" with their clients. Armed with user-friendly and easy-to-use functions such as accessing accounts and transferring funds, the one-stop-shop Internet service can provide clients with not only autonomy to prepare their own financial plans, but also assistance in executing the plan.

As the boundary and segmentation of software markets for the consumer public and professional financial planners become blurred, the financial planning software market will become more competitive. If the demand for content aggregation increases, an open information platform will take center stage, enabling financial planners to better manage and prepare financial plans for their clients. Companies providing financial planning services can analyze and aggregate client data at a corporate level for performance evaluation, and measure the performance of the in-house financial planners more effectively.

While financial planning firms and financial planners reap great benefits from embracing information technology, it must be emphasized that the more advanced the technology and the computer platform, the more training and higher skills the financial planner needs. Using software to generate output without understanding the limitations and the meaning of the analysis is as bad as not having the software at all. In short, technology is only an aid to the financial planner; it can never replace the financial planner's professional knowledge and integrity—the keys to the financial planner's success.

1.4   The CERTIFIED FINANCIAL PLANNER™ Mark

The Value of CFP® Qualification

Financial planning is a young and growing profession. In fact, financial planning is considered one of the top careers in the United States based on six criteria: environment, income, employment outlook, physical demands, security, and stress (Krantz 2001, 2002). As in many other professions such as the legal, medical, and accounting professions, the consumer public recognizes that professional qualification is an important indication of quality services. Obtaining a CERTIFIED FINANCIAL PLANNER™ (CFP®) qualification is the key to being a successful financial planner.

In financial planning, the CFP® mark represents the highest qualification that a financial planner can achieve. While one can debate endlessly on how to measure the quality and the level of a professional mark, one of the best indications is the level of acceptance from the industry, particularly by large financial institutions, and how they perceive the CFP® mark.

The Certified Financial Planner Board of Standards, Inc.[7]

The Certified Financial Planner Board of Standards, Inc. (CFP Board) is an independent certifying organization that owns and authorizes the use of the CFP®, CERTIFIED FINANCIAL PLANNER™, and CFP® certification marks (collectively "the marks") by the trademark law.[8] Formerly the IBCFP, it was jointly established by the College for Financial Planning and the ICFP on July 22, 1985 in the state of Colorado. On February 1, 1994, the IBCFP changed its name to the CFP Board.

In the early 1980s, there was a rapid growth in the number of financial planning practitioners in the United States, creating a huge demand for financial planning training and education. As a result, the responsibility for the maintenance and surveillance of the CFP® professional standard went beyond the capacity of the College for Financial Planning, then an educational institution for financial planning training and education. The IBCFP was thus set up and given the assignment of managing the CFP® designation. Since its establishment in 1985, the CFP Board has strived to make the CFP® mark a widely recognized professional certification.

---

[7] © July 12, 2005, Certified Financial Planner Board of Standards, Inc. (www.cfp.net/aboutus/mission.asp).

[8] The registered mark ® and "TM" are the proper marks in the United States for the CFP license. In some other countries and regions such as Hong Kong, due to different government regulations, the local laws require a "CM" mark for the intellectual property right protection.

In this regard, it is interesting to note that financial plannning has evolved to be one of the top jobs in the United States since then. In the 2001 *Jobs Rated Almanac* authored by Les Krantz (St Martin's Griffin), financial planning ranked the number one career in the United States. In the 2002 edition of *Jobs Rated Almanac* (Barricade Books, 2002), financial planning is still highly ranked, at number three. The ranking considers six criteria in its analysis: environment, income, employment outlook, physical demands, security, and stress.

The number of certificants also testifies to the popularity of the profession. By the end of 2007, there were 56,511 CFP® certificants in the United States, and another 54,354 internationally.

Besides being the certifying organization of the CFP® mark, the CFP Board also aims to foster higher professional standards in personal financial planning by enforcing the four "E" requirements for certification (education, examination, experience, and ethics), and establishing a comprehensive set of Code of Ethics and Practice Standards so that the public can value, access, and benefit from competent and ethical financial planning services.

In order to assist in establishing educational programs in financial planning, the CFP Board is working with the Academy of Financial Services on a model curriculum for university-level financial planning. When the development of the model curriculum is finalized, it will be offered, although not compulsory, as part of CFP®-registered programs.

The CFP Board is administered by a Board of Governors with 15 members, the majority of whom are CFP® certificants. The members serve a term of three years with the responsibility of establishing all policies relating to the financial planning profession and overseeing all the CFP Board activities. There are three subsidiary boards: Board of Examiners, Board of Professional Review, and Board of Appeals under the management of the CFP Board. Table 1.7 outlines the major events and contributions of the CFP Board since its establishment in 1985. It is worth noting that the CFP Board played an important role in helping to set up the FPSB in October 2004. An international standards-setting organization established by 17 non-profit associations outside the United States, the FPSB has since purchased the CFP® mark from the CFP Board. The FPSB has the following objectives:

1. To promote internationalization of the CFP® mark.
2. To oversee a global federation of organizations affiliated with the CFP® certification program.
3. To establish and uphold worldwide professional standards in financial planning services.
4. To maintain and enforce high standards for the affiliates that currently manage the CFP® certification program.

The Four "E" Requirements for CFP® Certification[9]

As an official member of the FPSB, the Institute of Financial Planners of Hong Kong (IFPHK) has adopted the four "E" certification requirements set by the CFP

---

[9] © July 12, 2005, Certified Financial Planner Board of Standards, Inc. (www.cfp.net/learn/knowledgebase.asp).

Table 1.7 Major events and contributions of the CFP Board between 1986 and 2007

Year	Event
1986	Became the certifying organization of the certification marks CFP®, CERTIFIED FINANCIAL PLANNER™ and CFP® certification marks Became responsible for testing and certifying CFP® certificants Established Code of Ethics, and Standards of Practice and Disciplinary Rules and Proceedings
1987	Adopted a registration system of financial planning educational programs of institutions other than the College for Financial Planning
1988	Established the continuing education and ongoing certification requirements
1989	Developed the delineation of experience, requirements, and certifying procedures
1990	Established the International CFP Council to promote global professionalism of CERTIFIED FINANCIAL PLANNER™
1991	Introduced a single comprehensive licensing examination
1992	Made extensive revisions to the Code of Ethics and Standards of Practice
1993	Introduced the new Code of Ethics and Professional Responsibility to replace the previous Code
1994	Changed name from IBCFP to the CFP Board Introduced a new CFP® mark for use by the currently authorized CFP® certificants to make differentiation between CERTIFIED FINANCIAL PLANNER™ certificants and financial planners Established a subsidiary board, the Board of Practice Standards, to start planning for the development and promulgation of Financial Planning Practice Standards for personal financial planning
1995	Reviewed the first exposure draft of Practice Standards Acquired the Registry of Financial Planning Practitioners certification mark from the International Association for Financial Planning (IAFP)
1996	Introduced a voluntary mediation program (administered by American Arbitration Association) to resolve financial planning disputes that may or may not involve ethics violations with IAFP, Institute of Certified Financial Planners (ICFP) and National Association of Personal Financial Advisors (NAPFA)
1997	Joined the IAFP to make a public recommendation that the financial planning practitioners should attain the CFP® certification
1998	Approved the Practice Standards Set up an office in the Washington, D. C. area to educate government regulators and public interest groups about the CFP Board Founded the Financial Services Advisory Council to study the evolving role of financial planning and CFP® certificants in the financial services profession
1999	Enforced the 100 series and 200 series Established the Consumer Advisory Council to solicit feedback from consumer representatives about the financial planning profession
2000	Enforced the 300 series Announced the lapse of the trademark registration of the Registry of Financial Planning Practitioners
2001	Enforced the 400 series
2002	Enforced the 500 series and 600 series
2004	Set up the Financial Planning Standards Board (FPSB)
2007	FPSB has members and associate members from 23 countries with more than 54,000 CFP® certificants outside the United States.

Sources: © July 12, 2005, Certified Financial Planning Board of Standards, Inc. (www.cfp.net/aboutus/mission.asp) and February 5, 2008, Financial Planning Standards Board (www.fpsb.org/site_docs/CertificantGrowth2007.pdf).

Board. According to the definition by the CFP Board, personal financial planning is a "process" of determining whether and how an individual can meet life goals through the proper management of financial resources. Financial planning is a lifelong and comprehensive process which evaluates all aspects of financial needs including consumption, income, wealth analysis, insurance protection, investment, retirement, employee benefits, tax planning, and estate planning.

Financial planning is different from other professions as the financial planning service adopts an integrated approach in a logical and consistent format for providing comprehensive and more targeted financial services in more than one specialized area of the financial lives of the clients. The financial planning industry has close connections with many other industries such as securities brokerage, insurance services, and tax consultancy. Financial planners may hold degrees and licenses in other disciplines such as finance, accounting, and tax. However, there is a unique feature of the financial planning profession. To obtain the CFP® designation, a financial planner has to fulfill the four "E" certification requirements imposed by the CFP Board: education, examination, experience, and ethics. The certification process is important for the profession as it assures the general public that all the holders of the CFP® designation are equipped with the minimum level of competence and training to provide adequate financial planning services. The four "E" requirements set the standard for the competent, qualified, experienced, and ethical financial planning professional.

Ongoing Certification Requirement[10]

CFP® professionals have to renew their licenses periodically, once a year or once every two years. Therefore, CFP® professionals must satisfy the ongoing certification requirement. While the four "E" certification requirements guarantee that all the holders of the CFP® designation have obtained the minimum level of competence and training to provide financial planning services, CFP® certificants have to update their knowledge and skills through continuing education, training, and development in order to enhance the value of the profession and to improve the image of the financial planning profession.

Regulation, Disciplinary Rules, and Procedures[11]

There are no specific rules and regulations governing the financial planning profession. However, there are rules and regulations monitoring the services provided by the financial planners. Since financial planners need to provide advice on securities investment, insurance, tax, and estate, they are subject to rules and regulations related to these areas.

As an example, in the United States, the Securities Act of 1933 and the Securities Exchange Act of 1934 regulate how, when, and by whom securities can

---

[10] © July 12, 2005, Certified Financial Planner Board of Standards, Inc. (www.cfp.net/learn/knowledgebase.asp and www.cfp.net/certificants/ce.asp).

[11] © July 2003, Disciplinary Rules and Procedures, Certified Financial Planner Board of Standards, Inc.

Table 1.8 Functions of the disciplinary bodies of the CFP Board

Disciplinary body	Function
Board of Governors	Exercises jurisdiction over all disciplinary matters and procedures
	Reviews and approves disciplinary rules and procedures
Board of Professional review	Carries out investigations
	Serves on Hearing Panel
	Reports to Board of Governors
Hearing Panel	Records findings of facts and recommendations
	Submits findings and recommendations to Board of Professional Review
Staff Counsel	Files requests for investigation
	Coordinates investigations
	Compiles documents to commence probable cause determination procedures
	Administers disciplinary enforcement proceedings
	Prosecutes charges of wrongdoing
Board of Appeal	Evaluates appeal cases

Source: © July 2003, Disciplinary Rules and Procedures, Certified Financial Planner Board of Standards, Inc.

be issued, registered, and traded. Securities brokers have to comply with the rules imposed by the National Association of Securities Dealers. Insurance agents must have their license approved by the state insurance commission in the respective states where the agents carry out the insurance business.

The duty of investigating, reviewing, and taking appropriate action with respect to the alleged violations of the Code of Ethics and Practice Standards is delegated to the Board of Professional Review, which is governed by the bylaws of the CFP Board. Table 1.8 exhibits the responsibilities of various disciplinary bodies of the CFP Board.

Grounds for Discipline

Article 3 of the Disciplinary Rules and Procedures imposed by the CFP Board spells out the following forms of misconduct which constitute grounds for discipline by the Board of Professional Review, regardless of whether the misconduct is carried out in the course of business or not:

1. Any act or omission which violates the provisions of the Code of Ethics, Practice Standards, and criminal laws.
2. Any act which is the proper basis for professional suspension.
3. Any act or omission which violates the disciplinary procedures and order of discipline.
4. Any failure to respond to a request by the Board of Professional Review.
5. Any false or misleading statement made to the CFP Board.

Table 1.9 shows the number of disciplinary cases opened and the number of hearing cases in 2005 and 2006.

Table 1.9 Disciplinary statistics 2005 and 2006

	2005	2006
Disciplinary cases	1,280	171
Hearing cases	66	96
Settlement offers	22	37

Source: © 2006, Annual Report, Certified Financial Planner Board of Standards, Inc. All rights reserved. Used with permission (www.cfp.net/Upload/Publications/AnnualReport2006.pdf).

CURRENT ISSUE

Consumer Demand for Financial Planning in Hong Kong and China

Surveying the Demand for Financial Planning in Hong Kong[12]

Since the establishment of the IFPHK in June 2000, the development of the personal financial planning profession in Hong Kong has been dramatic and encouraging. While there is no doubt that insurance companies and commercial banks are the major driving forces behind the formation of a high-quality financial planning standard in Hong Kong, they are not necessarily the only financial planning firms which should be interested in the financial planning business. Smaller firms can also be major players in the financial planning industry. In the United States, for example, traditional financial planning firms are small companies which may be affiliated with accounting firms or securities brokerage houses. Most of the top financial planners in the United States work for small firms. Only in the past few years were large corporations such as Ameriprise Financial, Charles Schwab, and Merrill Lynch keen to recruit professional financial planners and aggressively expand their businesses in financial planning.

In most Asian countries, it is the large corporations such as banks and insurance companies, not small professional firms, that are pushing for a professional financial planning standard. Initially, owing to the limitations of product types of these corporations, the consumer public may perceive financial planners as no more than high-end sales managers in these financial services companies. Under these circumstances, it is difficult for the concept of a truly independent financial planner to take shape. The result is that the financial planning profession is not given proper recognition by the consumer public. For this reason, the promotion of

---

[12] Previously published as "More Than Just Sales: A Survey of Demand for Financial Planning In Hong Kong," Cheng, L., *HK Financial Planner*, no. 1 (September 2002): 15–19. *HK Financial Planner* permits the authors to retain their own copyright when the article is published.

the CFP^CM mark in Hong Kong and the development of a professional and ethical code for financial planners are critical in providing the confidence and the recognition that financial planners deserve.

In order to perform a true financial planning function for an individual, the financial advisor has to understand that financial planning is a "process." Many traditional financial advisors think that financial planning is a "one-stop shop" which provides all kinds of products needed by the clients. This is only partially correct. Before the financial planner knows what product to recommend, a comprehensive evaluation of the financial status of the client is necessary to generate the right mix of products. Of course, this is easier said than done. In general, Chinese clients do not easily disclose private financial information to strangers, particularly when financial planners do not yet carry the same reputation that accountants, lawyers, and medical doctors do. Therefore, it would be extremely difficult for financial planners to get the financial data they need to do a good job in financial planning. That is why financial planners in Hong Kong as well as in many other Asian countries face a tough role ahead.

Fortunately, there is a trend in the United States where accountants are switching over to the financial planning profession. The IFPHK is interested in seeing more and more accountants becoming financial planners. As accountants have already earned the trust of their clients through their tax advising services, it would be much easier for them to extend comprehensive financial planning services to existing clients. The growing demand and continuous effort of the IFPHK and the financial services industries will instill confidence in the consumer public toward financial planning professionals. It may take a couple of years to see a sizable number of independent financial planning firms in Hong Kong. But with the growing maturity and increasing expectations of clients, the CFP^CM mark and a vigorous financial planning education are the only route to success for financial planners. In order to enhance public confidence in the financial planning profession and to ensure the service quality of practitioners, an increasing number of banks and insurance companies have imposed a compulsory requirement for their staff members to sit for the CFP^CM examination.

As personal financial planning becomes more widely accepted by the general public, there will be an obvious demand for quality financial planning services in Hong Kong. To appreciate the standing of financial planning in Hong Kong, we conducted a pilot study to survey the demand for financial planning services here. While the sample size is too small to make a strong statement from the results, the survey helps to shed some light on the perception of the consumer public of financial planning services in Hong Kong.

The Survey Sample

During the first six months of 2002, 245 people were surveyed by about 20 students of the Hong Kong Polytechnic University concerning their perception of and demand for financial planning services (Table 1.10 shows the distribution statistics). Respondents were asked about the importance of financial planning and their knowledge of it. The demand level for six areas of personal financial planning was also surveyed: short- and medium-term investment planning, long-term investment planning, insurance planning, tax planning, estate planning, and integrated personal financial planning.

Table 1.10 shows that the age and income distributions are not very even. First, there are significantly more people aged 30 and below, and relatively fewer people in the middle and over-50 age groups. Second, the range given for the income brackets is debatable. If we define high income as the ability of the client to pay for financial planning services, the cut-off point for the high-income level has to be increased substantially (e.g., to HK$50,000). In addition, there are relatively more low-income respondents, obviously due to the fact that many of the respondents are young and at the early stage of their careers. Therefore, there may be some limitations in our data analysis of the survey.

Table 1.10 Distribution and characteristics of 245 respondents in the survey

	Number of respondents	%
Gender		
Male	127	51.8%
Female	118	48.2%
Age		
30 and below	134	54.7%
31–40	46	18.8%
41–50	43	17.5%
Above 50	22	9%
Education		
Bachelor and higher	143	58.3%
High school and diploma	89	36.3%
Primary school and below	13	5.4%
Others		
Income		
Above HK$35,000	26	10.6%
HK$17,000–35,000	67	27.3%
Below HK$17,000*	149	60.8%

* Three respondents did not provide information about their income level.

Survey Results

Here, we shall focus on four aspects of the findings. The first pertains to the overall demand level for the six areas of personal financial planning, while the second, third, and fourth describe the demand level for these six areas by gender, age, and income, respectively.

Overall demand level   A 7-point scale is used to measure the demand level of the respondents for the six areas of personal financial planning services. Point 7 represents the highest demand and point 1 represents the lowest demand. In Figure 1.4 the results show that, among all six areas surveyed, insurance planning is the most vital with a demand level of 4.21 out of a 7-point scale. Integrated personal financial planning ranks second with a score of 4.15. Long-term investment planning (such as retirement planning) ranks third while short- and medium-term investment planning ranks fourth (note that combining the two types of investment may render it the highest in demand). Tax planning is relatively low in demand and estate planning is the least in demand with a score of only 3.16. These results are consistent with our expectations that the insurance profession would do an excellent job in educating the public that insurance protection is an important element in their lives.

Demand level (by gender)   When the sample is divided into subsamples of male and female for analysis (Figure 1.5), the results show that in four areas (short- and medium-term investment planning, long-term investment planning, tax planning, and integrated personal financial planning), male respondents have a slightly stronger demand, the differences ranging from 0.2 to 0.4 out of a 7-point scale. However, the overall pattern that emerges indicates that male and female respondents do not exhibit substantial differences in the demand level within any particular area of financial planning.

Figure 1.4 Overall demand level for six areas of personal financial planning

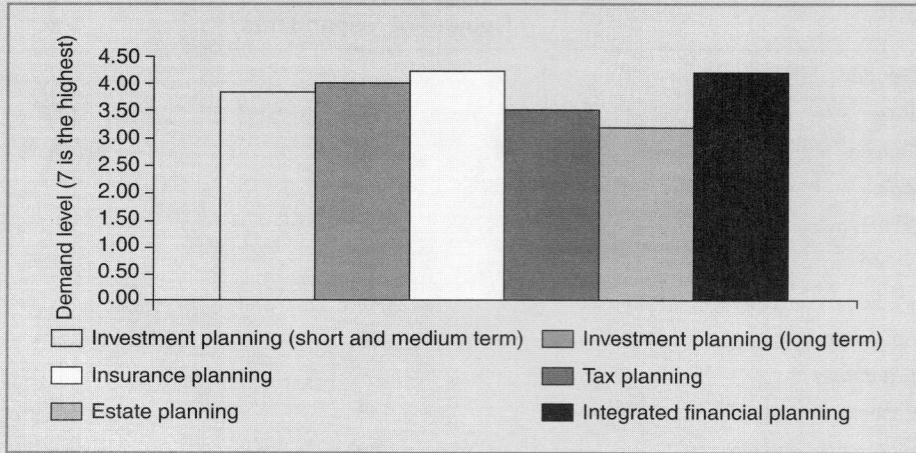

Figure 1.5 Demand level for six areas of personal financial planning (by gender)

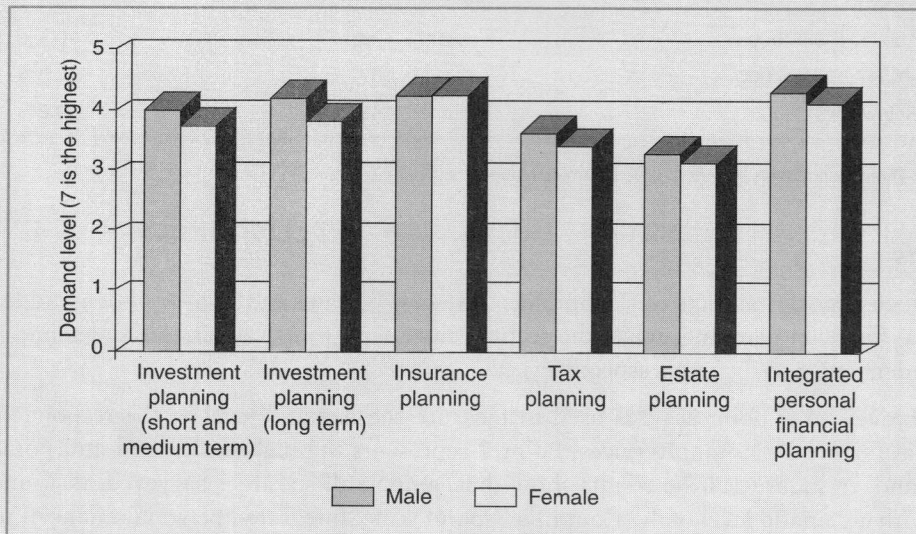

Demand level (by age) Dividing the sample into subsamples of different ages for analysis reveals significant differences in the demand level for selective areas of personal financial planning. As Figure 1.6 shows, the 31–40 age group has a higher demand than the other age groups for all areas of personal financial planning except estate planning. The oldest age group (above 50) demonstrates the weakest demand for all areas except estate planning. In fact, among the four age groups, the above-50 age group has the highest demand for estate planning. The results are consistent with our expectations that the middle age groups are more concerned about financial planning services, particularly in insurance, investment, and integrated personal financial planning.

Demand level (by income) In Figure 1.7, in terms of the three income groups, the middle-income respondents (HK$17,000–35,000) show the highest demand for all areas of financial planning. Compared to the high-income

Figure 1.6 Demand level for six areas of personal financial planning (by age)

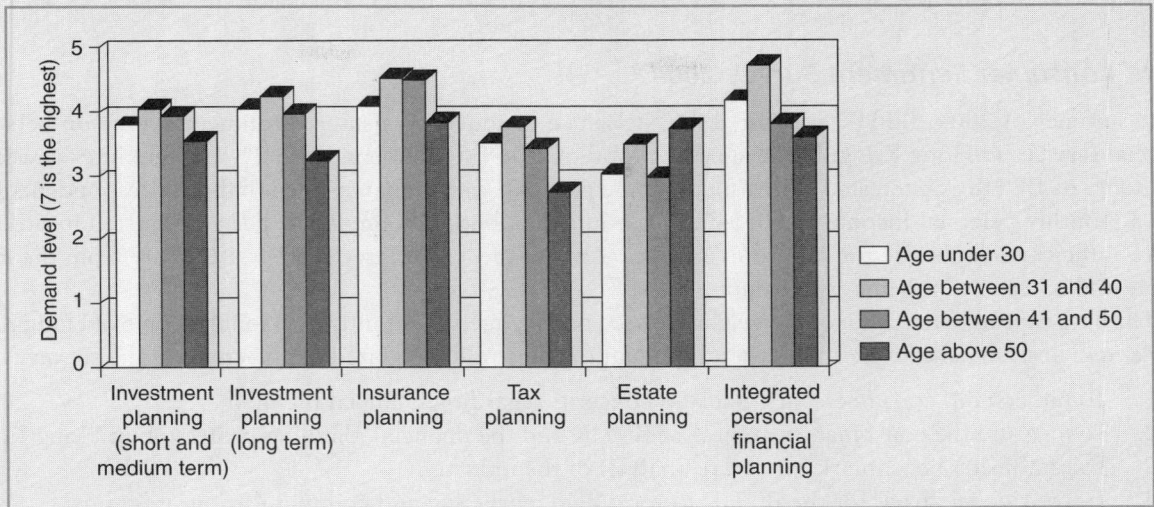

Figure 1.7 Demand level for six areas of personal financial planning (by income)

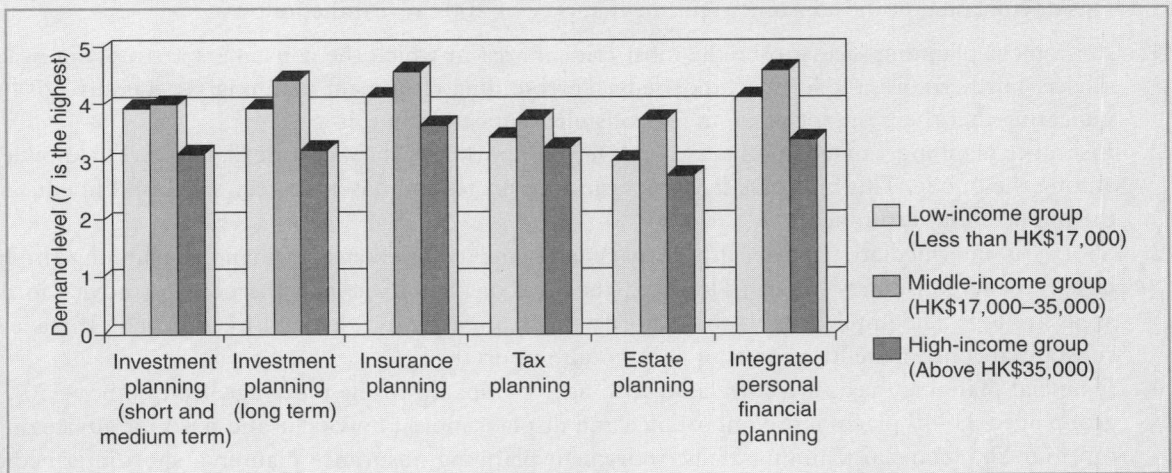

group, their needs appear to be significantly stronger in the areas of insurance, estate planning, investment, and integrated personal financial planning. The results for estate planning may not be accurate as there is only a very small subsample of the high-income respondents. Overall, the results reflect our expectations that there is a strong demand for integrated personal financial planning, insurance, and investment for the middle-income respondents.

Conclusion

The pilot study shows that (1) there is an obvious demand for quality financial planning services in Hong Kong; (2) there are no obvious differences between the male and female populations in terms of their needs for financial planning services; (3) age is an important factor in differentiating the needs for different areas of financial planning services; and (4) individuals of different income levels do exhibit different financial planning needs, but more research in this area is needed to draw a better conclusion.

IFPHK Consumer Sentiment Survey 2004[13]

In the summer of 2004, IFPHK appointed ACNielsen to conduct a consumer sentiment survey on personal financial services in Hong Kong. In the survey, a total of 1,068 respondents aged 21–60 were interviewed by telephone. As IFPHK is interested in investigating the personal wealth management habits of respondents who have a monthly personal income of HK$40,000 or above, a booster sample has been conducted in order to ensure sufficient sample size for subgroup analysis. Among the 1,068 interviewees, 1,003 are from the main sample and 65 are from the booster sample.

The data captured in this survey is weighted based on sex, age, and monthly personal income of Hong Kong people to give a fair reflection of the general population. The following are the objectives of the survey:

1. To understand consumers' attitude and concerns regarding financial planning.
2. To measure the consumer awareness of IFPHK and the financial planning profession in Hong Kong.
3. To establish a benchmark for future analysis of the industry.
4. To provide feedback for the IFPHK to formulate marketing and communication programs.

Executive Summary

The findings documented in the consumer sentiment survey of 2004 reveal the following:

1. Retirement planning seems to be the most critical area in which the consumers are most in need of advice. Furthermore, the level of knowledge surrounding retirement planning is generally not high, indicating that there is a lot of room for consumer education in this area.
2. Insurance planning, ranked number two in level of importance, shows a little higher level of knowledge among the public. This indicates that the insurance profession has been very successful in educating the public about insurance.
3. Short- or intermediate-term wealth management and comprehensive financial planning are also important in consumers' minds. However, the level of knowledge and the need for advice in both areas are low. The implication is that in order to create a greater demand for service in these areas, substantial consumer education is of paramount importance.
4. Financial planning needs are correlated with age. Compared to the older age group (above 50), the group aged 31–40 places more importance and displays more knowledge and need for advice on the top four key financial planning areas (retirement planning, insurance planning, short/intermediate-term wealth management, and comprehensive financial planning). This seems to indicate that the younger age group is more ready for financial planning services.
5. While the higher-income group recognizes the importance of financial planning, they already have relatively good understanding about it, and thus do not actively seek the services of financial planners. This suggests that the financial planning industry has to strengthen its services for the high-income group through stronger marketing campaigns and increased product choices for this group.

---

[13] The results reported here are retrieved from pages 5 and 6, *Background and Research Objectives and the Executive Summary of Consumer Sentiment Survey on Personal Financial Services* published by IFPHK, January 2005. The survey results have been produced by IFPHK under exclusive license by ACNielsen (China) Limited. The interpretations contained in this report have been provided by IFPHK and it is for reference only. IFPHK will not be held liable legally or otherwise for any losses made by anyone who has followed the recommendations.

6. Financial advice comes from four main channels: (1) personal banking (44%), (2) family/friends (21%), (3) media (20%), and (4) own effort (15%). Females show a higher dependency on personal banking and family/friends than males for financial advice, while males tend to rely on the media and themselves. Financial companies should take into account the choice of preferred channels in order to appeal to the intended gender group when promoting their products and services.

7. Consumers most prefer personal bankers to be their financial planner. In this respect, the higher-income group (22%) has a much stronger tendency to select a financial planner than the average public (5%).

8. The key attributes of a financial planner that a consumer considers most important are (1) professional knowledge; (2) trustworthiness; (3) quality and reliable services; (4) understanding their needs; and (5) professional qualification.

9. General awareness of the CFP[CM] qualification and the IFPHK is not particularly high with 16% of those surveyed having heard of the CFP[CM] qualification and 18% having heard of IFPHK. Significantly more people (47%) in the high-income group (above HK$40,000), however, have heard of the CFP[CM] qualification, and 32% in this group have heard of IFPHK. This is encouraging but it also means that IFPHK needs to do more in consumer education as financial planning is not just for the wealthy.

Surveying the Demand for Financial Planning in China[14]

In China, financial planning is an emerging industry. Various institutions including Bank of China, Citibank, and Ping An Insurance have recently introduced or expanded their personal financial services in order to better serve their high net-worth clients. Financial supermarkets are becoming more popular in China to meet the growing demand for personal financial planning services.

To investigate if there is a growing demand for financial planning services in China, IFPHK and Hong Kong Polytechnic University jointly did a survey in 2002 to find out the perception of the respondents in China on the importance of financial planning services in these areas: short-term investment planning, medium-term investment planning, retirement planning, insurance planning, tax planning, estate planning, and integrated personal financial planning. Respondents in four cities, Beijing, Shanghai, Shenzhen, and Wenzhou, were surveyed. The number of questionnaires sent out was 3,035 with a response rate of 83.1%. The final results were based on the responses of 2,490 valid questionnaires.

Table 1.11 shows the survey results. A 7-point scale is used to measure the importance level for the different areas of financial planning services. Point 7 represents the highest importance level and point 1 represents the lowest importance level. The survey results suggest that generally financial planning services are perceived as important. Disregarding integrated personal financial planning, the three specialization areas which receive the highest importance level (point 7 and point 6) are medium-term investment planning (14.5% for point 7 and 45.1% for point 6), retirement planning (17.2% for point 7 and 41.7% for point 6), and insurance planning (14.5% for point 7 and 47.6% for point 6).

To further explore the demand for comprehensive financial planning services in Hong Kong and China, another survey was conducted in 2002. A summary of the results is reported in Table 1.12. In the survey, the respondents were asked to provide answers to the following three questions:

1. Do you think that comprehensive financial planning services are important to you?
2. Do you have any knowledge (and/or experience) in comprehensive financial planning services?
3. Do you need any professional help on comprehensive financial planning services?

---

[14] Previously published as "China's Discerning Cosumers," Cheng, L. and Tang, E., *HK Financial Planner*, no. 2 (Spring 2003): 23–25. *HK Financial Planner* permits the authors to retain their own copyright when the article is published.

Table 1.11 Perception of the importance of financial planning services in China

	7	6	5	4	3	2	1
	Number of respondents (%)						
Short-term investment planning	341 (13.7%)	982 (39.5%)	656 (26.4%)	270 (10.9%)	130 (5.2%)	82 (3.3%)	24 (1.0%)
Medium-term investment planning	360 (14.5%)	1,118 (45.1%)	634 (25.6%)	208 (8.4%)	76 (3.1%)	66 (2.7%)	17 (0.7%)
Retirement planning	425 (17.2%)	1,030 (41.7%)	582 (23.5%)	262 (10.6%)	83 (3.4%)	59 (2.4%)	31 (1.3%)
Insurance planning	360 (14.5%)	1,182 (47.6%)	597 (24.0%)	196 (7.9%)	60 (2.4%)	67 (2.7%)	23 (0.9%)
Tax planning	168 (6.8%)	632 (25.5%)	755 (30.5%)	470 (19.0%)	170 (6.9%)	227 (9.2%)	55 (2.2%)
Estate planning	136 (5.5%)	474 (19.2%)	630 (25.5%)	654 (26.4%)	194 (7.8%)	292 (11.8%)	93 (3.8%)
Integrated personal financial planning	393 (15.9%)	991 (40.1%)	538 (21.8%)	311 (12.6%)	79 (3.2%)	127 (5.1%)	31 (1.3%)

Table 1.12 Demand level for comprehensive financial planning services in Hong Kong and Mainland China (survey period: January–December 2002)

	Mean score (1 = lowest; 7 = highest)				
		Mainland China			
	Hong Kong	Shanghai	Shenzhen	Beijing	Overall
(Number of respondents)	(244)	(548)	(937)	(620)	(2,470)
Do you think that comprehensive financial planning services are important to you?	4.9	5.6	5.4	4.8	5.3
Do you have any knowledge (and/or experience) in comprehensive financial planning services?	3.7	4.3	4.4	3.5	4.1
Do you need any professional help in comprehensive financial planning services?	4.2	5.2	5.1	4.7	5.0

In all the cities (Hong Kong, Shanghai, Shenzhen, and Beijing), approximately 5% of the respondents regard comprehensive financial planning services as important. Perhaps, owing to the fact that comprehensive financial planning services are still relatively new in Asia, the respondents also say that they do not have the knowledge and experience in comprehensive financial planning services and do need some kind of professional help. These statistics suggest that more promotion on financial planning services should be done in Hong Kong and Mainland China. In time, the rapid accumulation of personal wealth and the development of personal financial planning services by financial institutions would cultivate a sizable financial planning market for financial planners in China.

Key Terms

all-round knowledge   *12*

CFP® mark   *7*

four "E" requirements   *13*

high net-worth client   *10*

mass-affluent client   *10*

personal financial planning   *3*

total life planning   *5*

wealth management   *4*

References

Certified Financial Planner Board of Standards, First Annual CFP® Practitioner Survey 1999.

Friedman, G. H., "Q and A on Technology Fundamentals," *Journal of Financial Planning* (July 2003, www.fpanet.org/journal/articles/2003_issues/jfp0703-art6.cfm).

Krantz, Les, *Jobs Rated Almanac 2001* (St Martin's Griffin, 2001).

Krantz, Les, *Jobs Rated Almanac 2002* (Barricade Books, 2002).

McCarthy, E., "The Data Dilemma," *Journal of Financial Planning* (June 1998, www.fpanet.org/journal/articles/1998_issues/jfp0698-art2.cfm).

Punishill, J., "Grading Advisors' Planning Tools," *TechStrategy Report* (Forrester Research Inc., March 2002).

Starita, L., "Financial Planning Tools: The Next Milestone in E-Finance," Research Note (Gartner Group Inc., February 6, 2001).

Questions & Problems

Multiple-choice Questions

1. Which of the following statements is TRUE with regard to the job focus of a financial planner? It changes from _____.
    A. insurance planning to investment planning
    B. insurance planning to comprehensive advisory services
    C. product selling to comprehensive advisory services
    D. comprehensive advisory services to investment planning

2. To be a financial planner, one should possess which of the following key factors?
    I.   Comprehensive financial planning knowledge and skills
    II.   Trust from clients
    III. Excellent communication skills

    A. I only
    B. I and II
    C. I and III
    D. I, II, and III

3. The work of a financial planner is best described as developing a financial plan which _____.
    A. meets the financial goals set by his client
    B. meets the financial goals that he sets for his client
    C. thoroughly investigates the living standards of his client
    D. covers all aspects of his client's well-being and is mutually agreed on by the financial planner and the client

4. A fee-based compensation system for a financial planner is best described as _____.

    I.   a function of a service-based process
    II. a form of payment by hourly rate
    III. a payment for the risk that the client may question whether or not a product recommendation is influenced by the level of commission being paid

    A. I only
    B. I and II
    C. II and III
    D. I, II, and III

5. Based on the popular 80/20 principle, a financial planner who strives for success must be able to _____.
    A. reduce substantially the time spent on the 80% less profitable clients
    B. get rid of the 80% clients that bring 20% revenue
    C. understand how to assess a valuable client and learn interpersonal skills to say "no" when the client is not suitable for you
    D. increase the more profitable clients from 20% to 90%

Problems

1. Define personal financial planning.

2. What is the difference between financial planning and wealth management?

3. Describe the major changes in services and clientele in financial planning through time.

4. Describe the required knowledge and skills of a successful financial planner.

5. Describe the four "E" requirements for CFP® certification.

chapter **2**

Financial Planning: Basic Concepts, Professional Ethics, and Practice Standards

> ### Learning Objectives
>
> *After studying this chapter you should be able to:*
> 1 Understand the objectives of personal financial planning.
> 2 Understand the purposes of wealth management.
> 3 List the different planning areas of financial planning.
> 4 Understand the six-step financial planning process.
> 5 Understand the meaning of ethical behavior.
> 6 Describe professional and ethical responsibility.
> 7 Understand the challenges of ethical dilemma and best practices in financial planning.

In this chapter, we introduce the basic concepts and principles of financial planning. The objectives of financial planning are introduced in 2.1. In 2.2 we present the six steps of the financial planning process. The various theories of ethics are discussed in 2.3. In 2.4–2.6 we explain how to practice ethics and carry out professional responsibilities in the financial planning profession.

2.1   Objectives of Personal Financial Planning and Wealth Management

Personal Financial Planning

According to the Certified Financial Planner Board of Standards, Inc. (CFP Board), personal financial planning is *a process of determining whether and how an individual can meet life goals through the proper management of financial resources*. This definition clears several misconceptions about financial planning. First, financial planning is a *process* rather than a product. The ultimate product of the financial planning is the recommendation of a financial plan. Second, financial planners are not order-takers. Financial planners take an active role in the financial planning process to understand the financial concerns and formulate comprehensive plans to achieve the financial objectives of their clients.

Chieffe and Rakes (1999) employ the idea of an integrated financial planning model. They use the concept of a two-dimensional matrix and suggest that the financial planning process can be (1) divided into a current period (one to five years) and a future period (five years later), and (2) categorized into planned (expected) events and unplanned (unexpected) events. Such a classification allows us to have four core parts: money management and income tax planning for current planned events; investing for goals (goal-oriented investment) and retirement planning for future planned events; emergency planning for current unplanned events; and transference planning for future unplanned events.

Personal financial planning aims to provide professional and value-added services to fulfill the needs of clients. It helps to serve three major purposes: (1) improvement of living standards, (2) risk management, and (3) transfer of assets to the next generation.

Improvement of Living Standards

Since an individual's income and wealth distribution is uneven throughout his life, how to achieve financial security is a major concern. If he does not have well-prepared plans to establish his financial objectives in the early stages of his life, it is likely that he will overspend when money is plentiful and suffer a shortfall when he needs it. A good financial plan prevents a fall in living standards particularly in times when the income level is low (e.g., during retirement). Personal financial planning aims to provide a high living standard for clients at all times.

It is costly to maintain a high living standard. One way to achieve this goal is to generate returns on investment through proper portfolio asset allocation strategies. Investment planning requires professional skills and practical experience. Conservative investors are risk-averse and tend to put all their savings in the bank to earn interest. On the other hand, aggressive investors often underestimate the associated risks for high rates of return. Since not everyone has the time, knowledge, and experience to make good investments themselves, the role of financial planners becomes critical.

Risk Management

Financial planning helps to lessen the detrimental effects caused by unexpected events. From the viewpoint of personal financial planning, there are two main types of risks: risks at the micro level and risks at the macro level. Micro-level risks are those which are more closely related to clients such as unemployment, physical injuries (illness and disability), and accidents. Risks at the macro level are related to such macro factors as inflation, financial turmoil, and political and economic instability. Financial planning services can help to minimize risk and losses, and provide indemnity. Personal risk management employs various insurance products to manage the risk, for instance, an insurance product that can compensate for the loss of one's job due to physical injuries. Financial risk management employs investment techniques such as risk profiling and asset allocation.

Legacy Planning (Estate Planning)

Financial planners do not only provide services for clients but also help in making plans for their dependants. Clients' spouses and children can be viewed as part of their assets and liabilities. In devising overall financial plans, family members are relevant factors for consideration, for example, the living, educational, and medical expenses for the children may take up a large proportion of one's income. In addition, an estate plan is needed to help clients transfer their assets to the next generation upon death.

Wealth Management

In the previous section, we mention that personal financial planning involves mainly achieving the overall financial objectives of individuals. Wealth management is a closely related concept to personal financial planning and is defined as the practice of comprehensive financial planning with an emphasis on conducting and implementing investment management for clients. However, recently, there has also been an increasing emphasis on estate planning implementation in the wealth management of clients. Put simply, wealth management refers to financial plan involving large investment portfolios and estates.

Another common definition of wealth management is the categorization of wealth management activities into four separate functions: (1) wealth creation; (2) wealth accumulation; (3) wealth preservation; and (4) wealth distribution. These four activities of wealth management are closely related to the life-cycle of an individual. When a client is young and at the early stage of his career, most of his effort will focus on creating wealth (i.e., wealth creation). When the individual is more successful in his career, his salary and, consequently, his savings should increase accordingly, leading to the function of wealth accumulation. At a later life stage, the individual should have accumulated enough wealth. Thus, the main focus at this stage has shifted from wealth accumulation to wealth protection (i.e., wealth preservation). Finally, for wealthy individuals, legacy planning or estate planning is important when they are getting old. That is wealth distribution. In short, the four functions of wealth management fit nicely with the changing needs of an individual through his life-cycle.

In the practice of wealth management, the role of investment management must be emphasized. Traditionally, financial planners/wealth managers would, based on the estimated risk tolerance level of the clients, recommend a fixed asset allocation strategy. Unless major industry-specific or economic events occur, the asset allocation would not be changed. More recently, owing to the popularity of strategic and tactical asset allocation, hedged funds and other active market timing strategies, financial planners are more inclined to recommend a more frequent revision of asset allocation for clients. Under the comprehensive financial planning and total life planning that we advocate, the initial and continuous asset allocation strategies recommended must be closely tied to the financial goals of the clients. As making money is only the means but not the end, any investment strategy should aim to realize the financial and life goals of the clients.

Planning Areas of the Personal Financial Planning Process

A comprehensive personal financial planning process covers several **financial planning areas:**

1. **Consumption planning** (cash flow management).
2. **Taxation planning**.
3. **Insurance planning**/risk management.
4. Short- and medium-term **investment planning**.
5. **Retirement planning**.
6. **Estate planning**.

financial planning areas Consumption, tax, insurance, investment, retirement, and estate planning.

consumption planning Deals with clients' cash flow management and consumption behavior.

tax planning Deals with clients' tax liability and obligations.

insurance planning Deals with clients' insurance needs.

investment planning Aims to meet clients' short- and medium-term investment goals.

retirement planning Deals with clients' retirement needs.

estate planning Deals with clients' inheritance, estate management, and philanthropic needs.

Clients can obtain different financial planning services from different service providers. For example, they may seek investment advice from investment consultants or buy insurance policies from insurance agents. However, these various product providers do not consider the effects of the recommendations made on the overall financial status of their clients. Personal financial planners are different from the other financial service providers in that they must have the ability to devise a comprehensive plan by incorporating different planning areas for their clients. These planning areas will be explained at length in Chapters 4 and 5.

2.2   Steps in the Personal Financial Planning Process

In order to ensure the professional quality of the financial planning industry, financial planners have to comply with the practice standards imposed by the CFP Board. In the personal financial planning process, there are six steps:

1.   Establishing and defining the client-planner relationship.
2.   Gathering client data and determining goals.
3.   Analyzing and evaluating the client's financial status.
4.   Developing and presenting the financial plan.
5.   Implementing the financial plan.
6.   Monitoring the financial plan.

We briefly describe the six steps here; they will be discussed in more detail in Chapters 7–11.

Step 1: Establishing and Defining the Client-Planner Relationship

The financial planning practitioner and the client should define the scope of the engagement before any financial planning service is provided.[1]

One important key to success for financial planners is to develop and manage a good relationship with clients. Therefore, the first step of the personal financial planning process must be to establish a good client-planner relationship. This step is a crucial one as how well the relationship is established will affect later steps. Before any financial planning service is provided, the financial planning practitioner and the client should mutually define the scope of engagement. It is very important that the nature of the client-planner relationship and the scope of engagement are fully communicated and mutually understood. In short, step 1 is all about information disclosure and establishing a working (hopefully, also trusting) relationship with the client based on the mutually defining principle so that the client has some sense of the scope of the services expected.

---

[1] © July 2003, Financial Planning Practice Standards, Certified Financial Planner Board of Standards, Inc. All rights reserved. Used with permission.

Step 2: Gathering Client Data and Determining Goals

The financial planning practitioner should obtain sufficient quantitative information and documents about a client relevant to the scope of the engagement before any recommendation is made and/or implemented.

The financial planning practitioner and the client should mutually define the client's personal and financial goals, needs, and priorities that are relevant to the scope of the engagement before any recommendation is made and/or implemented.[2]

After a client-planner relationship is established, financial planners have to collect relevant data from them in order to devise a personal financial plan. Step 2 involves obtaining quantitative information and documents as well as determining a client's personal and financial goals, needs, and priorities. In the process of data collection, financial planners can have more chances to communicate and interact with their clients. Consequently, they will also have a better understanding of the financial goals and priorities of clients. The skill of managing clients' expectations in the goal-determining process is very important. Otherwise the financial planner will have a hard time in meeting the client's goals.

Step 3: Analyzing and Evaluating the Client's Financial Status

A financial planning practitioner should analyze the information to gain an understanding of the client's financial situation and then evaluate to what extent the client's goals, needs, and priorities can be met by the client's resources and current course of action.[3]

Having gathered the information from clients, financial planners are able to analyze and evaluate their financial status. The current financial status is the starting point for ultimate financial goals. Besides using the data (assets, liabilities, income, and expenses) collected in step 2 to analyze the financial status of clients, financial planners also have to gather and utilize information about the macroeconomic conditions (inflation rate, employment rate, fiscal and monetary policies, and market condition). With the information extracted from these different sources, financial planners are able to construct various analysis reports (balance sheet, income and expense statements, cash flow statement, and cash budget) to summarize the financial status of the clients. Here, the analysis of investment needs and risk profiling should be documented.

Step 4: Developing and Presenting the Financial Plan

The financial planning practitioner should consider sufficient and relevant alternatives to the client's current course of action in an effort to reasonably meet the client's goals, needs, and priorities.

---

[2] © July 2003, Financial Planning Practice Standards, Certified Financial Planner Board of Standards, Inc. All rights reserved. Used with permission.

[3] © July 2003, Financial Planning Practice Standards, Certified Financial Planner Board of Standards, Inc. All rights reserved. Used with permission.

The financial planning practitioner should develop the recommendation(s) based on the selected alternatives(s) and the current course of action in an effort to reasonably meet the client's goals, needs, and priorities.

The financial planning practitioner should communicate the recommendation(s) in a manner and to an extent reasonably necessary to assist the client in making an informed decision.[4]

Using the data gathered and analyzed in the previous steps, financial planners can identify and evaluate different alternatives for financial plans. They can select from these alternatives and develop appropriate recommendations as to the best financial plan for their clients. When they present their recommendations to clients, the clients will have to decide on what they want.

Step 5: Implementing the Financial Plan

The financial planning practitioner and the client should mutually agree on the implementation responsibilities consistent with the scope of the engagement.

The financial planning practitioner should select appropriate products and services that are consistent with the client's goals, needs, and priorities.[5]

When both clients and financial planners agree on and confirm the financial plan recommendation in step 4, financial planners have to execute the plan in step 5. There are three principles for the implementation responsibilities: accuracy, authority, and timeliness. In the implementation process, financial planners have to be very sure that the financial products and services executed are in accordance with those already specified in the previous steps. More importantly, the plan and any amendments to the plan implemented have to be supported by the absolute consent (authorization) of the clients. In addition, there should be a time schedule to ensure that the financial plan is implemented smoothly.

Step 6: Monitoring the Financial Plan

The financial planning practitioner and client should mutually define monitoring responsibilities.[6]

In the execution stage, the plan's progress should be monitored to make sure that the actual operation does not deviate from the designed plan too much. In the monitoring process, there may be a possibility that some or all the steps of the financial planning process have to be reinitiated due to the unexpected changes in external (e.g., changes in the macroeconomic conditions such as amendments in fiscal or monetary policies and financial market turmoil) and/ or internal (e.g., changes in the physical, psychological, and financial status of

---

[4] © July 2003, Financial Planning Practice Standards, Certified Financial Planner Board of Standards, Inc. All rights reserved. Used with permission.

[5] © July 2003, Financial Planning Practice Standards, Certified Financial Planner Board of Standards, Inc. All rights reserved. Used with permission.

[6] © July 2003, Financial Planning Practice Standards, Certified Financial Planner Board of Standards, Inc. All rights reserved. Used with permission.

the clients) factors. Consequently, the current scope of engagement, the current financial status analyzed, and the current financial planning recommendation implemented may have to be modified. In addition, financial planners have to agree on the monitoring responsibilities with the clients so that there is a mutual understanding of the scope of monitoring services the financial planners are able and willing to perform. In this step, regular communication between clients and financial planners is essential to constantly update information about the progress of the plan.

2.3   Ethics

What is Ethics?

Ethics has been defined as the understanding of what is good and right, bad and wrong; a set of principles of conduct governing behaviors; or a system of moral standards or values.

A code of ethics is essential in society to develop, maintain, and restore stability legally, economically, socially, and professionally. Business transactions can only be completed if the contracting parties keep their word. Economic stability needs a certain extent of ethical commitment (Arrow 1973). Social and interpersonal relationships require mutual trust and respect. Professional bodies have established codes of ethical conduct. Professionals and clients are in a fiduciary relationship. A fiduciary relationship means that professionals should act in the interests of their clients without conflict and bias. How should the clients rely on the performance of financial planners? The financial planning services operate through personal selling which creates numerous opportunities for abuse and misconduct. Financial planning professionals have to assure their clients that they will observe due care, and be diligent and competent in their conduct. Ethics is important. All of us need to be socially responsible and accountable for our behavior. We need to have socially responsible corporations and individuals. There are four components of social responsibility (Carroll 1979). They are (1) economic responsibility, (2) legal responsibility, (3) ethical responsibility, and (4) voluntary responsibility.

1.   Economic responsibility

Economic responsibility means that firms have to produce goods and services that are desired by the general public in the most cost-efficient and effective way. In this way, firms can earn profits for survival while the public can have the goods and services to satisfy their needs.

2.   Legal responsibility

Legal responsibility is the duty to obey the legislative rules and regulations. Non-compliance would lead to legal liability. For example, professionals are individuals who possess and exercise special skills and knowledge in the interest of others, and of whom a high standard of behavior and performance is expected. Professionals and professional bodies have a legal responsibility to discharge their duties well.

3. Ethical responsibility

Ethical responsibility includes behaviors and activities that are not codified into law but are expected from the public.

4. Voluntary (discretionary or philanthropic) responsibility

Voluntary responsibility is not legally required and ethically demanded but is desirable. A socially responsible individual is not compelled to do what is good for society, but does it of his or her own accord. Mellinger (2002) proposes that high net-worth individuals often include their personal philanthropic goals as part of a comprehensive wealth management strategy, and argues that philanthropy is a strategy for acquiring and serving high net-worth clients. Forward-thinking financial planners realize that such a desire for philanthropy provides them with the unique opportunity to combine social consciousness with smart business, resulting in a new trend in the financial planning profession to incorporate philanthropic products (for example, giving to charity, setting up private foundations) in the overall wealth management mix. So a win-win-win situation is achieved—what is good for the client is good for society and good for business.

Next, we discuss the many common myths about ethics (McDonald 1995).

Common Myths about Ethics

Myth 1: Ethics Is Morality

We usually relate ethics to morality. Morality refers to the standards of good and bad, right and wrong. Moral standards are the generally accepted rules and statements to describe what kinds of actions are morally right or wrong (moral norms) and what kinds of beliefs are morally good or evil (moral values). Examples of moral norms include *it is right to be punctual; it is wrong to be impolite.* Examples of moral values include *diligence is good; corruption is bad.* We all know that it is desirable to follow these standards. Looking at it from this point of view, we may think that ethics and morality are the same as these moral norms and moral values can become ethical norms and ethical values.

However, strictly speaking, they are not the same. Many ethical standards have their basis on moral standards, but not all. Ethics includes the process of making investigations into morality; morality is what is being investigated by ethics. Ethics is a normative study of moral standards and the moral decision-making process. In this study we would have a list of moral standards (with justifiable reasons) that can be reasonably applied to real situations; and suggested procedures for practical application of deciding right (versus wrong) and good (versus bad) actions and behaviors.

Myth 2: Ethics Is Legality

There are two misconceptions about the relationship between ethics and legality. The first is that ethics and legality are identical. This misconception may be due to the fact that many moral norms and values have been documented in legal rules and regulations. For instance, a moral individual should respect others and so will not kill, steal, lie, or cheat. The law has regulations against the immoral acts of murder, theft, and fraud. In this sense, ethics and legality are very similar. However, an action that we take may be legal but not necessarily ethical. For instance, respecting our parents by taking care of them when they are old is the ethical thing to do. However, as long as we do not abuse them, we would not be doing something illegal if we neglect our responsibility to take care of them and pay for their living expenses. Moreover, some laws are totally unrelated with morality. For instance, traffic rules dictate that we drive when the light is green and stop when the light is red.

In fact, obedience to the law is itself an ethical value. It is obviously right to follow legal rules and regulations. It is definitely wrong to do illegal acts. Therefore, ethics and legality are not identical but they are not completely different. We may say that ethics and legality overlap in some areas and ethics is of a larger scope than legality.

The second misconception is that the law should be a more relevant guide than ethics in our behavior. Paine (1994) argues that there is a misconception that law is more important than ethics. The reason for the predominance of law over ethics may be due to the myth that law and ethics govern two different spheres of influence: law is more likely for public life and ethics is more likely for private life. The law consists of a set of enforceable rules that are obligatory and compulsory for compliance. These rules are usually more precise. However, ethical rules are usually perceived as a set of moral guidelines. Conformity to ethical rules and principles is voluntary, optional, discretionary, and personal.

Myth 3: Ethics Is Business Ethics

Although there is a close relationship between ethics and business dealings, ethics is not only applied to business. The ethical concepts of good and right can be practiced in many different areas. Personal ethics includes the generally accepted principles and rules which individuals use in their personal lives. Accounting ethics and medical ethics are the codes of professional conduct for accountants and medical practitioners, respectively. Business ethics is just one of the numerous forms of applied ethics.

If ethics means our understanding of what is good and right, business ethics is the application of our ethical concepts (moral principles and moral decision-making process) to business, including business decisions, business transactions, and business management.

Myth 4: Business Should Be without Ethics

We have mentioned that economic responsibility is one component of social responsibility. By economic responsibility, it means that we need to provide goods and services that are desired by the general public using the most cost-efficient and effective means. Therefore, making profits from fulfilling the needs of the customers should be the major objective of doing business. From the business viewpoint, clients would be satisfied if the financial plans recommended by financial planners are profitable. Since the financial planning service is a business transaction between clients and financial planners, as long as the financial plans can benefit the clients economically, there should be no concern about ethics.

Does this imply then that financial planners can do whatever is necessary to benefit their clients—that they can use fraud, corruption, and insider trading to get the highest return or employ tax evasion tools to reduce tax liability for their clients? These unethical techniques may help increase the economic benefit for individuals but they create unfair distribution of welfare among all. Financial planners may have fulfilled their economic responsibility toward their clients, but they do this at the expense of the other components of social responsibility, i.e., legal, ethical, and voluntary responsibilities.

Therefore, business needs ethics. They are not contradictory. Although all business transactions are protected and regulated by legal agreements, we also need ethics to govern business activity. Otherwise, we may act unethically and break business contracts. Ethics is required to maintain business trust and stability. Good ethics can be a driving factor for good business (Collins 1994) and corporate culture.

Myth 5: Applying Ethics Is Always Costly

One of the main objectives of firms is to get higher profits. In the case of individuals, their objective is to earn higher incomes. The myth exists that it is easier to get extra monetary rewards by practicing unethical behavior. When we are facing an ethical dilemma, we are often tempted to choose rewards over ethics. Therefore, there are arguments against bringing ethical principles into a business situation as they may affect the pursuit of the highest profits for a firm and the best financial interests for an individual.

Of course, it is not true that unethical practice brings rewards while ethical behavior brings nothing. Unethical behavior may give you the chance to get immediate, easy, and short-term rewards. Nevertheless, habitual unethical practice is not a strategy for long-term survival. Consumers may be fooled by unethical service providers once, but not a second time. And these service providers will be jeopardizing their reputation and goodwill by following unethical practices. Reputation is an invaluable asset. The benefit from having a good reputation is immeasurable. Although it is harder to be ethical, as a smart financial planner, you should know that being ethical is an essential factor to make your clients loyal to you and to attract new clients. A reputation of being ethical helps build up your career in the industry gradually while a reputation of unethical behavior ruins your profession instantly. Therefore, the pursuit of ethics would lead to the pursuit of prosperity and hence monetary rewards. In this way, individuals with ethical responsibility tend to have optimization rather than maximization of profits as their objective. Therefore, ethical behavior is the best and the most appropriate long-term strategy.

Another point to bear in mind is that you need to be ethical not only to your clients, but also to other members of the financial planning profession and to your professional body. Your unethical practice may affect not only your mutual trust with your clients and hence your business, it could also ruin the confidence of thousands of clients in the whole financial planning profession.

Ethical Theories

In this section we introduce several ethical theories which are useful to help us understand what ethics is. Ethical theories are analysis tools to understand, evaluate, and solve ethical problems. There are various approaches to deal with ethical issues. Some are action-based (to evaluate if the performance is ethical) and some are character-based (to evaluate if the mind is ethical). Although there are many different sources of moral values and norms, some of these values may not be held for life; they may be discarded and replaced by new values adopted when we become more mature and get older. Our ability to tackle ethical issues and the level of our moral standards develop in different stages throughout our lives. Below we briefly discuss some ethical theories or approaches.

Utilitarian Approach

Utilitarianism is the analysis of benefits and costs (Bayles 1968; Sen and Williams 1982). The term *utilitarianism* is derived from *utility*. Benefit is positive utility and cost is negative utility. The utilitarian approach evaluates an action as right or wrong on the basis of the benefits and costs imposed on the society. If we use the utilitarian approach to deal with an ethical issue, the most appropriate solution is the one with the highest units of utility (that is the greatest net benefit or the lowest net cost).

Rights Approach

In the rights approach, the main ethical focus is on the *right*, which is an entitlement to something in order to pursue or protect certain interests such as the right to act in a particular way (Kant 1964; McCloskey 1965). The moral right, which is authorized and supported by moral norms and values, enables the right-holder to enjoy basic human rights consistent with the system of moral principles. These moral rights are also called natural rights or human rights.[7] Examples of moral rights are the rights to pursue love, happiness, interest, privacy, and liberty.

Justice Approach

Disputes and disagreements usually arise when there are injustice and unfairness. Examples of unfairness are unequal share of benefits, uneven distribution of costs, and asymmetric treatment.

One of the objectives of financial planners is to increase their client base. Therefore, a successful financial planner would have to serve a lot of clients. Among these many clients, some are "big" clients (that is, they provide more business). Financial planners have to consider their time allocation for each of

---

[7] The United Nations Universal Declaration of Human Rights specifies human rights as the right to have free speech, right to religion, right to own property, right to work, right to choose employment, right to protect against unemployment, right to just and favorable working conditions, right to just and favorable remuneration, right to form and join trade unions, and right to rest and leisure (www.un.org/overview/rights.html).

their clients if they have similar deadlines for the formulation of their financial plans. Should financial planners allocate more time and resources to the "big" clients than to the "small" clients? Is it just or ethical to give more time and resources to prepare the financial plan for "big" clients? In this ethical problem example, financial planners may use the distributive justice approach to solve the issue. In the first place, it is the free choice of financial planners to allocate their time and resources. As financial planners owe fiduciary duty to all their clients, all the clients deserve a share of the effort from the financial planners. According to the justice approach by Rawls (1971), as long as the financial planners do not neglect their professional duty to the "small" clients, it is ethical for financial planners to allocate their time and resources in proportion to the fee contribution of the different clients.

Ethics of Care Approach

Human beings are connected to each other by various types of relationships, for instance, parent-children relationship, employer-employee relationship, and buyer-seller relationship. Some of these are more intimate and some are more distant. The closeness of the relationship determines the degree of care and extent of obligation the parties have for each other. According to the ethics of care approach, we are obligated to exercise special care toward those with whom we have close relationships (Dillon 1992).

Financial planners and clients are in a fiduciary relationship. Clients rely on the financial planning services provided by financial planners. Therefore, financial planners owe a duty of care to their clients. According to the ethics of care, in this close relation of dependency, the financial planners should show compassion, concern, care, friendship, loyalty, and kindness to the clients.

Egoist Approach

In psychoanalytic terms, psychological health is the outcome of harmony among three personality substructures: *id, superego,* and *ego*. A person's ego is responsible for making appropriate responses to satisfy his needs and wants. We can equate the ego with self-interest. According to the egoist approach (Singer 1961), self-interest is the determining factor for behaviors. A selfish self-interest, for example, greed for money, may result in unethical behavior. A person's self-interest can override universal moral principles and standards. However, self-interest isn't always bad – for example, a desire to be good is an example of a self-interest that can lead to ethical behavior.

Mixed Approach

Each of the approaches we have discussed so far has its own value standards and moral reasoning. No single approach can give us the solution to an ethical problem. Sometimes we have to evaluate an ethical issue using several approaches. For example, suppose you have a very important client whom you have known for a long time. This client is very generous to you; he recommends many new clients to you and hence enables you to become the best financial planner of your firm. As you make adjustments to his financial plan, you discover that some of your client's business activities are illegal. For example, he uses poisonous raw materials for the manufacture of toys. So what should you do? Should you sacrifice your business to save strangers? Should you keep the illegal act secret and sacrifice the lives of many?

If you use the utilitarian approach, you may ask yourself whether the net utilitarian benefits of keeping it secret are larger than the net benefits of disclosing the illegal act (an action referred to as whistle-blowing). The utilitarian benefits of keeping what you know secret may be the continuous inflow of business. The benefits of disclosure may be the lives of many. You also need to ask whether these utilitarian benefits are more important than other values such as moral right (the right of the public to know, the right to privacy), justice (unequal distribution of benefits—only you and your client benefit if the secret is undisclosed; others will suffer) and costs (costs borne by the public if undisclosed), duty of care (breakdown of trust and confidentiality duty if disclosed), self-interest (fame, monetary rewards), and moral virtues (honesty, uprightness). Although these various approaches appear to give you conflicting values and rules of judgment, they provide you with guidelines and criteria to make the right choice. The final decision may not be an ethical one, but that decision is a justified one and the most appropriate one if you have used these various value standards.

2.4   Practicing Ethics and Carrying out Professional Responsibilities

Objectives of a Professional Code of Ethics

A professional code of ethics is a set of written statements on standards of behavior expected of professionals. Why do we need a professional code of ethics for professionals?

A Commitment to Serve Clients

A professional code of ethics is needed to ensure that the services provided by professionals are technically competent.

A Public Relations Statement to Assure the Public

Professionals have a duty to protect the public interest. A professional code of ethics is needed to assure the public that a code exists to govern professional activities.

A "Must" to Meet Rising Public Expectations

A better educated public and a larger number of corporate and financial failures have led to greater societal expectations of professionals. A code of ethics is needed to show that the profession takes its ethical responsibility seriously and is willing to meet rising public expectations.

A Guide to Distinguish Right from Wrong Practice

Besides satisfying societal expectations, a code of ethics provides a set of enforceable principles and rules for members to distinguish right from wrong practice.

A Guide to Improve Service

A code of ethics helps define the role and conduct of professionals. For instance, a professional must be objective (objectivity principle), fair (fairness principle), diligent (diligence principle) and exercise due care (due care principle). These guidelines help professionals to improve their service and be more accountable. In addition, the code of ethics alerts the professionals to possible ethical problems.

A Self-Regulation Mechanism

Another reason for a professional body to establish a professional code of ethics is to demonstrate its willingness, intention, and ability to self-regulate its members. This self-regulation mechanism indicates that professional bodies have their own monitoring system to scrutinize the behavior of their members without the need of public sanction. This self-surveillance enhances the value and credibility of the profession.

Components of a Professional Code of Ethics

The professional code of ethics is a system of norms, values, and standards that govern the practice of the members of a profession. In the code of ethics, there are two essential components: principles and rules. Principles are the moral concepts and notions that govern ethical behavior. These concepts and notions provide the reasons to justify why we have to follow the rules. Rules are the practical application of the principles and they specify the behavior expected of members.

Principles and rules are vital for each other. One cannot survive without the other. If the principle exists without the rule, we will not know when and how to apply the principle. If the rule exists without the principle, there is no meaning or justification for the rule. So principles provide the substance and rules make up the form of the professional code of ethics.

For example, if a rule tells a financial planner not to be personally involved with a client where money matters are concerned, he may ask, why? If a client is in need, why shouldn't we lend him a helping hand, especially if it is necessary to maintain a good client-planner relationship? However, the principles of integrity and objectivity give us the reason: we should avoid any situation where a potential conflict of interest may arise and affect our independent judgment.

Take another example: the competence principle tells us that we need to be competent in dealing with our clients. Does this then imply that we need to be experts in all planning areas of the financial plan, that we need to have a degree in finance to devise the securities investment plan and a degree in accounting to devise the tax plan? The answer is, no, we do not need to be an expert in all areas in order to be competent. The rules tell us that we are allowed to seek advice from other experts in those areas in which we are not that professionally competent in order to serve the best interests of our clients.

As learning the principles and rules of ethics without a subject matter or using a professional organization as an example can be difficult, we adopt Bayles (1989) to illustrate how these principles can be used as a requirement of fiduciary duty. In addition, we also use extracts from the CFP Board Code of Ethics and Professional Responsibility to illustrate how principles and rules can be written for financial planning practices (see Application Corner on page 62).

Fiduciary Duty of Professionals

Attributes of Fiduciary Duty

In a fiduciary relationship, a fiduciary (called an agent) is an entity who acts and undertakes to act on behalf of another (called the principal) in circumstances which give rise to a relationship of trust, confidence, and dependency. Owing to this relationship, the performance of the agent for the principal should be without bias and conflict of interest. Instead, the service should be done with due care, diligence, and competence. The high standard of quality of service expected of the agent requires him to demonstrate a number of characteristics (Bayles 1989). (Note that many of these attributes are part of the code of ethics for other professions.) The following list reflects the major attributes in upholding fiduciary duty.

1. Integrity: the ability to make independent judgment, and to avoid conflict of interest.
2. Objectivity: the ability to provide objective, reasonable, and prudent judgment for the interest of the principal, and an obligation to be impartial.
3. Honesty (duty of fidelity): the personality trait of being trustworthy and the ability to keep promises (explicit and implicit, written and verbal).
4. Accountability: the willingness to accept responsibility and the consequences of one's own behavior.
5. Competence: the possession of special and up-to-date knowledge and skill and the ability to exercise the knowledge and skill in the interest of the principal.
6. Pursuit of excellence: the enthusiasm to be as good, as diligent, as industrious, as committed, and as well-prepared as one can be and the ability to complete a task promptly to meet a deadline.
7. Discretion: the ability to keep secret all information related to the principal.
8. Duty of Disclosure: the duty to disclose sufficient and relevant information and potential conflict of interest so as to maintain mutual trustfulness.
9. Loyalty: the ability to be faithful and devoted.
10. Fairness: the ability to refrain from taking undue advantage of others.
11. Caring: the ability to treat others as an end in themselves rather than as a means to an end.

12. Respect: the ability to recognize the legal, moral, and human rights of others.

Fiduciary Relationships

Although the primary function of financial planners is to serve the interest of their clients, they have also to consider their responsibilities to other stakeholders. The four stakeholders are (1) clients, (2) employers, (3) the public, and (4) the profession.

Responsibility to Clients

Clients rely on the services provided by professionals. Bayles (1989) states that there are seven fundamental responsibilities to clients: (1) honesty, (2) truthfulness, (3) competence, (4) diligence, (5) loyalty, (6) fairness, and (7) discretion.

Responsibility to Employers

If you are not a partner of a professional agency, you are an employee. You then have a fiduciary relationship with your employers to act in their best interests. Your responsibilities to your employers are very similar to your responsibilities to your clients except for the fairness responsibility. Since you only have one employer to serve at a time, you do not need to comply with the fairness responsibility as there is no other employer to give different favors to. The six responsibilities to the employer are: (1) honesty, (2) truthfulness, (3) competence, (4) diligence, (5) loyalty, and (6) discretion.

Responsibility to the Public

There are three fundamental responsibilities to the public (Bayles 1989): (1) truthfulness (the obligation not to provide misleading and deceptive information), (2) nonmaleficence (the obligation to avoid injuries (physical, psychological, and financial)), and (3) fairness (the obligation not to show discrimination).

Responsibility to the Profession

As members of a professional body, professionals have certain responsibilities to it. There are three major types of responsibility to the profession (Bayles 1989): (1) social leadership (such as participating in charitable activities), (2) enhancement of professional knowledge and skill (such as organizing workshops and seminars to upgrade quality and participating in research activities), and (3) working for the public interest (such as updating the code of ethics and practice standards; more stringent monitoring and disciplinary mechanisms to check on the performance of the members).

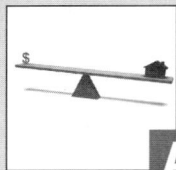

APPLICATION CORNER

Principles and Rules[8]

PART A   Code of Ethics and Professional Responsibility

The Certified Financial Planner Board of Standards (CFP Board) is a professional regulatory organization set up in 1985. For the ultimate benefit of the clients of financial planning services, CERTIFIED FINANCIAL PLANNER™ professionals should possess the four "E" qualifications. As have been mentioned in Chapter 1, the four "E" professional requirements are:

1. Education
2. Examination
3. Experience
4. Ethics

As "Ethics" is one of the professional requirements of financial planners, the CFP Board has identified the ethics standards, *Code of Ethics and Professional Responsibility* (*Code of Ethics*), which professional financial planners must comply with. The Code of Ethics applies to all persons who have been recognized and certified to use the CFP®, CERTIFIED FINANCIAL PLANNER™ and certification marks (collectively "the marks") in their performance of professional services. The ethical code provides a guideline to the CFP designees (current certificants, candidates for certification, individuals who have any direct or indirect entitlement to the CFP certification marks and who have been certified in the past and retain the right to reinstate their CFP certification without passing the current CFP® Certification Examination) actively involved in the practice of personal financial planning, in other areas of financial services, in industry, in related professions, in government, in education or in any other professional activity in which the marks are used.

Composition and Scope

There are two parts in the Code of Ethics: Principles (Part I) and Rules (Part II). The principles are statements expressing the ethical and professional ideals and recognition of the financial planning profession to serve the public, clients, colleagues, and employers in an ethically and professionally responsible manner in all professional services and activities. The comments following each principle further explain the meaning of the principle. The rules (Part II) present practical interpretation of the principles and set forth the standards of ethical and professionally responsible conduct expected from the CFP Board designees in particular situations.

Compliance

Implicit in the acceptance of these certification and authorization, each CFP Board designee must voluntarily ascribe to the code of ethics and additional requests of the CFP Board as mandated as well as all applicable

---

[8] © Code of Ethics and Professional Responsibilities, Certified Financial Planner Board of Standards, Inc.

laws and regulations. The voluntary decision empowers the CFP Board to take disciplinary action such as the permanent revocation of the right to use the CFP marks in case there is a violation of the code of ethics.

Part I: Principles

Introduction

These principles of the Code express the profession's recognition of its responsibilities to the public, to clients, to colleagues, and to employers. They apply to all CFP Board designees and provide guidance to them in the performance of their professional services. There are seven principles in the Code of Ethics set up by the CFP Board.

Principle 1: Integrity

A CFP Board designee shall offer and provide professional services with integrity.

Integrity includes the characteristics of honesty, candor, and uprightness which are required to decide what is right and just. The integrity principle does not preclude innocent error and legitimate difference of opinion, it simply means that integrity should not be subordinated to personal gain and advantage. Personal integrity is important to maintain and enhance public trust and confidence.

Principle 2: Objectivity

A CFP Board designee shall be objective in providing professional services to clients.

Objectivity requires intellectual honesty and impartiality. Regardless of the particular service rendered, a CFP Board designee should protect the integrity of his or her work, maintain objectivity, and avoid any bias in or subordination of his or her professional judgment that would be in violation of this code.

Principle 3: Competence

A CFP Board designee shall provide services to clients competently and maintain the necessary knowledge and skill to continue to do so in those areas in which the designee is engaged.

Sometimes, incompetence is used to excuse irresponsible behavior. Therefore, it is very important that financial planning services are provided by competent people. There are three major types of competence: physical, psychological, and technical. Physical competence means that financial planners should have sufficient physical power to act. Psychological competence suggests that financial planners should be emotionally stable to control their actions. Technical competence refers to the technical skills such as financial analysis that financial planners need to make recommendations for the financial plan.

A competent designee should have attained and maintained an adequate level of knowledge and skill and be able to apply the knowledge effectively to provide financial planning services for the clients. However, the designees should also have a continuing commitment to upgrade themselves through ongoing learning and professional improvement. In areas where the designees are not professionally competent, competence includes the wisdom to recognize the limitations of that knowledge, to seek expert consultation and to refer clients.

Principle 4: Fairness

A CFP Board designee shall perform professional services in a manner that is fair and reasonable to clients, principals, partners, and employers and shall disclose conflict(s) of interest(s) in providing such services.

Fairness demands a subordination of prejudicial feelings and personal desires in order to achieve a proper balance of conflicting interests. Designees should exercise impartiality and treat everyone in the same fashion and with the same intellectual honesty, and make full disclosure of any potential conflict of interests.

Principle 5: Confidentiality

A CFP Board designee shall not disclose any confidential client information without the specific consent of the client unless in response to proper legal process, to defend against charges of wrongdoing by the CFP Board designee or in connection with a civil dispute between the CFP Board designee and client.

The confidentiality duty helps to ensure that a CFP Board designee provide contemplated financial planning services effectively and that client privacy is protected. A client, by seeking the financial planning services of a CFP Board designee, may also be interested in creating a relationship of personal trust, confidence and dependence with the CFP Board designee. This type of relationship between the client and CFP Board designee can only be built upon the understanding that all the information supplied by the client to the CFP Board designee would be kept confidential.

Principle 6: Professionalism

A CFP Board designee's conduct in all matters shall reflect credit upon the profession.

A designee should take up the attendant responsibilities that come with the profession to behave with dignity and courtesy to those who use the financial planning services, fellow professionals, and those in related professions. As a member of the financial planning profession, each designee is obligated to work with fellow professionals to enhance and maintain the public image of the profession and to improve service quality.

Principle 7: Diligence

A CFP Board designee shall act diligently in providing professional services.

A designee should exercise diligence in the proper planning and execution of professional services in a reasonably prompt and thorough manner for the clients.

Part II: Rules

Introduction

As stated in Part I, the principles apply to all CFP Board designees. However, due to the nature of a CFP Board designee's particular field of endeavor, certain rules may not be applicable to that CFP Board designee's activities. The activities performed by CFP Board designees are indeed diverse. As a result, in considering the rules in Part II, the CFP Board designees must first recognize what specific services they are rendering and then determine whether or not a specific Rule is applicable to the services. To assist the CFP Board designees in making these determinations appropriately, the Code of Ethics includes a series of definitions of terminology used throughout the Code. Based upon the definitions, the CFP Board designees should be able to determine which services they provide and, therefore, which rules are applicable to those services.

Rules that relate to the Principle of Integrity

	The CFP Board designee should:
Rule 101	not solicit clients through false or misleading communications or advertisements.[9]
Rule 102	not engage in conduct involving dishonesty, fraud, deceit or misrepresentation, or knowingly make a false or misleading statement to a client, employer, employee, professional colleague, governmental or other regulatory body or official or any other person or entity.
Rule 103	have the following responsibilities regarding funds and/or other property of clients:

    a. in exercising custody of, or discretionary authority over, client funds or other property, a CFP Board designee should act only in accordance with the authority set forth in the governing legal instrument (e.g., special power of attorney, trust, letters testamentary, etc.); and

    b. a CFP Board designee should identify and keep complete records of all funds or other property of a client in the custody, or under the discretionary authority, of the CFP Board designee; and

    c. upon receiving funds or other property of a client, a CFP Board designee should promptly or as otherwise permitted by law or provided by agreement with the client, deliver to the client or third party any funds or other property which the client or third party is entitled to receive and, upon request by the client, render a full accounting regarding such funds or other property; and

    d. a CFP Board designee should not commingle client funds or other property with a CFP Board designee's personal funds and/or other property or the funds and/or other property of a CFP Board designee's firm. Commingling one or more clients' funds or other property together is permitted, subject to compliance with applicable legal requirements and provided accurate records are maintained for each client's funds or other property; and

    e. a CFP Board designee who takes custody of all or any part of a client's assets for investment purposes, should do so with the care required of a fiduciary.

Source: Certified Financial Planner Board of Standards, Inc.

Rules that relate to the Principle of Objectivity

	The CFP Board designee should:
Rule 201	exercise reasonable and prudent professional judgment in providing professional services.
Rule 202	act in the interest of the client.

Source: Certified Financial Planner Board of Standards, Inc.

---

[9] By Rule 101, a CFP Board designee should not make a false or misleading communication about the size, scope or areas of competence of the CFP Board designee's practice or of any organization with which the CFP Board designee is associated. In promotional activities, a CFP Board designee should not make materially false or misleading communications to the public or create unjustified expectations regarding matters relating to financial planning or the professional activities and competence of the CFP Board designee. The term "promotional activities" includes, but is not limited to, speeches, interviews, books and/or printed publications, seminars, radio and television shows, and video cassettes. In terms of representation of authority, a CFP Board designee should not give the impression that a CFP Board designee is representing the views of the CFP Board or any other group unless the CFP Board designee has been authorized to do so. Personal opinions should be clearly identified as such.

Rules that relate to the Principle of Competence

	The CFP Board designee should:
Rule 301	keep informed of developments in the field of financial planning and participate in continuing education throughout the CFP Board designee's professional career in order to improve professional competence in all areas in which the CFP Board designee is engaged. As a distinct part of this requirement, a CFP Board designee should satisfy all minimum continuing education requirements established for CFP Board designees by the CFP Board.
Rule 302	offer advice only in those areas in which the CFP Board designee has competence. seek the counsel of qualified individuals and/or refer clients to such parties in areas where the CFP Board designee is not professionally competent.

Source: Certified Financial Planner Board of Standards, Inc.

Rules that relate to the Principle of Fairness

	The CFP Board designee should:
Rule 401	disclose to the client: a. material information relevant to the professional relationship, including conflict(s) of interest, the CFP Board designee's business affiliation, address, telephone number, credentials, qualifications, licenses, compensation structure and any agency relationships, and the scope of the CFP Board designee's authority in that capacity; and b. the information required by all laws applicable to the relationship in a manner complying with such laws.
Rule 402	make timely written disclosure of all material information relative to the professional relationship in a financial planning engagement. In all circumstances and prior to the engagement, a CFP Board designee should, in writing: a. disclose conflict(s) of interest and sources of compensation; and b. inform the client or prospective client of his / her right to ask at any time for information about the compensation of the CFP Board designee. As a guideline, a CFP Board designee who provides a client or prospective client with the following written disclosures, using Form ADV, a CFP Board Disclosure Form or an equivalent document, will be considered to be in compliance with this Rule: – The basic philosophy of the CFP Board designee (or firm) in working with clients. This includes the philosophy, theory and/or principles of financial planning which will be utilized by the CFP Board designee; and – Résumés of principals and employees of a firm who are expected to provide financial planning services to the client and a description of those services. Such disclosures should include educational background, professional/employment history, professional designations and licenses held; and – A statement that in reasonable detail discloses (as applicable) conflict(s) of interest and source(s) of, and any contingencies or other aspects material to, the CFP Board designee's compensation; and – A statement describing material agency or employment relationships a CFP Board designee (or firm) has with third parties and the nature of compensation resulting from such relationships; and – A statement informing the client or prospective client of his/her right to ask at any time for information about the compensation of the CFP Board designee.
Rule 403	communicate in reasonable detail the requested compensation information related to the financial planning engagement, including compensation derived from implementation, upon request by a client or prospective client. The disclosure may express compensation as an approximate dollar amount or percentage or as a range of dollar amounts or percentages. The disclosure should be made at a time and to the extent that the requested compensation information can be reasonably ascertained. Any estimates should be clearly identified as such and based on reasonable assumptions. If a CFP Board designee becomes aware that a compensation disclosure provided pursuant to this rule has become significantly inaccurate, he/she shall provide the client with corrected information in a timely manner.
Rule 404	offer disclosure as described under Rule 402 or provide disclosure if requested at least annually for current clients.

Rule 405	request fair and reasonable compensation.
Rule 406	perform professional services with dedication to the lawful objectives of the employer and in accordance with this Code of Ethics.
Rule 407	a. advise his/her employer of outside affiliations which reasonably may compromise service to an employer; b. provide timely notice to his/her employer and clients about change of CFP® certification status; and c. provide timely notice to clients, unless precluded by contractual obligations, about change of employment.
Rule 408	inform his/her employer, partners or co-owners of compensation or other benefit arrangements in connection with his or her services to clients, which are in addition to compensation from the employer, partners or co-owners for such services.
Rule 409	disclose, in writing, the risks of the transaction, conflict(s) of interest of the CFP Board designee, and other relevant information, if any, necessary to make the transaction fair to the client, if the CFP Board designee enters into a personal business transaction with a client, separate from regular professional services provided to that client, the transaction should be on terms which are fair and reasonable to the client.

Source: Certified Financial Planner Board of Standards, Inc.

Rules that relate to the Principle of Confidentiality

	The CFP Board designee should:
Rule 501	not reveal – or use for his or her own benefit – without the client's consent, any personally identifiable information relating to the client relationship or the affairs of the client, except and to the extent disclosure or use is reasonably necessary (For purposes of this rule, the proscribed use of client information is improper whether or not it actually causes harm to the client):
	a. to establish an advisory or brokerage account, to effect a transaction for the client, or as otherwise impliedly authorized in order to carry out the client engagement; or
	b. to comply with legal requirements or legal process; or
	c. to defend the CFP Board designee against charges of wrongdoing; or
	d. in connection with a civil dispute between the CFP Board designee and the client
Rule 502	maintain the same standards of confidentiality to employers as to clients.
Rule 503	owe the CFP Board designee's partners or co-owners a responsibility to act in good faith. This includes, but is not limited to, adherence to reasonable expectations of confidentiality both while in business together and thereafter.

Source: Certified Financial Planner Board of Standards, Inc.

Rules that relate to the Principle of Professionalism

	The CFP Board designee should:
Rule 601	use the marks in compliance with the rules and regulations of CFP Board, as established and amended from time to time.
Rule 602	show respect for other financial planning professionals, and related occupational groups, by engaging in fair and honorable competitive practices. Collegiality among CFP Board designees shall not, however, impede enforcement of this Code of Ethics.

Rule 603	promptly inform CFP Board if the CFP Board designee who has knowledge, which is not required to be kept confidential under this Code of Ethics, that another CFP Board designee has committed a violation of this Code of Ethics which raises substantial questions as to the designee's honesty, trustworthiness or fitness as a CFP Board designee in other respects. This rule does not require disclosure of information or reporting based on knowledge gained as a consultant or expert witness in anticipation of, or related to, litigation or other dispute resolution mechanisms. For purposes of this rule, knowledge means no substantial doubt.
Rule 604	promptly inform the appropriate regulatory and/or professional disciplinary body if the CFP Board designee who has knowledge, which is not required under this Code of Ethics to be kept confidential, and which raises a substantial question of unprofessional, fraudulent or illegal conduct by a CFP Board designee or other financial professional. This rule does not require disclosure or reporting of information gained as a consultant or expert witness in anticipation of, or related to, litigation or other dispute resolution mechanisms. For purposes of this rule, knowledge means no substantial doubt.
Rule 605	make timely disclosure of the available evidence to the CFP Board designee's immediate supervisor and/or partners or co-owners if the CFP Board designee has reason to suspect illegal conduct within the CFP Board designee's organization. If the CFP Board designee is convinced that illegal conduct exists within the CFP Board designee's organization, and that appropriate measures are not taken to remedy the situation, the CFP Board designee should, where appropriate, alert the appropriate regulatory authorities, including the CFP Board, in a timely manner.
Rule 606	perform services in accordance with applicable laws, rules and regulations of governmental agencies and other applicable authorities; and applicable rules, regulations and other established policies of the CFP Board.
Rule 607	not engage in any conduct which reflects adversely on his/her integrity or fitness as a CFP Board designee upon the marks, or upon the profession.
Rule 608	disclose to clients the status of the CFP Board designee's firm as registered investment advisers. The Investment Advisers Act of 1940 requires the registration of investment advisers with the US. Securities and Exchange Commission and similar state statutes may require registration with state securities agencies. Under present standards of acceptable business conduct, it is proper to use a registered investment adviser if the CFP Board designee is registered individually. If the CFP Board designee is registered through his or her firm, then the CFP Board designee is not a registered investment adviser but a person associated with an investment adviser. The firm is the registered investment adviser. Moreover, RIA or R.I.A. following a CFP Board designee's name in advertising, letterhead stationery, and business cards may be misleading and is not permitted either by this Code of Ethics or by SEC regulations.
Rule 609	not practice any other profession or offer to provide such services unless the CFP Board designee is qualified to practice in those fields and is licensed as required by state law.
Rule 610	return the client's original records in a timely manner after their return has been requested by a client.
Rule 611	not bring or threaten to bring a disciplinary proceeding under this Code of Ethics, or report or threaten to report information to the CFP Board pursuant to Rules 603 and / or 604, or make or threaten to make use of this Code of Ethics for no substantial purpose other than to harass, maliciously injure, embarrass and/or unfairly burden another CFP Board designee.
Rule 611	comply with all applicable renewal requirements established by the CFP Board including, but not limited to, payment of the biennial CFP Board designee fee as well as signing and returning the Terms and Conditions of Certification in connection with the certification renewal process.

Source: Certified Financial Planner Board of Standards, Inc.

Rules that relate to the Principle of Diligence

	The CFP Board designee should:
Rule 701	provide services diligently.
Rule 702	enter into an engagement only after securing sufficient information to satisfy that the relationship is warranted by the individual's needs and objectives; and the CFP Board designee has the ability to either provide requisite competent services or to involve other professionals who can provide such services.
Rule 703	make and/or implement only recommendations which are suitable for the client.
Rule 704	make a reasonable investigation, consistent with the nature and scope of the engagement, regarding the financial products recommended to clients where such an investigation may be made by the CFP Board designee or by others provided the CFP Board designee acts reasonably in relying upon such investigation.
Rule 705	properly supervise subordinates with regard to their delivery of financial planning services, and should not accept or condone conduct in violation of this Code of Ethics.

Source: Certified Financial Planner Board of Standards, Inc.

Practice Standards[10]

In 1995, the CFP Board set up its Board of Practice Standards, with exclusively CFP® practitioners, to draft and revise practice standards for financial planners. As IFPHK has not developed its own Practice Standards yet, we adopt the US version here. Fortunately, due to the similarity of the Code of Ethics and Professional Responsibility between the two organizations (e.g., the code number for the ethical rules are virtually the same), we can still apply these standards using the ethical rules in Hong Kong. The aims of financial planning practice standards include: (1) to ensure that the practice of financial planning is based on the established norms of practice, (2) to advance professionalism in financial planning, and (3) to enhance the value of the financial planning process.

These practice standards establish the level of professional practice in the financial planning services. There is at least one related practice standard for each of the steps of the financial planning process. In each practice standard, there is a statement regarding an element of the financial planning process, an explanation of the standard, a description of its relationship to the Code of Ethics, and a detailed account of the potential impact on the public, the profession, and the practitioners. The meaning and purpose of the practice standards described in the explanation note provide a guideline for interpretation and application of the practice standards. There are close relationships between the seven principles of the Code of Ethics (integrity, objectivity, competence, justice, confidentiality, professionalism, and diligence) and the practice standards as the seven principles provide the moral reasons and justification for the practice standards.

It is mandatory for the CFP Board designees to comply with these practice standards when performing the tasks of financial planning. Financial planning professionals are encouraged to use the practice standards when carrying out the financial planning activities addressed by the practice standards. The content of the practice standards is authoritative and direct. The enforcement of the practice standards is based on the disciplinary rules and procedures imposed by the CFP Board and administered by the Board of Professional Review and the Board of Appeal. Although the main objective of the practice standards is to provide a framework for professional financial planning practice, noncompliance with the practice standards may give

---

[10] © July 2003, Financial Planning Practice Standards, Certified Financial Planner Board of Standards, Inc. All rights reserved. Used with permission.

rise to legal liability. Table 2.1 presents a summary of the practice standards and their relationships with the financial planning process.

Disciplinary Proceedings[11]

Although adherence to the Code of Ethics, individually and by the profession as a whole, is suggested, compliance is purely voluntary. Therefore, disciplinary proceedings are necessary to ensure a fair and reasonable process for a CERTIFIED FINANCIAL PLANNER™ professional against whom allegations of violating the Code of Ethics are brought.

Upon receipt of a written complaint, the CFP Board staff would review the allegations to examine if further investigation is necessary and grounds for discipline exist. Examples of the grounds for discipline are:

1. Violations of the Code of Ethics provisions of the CFP Board.
2. Violations of the criminal laws of any state.
3. Violations of the Disciplinary Rules and Procedures of the CFP Board.
4. Failure to comply with the request of the Board of Professional Review without good reasons.
5. Solicitation of false and misleading statements.

Depending on the severity of the misconduct, the forms of disciplinary action include a private written censure, a public letter of admonition, suspension of the right to use the CFP marks for a specified period of time (not exceeding five years) and permanent revocation of the right to use the CFP marks.

2.5 Practicing Professional Ethics in the Financial World

In this section, we discuss how ethical issues and best practices are dealt with in the financial world. We also present the decision-making models developed in the United States for solving ethical issues.

Ethical Issues

Life is full of choices. Occasionally these choices put us in a dilemma—in a position in which we have to face an ethical issue. The main source of many ethical problems is a conflict of interest between the decision maker (in this case, the agent or financial planner) and the stakeholders (clients, employers, colleagues, professional bodies, other professional members, and the public). The agent is under the fiduciary duty to act solely for the benefit and best interests of the principal in all matters connected with the agent-principal relationship. However, it is inevitable for the agent to have self-interest. In cases where the best interests of the principal are not congruent and do not match with the self-interest of the agent, a conflict of interest arises.

---

[11] © July 2003, Financial Planning Practice Standards, Certified Financial Planner Board of Standards, Inc. All rights reserved. Used with permission.

Table 2.1 Application of code of ethics and practice standards in the financial planning process

Step	Practice Standard series	Effective date	Code of Ethics	Purpose	Impact on public	Impact on profession	Impact on practitioner
1	100–1 Determining engagement scope	Jan 1, 1999 (revised on Jan 1, 2002)	Principle 4 Fairness Rule 402	Define scope of engagement mutually	Enhance mutual understanding	Enable more realistic and clearer expectations to be formed	Provide clearer focus for agreed objectives and tasks
			Principle 7 Diligence Rule 702	Disclose conflicts of interest, information right, and compensation in written form Provide competent services	Enhance likelihood of client satisfaction		Enhance potential for positive results
2	200-1 Gathering client data	Jan 1, 1999 (revised on Jan 1, 2002)	Principle 7 Diligence Rule 701 Rule 702 Rule 703	Obtain sufficient and relevant quantitative data to make suitable recommendations	Develop reputation of putting client's interest first	Promote reputation, value, and business for financial planning services	Facilitate development of appropriate recommendations
	200-2 Obtaining quantitative information and documents				Develop, maintain and increase public confidence		
3	300-1 Analyzing and evaluating client's information	Jan 1, 2000 (revised on Jan 1, 2002)	Principle 2 Objectivity Rule 201 Rule 202	Make objective, prudent, reasonable, and competent judgment for the financial planning analysis in a diligent manner	Arouse awareness of financial planning issues	Enhance recognition and appreciation for financial planning services	Establish the foundation to formulate recommendations
			Principle 3 Competence Rule 302 Principle 7 Deligence Rule 701		Increase likelihood of client satisfaction	Increase confidence in presentation	

Table 2.1 (continued)

Step	Practice Standard series	Effective date	Code of Ethics	Purpose	Impact on public	Impact on profession	Impact on practitioner
4	400-1 Identifying and evaluating financial planning alternatives	Jan 1, 2001 (revised on Jan 1, 2002)	Principle 1 Integrity Rule 102	Identify alternatives and develop recommendations with objective judgment, professional competence, and diligence	Satisfy goals, needs, and priorities	Enhance public perception of objectivity, value, and professional reputation	Establish foundation to formulate meaningful and responsive solution
	400-2 Developing the financial planning recommendations		Principle 2 Objectivity Rule 201 Rule 202	Present recommendations with objective and professional judgment without false and deceptive statements			Increase likelihood for recommendation acceptance
	400-3 Presenting the financial planning recommendations	Jan 1, 2002	Principle 3 Competence Rule 302 Principle 6 Professionalism Rule 607 Rule 609 Principle 7 Diligence Rule 701 Rule 703 Rule 704				
5	500-1 Agreeing on implementation responsibilities		Principle 2 Objectivity Rule 202	Get mutual agreement with client on implementation responsibility and financial product selection with professional competence and diligence	Increase likelihood of client satisfaction	Increase professional credibility	Enhance long-term client-planner relationship

Table 2.1 (continued)

Step	Practice Standard series	Effective date	Code of Ethics	Purpose	Impact on public	Impact on profession	Impact on practitioner
	500-2 Selecting products and services for implementation		Principle 3 Competence Rule 302 Principle 4 Fairness Rule 402 Rule 409 Principle 6 Professionalism Rule 606 Rule 609 Principle 7 Diligence Rule 701 Rule 703 Rule 704				
6	600-1 Defining monitoring responsibilities	Jan 1, 2002	Principle 7 Diligence Rule 702	Monitor performance of financial plan with diligence	Arouse mutual responsibility for monitoring performance	Enhance the reputation of high service quality	Increase potential for client satisfaction

Examples of situations where financial planners face conflicts of interest include the following:

1. Holding jobs in more than one company.
2. Having to choose between serving the best interests of the clients or the best interests of the employer.
3. Accepting and offering gifts.
4. Misuse of information and company assets.
5. Trading with insider information.
6. Facing time constraints (e.g., having to prepare for a certification exam and meet a client's deadline at the same time).
7. Having to choose between being loyal to previous employer or to existing employer.
8. Churning a client's account to generate a higher fee.
9. Twisting (replacing an older (insurance) policy with a new one).

In most circumstances, an ethical situation involves many stakeholders who have vested interests in the issue. Stakeholders can be categorized into two major types: primary and secondary, in terms of the intimacy with the decision maker. Primary stakeholders are those who are more directly affected by the decisions made by the decision maker. The stakeholders that a financial planner comes in contact with make up five types of environment:

1. Personal environment (e.g., family members, peers).
2. Work environment (e.g., employer, colleagues, business partners, clients, competitors (i.e., other firms providing financial planning services).
3. Professional environment (e.g., professional bodies like the Financial Planning Association, CFP Board, and FPSB).
4. Governmental environment (e.g., trade unions, taxing authority, and legislative authorities—Securities and Exchange Commission (SEC), Insurance Authority).
5. Social environment (the general public).

For instance, if you happen to obtain price-sensitive information about a public-listed firm from a client, should you use the information to make a profit? Before you make your decision, you would consider the different bi-directional influences and vested interests of your stakeholders, such as the living standards, moral principles and values of your family (personal environment); corporate culture of your firm (work environment); code of ethics and reputation of your profession (professional environment); legal rules and regulations (governmental environment); and public trust and expectations (social environment).

Decision-making Models

An ethical problem involves a dilemma which requires you to make a choice among different alternatives. As ethical problems can be complex, we need to have a more structured analytical framework to understand and deal with them. A systematic decision-making model enables the decision maker to come to a decision with a reasonable and rational justification. The final decision may or may not be ethical, but at least a decision has been reached after a thorough analysis. We introduce two commonly used decision-making models in this section: American Accounting Association (AAA) Model (May 1990) and Mary Guy Model (Guy 1990).

American Accounting Association Model

The American Accounting Association model uses a seven-step approach:

1. Identify the facts.
2. Identify the ethical problem.
3. List the principles, rules, values, and objectives: social responsibility, utility, rights, justice, code of ethics, legal requirements, self-values.
4. Identify alternatives to solve the ethical dilemma.
5. Analyze and compare the principles and objectives identified in step 3 with the alternatives identified in step 4 to determine if you can reconcile the principles and objectives with the alternatives.
6. Evaluate the consequences of the alternatives.
7. Make the choice most appropriate for the ethical problem.

Mary Guy Model

There are ten steps in the Mary Guy Model:

1. Identify the ethical problem.
2. Identify the intention and objectives.
3. Identify all the relevant facts (who are involved in the ethical problem and how the ethical problem came up).
4. Identify the alternatives for the problem.
5. Analyze the appropriateness of the alternatives (benefits, costs, risks, rights, justice, virtues, legal requirements, self-values, professional code of conduct).
6. Remove the costly alternatives (those inconsistent with the moral values (virtues, right, justice) of the decision maker, those with too much costs and risks to afford).
7. Prioritize the alternatives (by using different decision criteria such as utilitarian approach, rights approach, justice approach, ethics of care approach, egoist approach, and by matching the alternatives with the legal and professional requirements).
8. Choose the most appropriate alternative.
9. Work out an overall solution for the problem.
10. Implement the solution of the problem.

Common Professional and Ethical Challenges for Financial Planners and Wealth Managers

Some activities can be legal without being ethical. However, if activities are illegal, most likely they are also unethical. A financial planner or a wealth manager has to conduct his duties professionally. If he violates the code of professional conduct and exceeds legal boundaries at the same time, it may mean the end of his career and even imprisonment. Thus professional conduct related to legal licenses is a serious matter. Even if he does not do anything illegal, a financial planner or a wealth manager's conduct should be ethical. Financial services firms of high repute may still penalize an unethical planner through disciplinary actions. In the long run, the success of financial planners and wealth managers largely depends on their reputation, which is closely related to ethical standards. We will now look at some practices from ethical, professional, and legal aspects.

Gifting

Accepting and offering gifts may or may not be ethical. Whether the action of gifting is ethical depends on the intention. If a gift is offered with certain conditions, it may be unethical. For instance, if the financial planner accepts gifts from clients in return for special and favorable treatment, a conflict of interests arises as the act of accepting the gifts affects the objective and independent judgment of the financial planner (the integrity and objectivity principles). If the financial planner offers gifts to clients, this act can be perceived as unfair treatment of different clients (fairness principle). However, not all gifting actions are unethical. Gifting may be an action to show courtesy, respect, concern, and care, particularly on special events such as a birthday and Christmas. Rejection of gifts may be perceived as a negative response to the kindness of others which may jeopardize social relationships.

Therefore, the act of gifting may create an ethical dilemma for financial planners. Should the financial planner present gifts to clients on occasions such as a birthday and New Year as a signal of concern and care in order to cultivate a better client-planner relationship? Should the financial planner reject the kindness of clients by refusing gifts? Barry (1986) provides a list of factors to evaluate the appropriateness of accepting and offering gifts:

1. Value of the gift (whether the value is substantial enough to impose undue influence and affect independent judgment).
2. Purpose of the gift (whether the gift is accompanied with a request for a favor).
3. Timing of the gift (whether the gift is for a special occasion such as a birthday, an anniversary, Christmas or New Year).
4. Position of the donor and donee (a gift from a subordinate (superior) to a superior (subordinate) is more (less) likely to be for a favor; gifts between staff members of competing firms can be suspected of being bribes for employee theft).
5. Culture of the profession and industry (whether it is an accepted practice in the profession and industry to accept and offer gifts; whether there is a code of practice governing the issue of gifting).
6. Culture of the company (whether it is an accepted practice in the company to accept and offer gifts; whether there is staff policy governing the issue of gifting).
7. Rules and regulations (whether there is a law regulating the issue of gifting).

Proprietary Information

People are free to choose their employment. It is not uncommon to job-hop. Professionals usually switch jobs within competing firms in the same field. For instance, a financial planner may move from a job in an insurance company to a job in a bank. There is always a concern that proprietary information of competing firms will be disclosed when an employee switches jobs. Proprietary information refers to private information about a firm that may concern the firm's future plans, company strategies, and client records.

If the ex-employee uses the proprietary information to negotiate for employment terms, such as a higher position and a better remuneration package in the new firm, such an act, without the consent of the ex-employer, is unethical as it is similar to employee theft. This theft of company information is in breach of the confidentiality principle owed to the employer. The confidentiality duty does not end with the agency relationship. The duty continues as long as the information is acquired or given during the course of the agency relationship.

However, are the experience and technical know-how gained from being employed in a company regarded as company property? The answer is, no. An employee's experience and reputation are accumulated through the years and could have come from previous employment. Skills and experience acquired are not proprietary information as they are part of the human capital belonging to the employee rather than being a part of company property.

Insider Trading

Insider trading refers to the use of private or inside information to conduct securities trading. Inside information is price-sensitive private information about the firm which is not available to outsiders. As the information is price-sensitive, the use of inside information to trade in the securities market usually enables the insider to make a profit or to avoid a loss.

As financial planners possess clients' personal data, they may get access to inside information. If the clients are managers and directors of publicly listed firms, there might be leakage of price-sensitive information about the prospects of the listed firms. In some cases, the manager-client or director-client may use his inside information as a gift to exchange for a favor from the financial planner. If the financial planner uses the information to trade or pass the information to others to trade in the securities market, it is an offense. Insider trading is unethical as it creates informational imbalance and violates the moral principles of right and justice. In addition, if the financial planner obtains the inside information without the consent of the clients, the financial planner is in breach of his fiduciary duty to keep information confidential.

Data Privacy

Used in a broader sense, inside information can also refer to the personal information obtained on a client. Because we disclose a vast amount of our personal information to different sorts of organizations (e.g., governmental and business organizations) for many reasons, there is a need to protect the information from being misused. During the financial planning process, financial planners have to obtain personal and financial data from their clients. Due to the right to privacy, which is protected by regulation in many countries, financial planners can only collect data that is helpful for the financial planning process. Financial planners have the responsibility to keep the data confidential and allow only authorized persons access to the data. The use of clients' personal information for other purposes without their consent breaches their right to privacy, which is a basic human right.

Client data are a valuable asset. Unscrupulous financial planners may "sell" the personal data of their clients to competing firms for a profit; they may misuse the personal data of their clients for non-financial-planning-related activities, or they may trade their client database with credit card companies, banks, or mobile phone companies for promotional purposes.

Ways to Manage Conflict of Interests

We have seen that conflict of interests can result in unethical behavior. Some common ways to manage conflict of interests include the following:

Compliance   Firms have formulated company policies and professional bodies have established codes of ethics to help professional practitioners to address their ethical problems in practice. Compliance with the standards of the company policy and ethical codes can help professionals manage conflicts of interest.

Avoidance   One way to minimize the chance of being involved in conflict of interest is to avoid any situations that would give rise to it. For example, financial planners should not borrow money from or lend money to their clients. Financial planners should also avoid the practice of moonlighting.

Disclosure   If, however, the financial planner still finds himself involved in a situation where there is conflict of interest, the best thing to do is to disclose the problem so that other parties involved in the situation can be aware of it. Disclosure means an openness of information and greater transparency. For example, if your client asks for your personal opinion of an accounting firm to provide auditing service, and your spouse is a partner of one of the two accounting firms for selection, you should disclose your personal relationship to avoid being accused of using confidential information to help your spouse.

Best Practices in Financial Planning

It is common for any profession to have principles and rules for practitioners so that they can provide services of the highest quality. Such principles and rules are known as practice standards. Practice standards in financial planning are designed to guide financial planners and financial services firms in conducting their financial services in the best interests of society. In countries where financial planning is still a relatively new concept, these practice standards are still under development. In such cases, professional organizations and financial services firms may establish a best practices manual, which is based on their own experience and research, to provide some guidelines for financial planning professionals to follow. However, the standards that they develop may not be universally accepted by the industry, but serve as an important road map to reach that goal.

Just following a set of legal requirements would not be enough to formulate best practices; ethical principles must also be taken into account. While different professional bodies may have different practice standards peculiar to their profession, all follow similar ethical guidelines. Well-developed financial planning practice standards are evolved from centuries of general and profession-specific practices believed to be the best way to conduct financial planning and wealth management.

There are two opposing schools of thought regarding the formulation of best practices. The first is based on theoretical and academic studies. The second, championed by pragmatists in financial services, emphasizes the practical aspects— how best to implement something in the most efficient manner. Consequently, best practices guides of different institutions and professional bodies vary quite a lot, reflecting these opposing schools of thought. Judging from the fact that the CFP Board just published its first set of practice standards in 2004, a country would take years, if not decades, to formulate its own practice standards.

Following best practices may not lead to immediate financial gains for financial planners. On the contrary, it may mean incurring more costs. Some financial planners may truly believe that following best practices is worthy of the cost and effort. Others may consider it as just a requirement to stay in business. Either way, it is important that financial planning bodies take the time to formulate practice standards that would enhance the reputation of the financial planning profession as a whole.

2.6 Ethical Conduct and the Financial Planning Profession in Asia

Ethical principles and standards are derived from cultural values and norms. The fundamental values of ethics in different cultures should be basically the same, such as the principles against murder and theft. However, some ethical principles are different among Americans, Europeans, Africans, and Asians, due to differences in cultural values (Vogel 1992). For instance, an American, because of his strong belief in the rights of the individual, tends to use his or her own moral values and standards to determine what is right. A European is more likely to consult the advice of others to reach a group, rather than an individual, ethical decision. An Asian will relate moral principles and responsibilities with relationships. The greatest contrast exists between East and West.

Most of the systems in Asian countries are built upon relationships. The development and maintenance of long-term relationships is characterized by reciprocity (a system of returning favors in order to preserve a balanced relationship). In most cases, ethical standards are relative and situational rather than absolute and universal (Gundling 1991). Although there are ethical principles governing the rule of right and wrong, they are applied on a case-by-case basis after consideration of the relationship factor. Therefore, there is concern for the professional conduct of financial planners in Asia.

One important key to success for financial planners is to develop and maintain good relationships (*guanxi*) with customers. However, the kind of good customer relationship concepts practiced in the Western world is different from that in Chinese society. In the traditional Chinese business world, the development of *guanxi*-based relationship constitutes an effective marketing tool to conduct business, to cultivate mutual trust, and to maintain long-term relationships (Luo 1997; Luo and Chen 1997; Wong and Chan 1999). The philosophical and cultural differences in the concepts of business ethical practices and *guanxi* between the Westerners and Chinese have aroused the concern of financial planning professional bodies and practitioners. It is important for financial planning professionals to seek a balance between enjoying good *guanxi* with their customers while observing high ethical standards.

Understanding *Guanxi* and Ethical Practices in Mainland China[12]

Guanxi is defined as a special kind of relationship, characterized by implicit rules, both of obligation and reciprocity (Luo 1997). Such a relationship can cultivate a highly complex network constituting a "highly differentiated intricate system of overt and covert, as well as formal and informal social subsets governed by the unwritten law of reciprocity" (Wilpert and Scharpf 1990). By its definition, good *guanxi* is not necessarily unethical. However, Westerners tend to regard *guanxi* as giving rise to unethical behavior and the maintenance of good *guanxi* as leading to more unethical practices (Li and Wright 1999; Snell 1999; Standifird and Marshall 2000).

Many research studies have been conducted to examine the importance and impact of *guanxi* on ethical behavior in Chinese business operations (Luo 1997; Luo and Chen 1997; Wong and Chan 1999; Wright, Szeto and Cheng 2001). A recent survey research of 850 Chinese executives, titled "The Dynamics of *Guanxi* and Ethics for Chinese Executives" by Chan, Cheng and Szeto (2002), reports that there are three distinct ethics-related attitudes and two distinct *guanxi*-related attitudes for Chinese executives. The three ethics-related attitudes are (1) emphasizing own benefits than laws, (2) exploring legal loopholes for profits, and (3) resisting official governance and regulations. The two factors associated with *guanxi* are (1) emphasizing profits more than friendship, and (2) giving favor and doing business within the *guanxi* network. Chinese executives can be classified into three groups: (1) unethical profit seeker, (2) anti-governance *guanxi* cultivator, and (3) apathetic executive, by their ethics and *guanxi* orientation. Some demographic characteristics such as age and ownership structure are significant factors influencing the attitudes of Chinese executives toward *guanxi* and ethics. Executives who are younger in age and *guanxi*-oriented tend to work for privately owned firms and joint ventures. More ethical executives, who follow rules and are less aggressive in business networking, are likely to work for state-owned firms.

---

[12] Previously published as "China's Financial Planning Ethics under Scrutiny," Cheng, L. and Szeto, R., *HK Financial Planner*, no. 3 (Autumn 2003): 28–30. *HK Financial Planner* permits the authors to retain their own copyright when the article is published.

The implications of these studies suggest that the concept of *guanxi* is inherent in the cultural values and business practices of most Chinese. Therefore, it is almost impossible to ignore the special role played by *guanxi* in any business operation. Financial planners may have to incorporate this concept into their marketing strategy when working with Chinese clients. On the other hand, being members of the financial planning profession, they are obliged to comply with the Code of Ethics and Professional Responsibility established by the CFP Board. Consequently, the need to develop good customer relationships and at the same time to observe ethical standards create a lot of potential ethical dilemmas for financial planners.

The four essential elements in cultivating *guanxi*—trust, favor, dependence, and adaptation—often lead to insider-based decision making (Wong 1998). The entire process of developing *guanxi* involves such practices as giving face and exchange of benefits, favors, and information. The mutual relationship developed creates reciprocal obligations that are almost impossible to refuse (Wong and Chan 1999; Yi and Ellis 2000). It appears that an inappropriate application of these *guanxi* elements would be in conflict with the strict compliance of ethical principles.

More specifically, financial planners practicing principles that are directly in conflict with the *guanxi* culture (e.g., the principles of fairness, confidentiality, and diligence) will face an uphill battle in China. After all, *guanxi* implies favoritism, having an inside scope, and privilege. Consequently, it will be very difficult for a financial planner to be fair if certain clients demand favoritism; to keep information confidential if senior executives and influential clients demand to know confidential inside information; and to practice due diligence if it is acceptable for society to allow certain higher level individuals to enjoy privileges and not follow certain rules.

So it appears that practicing financial planning professionally and ethically in Mainland China is extremely difficult, if not impossible. Because of insufficient public awareness of the importance of ethical behavior and a lack of government regulations in upholding ethical and professional standards, financial planners in China will be very tempted to do what may seem acceptable (but is unethical or even illegal) to enhance their business. By doing so, there is no doubt that financial planners can start their business and expand their market share more quickly. Nevertheless, let us not forget that financial planning is a lifelong career. No matter how seemingly successful a financial planner is at the early stages of his career, what is more important is to be able to keep his business thriving till the end of his professional life.

We have seen many cases where successful, well-established financial services professionals lost everything due to some unethical practices conducted when they were young. Financial planners should not strive for short-term profit generated by unethical and unprofessional practices. They should instead focus on long-term prosperity. The reputation of a professional and ethical financial planning practitioner will eventually bring in a strong base of loyal clients and healthy income for the business. We are convinced that financial planners with high ethical standards will be the true winners in the profession.

APPLICATION CORNER

ISO Technical Committee TC/222 Standard on Global Financial Planning (Preliminary Edition)[13]

Ethics

According to the standards of the ISO Technical Committee TC/222 (draft ISO document section 5), ethical behavior, which goes beyond compliance with applicable rules and regulations, is at the core of the financial planning profession for the primary benefit of the clients. Ten ethical principles are suggested:

Principle 1: Behave with integrity

Characteristics of integrity include honesty, responsiveness, accountability, commitment to competence, reliability, fairness, and being open and responsible.

Principle 2: Put client's interest first

The legitimate interests of the clients should be paramount.

Principle 3: Exercise due care and diligence

The professional activities should be conducted with due skill, care, diligence, and competence.

Principle 4: Work within regulatory and legislative frameworks

The relevant rules, regulations, and standards of professional good practice should be observed.

Principle 5: Carefully manage conflicting interests

Conflicts of interest should be fully disclosed and fairly managed.

Principle 6: Communicate in a clear and appropriate manner

Information and recommendation about the financial plan should be conveyed in an understandable, effective, and constructive manner.

Principle 7: Provide suitable and objective recommendations

The recommended solutions should be objective to fit the needs of the clients.

---

[13] The information here is derived from the draft provided by the ISO Technical Committee TC/222 for public consultation during the summer of 2004. The content should be viewed as an indication of the direction taken by the ISO Technical Committee TC/222. The final ISO standard is now available for purchase at the ISO website.

Principle 8: Protect client confidentiality

The financial planners owe a duty of confidentiality to their clients unless they are subject to regulatory and legislative obligations.

Principle 9: Disclosure

Accurate and relevant information such as statement of qualification and credentials about the financial planners should be disclosed.

Principle 10: Appropriate competence

The financial planners should not accept and perform services of which they are incompetent unless they have the counsel of other qualified individuals.

Recognizing, valuing, and applying these suggested ethical principles in daily financial planning service is of fundamental importance to the professional life of a financial planner. Ethical decision-making ability can be developed and enhanced through experience and sharing.

Competence

According to the international standards of competence specified by the ISO Technical Committee TC/222 (draft ISO document section 6), there are three components of the competence requirement: core competence, demonstration of initial competence, and demonstration of continuing competence. These competence requirements ensure that the financial planners have the cognitive, understanding, application, analysis, and evaluation ability to perform qualified financial planning services.

There are general and specific requirements for core competence. The general requirements are that the financial planners must have a broad and general knowledge of the rules and regulations imposed by the legal and professional bodies; understand the scope of their engagement; render appropriate services; recognize their limitations; and seek the counsel of other professionals when necessary.

The specific requirements are that the financial planners must have the ability to apply their knowledge and skill to the various steps of the financial planning process. In the first step of the financial planning process (establishing client-planner relationships), the expected task of the financial planners is to assist their clients to establish reasonable expectations. For such a purpose, the financial planners need to understand the nature and scope of the engagement. In order to accomplish the expected task, the financial planners should have excellent communication skills to explain the mutual expectations of the engagement so as to build up a client-planner relationship.

In the next step of gathering client data and determining goals, the financial planners are required to collect both financial (past, current, and expected future income, expenditures, assets and liabilities) and nonfinancial (health, gender, age, lifestyle, occupation, marital status, family needs and priorities) data; relevant information for financial plans (insurance, investment, retirement, gifting, tax, and estate), and financial risk capacity and tolerance level of their clients so as to develop quantitative and qualitative goals in a comprehensive analysis. In order to establish and determine the goals, the financial planners need to have a broad general knowledge of data collection processes, financial and economic concepts, investment choices, and life-cycle stages. Therefore, the financial planners have to possess the ability of collecting data accurately, identifying objectives clearly, and explaining goals effectively.

In the third step, the data of the clients collected in step two are analyzed. The financial planners are expected to prepare a time-line for life events. They are to incorporate the economic, market, social, and tax factors to analyze the implications of current and projected net worth and cash flow statements of the clients in order to evaluate their needs in investment, risk management, insurance, tax planning, retirement, and estate planning. To handle the expected task, the specific requirements for core competence are that the financial planners should have the analytical competence to integrate the economic, market, and social factors with the individual financial strengths and weaknesses of the clients. Through the analysis process, the financial planners are able to evaluate the sufficiency of, or need for, current investment, risk management, insurance, tax planning, retirement and estate planning, and overall financial plans.

The fourth step is to develop and present the financial plan recommendations to the clients. Financial planners are expected to integrate the various financial plan components (investment decisions, risk management plan, insurance plan, tax strategies, retirement plan, and estate plan) and to obtain the properly informed commitment to proceed with the comprehensive financial plan. To accomplish this, the financial planners should possess knowledge of the relevant individual and corporate taxation laws, the concepts of risk management, insurance and personal financial risk tolerance, private, business and government retirement programs, and estate planning techniques. In addition, the financial planners need to have the ability to evaluate alternative proposals of various financial plan components professionally, to compile various components logically, to explain the most appropriate comprehensive financial plan effectively, and to obtain the clients' agreement to proceed with the recommendation.

When mutual agreement is obtained, the financial planners can prepare the necessary documentation to carry out the plan. In the fifth step, the financial planners have to be familiar with the various applicable legal and regulatory requirements, the implementation procedures and the means to seek counsel from other professionals. To achieve these expected tasks in the implementation step, the skills to communicate, coordinate, review, and reconcile the implementation strategies are essential specific requirements for core competence.

In the last step of the financial planning process, the financial planners are required to monitor the changes in market, economic, regulatory, legislative, and political environments as well as the changes in their clients' personal circumstances (needs, objectives, and risk tolerance level) on an ongoing basis. In the monitoring process, the financial planners need to possess the competence to recognize the impact of changes on the implemented financial plan. In some circumstances, the financial planners are expected to update and revise the financial plan accordingly and to explain the modifications to the clients.

The second component of the competence requirement is the ability to demonstrate initial competence. The certification bodies have to set up methods and indicators to measure the performance, knowledge, understanding, application, and skills of the financial planner. There are two principal assessment and evaluation means suggested by the ISO Technical Committee TC/222: third party assessment and evaluation process. The third party assessment can be in the form of a written examination, a multiple choice examination, or a portfolio of evidence (including individual performance measurements, random examination of complete files of current clients, case studies, oral assessments, client satisfaction surveys, work-based assessments, and scripted answer examinations). The performance of the financial planner can be ascertained through an evaluation process to check if the financial planner is compliant with the competence level proposed by the professional standards.

After the financial planners have met the requirements for core competence and initial competence, the last competence requirement is the ability to demonstrate continuing competence. Continuing competence can be expressed in the lifelong commitment to continuing education. There are various means by which the financial planners can demonstrate their ongoing commitment to continuously update themselves, e.g., by attending courses, conferences, seminars, workshops, group studies, and symposiums; and by writing professional articles and books.

Key Terms

consumption planning *48*

estate planning *48*

financial planning areas *48*

insurance planning *48*

investment planning *48*

retirement planning *48*

tax planning *48*

References

Arrow, K. J., "Business Codes and Economic Efficiency," Public Policy 21 (Summer 1973).

Barry, V., *Moral Issues in Business* (Belmont, CA: Wadsworth Publishing, 1986).

Bayles, M. D., *Professional Ethics* (Belmont, CA: Wadsworth Publishing, 1989).

Bayles, M. D., *Contemporary Utilitarianism* (Garden City, NY: Doubleday and Co., 1968).

Carroll, A. B., "A Three-dimensional Conceptual Model of Corporate Performance," *Academy of Management Review*, vol. 4 (1979): 497–505.

Chan, Y. K., Cheng, T. W., and Szeto, W. F., "The Dynamics of *Guanxi* and Ethics for Chinese Executives," *Journal of Business Ethics*, vol. 41, no. 3 (2002): 327–336.

Chieffe, N. and Rakes, G. K., "An Integrated Model for Financial Planning," *Financial Services Review*, vol. 8 (1999): 261–268.

Collins, J. W., "Is Business Ethics an Oxymoron?" (Editorial) (Cover Story), *Business Horizon*, vol. 37, no. 5 (September/October 1994): 1–8.

Dillon, R. S., "Care and Respect," in *Explorations in Feminist Ethics: Theory and Practice*, Cole, E. B. and Coultrap-McQuin, S., eds. (Bloomington and Indianapolis: Indiana University Press, 1992).

Gundling, E., "Ethics and Working with the Japanese: The Entrepreneur and the Elite Course," *California Management Review*, vol. 33 (1991): 25–39.

Guy, M., *Ethical Decision Making in Everyday Work Situations* (New York: Quorum Books, 1990).

Kant, I., *Groundwork of the Metaphysics of Morals*, Paton, H. J., trans. (New York: Harper & Row, 1964).

Li, J. and Wright, P., "The Issue of *Guanxi*: Discrepancies, Reality and Implications," BRC Working Paper 99036 (Hong Kong: School of Business, Business Research Center, Hong Kong Baptist University, Hong Kong, September, 1999).

Luo, Y., *Guanxi*: Principles, Philosophies and Implications, *Human Systems Management*, vol. 16, no. 1 (1997): 43–52.

Luo, Y. and Chen, M., "Does *Guanxi* Influence Firm Performance?" *Asia Pacific Journal of Management*, vol. 14, no. 1 (1997): 1–17.

May, W., *Ethics in the Accounting Curriculum: Cases and Readings* (Florida: American Accounting Association, 1990).

McCloskey, H. J., "Rights," *The Philosophical Quarterly*, vol. 15 (1965): 115–127.

McDonald, G. M., "Common Myths about Business Ethics: Perspectives from Hong Kong," *Business Ethics*, vol. 4 (1995): 96–101.

Mellinger, D. K., "Philanthropy: A Strategy for Acquiring and Serving High Net Worth Clients," *Journal of Financial Planning Association* (June 14, 2002).

Organizers of the Professional Ethics Program for the Securities, Futures and Investments Sectors, *A Practical Guide for Financial Practitioners*, English version (March 2004).

Paine, L. S., "Law, Ethics and Managerial Judgment," *Journal of Legal Studies Education*, vol. 12 (1994): 153–169.

Rawls, J., *A Theory of Justice* (Cambridge: Harvard University Press, The Belknap Press 1971).

Sen, A. and Williams, B., *Utilitarianism and Beyond* (New York: Cambridge University Press, 1982).

Singer, M. G., *Generaliztion in Ethics* (New York: Alfred A. Knopf, 1961).

Snell, R., "Obedience to Authority and Ethical Dilemmas in Hong Kong Companies," *Business Ethics Quarterly*, vol. 9, no. 3 (1999): 507–526.

Standifird, S. and Marshall, R., "The Transaction Cost Advantage of *Guanxi*-Based Business Practices," *Journal of World Business*, vol. 35, no. 1 (2000): 21–43.

Vogel, D., "The Globalization of Business Ethics: Why America Remains Distinctive," *California Management Review*, vol. 35 (1992): 30–49.

Wilpert, B. and Scharpf, S. Y., "Intercultural Management: Joint Ventures in the People's Republic of China," *International Journal of Psychology*, vol. 25 (1990): 643–656.

Wong, Y. H., "The Dynamics of *Guanxi* in China," *Singapore Management Review*, vol. 20, no. 2 (1998): 25–43.

Wong, Y. H. and Chan, R. Y. K., "Relationship Marketing in China: *Guanxi*, Favoritism and Adaptation," *Journal of Business Ethics*, vol. 22, no. 2 (1999): 107–118.

Wright, P., Szeto, W. F., and Cheng, T. W., "*Guanxi* and Professional Conduct in China: A Management Development Perspective," *The International Journal of Human Resource Management*, vol. 12, no. 8 (2001): 1–27.

Yi, L. and Ellis, P., "Insider-outsider Perspective of *Guanxi*," *Business Horizon*, vol. 43, no. 1 (2000): 25–31.

Questions & Problems

Multiple-choice Questions

1. The rule, "A Certified Financial Planner™ shall not solicit clients through false or misleading communication or advertisements," is related to which of the following principles of the Professional Code of Ethics of the CFP Board?
   A. Integrity
   B. Fairness
   C. Professionalism
   D. Diligence

2. The steps of the financial planning process include which of the following?
   I. Establishing client-planner relationships
   II. Analyzing and evaluating the client's financial status
   III. Putting strategies of financial planning together
   IV. Developing and presenting the financial plan recommendations
   V. Monitoring the financial plan recommendations

   A. I, II, and IV
   B. I, IV, and V
   C. I, II, IV, and V
   D. I, II, III, IV, and V

3. Which of the following are the principles that apply to all CERTIFIED FINANCIAL PLANNER™ certificants under the Professional Code of Ethics of the CFP Board?
   I.   Objectivity
   II.   Competence

III. Fairness
IV. Confidentiality
V. Loyalty
VI. Professionalism
VII. Diligence
VIII. Conservatism

A. I, II, III, IV, and VI
B. I, II, III, IV, VI, and VII
C. I, III, IV, VI, VII, and VIII
D. I, II, III, IV, V, VI, VII, and VIII

4. Which of the following are the key areas of the personal financial planning process?
I. Insurance
II. Consumption
III. Investment arbitrage
IV. Psychological fulfillment
V. Taxation
VI. Retirement
VII. Estate planning

A. I, V, VI, and VII
B. I, II, III, V, and VI
C. I, II, V, VI, and VII
D. I, II, III, IV, V, VI, and VII

5. Even if not required legally, a financial planner with high professional and ethical standards should disclose the following information:
I. Commissions
II. Restrictions relating to the ability to execute investment transactions
III. Potential financial interest between the advisor and the product provider
IV. Any cash rebate from recommending certain financial products

A. I and IV
B. I, II, and III
C. II, III, and IV
D. I, II, III, and IV

Problems

1. List the major planning areas of financial planning.

2. Describe the seven principles of the Professional Code of Ethics of the CFP Board.

3. What are the responsibilities to clients mentioned by Bayles (1989)?

4. Explain the challenges of practicing ethical financial planning in Asia.

5. Describe the concept of best practices in financial planning.

chapter **3**

Essential Concepts in Economics and Finance

Learning Objectives

After studying this chapter you should be able to:

1 Understand the relationship between major macroeconomic variables and financial planning.
2 Differentiate between money markets and capital markets.
3 Know the US stock markets and some major market indices.
4 Grasp the meaning of various investment vehicles.
5 Review the concepts of time value of money.

In this chapter we introduce some basic but critical economic and finance concepts that financial planners and wealth managers need to comprehend before they can conduct financial planning for clients.

3.1 Relationship between Macroeconomic Factors and Financial Planning

There is an important link between macroeconomic conditions and financial planning. When macroeconomic conditions change, the corresponding financial planning strategy must be modified. For instance, if long-term interest rate rises, the investment strategy on fixed income securities may need to be changed to capture the highest interest rate, leading to a reallocation of invested capital from other asset classes such as equity to long-term bonds. In other words, we should understand how macroeconomic factors and financial planning strategies are linked. While a more detailed discussion on this topic will be provided in Chapter 11 (Steps 5 and 6: Implementing and Monitoring the Financial Plan), we will briefly discuss this relationship here.

Economic conditions can be measured by different indicators. For instance, a recession driven by a substantial decline in exports for an export-oriented economy such as Australia and Japan can be damaging to the shipping and transportation industries in these countries. On the other hand, during recession and high unemployment, the education sector (especially vocational training programs and graduate programs) may benefit as people tend to believe additional education is needed to enhance the human capital during times of economic turbulence. Financial planners should try to understand how poor economic conditions affect different occupations so that they can evaluate their clients' financial plans better.

Very often, poor economic conditions are accompanied by poor stock market performance. Investors' confidence in the stock market and their risk tolerance level can be affected by their own job security and labor income. If clients have a lot of purchasing power in terms of investment and the overall market is devalued due to irrational sentiment, it is possible for these clients to invest more in undervalued securities. In short, financial planners should set up their own system for monitoring these variables and implement appropriate strategies for clients of different backgrounds and investment profiles.

Changes in government policies related to taxes on personal income, business income, property, and estate can directly affect the financial planner's strategies on tax planning, retirement planning, investment portfolio, and estate planning. They can also indirectly affect insurance strategies and consumption planning for clients as well. Monetary policies on interest rate and exchange rate can also affect inflation, property prices, investment returns, and the affordability of mortgage.

Where investment strategies are concerned, it is difficult to predict market conditions precisely. Financial planners should remember the principles of diversification and focus on long-term investment strategies. A continuous monitoring of market conditions to avoid substantial losses in a major market crash is much more important than speculating on the upside potential of the market.

In order to provide financial planning services to clients, financial planners and wealth managers, apart from knowing clients' personal financial situations, need to understand basic macroeconomic factors so that they can choose the most suitable investment portfolios for their clients in different economic environments.

While there are many economic variables affecting financial planning, it is not feasible for us to give a detailed explanation for all variables involved. In this chapter we will discuss eight macroeconomic factors that affect financial planning. They are (1) gross domestic product (GDP); (2) unemployment rate; (3) population demographics; (4) fiscal and monetary policies; (5) interest rate; (6) price level; (7) foreign exchange rate; and (8) business cycle.

Gross Domestic Product (GDP)

gross domestic product (GDP) The total market value of the production of goods and services within a geographic location during a specified time period.

Whether a country is prosperous or in bad shape economically has a huge impact on the personal income level, consumption level, and most important of all, confidence level of consumers in the future of their own wealth. Thus it is extremely critical for financial planners to know the general condition of the economy. A commonly used economic indicator for such a purpose is the **gross domestic product (GDP)**.

GDP is the total market value of the production of goods and services within a geographic location during a specified time period, usually a year. It is a common indicator used to determine the economic welfare of a country. A market with a growing GDP indicates that the economy of the country is expanding.

The growth in GDP indicates that there are increases in consumption expenditure, investment levels, government spending, and net exports. Increases in these factors are indicators of economic growth and consumer public confidence. As financial planners, we need to understand that the confidence of clients in their own financial future is an emotional but important input to consider in our construction of their financial plans.

In an economic recession, people will be more risk-averse. They become more uncertain about their future income and hence prefer to save more and reduce consumption and investment spending. In such a situation financial planners should make appropriate recommendations for clients. For instance, when clients are in need of money, financial planners may recommend that they withdraw the cash value of their insurance policies.

On the contrary, if the economy is strong, the consumer public is willing to spend and invest more. In preparing financial plans for clients, financial planners can take advantage of this sentiment and help them to set aside more money in savings and for their retirement needs. In good times when the stock market is rocketing, some clients may even suggest that their financial planners put a high percentage of their retirement money in risky investments. Such overoptimistic behavior of underestimating investment risk in bull market conditions is not uncommon; financial planners need to be aware of this and advise their clients accordingly.

Unemployment Rate

unemployment rate
Measures the percentage of the labor force that is out of work.

The **unemployment rate** measures the percentage of the labor force that is out of work and is seeking jobs actively. In terms of employment statistics, we can classify an individual into one of three categories: employed, unemployed, or not in the labor force. There are three major causes of unemployment: frictional unemployment, structural unemployment, and cyclical unemployment.

Frictional unemployment refers to the normal turnover of employees who are in the course of searching for new jobs. There is always an incentive among employees to look for better jobs. Frictional unemployment can never be eliminated, no matter if the economy is in prosperity or in recession.

In a situation where there is a mismatch between the skills possessed by employees and the job specifications required in the labor market, structural unemployment is the inevitable result. It is difficult to reduce structural unemployment unless the unemployed and redundant workers are retrained to equip themselves with the new skills and abilities required in the labor market.

Cyclical unemployment occurs because of changes in the economy. The employment rate is higher when the economy is good. However, in times of economic downturn, there may be insufficient job vacancies, thus causing a high rate of cyclical unemployment.

In addition, financial planners should understand that different industries have different industry life cycles, leading to different unemployment rates during the same time. For instance, traditional maturing industries such as chemical and petroleum firms in the United States may have a relatively stable employment outlook (keeping in mind that there are always seasonal fluctuations in the required labor force from year to year). Thus, a typical employee with an average performance working in these industries would not expect a fast-track promotion due to the expansion of the industry. On the other hand, right before the burst of the IT bubble, the average IT engineer in a medium-sized IT firm in Silicon Valley easily got a quick promotion and pay raise by simply moving around.

Financial planners should try to understand the effect of overall and industry-specific unemployment rates on their clients' job security. One major assumption of retirement plan calculation is that clients will enjoy a certain level of income from the planning year till retirement. Unexpected unemployment will cause a major problem in the accumulation of retirement funds.

Finally, the ability to maintain employment is also related to the personal ability and personality of the clients. Financial planners should remember that the employment status of clients is a key factor in financial planning.

Population Demographics

population demographics Reflect various aspects of consumers such as their gender, age, education level, and income level.

Population demographics reflect various aspects of consumers such as their gender, age, education level, and income level. All these characteristics are useful information for individual financial planners or financial planning firms to form their strategies in marketing and promoting their products. These demographic characteristics also help financial planners to identify their target market.

For instance, government and social welfare agencies may have difficulties in meeting the pension needs of an aging population. Countries with an aging problem need more pension funds to support the retired population. If the public pension system is not able to fund retirement properly, then financial planners should be aware of this issue when making financial plans for their clients. Proper research is needed to understand the demographics of the population so that effective strategies can be adopted by financial planners in promoting and implementing their services.

Fiscal and Monetary Policies

fiscal policy Refers to government spending patterns and tax initiatives in order to stabilize and manage the market and economy.

monetary policy Refers to the strategies related to money supply and interest rate changes implemented by the central bank to manage the market and economy.

The government can achieve a targeted budget position through two major means: by adopting a fiscal policy and a monetary policy. A **fiscal policy** refers to government spending patterns and tax initiatives so as to change the level of total national consumption and investment in order to stabilize and manage the market and economy. A **monetary policy** refers to the strategies related to money supply and interest rate changes implemented by the central bank, which determines the interest rate and the money supply in the market. The central bank in the United States is the Federal Reserve Bank.

As the economy expands, it is possible that it may become overheated, leading to inflation and high prices. In an economic recession, companies' earnings are generally down and the corporate sector is not willing to invest in capital stock. In view of this, the government may exercise various fiscal and monetary policies to bring the economy back to a healthier or more acceptable condition. Depending on the dominant school of thought employed by national economic advisors, a combination of tax, government spending control, money supply, and interest rate manipulation may be used by the central bank and government agencies to achieve the necessary economic objectives.

While the effects of some of these measures (such as a tax cut or government spending) would take a long time to realize, other measures (such as money supply and interest rate) may have a quicker impact on the economy. A financial planner's job is not only to assess the effectiveness of government policy on the economy, but he or she also needs to understand the effects of these policies on the cost of living, return on investment, and job security of clients.

Interest Rate

interest rate The opportunity cost of holding money or the compensation required by lenders for the use of money.

The **interest rate** is the opportunity cost of holding money or compensation required by lenders from borrowers for the use of money. The interest paid to lenders is to compensate for the late possession of money. Hence, interest rate can be interpreted as the earning power of money. The interest rate is determined by the demand and supply of money in the money market. The interest rate increases when the demand for money increases, and decreases when the demand for it decreases. On the contrary, the interest rate decreases when the supply of money increases, and increases when the supply of money decreases. Money can be used either for investment or for personal consumption. Therefore, there should be a cost for borrowing money and early consumption. In other words, the interest rate is the opportunity cost of holding money.

The interest rate is an important factor in financial planning. For instance, an increase in interest rate will immediately increase the cost of borrowing for both corporations and individuals, making loan payments higher for those who finance their home purchase through mortgage. On the other hand, a high interest rate also leads to a higher return on fixed-income securities. Thus, the net effect of an interest rate hike on clients would depend on whether they have more fixed-income assets or outstanding loans. While understanding the full impact of interest rates on financial planning requires advanced training in economics and finance, a competent financial planner should at least realize the fact that there is a close relationship between interest rate changes and financial planning deliverables. If financial planners are not comfortable in this area, they should acknowledge their limitation and seek additional help from other investment professionals so that appropriate recommendations can be given to clients.

Price Level

price level Reflects the general price level of goods and services, and is an indication of the cost of living.

The **price level** is determined by the overall prices of goods and services. Inflation is a time when there is a rise in the general price level for a certain period while deflation is a time when there is a fall in the general price level for a certain period. The inflation rate is the rate at which prices are increasing. If the inflation rate keeps on rising rapidly, the economic situation is called hyperinflation. There are some price indices measuring price levels in the economy. The consumer price index (CPI) and GDP deflator are two such indices.

The price level reflects the general price level of goods and services and is an indication of the cost of living. The estimation of the inflation rate using expected CPI changes is essential for predicting the amount of retirement funds needed for clients. Some assets such as real estate and gold are regarded as good tools to hedge for inflation. However, there is always a time lag between real estate prices and the economic cycle. Financial planners have to be very careful in employing the correct inflation rate for financial planning analysis. Most countries have financial institutions conducting inflation forecasts and making them available to the public, and financial planners should keep track of this information to make sure that up-to-date forecasts are used.

Foreign Exchange Rate

foreign exchange rate The ratio that reflects the value of the home currency relative to a foreign currency.

The foreign exchange rate is the ratio that reflects the value of the home currency relative to a foreign currency. The **foreign exchange rate** is important as it is one of the factors affecting the competitiveness of international trade between countries. As the foreign exchange rate fluctuates, the dollar price of the goods and services valued in foreign currency varies. For instance, in a trade between a European country and the United States, when the exchange rate of the euro against the US dollar decreases from 1 US dollar per euro to 1.25 US dollars per euro, the United States may be discouraged from importing goods from the European country as it needs to pay more for the same quantity of goods, other things being equal.

For high net-worth clients, it is not uncommon to invest in foreign currencies and overseas securities. In this case, financial planners would need to understand the effect of currency fluctuation on the value of clients' portfolios. They must hedge the currency risk for their clients. In fact, many mutual fund and portfolio managers acknowledge that one of the major reasons for their investments in overseas markets is to bet on the currency appreciation as well as the capital gains from securities. Consequently, financial planners can view buying foreign currencies as an additional investment channel for sophisticated and wealthy clients. On the other hand, exchange rate movements can also create problems for clients if they have overseas financial obligations such as college tuition fees. Financial planners should conduct a thorough investigation of the clients' goals, assets, and liabilities to better determine the exchange rate risk that clients face.

Business Cycle

business cycle Depicts the patterns of various economic conditions through time.

The **business cycle** depicts the pattern of various economic conditions through time. There are four different phases or transition points in the business cycle: trough, expansion, peak, and recession. The knowledge of business cycles is important for financial planners. Financial planners may have to adjust the financial plans for their clients under different stages of the business cycle. The business cycle affects financial planning in two ways. First, it affects the job security of clients. If the industry is phasing out in a certain city where clients are located, their employability may be in danger unless they are willing to move to another location. Relocation of clients may mean that a financial planner can no longer serve his or her clients as they may want a planner physically close to them. In addition, owing to the potential loss of jobs, the investment portfolios of clients may have to be restructured to a less risky asset allocation to reflect the risk of human capital. Financial planners will also need to communicate with their clients about the potential changes in their financial conditions under the different stages of the business cycle; hence the requirement for adjustments in their financial plans.

Second, the business cycle affects the performance of firms and therefore, the price of stocks. Equity prices are subject to the business cycle of the whole economy, the industry, and the firm itself. Securities analysis must take into account the effects of the business cycle on earnings of firms so that better investment choices can be identified for clients. For instance, financial planners may adjust the proportion of equity investment in the portfolio of clients when the business cycle is in the expansion or peak stage. If financial planners believe that stocks are overvalued during this expansionary period, they should adjust the equity portion downward. In contrast, if financial planners believe that stocks are undervalued and the prices hit bottom in times of recession, they may have to recommend making more investments in equity.

When financial planners prepare personal financial plans for their clients, they should take into account the relationship between macroeconomic conditions and financial planning inputs and deliverables. In this chapter we have briefly explained with some examples how macroeconomic factors such as GDP, unemployment rate, population demographics, fiscal and monetary policies, interest rate, price level, foreign exchange rate, and business cycle are concerns for financial planners in the financial planning process.

The relationship between financial planning and economic variables is extremely complicated. The relationship is so dynamic and integrated that it is almost impossible for financial planners to precisely predict the effects of the changes in these variables on the financial well-being of their clients. However, it is still the responsibility of competent financial planners to try their best to explore the potential effects and adjust their financial advice accordingly.

3.2 Financial Market Operation

The Global Financial Market

Currently, the US equity markets remain the largest in the world. However, the Asian markets are catching up fast. The market value of the largest stock exchange, the New York Stock Exchange, is approximately five times the size of the Tokyo Stock Exchange. In addition, the size of the Toronto Stock Exchange is similar to that of the Hong Kong Exchanges. The rapid expansion of the Hong Kong market is mainly due to the H-share IPO listings from huge Mainland firms. The improving market capitalization and liquidity of Asian markets allow US and European funds to trade Asian stocks without worrying about a liquidity problem.

For simplicity, we can divide the world into the developed market and the emerging market. This classification gives us a simple way to identify two equity asset classes with similar risk-return characteristics within a class while having very different risk-return characteristics across classes. Developed markets include the North American, Pacific and European regions. Currently, developed markets provide excellent returns within a relatively safe environment for investors. If an investor is willing to take additional risk, then emerging markets would definitely be a viable choice for long-term investment. Emerging Market Asia (including China, India, and Thailand), Emerging Market Eastern Europe (including Czech Republic, Hungary, Poland, and Russia), Emerging Market Latin America (including Argentina, Brazil, and Mexico) are good examples of emerging market segments. Currently, the returns for these emerging markets are extremely impressive. However, it is important to remember that the underlying risk for emerging markets is high.

No matter what markets we want to invest in, the investment vehicles and products in the different regions follow similar trading mechanisms and regulations. Since the financial planning process involves making investment recommendations for the clients in various types of financial plans (e.g., investment plans, education plans, and retirement plans), financial planners have to familiarize themselves with the financial market and various types of financial instruments such as stocks, bonds, treasury bills, mutual funds, and pension funds. A successful financial planner should have a clear understanding of these financial market terms so that a more appropriate personal financial plan can be devised. In this chapter we introduce the basic concepts and elements of the financial market.

Primary Market and Secondary Market

The stock market is composed of a primary market and a secondary market. The market for trading newly issued securities such as stocks or bonds is called the primary market or new-issue market. The usual players in the primary market are the government, financial institutions like investment banks, and the public. The newly issued securities in the primary market form the basis of the circulating market.

The secondary or stock circulating market is a market for trading securities that have been issued. The secondary market warrants the existence and development of the primary market and maintains the enthusiasm of the investors in capital turnover and flexibility in circulation.

The New York Stock Exchange is one of the largest secondary markets in the world, with the highest trading volume. In 2003, the average daily trading value of the New York Stock Exchange was over US$35,000 million. The major players in the secondary market are brokers and dealers. Brokers or dealers act as middlemen in the stock exchange; they match the requests of buyers and sellers for making deals at stated prices. The trading transactions in the secondary markets are usually traded over-the-counter (OTC). Trading over-the-counter means that securities dealers buy stocks from their clients and sell stocks to their clients at stated prices. Many different types of financial instruments can be traded on OTC markets, including stocks, government bonds, banker's acceptances, negotiable certificates of deposit, foreign currencies and federal funds.

Money Market and Capital Market

money market A network or platform for trading short-term financial instruments with maturity of equal to or less than one year.

The **money market** is a network or platform for trading financial instruments of short-term debt obligation of corporations and governments with a maturity of equal to or less than one year. Examples of financial instruments traded on the money markets are US treasury bills, negotiable bank certificates of deposit, and commercial paper. The money market is an ideal trading market for investors

capital market A network or platform for trading long-term financial instruments with maturity of more than one year.

with short-term surplus funds and a short investment horizon as investors can withdraw their capital within a short period of time: money market instruments are highly liquid. In addition, money market instruments are attractive investment alternatives as they yield a higher return as compared to the return from bank savings.

The **capital market** is a network or platform for trading financial instruments with maturity of more than one year. Financial instruments traded on the capital market include corporate bonds, stocks, government bonds, and residual mortgage. The capital market provides long-term investment opportunities for investors with a longer investment horizon. Capital market instruments usually yield higher returns than money market instruments. While money market instruments are more susceptible to the fluctuation of interest rates, capital market instruments are not. In addition, compared to the money market, the capital market is less volatile.

Major Stock Markets in the World

The market capitalization of the listed firms is often used as the indicator to determine the stage of development of a stock market. Table 3.1 shows the total market capitalization of listed firms in some countries as at June 30, 2007. The largest market capitalization of listed firms is in the US stock market. The value of market capitalization in the US is US$16,603,601 million, which is approximately 3.5 times the size of that in Japan. Hong Kong ranked fifth with a market capitalization of US$2,027,998 million.

Table 3.1 Market capitalization of some main stock markets as of June 30, 2007

Countries	Market capitalization (US$ million)
The United States (New York Stock Exchange)	16,603,601
Japan (Tokyo Stock Exchange)	4,681,046
Euronext (Comprises stock exchanges in Amsterdam)	4,240,062
The United Kingdom (London Stock Exchange)	4,036,986
Hong Kong (HKEx)	2,027,998
Canada (Toronto Stock Exchange)	1,980,839
Germany (Deutsche Börse)	1,956,079
China (Shanghai Stock Exchange)	1,693,017
Australia (Australian Securities Exchange)	1,355,556
Singapore (Singapore Exchange)	505,589
China (Shenzhen Stock Exchange)	490,464

Source: February 3, 2008, World Federation of Exchanges (http://www.world-exchanges.org/publications/EQU1107.pdf).

Stock Market Indices

In all stock markets, there are stock market indices. A stock index is a measurement indicator of the stock market. The function of a stock index is to provide a reference benchmark for the measurement of price changes in the stock market. With the aid of a stock market index, investors can observe and analyze the development dynamics of the stock market; they can study the investment trends of the market; and they can formulate investment strategies.

The New York Stock Exchange (NYSE) was established on May 17, 1792, and is one of the leading stock markets in the world. In June 2007, there were 2,782 listed securities on the NYSE. For the 21 trading days in June 2007, the total NYSE Group trading volume was US$1,934.2 billion. By the end of 2006, the market capitalization of all NYSE companies was valued at US$25 trillion. In the NYSE, there are three major indices showing the performance of the stock market: the NYSE Composite Index, the NYSE US 100 Index, and the NYSE International 100 Index. The NYSE Composite Index measures the performance and the change of aggregate value of all the listed common stocks on the NYSE. Table 3.2 reports the statistics of the top ten companies in the world in terms of market value as of March 30, 2006. Exxon Mobil, with a market value of US$362.53 billion, ranks at the top in terms of market value and is followed by General Electric, Microsoft, Citigroup, and BP.

The NYSE US 100 Index consists of the top 100 US stocks traded on the NYSE. The market capitalization of these companies represents 47% of the whole market capitalization in the US. These 100 companies come from ten different sectors: basic materials, consumer (cyclical), consumer (non-cyclical), energy, financial, healthcare, industrial, technology, telecommunications, and utilities. The NYSE US 100 Index is therefore highly representative. The NYSE International 100 Index includes the top 100 largest non-US stocks traded on

**Table 3.2 Top ten world companies in terms of market value
(as of March 30, 2006)**

Company name	Market value (US$ billion)
Exxon Mobil	362.53
General Electric	348.45
Microsoft	279.02
Citigroup	230.93
BP	225.93
Roval Dutch/Shell Group	203.52
Procter & Gamble	197.12
HSBC Group	193.32
Pfizer	192.05
Wal-Mart Stores	188.86

Source: February 3, 2008 (www.forbes.com/lists/2006/18/06f2000_The-Forbes-2000_MktVal.html).

the NYSE and is therefore an index providing information for investors making decisions for their investment portfolios globally. As of year-end 2004, the NYSE International 100 Index consisted of stocks from 18 countries.

The largest electronic stock market in the world is NASDAQ. There are more than 5,000 companies listed on NASDAQ. The commonly used indices of the NASDAQ are Nasdaq Composite Index and Nasdaq 100 Index. The Nasdaq Composite Index, similar to the NYSE Composite Index, includes US and non-US firms listed on the NASDAQ stock market. As at 2004, the index consisted of over 4,000 companies. Owing to the wide coverage, the Nasdaq Composite Index provides a general view of aggregate fluctuations on the stock market. The Nasdaq 100 Index was established in 1985, and includes the top 100 non-financial US companies listed on the Nasdaq National Market. The index shows the largest high-growth companies in major industries such as computer hardware and software, telecommunications, and retail/wholesale trade. Therefore, the Nasdaq 100 Index is useful for investors who are interested in making investments in shares of high-growth industries.

The Dow Jones Industrial Average (DJIA), set up by Dow Jones and Company, is a popular stock market index widely used in the world. DJIA includes 30 reputable blue chips US stocks, representing around 15–20% market value of the NYSE stocks. Examples of stocks included in the DJIA are International Business Machines Corporation (IBM), General Electric, and Exxon Mobil Corporation. Other widely used indices launched by Dow Jones and Company are the Dow Jones Wilshire 5000 Composite Index (full-cap) and Dow Jones STOXX 50.

In addition to the indices mentioned above, Standard and Poor's Corporation also maintains some broadly used indices such as the S&P 500 Index, the S&P Midcap 400 Index, and the S&P 100 Index. The S&P 500 Index is commonly used as the standard for evaluating the performance of large US companies. The composite constituents of the S&P 500 Index are leading firms in different industries, making the S&P 500 Index a representative market index and an ideal proxy for the US stock market. The S&P Midcap 400 Index reflects the performance of mid-sized companies. The S&P 100 Index, which is a modified version of the S&P 500 Index, measures the top 100 blue chips stocks in different industrial groups.

Although there are a number of indices available in the market, financial planners should be aware of using them correctly since different indices have their own implications. For instance, the S&P 500 Index is an index used to reflect the performance of large firms in particular. Therefore, although the S&P 500 Index is a representative index, it is not applicable for evaluating the performance of mid-sized firms; the S&P Midcap 400 Index may be more appropriate for this.

Stock Symbols

In order to save time inputting company names, a symbol system that changes the company name into an abbreviated form is adopted. In the United States, the symbols used are called stock market ticker symbols, and are in the form of capital letters. In Hong Kong, the stock code uses Arabic numerals instead of capital letters. Table 3.3 provides three examples of how the symbol system

Table 3.3 Examples of the symbol system on shares

Company name	Ticker (United States)	Code (Hong Kong)
Microsoft Corporation	MSFT	4338
Intel Corporation	INTC	4335
HSBC	HBC	0005

Sources: New York Stock Exchange website (www.nyse.com) and Hong Kong Exchanges and Clearing Ltd website (www.hkex.com.hk).

works. "MSFT" and "4338" are used to represent Microsoft Corporation in the US and Hong Kong stock markets, respectively. Therefore, if an investor is interested in the share price of Microsoft Corporation, the letters or numerals to be keyed in are "MSFT" in the US market and "4338" in the Hong Kong market.

Moreover, the application of the symbol system is not limited to shares. The symbol system can be used in mutual funds or stock indices. Examples of well-known stock indices are listed in Table 3.4.

Insurance Companies

In the financial market, we are more familiar with depository institutions such as retail banks. However, there are many other non-bank financial institutions which play an important role in the financial services industry, particularly in the financial planning field. Examples of nonbank financial institutions are insurance companies and investment banks.

The function of insurance is to pool and transfer risks. Insurance companies receive premium payment from clients and in return provide protection services for them. The premium is the cost of insurance paid by the policyholder for protection against different types of accidental events. There are various types of insurance products offered by insurance companies. Examples include life

Table 3.4 Examples of the symbol system on major US market indices

Index name	Symbol
Dow Jones Industrial Average Index	DJI
NASDAQ 100 Index	NDX
NASDAQ Composite Index	IXIC
NYSE Composite Index	NYA
NYSE International 100 Index	NIN
S&P 500 Index	SPX

Source: New York Stock Exchange website (www.nyse.com).

insurance, property damage insurance, general liability insurance and casualty insurance.

The insurance premium is the major source of revenue for insurance companies. When insurance companies receive the premium payment from their clients, they invest the premiums in the financial market to generate additional investment returns. Most life insurance companies invest their funds on long-term assets such as bonds (government bonds and corporate bonds), stocks, and mutual funds. Since it is relatively more difficult to predict the potential risk for property damage and casualty insurance, the companies selling property damage and casualty insurance products may choose to hold more highly liquid assets. Therefore, most property and casualty insurance companies invest mainly in highly liquid investment instruments such as treasury bills.

Pension Funds

The function of a pension plan is to provide income to retired employees. Employees and employers contribute funds into pension plans during the employment life of the employees. The pension funds are used to make investments to generate additional funds. When employees retire, they can get back their retirement income. There are two major types of pension plans: defined-benefit plan and defined-contribution plan. These two types of pension plans are discussed in detail in Chapter 5.

Pension funds can be run by private or public institutions. The contributions to the pension plan can be mandatory or voluntary. In the United States, both employees and employers are keen to participate in various types of pension plans and retirement plans (jointly sponsored by employers or separately sponsored by the employees) in order to provide sufficient retirement funds for the retired employees. Therefore, the financial institutions operating these pension funds are major players in the financial markets and the pension funds are a major source of capital for the financial markets.

3.3 Investment Vehicles

Due to differences in purchasing power and the level of wealth management services, investment vehicles used by high net-worth clients are more complicated than those suitable for mass-affluent clients. For instance, some high net-worth clients may have the purchasing power to play a part in alternative investments such as real estate, private equity investments, and non-listed hedge funds. However, our focus here is to cover basic investment products that are suitable for all clients. In general, even for very wealthy clients, their portfolios should not have more than 25% in alternative investments for the purpose of risk management. Thus we will only discuss mainstream investment vehicles that are commonly used.

Money Market Instruments

There are various types of financial instruments traded on the money market. In this section we introduce some of them: treasury bill, banker's acceptance, negotiable certificate of deposit, commercial paper, and repurchase agreement. Although these money market instruments are dissimilar in various aspects, the interest rates offered by these instruments are very close over time because of their relatively low risk and short-term nature. The relation between interest rate and length of time can be portrayed diagrammatically in a curve called the interest rate curve or yield curve. Theoretically, interest rate should be positively related to length of time. A positive relation means that the longer the time period to maturity, the higher the interest rate.

Treasury Bill (T-bill)

treasury bills (T-bills) Short-term US government debt obligations with minimum denominations of US$10,000 and a maturity currently equal to 3 months, 6 months, and 1 year.

If the US government is in need of money, it is the responsibility of the Treasury Department to look for various sources of finance. One way is to issue **treasury bills**. A more commonly used name for treasury bills is **T-bills**. T-bills are issued with the aim of financing the national debt of the US government. There are different maturity dates for T-bills. The maturity dates can be 28 days, 91 days, or 182 days. Unlike other money market instruments which pay interest as the investment return to the holders, the US Treasury Department does not pay interest on the T-bills but offers a discount rate to buyers. We illustrate how T-bills work with the example below:

Time to maturity : 91 days
Face value   : US$100,000
Discount rate   : 1.5%
Cost of T-bill   : US$100,000 × (1 − 0.015) = US$98,500

To buy T-bills, investors may either submit the bid in auction themselves or contact authorized brokers or dealers to make the purchase for them. The maximum amount and minimum amount of T-bills one can buy and sell at each bid are US$1 million and US$1,000, respectively. Upon maturity, the US Treasury Department redeems (buys back) the T-bills at face value from the investors who hold the T-bills until the maturity date. T-bill is a low risk or risk-free (free from default risk) investment option because the US government can print money to repay the debt when necessary. Therefore, the T-bill is an attractive and popular money market instrument in the United States.

Table 3.5 and Table 3.6 show some statistics on US T-bills. Table 3.5 shows that there is a decreasing trend in the discount rate of T-bills with a maturity of 13 weeks offered by the US Treasury Department through the years 2000 to 2003. Before 2001, the discount rate T-bills was maintained at a level of about 5%. However, by 2002, the discount rate had fallen drastically to less than 2%. If we compare the statistics of Table 3.5 with that of Table 3.6, we see that the investment yield for the T-bills with a longer time period to maturity (26 weeks) is higher than that for the T-bills with a shorter time period to maturity (13 weeks).

Banker's Acceptance

banker's acceptance A promise of future payment issued by nonfinancial institutions but guaranteed by a bank.

Although a **banker's acceptance** is a promise of future payment issued by nonfinancial institutions, the payment payable to the bearers is guaranteed

Table 3.5 Treasury bills with 13 weeks/91 days maturity (extract)

Issue date (year)	Discount rate (%)
1998	4.91
1999	4.78
2000	6.00
2001	3.48
2002	1.64
2003	1.03
2004	1.40
2005	3.22
2006	4.85
2007	4.48

Source: February 3, 2008, Board of Governors of the Federal Reserve System (www.federalreserve.gov/releases/h15/data/Annual/H15_TCMNOM_M3.txt).

Table 3.6 Treasury bills with 26 weeks/182 days maturity (extract)

Issue date (year)	Discount rate (%)
1998	5.02
1999	4.95
2000	6.17
2001	3.45
2002	1.72
2003	1.08
2004	1.61
2005	3.50
2006	5.00
2007	4.62

Source: February 3, 2008, Board of Governors of the Federal Reserve System (http://www.federalreserve.gov/releases/h15/data/Annual/H15_TCMNOM_M6.txt).

by banks. A banker's acceptance is issued usually for the purpose of financing international trade transactions. The banker's acceptance is quite popular in the money market because it can be bought and sold freely before the maturity date in the secondary market. Similar to T-bills, a banker's acceptance is sold at a discount rate which is set at a relatively low level due to its low risk.

Over the 10 years between 1994 and 2000, the middle rate of a banker's acceptance for a 3-month period was 6.6% at its highest in 2000. However, after

2000, the middle rate fell drastically to 3.67% in 2001 and to 0.9% in 2003. The substantial drop in the middle rate is due to the decline in interest rates in the market. Although the middle rate of a banker's acceptance is low, a banker's acceptance remains popular because of its low default risk.

Negotiable Certificate of Deposit (NCD)

negotiable certificate of deposit (NCD) A short-term marketable financial instrument issued by banks with a specified interest rate and maturity date.

A **negotiable certificate of deposit** (NCD), which is also called a bearer instrument, is a short-term marketable financial instrument issued by banks with a specified interest rate and maturity date. The interest rate paid on an NCD is determined between the banks and the investors. In most of the cases, the interest rate on the NCDs is slightly higher than that paid on T-bills because of the higher perceived risk of the NCDs. The maturity date of NCDs varies from 1 month to 6 months and the interest rate paid on NCDs usually fluctuates with the term of the maturity stated on the NCDs. Investors can hold NCDs until maturity and get back the principal and interest. If investors do not want to hold the NCDs until maturity, they can trade (buy and sell) NCDs in the money market before maturity. Although an NCD is not free of default risk, it is also an attractive money market instrument since it is rare and unlikely for large banks to default on their repayment.

Commercial Paper

commercial paper An unsecured promissory note with a maturity of less than 270 days issued by large, well-known companies.

Commercial paper is an unsecured promissory note with less than 270 days of maturity issued by well-known, large and creditworthy corporations. These large corporations may use the commercial paper as a short-term source of finance to pay for account receivables and inventories. The discount rate offered varies depending on the risk level of the issuing corporations and the maturity date. In some cases, the cost of finance through the issue of commercial paper is lower than by making bank loans. Examples of issuers of commercial paper are financial institutions such as banks and insurance companies. In order to eliminate the transaction fees for the issue of commercial paper, some issuers of commercial paper may bypass the dealers and sell the commercial paper directly to their clients Although commercial paper is not allowed to be traded in the secondary market, it is still a popular investment option for investors who have excess funds for investment on a short-term horizon and a financing vehicle for corporations which are in need of short-term funds.

Repurchase Agreement (Repo)

Repurchase agreements (repos) are very similar in nature to federal funds. While federal funds are short-term funds transferred among the depository institutions only, the transfer of funds using repos can be among banks and nonbank financial institutions (e.g., loan associations). A repo is a financial agreement between a seller and a buyer whereby the seller agrees to sell the securities to the buyer and promises to repurchase (buy back) the securities at a future date at a predetermined price. The common maturity dates of repos range from 3 to 14 days but some repos may have longer maturity dates ranging from 1 to 3 months.

Examples of securities which can be traded using repos are government bonds, commercial paper, and NCDs. Although the issuers of repos are mostly banks and nonbank financial institutions, some firms which are in need of short-term financing may also issue repos as a means to get funds, but usually these are issued with a shorter maturity. As for commercial paper, there is no secondary market for repos.

Capital Market Instruments

Capital market instruments are different from money market instruments in several aspects. The major difference between capital market instruments and money market instruments is the period of maturity. Capital market instruments have a longer maturity period than money market instruments. In general, capital market instruments have maturity periods equal to or more than 1 year. There are two major categories of capital market instruments: bonds and stocks. Since the level of risk in the capital market is relatively higher than that in the money market, the return yield of capital market instruments is higher than that of money market instruments. Interest rate fluctuations have a smaller impact on capital market instruments as compared with money market instruments. Here we explain the more common types of capital market instruments such as treasury notes and bonds, municipal bonds, corporate bonds, and stocks.

Bonds

bond A financial instrument which obligates the issuer to make periodic interest payments and to repay the principal to the bondholders at the end of the term.

Bonds, also called fixed-income securities, are just like IOUs. A **bond** is a financial instrument which obligates the issuer of the bond to make specified payments (periodic interest payments and bond principal) to the bondholders over a specified period (the life of the bond). A contract, called the bond indenture, is a formal written agreement between the bond issuer and the bondholder which states clearly the rights and obligations of the two parties, the par value (face value), coupon rate, and the maturity date. When the bond matures, the bond issuer has to repay the bond principal (also called par value, face value, or stated value) to the bondholder. The coupon rate is the annual interest rate which determines the annual interest payment per dollar of par value. The price of the bond is determined by the standing of the issuer, the coupon rate, and the time to maturity. The annual interest payment to the bondholder is the product of the coupon rate and the par value of the bond.

The example below explains how it works.

Par value of bond   : $10,000
Coupon rate (interest rate on bond) : 5%
Maturity   : 3 years

The par value is the price of the bond and so the bondholder needs to pay $10,000 to purchase the bond. The issuer of the bond needs to pay $500 ($10,000 × 5%) per year to each bondholder as the annual interest payment. At the maturity of the bond (that is, 3 years later), the issuer has to repay $10,000, the par value of the bond, to the bondholder.

In some cases, the issuer sells bonds with no coupon payment, or zero-coupon rate. This type of bond is called a zero-coupon bond. The bondholders of zero-coupon bonds receive no interest payment throughout the whole holding period. The return to the holder of a zero-coupon bond is in the form of price appreciation upon the maturity of the bond. One questions then, how bond issuers can attract investors to buy zero-coupon bonds—the answer is, zero-coupon bonds are usually issued at prices below the par value (that is, at a discount). Upon maturity, bondholders receive the payment of par value of the bonds. Therefore, the return for the bondholders of zero-coupon bonds is the difference between the discounted issue price upon purchase and the payment of par value upon maturity. Bonds can be traded (purchased and sold) in the bond market. The newly issued bonds are traded in the bond primary (or issuing) market. Others are traded in the bond secondary (or circulating) market.

Treasury Notes and Treasury Bonds

In the section on money market instruments, we discussed treasury bills, which are short-term financing means used by the US Treasury Department to finance national debt. The US Treasury Department has other means of getting finance (both short-term and long-term). Treasury notes and treasury bonds are two among the many. Besides having a longer maturity time, the interest rates of treasury notes and treasury bonds are higher than that of treasury bills because of the perceived risk level. As compared to other investment options, treasury bills, treasury notes, and treasury bonds are safe investments because they are supported by the taxing authority of the government. In the United States, the interest income on treasury bonds is not subject to state income tax.

Treasury notes have a maturity of between 1 and 10 years and **treasury bonds** have a maturity of more than 10 years. These two instruments offer a fixed interest rate and the interest is payable every 6 months. There are two kinds of treasury notes: fixed-principal treasury note and inflation-indexed treasury note. The difference between these two treasury notes is that the inflation-indexed treasury note incorporates the adjustment of inflation rates (which is based on the Consumer Price Index for All Urban Consumers (CPI-U)) in the calculation of interest payment. Although treasury notes and treasury bonds are low-risk investments, they are still affected by market interest rate fluctuations. If the market interest rate increases before the maturity date of the treasury notes and bonds, investors may suffer from financial loss due to the difference in the interest rates offered by the Treasury Department and the market. This is the interest rate risk.

The market interest rate is the major factor in determining the interest rate for treasury notes and bonds. The interest rates of treasury notes and bonds are normally higher than the market interest rate so as to attract risk-averse investors. In addition, the longer the time to maturity of the treasury notes or bonds, the higher is the interest rate offered. Therefore, notes and bonds are popular and attractive financial instruments for risk-averse investors to invest money in the capital market. Since October 2001, the issue of treasury bonds has ceased in the United States. However, notes and bonds remain attractive financial

treasury notes Medium-term US government debt obligations with a minimum denomination of US$1,000 and maturity of less than 10 years.

treasury bonds Long-term US government debt obligations with a minimum denomination of US$1,000 and a maturity of 10 to 30 years.

instruments for risk avoiders to invest money in the capital market. Table 3.7 and Table 3.8 show the interest rate of 5-year treasury notes and 20-year treasury bonds, respectively.

In the past, the bond market in Asia was less developed than that in the United States. Recently, however, the issue of bonds and trading activities in the bond market have become more popular in many Asian markets.

Table 3.7 Treasury notes with 5 years maturity (extract)

Issue date	Interest rate (%)
1998	5.15
1999	5.55
2000	6.16
2001	4.56
2002	3.82
2003	2.97
2004	3.43
2005	4.05
2006	4.75
2007	4.43

Source: February 3, 2008, Board of Governors of the Federal Reserve System (www.federalreserve.gov/releases/h15/data/Annual/H15_TCMNO M_Y5.txt).

Table 3.8 Treasury bonds with 20 years maturity (extract)

Issue date	Interest rate (%)
1998	5.72
1999	6.20
2000	6.23
2001	5.63
2002	5.43
2003	4.96
2004	5.04
2005	4.64
2006	5.00
2007	4.91

Source: February 3, 2008, Board of Governors of the Federal Reserve System (http://www.federalreserve.gov/releases/h15/data/Annual/H15_TC MNOM_Y20.txt).

Corporate Bonds

The issue of corporate bonds is an effective means for corporations to raise long-term funds. Occasionally, to increase the marketability of the corporate bonds, these corporate bonds may be backed by the securities of the bond issuers as collateral. To attract investors to buy corporate bonds, corporate bonds may have to offer higher yields because they carry a higher default risk than the bonds issued by the government. The maturities of the bonds are relatively longer and usually range from 10 to 30 years. The coupon (interest return from the bond) of corporate bond is paid twice a year. Such information as the maturity date, coupon rate, payment method, and collateral, if any, is specified clearly in the bond indenture. Corporate bonds are traded publicly. In order to increase the creditability of the bond issuers, the attractiveness of the bonds, and the confidence of potential buyers, the bond issuers usually make a sinking fund provision for the purpose of paying off a portion of the bond periodically and reducing the indebtedness of the bond issuers.

There are various types of corporate bonds, such as callable bonds or convertible bonds, depending on the terms and options attached to the bonds. If the issuers prefer to have greater flexibility in the redemption of bonds, they may add a call provision to the bond. Such a bond, known as a callable bond, allows the corporate issuers to redeem the bond at a predetermined call price during the call period before maturity. In practice, if the bond issuer exercises the call option to redeem the bond before maturity, he or she needs to pay a premium to the bondholder. Since there can be a call provision in the bond indenture providing a call option for the bond issuer of callable bonds to redeem the bond before maturity, there can also be a put provision allowing the bondholder to change the length of the bond holding period.

Putable bonds (or put bonds) provide an option for bondholders to swap the bonds, to sell the bonds back to the bond issuers, or to extend the holding period of the bonds at a specified date and put price (known as extendible bonds). As a general rule, the bondholders of putable bonds would exercise (would not exercise) the put option to extend the life of the bonds when the coupon rate of the bond is higher (lower) than the current market yields. The purpose of providing such a put provision is to protect bondholders against the loss of bond value due to the increase in interest rate and the deterioration of credit quality of the issuing corporations.

A convertible bond provides the bondholder with an option to convert the bond into a specified number of shares at a prestated price according to the terms in the bond indenture. The bond indenture of a convertible bond includes additional information about (1) the conversion ratio, which states the number of shares which can be exchanged by each bond, and (2) the conversion price, which is the ratio of bond par value to conversion ratio. The bondholder usually exercises the convertible option if the share price of the issuing corporation (bond issuer) is expected to rise in the near future. Therefore, the conversion value of the bond is the product of the market price of common stock to be exchanged and the conversion ratio specified on the bond indenture.

Bonds can be classified into secured bonds or unsecured bonds depending on whether the bond is backed by any assets of the issuing corporation in times of default. A secured bond is backed by collateral while an unsecured bond is backed by nothing but the creditworthiness of the bond issuers. Collateral can be any kind of assets (tangible or non-tangible assets) which are used to pledge against the default on a bond. Secured bonds can be backed by any kind of collateral; for example, mortgage bonds backed by a building or any kind of property; equipment obligation bonds backed by tangible property or assets such as machinery or equipment; and collateral trust bonds backed by financial assets such as stocks. The risk of secured corporate bonds is lower than unsecured bonds because bondholders have the right to liquidate the assets pledged as collaterals if the issuer cannot pay back the bond interest or principal.

A debenture is a kind of long-term unsecured bond (i.e., with no collateral) issued by corporations. Since the unsecured bond is not backed by collateral, it is relatively less attractive than the secured bond. Therefore, in order to attract potential investors for the unsecured bonds, the issuers of unsecured bonds have to offer higher coupon rates. A subordinated debenture is another type of corporate bond. The holders of subordinated debentures have a lower priority claim to the assets of the bond issuers in times of default and bankruptcy. This means that when the bond issuers become bankrupt, the subordinated debenture holders can get their money back only after the creditors, who have a higher priority claim, have made their claims. In order to increase the attractiveness of the subordinated debentures which have a lower priority claim, the coupon rates of such debentures are higher.

Although bonds are fixed-income securities which promise to pay a specified stream of income periodically, bond investment is not completely risk-free as the issuers of bonds may default on the obligation to pay or go bankrupt. Since there are so many bonds available on the market, how do financial planners decide on which bonds to recommend to their clients? Perhaps corporate bond credit ratings can help. Credit rating agencies perform analyses of the accounting and financial information of the bond issuers to assess the credit quality and repayment ability of the bond issuers. Examples of the commonly used indicators employed by credit rating agencies to evaluate bond quality are liquidity ratio (current ratio and quick ratio), profitability ratio (return on assets and return on equity), cash flow ratio (cash flow to debt ratio), leverage ratio (debt to equity ratio), and coverage ratio (ratio of earnings to fixed costs). The results of the credit analyses are used to construct corporate bond ratings. Moody's Investors Services and Standard and Poor's Corporation are two of the more well-known rating companies providing bond rating information to the public.

Table 3.9 provides some statistics on the rating systems of Moody's Investors Services and Standard and Poor's Corporation. Moody's Investors Services uses capital letters (e.g., "A"), small letters (e.g., "a") and Arabic numerals (e.g., "1") to indicate level of credit quality. For instance, a rating of "Aa1" is higher than "Aa3". Standard and Poor's Corporation uses "+" or "−" to show the different levels of credit quality within a grade. For instance, a corporate bond with "AA+" rating is better than a bond with "AA−". Bonds with a credit rating on or above "Baa" according to the rating system of Moody's Investors Services or "BBB" according to the rating system of Standard and Poor's Corporation are considered to be within a recommendable investment grade. These bonds

Table 3.9 The credit rating system of Moody's and Standard and Poor's

Moody's rating	Standard and Poor's rating	Description
Aaa	AAA	Highest quality
Aa	AA	Very high quality
A	A	High quality
Baa	BBB	Minimum investment grade
Ba	BB	Low grade
B	B	Speculative
Caa	CCC	Substance risk
Ca	CC	Very poor quality
C	D	Imminent default

Source: Yahoo Finance (http://bonds.yahoo.com/safety.html).

are called investment grade bonds. In contrast, bonds with a rating lower than "Baa" or "BBB" are considered to be speculative bonds and so are also called junk bonds. As the junk bonds have higher credit risks, the coupon rates of junk bonds are higher in order to attract investment. Although investing in junk bonds is a high-risk undertaking, junk bonds are a popular investment for speculators who prefer higher returns.

Stocks

stocks Represent the share of ownership of a corporation and a claim on its assets and earnings.

Stocks represent an entitlement to ownership interest and a claim on the assets and earnings of the corporation. The main difference between stockholders and bondholders is the entitlement of ownership. Bondholders are not the owners but the creditors of the firms. Bondholders invest in the firms by providing sources of funds. In return, bondholders get the promised cash flows in the form of interest payments (coupons) and principal. On the other hand, stockholders invest in the firms by buying the stock of the firms. Since the stockholders are the owners of the firms, their returns are in the form of dividends and capital gains. However, unlike the return for bondholders which is fixed and stated in advance, the amount and timing of dividend payments vary. Capital gains arise if the current market price is higher than the stock price at which stockholders bought their stocks. Stockholders have the voting rights for important issues such as the election of the chairman and directors. Although stockholders are the owners of the firms, they are the residual claimants. This means that stockholders can only claim back the outstanding stock amount, after the settlement of debts to creditors, if the firm becomes bankrupt. If the firm does not have anything left to settle the outstanding stocks of the stockholders, the stockholders may get nothing from the firm. While corporations may issue bonds which are callable, common stock cannot be callable.

There are two major types of stocks: common stocks and preferred stocks. Within the categories of preferred stocks, there are different classes: cumulative preferred stocks, noncumulative preferred stocks, participating preferred stocks, and convertible preferred stocks. All these various classes of stocks are a form of equity ownership. However, these classes of stocks are different in terms of dividend distribution, voting rights, and claim priority.

While bondholders receive their returns in the form of interest, stockholders receive their returns in the form of dividends. Dividends are usually declared annually (final dividend), bi-annually, and quarterly (interim dividend). Dividend distribution declared at other times is termed as special dividends. Dividends may be paid in the form of cash dividends or stock dividends. In terms of the priority to receive dividends, the stockholders of common stocks receive their dividends only after the stockholders of preferred stocks have made their claims. The stockholders of preferred stocks receive a fixed rate of dividend income as stated on the stock certificates while the stockholders of common stocks receive the residual of the dividend amount declared. Dividends are paid only if they are declared. Therefore, unlike bondholders who can receive interest as returns periodically, stockholders can receive their returns only when the firms make a declaration of dividend distribution. If a larger amount of dividend is declared, the stockholders of common stocks may receive a higher dividend value than the stockholders of preferred stocks. If no dividend is declared, the stockholders (of preferred stocks and common stocks) receive nothing as returns. The claim of dividends is not cumulative except for stockholders of cumulative preferred stocks. If no dividend is declared for the current year, the stockholders of cumulative preferred stocks have the right to receive the dividend in arrears cumulated (i.e., the fixed rate of dividends unpaid in the previous years) before the stockholders of noncumulative preferred stocks and common stocks receive their dividends if dividends are declared in the next year. Therefore, the stockholders of cumulative preferred stocks are protected by the cumulative provision and have the preferred right to be paid in full before other types of stockholders have their share of returns.

The stockholders of common stocks have the preemptive right to purchase the newly issued stocks to maintain the same percentage of ownership of the corporation. Unlike the stockholders of common stocks, no voting rights are given to the stockholders of preferred stocks except for the stockholders of participating preferred stocks. In addition, if the stockholders of preferred stocks are interested in becoming stockholders of common stocks, they may invest in convertible preferred stocks which entitles them to have an option to convert their preferred stocks into common stocks as stated on the stock certificates.

In terms of claim priority, as compared with the stockholders of common stocks, the term *preferred* for the stockholders of preferred stocks means that they have a higher priority to claim the assets of the firm in the event of bankruptcy or liquidation of the firm. The stockholders of common stocks have their claims to the assets of their firms only after all the other claimants (creditors and preferred stockholders) have received their shares. Therefore, the stockholders of common stocks are called the residual claimants of the firms.

Mutual Funds

mutual fund A financial intermediary through which small investors can put money together and form a sizable portfolio for investment.

Mutual fund investment has become a popular investment in the market since its first issue in 1924 in Boston. A **mutual fund** is a type of financial intermediary (a firm or a trust) through which the financial intermediaries operate their business by pooling funds and investing them for investors with a predetermined investment objective. A mutual fund investment consists of a portfolio or a basket of marketable assets and securities that allows investors to invest and achieve diversification in a cost-efficient and easy way. To become a shareholder of a mutual fund, the investor buys the shares which represent a portion of the holding of the mutual fund. Mutual funds are different from other types of funds or investments as the returns (net of expenses) of mutual funds in the form of interest and dividends are shared by the fund-holders.

The market value of mutual funds in the United States is the largest in the world. As of July 2006, members of Investment Company Institute (ICI), the national association of US investment companies, account for more than 8,000 open-end investment companies (mutual funds), more than 450 closed-end funds, and 100 exchange-traded funds. The total assets of these mutual fund companies exceed US$9 trillion. The market value of US mutual funds accounts for nearly half of that in the global market. The distribution of the net assets of mutual funds by fund category is shown in Table 3.10. Stock funds are the most popular funds in the United States. Investors there prefer making investments in capital appreciation funds or a combination of capital appreciation and money market funds which yield higher returns.

Large mutual fund companies in the United States include Fidelity Investments, Vanguard Group, and Charles Schwab Corporation. Many of these companies provide a variety of financial services and investment planning services to clients. They offer life insurance products and mutual fund products of many varieties, discount brokerage services, retirement services, and wealth management services.

Table 3.10 Distribution of net assets of mutual funds, December 2007

Category	Net assets (billions of dollars)
Stock funds	6,528.0
Hybrid funds	714.3
Taxable bond funds	1,305.5
Municipal bond funds	373.9
Taxable money-market funds	2,650.0
Tax-free money-market funds	467.6

Source: February 3, 2008, Investment Company Institute (www.ici.org/stats/n.f/trends_05_06.html).

3.4 Time Value of Money

time value of money
A concept which deals with how the value of money changes with time.

The **time value of money** is the single most important quantitative technique relating to personal finance. No other topic comes close in terms of relevancy to financial planning in both scope and depth.

For instance, most calculations involved in savings and investment return are based on the time value of money. If we use income smoothing to estimate the ideal consumption level and consequently the required life insurance protection, we have to calculate time value. Furthermore, two of the high priority goals in many families are to have sufficient savings to support the college education of their children and to buy a home. While the calculation of these two events are so critical to many families in financial planning, the computation involved in estimating the amount of savings and monthly mortgage payments is nothing more than a combination of several basic time value equations. Finally, most retirement planning calculations involve the estimation of savings for consumption after retirement. Once again, that is nothing more than time value calculation.

In this section, we first review the relevant equations. They are future value–single sum (FV), present value–single sum (PV), future value of an annuity (FVA), present value of an annuity (PVA), the two annuity due formulae (FVA^D and PVA^D), perpetuity (PV (Per)), and effective annual rate (EAR). After the equation review, we introduce scenarios of applications on financial planning using time value techniques so that you can fully understand how to apply these concepts in helping your clients.

We want to emphasize that while the calculations are relatively straightforward, and most financial services companies have computer programs and software which provide answers to these calculations by pushing or clicking a few buttons, our goal here is not to train you to become an expensive calculator. By asking you to go through these exercises, we hope that you can develop a sense of technical know-how about the sensitivity of certain inputs to the outcome. The estimation of your retirement income will mainly depend on the assumption of the inflation rate and return on investment. A competent financial planner should know the sensitivity of a client's estimated retirement income to the various interest rate inputs.

The ability to evaluate the potential negative effect or risk of using the wrong return inputs for your clients is extremely important in constructing a prudent retirement savings plan for them so that they can live the comfortable retired life they desire. This ability can be achieved by having a full understanding of the relationship between the input values and the output of the time value equations. We strongly encourage all of you to study our time value applications carefully so that you can make smart financial planning decisions for your clients.

Basic Techniques

We first review the four basic equations, FV, PV, FVA, and PVA. Then we go through the two annuity due equations, and finally, the perpetuity and the effective annual rate calculations.

Time Value of Money Equations

1. Future value – Single sum (FV)

    $FV = PV \times (1 + i)^n$

    $FV = PV \times FVIF_{i\%, n}$

2. Present value – Single Sum (PV)

    $PV = \dfrac{FV}{(1 + i)^n}$

    $PV = FV \times PVIF_{i\%, n}$

3. Future value of an annuity (FVA)

    $FVA = PMT \left[\dfrac{(1 + i)^n - 1}{i}\right]$

    $FVA = PMT \times FVIFA_{i\%, n}$

4. Present value of an annuity (PVA)

    $PVA = PMT \left[\dfrac{1 - \dfrac{1}{(1 + i)^n}}{i}\right]$

    $PVA = PMT \times PVIFA_{i\%, n}$

5. Annuity due (A^D)

    Ordinary annuity refers to the situation where payments occur at the end of each period. For annuity due, the payments occur at the beginning of each period.

    $FVA^D = PMT \times FVIFA_{i\%, n} \times (1 + i)$

    $PVA^D = PMT \times PVIFA_{i\%, n} \times (1 + i)$

6. Perpetuity (PV (Per))

    $PV\,(Per) = \dfrac{PMT}{i}$

7. Effective annual rate (EAR)

    $EAR = \left(1 + \dfrac{i}{m}\right)^m - 1$

Definition of Terms

i	= interest rate
n	= number of periods
PMT	= annuity payment
$FVIF_{i\%, n}$	= future value interest factor for i and n
$PVIF_{i\%, n}$	= present value interest factor for i and n
$FVIFA_{i\%, n}$	= future value interest factor for an annuity for i and n
$PVIFA_{i\%, n}$	= present value interest factor for an annuity for i and n
m	= number of compounding periods per year

Financial Planning Applications

Now that you have learnt the equations for time value, let us turn our attention to the application of these equations in solving financial planning problems. As we have mentioned earlier, time value techniques are very useful in solving consumption, investment, and retirement questions in financial planning. In fact, time value is also helpful in solving corporate finance and investment problems.

INVESTMENT QUESTIONS

Example 1 (simple investment)

If you have US$3,000 for investment today at an interest rate of 6% per year, what is the estimated amount you will get at the end of year 7?

Solution:

$$FV = PV \times (1 + i)^n$$
$$FV = \$3,000 \times (1.06)^7$$
$$= \$4,510.80$$

Example 2 (simple investment)

If a four-year fixed-term deposit will pay a total of US$4,222.40 for a principal amount of US$2,500, what should the annual interest rate be for the four-year fixed-term deposit?

Solution:

$$FV = PV \times (1 + i)^n$$
$$\$4,222.4 = \$2,500 \times (1 + i)^4$$
$$i = 14.00\%$$

Example 3 (simple investment)

You suggest to your client a savings plan to deposit US$7,500 a year in a savings account every December, starting from 2005. If the interest rate is 8%, compounded annually, how much will your client have at December 2007?

Solution:

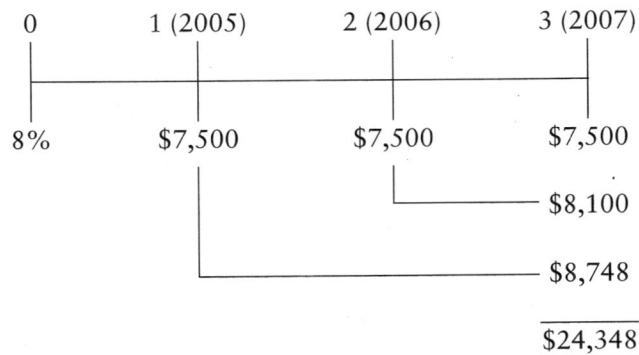

$$FVA = PMT \times FVIFA_{i\%, n}$$
$$= \$7,500 \times PVIFA_{8\%, 3}$$
$$= \$7,500 \times 3.2464$$
$$= \$24,348$$

Example 4 (simple investment)

Your client mentions to you that he will need US$13 million in 17 years to buy an apartment in Florida. The expected investment return should be 14% compounded annually. What amount will your client have to invest each year for the next 17 years to reach the US$13 million at the end of those years? (Assuming that the investment is made at the end of each year.)

Solution:

$$\$13,000,000 = PMT \times FVIFA_{i\%, n}$$
$$\$13,000,000 = PMT \times FVIFA_{14\%, 17}$$
$$PMT = \frac{\$13,000,000}{59.117}$$
$$PMT = \$219,902.9$$

Example 5 (home purchase)

You suggest that your client buy an office with a value of US$1,200,000 in Chicago. Your client has sufficient money to pay 25% as downpayment and has to borrow the remaining 75% from a bank. The client plans to repay the mortgage over a 25-year period. The interest rate for a 25-year mortgage is 15%. What is the annual mortgage payment?

Solution:

$$PVA = PMT \times PVIFA_{i\%, n}$$
$$1,200,000 \times 0.75 = PMT \times PVIFA_{15\%, 25}$$
$$\$900,000 = PMT (6.4641)$$
$$PMT = \frac{\$900,000}{6.4641}$$
$$= \$139,230.52$$

Example 6 (education)

You have a client, Jonathan, who is concerned about the college tuition fee for his daughter, Jessica. Jessica will start college in six years. The tuition fee will be US$55,000 per year for 4 years payable at the end of each year. Jonathan has already started investing US$4,500 per year 7 years ago and will continue to invest for 7 more years. Jonathan needs your advice on how much more he has to invest for the next 7 years in order to provide sufficient funds for the tuition fee for Jessica. The annual interest rate is assumed to be 10%.

Solution:

Present value of the tuition fee of US$55,000 per year:

$$PVA = PMT \times PVIFA_{i\%, n}$$
$$PVA = \$55,000 \times PVIFA_{10\%, 4}$$
$$= \$55,000 \times 3.1699$$
$$= \$174,344.5$$

Accumulated value of the annual investment of US$4,500:

$$FVA = PMT \times FVIFA_{i\%, n}$$
$$= \$4,500 \times FVIFA_{10\%, 14}$$
$$= \$4,500 \times 27.975$$
$$= \$125,887.5$$

Additional investment fund for the next 7 years:

Present value of tuition fee – Accumulated value of the annual investment
$$= \$\ 174,344.5 - \$\ 125,887.5$$
$$= \$\ 48,457$$

Additional annual contribution:

$$
\begin{aligned}
\text{PVA} &= \text{PMT} \times \text{PVIFA}_{i\%,\,n} \\
48{,}457 &= \text{PMT} \times \text{PVIFA}_{10\%,\,7} \\
48{,}457 &= \text{PMT}\,(9.4872) \\
\text{PMT} &= \frac{\$48{,}457}{9.4872} \\
&= \$5{,}107.62
\end{aligned}
$$

Example 7 (retirement planning)

Your client expects to receive a retirement income of US\$650,000 per year (at year end) for three years (from 2006 to 2008) from a special investment instrument you recommended to him in 2005. If the annual discount rate is 15%, what was the present value of this investment (at the end of 2005)?

Solution:

0	1 (2006)	2 (2007)	3 (2008)

8%   650,000   650,000   650,000

565,217.39 ——————

491,493.38 ——————————

427,378.53 ——————————————

$1,484,089.3

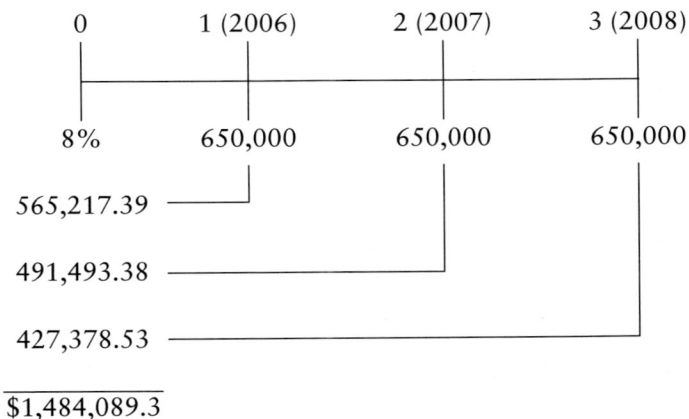

$$
\begin{aligned}
\text{PVA} &= \text{PMT} \times \text{PVIFA}_{i\%,\,n} \\
\text{PVA} &= 650{,}000 \times \text{PVIFA}_{15\%,\,3} \\
&= 650{,}000 \times 2.2832 \\
&= \$1{,}484{,}080
\end{aligned}
$$

Example 8 (retirement planning)

Your client has retired after working for 38 years. You have helped him in his retirement planning for some time and now his retirement fund has an accumulated value of US\$558,000. The life expectancy of your client is another 25 more years. Assuming that you can earn a 12% annual return for him, what will be his yearly annuity for the next 25 years?

Solution:

$$
\begin{aligned}
\text{PVA} &= \text{PMT} \times \text{PVIFA}_{i\%,\,n} \\
\$558{,}000 &= \text{PMT} \times \text{PVIFA}_{12\%,\,25} \\
\$558{,}000 &= \text{PMT}\,(7.8431) \\
\text{PMT} &= \frac{\$558{,}000}{7.8431} \\
&= \$71{,}145.34
\end{aligned}
$$

3.5   Investment Alternatives for a Recovering Market

If macroeconomic factors indicate that the market is in economic recession, financial planners should recommend an investment strategy with the aim of capital preservation. Usually, in such a situation, investments in highly liquid securities and low-risk financial instruments such as fixed-income securities are preferred. Investments in highly liquid securities provide investors with the flexibility to shift their capital to other securities when the market recovers from economic recession. Table 3.11 suggests some recommendations of investment strategies in a recovering stock market.

Table 3.11 Investment recommendations in a recovering stock market

Investment vehicle	Example	Risk	Return	Advantage	Disadvantage
Cash*		Very low	Very low	Liquidity	Low return
Notes/Bills**	Certificates of deposits, treasury notes, commercial paper	Very low	Very low	Liquidity	Liquidity
Bonds**	Treasury bonds, corporate bonds	Low	Low	Liquidity, acceptable return	Interest rate risk, default risk
Stocks***		Medium	Medium	Liquidity, acceptable return	Price risk
Managed portfolios***	Mutual funds, index funds	Medium	Medium	Acceptable return	Fees
Alternative investments*	Warrants, options, futures	High	High	Upside potential	High risk

* Reflects the appropriateness of the product in the recovering market, with one * indicating least appropriate.

Key Terms

banker's acceptance   *102*
bond   *105*
business cycle   *94*
capital market   *97*
commercial paper   *104*
fiscal policy   *92*
foreign exchange rate   *94*
gross domestic product (GDP)   *90*
interest rate   *93*
monetary policy   *92*
money market   *96*

mutual fund   *112*
negotiable certificate of deposit (NCD)   *104*
population demographics   *92*
price level   *93*
stocks   *110*
time value of money   *113*
treasury bills (T-bills)   *102*
treasury bonds   *106*
treasury notes   *106*
unemployment rate   *91*

Multiple-choice Questions

1. The implementation and impact of fiscal policy on the economy are often described as _____ and _____ direct, respectively.
    A. fast; less
    B. fast; fairly
    C. slow; less
    D. slow; fairly

2. Given that the nominal interest rate is 8% and the inflation rate is 3% per annum, what is the real interest rate per annum?
    A. 11%
    B. 8%
    C. 5%
    D. 3%

3. Which of the following economic/personal factors may affect the status and the financial plan of a client?
    I.   Divorce
    II.   Inflation rate
    III. Taxation law
    IV. Unemployment

    A. II and III
    B. III and IV
    C. I, II, and III
    D. I, II, III, and IV

4. When the economy is undergoing a deficiency in demand, it may result in _____ unemployment.
    A. cyclical
    B. frictional
    C. structural
    D. seasonal

5. The minimum investment grades for Moody's and Standard and Poor's ratings are:
    A. Baa, BB
    B. Ba, BBB
    C. Baa, BBB
    D. Caa, CCC

6. _____ is an unsecured promissory note with less than 270 days of maturity issued by well-known companies.
    A. Commercial paper
    B. Banker's acceptance
    C. Repurchase agreement
    D. Mortgage bond

chapter **4**

Financial Planning Components (Part I)

Learning Objectives

After studying this chapter you should be able to:

1 Compute the cash flow and cash budget of an individual.
2 Understand the key financial ratios for cash flow management.
3 Explain the use of consumption smoothing to determine the optimal level of consumption.
4 Describe the importance of tax planning.
5 List the tax planning principles.
6 Discuss tax planning strategies.
7 Demonstrate the international dimension of tax planning.
8 Explain the meaning of personal risk management.
9 Grasp the concept of basic risk control.
10 Know the definition and types of insurance.
11 Estimate the appropriate level of life insurance.

In this chapter we focus on three areas of financial planning: cash flow management (consumption planning), tax planning, and risk management (insurance planning). We discuss cash flow management first, since this concerns the basic needs of the client. Figure 4.1 shows the goal-oriented financial planning pyramid. Depending on the income level, the asset level, and the life stage of the client, the financial planner may not need to go through all levels of the financial

Figure 4.1 Goal-oriented financial planning pyramid

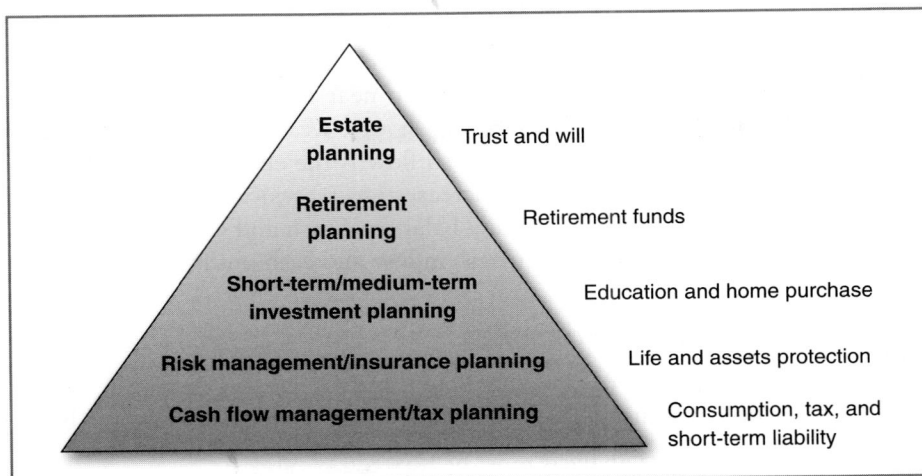

Estate planning — Trust and will

Retirement planning — Retirement funds

Short-term/medium-term investment planning — Education and home purchase

Risk management/insurance planning — Life and assets protection

Cash flow management/tax planning — Consumption, tax, and short-term liability planning pyramid. Of course, the priority and importance of each level to the clients may vary as well.

Assuming that the client is at the early stage of his life with some assets and a middle-level income, the very first thing the financial planner should check is the cash flow situation of the client. Unless the client is very rich, or at the very late stage of life with little obligation and liability, most clients face the challenge of effective consumption planning. With the power of the time value of money, effective cash flow management with an appropriate savings plan in place at the early stage can help most clients to achieve certain financial security and retire in comfort. Cash flow management deals with the cash inflow, which is income from employment for most clients; cash outflow, including daily household expenses; taxes and tax liabilities; and finally the net result of all these items: savings. As we will mention later, overconsumption is a major problem for most average clients in planning their finances.

If clients are unable to manage cash flow well, they would not have the financial resources to take care of the risk protection needs of themselves and their families. Everything else on the upper levels of the financial planning pyramid will be affected. Thus, it is important for financial planners to lay a good foundation and do a good job in consumption planning for their clients. We explain the fundamental concepts of cash flow management in 4.1. Tax planning is discussed in 4.2 and risk management and insurance planning in 4.3.

4.1   Cash Flow Management

cash flow management Aims to achieve a balanced or even a surplus cash flow.

Cash flow management aims to achieve a balanced or even a surplus cash flow. A balanced or a surplus cash flow means that there is always sufficient cash to pay for one's needs and wants. Ineffective management may lead to large fluctuations in cash flow, too little savings, and too much debt.

Before we learn how to manage cash flow, we need to know the meaning and purposes of cash. Cash and cash equivalents are current assets as they are short term, highly liquid, and readily convertible into cash within a short period of time (usually less than 12 months). They include coins and notes, current accounts, savings accounts, foreign currency accounts and short-term investments. The values of cash and cash equivalents are less subject to changes in the interest rate. These current assets are so near to maturity that their market values are unaffected by changes in interest rate. We need cash for consumption, investment, and financing activities. Cash flow is the change in the balance of the cash and cash equivalents. Cash increases (decreases) when the closing balance is greater (smaller) than the opening balance of cash and cash equivalents. Net cash flow is the difference between cash inflow and cash outflow.

Budgeting Principles

The purpose of a personal budget is similar to a corporate budget. Let us take a look at some of the budgeting principles related to personal budgeting.

- The analysis must be forward looking.
- The budgeting process must be well organized.

- The budget must be clearly presented.
- The budget must be used to compare with the actual expenses for evaluation.
- The budget should be used as a tool for improvement.

The budgeting procedure and components of a firm are different from budgeting for an individual. However, the concept and purpose are the same: prepare and plan for future finance-related activities by making forecasts in a systematic manner. There are obvious advantages in preparing a personal budget in personal financial planning. In preparing a budget, we first evaluate our financial situation and personal financial goals. Then after some data collection, the budget can be used to compare with the actual income and consumption figures for evaluation and better cash flow management. Consumption planning is the very first area to deal with in the financial planning process. Overconsumption due to lack of proper budgeting is the single most serious problem for many people in meeting their financial goals such as retiring comfortably. We should pay attention to personal budgeting to guarantee a good start in financial planning.

Cash Flow Management Techniques

Cash flow management aims to control matters relating to income and expenditure so that there is a surplus of income over expenditure to meet unexpected needs such as unemployment. When the expected expenditure and unexpected needs are met, the surplus of cash can be used for investment purposes. The two essential records in cash flow management are the cash flow statement and cash budget.

Cash Flow Statement

The cash flow statement is an account of the cash receipts and cash disbursements during a period. The purpose of preparing a cash flow statement is to evaluate the ability to generate positive cash flows to meet cash disbursement obligations and to see if there is a need for financing. The cash flow statement gives useful information for making decisions relating to consumption and investment activities.

When making an analysis of cash inflow and cash outflow for clients, financial planners have to evaluate the actual and expected cash receipts from the investment and cash payouts for the investment over different time periods. Two important factors are to be considered. Financial planners need to know the time between receipts and payouts of cash and the amount of the cash inflow and outflow. To ensure that the cash flow statement is fairly presented, it should be prepared, classified, and disclosed with valid, complete, timely, and accurate data. There are proper procedures for preparing a cash flow statement. It includes data collection on income and expenditures, data organization, identification of changes, data analysis, data checks, and adjustment. A sample cash flow statement for a household is exhibited in Table 4.1.

Table 4.1 Sample cash flow statement

Item	Examples	Amount ($)
Cash inflow from work	Income	
	Bonus	
	Allowance	
Cash inflow from investment	Dividends	
	Rental income	
	Bank interest	
	Bond interest	
	Capital gains	
	Sales of assets	
Other cash inflow	Retirement income	
	Social security	
	Gifts	
	Estate distribution	
Total cash inflows		
Cash outflow for consumption	Consumption expenses	
	Entertainment expenses	
	Medical expenses	
	Education expenses	
	Miscellaneous expenses	
Cash outflow for investment	Securities purchase	
	Real estate investment	
	Principal repayment	
Other cash outflow	Contribution to retirement fund	
	Contribution to education fund	
	Insurance premiums	
	Periodic repayment of loan/mortgage	
Total cash outflow		
Net cash flow		

Cash Budget

While the cash flow statement is an account showing past performance, the cash budget is a record of future cash inflow and cash outflow. Past performance of cash flows provides a good reference for making decisions and analysis for the future. With past information, clients can make a forecast of future income, spending, and investment. The cash budget can be used to provide information in advance on the ability and time schedule to generate more income and to make up potential cash shortages.

In order to monitor the ability of clients to control available resources with expected outlay for consumption and investment, the cash budget should be a balanced budget of cash inflow and cash outflow. A balanced budget is when cash inflow equals cash outflow. If the net cash flow is positive, the budget is in surplus; if the net cash flow is negative, the budget is in deficit. To ensure that the cash budget is useful and realistic, it should be prepared using accurate information on income and expenditure patterns. Table 4.2 presents a sample cash budget.

A cash budget is good for controlling the inflow and outflow of cash. Based on the projected information on the cash budget, financial planners and their clients can prepare a proforma cash flow statement periodically to plan ahead, allocate resources wisely, and accumulate sufficient cash to achieve future goals. A potential cash shortage is a signal of overspending. In case of potential cash shortages, financial planners would suggest more savings, more aggressive investment, and less consumption in the current period to reduce expenditure and to prepare sufficient cash for future use. If there is a surplus of cash, financial planners can propose using it for investments.

Variance is the difference between the budgeted and actual values of the cash flow items. Variance is used to measure the discrepancy between the projected and actual values of income and expenditure. A reasonable variance is acceptable. However, a large variance indicates a significant deviation of actual from the projected. Periodic review and revision of the cash budget are needed in order to improve the usefulness of the cash budget for cash management. When clients have an effective control over cash, income, and expenditure, their financial planners can use the predictable patterns of income and expenditure for better financial planning.

Financial Ratio Analysis

Financial planners employ financial ratios to help analyze the financial status of clients. The interpretation of ratios is based on both cross-sectional and time-series analyses.

Financial ratios are simple mathematical expressions of the financial relationship between the items on the various financial statements of clients.

Table 4.2 Sample cash budget

	Past actual	Current budget	Current actual	Variance
Cash inflow				
Item 1				
Item 2				
Cash outflow				
Item 1				
Item 2				
Net cash flow				

Financial ratios can be used to measure and reflect profitability of assets, liquidity position, debt repaying ability, risk preferences, living patterns, and values of clients. Therefore, financial ratio analysis enables financial planners to have a better understanding of their clients' current financial position so that they can select better financial planning strategies to devise better plans for their clients. Table 4.3 provides a list of commonly used financial ratios used by financial planners.

Financial planners have some rules of thumb that can be applied to the growth rate of the savings ratio or asset size to evaluate the financial performance of their clients. Outstanding performance is indicated by a growth rate of over 1.5 in the savings ratio or assets size. If the growth rate is between 1.0 and 1.5, the performance is regarded as good. Performance is acceptable if the growth rate ranges from 0.5 to 1.0. However, a growth rate of the savings ratio or assets size less than 0.5 is an indicator of poor performance.

If the performance is less than satisfactory, the suggested ways to improve the income, savings ratio and asset size are to increase working hours; to get salary increments through promotion and further education; to seek a better job with higher pay; to select investments with higher return; to reduce consumption expenses; and to reduce transaction costs. Financial planners may incorporate some of these suggestions in the financial plan in order to improve the current financial status of their clients.

Financial ratio analysis is more an art than a science. While there are many rules that financial planners can follow in analyzing these ratios, they must also use their experience and common sense in ascertaining the financial health of their clients.

Savings Plans

Besides preparing the cash flow statement and cash budget, another way to manage cash is to save. It is part of a financial planner's job to help formulate an

solvency ratio The ratio of net assets to total assets.

debt-to-total assets ratio The ratio of liabilities to total assets.

debt-to-income ratio The ratio of liabilities to income before tax.

liquidity ratio The ratio of current assets to monthly expenses.

savings ratio The ratio of surplus to income after tax.

investment assets-to-net worth ratio The ratio of investment assets to net worth.

Table 4.3 Selected personal financial ratios

Ratio	Formulae
Solvency ratio	$\dfrac{\text{Net assets}}{\text{Total assets}}$
Debt-to-total assets ratio	$\dfrac{\text{Liabilities}}{\text{Total assets}}$
Debt-to-income ratio	$\dfrac{\text{Liabilities}}{\text{Income before tax}}$
Liquidity ratio	$\dfrac{\text{Current assets}}{\text{Monthly expenses}}$
Savings ratio	$\dfrac{\text{Surplus}}{\text{Income after tax}}$
Investment assets-to-net worth ratio	$\dfrac{\text{Investment assets}}{\text{Net worth}}$

effective savings plan for their clients. The purpose of having a savings plan is to provide sufficient funds to fulfill consumption needs, to overcome unexpected cash shortages, and to achieve future goals. Many financial planners suggest that clients try to save about 10% of their total income.

In the United States, the financial institutions that deal in savings deposits include merchant banks, savings and loans associations, retail banks, and credit unions. There are two forms of savings and loans associations: partnership and company by shares. In a partnership, the depositors are the owners of the association and hence their income is in the form of bonuses rather than interest. If the association takes the form of a company by shares, the depositors receive interest as their income.

There are different choices of savings in the United States. Savings can be made in the current account, savings account, and money market deposit account. In addition, the savings can be used to buy negotiable orders of withdrawal, certificates of deposit, and treasury bills.

Constructing a Family Budget

When we prepare our personal budget, we may have to take a family perspective. For the life-stage of "married with children", a substantial portion of the expenses can be attributed to the children. Thus the family budget incorporates the income from the working couple and expenses for all family members including children. Key family budgeting items include family vacations, medical expenses (especially family with young kids or aging parents), and education expenses for children. The main challenge in constructing a family budget is to figure out a realistic consumption plan for each member. It is difficult enough to depict the consumption pattern for yourself, not to mention that of other people. Therefore, understanding the consumption habits and lifestyle preferences for each member is critical to reaching a consensus on the family budget.

While financial discipline is very important in implementing a family budget, it can only be attained when an individual has a proper financial value system, which is an integral part of the overall value system including cultural value, ethical value, and family value. Used properly, the family budget can be a great tool to establish financial discipline for children and to help them to take part in achieving family financial goals.

Theory of Consumption Smoothing

Based on the permanent-income hypothesis developed by Friedman (1957), financial planners can estimate the appropriate amount of consumption for their clients. The permanent-income hypothesis states that an individual's current consumption level is determined by the expected income in the future. In order to receive the highest lifelong overall satisfaction level through consumption, an individual tends to engage in a stable or slowly increasing consumption pattern, even though his income may be unstable through life. In other words, there is a tendency in human behavior to adjust and smooth consumption based on lifelong expected income.

For instance, we can observe that in general, medical students, law students, or accounting students on average will spend more money on daily consumption than liberal arts majors during their college life. This is due to the fact that students with higher job security and/or higher expected income after graduating are more willing to spend or borrow.

The implication for financial planners is that they should advise their clients to smooth their consumption patterns regardless of how much they earn in a particular year. Thus, clients should spend less and save more when their income is high. However, when income is low, they should withdraw money from their savings to maintain a stable consumption. In short, consumption smoothing provides a better overall satisfaction for individuals than the behavior of correlating periodical income with consumption.

If an individual's current consumption level is determined by future expected income, then there is an implicit tendency to spend or use all the money earned through our life, unless there is a desire to make bequests. Of course, making a bequest can be regarded as a form of consumption. Thus, the following equation can be written:

$$\text{Total lifelong income} = \text{Total consumption} + \text{Bequest}$$

To provide a simple model that can be used by financial planners in estimating the appropriate consumption level, we can use the following equation:

$$\begin{matrix} \text{Present value of annuity} \\ \text{(annual income)} \end{matrix} = \begin{matrix} \text{Present value of annuity} \\ \text{(annual consumption)} \end{matrix} + \begin{matrix} \text{Present value} \\ \text{(bequest)} \end{matrix}$$

By using this method, we can easily estimate the ideal annual consumption for clients. Of course, if the client has no bequests to make, they can spend all the money on themselves. This naive model has obvious problems. For example, irregular major consumption items such as home purchase, education, and even funeral expenses, are not taken into account. However, these problems can be easily solved by partitioning the lifelong consumption period into subperiods of equal consumption using the irregular major expenses as the break points. In addition, consumption is based on the per-capita assumption. If the number of members in the household varies through time, adjustments should be made to the combined household consumption to reflect the fact that some members like children may spend more or less than a regular adult, depending on the life-cycle stage they are in.

Consumption smoothing is a valid concept in estimating clients' ideal consumption level. It may be more appropriate for some clients than others. Financial planners should carefully consider all aspects of a client before dispensing consumption planning advice.

consumption smoothing A concept which suggests that an even consumption pattern throughout life would bring most satisfaction for an individual.

4.2   Tax Planning

In the United States and other well-developed countries where tax rates are relatively high, tax planning is one of the most important areas in financial planning, particularly for high net-worth clients as they are subject to the highest end of the progressive tax system. In Asia where personal tax rates are relatively low in most countries, tax planning may not be such an area of concern. However, as a significant percentage of wealthier clients in Asia may face tax consequences in North America, Europe, and Australia due to their multiple citizenship status and investments overseas, financial planners should not overlook the value of tax planning strategies in financial planning.

Every citizen has the legal and social responsibility to pay taxes to the government on time. It is illegal to evade paying taxes. Although it is important that we must carry out our tax obligations, it is also our concern to reduce our tax liability legally as much as possible. The challenge is for financial planners to maximize their clients' tax savings within the legal framework. In this section we discuss the significance of tax planning in the financial planning process. It is essential for a financial planner to be familiar with tax planning techniques so they can help clients meet their legal obligation to pay tax while minimizing tax payments.

Importance of Tax Planning

Tax planning is one of the planning areas in a personal financial plan. However, it should not be treated as a separate component. There are close relations between a tax plan and other planning areas of a personal financial plan, particularly the investment planning and the estate planning areas. Investment instruments and estate planning strategies come with tax implications.

For instance, investment choices may be affected by the client's tax bracket, tax credits, and deductions entitled to him. Financial planners should not consider investment returns net of cost only, but also net of tax. Clients in a high tax bracket should put capital in those investments which generate tax-free or tax-sheltered investment income. Otherwise, the clients may have a net loss after tax although the investment earns a before-tax profit. Table 4.4 illustrates how tax affairs are related to the financial transactions of other planning areas of financial planning.

The objective of a tax plan should be long term rather than short term. Financial planners should focus on the long-term total tax minimization objective over the whole life of their clients. In addition, the financial planners should not use the tax planning techniques to achieve objectives relating to tax affairs only; tax planning strategies can be utilized in a more comprehensive way to facilitate other financial goals. Tax elements can become factors for consideration in other plans. For example, when deciding whether to use borrowed funds for investment, the issue of whether interest expense is tax-deductible may be a relevant factor.

Role of Financial Planners

We have a social and legal responsibility to pay taxes. However, as taxpayers, we would like to pay as little tax as possible; particularly in countries where the tax rates are very high, income tax can be the largest expense item. Therefore, there is a great temptation to reduce tax liability as much as possible. There are many different ways to do this, but not all ways are legal. Unless clients are professional lawyers, certified accountants, or tax consultants they may not know which tax planning technique is appropriate, effective, risky, or unlawful.

Table 4.4 Tax implications of the financial plan

Type of financial plan	Transaction	Tax implication
Investment plan	Investment income (dividends, interest)	Salaries/income tax
	Transfer of registered shares	Stamp duty
	Transfer of registered debentures	Stamp duty
	Transfer of registered loan stocks	Stamp duty
	Capital growth returns	Capital gains tax
Real estate plan	Rental income	Property tax/profits tax
	Mortgage interest	Allowable deduction
	Conveyance on sale	Stamp duty
	Agreement for sale	Stamp duty
Insurance plan	Insurance premiums	Allowable deduction
	Insurance investment income	Salaries/income tax
Education plan	Tuition fee	Allowable deduction
Retirement plan	Pension income	Salaries/income tax
	Pension fund contribution	Allowable deduction
Estate plan	Transfer of estate	Estate duty/tax
	Receipt of estate	Inheritance tax

This is where financial planners come in. Financial planners should not only help in filing tax returns for their clients but also in devising a prudent tax savings plan. In order to do this, financial planners should have a clear understanding of the taxation system, its practical applications, and other legislation and regulations relating to tax. The primary objective of tax planning is to reduce or defer the tax liability of the clients. However, financial planners can also make use of tax planning strategies to achieve their clients' other financial objectives. In addition, in the whole tax planning process, financial planners should demonstrate their professionalism in complying with the ethical code of conduct and legal requirements and to remind the clients to observe their legal obligation too. Financial planners are socially irresponsible if they tempt, or become tempted by, their clients to conduct activities which are ethically inappropriate and legally unacceptable.

Tax Planning Principles and Strategies

Tax planning is an arrangement of taxation affairs in a legal and commercially realistic manner. The objectives of tax planning are to minimize the tax burden, defer tax payment, and shift tax liability, while utilizing legal means to do so. The outcome of the tax planning process should be the least costly, yet lawful.

Tax Planning Principles

As it is important for financial planners to make sure that their tax planning advice does not become tax evasion plots, they must observe the tax planning principles of lawfulness, prearrangement, timeliness, cost-effectiveness, all-roundness, and selectivity.

1. Lawfulness

It should be stressed that tax planning is a legitimate means to reduce or to defer tax liability. All tax planning techniques implemented should be within the legal limits. When financial planners provide tax-planning advice to their clients, they should also observe the professional and ethical code of conduct.

2. Prearrangement

Prearrangement means that the strategies in the tax plan must be executed before transactions are carried out. The minimization of tax should not be the sole or dominant purpose of the tax plan; there should be other benefits besides the purpose of saving tax. There are anti-avoidance or evasion provisions in most tax legislation. Therefore, in a tax plan, there should be a prearranged series of transactions for some other commercial and business purposes apart from the avoidance of tax payment.

3. Timeliness

The tax plan should be implemented on a timely basis. Financial planners should note the potential difference in the timing of the financial benefits and costs of the tax plan. In addition, the rules and regulations related to tax legislation can be refuted or amended. Financial planners should be aware of the impact of the changes in legislation and the potential risk of retrospective legislation on the tax plans.

4. Cost-effectiveness

The outcome of the tax planning process should be a tax arrangement which is the least costly. In the evaluation process, financial planners should offer alternative methods for their clients and discuss with them the feasibility of the choices financially and technically. However, neither financial planners nor clients should compare the tax benefits and costs only. The overall financial implications of the plan should be considered. The final choice selected should not be cost-effective in tax only but also in other aspects.

5. All-roundness

A good tax plan should not involve tax elements only as tax planning is part of the overall financial plan of clients. Therefore, in devising a tax plan, financial planners should consider other nontax factors and other planning areas. For example, financial planners may have to think about the taxability of the investment income such as dividends and capital gains. Other nontax transactions can facilitate the implementation of the tax plan.

6. Selectivity

Ideally, financial planners should arrange their clients' tax affairs in such a way that they are charged the least for every type of tax. For practical reasons, it is difficult to achieve this aim. To be cost-effective, in the process of evaluating different alternatives, financial planners usually focus on certain types rather than all types of tax. Some factors for financial planners to consider in their analysis include:

1. Nature of each type of tax including taxability (scope of charge), special features, tax rates.
2. Deductibility of each type of tax including exemption and allowable deduction.
3. Relative proportion of each type of tax in the overall tax liability of client.
4. Form of assessment such as separate assessment, joint assessment, personal assessment.

Here we use an example to illustrate how the form of assessment can affect the amount of net assessable income of a household.

In Year 1, the amounts of assessable income for husband and wife are $80,000 and $30,000, respectively. The allowable deductions are $100,000 for the husband and $100,000 for the wife. If the husband and wife do not have the choice to have joint assessment as a household, the following applies:

	Husband	Wife
Assessable income	80,000	30,000
Less: Allowable deduction	(100,000)	(100,000)
Net assessable income	–	–
Loss carried forward	(20,000)	(70,000)

In Year 2, the husband has an increase of income to $130,000. He is still entitled to allowable deductions of $100,000. There is no change in the wife's income and she does not enjoy allowable deductions for this year. If the husband and wife have the choice to have joint assessment as a household, the following applies for Year 2:

	Husband	Wife
Assessable income	130,000	30,000
Less: Allowable deduction	(100,000)	–
	30,000	30,000
Less: Loss brought forward	(20,000)	(30,000)
	10,000	–
Less: Loss transferred from wife	(10,000)	–
Net assessable income	–	–
Loss carried forward	–	(30,000)

On the other hand, if the husband and wife do not have the choice of joint assessment as a household in Year 2, the following applies:

	Husband	Wife
Assessable income	130,000	30,000
Less: Allowable deduction	(100,000)	–
	30,000	30,000
Less: Loss brought forward	(20,000)	(30,000)
Net assessable income	10,000	–
Loss carried forward	–	(40,000)

This example shows that for joint assessment, when there is an excessive loss in the assessable income of either husband or wife, the loss of one party can be used to offset the income of the other party, thus decreasing the total net assessable income of the household.

Tax Planning Strategies

Tax planning aims to minimize the tax liability of taxpayers. There are four basic strategies to do this: (1) decrease the taxable income, (2) increase the allowable deductions, (3) reduce the tax rate applicable, and (4) defer the tax payment. We will discuss two major types of tax planning techniques: general (applicable to all kinds of taxes) and specific (applicable to certain kinds of taxes only).

GENERAL STRATEGIES

Income and Profit Splitting

Most taxing authorities charge different categories of taxpayers (unmarried taxpayer, joint return for married taxpayer, separate return for married taxpayer and head of household taxpayer) different types of tax at different rates. Under such a taxation system, it is possible to reduce the total assessable income or profits by distributing income or profits among the taxpayers in different tax brackets. There are several income and profit splitting methods.

1. Split income between individuals to gain benefits of progressive tax rates

Some taxing authorities charge individual taxpayers a progressive tax rate. A progressive tax rate system means that a taxpayer with a higher level of income is charged a higher tax rate, while a taxpayer with a lower level of income is charged a lower tax rate. A way to take advantage of this is for the high-rate taxpayer to divert part of the income to a lower-rate taxpayer. Consequently, part of the assessable income can be charged at a lower tax rate (or zero tax rate). We use an example to illustrate this income splitting effect.

Take a family where the husband is the breadwinner and the wife is unemployed. The annual income of the husband is $200,000. The husband has a bank balance of $550,000 with an annual interest income of $55,000. The taxing authority grants no allowable deduction and charges tax on total income under a progressive tax system. The tax rates are 0% for income below $100,000, 5% for income between $100,001 and 200,000, and 15% for income above 200,000.

	Husband	Wife	Total
Salaries income	200,000	–	200,000
Interest income	55,000	–	55,000
Total income	255,000	–	255,000
Tax rate applicable	15%	–	
Tax payment	38,250	–	38,250
After-tax income	216,750	–	216,750

If the husband shifts part of the income, e.g., the interest income, to the wife:

	Husband	Wife	Total
Salaries income	200,000	–	200,000
Interest income	–	55,000	55,000
Total income	200,000	55,000	255,000
Tax rate applicable	5%	0%	
Tax payment	10,000	0	10,000
After-tax income	190,000	55,000	245,000

This example shows that under a progressive tax rate system, income splitting allows the tax rate applicable to be lower (15% versus 5%), the tax liability to be lower ($38,250 versus $10,000) and the after-tax income to be higher ($216,750 versus $245,000).

2. Split income between an individual and a partnership to gain the benefits of tax rate differential

The taxing authorities may charge individual taxpayers and corporation taxpayers different tax rates. For example, under the situation where individual taxpayers are subject to a progressive tax rate system while corporations come under a standard rate system, individual taxpayers can divide the total income in such a way that part of their assessable income would be charged at a different tax rate under a different tax category.

3. Split profits between partnerships and corporate partners to gain benefits from utilizing trading losses (i.e., make use of a loss-carrying company)

If profit splitting between firms is allowed, the losses of a partnership can be used to offset the profits of the corporate partners and their other companies. Consequently, the assessable income and profits can be reduced by the amount of losses.

4. Split income and profits between different territories to gain benefits from differences in territorial tax rates

Some regions (e.g., Hong Kong and Macau) adopt a territorial source concept in the taxation system. The territorial source concept means that only the income and profits sourced in the region concerned are taxable. If the taxpayer is able to divert part of the income or profits to an overseas territory where the tax rate applicable is lower, the taxpayer can enjoy the benefits from differential tax rates between different territories.

income tax Tax obligations related to personal income.

Salaries/income tax   If the individual taxpayer can structure the employment contract in such a way that part or all of the employment income is sourced offshore or overseas, that part of employment income from the overseas source may not be assessable locally.

profits tax Tax obligations related to business profits.

Profits tax   If the corporation attributes part or all of the profits to an overseas business source, that part of profits may not be assessable locally.

property tax Tax obligations related to property owned.

Property tax   The rental income of the taxpayer may not be assessable locally if the real estate investment is physically located overseas.

stamp duty Tax obligations arising from transactions related to asset sales.

Stamp duty   Stamp duty may not be payable locally if the documents are contracted offshore or overseas. In addition, some countries (e.g., Australia) authorize the states and territories to impose stamp taxes. Therefore, the rates for stamp tax vary, depending on where the documents and transactions are put into effect.

estate tax Tax obligations related to estate due to death of owner.

Estate tax   Estate tax may not be payable if the estate owner invests in overseas assets or shifts assets physically outside the taxable region.

5. Split income and profits between years of assessment to reduce tax liability or to defer tax payment

By this tax payment deferral technique, the taxpayer may defer the taxability of assessable income to reduce the tax burden for the current assessment year. Tax payment deferral can result in two possible benefits. First, as tax payment is reduced, the taxpayer retains the use of the money that was originally assigned for tax payment and enjoys the benefits of the time value of money. Second, in case there is a decrease in the tax rate or income in the next assessment period, the taxpayer can benefit from the reduction in tax rate or in tax payment. For instance, the taxpayer may fall in a lower tax rate bracket due to the decrease in income in the next assessment year. However, potential loss may be resulted if there is an increase in tax rate or income in the next assessment year.

6. Split income and profits based on different forms of tax

The taxpayer may plan the income and profits to be received in a nontaxable or less taxable form so as to reduce the tax burden. Income and profits can be arranged in the form of

- Off-shore income and profits by setting up a tax haven company. For instance, income tax is not imposed on individuals or corporations in the Commonwealth of the Bahamas and income tax is not imposed on individuals in Bahrain and Bermuda. Table 4.5 shows some examples of tax haven countries.
- Dividends and capital gains as the tax rates applying to dividends and capital gains are often lower than those applying to income.
- Some places like Hong Kong and Macau do not charge any tax on dividend income and capital gains, while some countries like Australia offer tax rebates on dividend income and capital gains.
- Royalties as royalty income can be less taxable.
- Nontaxable employee benefits that provide monetary rewards and are not included as part of assessable income.

Table 4.5 Examples of tax haven countries

Type of tax exempted	Name of country
Income tax on individuals	Commonwealth of the Bahamas, Bahrain, Bermuda, Brunei Darussalam, Cayman Islands, Kuwait, Oman, Paraguay, Qatar, Saudi Arabia, French Polynesia, United Arab Emirates
Income tax on corporations	Commonwealth of the Bahamas, Cayman Islands
Capital gains tax	Barbados, Bermuda, Bolivia, the British Virgin Islands, Chile, Fiji, Hong Kong, Isle of Man, Kenya, Lithuania, Macau, Mauritius, Swaziland
Tax on inheritance	The British Virgin Islands, Canada, Hong Kong, Isle of Man, Swaziland, Ukraine
Tax on gifts	The British Virgin Islands, Canada, Hong Kong, Isle of Man, Ukraine
Tax on wealth	British Virgin Islands, Hong Kong, Isle of Man, Lithuania

7. Gifting

Gifting is a common tax planning tool to reduce or to split assessable income, particularly in countries such as Australia, the British Virgin Islands, Canada, Hong Kong, Isle of Man and Ukraine, where gifting is tax-free. By gifting, the donor transfers the ownership of the income-earning assets to the donee gratuitously. That is, the donor transfers the assets to the donee for less than full consideration. However, gifting is not as simple as it appears to be. In order to make gifting as an effective tax-planning tool, the following conditions must be fulfilled:

- The ownership title of the income-earning assets must be passed to the donee before the income generated by the assets is assessable.
- The transfer of ownership is irrevocable (otherwise the income generated from the assets would still be included in the assessable income of the donor).

8. Family Trust

Another way of reducing or splitting assessable income is by setting up a family trust, in a discretionary trust format or a unit trust format. A family trust is a more effective income-splitting technique because of its flexibility. The trustee of the family trust collects the income and profits of all the family members. The income and profits are then divided among the family members in such a way that the total tax payable is a minimum. There are two major types of trusts: unit trust and discretionary trust. The beneficial ownership of the estate under a unit trust is divided into a number of units and the unit holders (beneficiaries) own the units rather the estate. While the trustee of a unit trust does not possess the discretionary power to distribute the estate, the trustee of a discretionary trust assigns the estate distribution to the beneficiaries. As family trusts are so widely used, many taxing authorities have imposed additional taxation rules restricting its practice for income splitting.

Making Use of Tax Deductions, Exemptions, and Relief

All taxing authorities provide tax deductions, tax exemptions, tax credits, and tax-relief items to taxpayers to reduce their tax liability. Financial planners should be aware of all these exemptions so as to reduce the net assessable income and profits for their clients.

Dividend Income and Capital Gains from Capital Investment

There are two sources of income from investments: dividends in the form of cash or stock and gains from capital growth. Different taxing authorities have different taxing policies on dividends. Dividend income is tax-free in Hong Kong but is taxable upon distribution in other countries such as the United States, Japan, and Australia. In countries where the dividend income is taxable, the taxing authorities in countries like Australia, Canada, France, and New Zealand grant tax credits or rebates on dividend income to avoid the double taxation on the distribution of dividends. The gains from capital growth (when the selling price is higher than the purchase cost) are taxed only when the investment is sold and the gains are realized. Therefore, the tax liability of gains from capital growth can be deferred to later years. In the tax-planning process, financial planners have to be sure:

1. If dividends and/or capital gains are tax-free or taxable in the place where the investment plans are launched. Financial planners may suggest investing in a place where dividend income and capital gains are not taxable.
2. About the relative tax rates of dividend income and capital gains between different investment markets. Financial planners will want to select an investment market where the taxability of dividend income and/or capital gains is the lowest.

Timing of Assets Sale

Financial planners should help clients smooth their income streams over the various assessment periods so that the income of one particular year will not become too excessive and be taxed at a higher tax rate under a progressive tax rate system. In an investment plan, the best timing for a sale of assets should be when the assets are at the highest price. However, when financial planners have to match the investment plan with the tax plan, they may have to time the sale of assets with the earning schedule of their clients. That is, the financial planners should smooth the revenue from the sales of assets with the pattern of income streams of the clients so as to prevent the total income from becoming excessively high, so incurring greater tax liability. For example, the best timing for the sale of assets in a tax plan would be during a year of tax losses when there are capital gains and tax losses to offset each other or during the retirement period of the client when the income level is low.

Gearing of Investment

It is not an uncommon practice for investors to borrow money for investment in securities or property, particularly when the interest rate is low. The investment gearing technique aims to make use of the borrowed funds to generate higher returns and the interest expense to claim tax deductions to decrease the tax burden because interest expense is an allowable deduction in some countries such as Australia. Below are examples to illustrate the two effects of investment gearing: positive gearing and negative gearing effects.

Example 1: Positive gearing
An investor puts in $200,000 in an investment portfolio, of which $100,000 are borrowed funds. The annual interest rate is 20%. The value of the investment portfolio increases to $400,000 after a year.

$$\text{Rate of return for the investment} = \frac{(\$400,000 - \$200,000)}{\$200,000}$$
$$= 100\%$$

$$\text{Dollar return for the investment} = \$400,000 - \$200,000 - (\$100,000 \times 20\%)$$
$$= \$180,000$$
$$\text{Rate of return for equity fund} = \frac{\$1800,000}{\$100,000}$$
$$= 180\%$$

Example 2: Negative gearing

An investor uses $200,000 to buy an apartment for rental purposes, of which $100,000 are borrowed funds. The annual rental income and interest expense are $10,000 and $9,600, respectively. Other miscellaneous expenses such as insurance for the apartment are $3,400.

$$\text{Total rental expense} = \$9,600 + \$3,400$$
$$= \$13,000$$
$$\text{Net rental income} = \$10,000 - \$13,000$$
$$= -\$3,000$$

Example 1 shows that investors can make good use of borrowed funds to earn returns. The rate of return for equity funds can be higher than the rate of return for whole investment funds. The use of borrowed funds to generate positive assessable income gives rise to a positive gearing effect. In countries where the interest expense for borrowed funds is tax-deductible, it can be used to offset the assessable income. In Example 2, the rental income is not sufficient to cover the interest expense for the borrowed funds. This is the negative gearing effect. The negative net rental income means that the rental income is not taxable. In addition, the rental loss can be used to offset the investor's other sources of assessable income.

Although the investment gearing technique appears to be a useful tax-planning tool, it can be used under certain conditions only:

1. When interest expense is tax-deductible.
2. When the opportunity cost of equity funds is low.
3. When financial planners have adequate knowledge of the financial market.

Therefore, the gearing investment technique should be used with care.

SPECIFIC STRATEGIES

Salaries Tax

A salaries tax is charged on income which is derived from employment. However, there may be some exemption items provided by the taxing authority. Therefore, financial planners may suggest that their clients reorganize their remuneration package so as to make use of the exemption rules. The setting up of service companies and partnerships is a common tax-planning tool to reduce tax liability. However, many taxing authorities are aware of the practice and have implemented some measures such as higher tax rates for service companies and partnerships.

Property Tax

Financial planners may suggest that clients buy properties for rental purposes in their financial plans. While pointing out the benefits of rental investment as being stable, profitable (there is potential for future capital gains from appreciation), and less risky, financial planners should remind their clients of the property tax that they would have to pay, and of the possibility of minimizing it.

Profits Tax

Transfer pricing has long been used by companies to shift profits from a high tax-rate country to a low tax-rate country. By the transfer pricing technique, an intermediate offshore company is set up, usually in a place where the tax rate is lower than that of the home country, by the home country purchaser. A vendor sells a commodity at a cost of $10 to the intermediate offshore company which resells the commodity at a price of $13 to the home country purchaser. The home country purchaser retails the commodity to customers at $15. Therefore, the home country purchaser can record a profit of $2 (the difference between $15 and $13, the cost charged by the intermediate offshore company) rather than $5 (the difference between $15 and $10, the cost charged by the original vendor) which would have been taxed at a higher rate. The $3 profit earned by the intermediate offshore company will be taxed at a lower rate. However, the widespread use of transfer pricing has aroused the attention of taxing authorities. Many taxing authorities impose an anti-avoidance provision to discourage the use of transfer pricing. The principle of the anti-avoidance provisions on transfer pricing is to deem the profits earned by the nonresident office to be derived in the name of the resident office if a close business connection is found between the nonresident office and resident office, and if the trading price is not set at arm's length transaction. Therefore, the pricing policy must be justified for transfer pricing to be used.

Besides using strategies to reduce the assessable profits, companies may restructure their expenses to maximize the amount of allowable deductions to reduce the tax burden. Many taxing authorities only allow interest expense to be tax deductible if the borrowed funds are used for business activities to generate assessable profits. Therefore, loans should be utilized for profit-making investments in order to maximize the interest deductibility. In addition, as management or accounting services can be regarded as profit-generating activities, professional service fees to external companies providing such services should be tax deductible. A business could set up consultancy companies in a foreign country (in a low tax-rate country, of course) to transform internal cost into external expense for tax deduction purposes.

International Tax Planning

As the market becomes more and more globalized, it is very likely that financial planners would have local clients having investments overseas or clients overseas trying to make investments domestically. Therefore, it is important for financial planners to have some knowledge of issues relating to international tax planning. Table 4.6 outlines a brief summary of the tax rates of 17 countries.

Many countries such as Japan, the United Kingdom, and the United States impose taxes on dividend income and interest income. However, some places such as Hong Kong do not have a capital gains tax on securities investment or a tax on interest income. Financial planners could advise their clients not to make investments in high-tax countries if similar investments are available in a low-tax or tax-free country.

In addition, it is important for financial planners to note whether their countries have a comprehensive tax treaty or agreement with other countries to avoid double taxation. Austria, France, Germany, Singapore, and the United Kingdom have entered into double taxation treaties with other countries. Residents in the United Kingdom are entitled to a tax credit through either the double taxation treaty or unilateral tax relief for foreign tax paid against the UK tax (income tax or capital gains tax) payable on foreign income or capital gains.

So far, we have focused only on the common tax types such as income tax, property tax, profits tax, stamp duty, and estate tax. However, there are many more types of tax. Financial planners may need to know other types of tax imposed by different countries. Table 4.7 gives a brief summary of these.

Tax Planning Risks

Both financial planners and their clients must bear in mind that it is their legal and social obligation to pay taxes to the government. Tax planning is a legitimate means of reducing tax liability. A good tax plan will inevitably have tax avoidance elements. However, care must be taken to ensure that the tax plan does not become an illegal tax evasion plan that employs deceit, subterfuge, and concealment. We need to be aware of the risks associated with tax planning.

Anti-Avoidance Provisions

To be sure that all our tax-planning techniques are "safe," we need to know the anti-avoidance provisions. Financial planners should not employ tax-planning strategies which would infringe on the anti-avoidance provisions as both they and their clients may be charged with fraud and willful evasion of tax. In case of unclear interpretations of the terms in the rules and regulations, professional advice from legal experts and tax consultants must be sought.

Risk from Legislative Uncertainty

Different sources of income such as pension, superannuation funds, and retirement funds are subject to various types of rules and regulations. In developed markets where the rules and regulations regarding social securities have been implemented for a long time, there are fewer uncertainties. In developing markets, changes to rules and regulations are more frequent. Financial planners have to keep abreast of these changes and amend their tax plans for their clients accordingly.

Table 4.6 Summary of Tax Rates of 17 Countries as at 2007

	Resident	Nonresident	Dividend	Capital gains tax	Examples of deduction	Husband/Wife	Tax bracket	Tax Rate
Australia	Worldwide basis, withholding tax	Australia source	Rebate for franked dividend	Yes	Business-related expenses, gift, medical expenses	No joint assessment	A$6,001–30,000 A$30,001–75,000 A$75,001–150,000 > A$150,000	15% 30% 40% 45%
Brazil	Worldwide basis, withholding tax	Brazil source		No but included as taxable income	Medical expenses, contributions to pension fund	Joint or separate	R$1,313–2,625 > R$2,625	15% 27.5%
Canada	Worldwide basis, withholding tax	Canada source	Tax credit for dividend	One-half of capital gains included as net income	Contributions to registered pension and savings plan, medical expenses, tuition fees	No joint assessment	C$0–37,178 C$37,178–74,357 C$74,357–120,887 > C$120,887	15% on excess 22% on excess 26% on excess 29% on excess
China	Worldwide basis, withholding tax	China source	Dividends are taxed in gross amounts received without deductions.	Included as other income and subject to tax in the same manner as income			RMB 0–475 RMB 476–1,825 RMB 1,826–4,375 RMB 4,376–16,375 RMB 16,376–31,375 RMB 31,376–45,375 RMB 45,376–58,375 RMB 58,376–70,735 > RMB 70,735	5% 10% 15% 20% 25% 30% 35% 40% 45%
France	Worldwide basis	France source (withholding tax)	Tax credit for dividend	Yes (except for sale of principal residence)	Pension contributions, charitable contributions	Joint assessment	€7,665–52,152 at geometrically progressive rates from 15% to 42%.	
Germany	Worldwide basis, withholding tax	German source (withholding tax)	Dividends are treated as part of total income.	Short-term capital gains included as taxable income and long-term capital gains are tax-exempt.	Social security contributions, insurance premiums	Joint unless one spouse requests separate		
Hong Kong	Hong Kong source	Hong Kong source	No tax	No	Charitable donations, home loan interest, recognized retirement scheme contributions	Joint or separate	HK$0–35,000 HK$35,000–70,000 HK$70,000–105,000 > HK$105,000	2% on excess 7% on excess 12% on excess 17% on excess

Table 4.6 (continued)

	Resident	Nonresident	Dividend	Capital gains tax	Examples of deduction	Husband/Wife	Tax bracket	Tax Rate
Japan	Worldwide basis, withholding tax	Japan source	Dividends are taxed and aggregated with other income, withholding tax	Included as other income	Social security contributions, medical expenses, charitable contributions, insurance premiums	No joint assessment	¥0–1,950,000 ¥1,950,000–3,300,000 ¥3,300,000–6,950,000 ¥6,950,000–9,000,000 ¥9,000,000–18,000,000 > ¥18,000,000	5% on excess 10% on excess 20% on excess 23% on excess 33% on excess 40% on excess
South Korea	Worldwide basis, withholding tax	Korea source	Tax credits for dividends, withholding tax	Included as taxable income	Business-related expenses, pension contributions, education expenses, medical expenses	No joint assessment	W 0–10,000,000 W 10,000,000–40,000,000 W 40,000,000–80,000,000 > W 80,000,000	8% on excess 17% on excess 26% on excess 35% on excess
Macau	Macau source, withholding tax	Macau source	Subject to complementary tax	No	Medical expenses, funeral expenses	No joint assessment	MOP 95,000–115,000 MOP 115,000–135,000 MOP 135,000–175,000 MOP 175,000–225,000 MOP 255,000–375,000 > MOP 375,000	7% on excess 8% on excess 9% on excess 10% on excess 11% on excess 12% on excess
Malaysia	Malaysia source, withholding tax	Malaysia source		Real property gains tax	Donations, mortgage interest, pension fund contributions, medical expenses	Joint or separate	RM 50,000–70,000 RM 70,000–100,000 RM 100,000–150,000 RM 150,000–250,000 > RM 250,000	19% on excess 24% on excess 27% on excess 27% on excess 28% on excess
New Zealand	Worldwide basis, withholding tax	New Zealand source	Imputation credits for dividend income	No but some capital gains may be included as income		No joint assessment	NZ$0–38,000 NZ$38,001–60,000 > NZ$60,001	19.5% on excess 33% on excess 39% on excess
Singapore	Singapore source	Singapore source	Taxable	No but some capital gains may be included as income	Business-related expenses, professional subscriptions, charitable donations, mortgage interest, pension fund contributions	Combined assessment is no longer available for married couples from 2005.	S$20,000–30,000 S$30,000–40,000 S$40,000–80,000 S$80,000–160,000 S$160,000–320,000 > S$320,000	3.5% on excess 5.5% on excess 8.5% on excess 14% on excess 17% on excess 20% on excess

Table 4.6 (continued)

	Resident	Nonresident	Dividend	Capital gains tax	Examples of deduction	Husband/Wife	Tax bracket	Tax Rate
South Africa	Worldwide basis, withholding tax	South Africa source	No tax on local dividend	25% of net capital gains are taxed at normal income tax rates	Business related expenses, pension fund contributions, charitable donations	No joint assessment	ZAR 0–112,500	18%
							ZAR 112,501–180,000	ZAR 20,250 + 25% in excess of ZAR 112,500
							ZAR 180,001–250,000	ZAR 37,125 + 30% in excess of ZAR 180,000
							ZAR 250,001–350,000	ZAR 58,125 + 35% in excess of ZAR 250,000
							ZAR 350,001–450,000	ZAR 93,125 + 38% in excess of ZAR 350,000
							> ZAR 450,001	ZAR 131,125 + 40% in excess of ZAR 450,000
Taiwan	Taiwan source, withholding tax	Taiwan source	Imputation credits for dividend income	Included as income	Charitable contributions, insurance premiums, medical expenses, mortgage interest	Joint return for married couples.	TWD 0–370,000	6%
							TWD 370,000–990,000	13%
							TWD 990,000–1,980,000	21%
							TWD 1,980,000–3,720,000	30%
							> TWD 3,720,000	40%
United Kingdom	Worldwide basis, withholding tax	UK source	Taxable	Yes	Pension fund contributions, charitable donations	No joint assessment	£0–2,230	10%
							£2,230–34,600	20%
							> £34,600	40%
United States	Worldwide basis, withholding tax	US source	Taxable	Included as income	Business-related expenses, medical expenses, charitable contributions	Joint or separate	US$0–7,300	10% on excess
							US$7,300–29,700	15% on excess
							US$29,700–71,950	25% on excess
							US$71,950–150,150	28% on excess
							US$150,150–326,450	33% on excess
							> US$326,450	35% on excess

Source: Various websites and *Individual Taxes: A Worldwide Summary* (New York: PriceWaterhouse Center for Transnational Taxation).

Table 4.7 Summary of other types of tax

Type of tax	Definition
1. Circulating tax	Charges on the turnover rate of commodity
2. Consumption duty	Charges on the sales of commodity
3. Value-added tax	Charges on the value added to the commodity in the production or operation process
4. Act tax	Charges on certain prescribed acts in some activities such as consumption, investment, or entertainment; examples of act tax are betting duty and stamp duty
5. Resources tax	Charges on the income derived from exploration and development of natural resources

Risk from Market and Economic Instability

There is a close association between tax planning and market conditions. Macroeconomic and microeconomic stability exerts great impact on earning power which in turn affects the tax-paying ability of clients. Some tax-planning techniques such as investment gearing make use of investment tools. In times of market instability when interest rates are high, clients using the investment gearing technique may not be able to earn sufficient income to repay the high interest. Although the risks due to the market and economic conditions are out of the control of financial planners, they should still obtain as much information as they can about the market to avoid or minimize their clients' losses.

Risk of Loss of Control

We have learnt that one strategy of reducing tax payment is for a high-rate taxpayer to transfer part of his income and assets to a low-rate taxpayer or to a person who is not subject to taxes (e.g., someone under the age of 18). However, such an arrangement implies that the transferors have to give up the ownership of the assets. Before using this assets-transfer technique, high-paid taxpayers should consider the following factors:

1. Legal constraints disallowing those under the age of 18 from being the transferee of assets.
2. Differential tax rates between the transferor and the potential transferee (e.g., in some countries, those under 18 may be charged at a higher tax rate).
3. Ability of the transferee to manage the assets.
4. Other types of tax charged (e.g., stamp duty or capital gains tax) on the transfer and sale of assets.
5. Transfer of assets being the potential cause of family conflicts.
6. Problems from marriage dissolution if a high-rate taxpayer transfers assets to his or her low-rate taxpayer spouse.

4.3 Risk Management and Insurance Planning

After taking care of consumption and tax planning, the next task for financial planners is to conduct effective risk management for clients through insurance planning. Risk management can go beyond insurance to employ advanced financial instruments such as options and futures to hedge the risk of investment and financial assets, but we will limit our discussion here to life and asset protection through insurance products.

Throughout life, we have to face a lot of uncertainties and risks—physical, psychological, and financial. Although we can do little to prevent the unexpected from happening, we can try our best to minimize financial losses, which is what risk management is all about. The purposes of risk management are to avoid risk, to reduce risk, and to transfer risk. For example, insurance is an effective risk transfer technique to compensate for financial losses due to the risk. As personal financial planning is a comprehensive process that evaluates all financial aspects of clients, a plan to manage risk and to compensate for financial losses must be one of the components of financial planning.

Role of Financial Planners

It may seem that identification of risk may not necessarily require the expertise of financial planners. After all, the consumer public knows how to buy life insurance to provide funds for their beneficiaries after death or health insurance to provide funds for their medical bills. However, there are many other unexpected risks in life, besides the common risks of death, illness, and natural disasters, which need to be protected against. Financial planners can help their clients to spot all the potential risks that can prevent them from achieving their financial goals.

Risk means uncertainty; it exists when the outcome of a set of circumstances or event is uncertain. There are many different definitions and types of risk. In finance literature, risk can be divided into diversifiable risk and non-diversifiable risk. In accounting terminology, risk is brought about by debt and is usually measured by the debt ratio. The higher the leverage, the riskier the firm is. In terms of investment strategy, risk usually refers to a situation where the consequences of the risk can result in either a loss or a gain, that is, speculative risk.

In the context of risk management and insurance planning, the risk we talk about is "pure risk." Pure risk is different from all other risks in that there is no possibility of making a gain out of pure risk. The consequences of pure risk are either a loss or no loss. In insurance, the three common pure risks are personal risk, property risk, and liability risk. Personal risk includes risk of early death, injury, or debilitating illness, and loss of income through incapacity to work. Property risk takes into account the loss or damage to property. Liability risk refers to the risk causing injury, damage, and financial loss to others. The job for financial planners in managing pure risk is to prevent pure risk from occurring or to minimize the loss due to pure risk. One effective means of dealing with pure risk is to obtain insurance coverage. However, not all pure risks are insurable.

Besides identifying risks for their clients, it is a financial planner's job to devise the most appropriate insurance policies to provide sufficient insurance coverage.

Risk Management Techniques

There are several risk management techniques. They are (1) risk control, (2) risk avoidance, (3) risk diversification, (4) risk retention, and (5) risk transfer.

Risk Control

Risk control means using every possible way to minimize risk. For example, in order to minimize the probability of fire in a laboratory, there should be warning signs such as "No smoking" or "Beware of fire" in the laboratory. If, however, a fire does break out, there should be precautionary measures to minimize the damage, such as installing smoke detectors, fire alarms, and fire extinguishers in the laboratory. Risk control techniques include tools, strategies, and processes that seek to avoid, prevent, reduce, or otherwise control the frequency and/or magnitude of loss and other undesirable effects of risks.

Risk Avoidance

Risk avoidance refers to utilizing all means to prevent risk or to keep away from all causes of risk. For instance, to avoid fires, we can use electricity rather than gas. However, in some cases, when we try to avoid risk, there are costs involved. Electricity may be more expensive than gas. Sometimes in the process of avoiding certain risks, other risks may arise. If we use electricity, we may reduce the chances of getting burnt but there is a higher probability for us to be exposed to electric shocks, which is another type of risk. Furthermore, some risks are unavoidable.

Risk Diversification

According to the portfolio theory (Markowitz 1952), if two loss exposures are perfectly and positively correlated, there is no gain through the use of pooling. When one exposure suffers from a loss, the other exposure suffers from an identical loss. However, when the two loss exposures have a zero correlation, there is much to gain from the use of pooling. By risk diversification, we mean spreading the risk burden and sharing the financial loss of risk among many parties so that the risk burden and the financial loss to be borne by one party can be substantially reduced. Or we can diversify or confront risk by combining the available resources (human resources, financial resources, or intelligence) of many parties. For instance, we can set up a partnership rather than a sole proprietorship, so that the financial liability can be shared among the partners. Also, the resources available for a partnership should be greater than for a sole proprietorship.

Risk Retention

When we use the three risk management techniques mentioned earlier to control risk, to avoid risk, and to diversify risk, we know that there are costs associated with them. For instance, there are costs involved in installing a smoke detector, fire alarm, and fire extinguisher, or in replacing a gas heater by an electric heater. The legal fee is higher for setting up a partnership than for a sole proprietorship.

If it is costly to control, avoid, or diversify risk, we may have to retain the risk and bear the loss.

Risk retention is a kind of self-insurance. As a simple example, we may consider purchasing a health insurance policy that provides full compensation for medical bills for only three out of these five illnesses: stomachache, headache, toothache, colds, and coughs. If the medical expenses for stomachache, headache, and toothache are higher than those for colds and coughs, we may choose to insure for the former three types of illnesses rather than the last two because the last two illnesses seem less severe. In such a case, we retain the risk of getting colds and coughs and bear the medical bills for these two illnesses. In other words, it is easier and simpler to bear the risk and the direct financial consequences of the risk (called risk financing) in some circumstances, particularly when the risk retained is acceptable, the financial loss suffered is manageable, and the other risk management techniques are unaffordable.

Risk Transfer

Risk transfer means shifting the risk and the loss of the risk to others. There are two main ways of passing on the risk to others: through a contract or through insurance. By using a contract, we can shift the risk and the associated financial loss to other parties. For instance, in a leasing contract, we have the right to use the asset while the lease holder retains the ownership of the asset and so we shift the property risk of the asset to the lease holder.

A more common means to shift risk is through insurance. In the risk-transfer process through insurance, the party which transfers the risk is the insured and the party which bears the risk is the insurer (insurance company). Similar to other risk management techniques, risk transfer is not without a cost. The policy holder has to pay a cost (the premium) to the insurer in exchange for sharing the risk transferred. When the insured suffers from the negative consequences associated with the risk transferred, the insurer has to compensate for the loss suffered. By the risk-transfer technique through insurance, the financial loss due to risk is compensated for.

Insurance is an effective means of transferring risk. In general, the consumer public buys insurance as they expect the insurance firms to provide them with the funds when they are in need. Insurance applies the concept of pooling so that the negative financial consequences of risk can be shared among many.

However, it is important to note once again that not all risks are manageable and not all pure risks are insurable. The use of insurance to transfer risk is effective but not always workable. The insurer only provides insurance service for insurable risk. There are three conditions affecting the insurability of risk:

1. **The risk must be nonspeculative**

In other words, only pure risk, a kind of risk which leads to either a loss or no loss (never to a gain), is insurable. The insurance company only provides insurance service to compensate for the potential loss but not to ensure potential profit.

2. The risk must be unscheduled and accidental

Unscheduled risk means that no one knows when and how the risk would take place, or whether the risk would lead to injuries. Accidental risk means that the risk should not be due to the intentional conduct or intentional omission of conduct of the insured. The insurance company provides insurance service for property risk. However, the insurance company would not compensate for property loss if we intentionally leave our property unattended.

3. The probability for the risk to take place is predictable mathematically and actuarially

Insurance is a business which provides compensation for losses due to risk. The insurers must be experts in managing risk. Insurers only provide insurance coverage for losses within predictable limits. The expected loss should be definite or determinate in time, place, peril (cause of a loss or risk), and amount so that the expected loss of an insurable risk is calculable over a reasonable operating period.

Principles of Insurance

Insurance is defined as the pooling of accidental and unexpected losses by transferring risk to the insurer (the party who agrees to indemnify the person being insured for the losses, to provide pecuniary benefits on their occurrence, or to render services connected with the risk). In a broad sense, insurance includes social welfare services provided by the government, such as social medical service, social elderly service, and unemployment benefits, as well as commercial insurance provided by privately run businesses to insure against such risks as the destruction of property or stock by fire, losses arising from fires or other causes, and the loss of human lives. The protection from risk provided by the government is termed *social insurance*. The protection from risk provided by commercial firms is termed *private insurance,* which falls into two broad categories: life and health insurance, and property and liability insurance. In the context of financial planning, obviously insurance is used in the commercial sense.

An insurance policy is a legally binding business contract between the insurer (or underwriter) and the policy holder. The insurance policy states all the necessary information agreed on between the insurer and the policy holder such as the respective rights and responsibilities of the insurer and the policy holder, the insurance object, insurance duration, premium, insurance benefit, and the beneficiaries. The policy holder pays the insurance premium amount (also known as *consideration*) as stated in the insurance policy to the insurer who then uses the premium to set up an insurance fund. This insurance fund indemnifies and compensates the insured for the financial loss due to insurable pure risk within the insurance duration.

Besides the insurer, there are three other parties in the insurance policy: the policy holder, the insured, and the beneficiaries. The policy holder, the insured, and the beneficiaries may or may not be the same person. The party who pays for the insurance premium is the policy holder. The party who is protected by the insurance policy is the insured. In the event of a covered loss, the insured can be reimbursed financially and/or receive other protection services. If an individual pays the insurance premium of a life insurance policy to insure against premature or accidental death of his own life, then the policy holder and the insured are the same person. The beneficiary is the assigned party who will receive the insurance benefit under the terms of the insurance policy. If an individual pays the insurance premium of a medical insurance policy to cover medical bills, then the policy holder, the insured, and the beneficiary are the same person.

The insurance policy may become invalid if there is no relevant insurable benefit arising from the insurance object for the policy holder and the insured. The insurance benefit is the amount paid to the beneficiaries when the insured suffers from financial loss under insurance cover. In general, the insurance benefit is computed based on the value of the insurance object. There are three essential conditions for insurance benefits:

1. **The benefit must be legal.** The benefit cannot be insurable if there are illegal elements and substances in the benefit.
2. **The benefit must be objective.** The benefit cannot be insurable if there are uncertain elements and substances in the benefit.
3. **The benefit must be measurable.** The benefit cannot be insurable if the benefit is not measurable mathematically. The insurable benefit must be measurable as the underwriter needs the information to estimate the insurance premium and insurance benefit.

In determining the insurance benefit, it is always easier to estimate the value of physical objects than personal objects. Examples of physical objects include home buildings, motor vehicles, furniture, and fixtures. Underwriters can use the economic or market value of these properties to determine the insurance benefit. Underwriters may need professional advice to assess the values of more valuable objects such as jewelry and antiques.

Unlike most physical objects which possess an economic or market value, the value of personal objects such as human life, human abilities, and earning power is difficult to quantify. Underwriters make an assessment of the insurance benefit for the personal object based on such parameters as gender, age, age of spouse, monthly income, monthly consumption, number and age of dependants, bank deposits, assets, investments, liabilities, interest rate, and inflation rate.

Functions of Insurance

The functions of insurance are categorized into basic function and derivative function:

1. Basic function

As we have discussed earlier, the basic function of insurance is to share, shift, and indemnify the insurable risk of the insured. By paying premiums to the insurer, the insured is able to get compensatory benefits. Through insurance, the financial loss due to uncertainty can be reduced.

2. Derivative function

There are two derivative functions: financing/investing and preventing disaster/loss.

Financing and investing The derivative functions of financing and investing serve two purposes. From the perspective of the insurer, since there is a time gap between the receipt of premiums from the policy holder and the payment of insurance benefits to the insured for compensation, the insurer can make use of the premium payments as investment funds to increase the value of the insurance fund. From the perspective of the policy holder, the policy holder can choose to allocate part of the premium as cash portion for investment purposes to increase the cash value of the insurance policy.

Function of preventing disaster and loss Through the insurance service, the insurer can provide loss management service for the insured. Besides providing actuarial estimates of the compensatory benefit, the insurer also makes professional estimates, and carries out analysis and assessment of the probability of potential risk. In addition, the insurer may make recommendations on precautionary measures and loss management.

Insurance Products

As the purpose of insurance is to provide funds to compensate for the various types of financial losses when necessary, insurance products can be categorized by the type of financial loss on the insurance objects. If the insurance object is a personal object (i.e., the lives and abilities of the insured), the insurer has to provide compensatory benefits in case the insured suffers from premature death, natural death, illnesses, physical and psychological disabilities, and loss in income earning power. Examples of physical objects are property and the economic value of the property. The property insured can be tangible such as land and buildings and motor vehicles, or intangible such as expected income.

Life Insurance

We are exposed to various personal risks of getting ill; becoming physically, psychologically, and financially incapable of supporting ourselves; and premature or accidental death. One of the immediate consequences of these personal risks is the loss or reduction of income or increase in expenses such as medical expenses and funeral expenses. Therefore, we need protection against negative financial consequences. One solution is to buy a **life insurance** policy. The insurance object of a life insurance policy is the life of an individual. Figure 4.2 provides an overview of various types of life insurance policies.

Before we discuss the different types of life insurance policies, we need to know about life insurance pricing. Major determinants of life insurance pricing include the probability of the insured event occurring, the time value of money, and loading. Insurers often use the probabilities of death for each age listed in mortality tables. Sometimes, insurers may modify the probabilities of death in the tables for their own pricing schemes. Some large insurers may have the financial

life insurance
Insurance policy that insures against premature or accidental death of a policy holder's life and provides financial compensation to the beneficiary of the policy holder.

Figure 4.2 Types of life insurance policies

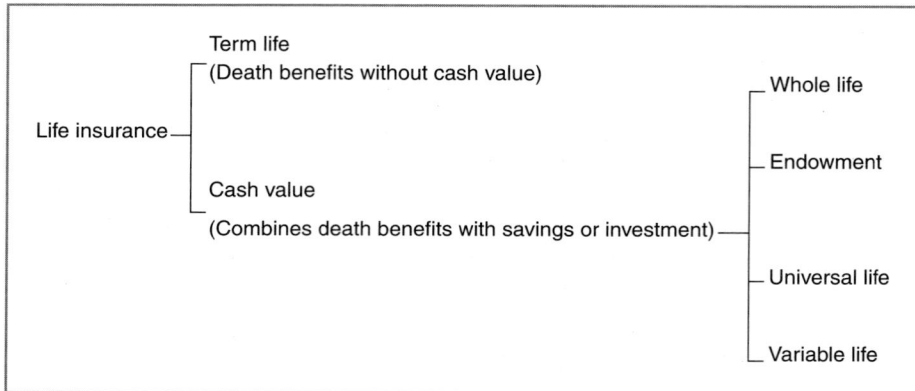

and human resources to construct their own mortality tables. Insurers must also try to earn investment returns on the premium revenue received from policy holders. The investment returns can be quite substantial as insurance policies may be in force for many years. The benefits promised according to the terms of the insurance policy are, of course, one of the determinants of the needed premiums. An extra charge known as *loading* is incorporated into the premium to cover expenses, taxes, normal profits, and contingencies of the insurance policy. Therefore, the gross premium rate is given by the following equation:

$$\text{Gross premium rate} = \frac{\text{Net premium rate (the discounted expected}}{\text{value of death benefits)}} + \text{Loadings}$$

Life insurance can be broadly categorized into two major types: term life insurance and cash value life insurance. Term life insurance provides death protection only, while cash value life insurance includes a savings element called the cash value with the death protection. Examples of cash value life insurance are whole life, endowment, universal life, and variable life.

In the history of insurance, term life insurance, whole life insurance, and endowment insurance were the more traditional products. During the 1970s, life insurance companies started to develop life insurance products that were much more sensitive to market conditions (particularly the financial market) than the long-established conventional products such as whole life and term life. There was an increased demand from the insuring public for higher flexibility in life insurance policies partly due to the changing inflation and nominal interest rates at that time. Consequently, new, more flexible products such as universal and variable life insurance were introduced into the life insurance market. These innovative life insurance products were aimed at reducing costs through making indeterminate-premium plans, introducing a more refined classification system, and providing provisions to encourage persistency.

Before we go into the details of each of these life insurance products, we need to get familiar with some terms:

Death benefit   Death benefit is the amount paid to the beneficiary upon the death of the insured.

Insurance premium   Insurance premium is payment in the form of a single lump sum or regular payment paid periodically throughout the term of the insurance policy for the insurance product.

Cash value   Cash value is the amount of the savings element in the insurance policy. Another name for cash value is *accumulation fund*.

Death protection   Death protection refers to the pure amount of insurance provided which is equal to the difference between the death benefit and the cash value.

Surrender/lapse   Surrender or lapse refers to the termination of the insurance policy. If the policy has a cash value, the amount received by the policy holder is called the surrender value. There may be surrender charges upon termination, thus the surrender value may be less than the cash value.

Face amount   Face amount is the stated amount of the insurance in the contract.

Policy loading   Loadings refer to policy expenses and can be in the form of back-end loads, front-end loads, or both. However, front-end loads are the most common.

Dividends   A life insurance policy which pays dividends is called a participating policy while one which does not pay is called a nonparticipating policy. Dividends from participating policies are not guaranteed and should not be counted as taxable income. Most whole life insurance policies are participating policies.

The purpose of life insurance is to insure against the premature or accidental death of a policy holder and provide financial compensation to the beneficiary upon the death of the policy holder, so that the beneficiary can maintain a certain living standard even after the death of the policy holder. There are various types of financial losses and costs upon the death of an individual, for instance, there is an immediate loss of the future earning power of the deceased for the surviving members. There are additional costs associated with death such as funeral expenses and estate tax. In order to protect the surviving members from the negative financial consequences, life insurance is needed. Factors that need to be considered before deciding on an appropriate life insurance policy include the following:

1. Duration of the insurance contract—term or whole life
2. Inclusion of investment element—cash value or noncash value
3. Responsibility to make investment decisions and willingness to bear investment risks
4. Universal life or variable life
5. Tax implications—life insurance proceeds for the beneficiary are free from income tax

Term Life Insurance

term life insurance
Insurance policy for a specific time period normally designed for at least 5 years up to 25 or 30 years.

Term life insurance is an insurance policy for a specific time period of at least 5 years up to 25 or 30 years. At the end of the specific time period, the term life insurance policy expires. If the insured dies during the specified period, there is compensation. There are several unique features of term life insurance. The premium for a term life insurance is relatively low. The annual premiums are based entirely on the mortality charges of that year. The exception to this rule are multiyear level premium plans in 5-year, 10-year, or 20-year terms.

Since there is a predetermined insurance duration, everything else being equal, the insurance benefits provided by term life insurance are relatively greater. Term life insurance only provides a death benefit without cash surrender or loan values. At the end of the term, the term insurance policy expires.

The expired term life insurance policy can be renewed for successive periods as long as the premium is paid. This is known as guaranteed renewability. Usually, no medical examination is required for a term life policy to be renewed. The policy holder can also convert the term life insurance policy to other types of life insurance policies such as whole life or universal life policies. However, such a convertibility option is only available if the insured has not reached the age of 65.

As the underwriter needs to bear substantial compensation liabilities as compared to the small insurance premium paid by the policy holder of term life insurance, the underwriter usually imposes certain restrictions and conditions on the purchase of term life insurance. For example, if the insurance benefit or the death benefit is too substantial, the underwriter may require the insured to undergo a complete and thorough medical examination before the premium amount and the terms of the insurance policy are determined. The insurance premium is a reflection of the insured's physical health and level of risk exposure (e.g., high risk of getting occupational injuries).

Whole Life Insurance

whole life insurance Insurance policy that insures the policy holder for his or her whole life, and that also contains a certain cash value after some minimum time period.

cash value The amount of cash savings in the insurance policy.

Unlike a term life insurance policy that insures the policy holder for only a short period of time, a **whole life insurance** policy insures the policy holder for his or her whole life. Whole life insurance policy is a form of permanent life insurance that contains a **cash value** after some minimum time period. Therefore, a whole life insurance policy is very similar to or can be regarded as an "endowment-at-100" policy. In the original form of whole life insurance, everything except dividends (if paid), is fixed. The annual premiums over the life of the policy and growth of cash values are fixed at the inception of the contract.

The fixed premium payment for whole life insurance is divided into two portions: (1) the premium to cover the death probability to provide for the minimum guaranteed death benefit; and (2) the cash portion, also called the accumulation fund or account, for long-term investment in securities, mutual funds, or bonds. In the early years of the policy, the cash portion is smaller. When the cash portion becomes larger in the later years of the insurance policy, the policy holder can use the accumulated cash value or the dividend income from securities investment and the interest income from savings investment to pay for the premium. In such a case, the net level premium method of the whole life cash value policy used to finance the whole life insurance provides for the overpayment of mortality charges in the early years of the policy and hence builds up a cash value as a savings element. The net amount at risk is reduced by the savings element so that the mortality charges are lower than they otherwise are. According to the terms of some whole life insurance policies, the policy holder may withdraw the cash value accumulated by borrowing from the insurance company under a loan provision or surrendering the insurance policy as partial surrender.

Endowment Insurance

An endowment insurance is a traditional insurance that pays the face value to the beneficiary upon the death of the policy holder or that pays the face value to the policy holder if he or she survives to the end of the term. The mechanics of **endowment insurance** are essentially the same as whole life insurance. The only difference is the time length of the insurance contract. For instance, an endowment-at-65 life insurance contract pays the death benefit when the insured dies before the age of 65 or pays the face amount when the insured reaches the age of 65.

Universal Life Insurance

Universal life insurance is a unique combination of term life insurance and whole life insurance. By blending the special features such as the protection of term life insurance and the cash value of whole life insurance, universal life insurance appeals to potential policy holders who favor more flexible arrangements for premiums and death benefits.

While the terms in a whole life insurance policy are more rigid, universal and variable life insurance policies are more flexible. In a universal life insurance policy, which is a cash-value policy, there are flexible terms for the premium payment, death benefit option, withdrawal means for cash value, and investment choice. The policy holder is required to pay the premium for the first year and then in later years, the policyholder has the option to increase or decrease the premium amount or to use the excess cash to offset the premium payment as long as the cost of keeping the insurance policy in force is covered. Such a policy is called a flexible premium policy. If the policy holder intends to increase the face amount of insurance policy, evidence of insurability is usually required by the underwriters.

The premium paid for a universal insurance policy is divided into two portions: (1) cash value fund or accumulation fund and (2) death benefit. The sources of growth in the accumulation fund of a universal insurance policy are new contributions and interest earnings. While the interest earnings are market-sensitive and fluctuate from year to year, they are subject to a minimum guarantee. The accumulation funds usually earn interest more than the guarantee. From the cash value fund, a mortality charge is deducted. The mortality charge is estimated using parameters such as the attained age of the insured and the net amount of risk which is the difference between death benefit and cash value.

There are two death benefit systems in a universal life insurance policy. Although there is no difference in the premium payment for the policies with

endowment insurance Insurance policy that would pay the face value to the beneficiary upon death of the policy holder or that pays the face value to the policy holder if he or she survives to the end of the policy term.

univeral life insurance Cash-value policy with flexible terms for the premium payment, death benefit option, cash value options at withdrawal, and investment choice.

different death benefit options, the first option provides a death benefit equal to the face amount (level death benefit) while the second option provides a death benefit equal to the sum of face amount and cash value (increasing death benefit). Another flexible feature of a universal life insurance policy is that the policy holder is allowed to withdraw the cash value accumulated by borrowing (loan provision) or surrendering the policy (partial surrender). While the excess cash of whole life insurance is usually invested in long-term market instruments, the cash value of universal life insurance is put in short-term money market instruments.

Variable Life Insurance

variable life insurance An investment unit-linked life insurance where the value of the policy is linked to the investment performance chosen.

While the investment decision for a whole life insurance policy rests on the insurance company, that for a **variable life insurance** policy is taken up by the policy holder. Variable life insurance, which is a unit-linked life insurance, is an investment-sensitive product. Variable life insurance was first offered in the United States in 1976. The reasoning behind this new innovative insurance product is to make life insurance more responsive to inflation rates by assuming that the securities returns in the stock market increase with inflation.

Like for a whole life insurance policy, the policy holder has to pay a fixed premium which provides funds to cover the death benefit and investment. A variable life insurance policy is variable or flexible in the sense that the investment option, the ultimate cash value, and the death benefit can vary. The policy holder is allowed to allocate investment funds in several investment options (investment subaccounts) designated by the insurance company. As the policy holder is the one who makes the investment decision, the policy holder bears the investment risks and returns. Consequently, there is no minimum guaranteed cash value. The cash value varies with the investment performance of the subaccounts to which the policy holder has allocated investment funds. For the death benefit, unless the policy holder takes up the responsibility to make up the shortfall for the premium to cover the death probability, the death benefit may be less than the coverage amount initially agreed on.

Health (Medical) Insurance

Insurance companies usually sell health insurance products with life insurance products rather than promote health insurance products separately. However, that does not imply that health insurance products are not important. There is an endless list of diseases and illnesses, known and unknown, curable and incurable, that a person may suffer from. It is impossible to provide health insurance coverage for all diseases. Understandably then, health insurance products are sold only after a thorough assessment is made of a person's medical history, level of occupational hazards, living conditions, and lifestyle.

The main purpose of health insurance is to provide funds for the insured to bear medical care costs. Medical care costs include costs for clinical treatment, dental treatment, pharmaceutical expenses, surgery, hospital care, medical examinations, nursing care, and administration.

Disability Income Insurance

We need health insurance to pay medical bills. However, if we become physically or mentally disabled, we will be unable to earn an income. Disability insurance provides funds to cover the loss of earned income due to physical or mental disability. It is a type of health insurance.

Property Insurance

If you own property, you are subject to property risk. Property risk refers to the possibility of property getting depreciated, damaged, or destroyed. There are two major types of property risk: risk of loss of the property (i.e., a direct loss) and risk of loss due to damage to the property (i.e., an indirect loss). Examples of property risks are fire, flood, earthquake, and theft. Property risk is directly related to the value of the property held.

There are two categories of property insurance. The *specified perils coverage* provides insurance for the specific causes of loss to the property included in the policy. The *all risks coverage* protects the property of the insured against all risks except those excluded in the property insurance policy. Examples of property insurance include the following:

Home building   Home building insurance provides cover for damage to the property or building due to fire, flood, earthquake, storm, and all other natural disasters.

Home content   Home content insurance provides cover for damage caused to the contents of a home due to fire, flood, earthquake, storm, and theft.

Comprehensive motor vehicle   Comprehensive motor vehicle insurance provides cover for damage to a vehicle due to fire, theft, collision, and third-party accidents.

Liability insurance

All of us are exposed to the risk of potential liability claims made by others. Liability risk refers to the liability that we need to bear for causing harm, injury, or financial loss to others. These risks may be due to negligent acts, failure to exhibit duty of care, recklessness, or non-conformance of contracts and laws. Examples of liability insurance include the following:

Third-party accident   Third-party accident insurance is compulsory for all owners of motor vehicles to cover the legal liability that may arise from the damage to a third party.

Public liability   Public liability insurance provides cover for the legal liability owed to those who are physically injured on the property of the insured.

Domestic workers' compensation   Domestic workers' insurance provides cover for the legal liability in relation to the injuries caused to domestic workers when working in the home of the insured.

Professional indemnity   Professional indemnity insurance provides cover for the legal liability in relation to the negligent advice given to clients when discharging professional duty.

Insurance Planning

We have now covered the basic insurance products marketed by insurance companies. In addition, several insurance products can be combined to create a more comprehensive insurance package. For instance, investment-linked life insurance products have become popular recently, particularly in Australia and Asia. This product combines the traditional life insurance protection with the benefits of investing in mutual funds and allows policy holders to participate in the securities market. Such an insurance innovation provides financial planners with more choices in meeting the insurance and investment needs of clients.

However, these products also demand a much stronger professional knowledge in comprehensive financial planning as such a hybrid product makes the traditional matching approach less effective. In the past, financial planners employed insurance products to meet insurance needs and investment products to meet investment needs. Nowadays financial planners can meet both insurance and investment needs of their clients by using a single product. Unfortunately, the percentage of insurance and investment components may not always match the clients' needs. Thus, financial planners may have to combine pure insurance products, pure investment products, and hybrid products together to properly meet their clients' financial needs. This requires advanced knowledge in quantitative analysis and a deeper understanding of the features of each product. In short, choosing the right insurance products to meet the clients' needs is not an easy task. Financial planners must be aware of the following factors that affect the insurance needs of their clients:

Age   We all go through different stages in our life cycle, and these life-cycle stages are age-related. Individuals at different life-cycle stages would have different protection needs. For instance, parents buy insurance products to protect their children in case of their premature or accidental deaths. A client's age also affects his ability to buy insurance products.

Number of dependants and marital status   When there are dependants (unemployed spouse and/or children) in the family, there is a need for the breadwinner to buy insurance to protect against his or her premature death. As the number of dependants increases, the need for insurance also increases.

Level of income and personal financial ability   The level of income and personal financial ability are significant factors determining one's insurance needs. Although there is a need for insurance protection, no insurance need can be fulfilled if there is no income.

Financial planners must determine the amount of insurance coverage that their clients need. The amount of insurance coverage varies from client to client, depending on the same factors (age, number of dependants, income level) that affect their insurance needs. There are a number of techniques to help insurance experts and financial planners to estimate the amount of insurance coverage. We will describe two such techniques: the rules of thumb approach and the needs approach.

Rules of Thumb Approach

rules of thumb approach A simple way to estimate a client's insurance needs based on subjective industry wisdom.

A simple way to estimate the insurance needs of the client is by using the **rules of thumb approach**. This approach is based on some subjective industry wisdom that the life insurance coverage should be a multiple of the annual income of the client. For instance, for whole life insurance, it is believed that 6–8 times the gross annual income should be sufficient. For term life insurance, a higher multiple such as 10–15 times the current annual income should be more appropriate.

On top of this, it is also believed that an emergency cash fund of at least 3–6 months of income should be available at all times. Of course, rules of thumb vary from country to country and from client to client, depending on many factors such as tax rates, lifestyles, asset levels, and the sense of security of the clients. One must be very careful in applying these rules to clients. Financial planners should always remember that life insurance should not be used as a lifelong financial protection for the surviving spouse and family members. As long as there is enough financial protection for them to survive the emotional period of grief and loss and learn to be independent financially, the insurance coverage is deemed to be appropriate. If clients demonstrate an unusually high level of insecurity, and demand an unusually large coverage of life insurance policies, financial planners should not just give in to their demands but pay more attention to their clients' personal and psychological profile to find out why they would want to overinsure themselves in this way.

Needs Approach

needs approach A more scientific way to estimate insurance coverage by predicting the lump-sum cash needed upon death to cover funeral expenses, liabilities, and ongoing consumption needs of the surviving spouse and family.

The **needs approach** is a better approach than the rules of thumb approach as it is more scientific. Using the needs approach, financial planners are required to come up with an estimate of the insurance coverage by predicting the lump-sum cash needed upon death to cover funeral expenses, liabilities, and more importantly, ongoing consumption needs of the surviving spouse and family. This approach requires an assumption of how much the surviving members really "need" for every year and for how long. *Need* can be a very abstract and subjective term. A lot of people think that they need a lot of stuff. However, what they really need may not be essential to their daily lives. In other words, what they think they need is actually what they *want* or *desire*.

Therefore, while the needs approach is more scientific in that it tries to estimate the consumption needs of surviving members and relate these to insurance coverage, the key issues of how much is necessary and for how long they should be protected are still "open" questions that financial planners will have to answer. Once these issues are resolved, hopefully with the support and understanding of the client, the calculation of the consumption amount and the estimation of the major expenses for the period become a mere exercise of time value of money calculation.

Using Consumption Smoothing to Estimate Life Insurance Needs

Earlier in the chapter we discussed how Friedman's permanent-income hypothesis can help to provide a useful consumption strategy for clients through consumption smoothing. The permanent-income hypothesis can also be used to estimate the amount of life insurance protection. The equation shown earlier on page 128 is repeated here:

$$\text{Total lifelong income} = \text{Total consumption} + \text{Bequest}$$

We can estimate the ideal annual consumption level for clients simply by assuming that clients would spend all their lifelong income on consumption. In this case, the total consumption would be determined by the income earned. Therefore, life insurance coverage should be related to lifelong income. To cater to the surviving family's needs, we can reduce the consumption level by the amount spent by the insured. After estimating the total consumption needs of the family in terms of present value, the financial planner can use that amount as the basis for the life insurance needed for the family. In theory, the calculation must be repeated annually—the reason being that, as the total lifelong consumption reduces through time, so does the insurance coverage. In practice, it is quite difficult to reduce the insurance coverage from year to year. Thus using a combination of term life and whole life insurance to create a matching pattern of the upward and downward trends in insurance needs in various life stages is an effective strategy to match cyclical insurance needs in a client's life cycle. In fact, there exist some life insurance products that provide a decreasing life insurance coverage through time. Such a decreasing term life insurance policy is a very useful tool in dealing with the declining insurance needs in the later stages of a client's life cycle.

So far, we have talked about how we can use the permanent-income hypothesis to estimate insurance needs. However, there are certain limitations of relating insurance needs to consumption smoothing. One of the major assumptions for consumption smoothing is that total lifelong income is a good indicator of the total consumption of an individual. There are cases where this assumption may not be valid. First, this assumption does not allow for the extensive use of debt with the intention of defaulting or using an insurance policy to cover the debt of the deceased. In this case, consumption can far exceed the income earned. Second, this assumption may not be valid as well if the income level of the client is too low or too high. We can divide clients into three major categories according to their incomes: (1) low income, (2) middle income, and (3) high income.

Individuals in the low-income group may not have enough money to buy proper insurance coverage. The high-income group may earn too much money for us to use the assumption that total income should be equal to total consumption, so the needs approach may be more suitable than the consumption smoothing approach. We can assume that the total lifelong income serves as a good benchmark of the total consumption for clients in the middle-income group. Thus, in order to estimate the insurance needs of clients, we can use the consumption smoothing approach with the total income as a constraint to estimate the ideal consumption level first, and then determine the proper insurance coverage.

Understanding the Risk Factors in Insurance Planning

Although the purpose of insurance is to manage risk by transferring risk to other parties, it does not mean that insurance planning is risk-free. There are three risk factors in insurance planning: insufficiency of insurance cover, overinsurance, and unnecessary insurance. These may be the result of inaccurate information about the client or insufficient understanding of the insurance products.

Insufficient insurance cover   There may be insufficient insurance coverage in terms of quality and quantity. The insurance products purchased may not be sufficient enough to cover all necessary needs of the clients, making some of the financial loss of the clients left uncovered, or the insurance duration may be too short.

Overinsurance   Some clients may assume that the more insurance products they purchase, and the higher the insurance premiums they pay, the higher the insurance payouts they would get should the inevitable happen. However, this is not really the case. In some circumstances, the clients may have paid more than they need. This is the risk of overinsurance. In addition, without knowing exactly what they have bought, the clients may have purchased products with overlapping insurance coverage. Therefore, without a comprehensive picture of the overall financial needs and the available insurance products in the market, an inappropriate mix of insurance products may create a situation where some risks remain uncovered and some risks are overprotected.

Unnecessary coverage   We talked about risk retention on pages 147–148. In some circumstances, it is too expensive to prevent, avoid, or transfer risk. Therefore, the easiest and simplest way is to retain the risk. Therefore, the clients have to decide whether some risks should be retained to reduce opportunity costs and to save on unnecessary premium payments for potential investment.

Key Terms

cash flow management   *122*
cash value   *154*
consumption smoothing   *128*
debt-to-income ratio   *126*
debt-to-total assets ratio   *126*
endowment insurance   *155*
estate tax   *135*
income tax   *135*
investment assets-to-net worth ratio   *126*
life insurance   *151*
liquidity ratio   *126*

needs approach   *159*
profits tax   *135*
property tax   *135*
rules of thumb approach   *159*
savings ratio   *126*
solvency ratio   *126*
stamp duty   *135*
term life insurance   *153*
universal life insurance   *155*
variable life insurance   *156*
whole life insurance   *154*

References

Friedman, M., *A Theory of the Consumption Function* (Princeton: Princeton University Press, 1957).

Individual Taxes: A Worldwide Summary (New York: PriceWaterhouse Center for Transnational Taxation).

Markowitz, H. "Portfolio Selection," *Journal of Finance*, vol. 7 (1952): 77–91.

Questions & Problems

Multiple-choice Questions

1. A financial planner can help manage the _____ risk for his or her client through using insurance products.
   A. pure
   B. business
   C. economic
   D. speculating

2. "An employee should not rely entirely on a combination of group term life insurance and social security benefits for their life insurance program." Which of the following support the above statement?
   I. Group term life insurance involves no savings.
   II. The benefits may be unavailable if the employee loses employment.
   III. The benefits may be inadequate to meet all financial needs and goals.
   IV. Group term life insurance allows less choice in designating beneficiaries.

   A. I and II
   B. II and III
   C. I, II, and III
   D. I, II, III, and IV

3. Which of the following are property insurance policies?
   I. Home contents
   II. Private motor car
   III. Personal income protection
   IV. Fire insurance
   V. Terminal illness

   A. I, II and IV
   B. I, III, and V
   C. II, III, and V
   D. II, IV, and V

4. Which of the following are elements of the needs hierarchy in financial planning services?
   I. Long-term and short-term investment goals
   II. Wealth management
   III. Insurance
   IV. Consumption
   VI. Permanent-income hypothesis

   A. I, II, and III
   B. II, IV, and V

C. I, III, and IV

D. II, III, and V

Problems

1. Describe the purposes of using ratio analysis.

2. Explain how consumption smoothing is used to determine the optimal level of consumption for clients.

3. Discuss the setting up of a family trust as a tax planning strategy.

4. Explain how an appropriate level of life insurance is estimated using the rules of thumb approach and the needs approach.

5. Explain how the concept of consumption smoothing is employed in determining insurance needs.

chapter **5**

Financial Planning Components (Part II)

5.1   Investment Planning

Investment planning is an important area in the financial planning process, and is in fact also involved in other planning areas such as retirement planning and even estate planning. Before we talk about the techniques involved in investment planning, we have to clarify the difference between regular investment practices and investment in the context of financial planning.

Misconceptions about Investment Strategies in the Context of Financial Planning

Owing to substantial interest among average consumers in making their own financial investments, clients probably understand the investment area more than they do the other areas of financial planning. This is especially true of Asian clients; they have a very strong incentive to earn more money through securities and real estate investments. Unfortunately, what they think they understand of investments may not be correct. Their misconceptions can prevent them from understanding the right approach to investment planning in the context of financial planning.

There are two major distinctions between regular investment practices and investment planning. First, the duration for regular investment practices can be relatively short if the investors aim to make short-term profits through high-frequency trading. It is possible that a sophisticated investor can buy and sell certain securities within one day to make arbitrage profit. However, in the context of financial planning, we should never conduct short-term trading such as this. In financial planning, short-term investment planning refers to investments that can give returns in about a year. Medium-term investment planning refers to investments that can give returns in 3 to 10 years. Anything more than 10 years can be classified as long term.

So in general, investment strategies in financial planning should not focus on short-term profit (of less than a year) in the securities market. Of course, there are always exceptions. If the financial planner is confident that the securities market is heading toward a major downward adjustment, or there is going to be a huge decline in value of certain mutual funds, then it is necessary to liquidate those investments to prevent significant losses. However, most investment advisors and wealth managers are not able to predict market directions accurately. Thus, adjustments like this should not happen frequently.

Second, all investments made by clients in financial planning should be related to some goals. Maximizing the return from investment is normally not a stand-alone goal for individuals. For instance, under consumption planning, clients should save some emergency cash in a bank account (which is a form of investment). Thus, the goal of this investment is for liquidity and for meeting unexpected personal needs.

It is common for couples with young children to invest money in college education funds. A prudent financial planner should recommend some suitable investment vehicles for these education funds. As the purpose of this investment is to provide college tuition, the risk of the investment choice should not be too high. If the tuition for certain colleges is very expensive and the only way to accumulate enough money is to invest in high-risk, high-return products, then the financial planners should persuade their clients to consider a less expensive college education instead of taking the unnecessary risk.

Financial planners should understand that they are not pure investment advisors only. The happiness of clients is not solely based on the amount of investment return but on how well their life goals can be met through following a proper financial plan.

Role of Financial Planners

There are many different types of investment instruments. Making an investment can be as simple as depositing money into a fixed deposit account or savings account to earn interest, or as complicated as investing in options, futures, or foreign currency. The risk and return parameters of these different investment instruments vary. The knowledge, ability, capital, and time required to monitor these investment options also differ. Does the average consumer really have the time to make investment decisions on his own, or the capital to make diversified investments, or the knowledge to guarantee profitable investments? When it comes to such a personal issue like one's own money, even a professional investor may not be able to stay calm and objective. A third-party financial planner may be able to provide more objective financial planning advice.

For financial planners to offer valuable investment advice, they must first understand the basic investment concepts, the investment products available in the market, and the expectation and risk tolerance levels of their clients. In determining the appropriate strategies, financial planners should also relate their investment recommendations to their clients' life goals. If the financial planners are not that competent in providing more advanced investment advice, they should seek professional help from investment specialists. It is important for financial planners to know their own limitations and not recommend investment products to clients without understanding their features.

Basic Investment Concepts

We will now explain some key concepts in conducting investment planning.

Return

The gain or loss from an investment is called the return. For securities return, there are two components. The first component is the cash received from the investment. For instance, cash dividend is the cash component of the return from a securities investment and interest is the cash component of the return from a loan investment. The second component is the capital gain or capital loss due to the difference in the prices at which the investment is purchased and sold. While there are many ways to measure return, we normally express return as a percentage. The percentage return is the total dollar value as a percentage of the original invested sum.

Risk

While there are many ways to measure and define risk, in the context of investment planning, we focus on financial risk related to investment. Commonly used risk measures are total risk (calculated as the standard deviation of return); market risk or systematic risk (measured by beta of the securities), and firm-specific or unsystematic risk (measured by the residual component of the variance). In order to attract investors to buy riskier securities, the market is willing to pay a compensation for the additional risk, called risk premium, which is the difference between the returns on a risky asset and a riskless investment. In an efficient market, the way to earn higher returns is to make investments with a higher level of risk.

In making investments, sometimes liquidity is also a concern, in addition to investment return. When the securities investment matures or is being sold, the market condition may have changed and the investment vehicle with the same risk-return trade-off may not exist when you want to reinvest the money. Reinvestment risk arises when the investment matures in times of low level of interest rate and reinvestment of the proceeds from the previous investment results in a lower market yield. The reinvestment risk is an important factor to be considered when making decisions on short-term investments.

It is important to select an investment strategy or asset allocation that yields the highest return with a tolerable level of risk. In order to construct a profitable asset allocation for their clients, financial planners have to perform risk and return analyses for various asset allocations.

Investment Horizon

Investment horizon is the length of time allowed to achieve the investment objective or the planned liquidation date of the investors. Investment horizon is a factor that affects the choice of investment instruments (long-term, intermediate-term, or short-term). Property investment is an example of long-term investment while securities investment can be relatively short-term. Investment in bonds and debentures can be of different investment horizons: 6-month, 1-year or 10-year. Investment horizon is also a factor for investment volatility which is an issue to be considered when making investment decisions.

Risk Tolerance

risk tolerance An indicator of the level of investment risk the investor is willing to bear.

Risk tolerance is an indicator of the level of investment risk the investor is willing to bear, and is a major factor in determining the risk-return trade-off and hence the type of investment instrument. In general, investors are risk-averse. They are not willing to make investments with a risk level that is above their tolerance level, no matter how high the return may be. In Chapter 6 we will introduce the concept of risk profiling—the procedure of evaluating the risk tolerance level of clients. It is important for financial planners to understand the techniques of risk profiling so that they can properly match the risk tolerance level of their clients to their investment portfolio.

Investment Policy Statement

investment policy statement Governs the overall direction, performance benchmarks, and boundaries of the investment strategies for clients.

Both financial planners and their clients should construct an **investment policy statement** that is mutually agreed on. There are several major reasons for such a statement: (1) to state the goals and objectives of the investment plan, (2) to provide an evaluation system for performance, (3) to set the boundaries for strategies and product purchases, and (4) to provide clear communication and better understanding of the investment policy, especially at times when there is a dispute or a change of investment advisors.

In general, the investment policy statement includes several major sections, including (1) the statement of purpose or an overview, (2) the investment objectives, (3) the roles and responsibilities of the investment advisors, and (4) the investment guidelines and boundaries. Investment objectives are extremely important as they spell out the medium-term and long-term performance targets of the plan. The objectives should also state the expected benchmark and return performance for each asset class if the portfolio is substantial, as well as the asset allocation strategies and the ranges of each asset class. In the guidelines and boundaries section, prohibited investments and undesirable strategies should be listed so that clients and investment advisors understand perfectly what investment vehicles and tactics should not be employed.

Finally, once the policy statement is drafted and agreed upon, both parties should follow and abide by the statement. The performance of the investment portfolio should follow a long-term view and the investment policy statement can help to ensure this.

Investment Strategies

There are many traditional and newly developed investment strategies used by financial services practitioners in handling the investments of clients. Most professional investment advisors and portfolio managers prefer active investment strategies to passive investment strategies. This implies a relatively high frequency of trading and asset turnover. Although there are additional transaction costs associated with active trading, most investment advisors and portfolio managers believe that the additional profits created by high-frequency trading more than make up for the additional transaction costs. Examples of popular active strategies are securities selection and market timing.

Securities selection aims to buy undervalued stocks before the price goes up or to sell overvalued stocks before the price goes down. Market timing is an investment strategy to conduct purchase and sale transactions in the market in expectation of price movements in the future. For instance, investors who use market timing would buy stocks that have a potential to rise higher than the market during an upturn. However, during an anticipated market downswing, investors should reconstruct the portfolio by selling securities that are expected to lose more than the market and buy securities that are expected to have a strong ability to resist market decline.

Market timing is usually used in conjunction with asset allocation. Financial planners have to adjust the weighting among different classes of investment assets. Examples of major asset classes are cash equivalents, equities, and bonds. If the financial planners are more sophisticated and the clients prefer a more advanced investment strategy, the equity class can be further subdivided into local stocks and overseas stocks. Local stocks include different subclasses such as high- and low-growth, industry-specific, and high- and low-dividend yield stocks. Additional asset classes such as real estate, foreign currency, and alternative investments (such as hedged funds, options, and futures) can be considered. For low-end financial planners and clients, the equity investment in individual stocks can be replaced by equity mutual funds. One must realize that buying bond mutual funds is not the same as buying bonds. For bonds, there is no interest rate risk if you hold the securities to maturity. But for bond mutual funds, owing to the active trading behavior of fund managers, the net value of the bond funds can go up and down and there is no guarantee that investors can get the principal back when they need the money.

Recently, asset allocation strategies such as strategic asset allocation (SAA) and tactical asset allocation (TAA) focusing on market timing of regional securities markets have become popular among high-end portfolio managers. In addition, the development of quantitative finance has also helped to popularize hedged funds among retail investors. Financial planners should at least understand these investment strategies and their limitations. As financial planners are not specialists in asset allocation strategies, it is not necessary for all financial planners to equip themselves with advanced investment knowledge and skills. However, if you want to be a successful wealth manager, investment management will be something that you have to master well.

Financial planners should advise their clients that they should not focus on short-term speculations in making investments. A passive investment strategy such as indexing with limited market timing should be more than sufficient for most average clients. However, if their clients require more sophisticated plans, financial planners have to evaluate the opportunity costs of their time spent on conducting investment analysis on their own or simply hiring investment specialists to do the job. For most financial planning firms, there must be enough economies of scale to either hire a full-time investment research analyst or outsource the job to external investment research firms to provide support to the financial planners. Financial planners should avoid the temptation to follow the investment advice of their clients in order to test their ability to make abnormal returns for them. Even though investment is a major area of financial planning, it is not the only thing that matters. Too much emphasis on investment returns may result in financial planners falling into the futile trap of investment competition.

Long-term Investment: Real Estate

Real estate refers to land, buildings, and structures, and all the equitable interests associated with these. In the United States, real estate includes single-family homes, condominiums, and cooperative apartments. Real estate is very different from other assets because of its unique characteristics of fixed location, long-term usage, and potential for appreciation. The returns of real estate investment may be in the form of capital gains (the selling price being larger than the acquisition price) and periodic rental income. When the real estate is sold, the investment can generate substantial cash inflow in terms of sales proceeds. The single most important factor in determining the price of real estate is location. The valuation model for real estate can be very similar to the discounted cash flow model. More advanced analysis uses the hedonic model in estimating housing prices.

There are differences between securities investments and real estate investments. Real estate is a tangible asset that normally brings a sense of security to investors because they can see and touch the asset or even live in it. Securities investments are intangible assets such as stocks, bonds, and other financial instruments which generate returns only. Certainly, a real estate investment enables the property owner to earn returns if the market price of the real estate is higher than the purchase price. Moreover, besides providing returns on the investment, real estate investment may offer other advantages such as potential cash inflow, tax benefits, and hedging against inflation.

Risk Assessment of Real Estate Investments

Real estate investment is a long-term investment with large initial investment capital (e.g., large outlay of cash as downpayment). Since real estate investment requires substantial initial outlays of capital, clients will have to take a loan to pay for the house or apartment. Before the client finalizes the mortgage decision, the financial planner needs to assess the client's investment objectives and repayment ability. To assess the client's repayment ability, the financial planner needs to estimate his or her personal net assets and cash flow position. In some cities where housing prices fluctuate quite substantially, the risks of real estate investments can be as high as that of the equity market. If substantial financial leverage is involved in the purchase, the risk in terms of return volatility of real estate can actually be similar to investing in stock options! Financial planners should make real estate investment recommendations with respect to the liquidity and the financial capacity of their clients.

The risk in real estate investment is mainly due to the deviation of the actual rate of return from the expected rate of return. Before financial planners can plan to manage the risk for real estate investment, they need to know the following risks inherent in real estate investment:

Price volatility   Like all other investments, real estate investment is subject to risks due to the political, social, economic, and investment market conditions as well as to changes in legislative rules and regulations. Owing to the unique features of real estate investment, it is also susceptible to demographic changes (e.g., population density and social structure).

Marketability and liquidity   Real estate is an irremovable asset. Its marketability and price level are restricted by its location. Real estate is also an illiquid asset. The purchase and sale transactions of real estate take a relatively longer time to proceed (as compared to other investments such as securities and derivatives). Although real estate investment can bring in large sales proceeds for the investor, it takes time for the investors to get it. Therefore, if investors are in quick need of cash, real estate investment is not a good choice. In some circumstances, the seller of the real estate may be pressured to lower the selling price to enhance the marketability and to speed up the selling process.

Interest rate movements   The value of real estate and interest rates are inversely related. The value of real estate is lower when the interest rate is higher. As real estate is usually acquired with borrowed funds or mortgaged for loans, the changes in interest rates have a great impact on the returns for the investors.

Physical deterioration   Real estate is subject to physical deterioration due to natural disasters (earthquake, storm, flood, hurricane, typhoon) and negligence (lack of maintenance and repair, fire, theft). The value of real estate can decline particularly if the real estate is not kept in good condition.

Medium-term Investment: Education

As early as the 1960s, economists have viewed the nurture, tending, and schooling of children as an economic or investment activity. Parents are willing to allocate part or most of their resources for their children so that they can receive the best education (primary, secondary, and tertiary) and develop their interests and full potential. In time, grown-up children may reward their parents for all the time and money invested in them. Rewards may not necessarily be monetary; nonmonetary rewards include pride and prestige in having well-educated children with distinguished occupations. Therefore, an education plan for one's children may be the most gratifying and rewarding plan among the investment components of the financial plan.

Importance of an Education Plan

An education plan is important because the need for higher education is increasingly fundamental for one's career and because the cost of higher education (tuition fees, books, equipment, and transportation) is growing. There are two major types of education plans: personal education investment and education investment for children.

Personal education investment refers to the education funds for the clients themselves. Clients may arrange an investment plan to provide funds for their own continuing education programs. In following their career paths, it may be a competitive advantage if they obtain relevant degrees and professional licenses. These degrees and professional licenses can be very costly.

Education investment for children refers to the education investment plan for the future education of the client's children, normally for college tuition fees. Such education investment plans are becoming more popular because most parents desire their children to receive a higher level of education to achieve a more favorable and prestigious position in the future.

In addition, the cost of education is growing fast and the financial assistance from the government is growing less. If parents do not plan ahead, the lack of sufficient funds may jeopardize the future of their children. Education planning can free the clients from the anxiety and financial burden of paying for the huge education expenses of their children.

Role of Financial Planners

Although clients may be keen to provide the best education for their children, they may not know how to do this. Uneducated clients, particularly, may find it difficult to pick appropriate colleges for their children. However, if the clients tell their financial planners that education for their children is a top priority, financial planners should be able to draw up an appropriate education plan to fund the education, and even help in selecting a suitable college or university, if necessary.

Estimating Education Expenses

There are many factors to consider in estimating the amount of education expenses:

1. **Level of education programs (primary, secondary, college, and graduate levels).** The tuition fees for college and postgraduate education are relatively higher than those for primary and secondary schools.
2. **Type of education programs** (commerce, accounting, business, dentistry, medicine, law, architecture, engineering).
3. **Duration of the programs.**
4. **Type of educational institutions (private or public).** There is a great difference in the tuition fees between public and private educational institutions. For instance, in the United States, the tuition fee of a private university ranges from US$40,000 to US$70,000 while that of a public university is around US$20,000.
5. **Location of educational institutions (domestic or overseas).** When children study overseas, there are additional expenses for transportation, boarding, medical insurance, and communication.

6. **Availability of financial assistance** (scholarships, government grants, government loans).
7. **Possibility of working part-time.**
8. **Number of children.**
9. **Age of children.** The younger the children are, the larger the resources that have to be allocated. On the other hand, when the children are older, the time for arranging and implementing the education plan is shorter. Therefore, the age of the children is a factor determining the size of investment funds and the form of investment strategy. If clients commence the education plan when the children are young, the clients may choose a long-term investment strategy and instruments.

Based on the information about financial objectives and financial conditions of their clients, and all the factors discussed above, financial planners can provide the most appropriate recommendation for the education plan.

Sources of Funding for Education

Financial planners need to be familiar with the available sources of funds for education as the availability of funds affects the type of financial planning strategies for the education plan.

Although most governments cannot provide free education, they do offer financial assistance in various forms such as loans, grants, and subsidies for those who are in need. However, not many are eligible to apply for and obtain this financial aid. The applicants have to be familiar with the terms and conditions of the application, duration and type of assistance, and repayment provisions. Since the government's allocated budget is limited and the number of applications is unlimited, those who can pass the assessment tests may not necessarily be able to obtain the assistance.

Scholarships Besides governments, many commercial enterprises, academic institutions, professional organizations, social welfare groups, religious associations, and universities offer scholarships to students who excel in academic work, social activities, and sports. These scholarships may be in the form of cash, reimbursement of tuition fees paid, and coupons for books and equipment.

Loans Many financial institutions offer low-interest loans to those in need. Although a loan can meet the immediate need of the client to pay for the children's education, the client has to bear the financial liability to repay the loan.

Part-time employment Some clients may let their children work part time to subsidize their tuition fees. Working part time is desirable as one can earn money and gain experience at the same time. However, finding appropriate part-time employment is not easy. The income from part-time employment can never be sufficient to cover the high cost of education. Besides, the study load together with the work load may be too much for students and may affect their studies.

Formulating the Education Plan

So while it is possible to get financial aid in the form of scholarships and loans, or to be able to subsidize tuition fees by working part time, it is better to have an education plan to ensure sufficient funds. There are four steps in the education plan:

1. Set a target of a preferred education program and get information about how much it will cost (tuition fee, administration cost, transportation, expenses for extracurricular activities, medical insurance cost, cost of books and equipment).
2. Set different scenarios of various inflation rates to estimate the expected costs of education under different circumstances.
3. Determine the option of one-time investment planning or multiperiod investment planning by comparing the present value of the amount needed for a one-off outlay investment and the present value of the periodic payments for multiperiod investment.
4. Select an appropriate investment instrument. When making recommendations for an appropriate investment instrument, financial planners have to bear in mind that the main purpose of education investment is to provide sufficient funds for education expenses rather than gaining profits. Security and liquidity are the main concerns. The investment strategies for an education plan can be of short-term or long-term horizon. When clients commence the education plan late, they may have to employ more short-term investment strategies. If they start early, they can employ long-term investment strategies. The tools for long-term education investment planning include personal savings, fixed coupon bonds, life insurance products, bonds (government or corporate), and mutual funds. It is also common to use mortgages and loans to achieve short-term education investment planning.

SAVINGS PLAN

Financial planners can suggest that clients set aside a certain proportion of their regular income in a savings account for education expense purposes. However, as personal savings can be used for other purposes and emergency needs such as death and unemployment, there is no guarantee that the personal savings can be left unused solely for the education expenses of the children. In addition, the investment duration of personal savings depends on the life span of the clients. If the clients die prematurely or accidentally, there will be no more savings.

BONDS

Clients can earn regular interest from bond investments. When they are in need of large amounts of capital, they can sell the bonds and enjoy the sales proceeds. In addition to coupon bonds that pay interest regularly, there are also zero-coupon bonds which pay no interest but allow the investor to buy at a deep discount. For instance, the US EE Series savings bond adopts a user-friendly approach to help individuals to save money for education purposes. The individuals who are interested in this kind of bonds can buy the bonds through the banks. The price of the bond is always half of the par value of the bond. The time to maturity for different interest rates is shown on the back of the savings bond certificate so the buyers can check when they can collect the money. If the bond money is used to pay for the education expenses of the buyer or the children of the buyer, the interest income earned from the bond is tax-free.

Treasury bills and government bonds are risk-free, highly marketable, and highly liquid (see a more detailed description of treasury bills in Chapter 3). There is the guarantee of periodic interest income and redeemable value upon maturity. Unlike treasury bills and government bonds, corporate bonds are more risky. However, investments in securities and corporate bonds yield a higher return.

LIFE INSURANCE PRODUCTS

Life insurance products can be used as an education investment instrument. If clients die prematurely or accidentally, according to the terms of the life insurance policy, the children who are assigned as the beneficiaries can get the death benefit and the cash value accumulated as compensation. If the clients are still alive and in need of money for education expenses, they can surrender the insurance policy partially to withdraw the cash values or use the insurance policy as a collateral for loans.

TRUST FUNDS

Clients can set up a trust and designate the purpose of the funds to be limited to education-related expenses for their children. The custodian bank and the trustee are responsible for monitoring the use of the funds according to the purpose. By doing so, the money in the education trust is tax-free. However, once the trust is set up, the funds cannot be used for other purposes. Thus, clients must consider carefully whether to set up a trust to fund their children's education.

MUTUAL FUNDS

Investing in mutual funds has the advantages of great variety and flexibility. Clients are allowed to swap their investment capital among various types of mutual funds. For instance, when the risk tolerance level of the clients is higher, they can put their capital into mutual funds which yield higher returns.

LOANS

Mortgage loans   Clients can mortgage their properties for loans to subsidize the cost of education. One of the advantages of a mortgage loan is the deductibility of mortgage interest, thus making the cost of mortgage loans lower. However, clients should be sure about their ability to repay the principal and interest before taking out a mortgage. Otherwise, they may lose their properties.

Low-interest-rate loans from educational institutions, government agencies, and approved financial institutions   In order to attract good students, educational institutions may offer low-interest-rate loans. Some government agencies and approved financial institutions also offer loans to help and encourage students to receive more education.

5.2   Retirement Planning

In most countries, people retire between the ages of 55 and 65. As living conditions have become better and medical technology has become more advanced, life expectancy has increased. If we assume the average expected life span to be 75, we will have 10 to 20 years of retirement. When we retire, we lose our income earning power. So how can we maintain or improve our living standards when we have lost our earning power during the retirement period? One way is to have a well-prepared retirement plan in place.

With the gradual maturity of the economy and the rise in living standards, middle-income individuals have become more interested in comprehensive financial planning and wealth management that can take care of all their financial needs. If possible, one should plan for retirement in the context of overall financial planning. As retirement planning is closely related to other areas of financial planning, we should also pay attention to these areas.

Many people think of retirement planning as simply investment with a longer horizon. This is not true. There is a lot more to retirement planning. An individual should have a clear understanding of his or her preferred lifestyle and life goals during the retirement planning process. Retirement planning involves achieving life's goals with financial freedom. Thus investment strategies for retirement should be very different from investment just to maximize returns. Return performance should not be the only indicator to judge the success of a retirement plan. After all, retirement can be viewed as the beginning of a second life that retirees can enjoy by pursuing activities that were not possible when they were working. With sufficient financial security through proper financial planning, and good physical and mental health, retirement can be an enjoyable period of life.

Importance of Retirement Planning

If an individual works 40 hours a week, 50 weeks a year, and 40 years for his or her whole life, he or she would have worked for a total of more than 80,000 hours. A comfortable retirement is what every employee dreams of, but it doesn't come without a cost. If we have to work so hard now in order to maintain current living standards, wouldn't that imply that we need to work even harder (more than 40 hours a week!) to save for the retirement period when we have no more income? It appears that a comfortable life now and in the future is hard to achieve. That is why retirement planning is so important.

Increase in Life Expectancy

Currently, the world's highest life expectancy is found in Singapore (81.6 years) and Japan (81.2 years). Medical and technological advances have increased the life expectancy of humans. However, a longer life can only be a good thing if it is comfortable. If we live longer and our retirement age remains the same, our retirement period gets longer. A longer retirement period means that we need to accumulate a larger amount of savings for retirement. Therefore, we need retirement planning.

Women generally have a longer life expectancy than men, and so they usually get less pension than men. The worldwide life expectancy for men is 62.7 years; for women it is 66 years. In North America and Europe, the difference in life expectancy between men and women ranges between 4 and 6 years. These statistics suggest that women are even more in need of retirement planning.

Early Retirement

Early retirement may be voluntary or unintentional. We can enjoy voluntary early retirement if we have sufficient financial resources. However, we may be forced to retire due to various reasons like work exhaustion or retrenchment. Whether voluntary or unintentional, we need to be prepared and have a retirement plan in place.

Insufficiency of Social Security and Retirement Pension Funds

Most governments provide social security schemes and services for the elderly. There are also various employer-provided retirement schemes, such as long-service plans, pension funds, and superannuation funds to help employees to save money for retirement. However, social security and pension schemes may sometimes go awry. In 2000, there was a great global market slump. It was the first time in 20 years that most of the pension schemes in the United States made a loss. There was a great reduction in asset size of retirement funds. For instance, the value of the well-known US 401 [k] plan shrank by US$72 billion. However, the market slump is just one of the reasons for the shortfall of retirement funds. Another reason is the aging problem. Since social security and employer-provided retirement funds may not necessarily be sufficient to provide for our retirement, we need retirement planning.

Role of Financial Planners

As retirement planning is so important, we need professional advice from the experts. Financial planners can help their clients to consider the following:

1. Desired retirement age.
2. Probability of early retirement (voluntary or involuntary).
3. Expected lifestyle and living standard in retirement.
4. Personal health condition.
5. Sources of retirement income (social security, superannuation)
6. Amount of accumulated income for retirement purpose.
7. Estimated income for retirement use.
8. Difference between actual retirement income and estimated retirement income.
9. Changes in medical insurance system.

10. Inflation and market interest rate fluctuations.
11. Periodic revision of retirement plan to adjust for the changes.

Problems in Retirement Planning

Planning Too Late

People have different financial goals throughout the various stages of their life cycle. In each stage, there must be some goals which are relatively more important than others. Many people have the misconception that a retirement plan is not important when they are young. Even worse, some people think that a retirement plan is only necessary when they retire! In actual fact, we need to make plans long before we retire.

When we are in our 20s or 30s, our more important goals may be luxury consumption, real estate investment, and preparations for a new family. After we have our own family, we are busy repaying financial liabilities and bringing up the children. We have no time and no resources to think about retirement plans and estate plans. Our excuse for ignoring these plans is that there is still a long time before we retire. If we postpone our preparations for retirement, there will be less capital allocated. If we have insufficient funds for retirement, we may have to defer our retirement. That is why it is so important to keep retirement planning in mind as early as possible. Financial planners should remind their clients about the importance of retirement planning in their overall financial plan.

Being Too Optimistic in Estimating Income and Expenses

Often clients overestimate their retirement income. They think that their retirement income from social security, employer-provided retirement plans, and individual retirement savings should be sufficient to maintain their living standard during retirement. In addition, they may overvalue their investment ability and assets. They may also underestimate their expected future expenditure, and think that they do not need to spend much. So they tend to allocate too little resources to retirement planning. Financial planners should remind their clients that their estimates for future income and expenses should be realistic rather than optimistic.

Investment Being Too Conservative

Most clients are aware that they can make use of investments to accumulate capital gains and returns for their retirement. But most prefer not to use too aggressive an investment strategy, being willing to sacrifice higher returns for higher investment security by conducting a less risky investment plan. As the most conservative and secure investment is making a savings deposit, more often than not, the retirement plan is actually a savings account rather than an investment account. Conservative investments may not be able to guarantee a positive real return (a rate of return which is higher than the inflation rate). Based on the risk-return trade-off preference of clients and risk-return analysis of the investment, a reasonable level of risk is acceptable.

Sources of Retirement Income

Social Security

In countries such as the United States, Canada, and Australia where there are well-developed social welfare systems and services, social security is an important source of retirement income. In some circumstances, the retirement income provided by social security is roughly 40–60% of the preretirement income. On average, the social security fund takes up a quintile or a quarter of total retirement income. Figure 5.1 shows the average composition of the different sources of retirement funds for a retirement plan in the United States. Social security income accounts for 22% of the total retirement income.

The US social security system provides benefits to millions of Americans. Employees contribute part of their income to the social security system during their employment period. All American citizens, including those with legal alien status, who work and pay contributions for 10 years, are eligible for pension benefits when they reach the minimum retirement age. Nevertheless, social security alone is not sufficient to maintain a desirable living standard during retirement in most countries; it is necessary to have additional supplementary retirement funds.

Annuity Plan

An annuity plan is one of the insurance products marketed by insurance companies (called the annuity providers) with the aim of providing a series of periodic and regular payments to clients (called the annuitants). Like other insurance products, the annuity plan can be bought by a lump sum payment or by a series of periodic payments over some years. There are two major types of

Figure 5.1 Average composition of retirement funds for retirement plans in the United States

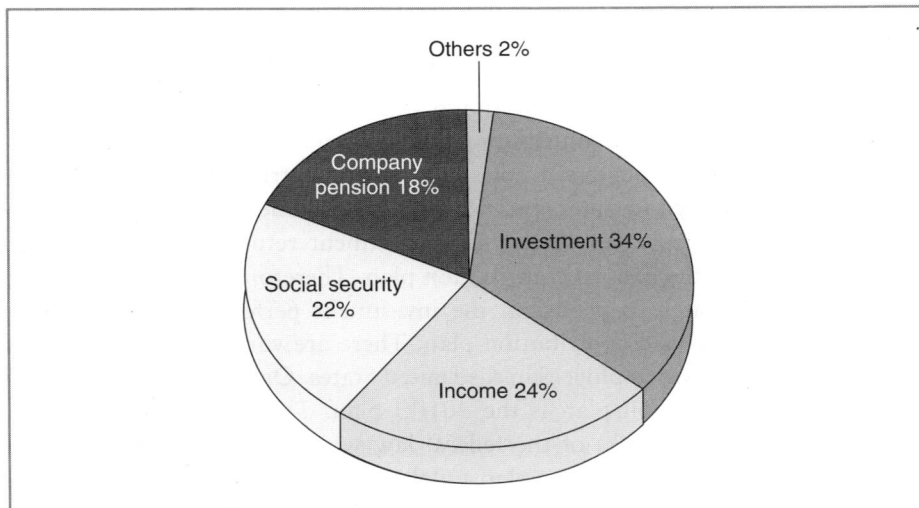

Source: US General Administration of Social Security.

annuity plans: temporary annuity and life annuity. The temporary annuity plan is payable for a fixed number of years.

Under a life annuity plan, the underwriter agrees to pay periodic annuities to the client as long as the client is still alive. Therefore, a life annuity plan can be used as a stable source of retirement income in the retirement plan. This type of retirement plan (life annuity plan) provides a guarantee to the retired that the retirement income will not be fully exhausted prior to death. Other miscellaneous types of annuity include single-premium annuity, deferred premium annuity, nonrefundable payment annuity, guaranteed payment annuity, certain period life annuity, fixed annuity, and variable annuity.

Most annuities are purchased through an insurance company and usually managed by a life insurance company. Therefore, a life insurance company is a major channel for the sale of annuities. Other sales channels include securities brokers and firms, mutual fund management companies, and banks. Since there are so many types of annuity plans and so many sellers of annuity plans, financial planners and their clients should consider the factors which are important for the selection. These factors include frequency of the annuity payments, term of annuity, method of payment, transaction costs and commissions, penalties for termination, or early withdrawal of the annuity plan.

Retirement Fund

A retirement fund is accumulated through continuous contributions, mostly from the income earned in employment. The retirement fund is invested and reinvested to provide retirement income for the retired. Retirement funds can be divided into two types: employer-provided retirement scheme and individual retirement scheme.

The employer-provided retirement plan, such as a pension plan, provident fund plan and long-service plan, is part of the remuneration package for employees. In the United States, a pension plan plays an important part in the corporate policy in relation to devising appropriate compensation plans for the employees and in the financial system by supplying a substantial amount of investment capital to the market. Pension plans make up the greatest proportion of the retirement income for the retired. There are two major types of pension plans: defined contribution plan and defined benefit plan.

defined contribution plan Provides retired employees a retirement payment based on the investment performance of the portfolio selected by the employees. Employees bear the investment risk.

A **defined contribution plan** is similar to a savings plan for retirees subsidized by the employers. Under the defined contribution plan, employers agree or are obligated to put a specified amount into the retirement fund of their employees. The employees receive the investment return as part of the retirement fund from the defined contribution plan. Therefore, how much the employees receive ultimately depends on the investment performance of the capital fund from the defined contribution plan. There are various qualified defined contribution plans for employees in the United States. One distinguished example of a defined contribution plan is the 401[k] plan. The 401[k] plan derives its name from Section 401(k) of the federal law which authorizes the implementation of the defined contribution plan and the responsibility of the employers to make specified contributions into the plan for employees. Under the 401[k] plan, employees are allowed to set aside the tax-deferred income from the contribution plan for retirement purposes. Another popular defined contribution plan is the employee stock ownership plan (ESOP). In an ESOP, the fund from the contribution has to be invested in the shares of the firms in which the employees are working. The main purpose of an ESOP is to motivate the employees to work hard as they can share directly in the capital gains when the stock price of the firm goes up.

defined benefit plan Provides retired employees a predetermined payment based on the salary and employment period of the employees. Employers or pension funds bear the investment risk.

While under a defined contribution plan, the employers agree to make a specified contribution to the retirement fund of the employees; under a **defined benefit plan**, the employers agree to provide the retired employees with a specified payment at the retirement date. Depending on the terms of the defined benefit plan, the specified payment may be a fixed amount or may be varied to adjust for the increased cost of living due to inflation. Conservative employees usually prefer the defined benefit plan because of the certainty of receiving a one-off payment at the retirement date.

In the United States, firms using the defined benefit plan as their chosen pension scheme have to follow one of two vesting schedules: the five-year rule or the three-to-seven-year rule. Being vested means that a worker has completed sufficient years of service and is entitled to receive accrued benefits under the plan. When an employee becomes fully vested, the employee is eligible to receive the accrued benefit, even if he or she leaves the company before retirement age. Under the five-year rule, employees become fully vested after five years of service. There is no partial vesting under this rule. However, there is partial vesting according to the number of years of service under the three-to-seven-year rule. For three years of service, 20% of the pension right can be vested. Subsequently, for each additional year of service, there is a further 20% increase in vesting (40% for four years of service; 60% for five years of service; 80% for six years of service; 100% for seven years of service). Consequently, the employees become fully vested after seven years of service. Table 5.1 presents the similarities and differences between a defined contribution plan and a defined benefit plan.

profit sharing plan The payment made by employers into the retirement fund varies with how much the employers earn from the business.

Besides the two major plans, there are other variations of pension-related plans. Under a **profit sharing plan**, payments made by the employers into the retirement fund are not fixed or defined but vary with how much the employers earn. Unlike a defined contribution plan, how much the employees receive ultimately does not depend on the investment performance of the retirement fund but depends on the corporate performance.

Another variation is the cash balance plan, which is a combination of the defined benefit plan and the defined contribution plan. Conservative employees would normally favor the certainty provided by the defined benefit plan while aggressive employees would normally prefer the potential of the growing asset value provided by the defined contribution plan and profit sharing plan. Under a cash balance plan, the employers provide an assurance for employees that there is a defined benefit in terms of a cash balance. In addition, the employers add to the cash balance amount by a certain percentage of salary (pay credit) or a certain percentage of investment return (interest credit).

Besides having employers provide retirement plans for employees as part of the remuneration package, employees can prepare their own retirement schemes for the future. Examples of these individual retirement schemes in the United

Table 5.1 Similarities and differences between defined contribution and defined benefit plans

	Defined contribution plan	Defined benefit plan
Input from employer to retirement fund	is a specified payment	is a specified payment
Amount of retirement income to employee	varies depending on the investment performance of the retirement fund	is fixed if the specified payment is not indexed to adjust for inflation
Investment risk	rests on the employee	rests on the employer
Purchasing power/inflation risk	–	rests on the employee if the specified payment is not indexed to adjust for inflation
Ownership of assets under the plan	belongs to the employee	belongs to the employer
Portability	is permitted	is restricted depending on whether the employers are of the same plan
Advantages to employers	As the periodic contribution is fixed, the employers do not need to increase the commitment although the investment performance of the fund is not satisfactory	Greater financial flexibility for the employers to allocate resources to fund plan particularly when the business is facing bad times
	The administrative cost of defined contribution plan is relatively lower than that of defined benefit plan	Greater tax-planning flexibility for the employers as the employers can adjust the fund contribution according to the earnings and tax liability

States are the Keogh plan and the individual retirement accounts. The Keogh plan (pension scheme for the self-employed) is a tax-deferred qualified retirement plan for self-employed individuals and the owners of unincorporated businesses. An individual retirement account (IRA) is a tax-deferred retirement account which permits individuals to allocate up to US$2,000 annually with income tax deferred until the individuals start to withdraw the savings at the age of 59.5 or later. If the savings are withdrawn earlier than 59.5, a 10% penalty may be charged.

Pension Plans: Terms and Concepts

The pension plan is a very important component of retirement planning. There are many types of pension plans. Financial planners need to know the different terms associated with the pension plan.

Vesting

vesting Refers to the right of the employees to receive retirement benefits when they leave the company.

Few of us remain in the same job our whole life. We change jobs and leave our employers whenever it is necessary. So can we get the retirement benefits provided by our former employers at retirement or even prior to retirement? **Vesting** is a term which defines the right of the employees to receive retirement benefits when they change jobs and leave their employers prior to retirement. The pension right is vested if the employees retain the right to receive pension benefits from their former employers prior to retirement and nonvested if the employees lose the right to do so.

Owing to the different costs and benefits of vesting for employers and employees, employers prefer pension rights to be nonvested while employees prefer pension rights to be vested. Defined contribution and profit sharing plans usually offer immediate vesting once employees participate in these plans. If employers are not willing to make pension plans provide immediate vesting, they may offer pension plans with deferred vesting.

By deferred vesting, it means that the time for the pension right to become vested is deferred. In the first few years of service, the pension right is nonvested. After the employees have remained in service for a number of years, the pension right becomes fully vested. When the pension right becomes fully vested, the employees can receive the pension benefits from their former employers even if they change jobs prior to retirement.

There are several benefits of deferred vesting particularly for the employers. In order to get the pension benefits, the employees have to work for a given period. Therefore, the deferred vesting pension plan helps retain employees in the firms for a given period and hence reduce the turnover of staff. In addition, if the employees change jobs before the pension right becomes fully vested, the employers can save the costs of pension plans for the early leavers. Although deferred vesting is beneficial for the employers as it reduces cost and staff turnover, earlier vesting is preferred by the employees. Firms which offer plans with earlier vesting are able to attract staff.

Portability

portability The right to carry the pension plan from the current employer to the next one.

Portability refers to whether the pension plan of the previous employer can be carried to the subsequent employer. A portable pension plan is one that allows an employee to carry the assets of the pension plan from one employer to another. As the assets of the pension plan are under the possession of the employees rather than the employers under a defined contribution plan, the defined contribution plan is portable. A defined benefit plan may not be portable unless the employers participate in the same plan. Since cash balance plans possess features of defined contribution and defined benefit plans, cash balance plans are usually portable.

Funding

If the pension plan is in the form of defined contribution, profit sharing, and cash balance plans, employees can be quite sure that the employers have fulfilled their responsibility to make periodic and guaranteed contributions. The asset values of these plans are known and held in the accounts of the employees. However, if the pension plan is in the form of a defined benefit plan, employers just give a promise to provide retired employees a specified amount in the future. Therefore, the future value of the assets of the plan is unknown. However, the present value of the expected future retirement benefit of the defined benefit plan can be estimated actuarially. The defined benefit plan is fully funded if the present value of the expected future benefits equals the current market value of the assets. The plan is underfunded if the present value of expected future benefits is greater than the current value of assets and overfunded if the present value of expected future benefits is smaller than the current value of assets.

Steps in Retirement Planning

Determine the Goals

At each stage of our life cycle, we have goals to achieve. Before we can determine our expected retirement income, we need to know our retirement goals, to which there are two aspects:

1. **Preferred retirement age.** The determination of the preferred retirement age is important because the retirement age is a parameter of the number of working years remaining. The financial burden is higher the earlier the retirement age.
2. **Standard of living.** A decent standard of living can only be supported by sufficient finances. If we want to have a longer retirement period, we may have to lower our living standards, everything else being equal. If we want to enjoy a higher living standard during retirement, we need to work harder and longer.

Develop Short- and Long-Term Retirement Plans

As most retirement funds are invested and reinvested in the securities market to generate more income, the expected retirement income is subject to changes in market conditions. Financial planners have to be aware of the impact of potential changes in the market on their clients' projected retirement income. In practice, the financial planners may employ both long-term and short-term strategies in drawing up the retirement plan. Long-term strategies usually last for 20 to 30 years until the retirement of the clients. In order to better control the long-term plan and make changes if necessary, financial planners may need to formulate some short-term financial benchmarks.

Since it is hard to monitor the progress of a long-term financial goal, financial planners should divide the long-term financial goals of the entire retirement plan into a series of short-term benchmarks. The short-term strategies are formulated to modify and update the information every three to five years. Periodically, the financial planners and the clients can review the performance of the short-term strategies with the short-term benchmarks. Based on the progress of the short-term plans, the financial planners and the clients can make adjustments and determine if their long-term plan can be achieved eventually.

Make Detailed Estimates and Forecasts for Retirement Income

Financial planners should exercise their professional judgment and competence in order to make a comprehensive retirement plan and an estimate of retirement income. Possible sources of retirement income are life insurance policies, annuity plans, subsidies to widows, investment returns, savings, income from part-time jobs, and income from sales of assets. Clients can sometimes be too optimistic and overestimate their future retirement income from social security and investments and underestimate their retirement spending. An overoptimistic estimation can result in insufficient retirement funds. To avoid this mistake, financial planners should collect as much information about their clients, investment strategies, and the market to perform a detailed analysis for the retirement plan.

Reconcile the Discrepancies and Formulate the Retirement Plan

A discrepancy can exist between the expectation of the client and that of the financial planner in the projected level of retirement income. Another discrepancy is the difference between the expected and the actual levels of retirement income. If the financial planners cannot reconcile and explain these discrepancies and provide remedies in time, there will be conflict between the clients and the financial planners.

In order to reconcile the discrepancies, financial planners should use the information collected about their clients, the investment strategies, and the market to further evaluate the overall appropriateness of the retirement plan. In the reconciliation process, financial planners should also invite their clients to express their opinions about the explanation, the remedies, and the adjustments. If necessary, financial planners should seek the consent of the clients on the following suggestions:

1. Increase the current savings to consumption ratio.
2. Extend the number of working years.
3. Reduce retirement spending.
4. Execute investment strategies with high returns.
5. Participate in extra pension schemes.

Risk Management in Retirement Planning

The major sources of retirement income are social security, employer-provided retirement plans, and individual investment income. These depend on various sorts of investments to generate income so they are subject to the same risks as those for investment and education plans. Some investments may be overexposed to risk leading to an unexpected loss of retirement income.

Financial planners should be cautious about changes in the market and in the individual circumstances of their clients. These variations may exert a negative impact on the estimated retirement income and expenditure. If financial planners do not make timely adjustments to the retirement plan, the retirement funds may be depleted.

The appropriate risk level of the investment portfolio should mainly depend on the risk tolerance level of the individual. Thus, we should not expect all individuals to have portfolios of the same returns as different individuals have different risk tolerance levels. Based on the risk tolerance level of clients, a long-term investment portfolio with an appropriate asset allocation mix should be constructed for the purpose of retirement investment. Figure 5.2 is an example of possible mixes of asset allocations for various risk tolerance levels. In theory, unless there is a predictable market downturn, or unless the client experiences some major life-event change, the asset allocation for a retirement portfolio should not be substantially or frequently changed. Of course, there is a wide spectrum of trading intensities appropriate for the retirement portfolio, depending on the preference of investment advisors and the clients. Thus, periodical portfolio rebalancing and changes of asset allocation are necessary to provide a suitable investment portfolio for the changing needs of clients, especially under a dynamic financial environment characterized by present-day conditions.

As we mentioned earlier, there are times where changes of asset allocation are required. An example of this is when the client makes the transition to retirement. In general, three years before retirement, financial planners should advise clients to start shifting some retirement money from risky to less risky asset classes. Gradually reducing the percentage of risky assets in the retirement portfolio avoids the unexpected losses due to a sudden market crash right before the retirement year. Figure 5.3 shows how this can be done.

No matter how risk averse the clients are, they should have some equities in their portfolio at the early stage of retirement (i.e., at 55–60). No matter how aggressive the clients are, there should be some cash and some bonds in the portfolio to maintain a certain liquidity and income for retirement.

In addition to risk tolerance level, there are other important factors affecting asset allocation for long-term investments such as retirement. The hedging effects

Figure 5.2 Matching risk tolerance level with asset allocation

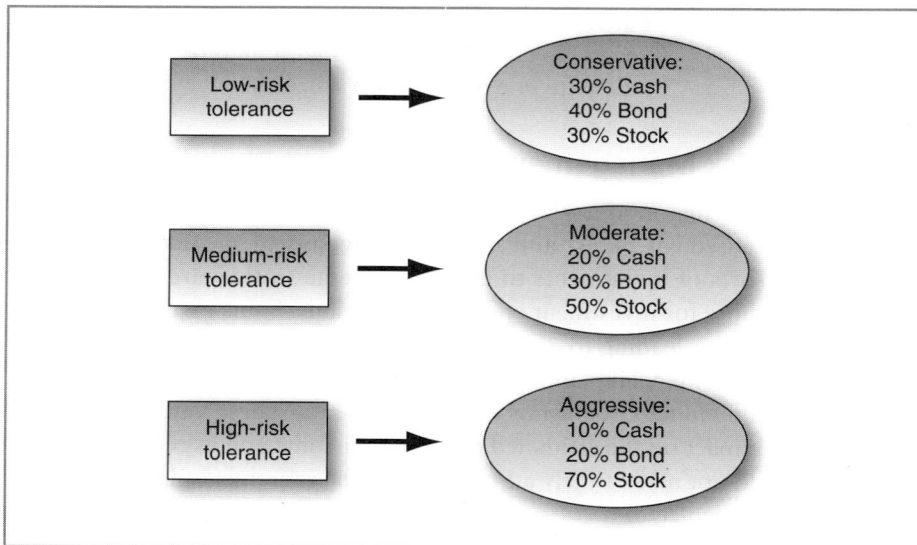

Figure 5.3 Portfolios in transition

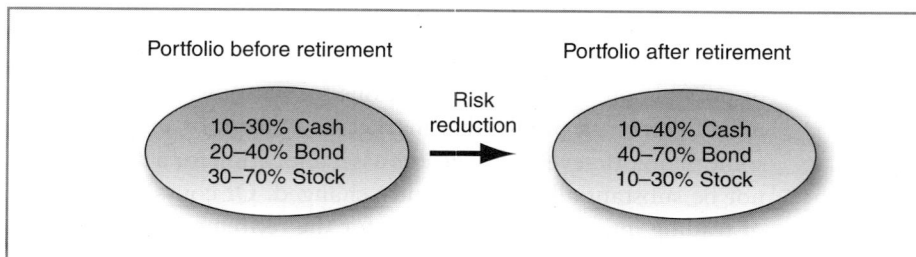

and labor supply flexibility of human capital are key factors in determining the riskiness of a portfolio. If clients are in a profession with a very stable income that is not related to stock market movements, then they can afford to invest in risky financial assets such as equities. Also, if clients are able to increase their income or delay retirement, they can also take higher risks in investment. Finally, if there is a long time before retirement, they can afford to take higher risks as well.

Retirement planning is such a major component in financial planning that almost all clients will expect in-depth advice in this area from planners. Once again, it is critical for financial planners to understand that retirement planning is *not* just long-term investment. A retiree needs more than money to enjoy his retirement. Financial planners should help clients to establish life goals after retirement, to achieve physical and mental health during retirement, and to maintain the financial discipline to work toward those retirement goals through the years. Retirement is a beginning, not an end.

5.3   Estate Planning

If clients have managed their wealth and assets well through financial planning during their lifetime, they should have a substantial amount of wealth and assets accumulated. As part of comprehensive financial planning services, financial planners should help their clients make arrangements for their wealth and assets to be distributed upon their death by drawing up an estate plan. Estate planning includes the management of an estate when the client is unable to handle their affairs for whatever reason, selection of estate planning tools, arrangement of assets and liabilities of the deceased, and achievement of the objectives of the deceased for the beneficiaries.

Importance of Estate Planning

Although estate planning is one of the planning areas of personal financial planning, it is often the planning area most neglected because old-fashioned clients are not willing to mention something related to death when they are still alive. Most clients have misconceptions about estate planning. They think that estate planning is too early for them, or they think that their estate will automatically pass on to the surviving spouse and children. Therefore, they think there is no need for estate arrangement and management. However, this is not true. If clients do not specify their objectives for their estate upon their death, the final arrangements may not necessarily be consistent with their objectives, or may even be very different from them.

Different countries have their own rules and regulations to administer the estate of the deceased. If the estate owner dies without a will specifying the arrangements for the estate, the court will appoint an administrator to manage the estate. In that case, the distribution of the estate may not necessarily be in accordance with the goal of the deceased estate owner. Worse, the estate may be left unmanaged or managed unwisely.

The goal of estate planning is to leave as much estate of the deceased as possible to the beneficiaries free of estate tax. Estate planning aims to help clients arrange and allocate their assets and liabilities and minimize tax liabilities associated with the estate. Estate planning should be flexible and versatile. Periodically, financial planners should help their clients to review and amend the estate plan according to the changes in objectives, expectations, investment preferences, and financial situation of the clients.

Estate planning involves arrangements to transfer the assets from one generation to the next. When drawing up the estate plan, financial planners should consider the following:

1. The drawing up of a formal will.
2. The purchase of life insurance.
3. The preferences and financial objectives of the estate owner.
4. The financial security of the beneficiaries.
5. The executor.
6. The number of beneficiaries.
7. The distribution of estate among the beneficiaries.
8. The distribution means.
9. The tax laws and tax minimization techniques for transferring the estate.
10. The most cost-efficient means to reduce administration costs for transferring the estate.

Basic Concepts of Estate Planning

The Estate

estate Includes all tangible and intangible assets and liabilities of the deceased.

The **estate** includes all assets and liabilities, tangible and intangible, of the deceased. Common examples of assets are land, buildings, property, cars, jewelry, bank deposits, securities, and life insurance policies. Examples of liabilities are loans, mortgages, medical fees, and tax payments.

intestate Refers to the situation where an estate owner dies without a valid will to give proper instructions on how to manage and distribute the assets after the death of the estate owner.

Intestate refers to the situation where an estate owner (or testator) dies without a valid will to give proper instructions on how to manage and distribute the assets after his or her death. The **probate estate** refers to the assets to be distributed by a personal representative when the estate owner dies. If the estate owner dies with a valid will, the probate estate will be managed by the executor designated in the will. If the estate owner dies intestate (that is without a valid will), the probate estate will be handled by an administrator appointed by the court.

probate estate Refers to the assets to be distributed by a personal representative when the estate owner dies.

An important issue concerning the estate is the title or the ownership of the estate. The ownership title affects the right of the estate owner to distribute the estate to the beneficiaries. In some cases, the estate owners themselves may not know whether they have the full ownership of the assets and liabilities under their management. Therefore, financial planners should remind their clients to be aware of the form of ownership they have of their assets and liabilities. There are two major forms of ownership: sole ownership and joint ownership.

Sole ownership

Sole ownership means that the estate owner has full ownership title to the estate. Since the estate owner has full control over his or her properties, the estate owner can sell them and distribute them to the beneficiaries. In general, it is easy to distinguish whether the property is solely owned or jointly owned. If there is only one name on the legal document stating the ownership of the property, there is no dispute. However, the issue of ownership may become complicated if the estate owner is married. In some cases, even if the legal document states that the estate owner is the legal owner of the property, the property may not necessarily be solely owned by the estate owner, but jointly owned by the estate owner and the spouse.

Joint ownership

Joint ownership means that the estate is jointly owned by more than one person. If the estate is jointly owned, the clients do not have full control over the estate. Therefore, the clients cannot distribute the estate as they would like if they had complete control. There are three categories of joint ownership:

Joint tenancy   Joint tenancy is the most common form of joint ownership. Joint tenancy means that the joint owners have equal share of ownership and control over the property. When one of the joint owners dies, the ownership of the property under the joint-tenancy arrangement passes to the other surviving joint owners unconditionally. Therefore, if the property is jointly owned under a joint tenancy arrangement, it can be passed to the surviving joint owners (or beneficiaries) automatically without the need of creating a will or power of attorney, hence saving the necessary legal and administrative costs and time to make the proper transference from estate owner to beneficiaries. In some countries like the United States where the legal procedure of making a will is timely and costly, a joint-tenancy arrangement may be preferable to a will.

Tenancy in common   Like in a joint-tenancy arrangement, the joint owners under a tenancy-in-common arrangement has a share (not necessarily equal share) of ownership and control over the property. However, a tenancy-in-common arrangement is different from a joint-tenancy arrangement in that the joint owners do not have the right of survivorship under the tenancy-in-common arrangement. That is, the ownership of the property does not pass to the surviving tenants in common unconditionally when one of the tenants in common dies. The ownership transference of the deceased tenant in common is executed in accordance with the terms of the will of the deceased. A tenancy-in-common arrangement is preferred for those joint owners who do not want to pass the ownership of the property to the surviving joint owners upon their death. This joint-ownership arrangement is appropriate for a partnership, in which case the deceased partner can pass the partnership share to the assigned beneficiaries rather than to the surviving partners.

Community property   The form of ownership of property particularly for a married couple is community property. The husband and wife have an equal share of ownership of the property. Like in the tenancy-in-common arrangement, the ownership of property under a community-property arrangement does not pass to the surviving joint owners unconditionally and automatically upon the death of one of the joint owners. Rather, the estate under a community-property arrangement is distributed to the beneficiaries according to the will of the deceased joint owner.

Since there are so many different forms of ownership, financial planners have to fully understand the impact of different forms of ownership on the value of the estate. Otherwise they cannot make an accurate estimate of the estate value, or be able to draw up the most appropriate estate plan. For instance, if the estate value is substantial, in order to save on taxes, and on the legal and administration costs for creating a will, financial planners may recommend a joint-tenancy arrangement with the right of survivorship as the form of ownership.

Will

will   A legally enforceable declaration and instruction of the estate owner on the estate when the estate owner dies.

A **will** is a legally enforceable declaration and instruction of the estate owner on the estate when the estate owner dies. A will only becomes effective upon the death of the testator. A will is an essential instrument of estate planning. Although a will is so important, it is often ignored. Not many people recognize its importance. Many think that they still have plenty of time before they really need it. Some fail to keep their will up to date to reflect any changes. Making a will helps to achieve and fulfill the objectives of the deceased and to enforce them legally.

There are three types of will: a formal will under the administration of an attorney, a written will, and an oral will. The formal will under the administration of an attorney is the most powerful as the procedure to formulate the will is formally drafted and witnessed by the attorney and signed by the testator. A written will is prepared and signed by the testator without the involvement of an attorney. As a written will is not drafted and witnessed by an attorney, it may not necessarily be valid legally. If the estate owner has not made a formal will, and is in critical medical condition rendering him incapable of writing, the only choice left is an oral will. However, to make an oral will legally enforceable, the oral statement should be witnessed by at least two bystanders. The witnesses must be over the age of 18 and cannot be the recipients of the estate. As a valid will is so important, financial planners should advise clients to make a formal will.

To allow amendments to be made to the will, financial planners may recommend that clients include codicils in the will. The inclusion of the codicil clause enables the testator to make changes in the will without drafting a new one. The testator should also include a residuary clause in the will. A residuary clause provides for the distribution of the remainder of the estate after all other specific bequests have been made.

Although financial planners cannot help clients formulate their wills, they can offer assistance in providing necessary information, suggestions, and explanations.

Executor

executor An individual appointed by the estate owner to be responsible for the distribution and settlement of the estate.

An individual who is appointed by the estate owner to be responsible for the distribution and settlement of the estate is the **executor** or the personal representative of the estate. An executor can be a professional such as a representative of a trust company or an attorney, or a nonprofessional such as a relative or friend of the estate owner. The executor and the trustee can be the same person if the estate owner sets up a trust for the estate. The responsibilities of the executor are to safeguard and manage the assets of the estate owner; to account for and pay for the cost of estate planning; and to make distributions of the estate among the beneficiary (beneficiaries) according to the will of the estate owner.

Trust

trust A fiduciary arrangement by which the creator of the trust transfers the estate under the management of the trustee.

A **trust** is a fiduciary arrangement by which the creator of the trust (grantor or settlor) transfers the estate under the management of the trustee (the fiduciary or the legal owner of the estate under the trust arrangement). The trustee handles the trust estate for the trust beneficiary (beneficiaries or equitable owners) according to the terms of the trust. A trust can be used as a supplement to a will, as a device to allow amendments in the estate plan, and as a tax-planning technique.

Based on the time when the trust is created, a trust can be categorized into two major types: a living (inter vivos) trust and a testamentary trust (trust under will). A living trust is created when the testator is still alive. For instance, the client can create a trust fund for the benefit of the surviving spouse and children during his or her lifetime. The surviving spouse and children are not the legal owners of the trust but the equitable owners (i.e., the beneficiaries) of the trust. The beneficiaries are entitled to the benefits in accordance with the terms in the deed of the trust. A testamentary trust is set up as part of the terms of a will. While the trustees of a living trust can be the grantors themselves, the trustees of a testamentary trust can never be the grantors as a testamentary trust can only be effective upon the death of the grantor. The fiduciary arrangement made by the grantor can be revocable or irrevocable. A revocable trust allows the grantor to make amendments to the terms of the trust. In contrast, the grantor of an irrevocable trust is not allowed to revoke the terms. The revocable trust is more popular because of its feature of revocability.

Power of Attorney

power of attorney The right of one person to act on behalf of another person as embodied in a deed.

Power of attorney is the right of one person to act on behalf of another person as embodied in a deed. It is a right to the donee of the power to discharge financial transactions and to assign the beneficiary (beneficiaries) to the estate which is subject to the power on behalf of the estate owner. By assigning the power of attorney, the estate owner authorizes a person to act as the will-maker on his behalf and to distribute estate directly under certain conditions. As the will can only be effective to provide instruction upon the death of the testator, the power of attorney can provide direction even when the donor of power is still alive.

Means of Estate Disposition

Estate owners can transfer their assets to their beneficiaries either during their lifetime or at death.

1. Transfer during lifetime
   - gifts inter vivos in irrevocable trusts or in custodianships
   - power of attorney
   - sales within family
2. Transfer at death
   - will
   - intestate distribution (when the estate owner dies without a valid will)
   - life insurance beneficiary or other beneficiary designation

Estate Planning Techniques

Estimate the Estate Value

The first step in estate planning is to obtain and collect financial data and information from the clients to make an estimate of the value of the estate. Financial planners need to know the following:

1. The categories of the items (e.g., tangible or intangible) making up the estate and the value of each item.
2. The taxability and deductibility of each item of the estate in order to devise the related tax savings plan for the estate.
3. The relevant factors (for instance, the location, marketability, and liquidity of the estate) in devising the most appropriate estate plan.

Financial planners can compile the financial data in a sample balance sheet as shown in Table 5.2. This balance sheet for estate planning contains some items that are not found on a normal balance sheet, for example, the death benefit of a life insurance policy, estimated medical expense, estate administration expense, and funeral expense. Using a balance sheet, the financial planners can easily categorize the different items of the estate of the client, estimate the net worth of the estate by subtracting the difference between the assets and liabilities, and assess the tax burden of the estate tax. With a clearer understanding of the financial value of the estate, the financial planner can better determine the objectives of the estate plan.

When filling in the financial data for the balance sheet, financial planners should:

1. Use the market value rather than the historical value to estimate the value of the assets and liabilities items.
2. Include all assets and liabilities items. Some items, particularly the intangible items, are more easily overlooked. If these items are omitted, the total value of the estate may not be the true one.

Table 5.2 Sample balance sheet for estate planning

Assets	Amount ($)	Liabilities	Amount($)
Cash and cash equivalents		Debt	
Bank deposit		Consumption expenses	
Savings account		Personal loan	
Foreign currency account		Mortgage	
Death benefit of life insurance		Life insurance premium payment	
Others		Others	
Subtotal		Subtotal	
Investment		Expenses	
Marketable securities		Estimated tax liability	
Bonds		Estate administration fee	
Mutual funds		Medical expenses	
Other investment gains		Funeral fee	
Subtotal		Subtotal	
Retirement income			
Pension fund			
Social security			
Individual retirement fund			
Other retirement income			
Subtotal			
Assets			
Property			
Antiques and collections			
Car			
Furniture and fixtures			
Jewelry			
Other assets			
Subtotal			
Assets total		Liabilities total	
		Net assets	

Determine the Objectives of Estate Planning

The second step of estate planning is to explore the objectives of the estate owner. Some common objectives of estate planning are:

1. Appropriate provision of the estate for surviving dependants (e.g., spouse and children) according to the will or objective of the estate owner.
2. Minimization of tax liabilities (estate tax/duty).
3. Protection of estate for beneficiaries with special needs.
4. Succession of nonestate assets.
5. Fulfillment and satisfaction of philanthropic objectives, if any, of the estate owner.

In collecting data on the objectives of the client, the financial planner may ask the client to fill in a questionnaire. However, owing to the unique features of an estate plan, it is better for the financial planner to conduct a face-to-face meeting with the client to explore the objectives.

Financial planners should note the differences in the financial objectives between estate planning and other financial planning areas. For other planning areas, the execution of the plans and fulfillment of the objectives are achieved during the lifetime of the clients. However, for estate planning, the objectives can only be fulfilled upon the death of clients.

Devise the Estate Plan

In devising the estate plan, the financial planners should note the following:

1. The variability of the estate plan

An estate plan should reflect the changes in the financial conditions and needs of the clients through the various stages of their life cycle. Financial planners have to allow for amendments in the estate plan in order to accommodate the changes. They can suggest that codicil clauses be included in the will or that an irrevocable trust be created.

2. The sufficiency of cash to pay for necessary expenses

In most countries, there is a tax levied on the transfer of estate from the deceased to the beneficiaries (estate duty or estate tax) or on the receipt of wealth by the beneficiaries (inheritance tax). The financial burden of the estate tax and inheritance tax can be substantial. Taxing authorities also require that the tax liability be paid before the estate is released to the beneficiaries. Therefore, beneficiaries need to pay first before they can enjoy the inheritance. In addition, there are other administration expenses such as medical expenses, funeral expenses, legal fees, accounting fees, and will execution fees to be paid. Only after all these fees have been settled, can the residual be shared among the beneficiaries in accordance with the terms in the will or deed of the trust. Consequently, if there is insufficient cash in the estate of the estate owner, the beneficiaries may have financial difficulties in meeting the liabilities. Financial planners should bear in mind the liquidity and sufficiency of cash in the estate of the clients. Cash and cash equivalents may come from bank deposits, death benefit of life insurance, and sale of marketable securities.

3. The taxability of estate tax or inheritance tax

One main job for financial planners in estate planning is to minimize the tax liability of the estate value. Therefore, financial planners need to know the tax laws, the tax rates, and the tax-saving techniques for the transfer and receipt of estate. For instance, in South Africa, the dutiable amount of estate tax of the deceased is calculated at a flat rate of 20% and an abatement of R 1,000,000 can be deducted from the net value to compute the dutiable amount.

As estate duty is a tax on the property of the deceased, a simple way to be exempted from the estate tax is to transfer the property to others by gifting during the lifetime of the deceased (gifts inter vivos). However, the technique of gifting is not as simple as it appears to be. Many taxing authorities are aware of this technique and impose additional rules for gifting to prevent the beneficiaries from getting the estate without paying the estate tax. In the United States, there is a tax called the gift tax on the gratuitous transfer of assets from the donor to the donee. Financial planners may suggest setting up a discretionary trust to manage the estate of the clients or an offshore company to own the assets.

Monitor and Make Periodic Revisions

Financial planners should periodically review the estate plan, preferably semi-annually or annually, particularly when there are changes in the following:

1. Marital status (marriage, separation, divorce, death of spouse).
2. Number of children (birth or death of children).
3. Health of the estate owner.
4. Financial condition of the estate owner.
5. Death of beneficiary (beneficiaries).
6. Death of executor.
7. Amendments in the legislative and taxation rules and regulations.

Risks in Estate Planning

When the clients die, no more amendments can be made to the estate plan. The following are risks that clients should look out for:

1. **Client plans too late.** If the estate plan is prepared too late, it may not be arranged well. The estate plan should be considered when clients are still in good physical and mental condition.
2. **Client dies without a valid will.** If the client dies without a valid will, the management of the estate will be handled by an administrator appointed by the court, and may not be according to the final wishes of the client.
3. **Client fails to grant an enduring power of attorney to another.** Without a proper and valid power of attorney, no one will have the right to assign the beneficiaries to the estate.
4. **The value of the estate is not accurately measured.** When financial planners do not make amendments to update the estate plan by inputting the latest changes in the values of assets and liabilities of their clients, the estate value may not be accurate.

Key Terms

defined benefit plan *181*
defined contribution plan *180*
estate *188*
executor *191*
intestate *188*
investment policy statement *168*
portability *183*

power of attorney *191*
probate estate *188*
profit sharing plan *181*
risk tolerance *168*
trust *191*
vesting *182*
will *190*

Questions & Problems

Multiple-choice Questions

1. Which of the following statements are correct with regard to defined contribution plans and defined benefit plans?
    I.   Under a defined benefit plan, the employer bears the investment risk.
    II. Employees are given a choice of where to invest funds under a defined benefit plan.
    III. A defined benefit plan can use an employee's past service prior to the implementation of the plan to calculate the annual retirement income.
    IV. Determining the annual employer contribution is easier under a defined benefit plan than under a defined contribution plan.

    A. I and III
    B. II and IV
    C. I, III, and IV
    D. II, III, and IV

2. Which of the following objectives of estate planning is true?
    I.   Protection of estate value
    II. Avoidance of lengthy probate
    III. Orderly succession of business

    A. III only
    B. I and II
    C. II and III
    D. I, II, and III

3. The key areas for a financial planner in examining the retirement goals of a client include _____.
    I.   Financial goal of the client
    II. Appropriate retirement age of the client
    III. Home purchase of the client
    IV. Estate arrangement of the client

    A. I and II
    B. I, II, and III
    C. I, II, and IV
    D. All of the above

4. What are the objectives of estate planning?
    I.   Protection of estate for beneficiaries with special needs
    II. Minimization of taxation liabilities
    III. Providing maximum benefits from the person's available financial resources
    IV. Appropriate provision for surviving dependants such as spouse and children
    V.   Maximum return with minimum risk
    VI. Succession of nonestate assets

    A. I, II, III, and VI
    B. I, II, IV, and V

    C. I, II, IV, and VI

    D. II, III, IV, and V

5. What are the types of asset allocation mix for a retirement portfolio?
   - I. Conservative
   - II. High-yield
   - III. Aggressive
   - IV. Moderate
   - V. Alternative investment

   A. I, II, and V

   B. I, III, and IV

   C. II, III, and IV

   D. III, IV, and V

Problems

1. Describe the problems of investing in real estate (in terms of marketability and liquidity).

2. Explain how bond investment is used as an appropriate investment instrument for an education plan.

3. Define a defined benefit plan.

4. Explain the meaning of vesting.

5. Describe how a will is useful in an estate plan.

chapter 6

Personal Profiling, Risk Profiling, and Life-cycle Analysis

In this chapter, we try to introduce a more general concept of client profiling. We suggest that risk profiling focuses on the financial risk values of clients while personal profiling evaluates all their other nonfinancial values. Combining the two together, we can come up with a comprehensive picture of the client's profile and value system, which is critical for financial planning analysis.

The other topic of discussion in this chapter, life-cycle theory, has long been examined by economists. The idea of a personal life cycle with classification of different life stages by age or certain human behaviors is also a well-known topic in the field of psychology and sociology. However, the application of life-cycle analysis in financial planning is more an industry practice than the results of academic research and studies. We will try to understand the concepts of risk profiling and life-cycle analysis in terms of their application to financial planning.

6.1   Personal Profiling

personal profiling
The process used to accurately analyze a person's nonfinancial background in order to construct an optimal financial plan.

Personal profiling is defined as the process of employing both quantitative and qualitative assessment methods to obtain an accurate analysis of the nonfinancial background of an individual in order to facilitate the construction of an optimal financial plan. While risk profiling measures how a client may embrace risk when dealing with investment, there are other aspects and values of clients which are also important in affecting their behavior. Personal profiling attempts to capture all nonfinancial but core values of the clients through observation and communication. For instance, parents with a deprived childhood are more likely to have a desire to provide more than necessary for themselves and their own children when they have money. In order to compensate for their past underprivileged experience, they may embrace a materialistic and extravagant lifestyle.

Personal profiling is an important conceptual framework and can be very useful in life-cycle analysis, establishing client-planner relationship (step 1 of the financial planning process), establishing goals for clients (step 2), analyzing financial status (step 3), monitoring the financial plan (step 6), and understanding the concept of total life planning. Personal profiling is useful in implementing total life planning as it considers the client's personality, family values, cultural values, lifestyle preferences, physical and psychological health, and experiences of major life events. Figure 6.1 illustrates the elements of personal profiling.

Personal Profiling and Financial Status Analysis

We have mentioned that personal profiling is related to analyzing the client's financial status (step 3 of the financial planning process). Figure 6.2 shows the relation between personal profiling and financial status analysis. Three separate components can be identified in analyzing the financial status of clients. First, we need to know more about the financial risk preferences of the individuals through risk profiling. Then we also need to evaluate the nonfinancial values of the clients such as cultural background, psychological condition, and family values by personal profiling. Finally, financial analyses of the clients' cash flow, assets, and liabilities are needed. By integrating the three components, we will

Figure 6.1 Elements of personal profiling

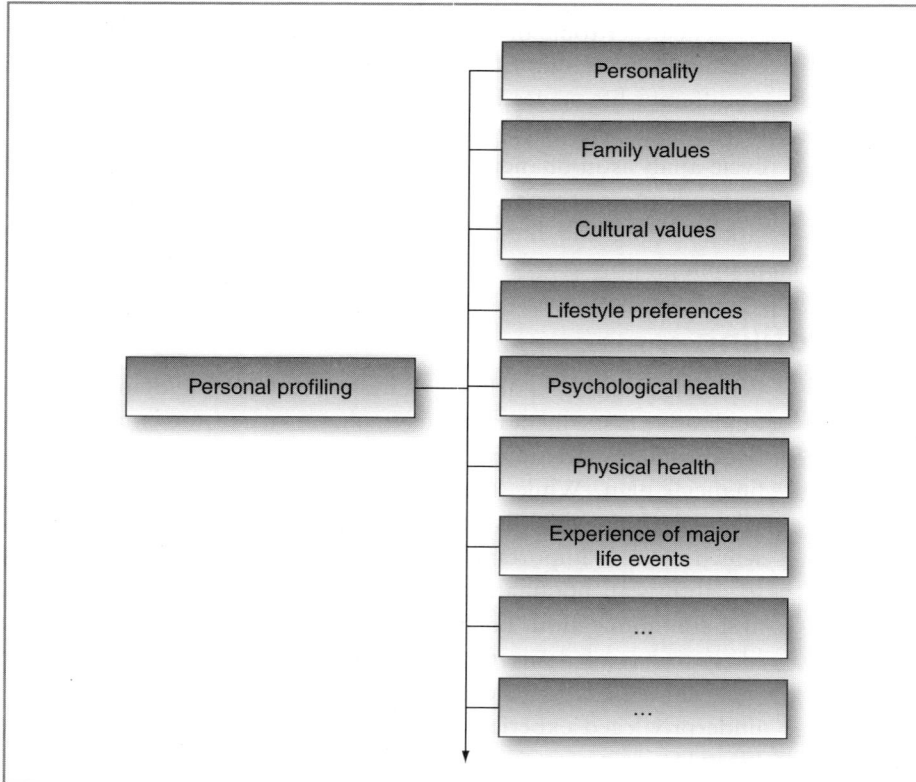

Figure 6.2 Role of personal profiling in determining the financial status of clients

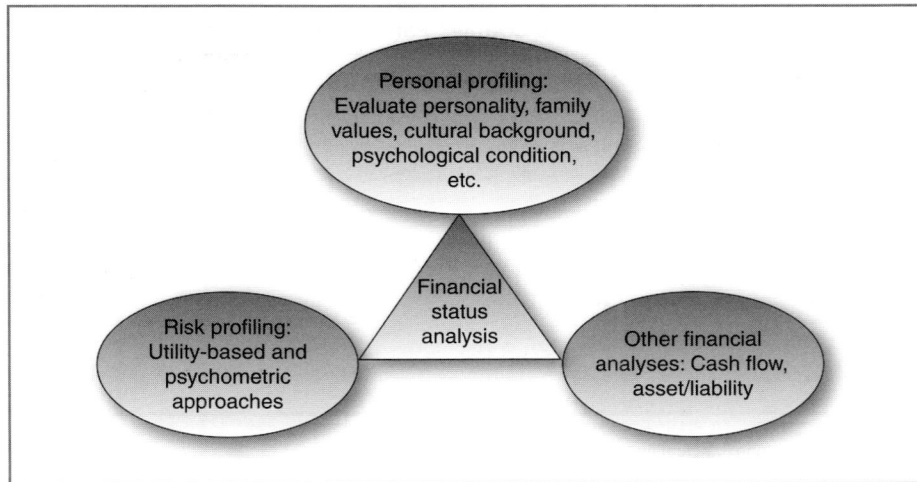

have a clear and comprehensive picture of how and why the clients have arrived at their current financial status. With this understanding, proper and effective recommendations can be provided to clients in order to improve their financial health and to help them work toward their life goals.

Personal Profiling, Life-cycle Analysis, and Total Life Planning

Each individual passes through different life-cycle stages from infancy to old age. Though it is true that we can categorize people by their life stages, each stage is unique to each individual so financial planners cannot apply the same recommendations to all clients of the same age.

Harold Evensky, principal of Evensky, Brown, Katz and Levitt in Coral Gables (recognized as the "father of financial planning" by some in the United States), has made it clear that applying life-cycle analysis blindly to clients without understanding the background and unique needs of the clients is a dangerous practice. It is important to integrate personal profiling, life-cycle analysis, and total life planning when conducting financial planning services for clients. Life-cycle analysis is nothing more than understanding the different physical, psychological, and financial needs of individuals at every stage of their life cycle.

Table 6.1 shows the various financial planning needs of clients at different life stages. For example, a financial planner should not emphasize the need for estate planning for a young male client with average income and wealth and with little financial obligations. After several years, if the same client is married with a young family, the financial planner must consider the physical and psychological health of this young male when designing the optimal financial plan. As the client gets older, estate planning becomes a more important issue.

In short, clients at different life stages have different needs, priorities, and objectives. Financial planners should know this and apply personal profiling in designing the financial plan; this means finding out about their client's

Table 6.1 Financial planning needs at different life stages

	Young adult	Newly married couple	Family with children	Preretirement period	Retired
Age	19–30	24–35	28–55	50–64	Over 60
Psychological health	**	***	***	**	**
Physical health	**	***	***	**	**
Financial health					
Consumption	**	***	***	**	**
Risk management	*	**	***	**	**
Investment plan	**	***	***	***	**
Retirement plan	*	*	**	***	**
Estate plan	*	*	*	*	**

* Denotes the level of importance, with one * indicating least important.

background, cultural values, lifestyle preferences, physical health, psychological wellness, and past experiences. Having this knowledge also helps the financial planner to develop and maintain a good client-planner relationship.

Financial planners should care not only about their clients' financial well-being, but also their personal desires. By helping their clients fulfill their personal desires, they are helping them in total life planning.

Using Personal Profiling to Match Financial Planners with Clients

Personal profiling can help to match financial planners with clients so that a trusting planner-client relationship can be established. Financial services companies should establish their workforce based on the different personal profiles of clients.

In Chapter 7, we will illustrate the principles of matching clients with financial planners. Depending on the sophistication of the clients and the maturity of the economy, different markets possess a different mix of client types. Therefore, financial planning firms should employ a mix of financial planners to meet the needs of the various clients.

6.2 Risk Profiling and Asset Allocation

Risk Profiling

A good financial planner chooses an investment plan that complements the risk profile of his client. A client's risk profile shows his risk tolerance, i.e., the extent of financial loss which he is willing to accept in order to pursue a certain level of investment returns. If a person is averse to losing money and uncomfortable with the volatility of returns, he has a low risk tolerance or high risk aversion. Risk tolerance is a familiar concept because throughout the financial planning process, financial planners need to gather information about their clients' risk tolerance level in order to conduct financial status analysis.

risk profiling The process of determining a person's risk tolerance level using utility-based or psychometric methods.

Risk profiling is defined as the process of determining the risk tolerance level of an individual using effective tools through a utility-based method or psychometric method (Roszkowski, Davey, and Grable 2005; Yook and Everett 2003). The methods may involve asking respondents a set of risk profiling questions with statement choices to choose from.

It must be said that risk profiling methods have their limitations. For example, human capital (the present value of future labor income) is conventionally *not* included as an asset in an investor's portfolio. Therefore, most of the risk profiling questions involve only a small amount of wealth from human capital when it is included in the assets, and as a result, respondents may indicate a higher risk tolerance than normal. In the case of Barsky, Kimball, Juster, and Shapiro (1997), who developed hypothetical situations in the investment arena by asking respondents to make their choices in investment gambles on lifetime income (human capital), a utility equivalent measure was used in the risk tolerance analysis to mitigate this bias toward higher risk tolerance.

Interpretation of respondents' answers is another gray area in risk profiling. Snelbecker, Roszkowski, and Culter (1990) found that there were substantial differences in the interpretation of the individual financial advisors of the same hypothetical statements of the clients, while some groups of financial advisors displayed some consistency in interpretation.

Risk profiling can be applied in other financial areas. For example, the past performances of clients' investments, embedded in the choices of risk profiling, can help to frame the expectations of the clients. Hence, risk profiling has become a tool for expectation management.

Risk Profiling Methods

UTILITY-BASED METHOD

utility-based survey Employs the utility theory to construct a series of questions to determine the client's equilibrium point which indicates his or her risk aversion.

The **utility-based method** employs the utility theory to construct a series of questions (gamble) with gradually increasing dollar amounts to search for the client's indifference (equilibrium) point in choosing the winning and losing amounts. The equilibrium point indicates the risk aversion or risk intolerance level of the individual.

Some researchers suggest that using a hypothetical gamble may not be easy for an individual to comprehend, leading to a less accurate answer. Consequently, it is recommended to use a commonly occurred life event involving a choice between two possible outcomes (one good and one bad), such as in the area of job opportunities, to determine the equilibrium point and obtain the risk tolerance data (Figure 6.3).

PSYCHOMETRIC METHOD

psychometric survey Employs life events and investment gamble involving various levels of risk in order to assess clients' risk tolerance.

The **psychometric method** is more common among practitioners as it is easily understood by clients. This method makes use of psychometric surveys which employ life events and investment gamble involving various risk tolerance levels

Figure 6.3 Example of a utility-based question

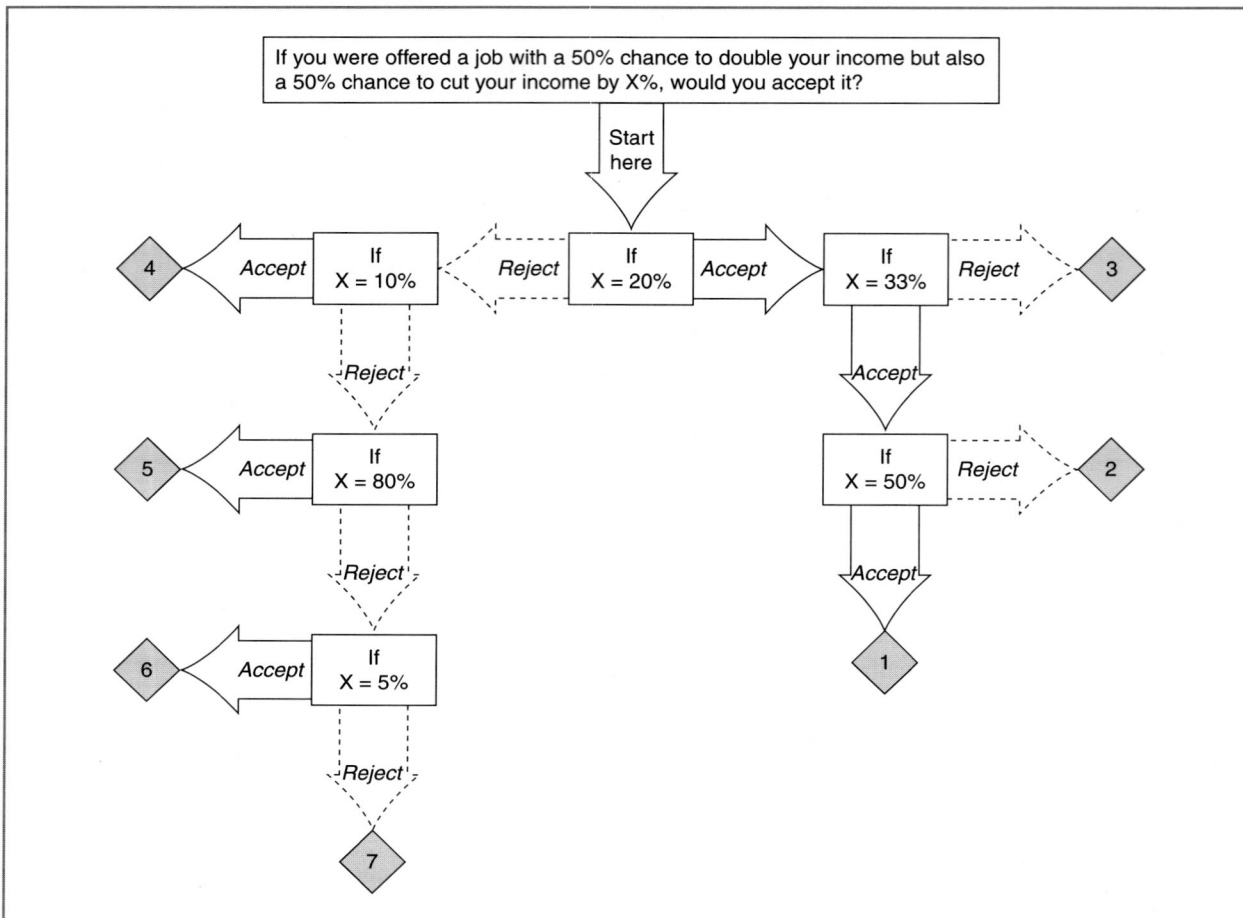

If you were offered a job with a 50% chance to double your income but also a 50% chance to cut your income by X%, would you accept it?

in order to assess the clients' risk tolerance level. Some of the questions asked of clients are indirect in order to assess their risk appetite in making nonfinancial decisions. All psychometric surveys have a number of questions with a score attached to each answer. By summing the scores for all the questions, clients receive a rating representing their risk tolerance level. Depending on the available choices of portfolio provided by the financial planner or wealth manager, the risk tolerance scores of the client are matched with a table consisting of three to seven ranges of scores, each corresponding with a recommended **asset allocation** mix.

Psychometric surveys are not without problems. MacCrimmon and Wehrung (1986) conclude that psychometric questions measure only a small part of the multidimensional nature of risk, and most people misstate their risk tolerance level in these situations. Therefore, the validity of many surveys using the psychometric method is in doubt.

While a psychometric survey is easily implemented, its accuracy is in question as there are no clear acceptable guidelines for financial services companies on how to select and construct questions in the survey. Consequently, many financial

asset allocation Refers to how investors spread their investment funds among various financial instruments

planners and wealth managers arbitrarily put together some questions at their convenience and use the survey as an instrument to assess the risk tolerance of their clients. Major problems of these psychometric questionnaires include using too many similar questions in one aspect (e.g., two questions asking a very similar life event such as a risky investment opportunity in gold mining and oil exploration) and not enough questions or no questions in some aspects (e.g., clients' reaction during a financial crisis to evaluate their ability to take losses in extreme cases). Using invalid and unreliable surveys creates a lot of suboptimal recommendations in investment strategies for clients.

Determining Risk Tolerance

Let's now look at how a risk tolerance questionnaire (Grable and Lytton 1999) can determine clients' risk tolerance level. Using the scores of the risk tolerance questionnaire, clients were categorized into one of the following five standard client profiles:

1. Extremely conservative.
2. Fairly conservative.
3. Moderate.
4. Fairly aggressive.
5. Extremely aggressive.

Clients were then recommended an investment portfolio which corresponds to their risk profile (Table 6.2). Table 6.3, based on historical data on investment return, shows the risk, return, and allocation of assets among three risk profiles. Figure 6.4 depicts the relation between risk and return of assets diagrammatically. Figures 6.5, 6.6, and 6.7 depict the asset allocation among the three risk profiles.

Effectiveness of Risk Tolerance Instruments

Yook and Everett (2003) evaluated the correlation of the ratings from six risk tolerance questionnaires[1] and found relatively low correlations among

Table 6.2 Risk profile and corresponding investment portfolio

Portfolio	Best return	Fair return	Worst return
Portfolio 1 (Extremely conservative)	9.9%	9.5%	8.2%
Portfolio 2 (Fairly conservative)	12.3%	10.0%	1.9%
Portfolio 3 (Moderate)	13.2%	10.5%	1.0%
Portfolio 4 (Fairly aggressive)	15%	11.0%	−2.6%
Portfolio 5 (Extremely aggressive)	17.1%	11.5%	−7.4%

[1] The questionnaires are (1) by Investment Technologies, Inc. (included in an article entitled "Bumpy Market Reminds Investors to Assess Their Risk Tolerance," *The Wall Street Journal*, July 14, 2000, (2) in an article entitled "Individual Investors," *Managing Investment Portfolios: A Dynamic Process*, Maginn, J. and Tuttle, D. (eds.) published by Warren, Gorham, and Lamont, 1990, (3) in the *Fidelity Focus* Spring 1992 issue, (4) on the website of A.G. Edwards and Sons Inc., (5) on the website of Scudder Kemper, and (6) on the website of the Vanguard Group.

Table 6.3 Risk, return, and allocation of assets

	Extremely conservative (1)	Moderate (3)	Extremely aggressive (5)
Return	9.50%	10.50%	11.50%
Standard deviation	8.32%	10.9%	13.5%
Allocation percentage			
Global stock	7.06%	10.29%	13.52%
Hong Kong stock	14.03%	18.66%	23.29%
Bonds	32.85%	45.86%	58.70%
Cash	46.07%	25.19%	4.31%

Using portfolio theory with the help of variance/ covariance matrix to generate the efficient frontier for portfolio choices

Figure 6.4 Risk and expected return

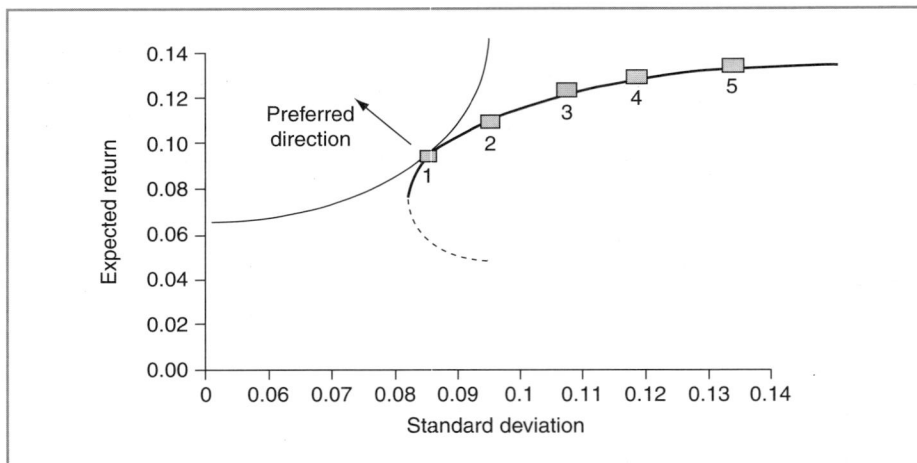

different questionnaires and a wide variation in both the significance levels and the coefficients of determination. The correlations of the rating among these questionnaires are between 0.31 and 0.78 with an average value of 0.56. Since the six questionnaires do not generate consistent ratings for the risk tolerance level of clients, it is highly possible that clients will receive different risk tolerance ratings depending on what instrument is being used for the evaluation. Consequently, financial planners and wealth managers may recommend different asset allocations for the same client. Some questionnaires can perform adequately in gauging risk

Figure 6.5 Extremely conservative portfolio (return = 9.5%; standard deviation = 8.32%)

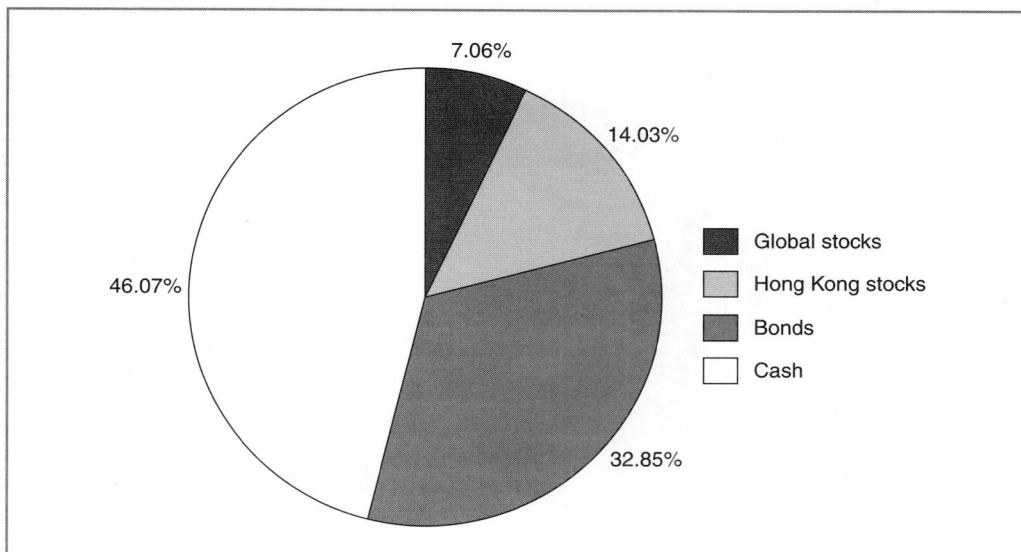

Figure 6.6 Moderate portfolio (return = 10.5%; standard deviation = 10.9%)

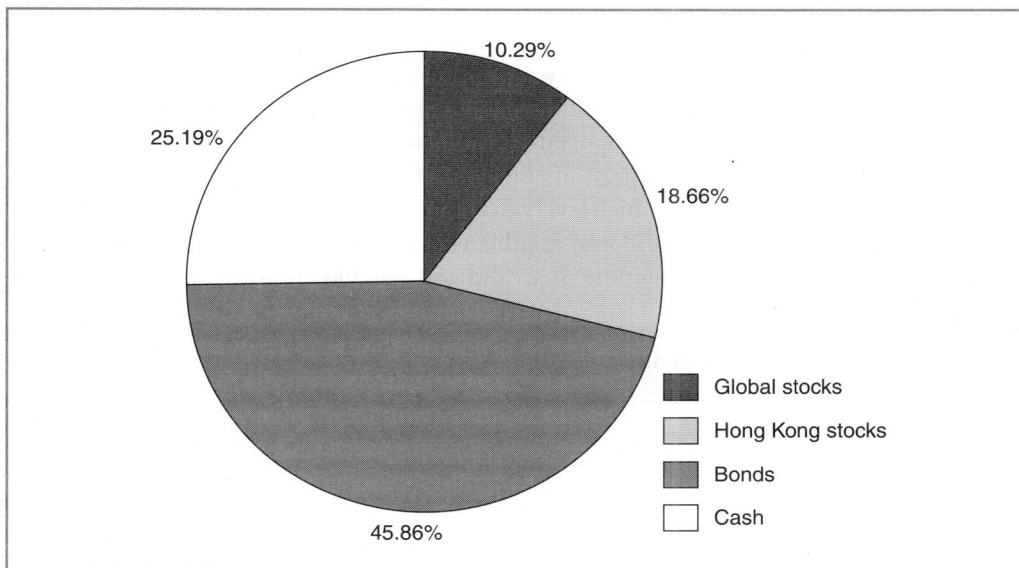

Figure 6.7 Extremely aggressive portfolio (return = 11.5%; standard deviation = 13.5%)

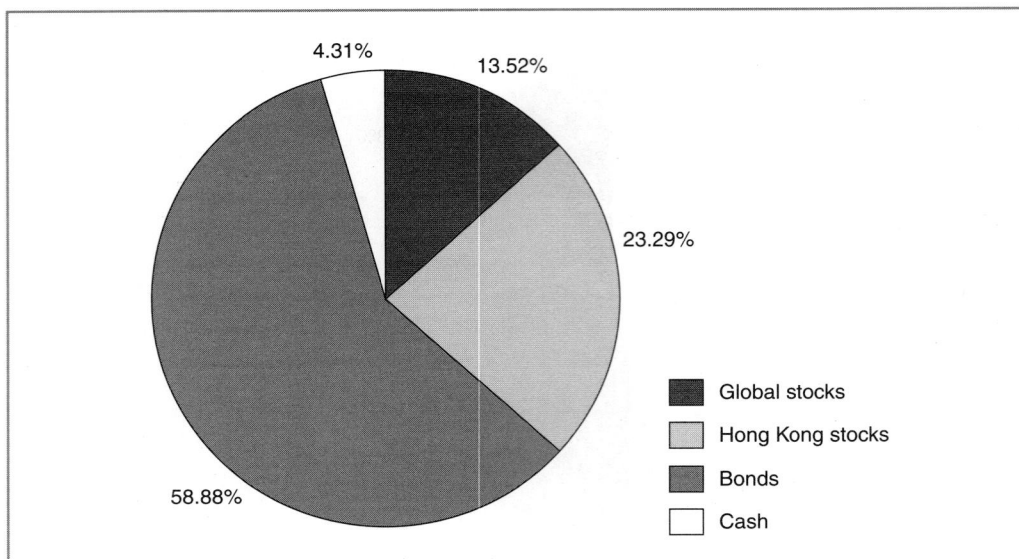

tolerance, whereas others cannot. In addition, Yook and Everett also warn financial planning practitioners that "it is not appropriate to attempt to assess the personal nature of risk aversion with some arbitrarily designed questions."

Roszkowski, Davey, and Grable (2005) followed up on the issue by explaining how to construct reliable and stable risk tolerance questionnaires, and how to choose and use rigorous psychometric assessments. There are two reasons for inconsistent ratings: invalidity and unreliability of the questionnaire. Therefore, if the risk tolerance level of clients is to be measured effectively, it is important to construct a valid and reliable risk tolerance questionnaire. Figure 6.8 shows the assessment outcome of a valid and reliable questionnaire.

Figure 6.8 Valid and reliable risk tolerance questionnaire

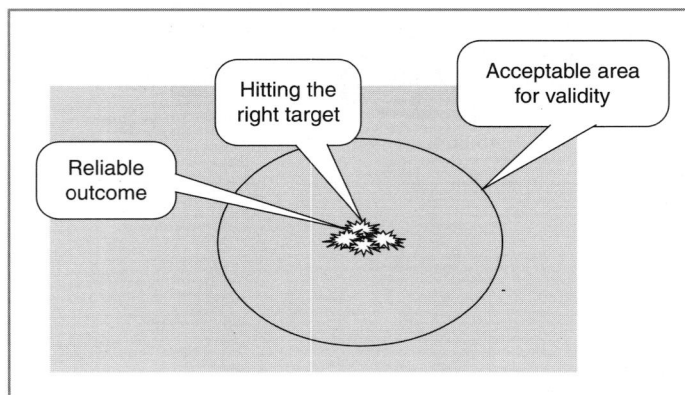

VALIDITY OF A RISK TOLERANCE QUESTIONNAIRE

validity A measure of how successful the instrument is in assessing outcomes.

Validity is a measure of how successful the instrument (questionnaire) is in assessing outcomes. It is similar to the accuracy of hitting the right target. Since the definition of accuracy varies, a so-called valid instrument can generate slightly different outcomes. As long as the risk tolerance ratings are within a certain boundary, it is regarded as a valid instrument. Since the same or similar client may get a slightly different assessment outcome with the same instrument every time, the questionnaire may not be reliable even though it is valid. Figure 6.9 shows such an assessment outcome.

RELIABILITY OF A RISK TOLERANCE QUESTIONNAIRE

reliability A measure of how persistent an outcome is generated by the instrument.

Reliability is a measure of how persistent an outcome is generated by the instrument. In other words, a reliable instrument must produce a very similar rating score for various clients of similar risk tolerance. Note that reliability does not necessarily imply accuracy (validity). A reliable instrument may be persistently wrong, i.e., it keeps generating the same "wrong" answer. Figure 6.10 shows such an assessment.

The following are some recommended solutions suggested by Roszkowski, Davey, and Grable (2005) to improve the effectiveness of risk tolerance instruments:

1. An instrument should contain at least 25 valid and reliable questions.
2. The instrument should be tested for overall validity (accuracy).
3. The instrument should be tested for overall reliability (consistency).
4. A good instrument for risk profiling should be able to detect the true risk tolerance level of clients, and clients of similar risk tolerance level should receive similar ratings every time they are being evaluated.

Figure 6.9 Valid but not reliable risk tolerance questionnaire

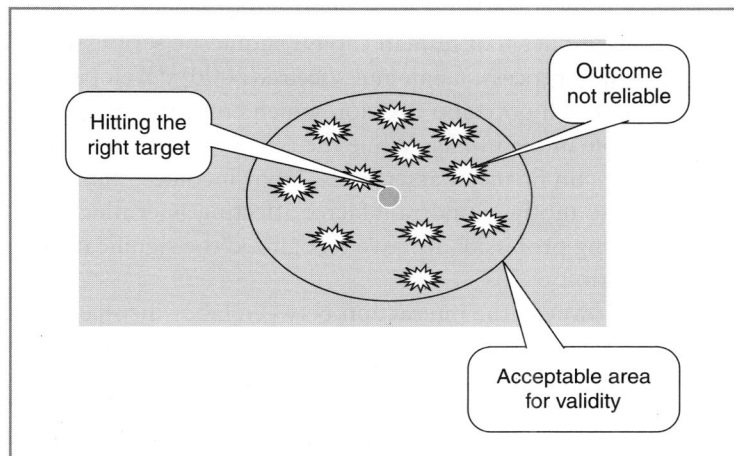

Figure 6.10 Questionnaire with reliable outcomes that do not hit the target

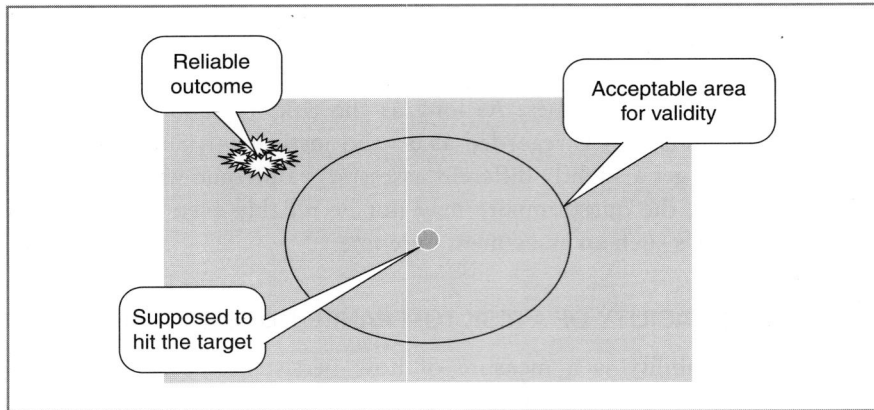

Human Capital in Asset Allocation

Financial planning professionals have some guidelines for investors on asset allocation, but academics criticize these guidelines as lacking sound evidence and strong theoretical support. Canner, Mankiw, and Weil (1997) examined asset allocation advice from major financial advisors in the United States and concluded that the suggestions of financial advisors cannot be completely explained by static modern portfolio theory that assumes investors are fully rational.

During the past four decades, academics have used different approaches to explain the conventional wisdom of asset allocation. Some academics have incorporated human capital into the model of optimal portfolio. Mayers (1972), Williams (1978), and Svensson (1988) studied the effect of human capital on optimal portfolio when human capital is considered as an exogenous nonmarketable asset.

Bodie, Merton, and Samuelson (1992) incorporated nonmarketable human capital as an endogenous factor into the model of optimal portfolio. Their result implies that human capital should be seriously considered in the financial planning process. Chan and Viceira (2000) developed a closed form solution for the optimal portfolio decision which considers human capital as an endogenous variable in the model. While the objective of traditional asset allocation analysis focuses on financial assets only, labor income—human capital—has increasingly become another important factor affecting asset allocation strategies, and financial planning professionals have recognized the significance of human capital in asset allocation.

However, the interaction between labor income and asset allocation has not been scientifically included in conventional financial planning practices. Unlike financial assets, human capital cannot be hedged perfectly because of the moral hazard problem. For instance, if an individual can find a tool or an insurance contract to hedge and guarantee his income level, then there is little incentive for him to work hard and perform as he already has a guaranteed level of income. In other words, hedging human capital in terms of labor income creates incentive to cheat and leads to a lower intrinsic value of human capital. While hedging in respect of human capital itself may not be easy, there exists a possible hedging or diversification effect between human capital and financial asset return in retirement portfolios.

Human capital, which may be considered the present value of future labor income, is analogous to the price of financial assets. The growth rate of labor income is similar to the return of financial assets, and both of them are uncertain. There exists a potential hedging effect between labor income and risky asset returns. For instance, a university professor with a fairly stable salary invests part of the income in the equity market for retirement. Since his labor income (human capital) is independent of the stock market performance, from the perspective of portfolio diversification, labor income and financial asset return for the professor exhibit the benefits of risk diversification. In other words, there is a hedging effect between the two assets.

On the other hand, imagine a client who is a stockbroker and who puts all his or her retirement money in a stock market portfolio. If there is a stock market crash, the stockbroker may not only suffer a huge decline in commission income due to the sharp reduction in trading activities, but may also face a substantial loss in his or her retirement portfolio. In this case, the human capital does not have any hedging effect against the financial asset. For this reason, stockbrokers should hold a lower percentage of less risky equity assets in their retirement portfolios.

A factor closely related to human capital which affects asset allocation is labor supply flexibility. People have the ability to vary ex-post labor supply depending on ex-ante investment performance. The ability to adjust labor supply ex-post is known as labor supply flexibility. The extra labor income generated from flexible labor supply ex-post provides a buffer for poor investment performance. Thus, investors can hedge against shocks to unfavorable stock returns by labor supply flexibility such as working more to make up for the losses, thus providing a cushion effect on asset allocation. The stronger the cushion effect of labor supply flexibility, the higher the risk tolerance and the riskier the portfolio.

Generally, investors with high-income risk (uncertainty in income) hold proportionately less risky assets in the portfolio. Where young people are concerned, some researchers think this group of people can have a riskier portfolio than old people because young people have higher risk tolerance, leading to the conclusion that risk tolerance is highly correlated with age. This is not necessarily true. Young people can take riskier portfolios because, in general, younger people have more labor flexibility than older people. Therefore, everything else being equal, if there are two clients, one young and one old, but with similar labor supply flexibility, then the two clients should have similar risk tolerance level despite the age difference.

In summary, as opposed to the traditional approach, the modified asset allocation analysis integrates two factors related to human capital:

1. Hedging effect of human capital against risky assets.
2. Labor supply flexibility.

Financial planners and wealth managers should quantify the effects of human capital on personal asset allocation by subjectively moving the risk tolerance level up or down, depending on the effects of human capital, to maximize asset allocation.

Challenges of Risk Profiling and Asset Allocation

The major difference between pure return maximization and financial planning is that return maximization pays little attention to the risk tolerance level of clients while financial planning emphasizes investment goals with the clients' risk tolerance level in mind. It is extremely difficult to convince clients to accept a lower expected return, especially when other financial planners or the mass media are publicizing a higher return performance for something else. The education background and expectations of the client are important in understanding and acceptance when the financial planner or wealth manager recommends a portfolio with a lower return but at a suitable risk level.

The key message to clients is this: the best portfolio for each is different, depending on how much risk they can bear without losing sleep or having emotional stress from the risk. The clients should know that their emotional state and financial discipline to employ the investment strategy recommended by financial planners or wealth managers are of utmost importance in meeting the targeted investment return. If a client takes on a portfolio with a higher expected return but a risk tolerance level beyond his acceptable level, when the volatility pushes the portfolio value down and the client suffers a huge loss, he or she may regret it and instruct the financial planner or wealth manager to cut losses and sell the losing assets. The client will then suffer an immediate loss, resulting in a suboptimal return. If the client can hold on to the losing portfolio, the volatility might eventually bring the portfolio value up. In the long run, the higher expected return could be achieved. There would be a higher chance of achieving long-term investment returns if he or she stuck to the recommended asset allocation and saw it through.

In conclusion, risk profiling helps to match clients' optimal portfolio to their risk tolerance level. Once the risk tolerance level is identified, financial planners and wealth managers should select the investment portfolio with the appropriate asset allocation in order to achieve the investment goals for the clients. Often a client may already have an existing portfolio which does not match his or her risk tolerance level. Thus, an adjustment in asset allocation is required. In some instances, clients may not trust their financial planners and wealth managers initially, and allow them to manage only part of their wealth. Financial planners and wealth managers need to know what other existing assets these clients have in order to come up with more investment strategies to complete the overall portfolio for each of them.

The Debate between the Practitioners and Academia

While risk profiling using standardized risk tolerance questionnaires is being adopted by many multinational financial institutions as a basic step in engaging wealth management clients for the purpose of portfolio construction, boutique and smaller wealth management firms in general do not depend on these risk tolerance questionnaires too much. In fact, many top financial planners who own smaller practices in the US and Australia have major concerns about the effectiveness of these survey instruments. They believe that in-depth interviews covering all aspects of clients' background and preferences may be a better way to assess the risk tolerance level of clients. It is possible that these planners are correct that their subjective assessment of the clients' risk preference is a superior choice for them as smaller firms normally take in fewer clients and standardization is not a big issue. However, for large firms, compliance efficiency, services quality consistency, and economies of scale are of greater concern. These financial institutions employ so many financial planning professionals with different skills sets to deal with clients of different levels of wealth. Controlling the quality of advice and maintaining professional standards are huge challenges. Thus using standardized risk tolerance questionnaires would be the only sensible option. Of course, these large firms have to realize that risk profiling is more than asking the clients to fill out some questionnaires and adding up the scores. Evaluating other aspects of clients such as their lifestyles and personalities through personal profiling is important to fully understand the clients' risk tolerance level. In this book, we take the view that the risk tolerance instrument is useful but not a magical tool that can do wonders. Financial planners must exercise extreme caution in using these instruments.

6.3   Life-cycle Analysis

Life-cycle Stages

The life of an individual is divided into several life-cycle stages. The exact number of life-cycle stages differs among individuals. There is also no theoretical consensus on how many stages should be used in financial planning. As financial planning focuses on clients who have income or wealth that they can use and control, we normally exclude the childhood stage and start with the young single. In general, five to six stages can be identified for the purpose of financial planning.

Young Single

The young single individual should have insurance protection against disability due to sickness and injury, which will affect their earning ability. As they are still young and their parents have not reached retirement stage, there is little need for financial protection against early death. In addition, if they have excess funds, they can also think about making investment and pension plans.

Newly Married

When young single individuals marry, their needs become substantially different. The needs and financial planning priorities of the newly married couple depend on their employment status. If both partners work, they would have more surplus funds to fulfill their financial planning needs. The couple will need to protect their earning ability against disability due to sickness and injury. There is also a need for life insurance to protect against the financial burden of an early and accidental death. If the couple has surplus funds, they may start making savings for retirement, setting up emergency funds for unexpected needs, and considering investment plans.

If only one partner works, the top priority is to protect against the financial consequences of early and accidental death of the breadwinner, so life insurance is important.

Married with Young Children

With the addition of children to the family, expenditure goes up, and the need for financial protection increases. The couple will have to provide for both the present physical needs and future educational needs of their children. There is also a possibility that one partner may have to sacrifice his or her job to look after the family. When there is a change in the employment status of the couple, the availability of funds for family expenditure may be affected. If there is surplus fund, the family may use it for investment and pension plans.

Married with Older Children

The couple should be in the middle of their careers by the time their children are older. The couple's earning power should have increased substantially and/or the unemployed partner may have returned to the workforce. This is the stage where the couple should have more surplus funds to invest. Investment income can be used to repay loans, to finance the educational expense of children, to pay for leisure, and to prepare for retirement.

Couple at Preretirement

In the preretirement stage, the children should have grown up. Therefore, the need for life insurance to protect the children against the financial consequences of early and accidental death of the parents is reduced. When the children become financially independent, the parents can put their first priority on retirement. They should try to maximize their investment income to supplement their retirement income.

Retired Couple

At this stage, the objective of the retired couple is to maintain their living standard. If there is a shortage of funds, they may have to invest more in order to generate additional income to supplement the shortage. If there is a surplus of funds, they may consider making arrangements for the disposal of their estates upon death. While tax planning should be done throughout the different life-cycle stages, during retirement, the objective of tax planning is to minimize the tax liability of the deceased when the estates have to be passed to the children.

We can see then that financial planning is important at every life-cycle stage of the individual. Table 6.4 shows the financial goals and activities for every life-cycle stage.

Table 6.4 Financial goals and activities at various life-cycle stages

Common financial goals and activities		
• Obtain appropriate career training.	• Accumulate an appropriate emergency fund.	• Evaluate and select appropriate investments.
• Create an effective financial recordkeeping system.	• Purchase appropriate types and amounts of insurance coverage.	• Establish and implement a plan for retirement goals.
• Develop a regular savings and investment program.	• Create and implement a flexible budget.	• Make a will and develop an estate plan.

Life-cycle stage	Specialized financial activities
Young, single (18–35)	• Establish financial independence. • Obtain disability insurance to replace income during prolonged illness. • Consider home purchase for tax benefit.
Young couple with children under 18	• Carefully manage the increased need for the use of credit. • Obtain an appropriate amount of life insurance for the care of dependants. • Use a will to name a guardian for children.
Single parent with children under 18	• Obtain adequate amounts of health, life, and disability insurance. • Contribute to savings and investment fund for college. • Name a guardian for children and make other estate plans.
Young dual-income couple, no children	• Coordinate insurance coverage and other benefits. • Develop savings and investment program for changes in life situation (larger house, children). • Consider tax-deferred contributions to retirement fund.
Older couple (+50), no dependent children at home	• Consolidate financial assets and review estate plans. • Obtain health insurance for postretirement period. • Plan retirement housing, living expenses, recreational activities, and part-time work.
Mixed-generation household (elderly individuals and children under 18)	• Obtain long-term health care insurance and life/disability income for care of younger dependants. • Use dependent care service if needed. • Provide arrangements for handling finances of elderly if they become ill. • Consider splitting of investment cost, with elderly getting income while alive and principal going to surviving relatives.
Older (+50), single	• Make arrangement for long-term health care coverage. • Review will and estate plan. • Plan retirement living facilities, living expenses, and activities.

Source: Kapoor, J. R., Dlabay, L. R., and Hughes, R. J., *Personal Finance* 7th ed., p. 11. © 2004, published by McGraw-Hill/Irwin, a business unit of The McGraw-Hill Companies, Inc. This table is reproduced with the permission of The McGraw-Hill Companies.

The Role of Family in the Life Cycle

It is a common assumption that an individual will get married and form a family. Therefore, many decisions in the financial planning process made throughout the different stages of the life cycle are made in the context of a family unit and throughout the stages of the family life cycle. The key elements in the family life cycle include the marital status of the individual, and the number and age of children.

The family life cycle is especially important when dealing with Asian clients because of the importance of family values and the extended definition of family which includes noncore relatives.

The Financial Life Cycle

The lifetime pattern of financial positions and earning power of an individual is referred to as the financial life cycle. One of the critical determinants of the earning power of an individual is the investment in human capital. The investment in human capital already exists during the dependent stage. The financial life cycle commences when an individual leaves his or her parents and starts to be independent.

In the very early stage of the financial life cycle, the consumption level of an individual is more likely to exceed the income level, particularly when the individual is making an investment in human capital. At this stage, financial help comes primarily from the parents and/or student loans. When the individual becomes more financially independent, he or she starts to spend money on more expensive consumption items like furniture and cars. At this stage, the individual may incur debts.

When the individual has worked for a certain number of years, his or her net worth begins to grow as earning power grows. The individual may have started a family by this time. The income earned by the individual at this stage would then be needed to cover the consumption expenses of the family unit, to pay off debt, to save, and to invest. As most of the income earned is used to cover the expenses of the family unit, the individual's net worth grows more slowly during this stage.

Once the children become independent financially and most of the debt is paid off, the individual should have surplus income and savings. The ability to save should be the highest at this stage of the life cycle. Consequently, there is a significant increase in the individual's net worth at this stage. When the individual retires, the earning power becomes very low or zero. The retired individual starts to draw upon his or her pension and to consume the accumulated savings. In the retirement stage, the savings rate is zero or negative and the individual's net worth declines.

The Role of Work in the Life Cycle

Work plays an important role as it affects both financial and nonfinancial aspects of the life cycle. Work is the single most important factor in one's financial life as work creates income. We need income to be self-sufficient financially and to provide the necessities and luxuries at different stages of the life cycle. The portion of income earned which is not used currently can be put into savings or investment for future use. In addition, we gain knowledge and experience through working, and this knowledge and experience from work is a valuable asset to get more future income and benefits.

Work affects our nonfinancial life as it helps to shape our social life through activities and relationships formed in the working environment. Work also determines the way we spend our leisure time. Some individuals prefer to engage in leisure-time activities which are as remote from work as possible. Other individuals, because of their involvement in their work, may be not interested in leisure activities as these individuals derive pleasure from work.

As the individual progresses through a well-planned working career, there is more leisure time and work creates more dollars available to be spent in leisure. Since work is important in both financial and nonfinancial aspects, it is necessary to look at it from a broader perspective. We should not only be concerned with what we may be doing today, tomorrow, or next week but also where our aspirations can lead us. We should examine how we can maximize the rewards and pleasures available to us through work.

The Life-cycle Model

The life-cycle model is the standard framework which economists use to think about the inter-temporal allocation of time, money, and effort. The model suggests that households should "smooth" expenditures. One of the strengths of the model is that it provides a single framework which integrates allocation at many different frequencies. Consumption smoothing suggests that consumption seldom varies with income. We engage in consumption smoothing from year to year through the various stages of the life cycle. Consumption smoothing is a forward-looking model which starts with the idea that people attempt to look ahead to their future income prospects when deciding how much to consume. They do not simply consider their current income.

Take the example of a young medical doctor who decides to take a year off from a high-paying suburban medical practice to do community service at little or no pay. Consequently, the income of the doctor may fall below the poverty line for a year. However, the doctor is unlikely to cut consumption to a fraction of the poverty level of income. The doctor makes his or her consumption decisions based on the expected income in the future. That is, the consumption decisions are based on the assessment of a more permanent income or a life-cycle income rather than a one-year income.

Here we futher illustrate the concept of consumption smoothing:

In a two-period model, an individual earns and consumes C_1 in period 1 and only consumes C_2 in period 2. Suppose the savings rate is 5% and the income in period 1 is $1,000. Then how can that individual allocate income in period 1 for consumption in both period 1 and period 2? The amount available for consumption is:

$$C_2 = (1,000 - C_1) \times 1.05$$

The amount spent in period 1 depends on the preference of the individual. Hence the amount available for period 2 is a result of the consumption in period 1. If the individual values the consumption in period 2 as much as the consumption in period 1, the individual most probably smoothes the consumption between period 1 and period 2, that is, $C_2 = C_1$. If $C_2 = C_1$, then

$$C_2 = (1,000 - C_2) \times 1.05$$
$$2.05 \times C_2 = 1,050$$
$$C_2 = 512.2$$

Friedman (1957) employed his permanent-income hypothesis to explain that, owing to declining marginal utility of consumption, an individual can maximize his lifelong utility by applying consumption smoothing. As a person prefers a steady (or gradually improving) life style, which requires a stable consumption pattern, he should avoid dramatic increases and decreases in consumption even if his income may vary significantly throughout his career. At the theoretical level, following this argument, a young person with low income would borrow money for consumption and repay the debt when he earns more in later years in order to maintain stable consumption. This hypothesis also suggests that an individual would save enough money in order to maintain a similar level of consumption after retirement. Numerous empirical research studies have expanded the concept of life-cycle savings or life-cycle investing.

In fact, life-cycle theory can be a very qualitative concept and require a lot of understanding in mathematical economics. We do not attempt to enter this area in this book. Renowned economics and finance scholars have done some significant research work in this area. Examples include Modigliani and Brumberg (1954); Friedman (1957); Ando and Modigliani (1963); Merton (1969); and Bodie, Merton, and Samuelson (1992). Other worthwhile readings on life-cycle savings include Hall (1978); Shefrin and Thaler (1988); Carroll (1997); Cocco, Gomes, and Maenhout (1998); Campbell, Cocco, Gomes, and Maenhout (1999); Browning and Crossley (2001); Johnson, Kotlikoff, and Samuelson (2001); and Börsch-Supan (2003).

In this book, we take the simplest form of the life-cycle concept and explain the life-cycle model as the predetermined relationship between personal consumption (and its derivatives such as insurance, savings, and investing decisions) and age, or life stages, of an individual.

In practice, the life-cycle concept has a significant implication for financial planning practices, particularly on consumption advice, required insurance protection, and long-term savings for retirement purposes. If financial planners adopt the life-cycle approach in financial planning, they will first estimate the life-long income (i.e., human capital) in terms of the present value of their clients through their financial life cycle.

Since in general we can assume that clients can only spend as much as what they earn, the financial planner can equate the sum of the present value of total lifelong income and current asset value to the sum of the present value of lifelong consumption and bequest. Applying this rule with consumption smoothing (that is, identical consumption per year excluding extraordinary items and mortgage payment), the financial planner can estimate the funds available for savings and investment to achieve the goals of clients, or the extra funds/income needed to meet the ends. At this point, the needs and unique characteristics of various life stages should be considered in the financial planning analysis to make sure that proper consumption, insurance protection, and savings for short-term and long-term goals are considered.

When applying this concept to financial planning, however, we need to take into account some assumptions and limitations.

Assumptions and Limitations of Applying the Life-cycle Model to Financial Planning[2]

The life-cycle model is very useful in providing some generalizations of clients' needs in financial planning. However, there are certain assumptions and limitations that financial planners have to consider when using life-cycle analysis for their clients.

Cultural Effects

The consumption and savings behaviors are dependent on the culture of a people. It is believed that Asians, for example the Chinese, generally save more than they consume compared with their Western counterparts. Thus, a financial planner should not adopt the financial planning strategies concerning consumption and savings level for clients strictly from evidence documented for another country without understanding the potential **cultural effects**.

cultural effects The influence of cultural values on people's savings behaviour throughout their life cycle.

cohort effects The effect of generation-specific values on people's savings behaviour throughout their life cycle.

Cohort Effects

Börsch-Supan and Lusardi (2003) suggest that different cohorts (i.e., different generations) demonstrate different savings behaviors. These **cohort effects** are due to different generations being subject to different economic conditions and potentially different pensions and tax systems, so financial planners should be careful in comparing consumption and savings behaviors of consumers in the same age category but from different generations. Thus, empirical research using data from different cohorts to generalize the consumption and savings patterns through various life stages for a given clientele could be subject to bias.

Wealth and Income Effects

The idea of consumption smoothing is somewhat related to the assumption that the wealth and income of an individual are limited resources, and the individual has to make an effort to earn an income and save for the future. Thus, for extremely wealthy people, the concept of consumption smoothing using income smoothing as the underlying assumption may not be as critical, as they will not need to spend all their wealth to maintain a comfortable life style.

For extremely poor and low-income people, assuming lifelong income equals lifelong consumption may not be practical either. For example, insurance planning using income smoothing assumption is not practical as these people never earn enough to reflect the minimum level of life insurance protection needed to meet their financial obligations. In short, the application of the life-cycle model derived

---

[2] For some of our discussion of life-cycle analysis, we use some material from Life-cycle Savings and Public Policy, A. Börsch-Supan (ed.) (2003). For a more detailed description of global life-cycle savings and public policy of different countries, refer to this book.

from the permanent-income hypothesis is most appropriate for middle-income and high-income people.

Uncertainty about the Future

One assumption of the permanent-income hypothesis is that we have a reasonable idea of the expected income of an individual. For example, the permanent-income hypothesis predicts that a medical student will spend more money on leisure compared to a history major because the medical student's expected income will be higher than that of the history major after they graduate. However, such a conclusion assumes that the medical student has confidence that he will be employed as a medical doctor. In some cases, owing to unexpected disequilibrium in supply and demand, some medical school graduates in certain societies may not receive full employment after they graduate, leading to the uncertainty of income level and therefore an inability to spend at a higher level during college as predicted by the theory.

Unique Characteristics of Individuals

Every client has his own unique background and timing of different life stages. Thus, even though we can generalize and categorize people by life stages, we cannot treat our clients as a uniform object and apply the same recommendation to all clients of the same age without first understanding their unique backgrounds needs.

Integrating Life-cycle Analysis into Financial Planning Areas

Financial planners should take into account the unique characteristics of the various life stages of clients when formulating the financial plan. We will now discuss each financial planning area in the context of the various life stages. For convenience, we will consider a typical client going through the various life stages shown in Table 6.5 (i.e., getting married and having children within the predefined age range) and earning middle-level income (e.g., US$100,000 to US$250,000 of annual household income) throughout the whole career.

Table 6.5 Importance of financial planning areas by life stages

	Young adult Age: 19–30	Newly married couple Age: 24–35	Family with children Age: 28–55	Preretirement period Age: 50–64	Retired Age: Over 60
Consumption planning	**	***	***	**	**
Tax planning	*	**	**	**	**
Insurance planning	*	**	***	**	**
Investment planning	**	***	***	***	**
Retirement planning	*	*	**	***	**
Estate planning	*	*	*	*	**

* Denotes the level of benefits received, with one * denoting the least benefit.

Consumption Planning for Different Life Stages

In general, for a single young adult with only a few years of working experience, income is generally low but consumption needs can be relatively high. It is a time when consumption exceeds income. In these early years, a typical client (i.e., assuming a middle-income family background without an expectation of huge inheritance) settles into a certain lifestyle gradually. While savings and the ability to invest at this stage are very limited, proper consumption planning and financial discipline are very important at this stage as these two aspects will have a strong impact on how the clients will be able to exercise the required financial discipline to achieve their financial goals in the future. Consequently, proper cash flow management, income-based consumption (i.e., not spending more than what one earns), and having the right attitude toward consumer debt (e.g., credit card use), are important factors in financial planning for this early stage in the life cycle.

When the clients mature in the second and third stages (i.e., just married and having children, respectively), consumption planning becomes even more important as the clients' financial burden becomes much heavier due to the higher expenses involved in maintaining a family. If additional members to the family are expected in the near future, then adjustments will have to be made to consumption and lifestyle. Proper life goals related to education needs and living conditions expected should be determined as soon as possible at these stages so that more time is available for the accumulation of the required funds. We can easily find numerous examples in life where the parents or the children have to incur an enormous amount of debt in order to realize their education goals or other short-term goals due to the lack of proper consumption planning at these stages.

In the last two stages, where the clients have become more financially independent and later on retire, their lifestyles follow a well-defined pattern. There is not much room for substantial changes, especially by reducing expenses, without inflicting a lot of pain to the clients. Consumption planning in general should not be a major issue for most clients at this stage. Unfortunately, in reality, we see a lot of retired clients having to struggle with consumption control due to unexpected negative life events such as job losses or investment losses at a very late life stage.

Tax Planning for Different Life Stages

Tax planning strategies such as income splitting, timing of asset sale and gearing of investment, work best only when the client reaches a certain level of income. As income is largely a function of the life stage, it is obvious that tax planning is not really a big concern for clients in earlier and later stages of their life.

Insurance Planning for Different Life Stages

Insurance planning is closely related to the life-cycle theory if one believes that a person should not spend more than what he earns and accepts the idea of consumption smoothing. In this case how much life insurance one needs will be closely related to a person's lifelong income. The need for life insurance as protection for the family is the present value of expected future financial burdens and liabilities, which are determined by the consumption level and other specific events. The amount of life insurance coverage varies as the client moves through the different stages of his or her life cycle.

Because clients' risk increases when the financial responsibility becomes heavier, an analysis of insurance needs using the life-cycle approach with income smoothing will result in an increase in life insurance when the clients move from the first stage to the second and third stages. Following the same logic, the insurance needs will then gradually decline when the clients are in the last two stages as their financial obligation decreases.

In order to allow their clients to maintain flexibility in increasing and decreasing insurance protection through the various life stages, financial planners have to estimate the permanent and variable components of their clients' insurance needs. For the permanent component, it will be ideal to purchase a whole life or universal life insurance contract with or without an investment-linked feature. For the variable component, one or more term life contracts will be sufficient. Recently, some insurance companies have tailored new life insurance products to meet the declining insurance needs of clients as they grow old by allowing a declining coverage (i.e., face value) and charging a lower insurance premium than the other contracts with a constant coverage.

Investment Planning for Different Life Stages

The investment planning we discuss here concerns short-term and medium-term investment, as long-term investment is covered as part of retirement planning. A single adult will likely save or invest to pay off major consumption items like wedding expenses, vacations, home purchase, and car purchase. For a young family unit, education expenses for the children are major items for medium-term investment. The life-cycle model is critical to the process of determining the risk/return trade-off of clients for investment planning. For instance, younger investors are more willing, relative to older investors, to bear higher risk for higher returns. In short, financial planners should consider the life stage characteristics of the clients while keeping in mind the limitations discussed earlier, in designing appropriate investment strategies for their clients.

Retirement Planning for Different Life Stages

For retired people, investing in a portfolio generating a stable income is of major importance. Even though the power of the time value of money tells us that we should save for retirement as early as possible, young adults have too many other immediate concerns to worry about saving for retirement. Thus, retirement planning in general is not a high priority for the first two stages but becomes a more important issue when the clients enter into the third stage (i.e., family with children). Nevertheless, it is important that a planner should encourage a client with sufficient income to start the habit of saving for retirement early so that the clients will develop a strong financial discipline to save for the future at an early stage.

Estate Planning for Different Life Stages

For wealthy clients desiring to establish a trust for family members or for charity purposes, it is important to have an investment plan allowing a sustainable income from the trust to support their preferred funding activities. However, whether rich or not, all clients should establish a will so that an orderly and efficient execution of estate distribution can be performed. In most cases, estate planning is not a concern until clients reach the last stage of their life cycle.

Key Terms

asset allocation *204*

cohort effects *219*

cultural effects *219*

personal profiling *199*

psychometric survey *203*

reliability *209*

risk profiling *203*

utility-based survey *203*

validity *209*

References

Ando, A. and Modigliani, F., "The Life Cycle Hypothesis of Savings: Aggregate Implications and Tests," *American Economic Review*, vol. 53, no. 1 (1963): 55–84.

Barsky, R. B., Kimball, M. S., Juster, F. T., and Shapiro, M. D., "Preference Parameters and Behavioral Heterogeneity: An Experimental Approach in the Health and Retirement Study," *Quarterly Journal of Economics*, vol. 112, (1997): 537–579.

Bodie, Z., Merton, R. C., and Samuelson, W., "Labor Supply Flexibility and Portfolio Choice in a Lifecycle Model," *Journal of Economic Dynamics and Control*, vol. 16, no. 3/4 (1992): 427–449.

Börsch-Supan, A. and Lusardi, A., "Savings: A Cross-National Perspective," in *Life-cycle Savings and Public Policy,* Börsch-Supan, A., ed. (London, UK: Academic Press, 2003): 1–28.

Browning, M. and Crossley, T. F., "The Life-cycle Model of Consumption and Savings," *Journal of Economic Perspective*, vol. 15, no. 3 (2001): 3–22.

Campbell, J. Y., Cocco, J. F., Gomes, F. J., and Maenhout, P. J., "Investing Retirement Wealth: A Life Cycle Model," NBER Working Paper Number 7029 (1999).

Canner, N., Mankiw, N. G., and Weil, D. N., "An Asset Allocation Puzzle," *American Economic Review*, vol. 87 (1997): 181–191.

Carrol, C. D., "Buffer-stock Savings and the Life Cycle Permanent Income Hypothesis," *Quarterly Journal of Economics*, vol. 112, no. 1 (1997): 1–55.

Chan, L. Y. and Viceira, L. M., "Asset Allocation with Endogenous Labor Income: The Case of Incomplete Markets," Working Paper, Harvard University (2000).

Cocco, J. F., Gomes, F. J., and Maenhout, P. J., "Consumption and Portfolio Choice over the Life Cycle," Working Paper, Harvard University (1998).

Friedman, M., *A Theory of the Consumption Function* (Princeton: Princeton University Press, 1957).

Grable, J. and Lytton, R. H., "Financial Risk Tolerance Revisited: The Development of a Risk Assessment Instrument," *Financial Services Review*, vol. 8 (1999): 163–181.

Hall, R. E., "Stochastic Implications of the Life Cycle Permanent Income Hypothesis: Theory and Evidence," *Journal of Political Economy*, vol. 86 (1978): 971–987.

Johnson, S., Kotlikoff, L. J., and Samuelson, W., "Can People Compute: An Experimental Test of the Life Cycle Consumption Model," in *Essays on Savings, Bequests, Altruism and Life Cycle Planning*, Kotlikoff, L. C., ed. (Cambridge, MA and London, UK: MIT Press, 2001): 335–385.

MacCrimmon, K. R. and Wehrung, D. A., *Taking Risks: The Management of Uncertainties* (New York: Free Press, 1986).

Mayers, D., "Nonmarketable Assets and Capital Market Equilibrium under Uncertainty," in *Studies in the Theory of Capital Markets*, Jensen, M. C., ed. (New York: Praeger Publishers, 1972): 223–248.

Merton, R. C., "Lifetime Portfolio Selection under Uncertainty: The Continuous-Time Case," *Review of Economics and Statistics*, vol. 51, no. 3 (1969): 247–257.

Modigliani, F. and Brumberg, R., "Utility Analysis and the Consumption Function: An Interpretation of Cross-section Data," in *Social Cognitive Development Frontiers and Possible Futures*, Flavell, J. H. and Ross, L., eds. (Cambridge, NY: University Press, 1954).

Roszkowski, M., Davey, G., and Grable, J., "Insights from Psychology and Psychometrics on Measuring Risk Tolerance," *Journal of Financial Planning*, Article 8 (April 2005).

Shefrin, H. M. and Thaler, R. H., "The Behavioral Life Cycle Hypothesis," *Economic Inquiry*, vol. 26 (1988): 609–643.

Snelbecker, G., Roszkowski, M., and Culter, N., "Investors' Risk Tolerance and Return Aspirations and Financial Advisors' Interpretations: A Conceptual Model and Exploratory Data," *Journal of Behavioral Economics*, vol. 19 (1990): 377–393.

Svensson, L. E. O., "Trade in Risky Assets," *American Economic Review*, vol. 78 (1988): 375–394.

Williams, J. T., "Risk, Human Capital and the Investors' Portfolio," *Journal of Business*, vol. 51 (1978): 65–89.

Yook, K. and Everett, R., "Assessing Risk Tolerance: Questioning the Questionnaire Method," *Journal of Financial Planning* (August 2003): 48–55.

Questions & Problems

Multiple-choice Questions

1. Which of the following is the best tool used in risk profiling to determine the risk tolerance level?
   A. A questionnaire
   B. A short phone interview
   C. A background check of the education of the client
   D. The career development of the client

2. The permanent-income hypothesis of Friedman (1957) suggests that an individual, by applying _____ can maximize _____.
   A. portfolio theory; return
   B. comprehensive financial planning; happiness
   C. consumption smoothing; lifelong utility
   D. risk control; lifelong utility

3. Which of the following is not one of the aspects to be evaluated in personal profiling?
   A. Personality
   B. Psychological health
   C. Family value
   D. Securities transactions for the past six months

4. Which of the following statements concerning insurance planning for different life stages are true?
   I. As the client moves from one stage to another stage of the life cycle, the amount of life insurance coverage varies.
   II. As the financial obligation of the client changes in the last two stages of the life cycle, the insurance needs gradually increase.
   III. Financial planners have to tell their clients to buy maximum insurance coverage in order to enable them to maintain sufficient insurance protection.
   IV. As the financial obligation of the client decreases in the last two stages of the life cycle, the insurance needs gradually decline.
   V. Financial planners have to estimate the permanent component and the variable component of the insurance needs of the clients so as to allow the clients to maintain flexibility to increase or to decrease insurance protection.

   A. I and II
   B. I, II and III
   C. I, III and IV
   D. I, IV and V

5. Which life-cycle stage best corresponds to the statement "When the children leave home or become financially independent, the parents' income level increases"?
   A. Young married
   B. Preretirement
   C. Young adult
   D. Retired

Problems

1. Describe the impact of the cultural effect and the cohort effect on applying the life-cycle model in financial planning.

2. Define personal profiling.

3. Define risk profiling.

4. Describe how to use a psychometric survey to gather information on risk profiling.

5. Suggest some ways to improve the effectiveness of a risk tolerance questionnaire.

PART II

The Financial Planning Process

Step 1: Establishing Client-Planner Relationship

> **Learning Objectives**
>
> *After studying this chapter you should be able to:*
> 1 Explain the meaning of Reverse MIRAGE.
> 2 Describe the relationship between the six-step process and practice standards.
> 3 Explain the value of the scope of engagement.
> 4 Know the importance of mutually defined principles.
> 5 Know how to prepare an interview with clients.
> 6 Understand communication techniques.
> 7 Know how to classify clients.
> 8 Understand the principles of matching clients with planners.
> 9 Know how to promote financial planning services.

To be a successful financial planner, strong communication and interpersonal skills are required. This is particularly important when the financial planner is acquiring personal information about their clients in seeking to understand their financial goals. In this chapter we discuss the ways in which financial planners can develop their interpersonal skills so as to establish a solid professional relationship with their clients. But first let us recap what we have learnt about the six-step financial planning process, and explain it a little more.

7.1   The Six-step Financial Planning Process and the CFP Board Practice Standards

The six-step financial planning process follows the logical sequence of completing a project in the corporate world. And like any project, it can be broken down into several phases. Phase 1 deals with fact finding and analysis and comprises step 1 (establishing client-planner relationship), step 2 (determining goals and gathering client data), and step 3 (determining client's financial status). Phase 2 deals with recommendations and actions and comprises step 4 (developing and presenting financial planning recommendations) and step 5 (implementing the financial planning recommendations). Finally, the last phase deals with reviewing the situation and making appropriate adjustments and improvements. In the financial planning process, this is step 6 (monitoring the financial plan).

Bill Moran, Vice President of Financial Planning Operations, Ameriprise Financial, has developed a very easy way to memorize and interpret the six-step financial planning process. Bill calls the six-step process *Reverse MIRAGE.* MIRAGE spelt backwards gives us the acronym *EGARIM*, which stands for (1) Engage, (2) Gather, (3) Analyze, (4) Recommend, (5) Implement, and (6) Monitor. Thus, EGARIM, or Reverse MIRAGE, is a summary of the actions for the six-step process. Moreover, Bill provides an intuitive explanation of why Reverse MIRAGE is especially relevant for financial planning. A mirage, as we all know, is an illusion of something desirable, just like the financial freedom that an individual desires but is not necessarily realistic with his or her present financial condition and lifestyle. Employing effective financial planning can help an individual to convert this mirage into a real thing. Reverse MIRAGE helps individuals make their dream come true and is the essence of financial planning.

In a well-developed economy, financial planners must be aware of what clients expect from them, and they should do everything they can to meet those expectations. Clients expect their financial planners to (1) have good educational background, (2) have adequate experience in financial planning, (3) have effective communication skills, and (4) fully disclose their fees and commissions.

Adopting good practice standards helps to meet these client expectations. In Chapter 2, we introduced you to the CFP Board's practice standards. These practice standards set the benchmark and establish the boundaries for practicing financial planning. Practice standards can also help financial planners to maintain consistency and quality of services provided. In the long run, good practice reduces complaints from clients and enhances the reputation of financial planners. The practice standards are designed to go hand in hand with the six-step process. Thus, each step has one or more related practice guidelines. Table 7.1 describes the related practice standards for the six steps.

Remember, the key to success in establishing a strong and long-lasting relationship with clients is to gain their trust. Having a good reputation by following the practice standards is a necessary ingredient in gaining trust from clients. Each practice standard has an explanatory statement that provides a guideline for the interpretation and application of the practice standard. Although the related practice standards are associated with particular steps of the financial planning process, it does not mean that each practice standard should be considered alone. For example, the 100 Series lays the foundation for

Table 7.1 The financial planning process and related practice standards

Financial planning process	Related practice standard
1. Establishing and defining the relationship with a client	100-1 Defining the scope of the engagement
2. Determining goals and gathering client data	200-1 Determining a client's personal and financial goals, needs, and priorities 200-2 Obtaining quantitative information and documents
3. Analyzing and evaluating the client's financial status	300-1 Analyzing and evaluating the client's information
4. Developing and presenting financial planning recommendations	400-1 Identifying and evaluating financial planning alternatives 400-2 Developing the financial planning recommendations 400-3 Presenting the financial planning recommendations
5. Implementing the financial planning recommendations	500-1 Agreeing on implementation responsibilities 500-2 Selecting products and services for implementation
6. Monitoring the financial plan	600-1 Defining monitoring responsibilities

all six steps and all subsequent series are in some way connected to the practice standards guidelines for their previous steps. Financial planners should carry out the practice standards for the related steps as an interactive and continuous process.

7.2   Practice Standards 100 Series

In the first step of the financial planning process, financial planners have to establish a relationship with their clients. It is important that the financial planners and their clients define the scope of the engagement. Therefore, Practice Standard 100-1 of the CFP Board states that

> **The financial planning practitioner and the client shall mutually define the scope of the engagement before any financial planning service is provided.**

scope of engagement
The mutually agreed upon declaration that lists the responsibilities, compensation, and limitations of the financial planner, and the responsibility of the client.

It is important for financial planners and their clients to determine the **scope of engagement** and what activities may be necessary to proceed with the engagement. The mutually defined scope of engagement helps to establish realistic expectations for clients and financial planners. Examples of the issues and activities to be defined include identifying the services to be provided; disclosing any possible conflict of interest of the financial planner; disclosing the financial planner's compensation arrangement; determining the respective responsibilities of the client and the financial planner; setting the duration of the engagement; and providing any information necessary to define or limit the scope. Specifying the limitations of the financial planner is also important, especially when the clients did not disclose all necessary information for the planners to conduct accurate financial planning. In this case, listing the limitations and disclaimer in the engagement letter can help to avoid unnecessary legal and financial liabilities.

In many cases, the scope of engagement is limited to specific planning areas. If the financial planner provides a commission-based instead of fee-based service, the scope of engagement for product implementation can actually be dealt with at a later stage in step 4. This is because the client and financial planner may not be interested in signing the scope related to products unless the client accepts the strategies and the advisory aspects of the financial plan first. Consequently, it may be more convenient for commission-based financial planners to sign the scope of engagement for implementation as an authorization to proceed after the client accepts the fully developed plan in step 4. Although this practice standard does not require the scope of the engagement to be in writing, there may be certain disclosures of material information (such as disclosure of conflict of interest or sources of compensation) that are required to be in writing. The scope may change by mutual agreement as the relationship between financial planner and client continues.

Having a mutual agreement on the engagement scope between financial planner and client is important since the clarity of the scope of the engagement enhances the likelihood of achieving client expectations. From the perspective of the public, better service is provided if the financial planner-client relationship is based upon a mutual understanding of the engagement. The improved service provided by financial planners enhances the satisfaction level and hence the reputation of financial planners and the financial planning profession.

Financial planning practitioners can also benefit from the practice standard as a mutually defined scope of the engagement provides a framework for the financial planning process by focusing both the client and the practitioner on the agreed-upon tasks. A clear agreement between financial planner and client enhances the building of a more solid foundation for a trusting relationship. If clients have clear and realistic expectations of the financial planning process and the services provided, they will be happier clients, leading to a higher retention rate of clients and a lasting client-planner relationship.

Practice Standards 100 Series implies that a financial planner must be honest. In the fiduciary relationship with the client, a financial planner, being the agent of the principal (the client), has to provide financial planning services with honesty and professionalism. If the financial planner cannot give the impression that he or she is honest and professional at the very first meeting, he or she may lose the client.

Being honest means that financial planners should not exaggerate their qualifications, abilities, or track records; they should not misrepresent what their firms can do for clients; and they should not misrepresent their firms. Based on the 100 Series, we suggest several ways in which financial planners can show their honesty to their potential clients at their first meeting:

1. Be honest about what you can or cannot do

Having CFP® certification does not imply that a CFP® certificant is a financial planning "superman." Therefore, financial planners should not boast that they can help their clients achieve all their goals with no outside help. For example, you can give advice on estate planning to your clients, but you may need a lawyer to help your clients in writing wills.

2. Present a complete picture of your track record to clients

Not only should an honest financial planner present a good track record, but he or she should also not hide a bad track record. Among the many clients you have in your career, you are bound to have some clients showing excellent investment returns while others having unsatisfactory results. You cannot just present the best results to your clients or potential clients.

3. Be neutral when recommending products manufactured by your firm

Many financial services companies manufacture their own products and expect their planners to promote these products. Financial planners with integrity and professionalism should advise their client to use the best products no matter who the manufacturers are. Clients would be impressed if you provide impartial and fair recommendations.

4. Be honest about the limitations of your firm

If your firm is not licensed to perform certain functions in financial planning, you must explain this clearly to clients in advance.

5. Be honest about your relationship with other professionals

Sometimes you need to refer your clients to other professionals. You should inform your clients what kind of relationship you have with these professionals, particularly if you receive any referral fees.

7.3 Establishing Client-Planner Relationship

Obtaining the proper financial information about the client is an essential component in financial analysis and financial plan development. In order to obtain valuable, but often sensitive, information, the first step is to establish a closer relationship with the clients. In fact, the success of the relationship largely depends on the interpersonal and communication skills of the financial planner. We will now discuss how to conduct interviews with clients.

Preparing the Interview

Conducting an interview is an effective method to communicate with clients and understand their needs. It is also useful to help financial planners determine whether their clients are likely to establish a cooperative relationship in the future or not. Therefore, at the first meeting, the goal of the financial planner should be to find out their clients' financial goals, investment preferences, and other basic information. More importantly, the financial planners should use the interview as the opportunity to explain the benefits, commitment, and fees involved in financial planning to the clients.

Before an interview, the financial planner should:

1. **Develop a "meeting outline" that defines the objectives and sets the details for the meeting (e.g., prepare the appropriate questions to obtain key information from the client).** Two objectives should be achieved in the first interview: gaining an understanding of the client's basic financial situation and determining whether a fruitful client-planner relationship can be established. Developing an effective meeting outline can enhance the quality of the interview and help ensure that these objectives are attained.

2. **Prepare in advance relevant economic data (e.g., some basic macroeconomic and financial market data).** Two copies of the materials should be made, one for the client and the other for the financial planner.

3. **Select an appropriate time and venue and estimate the duration of the interview (e.g., the time required for the client to fill in data forms).** Generally, the office of the financial planner is the best venue. This arrangement can bring three benefits. First, it allows the financial planner to control the environment and minimize the possibility of external disturbances. This enables the financial planner to have better control of the interview. Second, it ensures that the relevant information about the financial planning services can be provided to the client. Finally, a proper meeting room can project a strong professional image of the financial planner and the company to the client, thus enhancing trust.

4. **Make sure that the client is aware that the financial planner is only the advisor of the client and that the client will not lose control of his or her assets (i.e., the client still makes all final financial decisions).** The financial planner should stress to the client that his or her role is one of advisor to the client. As many financial decisions are difficult, the financial planner can help organize and explain the relevant information to assist the client in the decision-making process. The responsibility of the financial planner is to make suggestions and recommendations while the responsibility of the client is to make the final decisions.

5. **Remind the client to bring relevant documents (e.g., insurance policies, tax statements, and securities holdings).** Since these documents can provide detailed information about the client, obtaining the information from these documents is more convenient and accurate than asking the client to recall the information from memory. The financial planner should prepare a list of documents generally considered relevant as the client may not know which documents are relevant and which are not.

6. **Prepare recording tools in advance (e.g., different kinds of forms).** Proper recording of all relevant information is an indispensable step for two reasons. First, when developing the financial plan for clients, it is unwise to rely on the memory of the financial planner for the information. Therefore, recording of information is necessary. Second, in the event of any future dispute between the client and the financial planner, these records can provide proof of the information provided to and by the client.

7. **Request that the clients not engage in any other activities or business (e.g., phone calls) during the interview.** It is important to ensure that the interview is not disturbed. Ensuring this conveys a clear message to the client that the service to the client is very important to the financial planner. This helps create trust and open the channels of further communication.

Besides preparing the paperwork and necessary documents for the interview, financial planners should prepare themselves to give a good impression to clients at the first meeting. Certainly, punctuality is very important; it is better to be at the interview 10 minutes early. It is also possible that clients may raise questions to test the financial planners. Therefore, financial planners should be well prepared for the questions from the clients. The key is to understand the expectations of the clients. Table 7.2 shows the consumer public's common misconceptions about financial planners and financial planning, and some suggested responses by financial planners.

Financial planners may also have misconceptions of their own regarding their clients, especially when they get clients who are quiet and uncommunicative. Financial planners should remember that just because clients do not express a different opinion to theirs, it does not necessarily mean that they are agreeing with the financial planners. Financial planners should not assume that clients' expectations match theirs. Clients can still be dissatisfied even though the financial planners think their financial plans are excellent. Thus it is important for financial planners to probe and ascertain what their clients really think.

Table 7.2 Common misconceptions and suggested responses

Common misconceptions	Suggested responses
1. Clients think that financial planning services are not necessary; personal financial planning can be conducted by themselves.	Inform clients that you, as a financial planner, can provide various professional services. You can: • Provide objective risk management. • Deal with tedious paperwork. • Decrease their tax burden. • Offer consumption planning. • Provide professional investment advice and retirement planning.
2. Clients have wrong ideas about what constitutes good financial planning services.	• Be patient with clients. • Listen to clients to get more insights into how they think. • Don't directly attack clients' wrong ideas as this may undermine rapport and cause mistrust. • Provide specific examples to show clients what financial planning services really means, in contrast to clients' misconceptions.
3. Clients think that financial planners know everything.	• Explain clearly the objectives of financial planning services and the role of financial planners. • Don't mislead clients about your ability, qualifications, and reputation. • Help clients to form realistic expectations gradually.
4. Clients have unrealistic expectations about investment return.	• Explain clearly that there are risks associated with financial investment. Emphasize that investment planning for clients must focus on achieving life goals instead of purely maximizing returns. • Inform clients that investment return is affected by factors such as the general market and economic conditions, risk tolerance levels, and investment horizon. Thus, clients should not blindly compare their portfolio returns with those of their friends without considering these factors.

Information Disclosure

In the financial planning process, most clients are eager to know how much they can get and what the risk level is if they follow the financial plans suggested by financial planners. Therefore, it is the duty of the financial planners to provide the basic knowledge to their clients, in order to help them understand the benefits and risks of financial planning. Impractical and unrealistic expectations and goals should be avoided in the financial plan. If financial planners can provide relevant and sufficient information to enable clients to have a better understanding of financial planning, it helps to establish the professional image of the financial planners and to create an atmosphere of candor between clients and financial planners.

First, financial planners need to explain the six-step financial planning process to their clients. The introduction of the whole process is significant as it allows clients to understand the professionalism and standardization of the financial planning services. Financial planners must employ effective communication skills at this point in order to help clients to fully understand the relevant issues. Financial planners should always bear in mind that clients with little or no background in the financial planning process will need more detailed explanations than clients with some experience or knowledge.

Second, financial planners need to explain the respective roles of financial planner and client in the financial planning process. The scope of engagement using the mutually defined principles in the Practice Standards 100 Series helps to communicate the responsibilities of both parties. This document can be important if clients dispute the services provided. Financial planners should also disclose the fees that they will receive directly or indirectly. While regulations of fee disclosure vary in different countries, financial planners with the highest practice standards should try their best to disclose their financial interest in dealing with clients even if this may require them to go beyond the requirements of the local regulations.

As required by the practice standards, financial planners should adopt a high standard of business ethics, follow professional procedures, and use the proper tools in order to formulate a practical and integrated financial plan in accordance with the financial needs of their clients. However, in China and other Asian countries, financial planning is still in the early stages of development. The general public in these countries tends to perceive financial planners as investment consultants or insurance agents whose jobs are to market different investment products. In such a case, it is particularly important for the financial planners to explain the differences and the relationship between financial planning services and other financial services. Moreover, the clients need to understand the functions of financial planning. Theoretically, financial planning helps clients achieve their financial goals, but, in fact, not all financial goals can be achieved. For instance, a client with an average income of $100,000 may want to have an investment plan that can result in $5,000,000 in five years. This is obviously impractical. Other financial goals, even if theoretically feasible, may require the clients to take very high risks. In short, a financial plan cannot attain *all* goals. The main objective of financial planning is to assist clients to improve their current financial management and accumulate more financial resources for the future. This task of giving clients the true picture of reaching their financial goals is an important part of managing client expectation in the early stages.

An effective way to handle information disclosure is to prepare a set of questions and answers. If time permits, financial planners can go through these questions and answers verbally with their clients. If not, a leaflet can be given to the clients for further reading. Here are some clients' commonly asked questions:

1. What are the experiences and qualifications of the financial planner?

Clients are generally concerned about whether financial planners have the ability to provide high quality services for them. They need to know the qualifications and experience of the financial planners. Financial planners should be prepared to provide information about their credentials and qualifications to their clients upon their request. If financial planners have little experience in the financial planning profession, they should focus more attention on the qualification and the experience of their firms.

2.   What are the fees for financial planning services?

The fee issue is very important to most clients. Financial planners should explain in detail the charges of the different categories of financial planning services. Clients and financial planners should have a mutual agreement on the fee issue. To avoid any potential disputes, a written agreement is better than a verbal agreement.

3.   What are the investment strategies that will be used?

Most clients lack knowledge in the area of making investments, and would naturally like to know more about the investment strategies of financial planners. Financial planners need to explain to their clients in detail the investment instruments selected and the investment strategies employed.

4.   What computer software will be used in formulating the financial plan?

To reduce workload and improve accuracy, financial planners may need to make use of computer software to develop the financial plans. Some clients may be interested in knowing how the software operates, so financial planners should explain to clients the nature of the software and why the software is selected for use. It may be helpful to illustrate the software operations and give some examples.

5.   What is the role of other professionals in the financial planning process?

The duties of other professionals, such as accountants, lawyers, and insurance agents should be explained. If clients know that their financial planners are in close contact with other professionals, clients can consult other professionals in case they need their help during the financial planning process.

6.   What follow-up services are provided?

Financial planners and their clients should, periodically, reevaluate the financial plan. This is important to determine if the economic and financial situations of the clients have changed. Financial planners can then make the necessary adjustments to the current financial plan.

7.   What investment returns can I expect?

The investment plan is, unquestionably, an important part of the overall financial plan. In some cases clients may expect their investments to provide unrealistically high returns. Financial planners should explain to their clients that the investment plan is only one part of the overall financial planning process and high rates of return should not be the single objective of a well-developed investment plan. Other factors like liquidity, stability, and security of the investment should also be carefully considered. Financial planners should make their clients understand this before trying to quantify their life goals and set the financial targets.

Interview Objectives

After explaining the important issues to clients and acquiring the necessary financial information from them, the initial interview comes to an end. Financial planners should by this time have a fair understanding of the financial planning objectives, financial goals, and investment preferences of their clients. Before the conclusion of the interview, financial planners should reconfirm with their clients that all information given is correct.

The main purpose of the initial meeting is to obtain clients' basic information. Certainly, it is not possible to collect all relevant information in one meeting. Indeed, if the clients decide to employ the financial planners, data collection forms (in hard copy or electronic format) should be used. This can save a lot of time in collecting information. In addition, the letter of engagement should be explained and signed (if possible). Finally, financial planners should arrange for the next meeting with their clients before the end of the interview.

7.4 Communication Techniques for Financial Planning

Financial planners should have excellent interpersonal skills. Clients may feel nervous and anxious about disclosing personal information to financial planners. Therefore, financial planners should first try to make friends with the clients, showing true concern for them while trying to understand their financial expectations and goals.

The major objectives for meeting with clients are to establish the client-planner relationship and to obtain relevant financial information. During the meetings, the level of communication skills can directly affect the quality and quantity of the required information to be collected, as well as clients' perception of the financial planners' competence. Therefore, based on the personality profile of the clients, financial planners should choose a suitable communication tactic to approach them. Only clear and effective communication will enable financial planners to convey a positive image to their clients.

Before we discuss the various communication techniques, we will first examine some obstacles to good communication. Good communication requires both effective sending and receiving of messages. However, not all of us are good listeners. It is estimated that only about 60% of spoken information is accurately received. There are a number of reasons why messages are not well conveyed between the sender and receiver:

1. The message sent is unclear or not specific enough, causing the receiver to make assumptions.
2. The receiver is not paying attention due to lack of interest in the subject matter.
3. The receiver is preoccupied with other matters.
4. The sender is not saying what the receiver wants to hear.
5. The receiver is busy formulating a rebuttal to something the sender said previously.

Projecting a Professional Image

Most clients would form their opinions about their financial planners in the first few minutes of the initial meeting. Clients may make their judgments based on what they observe from the appearance, attire, language, and manners of the financial planners, or even the surroundings of the company (e.g., the office of the financial planners). If the financial planner is perceived as being impolite, being indecisive, or having poor morals, the client may suspect his or her ability and ethical conduct. On the other hand, a strong professional image will help financial planners to gain the trust of their clients.

Another point to note is that the office of the financial planners is the most suitable venue for meetings with the clients. Nevertheless, a large desk or a big empty room may make clients feel uncomfortable or make it difficult for them to relax. Therefore, if possible, financial planners should consider placing a coffee table and a small sofa in their office, which can induce a more friendly environment for the meeting.

Communication Strategies

The primary communication vehicle in the first interview should be direct personal conversation. Direct personal conversation between financial planner and client gives each party the opportunity to learn about each other and hopefully, enables a bond of trust to be developed.

At the same time, clients can be given data collection forms to fill out. However, since most clients do not have professional knowledge, they may not be able to provide correct answers for the questions on the forms. Therefore, data forms, although important, should not be the only communication technique to be used to get information from clients.

Many clients do not fully understand their financial status and goals in the first interview; some do not even know the role of financial planning. This may be why clients may feel uncomfortable when meeting with financial planners for the first time. Financial planners need to create a comfortable environment and give clients the opportunity to participate in the discussion. That is, financial planners should not do all the talking; rather, they should encourage clients to talk. For example, financial planners can ask their clients if they want something to drink, and then take some time to discuss other topics, for example their family, their job, their children, and their investment experiences. In addition, if financial planners do not focus on topics related to financial planning only, clients may have the impression that the financial planners are concerned about them as individuals, and not just as business opportunities.

Certainly, after the warm-up conversation, financial planners should direct the conversation toward relevant financial planning topics. Financial planners must present ideas and ask questions in a logical way. They should give their clients time to think of and ask questions if they have any.

Active Listening

The communication process consists of speaking and listening. Some people think that when they are speaking, they are in control of the process, and when they are listening, they relinquish control to the other party. This is only true if the listener is a passive listener. Passive listeners only take an active role in communication when it is their turn to speak, leaving the process beyond their control at least half the time. Taking 100% responsibility for communication requires you to be specific and articulate in your own speech, and to actively facilitate the quality of the other party's communication when you are listening. This facilitation is known as **active listening**. By taking part in active listening, the listeners show their respect and appreciation for the speakers. It can be frustrating if clients perceive that their financial planners are not really listening to them. Clients are most likely to feel this way when the financial planners are passive listeners. There is nothing that destroys rapport faster than having clients believe that their financial planners do not care about what they say.

active listening The proactive method in listening to and understanding clients.

During the interview, financial planners need to be good active listeners. Asking questions and taking notes are essential but not sufficient for an effective financial planning interview. Whenever appropriate, financial planners should also provide short comments from time to time. Here is an example of active listening:

Client:	I have a property insurance policy purchased from the ABC Insurance Company and I expect the premium to be increased next year.
Financial planner:	You do? Why?
Client:	Well, my flat has a lot of cracks. In fact, my wife and I want to buy a new flat.
Financial planner:	Oh, I see. So how much does the ABC charge you for the premium now?

From this simple example you can see that when financial planners make responses to clients' statements, clients will realize that the financial planners do listen carefully and try to understand clients' expectations. Whenever financial planners are not sure about the information, they should repeat the answer for confirmation. Financial planners should also bear in mind that they should not disturb their clients by abruptly raising questions or making conclusions when the clients are talking.

Being an active listener results in the following benefits:

1. Enables accurate exchange of information. This is critical for you to serve the client properly.
2. Reduces misunderstandings. This helps increase client satisfaction with your services.
3. Increases rapport. When clients feel you understand them, it creates greater rapport and trust.
4. Differentiates you from others. Since most people are poor listeners, good listening skills will make you stand above the crowd.

Nonverbal Communication

Financial planners should learn how to "read" their clients' body language in order to know what they really think and need. Some clients may not express themselves clearly when answering the questions of their financial planners. Occasionally, what clients say may not be consistent with what they think. In such cases, financial planners need to pay attention to their clients' non-verbal cues in order to understand them better.

The nonverbal cues of a person refer to his or her body language, which include eye contact, facial expressions, postures, and gestures. Body language is a subtle, yet important, way of transmitting information. **Nonverbal communication** skills are no less important than verbal communication skills. In fact, according to Figure 7.1, body language is the most important means of conveying information to clients.

Therefore, when meeting with their clients, financial planners should pay attention to several points related to nonverbal communication:

1. Maintain eye contact with clients during the conversation. Making eye contact signals to clients that the financial planners are listening attentively to them. Financial planners should not look around or lower their heads because such actions give clients the impression that the financial planners are not paying attention.
2. Use appropriate facial expressions. When clients are talking, it is not appropriate to interrupt. However, financial planners can use facial expressions to show their feelings instead. For example, whenever

nonverbal communication
Communication that doesn't use words but body language, including facial expressions and gestures.

Figure 7.1 **Factors affecting transmission of information**

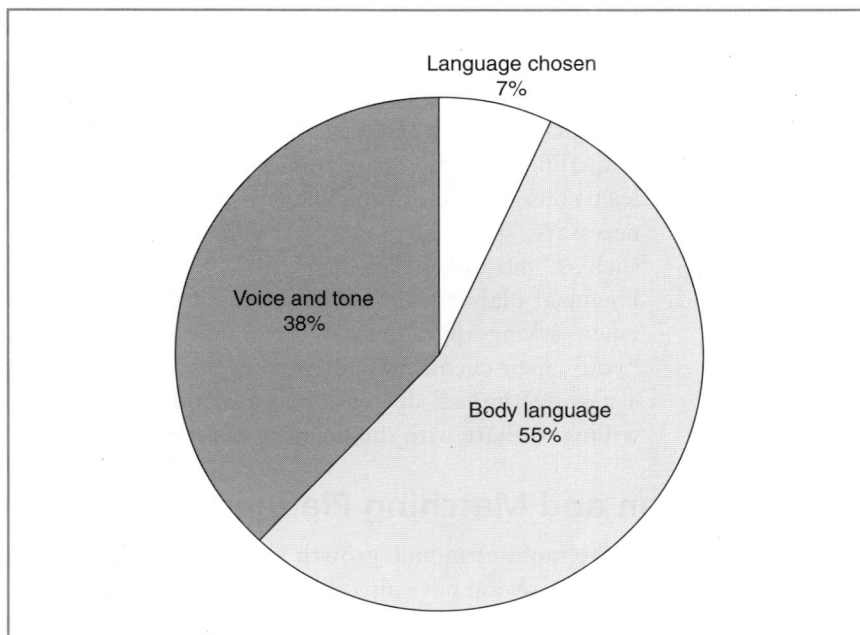

Source: Wood, G., *Customer Communications in Marketing 2000–2001*, Butterworth-Heinemann, p. 19.

financial planners agree with something that their clients have said, they can smile or nod their heads. Indeed, financial planners should use facial expressions to show their understanding and sympathy particularly when the clients mention some unhappy experience.

3. Sit properly. Proper posture conveys a positive professional image. On the contrary, if financial planners lounge in a very casual manner, clients may question their professionalism and abilities. Sitting up straight while leaning forward slightly indicates that you are actively listening to clients.

4. Use effective gestures. Financial planners can use different kinds of gestures when expressing their ideas. However, they should bear in mind that some gestures, such as clenched fists, have negative connotations and should be avoided. They should also avoid annoying gestures such as shaking their legs.

Using Words Carefully: Legal Liability

Financial planners are providers of professional services so it is acceptable to use technical terms or jargon at the interview. However, financial planners should explain the technical terms to clients when necessary. It is always unwise to make promises that cannot be kept. For example, financial planners should not make misleading statements that would imply that certain investment plans can earn high returns for their clients. Here we highlight some words that financial planners should be careful of using:

1. When talking to their clients, financial planners should use "we" instead of "I." "I" refers to the financial planner alone, while "we" refers to the entire company that the financial planner represents. If a dispute should occur, any legal liability should rest with the company, not with the financial planner.

2. Financial planners should not use words like "promise", "certainly," or "guarantee" when discussing issues beyond their control. These unqualified words can have a legally binding effect and can result in legal consequences for the financial planners and their companies. When necessary, financial planners should use words with some ambiguity such as "most likely" or "optimistic."

3. Financial planners should avoid using the word "you" too frequently when asking questions. If the financial planners overuse the word "you", their clients may feel greater personal pressure which may create a negative impact on the amount of information the clients would be willing to share with the financial planners.

7.5   Client Segmentation and Matching Planners with Clients

Following the rapid economic growth in Asia, the behavior and expectation of consumers in the region have also changed substantially. Christina Hui, Regional General Manager (Asia) of Charles Schwab, uses an excellent story to illustrate the change of clientele for financial services firms. Christina explains that in the past, most financial planning clients behave like owners of luxurious Rolls-Royce sedans, who sit at the back of their cars and ask their drivers to take them to their destinations by the safest and quickest way. The owner of the Rolls-Royce is not interested in the details of the route the driver uses. The car owner represents the wealthy client and the driver represents the financial planner. As long as the financial planner achieves the financial goals for the client, the client is not interested in the details of the investment strategies and the products used.

Nowadays, though, clients are more like BMW owners. The Rolls-Royce is famous for its comfortable back seats, so most Rolls-Royce owners prefer sitting at the back instead of driving in front. However, the BMW sports car owner is more interested in driving than sitting at the back of the car. The new breed of financial planning clients is in general younger, more aggressive, more knowledgeable in finance, and most importantly, more interested in participating in the financial planning process. They want to be involved in the decision-making process, and they are willing to take some responsibility for the outcome, whether it is a success or a failure. The new kind of client prefers to drive his or her own BMW. The financial planner has become the co-driver sitting beside the driver in the front. The role of the financial planner has changed from one of making all the decisions to one of providing technical support and giving advice. Of course, it is not necessarily easier to be a co-driver, especially if the clients are very knowledgeable and demanding.

If a financial planner is interested in serving the new clientele, then a different business model and different skills set are required to be successful. While the number of this new clientele varies, depending on the local economy and education level, a financial planner must be ready for the challenge as this new clientele will increase and will eventually become the dominant group among financial planning clients.

Client Segmentation

Financial planners frequently need to meet clients with different cultural, educational, and social backgrounds. All of these factors affect the investment preferences and financial goals of the clients. Although some clients have similar financial status, their preferences and goals may be very different; so financial planners should develop individualized financial plans according to their clients' specific characteristics. Financial planners need to gather all appropriate information during the interview with their clients and then segment their clients accordingly. The main purposes of client segmentation are to derive an appropriate communication strategy to establish a better relationship and to identify an appropriate financial planner to deal with the clients.

Client segmentation is the process of dividing clients into distinct subsets using certain characteristics. The first step in developing a strategy is to select the most appropriate way to segment the clients. The most common methods are:

1. Psychological segmentation (e.g., personality, perception, and attitude).
2. Demographic segmentation (e.g., age, sex, marital status, income, education, occupation).

3. Geographic segmentation (e.g., region, city size, density of area, and climate).
4. Sociocultural segmentation (e.g., culture, religion, race, social class, and family life cycle).

We can also use the technique of personal profiling to assess the overall personal background of the clients. Personal profiling involves examining the client's personality, family values, cultural values, lifestyle preferences, psychological health, physical health, and experience of major life events.

Numerous studies have been conducted to identify the psychological variables of potential interest to financial planners. These studies assist financial planners in understanding the personalities, lifestyle, and behaviors of their clients. For more details of these models, please refer to Phillips and Bergquisst (1999) and Keirsey and Bates (1984).

Techniques for better communication and relationship development can help financial planners to classify their clients into specific categories of personality traits. However, it isn't easy to classify some clients—some have a mixture of personality traits. Therefore, it is essential to observe more thoroughly, listen more actively, and prepare more carefully. More importantly, financial planners should remember that effective communication not only brings mutual success but also facilitates a harmonious long-term relationship with their clients.

Matching Planners with Clients

client orientation The style of client in handling financial planning-related requests and tasks.

Depending on the sophistication of the clients and the maturity of the economy, different markets possess a different mix of client types. Financial planning firms should employ a mix of financial planners to meet the needs of various clients. In addition to using personality traits to classify clients, financial planning firms also classify clients according to three factors: **client orientation** (relationship-oriented or analysis-oriented), asset size, and income level. Clients can be divided into high net-worth clients and non-high net-worth clients based on their minimum asset size and income level. Then clients are classified again by client orientation. The head financial planners will then match the appropriate financial planners to clients according to these three criteria. Figure 7.2 shows the matching criteria mentioned above. While this is not an exact science, financial planning firms should try to match their financial planners with clients as best as they can.

The personal profile of clients reflects the nonquantitative (soft aspect) of client orientation. The financial profile reflects the quantitative aspect (hard aspect) of client orientation. By combining the personal profile and financial profile of clients, we can categorize them into two orientations: relationship-oriented and analysis-oriented (Figure 7.3). Relationship-oriented clients are not interested in numbers at all. They have stronger psychological needs and their behaviors are more easily affected by their emotions. In dealing with relationship-oriented clients, financial planners must try to understand their feelings and address their emotional needs. As relationship-oriented clients can sometimes be irrational, financial planners should be more sensitive to their life goals and be more forgiving if their requests are not logical. Once their psychological needs are satisfied, this client type will generally become very loyal customers. Relationship-oriented

Figure 7.2 Principles in matching financial planners with clients

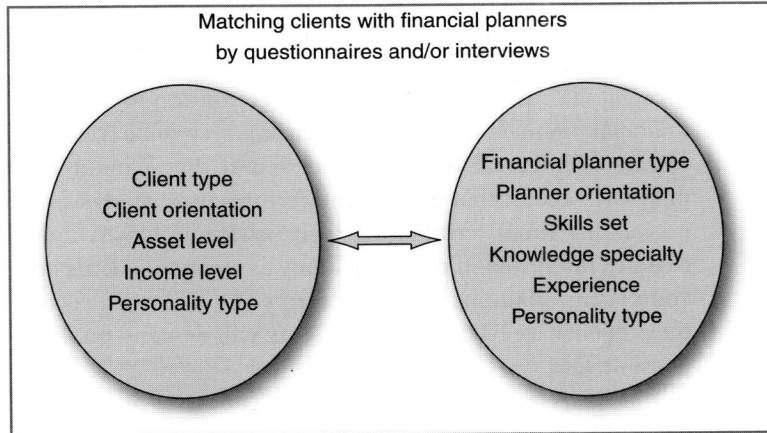

Matching clients with financial planners
by questionnaires and/or interviews

Client type
Client orientation
Asset level
Income level
Personality type

Financial planner type
Planner orientation
Skills set
Knowledge specialty
Experience
Personality type

clients are usually less critical about their investment returns. Thus, it is actually easier to maintain a long-term relationship with relationship-oriented clients. Financial planners should have a strong emotional quotient (EQ) and excellent communication skills to deal with this client type. Relationship-oriented clients don't generally ask too many technical questions or care about numbers; they value human relationships more. The ability of the financial planners to explain how their financial goals can be related to their life goals is critical to make the relationship-oriented clients satisfied. If the financial planners can do this, they will be able to earn total trust from their clients, leading to a successful and long-lasting relationship.

Figure 7.3 Client types in terms of client orientation

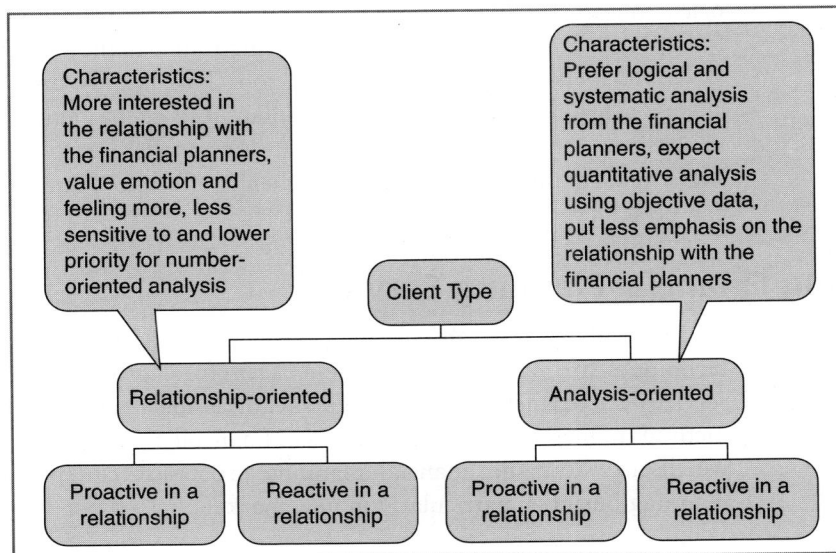

Characteristics:
More interested in the relationship with the financial planners, value emotion and feeling more, less sensitive to and lower priority for number-oriented analysis

Characteristics:
Prefer logical and systematic analysis from the financial planners, expect quantitative analysis using objective data, put less emphasis on the relationship with the financial planners

Client Type

Relationship-oriented

Analysis-oriented

Proactive in a relationship

Reactive in a relationship

Proactive in a relationship

Reactive in a relationship

Analysis-oriented clients, on the other hand, generally place more emphasis on quantitative, systematic analysis and are less interested in a deeper friendship with their financial planners. To deal with these clients, financial planners should have strong knowledge in financial analysis, updated market intelligence, and a professional image with a logical presentation style. It is still important for the financial planners to build a rapport and try to be friends. However, the financial planners should also understand that if they cannot deliver a sound financial plan with acceptable investment performance, analysis-oriented clients will have no qualms about terminating their service and switching to another firm. Firms that are interested in targeting analysis-oriented clients have to maintain a highly competitive planning service in terms of cost structure and services provided. As these clients are bargain hunters, they will demand quality service with the lowest possible fees.

Both relationship-oriented and analysis-oriented clients can be either proactive or reactive in establishing a relationship with their financial planners. Financial planners should employ appropriate communication tactics so that the clients will not feel that the planners are being either too aggressive or too laid-back in dealing with them.

Based on the concepts mentioned in Figure 7.2 and Figure 7.3, let us now look at an example of how the financial planner is matched with the client. Figure 7.4 shows how clients are divided into two orientations and two asset/income levels. Thus, there are four groups of clients in terms of their personal profile and financial profile: relationship-oriented client with high asset size and high income level, relationship-oriented client with low asset size and low income level; analysis-oriented client with high asset size and high income level and analysis-oriented client with low asset size and low income level. Head financial planners will then assign appropriate financial planners to serve these different clients. Financial planners should effectively serve two different categories of clients. For instance, planner A can serve quadrants 1 and 3 (i.e., relationship-oriented clients) while planner B can serve low asset/income clients. It is not wise to expect one planner to serve all four quadrants as they demand very different skills and personalities to do a good job. This is only one way to categorize clients; a firm can use other demographics and client characteristics to classify their clients for the matching process. As long as there are planners with different skills to serve different categories of clients, effective financial planning services can be achieved.

7.6   Promoting Financial Planning Services

Financial planning is an emerging business. Its basic concepts, functions, and techniques are new to most people. Therefore, promoting financial planning services is extremely important. Financial planners can use different promotion methods to increase public awareness of financial planning services. In this section we discuss how the financial planning profession can promote the financial planning business, particularly in new markets.

Figure 7.4 Matching financial planner with client by client orientation, asset size, and income level

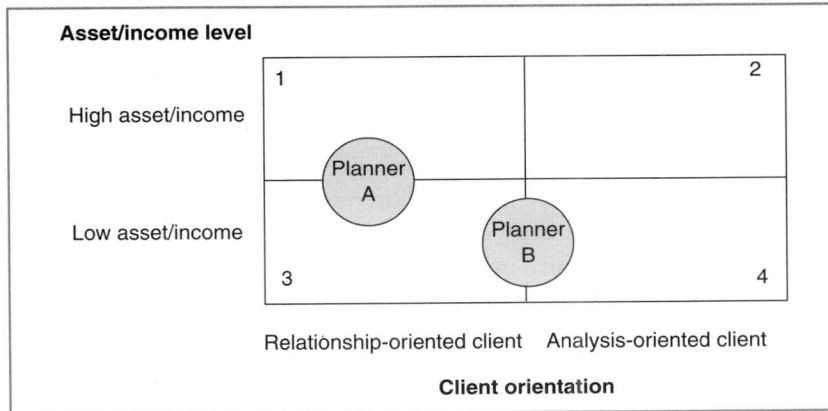

Channels of Promotion

Public Speeches

Giving public speeches and lectures are effective ways for financial planners to promote themselves. The audience can learn more about financial planning and understand its professional concepts and functions. Furthermore, the cost involved is not high. The main expenses for making public speeches and lectures are the cost of your time, the cost of booking the venue, advertising costs, and some administrative expenses.

New financial planners with little training or no experience may feel nervous about giving a public speech. Inexperienced speakers can get help through books and audio-visual material on developing public speaking skills or they can join clubs which focus on public speaking. They can then start by giving presentations to small, private groups of friends and relatives. The content of the speech is as important, or more so, than the presentation style. The audience will not be interested in the speech unless the topic appeals to them.

There are several points that financial planners should pay attention to when giving a speech:

1. Financial planners should speak at an appropriate speed. They should use different words and phrases to repeat the important ideas two or three times. Generally, it is not easy for the audience to remain attentive throughout the entire speech. Therefore repeating the contents, particularly when new concepts are introduced, is essential.

2. It is better not to recite or read from a script when giving a speech. As they speak, financial planners can walk down the stage and get closer to the audience. This creates a more informal, lively atmosphere and is an effective way to keep the attention of the audience.

3. Financial planners may raise questions during the speech, ask if the audience has any questions, or provide examples to illustrate a point.

Interacting with the audience like this helps to arouse and maintain the interest of the audience in the topic.

4. During the speech, financial planners should use different tones, gestures, facial expressions, or postures to express their ideas. Remember, appropriate body language can enhance the power of the speech. However, financial planners should avoid making exaggerated statements and actions.

5. The duration of the speech must be considered. If it is too long, the audience may lose interest. A break may be given if the speech is to last more than one hour. The speaker should pay careful attention to the audience and shorten the speech if there are signs that the audience is getting restless.

6. Financial planners can make use of audio-visual aids. This helps to hold the attention of the audience and hence create deeper impressions.

7. An outline or handout should be given to the audience before the speech. The purpose of the outline or handout is to let the audience know what they will learn from the speech and to minimize note-taking activity which can distract the attention of the audience during the speech.

Using the Mass Media

Besides having face-to-face communication with the audience, financial planners can also promote their services through the mass media.

Radio and television   Promotion through radio and television allows the consumer public to learn in a passive mode. The consumer public just listens to or watches the program but cannot interact with the financial planner. However, radio and television broadcasts may be able to reach a wider audience. The drawback is that the cost of promotion through radio and television can be quite high.

Newspapers and magazines   Financial planners can write articles, books, or brochures about financial planning, and sell them to the public or provide them free of charge. Through publications, the consumer public can learn more about the financial planning process and decide whether or not they need the service. Interested members of the public may want to consult the financial planners for further information. Therefore, the financial planners should put their contact numbers and e-mail addresses in the publications.

The Internet   The Internet is an effective way to convey information. Financial planners can establish personal home pages or websites to release information about financial planning to the consumer public. This method has been adopted widely in the financial planning sector in the United States.

Key Issues in Promotion

Observing Local Regulations When Conducting Seminars Related to Products

While giving seminars and speeches to the public is an effective way to promote the financial planning practice, it is important for financial planners to know the legal boundary of these activities. For instance, The Securities and Futures Commission (SFC) in Hong Kong gives clear guidelines for financial planning and investment professionals to follow when engaging in these activities:

- When a public seminar (currently defined as a seminar with more than 50 attendees) involves the introduction of an investment instrument or opportunity, it is regarded as a marketing activity, and prior authorization is required. Of course, if only a general market outlook is being discussed in the seminar, then this is treated as purely "advising" and no prior approval is necessary. However, if the seminar explicitly promotes certain products, then authorization is needed. Such a regulation applies to all financial intermediaries and banks.
- Currently, the "private placement" regulation is still under consultation by the SFC (as of September 13, 2005). For the time being, promotion of products for no more than 50 persons is considered as a private placement and not public. Thus, no authorization from the SFC is required, whether the products themselves are authorized by the SFC or not.
- Consequently, financial planning firms should avoid holding a seminar to market their practice and introduce products at the same time. Without getting an appropriate license, it is an offense under the Securities and Futures Ordinance.

Using Resources within the Company

If financial planners are employed by a financial planning company, they can make use of the capital and reputation of the company to gain the competitive advantage in the market. Generally, financial planning companies may launch several promotion campaigns each year to increase publicity and to widen the client base. In this way, the financial planners do not need to use their own personal resources to exploit new clients.

Importance of Business Ethics

Sound business ethics is also the basis of a successful financial planner. Financial planners should access, use, and keep the confidential and personal information of the clients carefully during the financial planning process. All the decisions should be in the best interest of the clients as the clients rely on the professional advice provided by the financial planners. The topic of business ethics is discussed in Chapter 2.

Working Together with other Financial Planning-related Services

Financial planning is a business with great potential of development worldwide, particularly in the developing countries. Therefore, financial planners should seize the opportunity to find new markets and new clients. In China, as personal and household incomes increase, many people have started to consider making investments in order to accumulate more wealth for the future. Currently, there are many financial and nonfinancial institutions, like accounting firms, insurance companies, and banks providing personal financial services.

However, personal financial services are not the core business of these institutions. The financial services provided by these institutions are limited and the employees in these institutions offering the services are not financial planning professionals and so they may not be able to satisfy the needs of the clients. Financial planners can work with these institutions and help to develop financial planning services in these institutions. In addition, financial planners can also make use of their professional skills and high-quality services to set up consultancy companies providing financial planning services, thus attracting new clients and competing with the other institutions. At the same time, financial planners should also develop alliances with related industries such as law firms, so as to offer more comprehensive services for the clients.

FINANCIAL PLANNING IN PRACTICE

Interview with Guy Cumbie, Chair of the Financial Planning Association 2002

Can you give some comments on step 1 of the six-step financial planning process?

This step is a crucial one and one that was added several years ago when its import to all that is to follow was duly recognized by the CFP Board. Prior to the addition of this step, the process jumped right into data gathering and left to assumption, or perhaps one might even say presumption, that the nature of the client-advisor relationship and the scope of the engagement were somehow fully communicated and mutually understood. Fortunately for clients and financial planners, it was eventually recognized that this was probably a very weak assumption. The reality is that mutual clarity with respect to both the nature of the relationship and the scope of the engagement is truly foundational to the success of the endeavor.

It could be said that step 1 is all about the management of expectations —to some extent the expectations of both the client and the advisor.

Some key aspects of the relationship

- It is a professional advisory and consulting relationship.
- The patron is considered to be and is served as a client, rather than as a customer.
- The relationship is fiduciary (trust-based) by its very nature.
- The financial planner is an advocate for the interests of the clients and places the interests of the clients ahead of self-interest.
- The financial planner is generally compensated for the services provided.
- Timely reciprocal disclosure resides at the heart of a trust-based relationship.

- The relationship tends to be very different from traditional retail financial services.
- The relationship is guided by process and constrained by practice standards.
- Multiple face-to-face meetings (with both spouses present) may be indicated.
- Significant effort on the part of the client(s) is required.
- Identification of all key contact persons and communication methods is to be made.

Defining the scope of the engagement

- It may be close-ended (in which case it would typically be perhaps annually-renewable), or
- It may be open-ended (or "evergreen" or self-renewing at some specified interval).
- The engagement may be for full-blown comprehensive planning, or
- It may be more limited in scope as in "modular" or "focus" planning engagements.
- Multiple face-to-face meetings will typically be required.
- Expected timeframes and expected charges need to be outlined clearly.
- How much implementation support is within the scope.
- The guaranteeing of outcomes is seldom within the scope of the financial planning engagement.

Common challenges

- Many clients do not recognize that communicating effectively in step 1 is a crucial and substantive part of the process and as such is as fully billable as any other part of the process.
- The relationship is so radically different from traditional retail financial services sales relationships that it is very difficult for many new clients to readily make the translation from the old to the new.
- In American culture it is inherently difficult to look a client in the eye and say "trust me"—yet that is the essence of the financial planning relationship and it will be dysfunctional until that trust exists.
- Trust typically has to be earned by the financial planner over time which impairs effectiveness of the early stages of the engagement during which the relationship is relatively "unseasoned" and clients may be wary.
- The value of personal financial planning resides largely in its holistic and integrative nature and the long-term peace of mind that the applied holism can bring about. Accordingly, a huge challenge that begins before step 1 and typically continues beyond it is near term value perception and recognition by the client.
- Clients often tend to underperceive the amount of time and effort they may need to put into the engagement in order to get all they're expecting out of it.

Key Terms

active listening *240*	nonverbal communication *241*
client orientation *244*	scope of engagement *231*

References

Keirsey, D. and Bates, M., *Please Understand Me: Character and Temperament Types* (Del Mar, CA: Prometheus Nemesis Book Company, 1984).

Phillips, S. R. and Bergquisst, W. H., *The Six Principles of Successful Self-Management: A Guidebook for Using the Personality Preference Profile,* 2nd ed., (Amherst, MA: HRD Press, 1999).

Multiple-choice Questions

1. In order to accomplish the process of mutually defined scope of engagement
    with his or her client, a financial planner must _____.
    I.   disclose any conflicts of interest
    II. disclose the compensation structure
    III. establish the length of the engagement
    IV. determine the client's constraints and limitations
    V.   define the responsibilities of the planner and client

    A. I, II, and III
    B. I, II, III, and V
    C. I, III, and V
    D. I, II, III, IV, and V

2. In preparing an interview with the client, a financial planner should
    _____.
    I.   determine the objectives and details of the meeting
    II. prepare several financial plans for the client to choose from
    III. estimate the duration of the interview
    IV. restate the rights of the client

    A. II and III
    B. I, II, and III
    C. I, III, and IV
    D. I, II, III, and IV

3. When the financial planner meets his or her client for the first time, the
    financial planner must _____.
    I.   define the responsibilities of the client
    II. collect the client's financial information
    III. disclose his financial status to the client
    IV. disclose the arrangement of compensation to the client
    V.   explain the whole financial planning process to the client
    VI. understand the client's financial goals and risk preferences

    A. II, IV, and VI
    B. I, IV, V, and VI
    C. II, III, IV, and VI
    D. I, II, IV, V, and VI

4. In the process of financial planning, a financial planner should disclose which
    of the following information to his or her clients?
    I.   The planner's financial status
    II. The planner's professional qualifications
    III. The planner's experience in providing financial planning services
    IV. The fees, commission and rebates received by the planner
    V.   Regulatory limitations that the financial planner is subjected to
    VI. Related software used by the planner

    A. I, IV, and V
    B. II, III, IV, and V

C. II, IV, V, and VI

D. II, III, IV, V, and VI

5. The objectives of having an interview with the potential client include

_____.

I.   obtaining the client's basic information

II. understanding the client's financial planning objectives, financial goals, and investment preferences

III. concluding the interview and reconfirming the client's information

IV. explaining the letter of engagement to the client

V.   arranging the second meeting with the client

A. I, II, and V

B. II, IV, and V

C. I, II, IV, and V

D. I, II, III, IV, and V

Problems

1. Explain the reasons why it is important for financial planners to practice active listening.

2. Describe the personality of relationship-oriented clients and how financial planners should deal with them.

chapter **8**

Step 2: Determining Client Goals and Expectations and Gathering Client Data

> ### Learning Objectives
>
> *After studying this chapter you should be able to:*
>
> **1** Explain Practice Standards 200 Series.
> **2** Understand how to manage clients' expectations.
> **3** Understand the concept of goal prioritization.
> **4** List common goals and objectives of clients.
> **5** Describe the financial planning pyramid.
> **6** Design a data collection form.

8.1 Practice Standards 200 Series

In the Practice Standards 200 Series, Practice Standard 200-1 specifies the importance of determining a client's personal and financial goals, needs, and priorities while Practice Standard 200-2 is a guideline for financial planners on the collection of data from clients.

The quality of service provided for clients can be further assured if financial planners do not only comply with the Practice Standards but also the Code of Ethics and Professional Responsibility. The principles particularly related to Practice Standards 200-1 and 200-2 are Principle 5 (confidentiality) and Principle 7 (diligence).

200-1: Determining a Client's Personal and Financial Goals, Needs, and Priorities

> The financial planning practitioner and the client shall mutually define the client's personal and financial goals, needs, and priorities that are relevant to the scope of the engagement before any recommendation is made and/or implemented.

Practice Standard 200-1 suggests that prior to making recommendations to their clients, financial planners and clients should mutually define the personal and financial goals, needs, and priorities of the clients. We saw earlier in Practice Standard 100-1 that financial planners and clients should first mutually define the scope of the engagement which includes determining what activities may be necessary to proceed with the engagement. When financial planners and clients have accomplished this first step, they have to start to prepare the financial plan for their clients. In order to do this, financial planners have to understand the goals, needs, and priorities of their clients. Understanding clients' goals, needs and priorities helps to set the foundation for the whole financial planning process. Financial planners need to explore their clients' values, attitudes, expectations, and time horizons as these affect their goals, needs, and priorities.

Goals are important because they provide focus, purpose, vision, and direction for financial planners in the financial planning process. Financial planners will have to assist clients to set realistic goals. It should be noted, though, that financial planners cannot always do a good job because the information given by clients is sometimes too sketchy or subjective. The success of the task is limited by what the clients are willing to reveal to their financial planners.

200-2: Obtaining Quantitative Information and Documents

The financial planning practitioner shall obtain sufficient quantitative information and documents about a client relevant to the scope of the engagement before any recommendation is made and/or implemented.

Practice Standard 200-2 states that, prior to conducting analyses and making recommendations, financial planners should follow the scope of the engagement and determine what necessary quantitative information and documents are needed from the clients for the development of a financial plan. The information may be obtained directly from the clients in the interview, by inviting the clients to fill in data collection forms and questionnaires, and by asking the clients to provide personal and financial records.

The information requested by financial planners is important for the success of developing a good financial plan. However, as the information requested is private, personal, and confidential, clients may have reservations in doing so, especially if the clients do not trust their financial planners at the early stage of the relationship. Financial planners must emphasize that incomplete or inaccurate information may result in improper conclusions and recommendations in the financial plan.

If financial planners are unable to obtain sufficient and relevant quantitative information and documents to form a basis for certain recommendations, they may have to restrict the scope of the engagement to those matters for which sufficient and relevant information is available. In the worst case scenario, the financial planner may have to terminate the engagement as the financial plans cannot be developed without some critical information.

8.2   Determining Financial Goals and Objectives

needs The expenses that must be incurred for daily necessities.

wants Desires which people have but which may not be essential for survival.

In trying to determine clients' personal and financial goals and needs, it is important to distinguish the difference between **needs** and **wants**. In general, *needs* include the expenses that must be incurred for daily necessities. *Wants* are desires which the clients have but which may not be essential for survival. It is natural for all of us to have wants. However, too many goals that are unrealistic or expectations that are too high may lead to disappointment and frustration. Thus, an effective financial planner must learn to manage a client's expectations.

Managing a Client's Expectations and Goal Prioritization

Harold Evensky, principal of Evensky, Brown, Katz and Levitt, has asserted that managing a client's expectations is a very important skill in conducting financial planning successfully. When a client has unrealistic expectations about the financial planner's ability in generating investment returns for his or her portfolio, the client's disappointment may result in dissatisfaction with the financial planner. In other words, if a client is given a rosy picture, either by his own false expectations or by being fed false hopes by the financial planner, the financial plan is bound to fail. Professional and ethical financial planners should have a clear understanding of their clients' expectations, especially about their financial goals and their ability in reaching these goals. In addition, managing clients' expectations by continuously communicating and educating them throughout the whole planning process is very crucial to the success of the relationship.

Using skillful communication techniques with the help of effective visual aids in conveying the message about clients' unrealistic expectations can help to reduce embarrassment or prevent clients from losing face. Bluntly announcing to the client that it is impossible to reach his or her goals may damage or even kill the client-planner relationship. Nevertheless, honesty must be the main priority in any communication strategy used in managing a client's expectations.

When all the goals and objectives are mutually defined, the next step is to set priorities for these goals and objectives. If there are unlimited time and resources, all realistic goals can be realized. However, clients usually want to achieve more goals than their resources will allow them to achieve. In addition, some goals are more important than others. Financial planners should help clients to list and then identify as many feasible goals as possible.

goal prioritization
The process of guiding clients to give priority to more important goals and objectives.

If both clients and financial planners understand that not all goals can be realized, using the mutually defining principle, financial planners must help their clients to prioritize the goals listed. This process is called **goal prioritization**. Goal prioritization is critical and can be successful only if clients agree and commit to the predetermined goal prioritization plan. Here, in the context of financial planning, goals are related to the financial well-being of clients. However, financial well-being, together with psychological and physical well-being, should be considered as part of total life planning. Therefore, in a broader scope, financial goals should be determined and prioritized while considering other nonfinancial goals in the context of a balanced lifestyle.

Formulating Financial Goals and Objectives

Figure 8.1 shows the financial planning pyramid which demonstrates how to prioritize clients' financial planning needs by the different financial planning areas. This financial planning pyramid is very similar to Maslow's hierarchy of needs (1968) in which the needs of individuals are arranged in order of urgency. For an average client who has limited income and wealth, the financial planner should first deal with the client's consumption behavior. Financial planners should look at the consumption pattern and cash flow and advise the client on consumption planning as well as tax planning.

Once the consumption area is taken care of, the area of risk management through proper insurance protection is next. For example, for a young family with children and a sole breadwinner, life insurance and health insurance are critical. Once insurance planning has been taken care of, the financial planner should focus on the client's short-term and medium-term investment-related goals.

Figure 8.1   Financial planning pyramid

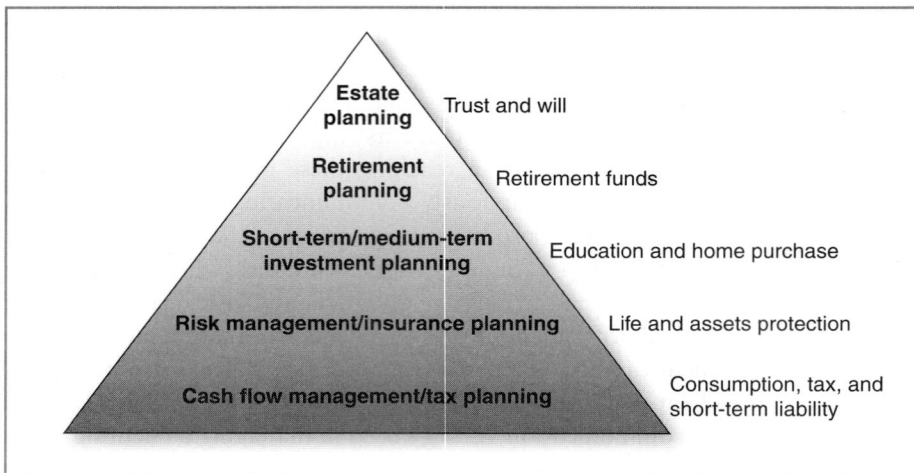

These goals are normally related to major expenditure in life such as wedding expenses, down payment for home purchase, and education for the children. To achieve these goals, savings and investment plans must be formulated. Thus, we can classify these goals under the area of investment planning, or investment for goals.

Retirement planning is next. A lot of people think that retirement planning simply means long-term investment. This is not true. In a wealthy society, many would-be retirees have already got some basic pension plan. Thus, proper investment may help them to live more comfortably after retirement. However, there are a lot more challenges in retirement than having an optimal investment portfolio and proper insurance. For instance, how to make their lives more interesting and spend their time on meaningful activities is a big concern for many retirees. Because of advances in health care, people are now living longer lives. Thus, retirement planning no longer focuses on investment alone but also on how to spend the financial resources wisely to give retirees a high-quality life. Of course, investment planning is still a major part of it as there is little you can do if you do not have much money to go around. In short, proper retirement planning goes beyond long-term investment and includes advice on lifestyle consumption, career development after retirement, and the development of hobbies and interests.

Finally, while it is almost a taboo in Asia, a financial planner has to address the issue of estate planning. Estate planning involves wealth protection and wealth transfer. For high net-worth clients, estate planning is a very complicated matter. The financial planner has to understand the client's life goals in this area.

The financial planning pyramid is a logical theoretical framework. In real life, clients at different life stages may have different priorities and the order described in the framework may not always apply to every client. For instance, a wealthy client may not have an issue in consumption planning or even insurance protection. So the financial planner may want to do a quick check in these two areas and go straight to investment management and estate planning. For a young husband with a homemaker spouse and three young kids, retirement planning and estate planning would be a low priority. In addition, while the logic is to move from the bottom to the top of the pyramid, we are not suggesting that the financial planner should deal with one area at a time this way. Multitasking and simultaneous executions should be considered if possible. There is no reason why a planner cannot help the client to work on his consumption planning while taking care of his insurance needs at the same time. The planning order as indicated by the financial planning pyramid is just to remind the financial planner of the relative immediacy of different financial needs. The financial planning pyramid is a useful guide for the financial planner in meeting the more basic financial needs of the clients before moving on to a higher level of financial goals.

We have mentioned before that managing a client's expectations is a very critical element in financial planning. In the process of identifying clients' goals, financial planners should make a quick assessment to see if they are reachable. If not, the financial planner should start the process of managing the client's expectations so that the client will not have the wrong picture. On the other hand, if the client has an unrealistic expectation of investment returns generated from the portfolio recommended by the financial planner, the financial planner should educate the client that investment planning is not only about maximizing returns. The financial planner has to let the client know that financial planning deals with how to achieve financial goals, and that includes both making and spending money. Maximizing returns and wealth is not the job of a financial planner, but of an investment specialist. In short, managing clients' expectations through proper coaching and education is an integral part of successful financial planning.

Figure 8.2 illustrates the seriousness of improper consumption. In this case, the actual consumption far exceeds the optimal consumption of the client. If the client is not informed at an early stage about the problem of overconsumption and advised to change his or her consumption behavior, no resources will be available to deal with other financial goals. In other words, helping clients to deal with basic financial needs properly is the prerequisite for conducting financial planning for higher-level needs. Managing client's expectations in achieving higher-level financial goals through proper consumption planning is the key element of goal prioritization.

We have mentioned earlier that financial planners need to study the personal profile of their clients. Sometimes it may be convenient to classify a client's objectives by time horizon. Short-term objectives refer to those objectives that are formulated and amended by clients once a year and are expected to be achieved within 5 years. Medium-term objectives are those objectives that are adjusted only if necessary after they have been formulated and are expected to be accomplished within 6 to 10 years. Long-term objectives are put forward as confirmed goals and are expected to take a longer time (more than 10 years) to achieve. However, it is dangerous to use time horizon as the only criterion in formulating investment strategies. In addition to time, there are many factors that are also important to consider when making investment decisions. These factors include the nature of the goals, risk tolerance of the clients, and macroeconomic conditions.

Figure 8.2 Managing client's financial needs

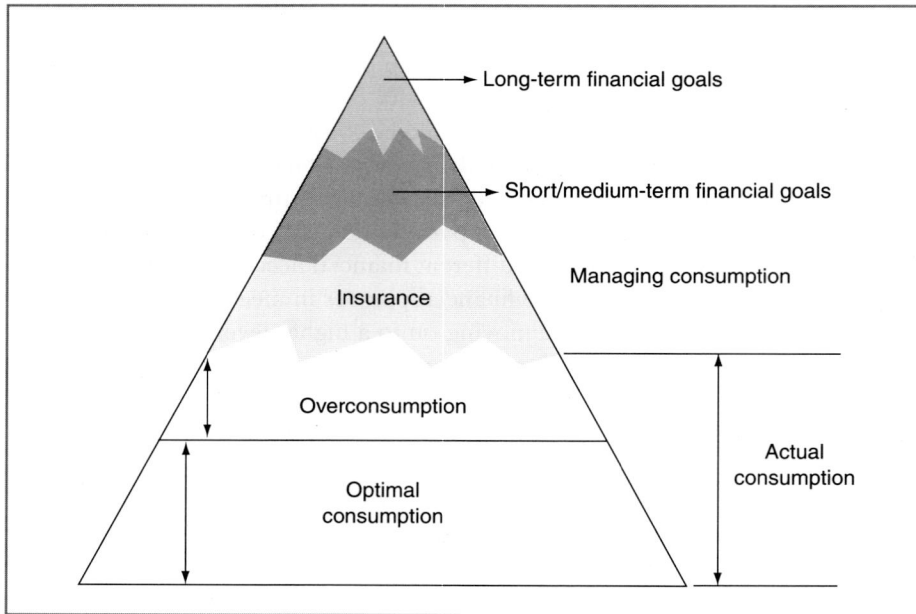

The following factors should be considered when formulating goals and objectives:

1. Goals should be concrete, reasonable, and achievable.
2. A common objective is to improve the financial well-being of the clients.
3. Financial planners and their clients should not just focus on investment. Proper risk management such as cash reserves for emergency use should be employed in all circumstances.
4. Goals and objectives should be prioritized in the order of importance. The financial planning pyramid is a good guideline to follow in this case.
5. For whatever reason, if financial planners have to amend the priorities of the objectives during the financial planning process, the financial planners must inform their clients and obtain their consent before any amendments can be made. The amendments must also be within the boundaries stated in the scope of engagement.

Under the framework of total life planning, there are three distinctive but related areas of needs for an individual: psychological, physical, and financial needs. All life goals must be anchored to one or more of these three aspects. The financial planner's job is to convert these life goals into measurable and executable financial goals. The financial planning pyramid provides a useful guide to how financial needs can be classified and prioritized based on their immediacy. Some clients may have stronger psychological or physical needs. In this case, the financial planner needs to pay more attention to achieving a balanced lifestyle for the client and financial goals such as wealth accumulation and estate planning may take a back seat in the overall plan.

Table 8.1 provides some examples of life goals and their corresponding financial goals.

8.3 Gathering Client Data

Gathering high-quality client data is critical for the development of a successful financial plan. The information gathered has to be accurate, complete, relevant, reliable, and timely. Without appropriate and accurate financial information about clients, financial planners cannot form a complete picture of their current financial situation or produce an accurate forecast of their future financial situation. We have seen that in step 1, financial planners must first collect some preliminary personal data. In step 2, the data collection process focuses on quantitative data.

If clients are not willing to provide the necessary information, financial planners have to inform their clients that the success of the financial plan is dependent on the information available. If the clients still refuse to provide the data, financial planners can choose to terminate their services so as to avoid the potential disputes and liability which may arise due to the failure of the financial plan.

Types of Information

There are many ways to classify information needed from clients. First, we can divide information into personal information and macroeconomic information. We can also refer to personal information as primary data and macroeconomic information as secondary data. For the purpose of data collection and subsequent data analysis, personal information can be divided into two categories, financial and nonfinancial. Financial information refers to the basic financial and quantitative details of the clients, which include assets, liabilities, cash flow, income, and expenses. This information helps the financial planners to evaluate if the financial objectives and expectations are reasonable and gauge the probability of success. Nonfinancial information consists mostly of clients' qualitative data such as social status, age, and investment preferences. Macroeconomic information

Table 8.1 Examples of life goals and corresponding financial goals

Life goals	Corresponding financial goals
1. Provide for the financial needs of the family	• Maintain sufficient level of savings • Protect income and wealth
2. Protect the family financially if something bad happens	• Purchase sufficient insurance coverage • Maintain a certain level of savings and wealth
3. Have a worry-free retirement	• Have sufficient savings for retirement • Pay off mortgage
4. Provide good education for children	• Have tuition money ready when needed

includes information about the general economy and the market, price level and inflation rate, financial market regulations, personal taxation system, and social security system. Macroeconomic information is important as macroeconomic factors affect clients' current and future financial situations.

It is important for financial planners to understand that it may take a lot of time and effort to collect and compile the data about their clients. Clients come from different cultural and educational backgrounds, and therefore have different **risk tolerance levels**, and different financial goals and expectations. The provision of financial planning services cannot be accomplished without obtaining all these relevant data.

Information can also be classified into quantitative and qualitative information. Quantitative information describes clients' characteristics in numerical form, for example, income and age. Qualitative information is subjective and cannot be expressed in numbers easily; it usually describes clients' attitudes, for example, their risk tolerance levels and career prospects. Qualitative information is more difficult to collect as compared to quantitative information. Financial planners need to collect both types to be able to give objective advice tailor-made for their clients.

Table 8.2 gives examples of quantitative and qualitative information offered by clients.

It is not difficult to distinguish these two types of information. Qualitative information usually needs the financial planner to make an educated guess after understanding the situation. At the same time the financial planner should carefully design interview questions so that guessing can be minimized wherever possible.

risk tolerance level
An indicator of the level of investment risk the investor is willing to bear.

Tools for Collecting Data

Using Questions Effectively

During their interview with clients, financial planners should ask as many questions as they can to obtain more information. Direct and appropriate questions do not only lead the clients to provide more accurate and comprehensive answers, but also help to establish a better relationship between clients and financial planners.

The first rule of good communication is to ask relevant questions. This is a simple process where you listen carefully to the content and then ask questions that seek clarification, verification, or motivation:

Table 8.2 Types of information provided by clients for investment preference and risk tolerance

Types of information	Response of client
Quantitative information	"My annual salary is about US$100,000 and I expect to have a 3% pay raise per year in the future."
Qualitative information	"I do not want to have high-risk stocks in my investment portfolio."

Source: *Introduction to Financial Planning* (DFP1), p. 2.4, published by Deakin University on behalf of the Financial Planning Association of Australia Limited.

1. **Clarification.** Clarifying questions are asked when there are inconsistencies or unclear messages in the conversation.
2. **Verification.** Verifying questions are asked to verify that the information has been correctly received.
3. **Motivation.** Motivational questions help provide understanding on why people behave in a certain way.

Several types of questions can be used under various circumstances:

1. **Open-ended question.** This kind of question requires clients to describe a situation or express their opinions in detail. For instance, "What do you think about your present financial status?"
2. **Close-ended question.** This kind of question solicits factual information, usually in the form of a yes/no answer. For instance, "Have you asked anybody else to manage your money?"
3. **Reconfirming question.** This kind of question is used to confirm a previous statement made by the clients. For instance, after a client indicates a desire to avoid investments in risky stocks during the interview, the financial planners should reconfirm this at the end of the interview by asking, "I just want to make sure that you do not prefer risky investment in stocks, right?"

If open-ended questions are used, financial planners will get more information from clients' answers. Consider these two questions: (1) "Can you describe some of your investment choices at the present time?" and (2) "Do you invest in stocks, bonds, or mutual funds?" Question (2) requires only a "yes" or "no" answer for each type of investment choice and provides limited information for financial planners.

Nevertheless, some clients may think that open-ended questions are more difficult to answer. One way to assist clients is to provide some suggested answers or references. If financial planners want to know the investment preferences of their clients but the clients do not know what the question means, the financial planners may suggest some answers like "high return," "low risk," "stocks," "bonds," or "options," in order to guide the clients to provide information. Another method is to change the open-ended question to a close-ended question, and then lead clients to give more specific answers.

Financial planners should choose the type of questions to be asked carefully. In areas where only factual information is required, close-ended questions should be used instead of open-ended questions because close-ended questions solicit facts, not opinions, and are answered more quickly. Close-ended questions allow financial planners to have better time control.

Financial planners should pay attention to the following points:

1. Unclear answers provided by clients may lead to misunderstandings or mistakes in the construction of the financial plan. Therefore, financial planners should repeat the questions to clarify the answers at the appropriate time. However, some clients may not like to answer repeated questions. In such a case, financial planners should rephrase the question.

2. Clients' conversation habits or style may affect the ability of the financial planners to assimilate and record the information. For example, clients may talk too fast or too much. If financial planners have difficulty in recording the information, they can try to get clients to speak more slowly.

3. If clients agree, financial planners can use tape or digital recorders to record the details to be accurately transcribed later.

4. Financial planners should always maintain a gentle and polite manner and avoid any rude behavior. This helps to enhance the quality of the information received.

Using Data Collection Forms

Financial planners may make use of data collection forms to gather the necessary information regarding clients' personal backgrounds and financial positions (i.e., primary data). Using data collection forms is efficient and effective if clients answer all the questions on the form accurately. In addition to the data collected from clients, financial planners may need to obtain relevant information from clients' lawyers, accountants, and insurance agents. In such a case, financial planners have to request that clients write and sign an authorization letter for them to collect information from these professionals. Macroeconomic or market information (i.e., secondary data) can easily be obtained from governmental departments, financial institutions, and the Internet.

Financial planners should design the data collection form carefully. A badly designed form reflects badly on the organizational ability of the financial planner.

A good data collection form should:

1. Be written in simple and easy-to-understand language.
2. Be in a user-friendly format.
3. Be logical.
4. Ask for relevant information only.
5. Have similar information grouped under the same headings.
6. Have questions following a sequence from a general category to a specific category of information.
7. Not be too long.

Sample Forms for Collecting Data[1]

While there are many ways to design a data collection form, here we will illustrate the key features and categories of a standard data collection form by modules. The forms can be in an electronic format or hard copy.

---

[1] I want to thank Joseph K. S. Chan for providing the computer screen pictures for data collection in this chapter.

MODULE 1: PERSONAL BACKGROUND

Table 8.3 lists the key and optional data when designing the form for collecting personal background data from the client. Figures 8.3 and 8.4 are examples of a computer input screen for the same data.

Table 8.3 Data form for module 1: Personal background

		Client	Spouse	Child 1	Child 2
Key data					
1.1	Name				
1.2	Gender				
1.3	Date of birth				
1.4	Education level				
1.5	Occupation				
1.6	Marital status				
1.7	Expected retirement age				
1.8	Life expectancy				
Optional data					
1.9	Job security				
1.10	Place of birth				
1.11	Health condition				

Figure 8.3 Example of input screen for personal background: Client/spouse

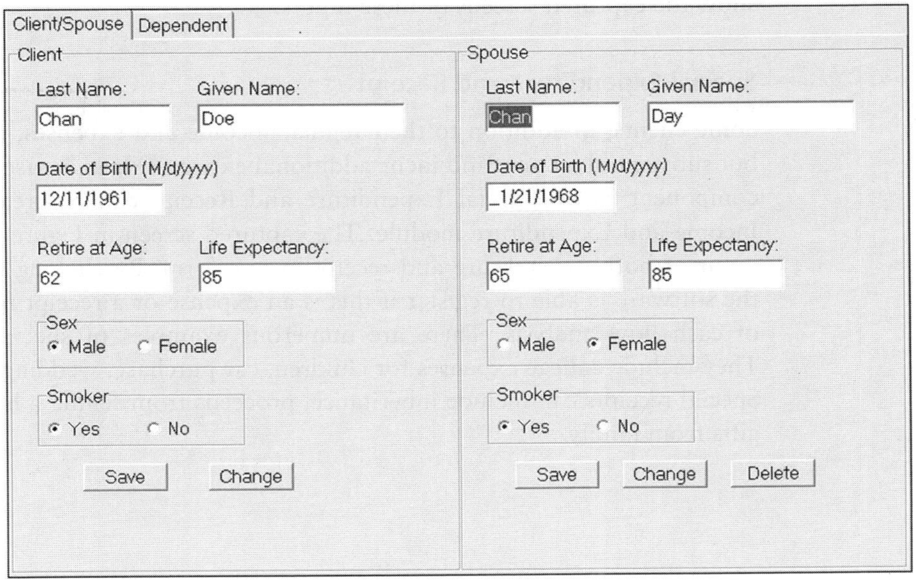

Figure 8.4 Example of input screen for personal background: Other dependants

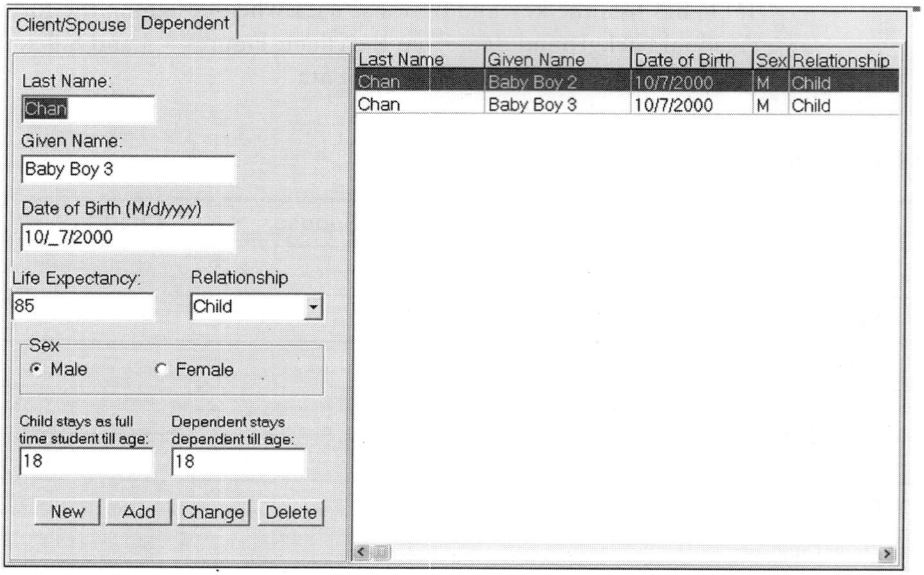

MODULE 2: INCOME AND EXPENDITURE

Regular Income and Expenditure

The financial planner should next collect financial data from the client. While there is no definite sequence to the collection of financial data, we suggest starting with something easy to deal with: income and expenditure. The collection form here is a simplified one which only seeks annual data from the client. For some clients, monthly expenses may be needed in order to prepare a cash budget. Table 8.4 shows a list of common items in income and expenditure. Figures 8.5 and 8.6 show the captured screens of these inputs.

Special Expenditure and Receipt

Some clients, in addition to their regular income and expenses, enjoy irregular but substantial income and incur additional expenses. In this case, an additional component called Special Expenditure and Receipt can be created under the Income and Expenditure module. The captured screen in Figure 8.7 allows the input of both expenditure and receipt in one form. By clicking the right item, the software is able to register if this is an expense or a receipt for the purpose of cash flow analysis. There are numerous examples of special expenditure. They include college expenses for children, car purchase, wedding expenses, etc. Special receipts can include inheritance, proceeds from selling a house, or major gifts from family.

Table 8.4 Data form for module 2: Regular income and expenditure

		Annual dollar amount ($)
Regular income		
Key data		
2.1	Annual salary	
Optional data		
2.2	Investment income	
2.3	Other income (specify)	
Regular expenditure		
Key data		
2.4	Food	
2.5	Rent	
2.6	Clothing	
2.7	Transportation	
2.8	Insurance premium	
2.9	Medical expenses	
2.10	Child care	
2.11	Entertainment	
Optional data		
2.12	Annual vacation	
2.13	Gifts	
2.14	Miscellaneous	

MODULE 3: MORTGAGE

While some may think that mortgage payment is an expense, in fact, part of mortgage payment actually becomes equity for your property. Mortgage is such a major asset for most households that it deserves a separate module to deal with the data. Information needed for the mortgage is listed in Figure 8.8. The items needed include remaining balance, remaining terms of payment, and interest rate. The purpose of the mortgage module is to compute the monthly payment and the accumulation of the equity for the property. In situations where the interest is tax-deductible, the total interest for the year can also be estimated from this module.

Figure 8.5 Example of input screen for regular income

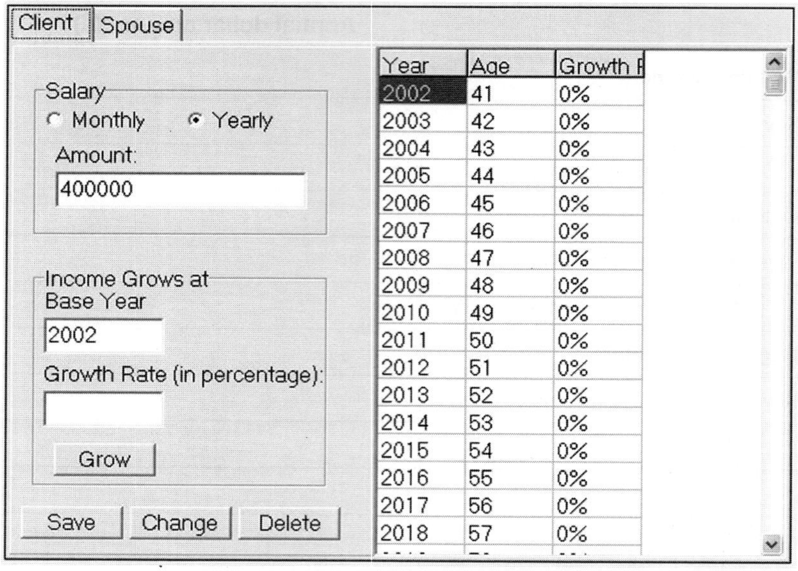

Client	Spouse

Salary		
○ Monthly	● Yearly	

Amount:

400000

Income Grows at
Base Year

2002

Growth Rate (in percentage):

[Grow]

[Save] [Change] [Delete]

Year	Age	Growth F
2002	41	0%
2003	42	0%
2004	43	0%
2005	44	0%
2006	45	0%
2007	46	0%
2008	47	0%
2009	48	0%
2010	49	0%
2011	50	0%
2012	51	0%
2013	52	0%
2014	53	0%
2015	54	0%
2016	55	0%
2017	56	0%
2018	57	0%

**Figure 8.6 Example of input screen for regular
expenditure**

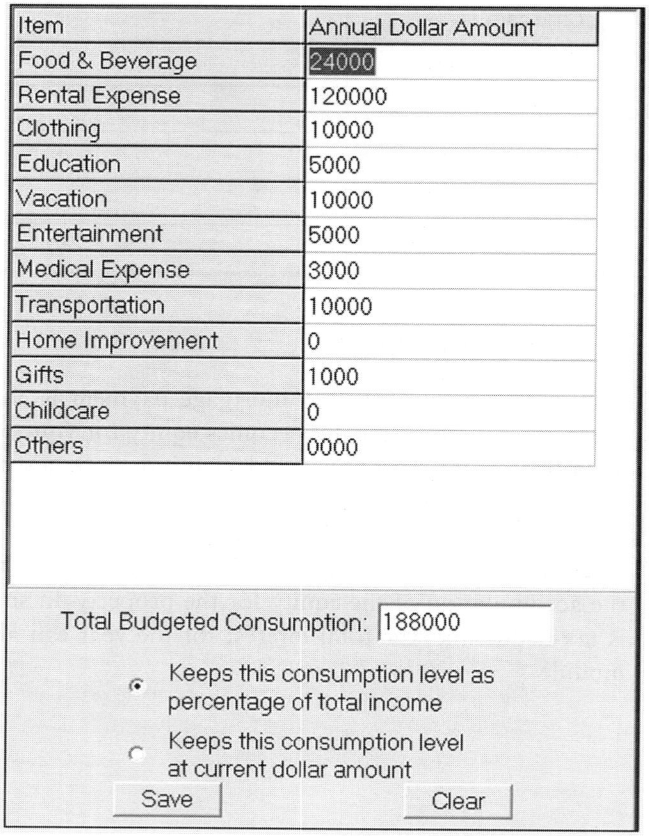

Item	Annual Dollar Amount
Food & Beverage	24000
Rental Expense	120000
Clothing	10000
Education	5000
Vacation	10000
Entertainment	5000
Medical Expense	3000
Transportation	10000
Home Improvement	0
Gifts	1000
Childcare	0
Others	0000

Total Budgeted Consumption: 188000

● Keeps this consumption level as
   percentage of total income

○ Keeps this consumption level
   at current dollar amount

[Save]   [Clear]

Figure 8.7 Example of input screen for special expenditure and receipt

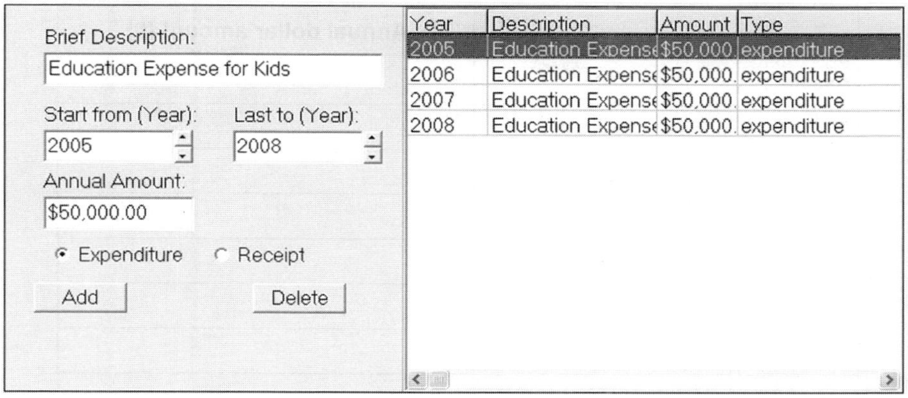

Brief Description:
Education Expense for Kids

Start from (Year): 2005   Last to (Year): 2008

Annual Amount:
$50,000.00

◉ Expenditure   ○ Receipt

[Add]   [Delete]

Year	Description	Amount	Type
2005	Education Expense	$50,000.	expenditure
2006	Education Expense	$50,000.	expenditure
2007	Education Expense	$50,000.	expenditure
2008	Education Expense	$50,000.	expenditure

Figure 8.8 Example of input screen for mortgage

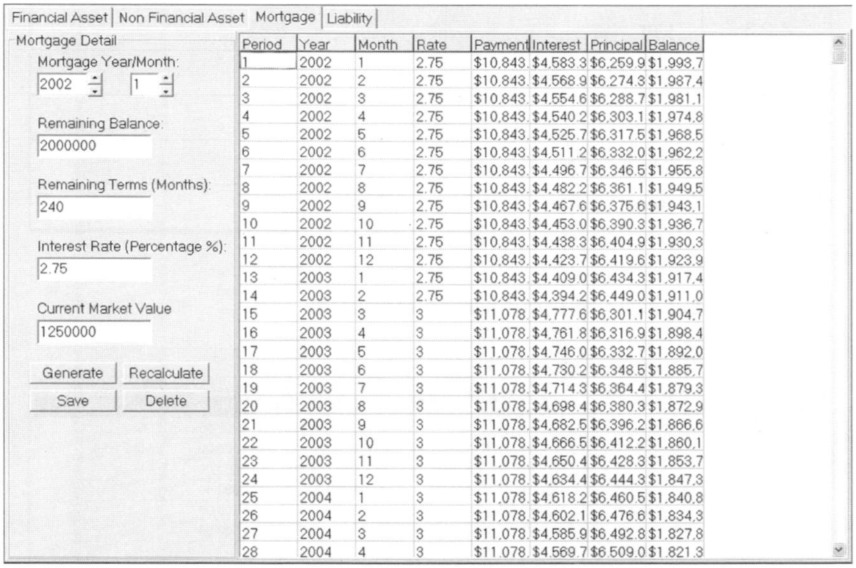

Financial Asset | Non Financial Asset | Mortgage | Liability

Mortgage Detail

Mortgage Year/Month: 2002 1

Remaining Balance: 2000000

Remaining Terms (Months): 240

Interest Rate (Percentage %): 2.75

Current Market Value: 1250000

[Generate] [Recalculate]
[Save] [Delete]

Period	Year	Month	Rate	Payment	Interest	Principal	Balance
1	2002	1	2.75	$10,843.	$4,583.3	$6,259.9	$1,993.7
2	2002	2	2.75	$10,843.	$4,568.9	$6,274.3	$1,987.4
3	2002	3	2.75	$10,843.	$4,554.6	$6,288.7	$1,981.1
4	2002	4	2.75	$10,843.	$4,540.2	$6,303.1	$1,974.8
5	2002	5	2.75	$10,843.	$4,525.7	$6,317.5	$1,968.5
6	2002	6	2.75	$10,843.	$4,511.2	$6,332.0	$1,962.2
7	2002	7	2.75	$10,843.	$4,496.7	$6,346.5	$1,955.8
8	2002	8	2.75	$10,843.	$4,482.2	$6,361.1	$1,949.5
9	2002	9	2.75	$10,843.	$4,467.6	$6,375.6	$1,943.1
10	2002	10	2.75	$10,843.	$4,453.0	$6,390.3	$1,936.7
11	2002	11	2.75	$10,843.	$4,438.3	$6,404.9	$1,930.3
12	2002	12	2.75	$10,843.	$4,423.7	$6,419.6	$1,923.9
13	2003	1	2.75	$10,843.	$4,409.0	$6,434.3	$1,917.4
14	2003	2	2.75	$10,843.	$4,394.2	$6,449.0	$1,911.0
15	2003	3	3	$11,078.	$4,777.6	$6,301.1	$1,904.7
16	2003	4	3	$11,078.	$4,761.8	$6,316.9	$1,898.4
17	2003	5	3	$11,078.	$4,746.0	$6,332.7	$1,892.0
18	2003	6	3	$11,078.	$4,730.2	$6,348.5	$1,885.7
19	2003	7	3	$11,078.	$4,714.3	$6,364.4	$1,879.3
20	2003	8	3	$11,078.	$4,698.4	$6,380.3	$1,872.9
21	2003	9	3	$11,078.	$4,682.5	$6,396.2	$1,866.6
22	2003	10	3	$11,078.	$4,666.5	$6,412.2	$1,860.1
23	2003	11	3	$11,078.	$4,650.4	$6,428.3	$1,853.7
24	2003	12	3	$11,078.	$4,634.4	$6,444.3	$1,847.3
25	2004	1	3	$11,078.	$4,618.2	$6,460.5	$1,840.8
26	2004	2	3	$11,078.	$4,602.1	$6,476.6	$1,834.3
27	2004	3	3	$11,078.	$4,585.9	$6,492.8	$1,827.8
28	2004	4	3	$11,078.	$4,569.7	$6,509.0	$1,821.3

MODULE 4: ASSETS AND LIABILITIES

Assets and liabilities are important data for financial planning. Unfortunately, most clients would have a hard time remembering their assets and liabilities. Financial statements from clients would be helpful in preparing this data. Table 8.5 lists some major items in assets and liabilities. Figure 8.9 is an example of the input screen for assets. For simplicity, it is possible that the input screen looks at only net assets (i.e., assets minus liabilities) so that there is no need for a separate input screen for liabilities. One may ask: What if a client has more liabilities than assets? The input screen using net assets will not work because the values will be negative. In this case, the financial planner should strongly ask himself why he thinks the client is appropriate for comprehensive financial planning at all!

Table 8.5 Data form for module 4: Assets and liabilities

		Annual dollar amount ($)
Assets		
4.1	Financial assets	
4.1.1	Stocks	
4.1.2	Bonds	
4.1.3	Savings certificate	
4.1.4	Savings deposit	
4.1.5	Mutual funds	
4.2	Real assets	
4.2.1	Equity value of home	
4.2.2	Vacation home	
4.2.3	Car	
4.2.4	Expensive jewelry	
Liabilities		
4.3	Credit card	
4.4	Personal loan	

Figure 8.9 Example of input screen for assets

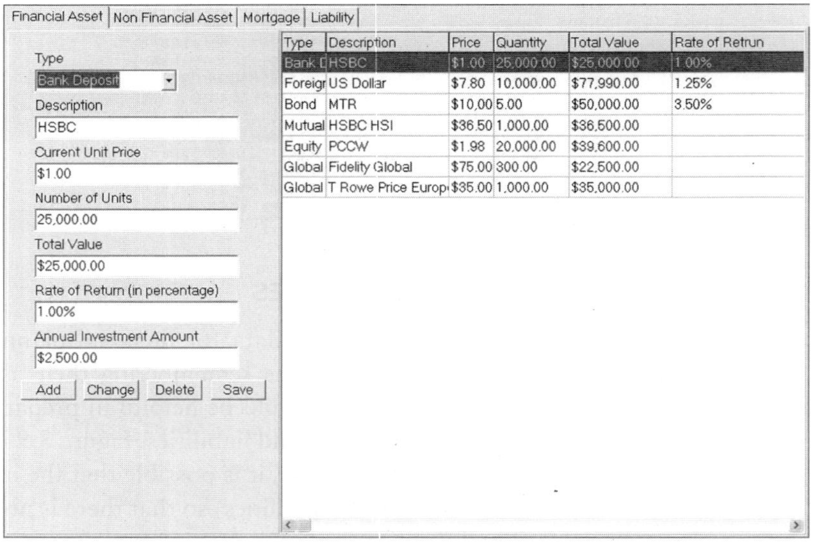

MODULE 5: RISK PROFILING

Risk profiling is a very important step in determining the risk tolerance level of the client. The sample questionnaire shown in Figure 8.10 is a psychometric instrument based on the article by Grable and Lytton (1999). We have modified the questionnaire using a larger dollar amount to create a more realistic risk-return dilemma for more affluent clients.[2]

Financial planners will need to take time to help clients fill in the questionnaire, depending on clients' education level and investment experience. While a clear understanding of the questions is necessary, clients do not need to think too hard in giving an answer to these questions. A psychometric instrument works reasonably well on the basis that the respondent gives an intuitive answer without too much rational thinking to derive the answers. A quick and direct response normally reflects the psychology of the client. Going through additional analyses and rational decision processes may make the answer less truthful, thus rendering the client's risk tolerance level less accurate. In short, the financial planner should give the client some time to fill the questionnaire and make himself or herself available when needed. Financial planners should fully understand the instruments and be able to provide appropriate examples and explanations for the questions.

For each of the 13 questions, a score is attached to each answer. Table 8.6 provides these scores for the purpose of computing the total risk tolerance scores for clients. Table 8.7 is the classification table identifying the risk tolerance level of clients. Five categories of risk level are used. They are (1) extremely aggressive, (2) moderately aggressive, (3) moderate, (4) moderately conservative, and (5) extremely conservative.

For a more detailed discussion of the interpretation of the risk tolerance score, refer to Chapter 6.

MODULE 6: PENSION AND RETIREMENT BENEFITS

The module for pension and retirement benefits includes information on all possible pensions for clients and their spouses from current and previous employers. There are different forms of pensions such as defined benefits, defined contribution, lump sum payments or annuity after retirement. Thus, it is quite difficult to design a standardized form to collect all these data. In general, the data form should ask for the market values of all pensions if they are investment-linked; the annual retirement benefits if they are defined benefits and cannot be withdrawn as a lump sum before retirement; and the lump-sum benefits upon retirement if applicable. Other information such as retirement age and expected return should be included. Figure 8.11 shows an example of the input screen for the pension and retirement benefit module.

---

[2] Since we have modified the questionnaire, the validity and reliability of the original questionnaire described by Grable and Lytton may not be applicable here. We are responsible for any remaining errors. However, we are not liable for any damages or losses incurred by anyone as a result of using this instrument. Readers should use this as an illustration of what a typical questionnaire would look like. Please be reminded that it will be inadvisable to adopt this questionnaire for professional use without conducting statistical testing for its validity and reliability.

Figure 8.10 Data form for module 5: Risk profiling

1. In general, how would your best friend describe you?
    (1)   An aggressive risk taker
    (2)   Willing to take risks after completing adequate research
    (3)   Cautious
    (4)   A real risk avoider

2. You are on a TV game show and can choose one of the following. Which would you take?
    (1) $10,000 in cash
    (2)   A 50% chance at winning $50,000
    (3)   A 25% chance at winning $100,000
    (4)   A 5% chance at winning $1,000,000

3. You have just finished saving up for a once-in-a-lifetime vacation. Three weeks before you plan to leave, you lose your job. What would you do?
    (1)   Cancel the vacation
    (2)   Take a much more modest vacation
    (3)   Go as scheduled, reasoning that you need the time to prepare for a jobsearch
    (4)   Extend your vacation, because this may be your last chance to go first-class

4. If you unexpectedly received $200,000 to invest, what would you do?
    (1)   Deposit it in a bank account, money market account, or an insured CD
    (2)   Invest it in safe high-quality bonds or bond mutual funds
    (3)   Invest it in stocks or stock mutual funds

5. In terms of experience, how comfortable are you investing in stocks or stock mutual funds?
    (1)   Not at all comfortable
    (2)   Somewhat comfortable
    (3)   Very comfortable

6. When you think of the word *risk*, which of the following words comes into your mind first?
    (1)   Loss
    (2)   Uncertainty
    (3)   Opportunity
    (4)   Thrill (Exciting)

7. Some experts predict that the prices of assets such as gold, jewels, collectibles, and real estate (hard assets) will likely increase in value, and that bond prices may fall. However, they tend to agree that government bonds are relatively safe. Most of your investment assets are now in high-interest government bonds. What would you do?
    (1)   Hold the bonds
    (2)   Sell the bonds, put half the proceeds into money-market accounts, and the other half into hard assets
    (3)   Sell the bonds and put the total proceeds into hard assets
    (4)   Sell the bonds, put all the money into hard assets, and borrow additional money to buy more

8. Given the best and worst case returns of the four investment choices below, which would you prefer?
    (1) $2,000 gain best case; $0 gain/loss worst case
    (2) $8,000 gain best case; $2,000 loss worst case
    (3) $26,000 gain best case; $8,000 loss worst case
    (4) $48,000 gain best case; $24,000 loss worst case

9. In addition to whatever you own, you have been given $10,000 with two possible consequences. You are now being asked to choose between the two consequences:
    (1)   A sure gain of $5,000 (i.e., certain gain of $15,000)
    (2)   A 50% chance to gain $10,000 and a 50% chance to gain nothing

10. In addition to whatever you own, you have been given $20,000 with two possible consequences. You are now asked to choose between the two consequences:
    (1)   A sure loss of $5,000 (i.e., certain gain of $15,000)
    (2)   A 50% chance to lose $10,000 and a 50% chance to lose nothing

Figure 8.10 (continued)

---

11. Suppose a relative left you an inheritance of $1,000,000, stipulating in the will that you invest ALL the money in ONE of the following choices. Which one would you select?
    (1) A savings account or money-market mutual fund
    (2) A mutual fund that owns stocks and bonds
    (3) A portfolio of 15 blue chip stocks
    (4) Commodities like gold, silver, and oil

12. If you had to invest $200,000, which of the following investment choices would you find most appealing? High-risk investments are futures or options; medium- risk investments are stocks or stocks funds; low-risk investments are bonds or bond funds.
    (1) 60% in low-risk investments, 30% in medium-risk investments, 10% in high-risk investments
    (2) 30% in low-risk investments, 40% in medium-risk investments, 30% in high-risk investments
    (3) 10% in low-risk investments, 40% in medium-risk investments, 50% in high-risk investments

13. Your trusted friend and neighbor, an experienced geologist, is putting together a group of investors to fund an exploratory gold mining venture. If they succeed, the venture could pay back 50 to 100 times the investment. If the mine fails, the entire investment will be worthless. Your friend estimates that the chance of success is only 20%. If you had the money, how much would you invest?
    (1) Nothing
    (2) 1 month's salary
    (3) 3 months' salary
    (4) 6 months' salary

Table 8.6 Scoring table for calculating risk tolerance level

1.	(1) = 4	(2) = 3	(3) = 2	(4) = 1
2.	(1) = 1	(2) = 2	(3) = 3	(4) = 4
3.	(1) = 1	(2) = 2	(3) = 3	(4) = 4
4.	(1) = 1	(2) = 2	(3) = 3	
5.	(1) = 1	(2) = 2	(3) = 3	
6.	(1) = 1	(2) = 2	(3) = 3	(4) = 4
7.	(1) = 1	(2) = 2	(3) = 3	(4) = 4
8.	(1) = 1	(2) = 2	(3) = 3	(4) = 4
9.	(1) = 1	(2) = 3		
10.	(1) = 1	(2) = 3		
11.	(1) = 1	(2) = 2	(3) = 3	(4) = 4
12.	(1) = 1	(2) = 2	(3) = 3	
13.	(1) = 1	(2) = 2	(3) = 3	(4) = 4

MODULE 7: ESTATE PLANNING

The final module for data collection is estate planning. In this section, bequest and funeral expenses are key items. Of course, for wealthier clients, estate planning also includes information related to the establishment of a trust, and to the writing of a will. Figure 8.12 shows an example of the input screen for the estate planning module.

Table 8.7 Risk tolerance classification

	Lower bound	Upper bound
Extremely aggressive	36	47
Moderately aggressive	30	35
Moderate	24	29
Moderately conservative	19	23
Extremely conservative	13	18

Figure 8.11 Example of input screen for pension and retirement benefits

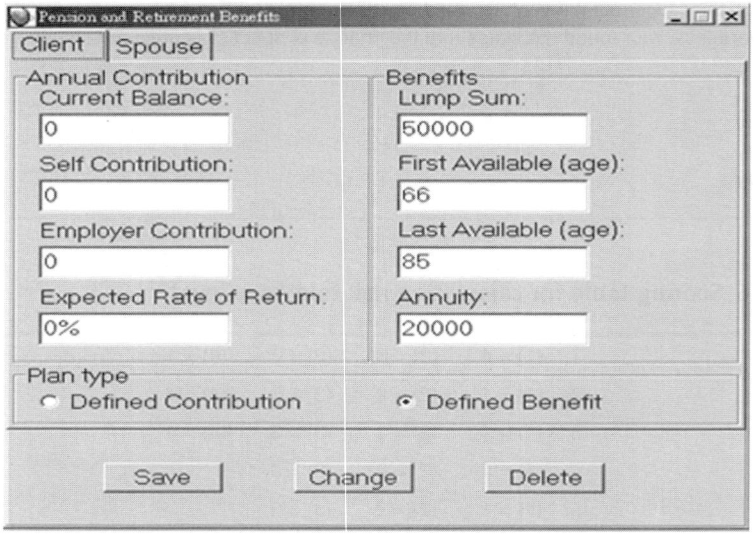

When the client has filled in all the information on the data collection form, both the financial planner and the client should check to see whether there is missing, incomplete, or incorrect information. If the client agrees with the service fee charged by the financial planner, the financial planner may ask the client to verify the data with written confirmation.

Confidentiality of Client Information and Data Privacy Protection

As clients have provided their personal data to financial planners for financial planning purposes, it is the responsibility of the financial planners to keep the data confidential and protect the privacy of the clients. This confidentiality duty is one of the ethical responsibilities of financial planners. It means that financial planners should not use the data for nonfinancial planning purposes and should not disclose the personal data without the consent of the clients during the course of work with the clients (unless under proper legal procedures).

Figure 8.12 Example of input screen for estate planning

Besides having to comply with the Code of Ethics, financial planners must also follow the principles of data protection. Examples of personal data protection principles are listed below:

- Principle 1: Purpose and manner of collection
- Principle 2: Accuracy and duration of retention
- Principle 3: Use of personal data
- Principle 4: Security of personal data
- Principle 5: Information to be generally available
- Principle 6: Access to personal data

Therefore, financial planners must ensure that clients' personal information be used for financial planning analysis only and not for other commercial use. Financial planners should also bear in mind that this confidentiality duty does not end even if the financial planners have terminated their engagement with their clients.

FINANCIAL PLANNING IN PRACTICE

An Interview with Guy Cumbie, Chair of the Financial Planning Association 2002

Can you give some comments on step 2 of the six-step financial planning process?

If step 1 of the six-step process is, as I have suggested, the foundation of the process, then step 2 is where the sleeves get rolled up and the really serious work begins. This is typically true for both the client and the planner.

With respect to the gathering of hard data, planners usually begin by presenting the client with questionnaires and checklists of required documents. Considerable follow-up and facilitation are usually required to complete this typically fairly arduous chore. Having a patient, persistent, and helpful assistant or paraplanner can prove invaluable here. It's also useful to recognize instances wherein the planner or their staff can support the client in this effort by becoming authorized to request information directly, on behalf of the client, from other service providers and financial institutions.

On the soft side, ascertaining who the client really is as a unique human being and what clients really want, the work is much more subtle yet often every bit as difficult if not more so. When it comes to identifying their real purpose, their vision, and their values, and accordingly identifying and prioritizing all the attendant goals, many clients haven't really given it much thought. When first broaching this area, it's pretty common to hear simplified generalizations like "I really would like to be able to retire some day." On the other hand, some clients are amazingly self-actualized and have given a great deal of thought to who they are and specifically what they want. These clients can be quite exciting and rewarding to work with and the creative strategic planning we are able to employ as professional planners in these more "advanced" engagements can quickly move to a level we have come to refer to in our practice as "thinking beyond solutions."

Some Common Challenges Related to Step 2a

- Clients often confuse goals with objectives.
- Clients sometimes consider this deeply personal, values-based aspect of the planning process to be overly personal to the point of being inappropriately intrusive.
- Because there is typically little familiarity with the work of developing personal and professional "vision," clients often encounter a very steep learning curve here.
- This step often requires lots of skillful facilitation and patience by the planner.
- Clients frequently question the relevance of this "soft side" discovery work. This is especially ironic since what's being sought is what "really matters."
- Few clients are grounded in the basics of strategic planning and strategic thinking methodologies and this creates a tendency to want to move too quickly to implementation.

Some Common Challenges Related to Step 2b

- Clients are sometimes shocked and frustrated at the level of detail required.
- Planners need to be careful accepting and relying on verbal or written answers to important questions where source documents really should be obtained.
- Keeping the data sufficiently current to be useful can be an ongoing challenge.
- Financial terminology and jargon can impair communications in this step.
- Clients and sometimes the planners can be overwhelmed with data and documents.

Key Terms

goal prioritization   *257*
needs   *256*

risk tolerance level   *262*
wants   *256*

| **References** | Grable, J. and Lytton, R. H., "Financial Risk Tolerance Revisited: The Development of a Risk Assessment Instrument," *Financial Services Review*, vol. 8 (1999): 163–181. |
| | Maslow A. H., *Toward a Psychology of Being*, 2nd ed. (New York: Van Nostrand Reinhold, 1968). |

Questions & Problems

Multiple-choice Questions

1. The role of the financial planner in determining a client's personal and financial goals, needs, and priorities is to _____.
   A. define the financial goals for the clients
   B. explore the personal values and attitudes of the clients
   C. persuade the client that certain goals and objectives are unachievable
   D. facilitate the goal-setting process in order to clarify the goals and objectives with the client

2. In setting the financial goals of the clients, a financial planner should differentiate between the _____ and _____ of the clients.
   A. attitudes, expectations
   B. needs, wants
   C. needs, priorities
   D. wants, priorities

3. Which of the following factors should be considered in formulating financial goals for clients?
   I.   Following the mutually defined principles
   II. Preparing emergency cash
   III. Helping clients prioritize their goals
   IV. Encouraging clients to maximize returns during the retirement stage

   A. I, II, and III
   B. II and III
   C. I, III, and IV
   D. I, II, III, and IV

4. Which of the following statements with regard to collecting client information is TRUE?
   I.   It helps to understand the client's financial situation and objectives.
   II. Collecting client information enables the financial planner to suggest a reasonable and practical financial plan to the client.
   III. The relevant information can be collected by the financial planner while undergoing financial analysis and planning.
   IV. A financial planner should stop providing financial service to the client if the client cannot provide a certain part of the necessary information.

   A. I and II
   B. I and IV
   C. I, II, and III
   D. I, II, and IV

5. Which of the following are the inputs of the data form for regular income and expenditure?
    I.   Bonds
    II.   Interest income
    III. Insurance premium
    IV.   Securities
    V.   Personal loan
    VI.   Gifts
    VII. Occupations

    A. II and III
    B. II, III, VI, and VII
    C. I, II, IV, and V
    D. II, III, and VI

Problems

1. Describe the purpose of the financial planning pyramid in the financial planning process.

chapter **9**

Step 3: Determining Client's Current Financial Status

9.1   Practice Standards 300 Series

300-1: Analyzing and Evaluating the Client's Information

A financial planning practitioner shall analyze the information to gain an understanding of the client's financial situation and then evaluate to what extent the client's goals, needs, and priorities can be met by the client's resources and current course of action.

In step 2, we discussed how to determine goals and collect the necessary information from clients. In step 3, the financial planner has to analyze and evaluate the information collected based on the mutually defined goals and expectations within the boundary of the scope of engagement.

Analysis and evaluation activities form the foundation for determining the strengths and weaknesses of clients' financial positions. During the analysis, if financial planners discover that certain data are missing or are inconsistent, they should seek clarification with their clients. In case the clients refuse to comply or the new data reveal new information that leads to a change in the scope of engagement, financial planners should act accordingly.

The principles of the Code of Ethics and Professional Responsibility which are related to Practice Standards 300 Series are objectivity (Principle 2), competence (Principle 3), and diligence (Principle 7). The objectivity principle requires that financial planners provide professional services free of bias. The two rules of the objectivity principle state that financial planners should exercise reasonable and prudent professional judgment in providing professional services (Rule 201) and act in the interest of the client (Rule 202).

Financial analysis and evaluation require a certain level of competence from financial planners. According to Principle 3, financial planners are obliged to provide services to clients competently and maintain the necessary knowledge and skill to continue to do so in those areas engaged. Financial planners need to have technical skills in financial analysis to make recommendations for the financial plan. If they are not professionally competent to do this, they should seek expert advice or refer clients to other professionals (Rule 302).

Principle 7 sets down the rules that financial planners should act diligently in providing professional services. The financial planner may be objective and competent in carrying out the analysis and evaluation tasks, but he or she must also be diligent in performing the analysis in order to develop an appropriate financial plan and to implement recommendations in the interests of the clients.

Practice Standard 300-1 serves as a commitment of the financial planning profession to assure the clients and the public of the quality service provided by financial planners. The quality of financial planning services is guaranteed if the financial planning recommendations presented are based upon objective and competent analysis of the information collected. If the financial planners have complied with the Practice Standards 300 Series and the Code of Ethics to be objective, competent, and diligent in performing the task, the financial planners can be confident in presenting the financial planning recommendations for the clients. The likelihood of achieving the goals and objectives of the clients is increased.

9.2   Maintaining a Holistic View

Measuring Financial Health in the Context of Total Life Planning

The total well-being of clients depends on the satisfaction of three separate but related dimensions of human needs. These are financial needs, psychological needs, and physical needs. While financial planners may not be qualified to fulfill or even properly address clients' psychological and physical needs, financial planners have to take these two nonfinancial needs into consideration when evaluating clients' financial health. The reason is that if clients are not well psychologically or physically, it is likely that their financial condition is not good either.

Table 9.1 shows the relative importance of the different components of total well-being through the various life stages of a client. We are not saying that an older client's psychological or physical health is not as important as that of a client with children. We try to illustrate the importance of the health condition of the client from the perspective of a planner. For example, a three-star rating given to financial health for a newly married couple indicates to the planner that, if this client at this particular life stage has a bad financial condition (e.g., poor income with a lot of debt), then the effects of these financial problems on the client's life are much more damaging than the effects of the same problem on a retired client. As clients at different life stages have different priorities in their needs and objectives, financial planners should understand the clients' personal profile in the context of total life planning in conducting financial analysis.

Table 9.1 Relative importance of the components of total well-being by life stages

	Young adult	Newly married couple	Family with children	Couple during Preretirement period	Retired couple
Age	19–30	24–35	28–55	50–64	Over 60
Psychological health	**	***	***	**	**
Physical health	**	***	***	**	**
Financial health	**	***	***	**	**

* Denotes the level of importance, with one * denoting the least important.

Analyzing Financial Needs Using the Life-cycle Approach

Clients have unique needs at different stages of their life cycle, and these should be taken into account and integrated into financial status analysis. We have also seen that clients' life stages, lifestyle, personal profile, and financial conditions are all interrelated. Together, these factors determine clients' current financial well-being and future financial needs.

For example, for a client who has a nonworking spouse and two young children, a shortfall in life insurance protection is a critical and immediate concern. For a client who is a retiree with a working spouse, the same shortfall in life insurance protection would be a less serious issue. Thus the results of financial status analysis must be interpreted in the framework of life-cycle analysis so that proper recommendations can be made.

Paying Attention to Personal Profile When Analyzing Financial Needs

We have seen that personal profiling is the process of employing both quantitative and qualitative assessment methods to obtain an accurate analysis of the nonfinancial background of an individual in order to facilitate the construction of an optimal financial plan to meet the individual's needs and objectives. Every client is unique; though they may be at the same life stage, due to their different personal and cultural backgrounds, they may have different financial needs. Thus, though we can generalize and categorize clients by life stages, we cannot make identical recommendations for clients in the same life-stage category. The personal profile of the client must be considered in conducting financial status analysis and formulating action plans.

9.3 Impact of Economic and Financial Environments

Financial planners also need to take into account economic and financial conditions when evaluating the financial status of clients as these may have an impact on clients' income, investment horizon, and retirement ages. With a more solid understanding of the relation between these external factors and the financial status of their clients, financial planners can conduct a more objective financial analysis. In addition, economic and financial conditions change through time. Constant monitoring and review with corresponding adjustments to clients' financial plans are essential.

Understanding Financial Market Systems

The government and related governmental authorities play a vital role in financial market operation by imposing financial market regulations, setting up social security and taxation systems, and implementing fiscal and monetary policies. The government performs the role of market regulator by imposing various financial market regulations to legalize market trading and to provide an equitable playing field.

When conducting financial status analysis for clients, financial planners have to be aware of the financial system and the markets in which they provide their service. Regulations and operational procedures of the financial market can affect the conclusions of financial status analysis. For instance, in a regulatory regime which does not allow the earlier withdrawal of pension money before the mandatory retirement age, the analysis of retirement savings needed is more straightforward. However, if pension money can be withdrawn as a lump sum for immediate use when the client changes jobs or leaves the country for a long while, retirement analysis can be more complicated as the pension money can be used for other purposes by the clients before actual retirement. A competent financial planner should take these local market characteristics into consideration when conducting financial analysis.

The social welfare system and the quality of health care services in a country also affect financial analysis of clients' retirement and insurance protection needs. Financial planners should be familiar with the pension fund system; mandatory retirement plan; welfare system for families, children, and the elderly; unemployment assistance; assistance for the disabled; medical policies; educational subsidies for children; and the availability and standard of public schools. Information about the pension fund system, mandatory retirement plan, and welfare system for the elderly is essential for the analysis of retirement planning. Availability of educational subsidies and the standard of public schools are relevant inputs for education planning.

Financial planners also need to understand the tax regulations related to the financial status of their clients. There are various types of tax for individual tax payers such as income tax, capital gains tax, and property tax. In countries where tax rates are relatively high, the estimation of taxes to be paid when the clients make more money in the future can make a difference to the savings balance and to the recommended consumption behavior.

Economic and Financial Indicators

Two major determinants of the future financial well-being of clients are the assumed return for investment and cost of living. In turn, these determinants are related to other macroeconomic and financial indicators such as interest rate, securities market performance, business cycle, inflation rate, and employment levels.

The government can affect the financial and macroeconomic conditions through its fiscal and monetary policies. Through different types of fiscal policies, contractionary and expansionary, the government can underspend or overspend, respectively, to affect the gross domestic product (GDP) of the economy. The government can also influence the economy through its monetary policy. One of the most common tools of monetary policy is interest rate policy. The government can use interest rate policy to influence the level of spending in the economy. Based on basic economic principles related to the production possibility curve (PPC), if the interest rate is high, there is a higher tendency for the public to spend less now and save more for the future. If the interest rate is low, there is a higher tendency for the public to spend more on consumption now as the return rate on savings is lower than the expected level.

Interest rate is determined by the demand and supply of money in the market and is an important indicator of the market. It is a commonly used benchmark for the evaluation and measurement of the expected rate of investment return in the money and capital markets. In addition, the rate of return of various financial instruments, such as fixed-income securities, fluctuates against the market interest rate. Since many planning components of the financial plan, particularly the investment planning and retirement planning components, involve investments in the market, financial planners should be aware of market interest rate fluctuations and their impact on the financial plan. Occasionally, adjustments to the financial plan may be necessary due to the change in interest rate.

In Chapter 3 we explained that the business cycle depicts the recurring patterns of economic good times and bad times. It is important for financial planners to have knowledge of the business cycle so that they can adjust the financial plans for their clients under different stages of the business cycle.

The price level and inflation rate are indicators of the income and consumption levels of the consumer public. In a market where the income and consumption levels are high, the price level is also high. For instance, in China, the average income of citizens in Shenzhen is four times higher than that of the residents in the western area. Hence, the price level of the southeastern coastal area is generally higher than that of the middle-west area. Therefore, financial planners should consider the general price levels of the areas where the clients live as the price level affects the consumption pattern of the clients.

The employment level is measured by the unemployment rate (discussed in Chapter 3). The employment level is closely related to the business cycle. In good economic times, the market has a great demand for labor, and hence the unemployment rate is low. Generally speaking, when the market condition is good and the employment level is high, clients become more optimistic about the future, and their attitude toward risk is moderately aggressive or aggressive. When the economic and market conditions are stagnant, the unemployment rate is relatively higher. Therefore, there is a fear of losing jobs or suffering salary cuts. Of course, a client's job security is also related to the industry he or she is in. If the industry is declining, no matter how competent an employee the client is, his or her job security is still uncertain. In such a case, the financial planner should pay extra attention to insurance protection and savings plans.

Keeping in mind, then, that financial status analysis is related to such factors as clients' physical and psychological health, life stages, and personal profiles, as well as economic and financial indicators, we now focus on how to carry out the actual financial status analysis. We will first look at clients' personal financial statements.

9.4   Analysis of Financial Statements

flow The measurement of accounting and financial conditions through a period of time.

stock The inventory or balance of financial indicators at a given point in time.

Financial statements can be classified into two major categories based on the *flow* and *stock* concepts. **Flow** refers to the measurement of accounting and financial conditions through a period of time. The income statement and cash flow statement belong to this category. The main purpose of such statements is to measure the financial activity of the subject over a certain period of time. Based on the figures in these statements, we can understand the subject's average performance and behavior. **Stock** looks at the inventory or balance of financial indicators at a given point in time. The balance sheet belongs to this category. A balance sheet reflects the financial strengths and shortcomings of a client at a particular moment. However, it does not say anything about the client's financial activity before or after that particular date. While the stock indicator is a more specific indicator of financial status than the flow statement variables, flow variables give us an overall picture of financial performance throughout a period. A financial planner has to use both flow and stock indicators together in assessing the client's financial status. These two categories of financial indicators complement each other. Being used together, a complete financial picture can be revealed.

In financial status analysis, financial planners first employ clients' financial data gathered in step 2. Using the information from the various financial statements, the financial planners can perform various analyses, such as asset analysis, liabilities analysis, and cash flow analysis for clients. Financial ratios can be calculated using the information on the financial statements to evaluate the financial health of the clients. These analyses are needed to generate specific recommendations for various planning components such as consumption planning, insurance planning, and investment planning.

The Income Statement

The income statement reflects the income and expenditure of an individual. Since the actual income and expenses may vary month by month, we normally prepare an income statement for a period of one year. Usually the one-year period follows the tax assessment period (e.g., January to December in the US and China, July to June in Australia, and April to March in Hong Kong) for ease of calculating taxes.

The main purpose of the income statement is to give the financial planner and the client an idea of the average levels of income, expenses, and savings per year. The financial planner has to understand that an annual income statement cannot capture the seasonality of expenses. Thus, savings may not be accumulated equally month by month throughout the whole year.

While the source of income is usually limited and less likely to be unexpected, the list of expenses seems to be endless. Expenses can be divided into regular expenses and irregular expenses. Common examples of regular expenses are food consumption expenses, transportation expenses, income tax and property tax, medical expenses, mortgage repayment, insurance expenses, and educational expenses. Irregular expenses may include house remodeling expenses, major gifts for special occasions, and wedding expenses.

Table 9.2 shows an example of an income statement for a middle-aged married client with children. Peter Brown is a senior executive working in the United States with a homemaker spouse and two young children (6 and 9 years old). All the figures in the income statement are based on typical expenses in a large city in the United States.

A lot of people think that entertainment and vacations are not regular activities. This is a wrong assumption. For middle-income and high-income clients like Peter Brown who live in developed countries, taking annual vacations is a permanent part of their lifestyle. Second, many people also think that medical expenses are not regular as people do not get sick all the time. However, for a family of four with two young children, the chance of one of them being sick in a given month is quite high. Thus, medical expenses are also unavoidable.

It looks like Peter Brown is making a handsome income. When we look closely at the expenses, most of them are quite reasonable and there is not much room for cutting back. There are two exceptional expense items. First, the wedding gifts for Peter's brother and the house remodeling took away most of the savings for the year. Second, the children's education includes private school tuition fees for one of them. While most of the other expenses are for consumption goods, some money from the life insurance premium and mortgage payment goes into the cash value of a whole life policy and equity of the house. These investments will show up in the balance sheet as assets. Finally, while there is a surplus of $2,993, it does not mean that they can add this amount to the savings account at the end of the year. As expenses can be paid by credit card, it is highly possible that the cash balance in the bank appears to be more than the actual savings when the client looks at the statement at the end of the year.

The income statement for clients at different life stages may look quite different, especially for the expense items. For Peter Brown and his family, the mortgage payment, insurance premium, and education expenses are quite unique to their life stage. For an empty nester, these three items would most likely be less significant. Financial planners should look at the income and expenses of their clients in the context of their life stages when evaluating their optimal consumption and savings.

The Cash Flow Statement

In most cases, the items and amounts involved in the cash flow statement (see Table 9.3) are very similar to those in the income statement. The only difference is that when consumers are paying for bills with credit cards, the amounts in the cash flow statement for selective items may be different. In addition, in the cash flow statement, there may be a credit card payment for the last year's expenses.

Table 9.2 Income statement of Peter Brown, January 1–December 31, 2004

	(US$)	%
Income		
Regular income		
Salary	180,000	96.2%
Dividend[1]	2,000	1.1%
Bond interest[2]	5,000	2.7%
Savings deposit interest[3]	100	0.1%
Total regular income	**187,100**	**100.1%[8]**
Irregular income	0	0
Total irregular income	**0**	**0.0%**
Total income	**187,100**	**100.1%**
Expenses		
Regular expenses		
Food	24,000	13.0%
Utility and phone	7,200	3.9%
Children's education[4]	12,000	6.5%
Income tax (Federal and State)[5]	63,000	34.2%
Medical expenses	2,400	1.3%
Insurance premiums (life and health)	7,200	3.9%
Insurance premium (property and auto)	2,000	1.1%
Mortgage payment[6]	17,437	9.5%
Entertainment and annual vacation	7,000	3.8%
Car payments (two cars)	11,870	6.4%
Gasoline	6,000	3.3%
Miscellaneous[7]	6,000	3.3%
Total regular expenses	**166,107**	**90.2%**
Irregular expenses		
Wedding gifts for brother	3,000	1.6%
House remodeling	10,000	5.4%
Down payment for a car	5,000	2.7%
Total irregular expenses	**18,000**	**9.7%**
Total expenses	**184,107**	**99.9%[9]**

$187,100 (Total income) – $184,107 (Total expenses) = $2,993 (Surplus)

1. 100,000 (stock value) × 2% (dividend yield)
2. $100,000 (par value of bond) × 5% (interest)
3. $10,000 (savings deposit) × 1% (interest)
4. Assuming one child goes to private school and the other attends public school.
5. 35% of salary.
6. Assume 6% annual percentage rate, 20 years, $200,000 original loan amount.
7. Includes capital gains and dividend tax.
8. Due to rounding error, the sum of the percentage column equals 100.1% instead of 100%.
9. Due to rounding error, the sum of the percentage column equals 99.9% instead of 100%.

These changes would affect the cash balance, leading to a different figure between the surplus or deficit in the income statement and cash balance in the cash flow statement for the year. If there is a huge amount in the credit card balance, it would be difficult for clients to accurately assess their consumption for a given period. In order to help clients to understand their consumption behavior, it is advisable to ask them to spend money on a cash basis for a period of 3 to 6

Table 9.3 Cash flow statement of Peter Brown, January 1–December 31, 2004

	(US$)	%
Cash inflow		
Cash inflow from regular income		
Salary	170,000	91.6%
Dividend	1,900	1.0%
Bond interest	13,500	7.3%
Savings deposit interest	90	0.0%
Total cash inflow	**185,490**	**99.9%[2]**
Cash outflow		
Cash outflow from regular expenses[1]		
Food	22,000	12.2%
Utility and phone	6,600	3.7%
Children's education	10,800	6.0%
Income tax (Federal and State)	59,500	33.0%
Medical expenses	2,200	1.2%
Insurance premiums (life and health)	7,200	4.0%
Insurance premium (property and auto)	2,000	1.1%
Mortgage payment	17,437	9.7%
Entertainment and annual vacation	6,000	3.3%
Car payments (two cars)	11,870	6.6%
Gasoline	5,500	3.1%
Miscellaneous	5,000	2.8%
Credit card payment for December of last year	6,000	3.3%
Total	**162,107**	**90.0%**
Cash outflow from irregular expenses		
Wedding gifts for brother	3,000	1.7%
House remodeling	10,000	5.6%
Down payment for a car	5,000	2.8%
Total	**18,000**	**10.1%**
Total cash outflow	**180,107**	**100.1%[3]**

$185,490 (Total cash inflow) – $180,107 (Total cash outflow) = $5,383 (Net cash flow)

1. Selective items in the expenses are assumed to have 10% of the annual amount paid by credit card, leading to a smaller cash outflow than the expenses shown in the income statement in Table 9.2.
2. Due to rounding error, the sum of the percentage column equals 99.9% instead of 100%.
3. Due to rounding error, the sum of the percentage column equals 100.1% instead of 100%.

months so that the cash flow for the period would better reflect actual expenses incurred. If there is a net cash outflow in the short run, clients can use their savings to cover this shortfall. However, if the deficit continues, the client may have to seek long-term solutions such as increasing income, reducing expenses, or even selling part of their assets in order to cover the expenses for the family.

Combining the Income Statement with the Cash Flow Statement

As you can see, the income statement and the cash flow statement are very similar. In fact, as most incomes are received on a cash basis, there is a very high chance that the income figures and cash inflow figures are identical. Thus, the only differences are for those expense items partially paid by credit card. To save time and paperwork, we can skip the income statement and prepare the cash flow statement only. For clients who have a predictable payment pattern using the credit card, it would be easy to estimate the actual expenses from the cash flow statement without creating a separate document.

The Balance Sheet

The balance sheet is a financial statement that reports what an individual owns (assets) and owes (liabilities). Assets include liquid assets (e.g., savings deposit), longer-term financial assets (e.g., stock and bonds), nonfinancial personal assets (e.g., valuable items such as jewelry), and real estate. Examples of liabilities are credit card balances, personal loans, and mortgage. In terms of time horizon, liabilities can be divided into two types: short-term liabilities (obligation to be paid within 3 years), and long-term liabilities. Net worth is the difference between total assets and total liabilities. The financial planner should be careful about the source of contribution to the net worth of the client. If the main source of net worth comes from the equity of the home, then the burst of the real estate bubble may wipe out most of the net worth of the client. On the other hand, if the net worth comprises many different sources of similar values (e.g., 30% cash, 30% stocks and bonds, and 40% home equity), then the risk of a substantial devaluation of the net worth will be low.

Table 9.4 shows the balance sheet of Peter Brown. It indicates that he is very strong financially, with a net worth of over half a million dollars. As his liabilities are not substantial, even an unexpected devaluation of property price and a collapse in the securities markets would not cause any major financial difficulties for him.

9.5   Analysis of Financial Ratios

A financial ratio is a simple mathematical expression of the financial relationship between various items on the financial statements of clients. Financial ratios can be used to measure and reflect the profitability of assets, liquidity position, debt repaying ability, risk preference, and living patterns and values of the clients. We have seen that the purpose of financial statement analysis is for the financial planner to evaluate the current financial health of the client. **Financial ratio analysis** can be used to predict the client's future financial behavior, assuming the same pattern persists. Table 9.5 provides a list of commonly used financial ratios for analysis.

financial ratio analysis The technique of using financial ratios to evaluate the financial strength of a client.

Before we go into the interpretation of financial ratios, we first have to set some boundaries. In order to provide some guidance, we attempt to give a reasonable range of the possible values of the ratios. As the ratios are calculated by dividing a numerator by a denominator, we also give the boundary of both variables by using symbols (–, 0, +). We have to state clearly that the ranges given are based on reasonable expectations, *not* on mathematical possibilities. In theory, the value of assets can be zero or even negative.

For instance, in big cities like San Francisco, Tokyo, and Hong Kong where real estate price has gone through a long-term appreciation and is then followed

Table 9.4 Balance sheet of Peter Brown as at December 31, 2004

	(US$)	%		
Assets				
Liquid assets				
Checking account	2,000	0.3%		
Savings account	10,000	1.5%		
			12,000	1.8%
Long-term investment assets				
Stock mutual funds	100,000	14.6%		
Cash value of whole life policy	5,000	0.7%		
Bonds	100,000	14.6%		
Mutual funds in 401K (pension)	200,000	29.2%		
			405,000	59.1%
Personal items				
Automobile	30,000	4.4%		
Household items	8,000	1.2%		
Jewelry	10,000	1.5%		
			48,000	7.0%
Real estate				
Market value of home	220,000	32.1%	220,000	32.1%
Total assets			685,000	100%
Liabilities				
Short-term liabilities				
Credit card	6,500	0.9%		
Auto loan	15,000	2.2%		
			21,500	3.1%
Long-term liabilities				
Mortgage	100,000	14.6%	100,000	14.6%
Total liabilities			121,500	17.7%
Net worth			563,500	82.3%

by a sudden collapse, wealthy clients can suffer from negative equity in property, leading to a negative value for net worth or even total assets. However, in general and for the long run, this situation should not be common for financial planning clients. In fact, if a financial planner has a client like this, what the client really needs is debt restructuring. There will be no money for other financial planning needs, making this client a very undesirable candidate for long-term comprehensive financial planning. In addition, in designing the boundaries, we also assume that our clients do not exhibit extremely aggressive investment behavior such as using substantial margin trading (i.e., high leverage in financial investments) which may result in negative value in investment asset. Thus, we exclude negative values as a reasonable region for the boundary of all financial variables related to assets.

Furthermore, in theory, assets can also be zero. In practice, a planner will be crazy to take on a client with zero assets (that means, the client does not even

Table 9.5 Financial ratios

Ratio	Formulae	Comment	Reasonable range
Solvency ratio	$\dfrac{\text{Net worth } (+)}{\text{Total assets } (+)}$	"+" Net worth/Total assets; No "−" by excluding negative equity for property and aggressive investment behavior; no "0" because it is practically unlikely.	Positive to 1
Investment assets to net worth ratio	$\dfrac{\text{Investment assets } (+)}{\text{Net worth } (+)}$	"+" Investment assets/Net worth; no "−" by excluding negative equity for property and aggressive investment behavior; no "0" because it is practically unlikely.	Positive
Debt to total assets ratio	$\dfrac{\text{Total liabilities } (0, +)}{\text{Total assets } (+)}$	"+" Total assets: same as above.	0 to less than 1
Debt to income ratio	$\dfrac{\text{Total liabilities } (0, +)}{\text{Income before tax } (-, +)}$	"−" Income before tax is possible; business expenses exceeding revenue is quite common for self-employed professionals.	Negative to infinity
Liquidity ratio	$\dfrac{\text{Liquid assets } (-, +)}{\text{Monthly expenses } (+)}$	"−" Liquid assets are possible; assuming stocks and bonds are excluded from liquid assets, then liquid assets can be negative at times when overdraft is used for business or investment.	Negative to positive
Savings ratio	$\dfrac{\text{Surplus } (-, +)}{\text{Income after tax } (-, +)}$	"−" Income after tax; business expenses exceeding revenue is quite common for self-employed professionals.	Negative to positive*

* Assuming that both surplus and income after tax cannot be zero at the same time, otherwise the value of the ratio becomes undefined.

have a few dollars in a savings account!). Thus, to provide useful guidance, we set the boundary indicator for total assets as "+" instead of "0."

For income variables, one may assume that it cannot be negative. This is true if the client is an employee receiving a salary and commission. However, for self-employed professionals and business owners, it is possible that, in a given year, their operating or business expenses exceed their gross income, resulting in a loss. Thus, we allow income-related variables to be negative.

There are different definitions of liquid assets. Here we adopt a narrow definition, which excludes stocks and bonds. Thus, it is possible that liquid assets can be negative at times when overdraft is used for business or investment. A similar logic applies to all ratios.

Using Peter Brown as an example, Table 9.6 provides the calculation of the financial ratios for analysis. Judging from the financial statements of Peter Brown, we should be able to have an overall understanding of his financial health. Ratio analysis helps to confirm these findings by giving us more precise indicators. However, we have to be reminded that the interpretation of ratios is more an art than a science. The rules derived from ratios can be too systematic and may lead to wrong conclusions. Thus, a financial planner should use experience, knowledge, and specific personal details of the client together to perform accurate financial analysis.

Based on the solvency ratio, investment assets to net worth ratio, and debt to total assets ratio, Peter's long-term financial health is good. Debt is low, and the assets ratios are in good shape. In terms of income strength and short-term

Table 9.6 Financial ratios of Peter Brown

Ratio	Formulae	Peter Brown	Peter Brown
Solvency ratio	$\dfrac{\text{Net worth}}{\text{Total assets}}$	$\dfrac{\$563,500}{\$685,000}$	0.8226
Investment assets to net worth ratio	$\dfrac{\text{Investment assets}}{\text{Net worth}}$	$\dfrac{\$12,000 + \$405,000 + 220,000_{\,1}}{\$563,500}$	1.1304
Debt to total assets ratio	$\dfrac{\text{Total liabilities}}{\text{Total assets}}$	$\dfrac{\$121,500}{\$685,000}$	0.1774
Debt to income ratio	$\dfrac{\text{Total liabilities}}{\text{Income before tax}}$	$\dfrac{\$121,500}{\$187,100}$	0.6494
Liquidity ratio	$\dfrac{\text{Liquid assets}}{\text{Monthly expenses}}$	$\dfrac{\$12,000}{\$166,107/12}$	0.8669
Savings ratio	$\dfrac{\text{Surplus}}{\text{Income after tax}}$	$\dfrac{\$2,993}{\$187,100 - \$63,000}_{\,2}$	0.0241

1. Investment assets here include liquid assets, long-term investment assets, and real estate, but exclude personal items in the balance sheet in Table 9.4.
2. When calculating income after tax for the savings ratio, to make it simple, we use only the salary to calculate the income tax (footnote 5 from the income statement in Table 9.2). We exclude other income such as dividend and interest because the tax rates for these incomes vary and can be different from the income tax rate, depending on the type of securities (tax deferred or not) and the applicable tax regulation during the period.

liquidity, Peter is also very healthy financially, as indicated by the debt to income ratio and liquidity ratio. The only area of concern is reflected in the savings ratio, which has a value of 2.4%. Given his relatively high income, it seems that Peter is not saving as much money as he should. However, if we look closely at the income statement (Table 9.2), we realize that the irregular expenses, especially the $10,000 house remodeling, are the major reason that the savings ratio is particularly low for the year. It is reasonable to expect that irregular expenses for future years should be around half of the actual amount this year (e.g., $9,000), leading to a much healthier savings ratio (9.7% = $11,993/$124,100). In short, Peter is in good shape overall financially. Nevertheless, it is too early to draw the conclusion that Peter can reach all his financial goals from the result of our financial status analysis. As meeting goals depends on client's expectation in all financial planning areas and the preferred lifestyle after retirement, additional analyses on matching the quantified goals with financial resources are needed before any conclusion can be drawn on recommendations.

We can also employ cross-sectional and time-series analyses in understanding a client's financial status. These analyses are done when evaluating financial ratios. Cross-sectional analysis means the usage of certain benchmarks and rules of thumb in judging the financial health of the client in a given period. Time-series analysis refers to the practice of detecting the trends and fluctuations of financial health through time. Conducting these analyses for personal financial planning, however, can be relatively difficult due to the problem of a lack of benchmark and norms for comparison.

Financial ratio analysis has long been used by financial planners to evaluate the financial position of clients. Through the years, financial planning practitioners have accumulated some insights into financial ratio analysis:

1. Financial ratios are closely related to changes in the financial and economic market conditions.
2. Wealth accumulation and age are positively related.
3. The financial position, as reflected by financial ratios, for a family made up of a more mature couple with higher household income is better than that for a family made up of a young couple with lower household income.
4. Some rules of thumb have been formulated using the growth rate of the savings ratio and assets size to evaluate the financial performance of clients.
5. Outstanding performance is indicated by a growth rate of over 1.5 in the savings ratio or assets size. If the growth rate is between 1.0 and 1.5 (0.5 and 1.0), the performance is regarded as good (acceptable). However, a growth rate of the savings ratio or assets size of less than 0.5 is an indicator of poor performance.

If the performance is less than satisfactory, suggested ways to improve the income, savings ratio, and asset size are to increase working hours; to get salary increment through promotion and further education; to seek a job with higher pay; to select investments with higher returns; and to reduce consumption expenses. The financial planners may incorporate some of these suggestions in the financial plan in order to improve the future financial status of their clients.

9.6 Relating Financial Status Analysis to Financial Needs

After studying the client's current financial status, the next step is to use the knowledge to meet the client's financial needs. The matching exercise between existing financial resources and life goals can be very complicated. Nevertheless, the financial statements and ratios provide useful insights into consumption needs, insurance needs, investment needs, retirement needs, and even estate planning needs. These insights are then used as the basis for making recommendations in the overall plan in step 4 (see Chapter 10).

Based on the client's financial statements and financial ratios, financial planners should produce some estimation of what the financial resources and accumulation of wealth and assets should be after 5 years, 10 years, and before and after retirement if the same consumption and investment patterns continue. This is known as **status quo financial analysis**. These status quo financial analyses are different from the forecasts based on recommendations made by financial planners involving changes of current consumption and investment behavior.

status quo financial analysis The evaluation of the future financial status of clients assuming that current consumption and investment behavior persists.

Several areas of financial projection should be made in the status quo analysis. First, using the current savings rate with a long-term adjustment for a more reliable average rate, the financial planner should produce a year-by-year cumulative savings chart for the client. Using the existing investment composition and return rate, a projection of the financial wealth through the years should be estimated. Of course, major life events with the implication of significant expenses should be considered in the analysis to reflect the potential shortfall of savings and cash flow. These analyses give the planner some important indicators and valuable inputs to design proper planning strategies in the next step.

Figure 9.1 shows how financial status analysis is related to financial planning needs. In conjunction with the assessment outcomes from step 2 on goals and expectations, personal profiling, and so forth, the output from financial status analysis can now be used together to evaluate whether the financial needs of the client can be met by the existing financial resources with the current consumption and savings pattern. Following this matching exercise, the financial planner should generate conclusions in various financial planning areas. These conclusions should answer the following questions: Is the client overspending as he or she follows the existing consumption pattern? Is the savings rate acceptable? Is there enough insurance protection? Does the risk level of the existing investment portfolio match the risk tolerance level of the client? Are there sufficient investments for various financial goals? And finally, is there a proper arrangement for estate planning needs? The financial planner will need the answers to these questions so that he can provide appropriate recommendations and action plans in step 4.

Figure 9.1 Relating financial status analysis to financial planning needs

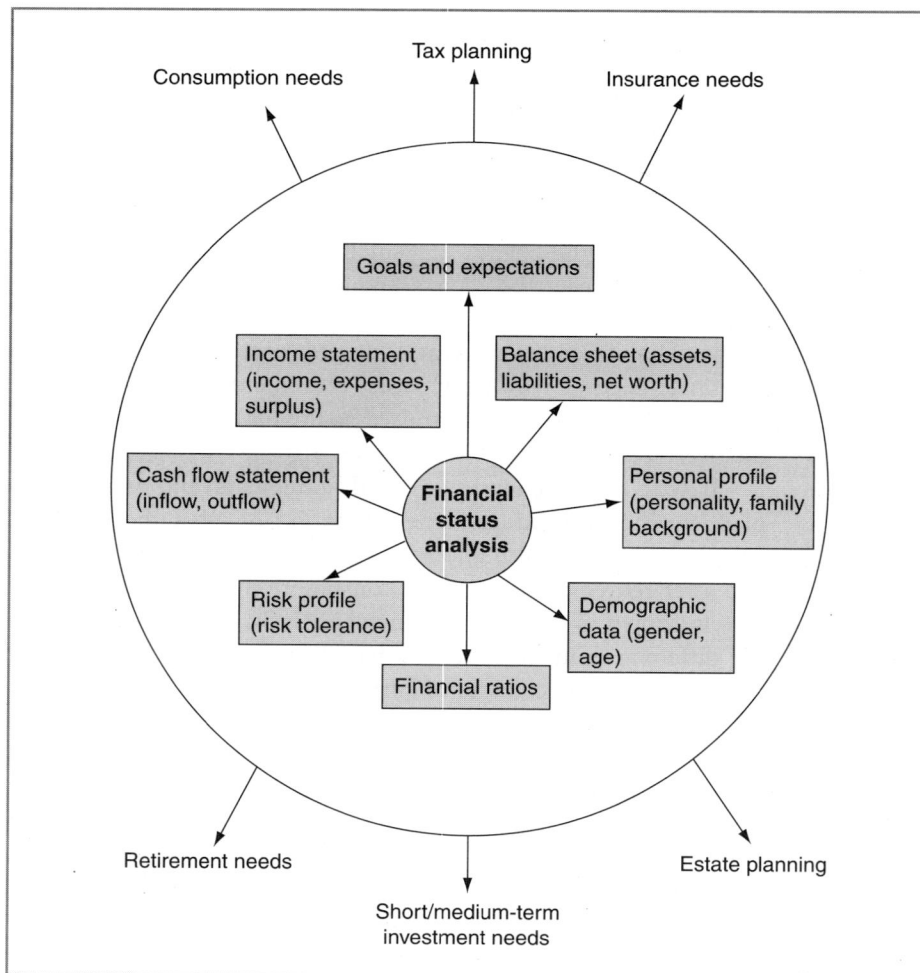

FINANCIAL PLANNING IN PRACTICE

An Interview with Elaine Bedel, Chair of the Certified Financial Planner Board of Standards 2002

Can you give some comments on step 3 of the six-step financial planning process?

This step is a very important part of the financial planning process. This is the step in which the planner gets a full understanding of the client's current financial situation. Without this knowledge, the planner cannot make recommendations for future actions. Within this step, the planner will determine whether the client's current actions are sufficient to meet his or her goals. If the current situation and the clients' current actions will allow them to meet their goals in the most efficient and effective manner, then the planner will only be validating the current actions. If, however, the planner determines that clients cannot achieve their goals with their present financial situation and current actions, or the planner determines their current actions are not the most efficient and effective means of accomplishing the goals, then the planner continues with step 4.

An Interview with Robert Barry, President of the Financial Planning Association 2002

General Observations

I believe that this is one of the most critical steps in the financial planning process and one that is central to the development of client goals and objectives. In our firm we refer to the printed reports and attendant meetings that we hold during this stage of the process as the "critical factors" phase because we feel that this codification of monetary and philosophical issues is so central to the development of a sound and cogent planning effort.

There are many components of the financial plan that can be tested and evaluated at this stage of the process. Advisors should pay close attention to the responses that they received early in the discovery process to see if there is a correlation between the client's responses to certain questions and the data that is uncovered. As an example, we just completed a critical factors report for a couple that only recently engaged our firm for financial planning. The initial cash flow reports showed that the clients had considerable positive cash margins in the current period and in the ensuing four or five years.

During the discovery phase, the clients noted that their history of earnings had been both stable and steadily increasing. They commented that they were good savers and had more of a propensity to live frugally than they did to spend money on frivolous items of personal enjoyment. Yet, when one looked to the client's balance sheet there was a total lack of any meaningful investment or cash equivalent assets beyond what was deposited as a result of employer plans and a nominal commitment to savings.

This outcome raised two important questions: (1) Where did the money go to, and (2) Why was it that the clients saw themselves as savers yet so obviously didn't have any investment or cash commitments to speak of?

Often it is that gap between "knowing" and "doing" that confuses clients. Knowing that you can save because you have the discretionary funds to and actually saving the money are often confused as the same thing. This "knowing/doing" gap presents itself at various stages of life as well as in the planning process. How many of us as advisors and business owners have been content to simply understand what it is that we are supposed to do yet have little actual application of that knowledge to back it up?

The determination of the client's financial status also gives us a chance to test for debt to equity ratios, debt service ratios, and a host of other more defined benchmarks of financial success. Statistical analysis is important at this stage. Early testing of the "theory" which we'll define here as the client's articulated desires matched against the current array of assets that they believe can help them to attain them, is a critical step.

It also pays, if you want to dig deeply into the reasoning behind the client's motivations, to ask many "why" questions. When we review cash flow statements with clients we give them some time to review the information as we've compiled it and then simply ask them, "Why do you spend your money the way you do?" It can be an empowering conversation about the people that you're planning for. And, in the end, it's the people that you plan for, not their finances. That may be the most appropriate perspective on the issue when one considers that in the final analysis it's the clients who choose to retain you and keep you as their trusted advisors. Their finances don't care very much about who it is that is managing them.

Challenges in Determining the Client's Financial Status

Many of the impediments to clear conclusions during this phase are what you would imagine that they'd be. Did you gather the right information? Is it entered into your computer program or spreadsheets correctly? Have you used the right assumptions about growth of assets, inflation rates, spending patterns, and changes in the client's circumstances? Tough questions, but questions which we all find a way to answer.

The larger questions, however, are likely to lie at the heart of the relationship itself.

Are both parties equally engaged in the effort? Are you looking at finances that were accumulated by the spirit and will of two people or are you looking at the manifestation of the breadwinners' view of the world and the silent partners' abdication in that they've been told that they don't really make that much of a contribution anyway? Are the goals realistic? Do they reflect the client's values? Do you have two people telling you that they don't need that much insurance because their children would just have to settle for less and not attend that expensive university if anything happened to them?

Perhaps most importantly, how do you get people to articulate their dreams, to share with you their view of the life that they'd like to lead rather than the one that they are leading? And, if you've been successful in that process, do the current allocation of funds, cash flow considerations, and estate planning documents reflect a life as rich and full as the one that they are telling you that given their druthers, would be the one they'd lead? Simple. Ask.

At the point where we are evaluating the current financial status of a client we have a myriad of opportunities to see if we have clients who are controlling their finances with their life or are allowing their life to be controlled by their finances. When do we start to live the dreams that we have? Shouldn't the role of a trusted advisor be, at the very least, to point clients in the direction of those goals? Reorientation is a simple dynamic: state the facts, measure the realities, and then redirect the effort. In sum and total that's pretty much the financial planning process.

Returning to the why questions presents opportunity and with it, the challenge to turn that opportunity into a value. Why did you select the investments that you did? How did you select them? Who and/or what do you rely on for financial insight when you make a major investment decision? Better that you know the sources now so that you can consider them as you build for the future. And, it also helps to know where your clients are going to be looking for answers when they're not talking with you.

And of course, the age-old and time-honored problems rear their head at this point as well. What numbers do we use to estimate capital market returns on equities and fixed income? What assumptions do we make about providing estate-planning guidance? Do we show clients hypothetical illustrations that depict a mega million-dollar scenario at a point in the distant future or do we pick a mid point as a reference guide and build a more realistic hypothetical scenario that we believe we can get the client to act on? And through it all, the issues of personal values and goals will come up, over and over and over again.

If there is a challenge in this step of the financial planning process it is the challenge of life. What is important to us, how do we plan to achieve that end state, and what compromises and trade-offs are we willing to make along the way? The recommendations that you'll make as a financial planner are in most cases subtle. It's the change on the margin and it's highly unnoticeable to most clients. Do clients ever really feel the problem that you helped them avoid? If they don't experience the negative implications of something by the work of your own hand, do they really sense that you've saved them from some great harm? Unlikely. But, I'll contend that clients do know when you've played a role in helping to shape not only their finances but their lives.

As you do your work, remember that the challenges in each step of the financial planning process lie equally with you as advisor and your client. If we ask the right questions, we can elicit the right answers and taking those answers, we can craft a strategy that moves the lives of people forward. Financial planning is about building the lives that we want and the numerical and statistical challenges aside, the greatest one that we face is in helping our clients to be the living embodiment of the very best that they can be. Your challenge will be as artist not as scientist. Train hard—it will be worth it in the end.

Use this step in the process to ask "Why?" Ask yourself frequently, ask your client as often as you can, and I think that both you and the people that you serve will be happy with the answers.

Key Terms

financial ratio analysis *289*	status quo financial analysis *293*
flow *285*	stock *285*

Questions & Problems

Multiple-choice Questions

1. An income statement can be divided into three parts/items including the following:
   I.   Assets
   II. Income
   III. Expenses
   IV. Liabilities
   V.   Balance sheet
   VI. Surplus/deficit

   A. I, IV, and V
   B. I, IV, and VI
   C. II, III, and V
   D. II, III, and VI

2. Which of the following statements regarding financial ratio analysis is true?
   I.   Wealth accumulation and age are unrelated.
   II. Financial ratios are closely related to macroeconomic changes.
   III. The savings ratio of an individual with a growth rate of less than 0.5 is described as poor.
   IV. The financial ratio for a more mature family should be better than a younger family.

   A. I and II
   B. II and IV
   C. I, II, and III
   D. II, III, and IV

3. Which of the following principles under the CFP Board's Code of Ethics and Professional Responsibility relate to the practice standard in analyzing and evaluating the client's information?
   I.   Principle of integrity
   II. Principle of objectivity
   III. Principle of competence
   IV. Principle of professionalism
   V.   Principle of diligence

   A. I, II, and IV
   B. II, III, and V
   C. I, II, III, and V
   D. II, III, IV, and V

4. The lowest living standard in forecasting the expense of a client is defined as
   _____.

   A. the living standard that the client currently has
   B. the lowest living standard that the client had in the past
   C. the living standard with just enough food and clothing
   D. the living standard with just enough food and clothing after taking inflation into consideration

The following table provides the information for questions 5 to 7. The information is for a 1-year period.

Total regular income	$269,000
Total regular expense	$119,850
Income tax	$47,300
Liquid assets	$14,500
Long-term investment assets	$554,000
Personal items	$35,000
Real estate	$246,000
Short-term liabilities	$35,900
Long-term liabilities	$130,000

5. Compute the solvency ratio.
   A. 0.1953
   B. 0.6728
   C. 0.6167
   D. 0.8047

6. Compute the investment assets to net worth ratio.
   A. 1.4518
   B. 1.1915
   C. 0.8047
   D. 0.1953

7. Compute the liquidity ratio.
   A. 1.4518
   B. 1.1915
   C. 0.6167
   D. 0.8047

chapter 10

Step 4: Developing and Presenting the Financial Plan

> ### Learning Objectives
>
> *After studying this chapter you should be able to:*
>
> 1 Explain Practice Standards 400 Series.
> 2 Understand the construction of recommendations for various planning areas.
> 3 Construct a written financial plan.
> 4 Understand the core content and other content of the financial plan.
> 5 Understand the skills for presenting the plan.

10.1 Practice Standards 400 Series

The Practice Standards 400 Series addresses three related questions: (1) What is possible? (Practice Standard 400-1), (2) What is recommended? (Practice Standard 400-2), and (3) How is it presented? (Practice Standard 400-3). Practice Standard 400-1, titled "Identifying and Evaluating Financial Planning Alternatives," is the first part of step 4. Before financial planners can present the most appropriate financial plan for their clients, they need to identify and consider the possible alternatives. They then proceed to the second task of "Developing the Financial Planning Recommendations" (400-2). Financial planners perform the first two tasks without the presence of the clients. Once the most appropriate financial planning recommendation is developed from a list of possible alternatives, they proceed to Practice Standard 400-3, titled "Presenting the Financial Planning Recommendations."

The principles of the Code of Ethics and Professional Responsibility related to the Practice Standards 400 Series are integrity (Principle 1), objectivity (Principle 2), competence (Principle 3), professionalism (Principle 6), and diligence (Principle 7). The integrity principle states that financial planners should offer and provide professional services with integrity. The characteristics of integrity are honesty, candor, and uprightness. Integrity implies no subordination to self-interest, personal gain, or advantage and is important to maintain and enhance public trust. When financial planners present the recommendations to their clients, they should not knowingly make false or misleading statements (Rule 102) for the purpose of deceiving the clients to agree to the recommendations.

The objectivity principle requires the financial planners to provide unbiased professional services to clients. Rule 201 suggests that financial planners should exercise reasonable and prudent professional judgment in providing professional services. Rule 202 requires the financial planners to act in the interest of the client.

The identification of possible alternatives and the development of recommendations require a certain level of competence from financial planners.

According to Principle 3, financial planners should provide services to clients competently and maintain the necessary knowledge and skill to continue to do so in the advisory process. In the first part of step 4, they need to have a creative mind and exercise the professional judgment to select the most appropriate recommendations among the alternatives. If they lack the professional competence to do so, they should seek external advice and/or refer clients to other experts (Rule 302).

Principle 6 requires financial planners to provide professional advice to clients. Being professionals, financial planners should behave with dignity and courtesy to those who use their financial planning services, to fellow professionals, and to other related professionals in the advisory process. As financial planning services require certain expertise and regulatory licenses, financial planners should not provide the services unless they are licensed as qualified by law (Rule 609). In addition, Rule 607 requires that financial planners should not engage in any conduct that compromises their integrity.

Principle 7 (diligence) requires that financial planners should act diligently in providing professional services. Although financial planners can be objective and competent, if they are not diligent, they may not be able to satisfy the purpose of developing recommendations which are suitable for their clients (Rule 703). In addition, Rule 704 suggests that financial planners should make a reasonable investigation into the financial products recommended to their clients, particularly during the development of recommendations stage.

The Practice Standards 400 Series serves as a commitment of the financial planning profession to serve the clients. When the recommendations are presented and communicated to the clients, the clients should recognize the competent and diligent services provided by financial planners. In addition, the Practice Standard 400 Series reinforces the practice of putting the interest of the clients first at all times when developing and presenting the financial planning recommendations. Hence, the likelihood of achieving the goals and objectives of the clients is enhanced.

This practice standard serves as a guideline to encourage financial planners to commit to a higher quality of service. Such a commitment contributes to the client's satisfaction and increases the likelihood of clients accepting the recommendations. With such a commitment to quality service, the perception of the public about the value of the financial planning profession is enhanced.

400-1: Identifying and Evaluating Financial Planning Alternatives

> The financial planning practitioner shall consider sufficient and relevant alternatives to the client's current course of action in an effort to reasonably meet the client's goals, needs, and priorities.

Before financial planners are able to present the recommendations, they have to identify and evaluate all the possible alternatives. In this task, financial planners need to have creative and analytical minds to spot the alternatives and to exercise professional judgment to evaluate the effectiveness of each of the alternative actions in meeting the objectives of the clients. This evaluation process requires financial planners to consider multiple assumptions and scenarios, to conduct research, and to assess the conditions in which the identified course of action can reasonably meet the clients' goals, needs, and priorities.

400-2: Developing the Financial Planning Recommendations

The financial planning practitioner shall develop the recommendations based on the selected alternatives and the current course of action in an effort to reasonably meet the client's goals, needs, and priorities.

Once financial planners have identified and evaluated the alternatives for the course of action, they can develop the financial planning recommendations expected to reasonably meet the goals and priorities of the clients. The recommendation may be an independent action or a combination of actions that may need to be implemented collectively. Before the developed recommendations can be presented to their clients, financial planners have to make sure that the recommendations are consistent with the scope of the engagement and the goals of the clients.

Financial planners should address the assumptions made (e.g., inflation, interest rate, life span) and constraints (e.g., financial, emotional, health) as provided by their clients in the presentation. If possible, financial planners should also make references or justifications to the assumptions made, and state alternatives if some of the constraints are altered or removed.

400-3: Presenting the Financial Planning Recommendations

The financial planning practitioner shall communicate the recommendations in a manner and to an extent reasonably necessary to assist the client in making an informed decision.

When the recommendation is presented, financial planners should make a reasonable effort to assist the clients in understanding their current financial position, the recommendations, and their effectiveness in meeting the goals and needs. In order to enable clients to better understand the recommendations, financial planners need to communicate the economic assumptions, advantages, disadvantages, risks, and time sensitivity of the recommendations to the clients. It is important for clients to understand that the best recommendations may vary due to changes of economic conditions, legislation, family status, career, investment performance, health, and so on.

In summary, the Practice Standards 400 Series serves as a guide to financial planners to (1) provide alternatives for the financial plan; (2) develop recommendations based on the alternatives; and (3) communicate recommendations to clients; all in the context of meeting the clients' goals and within the boundary of the scope of engagement. In addition, in the meeting to present the recommendations, if there are conflicts of interest that have not been previously disclosed, financial planners should address these conflicts and consider what impact the conflicts will have on the recommendations. Furthermore, presenting the recommendations to the clients provides the opportunity for the financial planners to assess whether the recommendations can meet the goals and expectations of the clients, whether the clients have the willingness to act on the recommendations, and whether modifications for the recommendations are needed.

10.2   Developing a Financial Plan

Checking the Steps for Plan Development

Before the financial plan and strategies are developed for the clients, the financial situation and expected objectives of the clients must be reviewed.

1.   Ensure all relevant information is ready

Before financial planners start to develop the financial plan, they have to be sure that the data collected in step 2 are valid, complete, and accurate. Although financial planners should have collected sufficient data from their clients, they may still have to keep in touch with the clients during the development stage of the financial plan in case more updated information is required.

2.   Ensure the validity of clients' objectives and needs

Financial planners should list all the objectives of their clients. Objectives can be categorized into different types in terms of the time horizon: short-term objectives (e.g., vacation, new car), intermediate objectives (e.g., housing mortgages) and long-term objectives (e.g., retirement). Objectives can also be classified by their immediacy (e.g., more urgent needs include life insurance or health insurance). Common objectives are income and asset protection, liabilities reduction, education funds, retirement, and asset transfer (particularly upon death).

3.   Ensure validity of the results of the analysis and develop the planning strategies

When the objectives of their clients are confirmed, financial planners can use the results from their analysis to form the recommendations to achieve the various financial objectives of the clients.

Developing Recommendations for Each Planning Area

The financial planner should have obtained a clear picture of the financial status and the shortfalls in each financial planning need in step 3. For example, the analysis in step 3 should be able to provide answers to some important questions (e.g., How much additional money is needed for education funds? Is there an overconsumption problem? Is there a need for additional insurance?). In step 4, financial planners have to formulate recommendation alternatives based on the answers to these questions. In providing recommendations, it is important for planners to provide financial forecasts for savings, expected returns for investments, and wealth level through time under different alternative recommendations and assumptions. If possible, a range of forecasts for key financial goals should be provided so that the clients will understand that the final outcome may vary, depending on the net effects of many factors combined together.

The planner has to realize that, owing to the financial situation and needs of the client, it may not be necessary to provide recommendations that lead to actions in each possible financial planning area. Nevertheless, it is a good practice to communicate to the clients your assessment for each area so that the client will better understand why there is no action recommended in some areas. This practice will strengthen the concept of comprehensive financial planning in the client's mind.

Finally, the financial planner is encouraged to provide alternative recommendations. There are two major reasons for this. First, in the dynamic financial world, conditions may change quickly and what is a sound recommendation for this moment may not necessarily be the best after a few weeks. It is a prudent practice in financial planning to provide different alternatives that can be optimal, depending on some financial and personal assumptions related to the market and the clients, and to provide different scenarios of economic conditions. Second, in certain countries where consumer protection is strong, providing alternative recommendations can also be a compliance issue at the institutional or even regulatory level.

Consumption Planning

For the average client, overconsumption can be a common problem. If the problem involves other core members of the family, then it is even more difficult for the client (assuming he or she is the head of the household) to control the budget. From the client's financial statement analysis and financial ratio analysis in step 3, the financial planner can provide reasonable recommendations for consumption planning and cash flow management. Of course, clients' cooperation in changing their consumption behavior is critical to the success of meeting the investment goals. Managing clients' expectations and educating them on consumption behavior is an integral part of the recommendation. These activities should continue in step 6 as a constant reminder and encouragement in shaping a new consumption pattern for clients.

As consumption planning normally focuses on behavioral changes of clients and does not involve the purchase of products, it is less tangible to the clients. It is also more difficult for financial planners to influence the outcome, and therefore the success, in consumption planning. Consequently, it may also be more difficult to practice consumption planning for commission-based planners where product selling is important to their income. In fact, there exists a challenge for insurance professionals in working with clients who depend on their monthly savings to pay for the premium for their whole life policy or investment-linked plan. Owing to the inability in controlling consumption as expected, clients in the earlier life stages may find it difficult to keep paying the annual premium for these plans and consequently drop out of the policy. If proper consumption planning is conducted for these clients, their ability in paying the premium for future years can be better assessed and the dropout rate can be substantially reduced. Even though consumption planning may not involve financial products and does not generate income directly, professional and ethical financial planners should not take this task lightly as proper consumption planning recommendation sets the right foundation for other financial planning areas.

RECOMMENDATIONS RELATED TO CONSUMPTION

Spending too much money is not a problem only for people with limited income. It is also very common for high-income professionals such as medical doctors and investment bankers to spend more than they should. In some extreme cases, they spend more than they earn and wind up with a huge debt. On the other hand, it is also possible that some older clients in Asia, especially those who have a lot of money but insist on living on a pitiful budget, do not spend as much as they are able to. Nevertheless, insufficient spending may result in less than optimal satisfaction but does not lead to any spillover problem to family members or to society due to financial liability and bankruptcy. Thus our focus here is only on dealing with overconsumption and establishing a saving habit. In designing the recommendations for consumption, financial planners should pay attention to the following issues:

1. Changing consumption behavior is tough. It requires courage, endurance, cooperation of family members, and continuous support from the financial planner.
2. To make sure that all these efforts are for a worthy goal, the analysis and the recommendations of consumption planning must be appropriate and feasible.
3. An appropriate strategy to reduce consumption or increase savings does not mean that it has to focus on cutting expenses alone. The client should feel comfortable in meeting the consumption targets, and not feel that he or she is under constant pressure to cut down on spending.
4. While using financial ratios and quantitative benchmarks for clients is helpful, managing human behavior is not an exact science. It is very difficult to make an accurate forecast of outcomes that are solely due to a long-term voluntary effort of an individual. An appropriate consumption strategy should provide certain flexibility for the client to adjust to a tighter budget through time.
5. As financial discipline can be built through education and training, it is not a bad idea to educate clients in this concept at an earlier stage, so that they can better control their consumption level at the retirement age if needed.
6. Often a change of consumption pattern means a corresponding change in lifestyle. Clients have to fully understand the effects of such a change, and must be willing to make some sacrifices in order to fulfill a more important goal.
7. When the recommendations involve a sale of major personal assets such as a vacation home, a luxury car, and expensive jewelry, careful consideration about the sentimental value and emotional attachment of the client to these items must be given.

8. The monthly savings due to lower spending should be channeled to appropriate investments immediately to establish a sense of achievement.

9. For clients who have difficulty in leaving their savings alone, the savings can be invested in pension funds or long-term savings plans under which early withdrawal may require additional paperwork and be subject to a penalty. This helps to prevent the client from spending the money on impulsive and unnecessary major purchases.

10. Through the years and at different life stages, an individual may have different life goals, leading to different optimal consumption levels. The financial planner should closely monitor the client and make sure that the consumption and savings plans meet the current goals of the client.

Tax Planning

While the financial planner may not have the expertise in giving detailed tax planning advice to clients, it is still reasonable to expect some overall observations and directions related to the tax area. However, if the financial planner is not a qualified accountant or tax expert, a proper disclaimer and reminder of this must be given to the clients verbally and in written form.

Tax planning recommendations can involve professional services with or without financial products. As the relationship between the benefits and the recommended tax strategies is more predictable, clients are more able to appreciate the effects in tax planning. In addition, in most cases, tax planning strategies work for a longer period, normally at least for the whole year, assuming that the financial status and the income do not change. Thus, the monitoring aspect of tax planning strategies is less important than other areas such as investment and consumption.

RECOMMENDATIONS RELATED TO TAXATION

Tax issues are generally of more concern to wealthy clients and businessmen than to middle-income salary earners. Thus, a more detailed strategy in the financial plan should be expected for a wealth manager that deals with high net-worth clients. Some issues related to recommendations on tax strategies are listed below:

1. The planner should stress that tax planning begins *before* each assessment year, not after receiving the invoice.

2. A major goal for tax planning is to reduce tax liability legally.

3. Other possible benefits from tax planning include better timing of tax payment in order to match the consumption and investment activities of the clients.

4. Reducing variations in the amount of taxes paid from year to year can be a benefit in terms of risk management.

5. When considering strategies for reducing taxes, financial planners should provide some estimates on potential tax savings.

6. If the tax savings are related to estate planning, other qualitative factors such as flexibility in wealth distribution and transfer using trusts should be considered. Often, there are some potential drawbacks related to money withdrawal in using tax-sheltered or tax-deferred vehicles to handle income and wealth. Financial planners must balance all tax and nontax factors in making tax recommendations.

7. In Asia, many wealthy clients are also small- and medium-sized business owners. Tax savings strategies may involve some business tax arrangements. A financial planner must be able to assess the overall situation for both personal and business tax liability when making recommendations.

Insurance Planning

Insurance planning is related to consumption planning as most analyses in insurance needs require input from the consumption of clients. In addition, insurance premiums are normally paid on a regular basis, either monthly, quarterly, semi-annually, or annually, which can be affected by clients' consumption and savings. Except for the case of proper insurance coverage, insurance planning most likely involves the recommendation of either buying or dropping certain insurance products. In addition, owing to the different areas of insurance needs (e.g., general insurance and life insurance), the recommendation normally involves more than one product. As there are different methods in computing insurance needs, and different combinations of products to meet the same need, insurance recommendations from different financial planners can vary substantially in terms of actual products being used. The recent popularity of investment-linked insurance policies adds substantial complexity and flexibility in insurance product recommendation.

Financial planners should therefore explain clearly to their clients that while the types of insurance needs can be easily assessed, there can be many possible combinations of insurance products to meet those needs. Consequently, planners should reserve ample time in communicating insurance recommendations to clients so that clients can make an educated decision in the final selection of insurance products. In addition, owing to rapid insurance product innovations and changing personal needs of clients, a periodical review of insurance needs is critical for the success of insurance planning.

RECOMMENDATIONS RELATED TO INSURANCE

While there are many insurance products covering life, property, automobile, travel, and health, financial planners normally focus more on life insurance. When providing insurance recommendations, you should pay attention to the following issues:

1. While the financial planner may have a lot of experience in estimating the insurance needs of a typical client, it is important for the planner to take the time in explaining the process of estimating the insurance needs in the plan in order to educate the client. The better the client

understands the importance of insurance protection and the amount needed, the lower the chance that the client will drop out of the policy.

2. When using the needs approach to come up with the recommendation for insurance needs, there are many subjective factors involved in the estimation process. For instance, when estimating the income needs during the readjustment period (which is the immediate period following the death of the insured), the planner should take into consideration the emotional strength of the surviving family members. Some may take a year to recover emotionally; others may take two to three years to heal. The estimation of income needs during the dependency period (the time it takes the youngest child to reach an independent stage financially) can also vary substantially. If the clients want to include college education and the corresponding living expenses for the children, then the amount needed would be much larger than the one required to support them through high school only. Finally, the income needs for the surviving nonworking spouse also depend on how fast the spouse can rejoin the labor force. Sometimes the spouse may need to go back to college or acquire some education before becoming employable. Thus, the financial planner should include all these factors in estimating the insurance needs of the client.

3. When the human capital approach (present value of future income of the client) is used, the major unknown is the ability of the client to get promotion at work or stay employed. As industries and firms experience life cycles differently, the employability and the income level of the client are subject to both external and internal factors. Estimating the human capital of the client is nothing more than an educated guess. The planner should look carefully into these economic and industry factors as well as the professional competence of the clients when assessing their future income. Of course, when the time is closer, and the picture becomes clearer, proper evaluation and adjustments to these estimations must be made periodically so that the client receives adequate (and not excessive) insurance coverage at all times.

4. Whatever approach is used to estimate the life insurance needs, the financial planner must also evaluate the ability of the clients to meet the monthly or annual premium payment. Insurance should be used as a tool for risk management, not a quick way to get rich. Some clients tend to buy excessive insurance to compensate for their sense of insecurity. The financial planner must point out the financial costs of paying for insurance they do not need instead of taking advantage of their emotional weaknesses to sell more insurance.

5. As we have mentioned before, there are different ways to provide life insurance coverage for a client. Alternative recommendations should be provided for clients if possible. First, depending on the financial conditions of the clients, different levels of coverage should be recommended so that clients can have an option to start off with something that they feel more comfortable with. Second, given the amount of coverage, different types of products should be recommended. For example, the financial planner

can recommend a whole life policy, a term life policy, or a combination of whole life and term life policies to provide a US$500,000 life insurance for a 30-year-old nonsmoking male. Of course, whole life instruments have cash values and other features that term life products do not. However, the periodical payment for a whole life policy is also much higher than that for term products. Financial planners should consider products that best meet the insurance needs of the clients instead of looking at the size of the commission attached to the products.

6. To provide insurance coverage for clients at different life stages, the insurance recommendations may be implemented at different times. For example, if the financial planner is providing a recommendation for a 30-year-old client with a nonworking spouse and two young kids, the insurance needs at present are relatively greater than 20 years from now. Thus, the financial planner can consider a permanent component of insurance coverage using whole life with a temporary component using a 20-year term policy. In addition, some companies actually have some term life policies with a declining life insurance coverage. While the financial liability and obligation remain about the same, the client's own savings and wealth accumulated through time can be used as emergency cash and funds for the surviving spouse. Thus, the need for external insurance coverage would decline. Such a product can meet the changing insurance needs as the client gets older, and the declining coverage makes it cheaper as well. In this case, the client would not face the problem of excessive coverage when he is 50 years old. A strategy like this should be planned when the client is still young. Of course, if there are changes in the client's insurance needs, the financial planner can always recommend more coverage in the future.

7. When the recommendation involves an investment-linked policy, the financial planner has to understand the investment performance of the products and how these products help to meet the investment goals of the clients. While there are many high-quality investment-linked insurance products, there are also drawbacks, including their relatively long-term payment period, penalty for early withdrawal, and complicated fee structure. Obviously, for certain clients, an investment-linked product is a great invention that helps them to meet various needs in one package. Other clients may be better served by the more traditional insurance products. Financial planners should provide alternative recommendations involving both investment-linked and pure insurance products so that the clients can compare these and select the ones they prefer.

Investment Planning

Investment planning here refers to investment for medium-term goals such as education funds and home purchase. Understanding that most clients, especially in Asia, will not disclose all their wealth and financial assets to financial planners, financial planners have to be careful about the potential effects of their recommendations on investment strategies and products used. One way to solve the problem of giving advice for partial wealth of clients is to ask the client (or his investment advisor for the remaining wealth) to at least tell you the riskiness of the unknown portfolio and the value of that portfolio relative to the known portion that you are aware of. In this case, you can try to come up with a complementary portfolio to serve the overall goals of the client.

Another way to deal with the existence of unknown financial assets of clients is to design a portfolio to focus on your portion of the wealth/income to achieve a special life goal, such as education funds for children. In this case, you have a very specific goal with a known investment horizon and risk level. Dividing the money up into different portfolios based on the investment goals seems inefficient from the administrative and cost perspectives. However, there are some advantages of doing so for the client in terms of managing his or her expectations and giving a proper evaluation of your performance. By directly relating the investment portfolio with a specific goal, it is much easier to educate clients about the appropriate risk-return trade-off, the reasons for the asset mix, and the optimal duration of the investment. This is especially true when the financial planner handles only part of the wealth. This goal-specific portfolio approach will give the client a clear linkage between your advice and the performance of your suggested portfolio.

As we have mentioned, the information on existing investments is important for the financial planner to decide how the investment goals of the client should be achieved. In most cases, some changes in the investment vehicles and asset allocation would be necessary. In the case of using savings per month for investment, the financial planner should consider investment plans that have minimum cost. As the execution of new investment plans may involve selling existing securities, the timing of the implementation can be tricky and the financial planner should consider the impact of timing uncertainty on implementation when forming the new investment portfolio strategies. A more comprehensive coverage of asset allocation analysis and recommendations using the results from risk profiling is found in "Investment Strategy Recommendations" in Chapter 14.

RECOMMENDATIONS RELATED TO INVESTMENT

Financial planners should always provide alternatives for their investment choices, and explain clearly the pros and cons of the risk-return trade-off for each major investment vehicle recommended. They should also educate their clients on the importance of long-term asset allocation and the shortcomings of short-term speculative activities. Due to a greater interest in investment among Asians, financial planners working for Asian clients should equip themselves with sufficient investment knowledge so that proper answers can be given when clients question their recommendations. In addition, continuous monitoring of the securities markets is required to detect investment opportunities.

Financial planners should follow a consistent investment philosophy in forming their investment recommendations. This is because for any investment technique to work, it must be applied many times and for a long period. Research results for any investment strategy are based on a large sample and many years of data. To achieve the results stated in textbooks or research reports, the techniques must be used on many clients for an extensive period of time. The average outcome of all the clients combined will resemble the findings reported in the readings. Financial planners have to stay rational and objective in forming investment recommendations for clients. Blindly chasing after so-called insider information and market intelligence for investment choices can be disastrous for both financial planners and clients.

Retirement Planning

On top of investment strategies, retirement planning involves other important elements such as preferred lifestyle and optimal consumption level after retirement, postretirement activities, and health-related issues. From the investment aspect, emphasis on the long-term investment horizon and dollar-cost averaging is important. The existing pension funds and retirement savings obtained in step 3 are valuable inputs in determining how to form the retirement investment plan for the client. As investment choices in an approved retirement fund or pension system are regulated, whatever the client has chosen in the existing portfolio should not be too damaging or way off the mark. Thus adjustments in the asset allocation for retirement funds can be implemented through a period of time (as long as a few months). In addition, the monthly pension contribution can be altered easily to fit the proper risk-return profile of the client. In short, while the data and results from previous steps are critical for developing the retirement planning recommendations, forming the actual recommendations should not be too difficult.

The basic techniques and issues involved in the asset allocation for the retirement portfolio are the same as those for medium-term investment planning. Financial planners should remind their clients that retirement investment is for the long term. Once the plan is in place, clients should stick with it. Financial discipline, not return maximization, is the key to success for any long-term investment plan.

DIFFERENTIATING BETWEEN PRERETIREMENT AND POSTRETIREMENT PLANNING ACTIVITIES

Retirement planning can be one of the longest-lasting planning areas (after estate planning) in terms of time coverage. In fact, there are some differences between preretirement and postretirement planning activities. The former includes activities for the purpose of achieving certain financial goals and benchmarks to prepare for an optimal retirement. These goals and benchmarks must be reached before or at retirement to accumulate the financial resources to achieve the preferred lifestyle.

The latter focuses on planning activities for the purpose of preparing clients for a postretirement lifestyle. Postretirement planning includes many nonfinancial elements. Financial planners should provide information on available choices so that their clients can make informed decisions when choosing an optimal lifestyle and engaging in postretirement activities. While planners should focus on financial needs of clients, these financial needs must be related to consumption behavior and lifestyle activities. An all-round financial planner practicing total life planning needs to consider these personal issues when designing the retirement plan for clients.

While both preretirement and postretirement components contain an investment element, the focus switches from wealth accumulation to income generation. Thus, during the few years before retirement (sometimes called the preretirement stage, which should not be confused with preretirement planning activities), the retirement portfolio should be gradually moved from a more risky asset allocation to a more conservative one.

RECOMMENDATIONS RELATED TO POSTRETIREMENT PLANNING

Recommendations for retirement planning related to the investment portfolio will be discussed later in "Investment Strategy Recommendations." Our discussion here focuses on the noninvestment issues of postretirement planning:

1. Retirement can be viewed as a change of lifestyle or career. Financial planners should help their clients in postretirement activities such as hobby development, appropriate volunteer work, part-time job opportunities, and study opportunities. While young clients would not be interested in these in their financial plans, near-retirement clients would appreciate information in these areas as an appendix attached to the regular plan. In addition, understanding clients' postretirement activities is important for financial planners to estimate the consumption and insurance needs for the postretirement period.

2. Medical and health-related issues are a big concern for retirees. If possible, understanding the health conditions, diet preferences and exercise habits of clients now can provide valuable insights into clients' postretirement preferred lifestyles. In the United States, some successful financial planners have established a very profitable practice focusing on retirees. In this case, knowledge on medical insurance, home care services, and elderly homes is useful.

3. Retirement is a major goal for most clients. However, retirement is also a very vague concept, which means different things to different people. In providing recommendations for retirement, financial planners must have a clear understanding of their clients' retirement goals. Simply constructing a retirement portfolio to meet the daily financial needs is only a part of the job. Helping clients to fund their retirement "dreams" is just as important.

4. If the financial planner is successful, the client will most likely stay with the planner even after his or her retirement. In reality, a client maintaining such a long-term relationship with his or her financial planner must possess a certain wealth (otherwise the client would have dropped out or the planner would have transferred the client to a junior planner). These older and wealthier clients are a treasure to the financial planner. They normally have total trust in their planners and allow them to invest their money without much constraints. These loyal clients serve as an important income base for most successful planners.

Estate Planning

Similar to tax planning, estate planning is a well-defined area requiring professionals such as lawyers and accountants to facilitate the implementation. The financial planner can gather some idea of the estate planning needs of the clients from their personal background, life goals, and financial status. However, the actual recommendation and the ways to implement these recommendations should be validated by licensed legal and accounting experts. Most general financial planners do not give detailed recommendations unless they are licensed legally to do so, or have someone qualified in their team for such a task. Nevertheless, the financial planner should at least know enough to conduct an overall analysis (e.g., establishing a will or a trust) and point the client in the right direction.

RECOMMENDATIONS RELATED TO ESTATE PLANNING

1. Basic estate planning advice would include preparing a will. While there are professional services available which provide will-writing at a very affordable cost, financial planners can help by understanding the life goals of their clients and advising them on how to protect their wishes through a legal procedure.

2. In the process of preparing a will, family secrets and conflicts among family members may surface. The financial planner must be discrete and make sure that all information is kept confidential. Recently, some accounting and legal firms have used will-writing as an entry point to establish client relationship for further financial planning services. Recommendations on estate planning must involve the clients or even their beneficiaries so that the arrangement is acceptable to everybody. This can reduce the problem of future family conflicts and disputes. Of course, in real life most wills are based on the sole decision of the clients and making everybody happy is impossible. In this case, financial planners have to prepare themselves psychologically for endless complaints and lobbying from family members who are not happy with the will.

3. When a trust is involved in estate planning, the focus is normally on tax benefits and confidentiality. A trust is also related to legacy planning and the implementation of systematic charitable donations. Recommendations in this area normally require legal and accounting expertise. The financial planner's role may be limited if he is not licensed in this area. The financial planner should also point out the drawbacks of using trusts in their recommendations. In some cases, the trusts are irrevocable. The inflexibility of trust arrangements should be clearly understood by clients.

4. When the recommendations are related to taxation, the financial planner should evaluate the overall benefits of the estate planning recommendations and the tax planning recommendations so that an integrated conclusion can be reached for these strategies.

10.3   Presenting a Financial Plan

The Financial Plan in Written Form

It is important that the financial plan be presented in written form. A written plan helps financial planners to go through all the recommendations, one by one, to make sure that they are valid.

Since financial planners need to present a lot of information to their clients, the clients need time to go through the plan to understand it. A written plan allows time for clients to read the information more carefully before, during, and after the presentation. In addition, a document in black and white provides legal protection to both parties. Particularly when there is a dispute, a written document can be used as a piece of evidence. You should always mark "Private and Confidential" on the cover of the financial plan to protect your client's privacy.

The Content of a Financial Plan

core content Refers to the essential components of the financial plan which may include the executive summary, scope of engagement, financial objectives and current financial status, assumptions, financial planning strategy, specific recommendations, and forecast.

Here, we divide the content of a financial plan into core content and other content. **Core content** refers to the necessary and essential components of the plan in terms of allowing the clients to understand the key issues. Material in the other content section may still be important but not critical in the presentation process. It does not mean, however, that it is less important than the core content. In addition, the various sophistication levels of the clientele from different countries may require a different mix of core content and other content. Below we provide a list of core content and other content based on the assumption of a sophisticated financial planning industry where fee-based advisory exists.

Core Content of a Financial Plan

The core content includes the necessary information for the clients to know before they can understand and act upon the financial planning recommendations in the financial plan. The core content of a financial plan consists of, but is not limited to, the parts suggested here:

1.   Executive summary

The executive summary of the full written plan should not exceed 400–500 words, and should ideally fit one page. The purpose of the summary is to list the key recommendations and potential outcomes of the plan.

2.   Scope of engagement

For a well-developed financial planning industry with educated clients willing to accept fee-based financial planning, it is acceptable to provide the scope of engagement as part of the core content. The scope of engagement is a major component in the Practice Standards 100 Series (step 1). It states the boundary of services, responsibilities for both the client and the planner, and reward system under the mutually defined principle. If possible, it should also provide a discussion on the frequency and the nature of monitoring activities (step 6).

If the financial planning service is at least partially fee-based, it would be easy to spell out the scope of engagement. However, if the financial planning services are being practiced in a less developed market, where commission-based planning is the mainstream practice, then some of the content in the scope of engagement cannot be determined until the clients accept the recommendations which are mostly tied to product implementation. In this case, it may make more sense to defer the scope of engagement to a later section or even to the end of the plan in the form of an authorization to proceed or scope of engagement for implementation.

3. Financial objectives and current financial status

In the Practice Standards 200 Series (step 2), the planner is required to help the client to identify and prioritize his goals. Client data are also collected in this step. Thus, it is logical to include these findings in the core content. It helps clients to review their goals and data before the analysis is shown to them. This section reports the current financial situation, financial goals, and risk profile of the clients.

4. Assumptions

Besides using the data from the clients, financial planners need to make assumptions of various factors in order to complete the analysis. Therefore, financial planners should state the assumptions and explain to the clients what may happen under different circumstances. The usual assumptions include inflation rate, income level, investment return, retirement contribution, consumption level, and tax rate.

5. Financial planning strategy

In a financial plan, there should be a section describing the strategies to help the clients in achieving the financial objectives. The strategies serve as a framework to form the specific recommendations. A major item in this section is the investment policy statement.

6. Specific recommendations

Owing to the technical nature and the length of the documentation, the analysis of the client's current financial status in step 3 is deferred to other content as reference. Here, we move to step 4; the Practice Standards 400 Series requires the provision of recommendation alternatives, preferably alternatives under different scenarios. The specific recommendations include cash flow planning (income/expenditure planning), investment/savings recommendations, retirement planning, insurance planning, estate planning, and financial calculations. For simplicity, we suggest that financial planners provide a summary of the main points of the recommendations, preferably in bullet-point form. A brief summary enables the clients to have a quick review of the advice in the financial plan.

7. Forecast

The forecast is a result of the financial analysis and recommendations. Since the financial plan is devised to achieve the financial objectives of clients, financial planners need to illustrate how the clients can achieve their objectives in the future using the forecast. Also, financial planners have to explain clearly to their clients the implications of the forecast under different assumptions.

Other Content of a Financial Plan

The other content of a financial plan includes the information which is important but not necessarily critical for clients to understand. The other content may be composed of, but is not limited to, the parts suggested here:

1. Authorization to proceed (product implementation)

authorization form
An engagement letter for implementation which formalizes the fiduciary relationship between clients and financial planners and establishes the basis upon which the financial planning services are to be provided.

If the financial planning recommendations presented are accepted, the clients should sign an **authorization form** (engagement letter for implementation) or document which formalizes the fiduciary relationship between clients and financial planners and establishes the basis upon which the financial planning services are to be provided. This authorization form or document, included as part of the other content of the financial plan, serves as an authorization to proceed. The form, once signed by the clients, represents the written instructions from the clients to allow the financial planners to proceed to implement the financial plan.

The letter of engagement should have been prepared and written in step 1 of the financial planning process when financial planners and clients mutually define the scope of the engagement. In step 4 the clients should sign the authorization to proceed or letter of engagement formally in the financial plan if they have not signed anything in step 1, or they should sign again the instruction for implementation if they have already signed once the letter of engagement prepared in step 1.

2. Disclosure of fees and commissions

The plan must contain a clear description of the services provided by the financial planner, and the exact amount of fees and commissions charged by the financial planner. According to the Code of Ethics and Professional Responsibility, financial planners should provide services with integrity. Therefore, the financial planners should not mislead the clients about the types of services provided and the amount of fees charged. In addition, clients have the right to know the full cost of implementing the financial planning recommendations suggested in the financial plan. This information should be clearly disclosed in the main body of the written plan rather than being camouflaged or disclosed in the form of notes, appendices, or at the very end of the written report.

3.   Disclosure of potential conflict of interests and limitations

Financial planners, being the agents of the principals (clients), owe a fiduciary duty to their clients which includes a duty of disclosure. The duty of disclosure is the responsibility to disclose sufficient and relevant information about any potential conflict of interest to the clients in order to maintain mutual trustfulness. Examples of the information to be disclosed to clients include fees and commissions that relate to the investments recommended and restrictions on the advice that financial planners can provide.

4.   Disclaimers

disclaimer A statement
which expresses the
limitation of the liability
of the financial planner
to the client.

A **disclaimer** is a statement that expresses the attempt of the financial planners to restrict or limit their liability to the clients. The inclusion of the disclaimer in the written financial plan is a method of notifying the clients that the financial planners engaged cannot be held responsible for all the events that are outside their control.

5.   Supporting documentation

In order to provide evidence for the clients that the financial planning recommendations are the result of complete, competent, and detailed analysis about the clients (e.g., the use of financial calculations, economic indicators, scenario analysis), financial planners should include the supporting documents to show how they came up with the financial planning recommendations in the written financial plan. This supporting documentation part should be positioned at the rear section of the written report following the disclosure and disclaimer sections. The supporting documents may be in hard or soft copy.

Preparatory Work Before, During, and After the Presentation

As financial planners focus on the financial planning recommendations, such as whether the recommendations are good enough to persuade the clients to act upon them; whether the forecast is realistic and accurate enough to predict the future position; or whether the strategies are practical enough to achieve the financial objectives, they may neglect some seemingly less important issues. These include a proper meeting venue and time (so that clients and planners will not be disturbed); advance preparation so that a smooth and clear presentation can be delivered; and optimal timing and amount of information (so that clients will not be overloaded with unnecessary information). The ability to handle these points, although minor, may also affect the impression clients have of the financial planners. Therefore financial planners should also bear in mind the following points which, although not directly related to the financial planning recommendations, may influence the impression that clients have of the financial planners:

Before the Presentation

Before financial planners present the financial plan to their clients, financial planners should double-check to see if the correct name of the client is printed on the front cover of the report, that the document is organized in the right sequence, and that the presentation aids and auxiliary equipment are ready to guarantee a smooth presentation.

When the financial plan is ready, financial planners should do some preparatory work on the venue for the meeting with the clients. These include making sure that the room is tidy, that the client's chair is positioned with a clear view of the computer screen, and that the room temperature is comfortable enough. The environment of the meeting room should be comfortable and quiet so that the client will not be distracted. These preparations before the presentation should help minimize the mistakes made by financial planners. With fewer mistakes, the likelihood of having the clients accept the financial plan can be enhanced.

During the Presentation

In the meeting, when financial planners need to present the financial plan to the clients, financial planners should explain the content in the financial plan clearly. To increase the likelihood of acceptance, financial planners have to make sure that the clients fully understand the financial plan. Financial planners should not give any misleading or false information in an attempt to deceive the clients into accepting the financial plan. They should inform the clients about all the necessary costs, expenses, and fees of the services associated with the execution of the financial plan. Preferably, all these costs and fees should be explicitly documented on paper.

During the presentation, financial planners should from time to time invite and encourage clients to ask questions. This kind of client-planner interaction enables financial planners to know whether the clients are interested in the financial plan and whether they understand it. It may be helpful for financial planners to make a bullet-point list of the main issues. Particularly when the more complicated aspects of the financial plan are to be addressed, financial planners have to be careful not to lose the attention and interest of the clients as many clients lose patience when they do not understand something. Financial planners can maintain the attention of the clients by taking short breaks and being precise and brief.

It is very important that financial planners should avoid pushing the clients too aggressively to accept the financial plan. For many clients who have limited knowledge about investment, retirement, and tax issues, the financial plan is a complicated and technical document. Financial planners should give sufficient time for the clients to digest the details of the financial plan.

Financial planners may suggest that the clients take the financial plan home to discuss it with other family members and to consult the advice of other professionals such as their tax accountants, insurance agents, and lawyers. If clients hesitate to accept the financial plan, the financial planners should offer to arrange another meeting for further discussion, perhaps in two weeks' time.

If clients eventually accept the financial plan, financial planners should obtain a written consent from the clients.

After the Presentation

After the presentation, clients may have a lot of questions about the financial plan. Financial planners should answer the questions clearly and patiently. Since there is a time period between the collection of clients' data and the development and presentation of the financial plan, the information used by financial planners to formulate the recommendations may change. In addition, there are times that the clients may have expressed their financial objectives incorrectly or the financial planners may have misinterpreted the financial objectives. In such a case, the financial planners may need to make amendments to accommodate the more updated information.

Financial planners should make a detailed record of the meeting. It is essential that they inform their clients that any changes will be verified by the clients in writing. A confirmation letter should be given to the clients including the amendments of the plan and a request for a signed statement for the amendments.

client declaration form A form signed by the client which represents a formal approval of the financial plan by the client.

When clients fully understand the financial plan and are satisfied with the recommendations, financial planners should obtain a formal approval of the financial plan from the clients through a **client declaration form**. In the client declaration form, the clients may declare that (note that the list of things to be declared suggested here is not exhaustive):

- The information connected with the financial status and the objectives in the financial plan is accurate and real.
- Any important information is not missing.
- The financial planner has already explained the relationship between risk and return of the recommended portfolio, the assumptions used, and the recommendations.
- The clients understand and know about the disclosed expenses and commission.

Besides the client declaration form, another form the financial planners must obtain from the clients is the authorization to proceed form. This represents the instruction of the clients for the financial planners to commence the implementation of the financial plan. In some cases, the authorization to proceed is incorporated in the letter of engagement.

FINANCIAL PLANNING IN PRACTICE

An Interview with Elaine Bedel, Chair of the Certified Financial Planner Board of Standards 2002

Can you give some comments on step 4 of the six-step personal financial planning process?

This step may represent the "heart" of the financial plan. During this step, the planner develops strategies that will allow clients to meet their goals. Multiple strategies or alternatives may be developed. The planner must then communicate the strategies in a manner that allows the client to have a full understanding of the actions that need to be taken and the potential outcomes. If the client does not understand the strategies, he or she may be reluctant to move into the implementation stage. When there are several strategies or alternatives that would allow the client to achieve his or her goals, the planner needs to discuss the pros and cons of each strategy with the client. The client's input will be needed to determine the most appropriate strategy to recommend.

In some cases, the planner may determine that there is no suitable strategy that will allow the client to achieve his or her goals. In this case, the planner must be ready to discuss with the client the need to be more realistic and to revise his or her goals. An example would be retirement. Perhaps the client wants to retire at an early age with a specific level of lifestyle, e.g., to be able to spend freely. The planner may have to discuss more appropriate or realistic alternatives with the client, such as either retiring at a later age or reducing desired spending.

Key Terms

authorization form   *317*

client declaration form   *320*

core content   *315*

disclaimer   *318*

Questions &Problems

Multiple-choice Questions

1. The financial planning practitioner shall consider sufficient and relevant alternatives to the client's current course of action in an effort to reasonably meet the client's _____.
   A. total satisfaction
   B. goals, needs, and priorities
   C. minimum expectation of fees
   D. wants

2. The financial planning practitioner shall communicate the recommendations in a manner and to an extent reasonably necessary to assist the client in _____.
    A. pursuing his dreams
    B. meeting the client's budget
    C. making an informed decision
    D. maximizing client's utility

3. Which of the following make up the core content of a financial plan?
    I.   Forecast
    II.   Executive summary
    III. The client's existing portfolio details
    IV.   Statement of current situation and financial objectives
    V.   The past performance of investment recommended by the financial planner

    A. I, II and IV
    B. II, III, and IV
    C. I, III, IV, and V
    D. II, III, IV, and V

4. It is important to present a financial plan in written form because _____.
    I.   it provides clients with ample opportunity to consider the advice
    II.   it gives legal protection and a sound basis for future planning
    III. it provides legal protection to the licensee
    IV.   it serves as a proof that the financial planner has delivered the financial planning service to the client

    A. I and II
    B. I, II, and III
    C. I, II, and IV
    D. II, III, and IV

Problems

1. In developing recommendation for clients, why it is important to provide alternative recommendations?

chapter 11

Steps 5 and 6: Implementing and Monitoring the Financial Plan

11.1 Practice Standards 500 Series and 600 Series

There are two sections in the Practice Standards 500 Series for implementing the financial planning recommendations: 500-1 and 500-2. There is only one section, 600-1, in the Practice Standards 600 Series for monitoring the financial planning recommendations.

Practice Standards 500 Series

After the financial plan is developed, presented, and accepted, financial planners have to implement the recommendations suggested in the financial plan. The Practice Standards 500 Series serves as a guide for financial planners to know how to implement the financial plan for clients in accordance with the Code of Ethics and Professional Responsibility of the CFP Board.

The Principles of the Code of Ethics and Professional Responsibility which are related to the Practice Standards 500 Series are objectivity (Principle 2), competence (Principle 3), fairness (Principle 4), professionalism (Principle 6), and diligence (Principle 7).

According to the objectivity principle, financial planners should be free from bias when providing professional services to clients. Therefore, when implementing and executing the financial plan, particularly when selecting the products and services for the clients, financial planners should act in the interest of the clients (Rule 201).

Financial planners should implement and execute the financial plan for the clients competently and maintain the necessary knowledge and skill to continue to do so in those responsibilities mutually agreed on. In the first part of step 5, the responsibilities of the financial planners include identifying activities necessary for implementation and selecting and securing products and services. If the financial planners lack the professional competence to implement the financial plan and to select strategies, they should seek help and/or refer clients to other experts (Rule 302). In such a case, the financial planners should coordinate with other professionals for executing the financial plan.

The principle of fairness requires financial planners to perform professional services in a manner that is fair and reasonable to clients. According to Rule 402, financial planners should make timely written disclosure of all material information relative to the professional relationship. In particular, financial planners should, in writing, disclose conflicts of interest and sources of compensation.

The principle of professionalism requires that the conduct of financial planners should bring credit to the profession in all matters. In order to enhance their professional image, financial planners should behave with dignity and courtesy to the clients, fellow professionals, and other related professionals. Financial planners should only provide services for which they are qualified and are licensed as qualified by local regulations (Rule 609). Financial planners can only be perceived as professionals if they use their professional judgment in selecting the products and services that are in the interest of the clients. Professional judgment incorporates both qualitative and quantitative information. In addition, Rule 606 requires the financial planners to perform services in accordance with the applicable laws, rules, and regulations of governmental agencies and other applicable authorities.

As in all the four previous steps of the financial planning process, financial planners should act diligently in implementing the financial plan for clients. Rule 703 of the diligence principle states that financial planners should implement the recommendations that are suitable for clients. In addition, Rule 704 suggests that financial planners should make reasonable investigations regarding the products and services to be selected for the execution of the financial plan.

Compliance with the practice standards is one way to increase the value of the financial planning profession in the eyes of the public. Implementing the financial planning recommendations using the appropriate products and services for the clients increases the credibility of the financial planning profession over time.

500-1: Agreeing on Implementation Responsibilities

> The financial planning practitioner and the client shall mutually agree on the implementation responsibilities consistent with the scope of the engagement.

The clients are the ones who are responsible for accepting or rejecting the financial planning recommendations. If clients accept the financial plan, the clients and financial planners have to mutually agree on the services, if any, to be provided by the financial planners. It is at this time that the clients and the financial planners know exactly what kinds of financial planning services are provided. Therefore, if the kinds of services agreed on mutually by clients and financial planners in step 5 are different from the scope of engagement originally and mutually defined in step 1 in accordance with Practice Standard 100-1, the scope of engagement should be modified accordingly.

Practice Standard 500-1 specifies the responsibilities of the financial planners. These include identifying activities necessary for implementation of the financial plan; determining division of activities between the financial planners and the clients; referring the clients to other professionals; coordinating the services and activities with other professionals; sharing information as authorized by the clients; and selecting and securing products and/or services.

If there are conflicts of interest, sources of compensation, or material relationships with other professionals or advisors that have not been previously disclosed, the financial planners should disclose them at this time before the financial plan is implemented. If the financial planners are not that competent to implement the responsibilities as mutually agreed on, they may need to refer the clients to other professionals or advisors. When referring their clients to other professionals, they should tell their clients on what basis they have chosen these professionals.

500-2: Selecting Products and Services for Implementation

> **The financial planning practitioner shall select appropriate products and services that are consistent with the client's goals, needs, and priorities.**

Once clients have delegated the implementing responsibilities to the financial planners in accordance with Practice Standard 500-1, the financial planners can execute the financial plan. According to Practice Standard 500-2, financial planners should select the products and services that reasonably address the needs of their clients. The financial planners must bear in mind that the products and services selected to implement the financial planning recommendations must be suitable to the financial situation of the clients and consistent with the goals, needs, and priorities as mutually defined in step 2 of the financial planning process.

According to Practice Standard 500-1, financial planners are allowed to refer the clients to other professionals to seek advice. However, the products and services selected by the financial planners may differ from those selected by other professionals. In implementing the financial plan, more than one product or service may exist that can reasonably meet the goals, needs, and priorities of the clients.

Practice Standards 600 Series

The last step of the financial planning process is to monitor the financial plan to make sure that it is carried out properly.

The Practice Standards 600 Series relates to the Code of Ethics and Professional Responsibility through the Principle of Diligence and Rule 702. Rule 702 requires financial planners to enter into an engagement only after sufficient information is obtained to satisfy that the relationship is warranted by the goals and objectives. In addition, financial planners should have the ability to either provide requisite competent services or to involve other professionals to provide such services.

By complying with the Practice Standards 600 Series, financial planners and clients mutually agree on the monitoring responsibilities. Such a mutual agreement increases the potential for client satisfaction. The chances of a misunderstanding between financial planners and clients can be minimized if the responsibilities are clarified. As the Practice Standards 600 Series also promotes the awareness that financial planning is a dynamic process rather than a static process, it is also the responsibility of the financial planners to modify the financial plan whenever necessary.

600-1: Defining Monitoring Responsibilities

The financial planning practitioner and client shall mutually define monitoring responsibilities.

The purpose of the Practice Standards 600 Series is to clarify the role of the financial planners in the monitoring process of step 6. By clarifying and mutually defining this monitoring responsibility, the expectations of the clients are more likely to be in alignment with the level of monitoring services to be provided by the financial planners. Financial planners should make a reasonable effort to define and communicate to their clients the monitoring activities that the financial planners are able and willing to provide. Financial planners are to explain to their clients what is to be monitored, the frequency of monitoring, and the communication method. In doing so, clients can have a better understanding of the monitoring service to be provided.

Throughout the monitoring process, there are times when financial planners need to reinitiate the steps of the financial planning process because financial planning is a dynamic process rather than a single process. The financial situation of the clients may change. The economic and market conditions may change. The goals and objectives of the clients may change. If there are changes in the financial planning process, the current scope of the engagement and the financial plan may have to be modified accordingly to accommodate the changes.

11.2 Step 5: Implementing the Financial Plan

Important Issues in Implementing the Financial Plan

According to the Practice Standards 500 Series, the implementing responsibilities of the financial planners include selecting financial products and services; identifying the duties of financial planners and clients under the action plan, and coordinating with other professionals with the authorization of the clients. From time to time, financial planners and clients may have to evaluate the success of the implementation plan. The success may be measured by the accuracy or appropriateness of the selection of asset allocation and investment strategies; effectiveness of the strategies to achieve the financial objectives of the clients; and timeliness of implementing the strategies.

Timing of Implementation

Since there are so many goals and objectives to be achieved, financial planners may categorize the goals and objectives in terms of immediacy. The action plan is executed according to the immediacy of the objectives. The recommendations which are easily affected by the timeliness of the transactions should be implemented first and those for which timing is not important can be executed later.

Communication with Clients

After the action plan is formulated, financial planners should explain the procedures and strategies of each step to achieve the objectives and discuss with the clients if any amendments are needed. In addition, financial planners can ask if the clients have any other requests that the financial planners can fulfill. Finally, although the financial plan has been accepted, financial planners should continue to keep in contact with their clients.

Coordination with other Professionals

When financial planners need to implement the strategies as documented in the financial plan, these strategies may be related to some area of expertise in which the financial planners may not be that competent. Although professional financial planners have all-round knowledge in many areas including accounting, tax matters, finance, investment, and insurance, it is unrealistic to assume that the financial planners possess more specialized know-how than the experts who hold educational and professional qualifications and working experience in these areas. Therefore, when financial planners need to implement strategies in areas where they are not professionally competent, they are allowed to seek help from qualified experts (Rule 302).

Maintenance of Records

Financial planners have to obtain personal and financial data from clients throughout the financial planning process. All financial planning firms should have guidelines for the financial planners to follow for maintaining the records of clients.

Financial planners have a fiduciary relationship with their clients. One of the fiduciary duties is the responsibility to keep information about the principals (clients) confidential. The disclosure of information, intentional or unintentional, without the consent of the clients, no matter whether the information is confidential or material, intrudes the privacy rights and violates the discretion duty (Principle 5 of confidentiality of the CFP Board's Code of Ethics and Professional Responsibility).

In addition, financial planners can only collect data that is essential for the financial planning process. Financial planners are not allowed to let unauthorized persons access to the data; to disclose the data; and to use the data on non-financial planning-related activities without the prior consent of the clients. One of the principles for the use of client data is the security of personal data. It is important that financial planners use appropriate security measures for the access and processing of personal data. Therefore, financial planners have to maintain clients' data properly. Such a commitment to maintain good records of the clients is critical for maintaining a long-term relationship with the clients and to enhance the professional image of financial planners in the eyes of the public.

The records may be kept in paper documents or in electronic format. Therefore, maintenance and security measures should be for both paper and electronic records. For example, paper files of client data should be locked in a drawer. Computer files of client data should be accessed by authorized persons only using passwords.

One may ask, what about the records of "incomplete clients" (individuals who started the financial planning process but gave up in the middle)? Do

incomplete client
Someone who has a partial relationship with, but is not a formal client of, the financial planner.

financial planners need to maintain good records of these incomplete clients as well? Occasionally, these **incomplete clients** may have provided some personal and financial data to the financial planners before they decided to say "no" to the services. In such a case, the financial planners should still keep good records of these incomplete clients. Although these incomplete clients do not have any business relationship with the financial planners yet, there is a possibility that they may come back and ask the financial planners for financial planning advice again in the future. Keeping good records of these incomplete clients is one way to give a good impression of the financial planners to the incomplete clients. In addition, if there are legal disputes from the incomplete clients regarding the financial planners and the financial planning firms, these records can be part of the evidence to protect them in court.

11.3   Step 6: Monitoring the Financial Plan

Sources of Changes and the Corresponding Strategies

macro-level factors
Major economic events that affect the planning needs of a client.

micro-level factors
Major personal events that affect the planning needs of a client.

Financial planners need to monitor the implemented financial plan constantly to check if there are changes affecting the achievement of the financial plan. Changes can be categorized into two types in the context of financial planning: changes at the **macro-level** and changes at the micro-level (or personal level). **Macro-level** changes include changes in interest rate, inflation rate, economic conditions, tax regulations, and social security system. Examples of changes at the personal level are changes in wages, annual living expenses, employment status, lifestyle, marital status, and birth or death of family members. Both macro- or micro-level changes exert an impact on the development, implementation, and achievement of the financial plan. Therefore, the monitoring responsibilities should include a review of the financial planning strategies embodied in the financial plan.

Changes in Macro-level Factors

In Chapter 3, we introduced you to some macroeconomic factors and their impact on financial planning. Here we review some of these macroeconomic factors and examine how they should be monitored and what appropriate action needs to be taken.

Economic conditions can be measured by different indicators. Well-known leading indicators include money supply, stock prices, and consumer confidence. Some examples of lagging indicators are prime rate, duration of unemployment, and commercial and industrial loans outstanding. When the economy has shown signs of recession (either based on evidence of significant decline in output, income, employment and trade for 6 months to a year, or on the technical definition of two consecutive quarters of real GDP decline), financial planners have to examine the potential impact of a weak economy on clients' job security, income level, investment returns, and risk tolerance level. As different industries and different occupations within the industry can be affected differently by an economic downturn, financial planners should not assume that bad economic conditions would exert similar influence on clients.

For instance, a recession driven by a substantial decline in exports for an export-oriented economy such as Australia and Japan can be damaging to the shipping and transportation industries in these countries. However, during recession and high unemployment, the education sector (especially vocational training programs and graduate programs) may benefit as people tend to believe additional education is needed to enhance the human capital under economic turbulence. Financial planners should try and understand how the poor economic conditions affect different occupations so that they can evaluate their clients' financial plans better.

Very often, poor economic conditions are accompanied by poor stock market performance. Overall investors' confidence in the stock market and their risk tolerance level can be affected by their own job security and labor income. Financial planners should talk to their clients and ascertain if the feeling of insecurity is valid. In addition, if clients have a lot of purchasing power in terms of investment and the overall market is devalued due to irrational sentiment, it is possible for these clients to invest more in undervalued securities. However, if the market conditions are good, it is recommended that financial planners should not aim at getting short-term gains by active trading activities. Some aggressive clients may actually urge the planners to trade more. Financial planners should be prepared to educate their clients about the long-term nature of their investment portfolio in financial planning.

In short, economic conditions have a dynamic relationship with financial planning. Financial planners should set up their own system for monitoring these variables and implement appropriate strategies for clients of different backgrounds and investment profiles. Experience tells us that financial planners normally get more business and attention from the media when the stock markets perform poorly. It is because less active or longer-term investment portfolios are normally diversified, and are less sensitive to market declines than the more active and aggressive portfolios, which tend to make more money in good times, but also lose more in bad times.

Changes in government policies related to taxes on personal income, business income, property, and estate can directly affect the financial planner's strategies on tax planning, retirement planning, investment portfolio, and estate planning. They can also indirectly affect insurance strategies, and consumption planning for clients as well. Monetary policies on interest rate and exchange rate can also affect inflation, property prices, investment returns, and the affordability of mortgage. Financial planners should closely monitor the relevant aspects of the clients' financial plans and study how they are affected by the changes in these policies and financial variables.

Where investment strategies are concerned, it is difficult to precisely predict market conditions. We can only guess what is more likely to happen in the securities market. Financial planners should remember the principles of diversification and focus on long-term investment strategies. Capturing undervalued stocks and shifting assets under the right timing may sound good, but such strategies are not the focus of a financial planner. A continuous monitoring of market conditions to avoid substantial losses in a major market crash is much more important than speculating on the upside potential of the market.

Changes in Micro-level Factors

While there are many micro-level or personal factors that can lead to changes in the financial plan, it is not possible to capture all of them. Some of the key factors are listed here.

Employment

Employment can be affected by both macro-level or personal factors. The accumulation of savings is based on the assumption of a continuous income till retirement. If there is a risk of unemployment, financial planners should assess what it would do to their clients' financial health. Nowadays, owing to globalization, international trade, and development of information technology, jobs are more uncertain than ever. Even if clients can stay employed, their income can vary substantially at different life stages. Financial planners have to keep an eye on the rise and fall of various industries and occupations in the local economy so that a more accurate assessment of employability and income level of clients can be made. Of course, employment is also subject to personal factors that are totally unpredictable. Financial planners should have a contingency plan ready to handle sudden unemployment of clients in order to meet their immediate consumption needs and their long-term financial needs.

So far, we have focused on the effects of employment on future income and savings. Sometimes, employment issues affect more than the financial needs of the client. For instance, job relocation goes beyond income changes and affects other needs of clients as well. Due to globalization of businesses and consequently the labor market, especially for managerial and highly skilled jobs, job relocation to another city or country is getting more common. The actual disposable income and savings can be higher or lower, depending on the net effect of many factors including cost-of-living adjustments, income adjustment, tax burdens, education allowances for children, and the decision of whether the immediate family members would move together or not. In addition, the amount of insurance coverage and education funds needed may also be affected. As the client is moving far away, the planner has to figure out a way to maintain the planning relationship, or prepare for transition of certain aspects of the clients' services to other planners who are located at that geographical location. Finally, job relocation for a considerable time period can actually change one's life goals. Financial planners have to advise their clients facing relocation about their options and potential challenges related to their financial needs.

Marriage

At the personal level, getting married is a cause for joy. However, the related current and future financial responsibilities must be properly addressed. The immediate needs include wedding expenses, additional expenditure or investment for a bigger home, and additional life insurance and medical insurance. There is no fixed formula to calculate how much money is needed, but one thing is certain—there will be a change in consumption and savings behavior. Financial planners should go through the financial implications of getting married with their clients. In addition, they can provide careful suggestions for the wedding budget, always keeping in mind that their role is to design the financial plan to fulfill the clients' goals. They should never impose their personal judgment on what those life goals should be or the appropriate levels of expenditure in fulfilling the goals.

Children

Just like marriage, having children brings joy and fulfillment, but along with it come substantial financial responsibilities. For clients who want to provide private school education for their children, the financial commitment can be as high as the amount needed for their retirement. Consumption needs, insurance needs, and investment needs will be affected. Some clients may be interested in exploring the financial commitment of having kids with their financial planners. It is a good idea for financial planners to introduce the topic and briefly advise clients on the financial commitment of having children during a regular session. If the clients are interested, additional consultation sessions can be arranged.

Death of Immediate Family Members

The emotional distress of losing a loved one can be substantial. A caring and considerate financial planner should provide emotional support to the bereaved client. The financial planner should help the client to deal with the paperwork for the insurance or even some aspects of the funeral arrangements if necessary. It is also possible that some clients would want a change in lifestyle after experiencing such a personal loss. The financial planner should keep an eye on the client for a period of time in order to determine if changes in other planning areas are needed.

Major Health Problems

Health insurance may not be able to cover all the medical expenses if the health problem is a long-term one. A substantial portion of the client's savings may be used up to pay the medical bills. And even if the client is fully recovered physically, it may take longer for the client to heal psychologically. Major health problems affect insurance needs, consumption needs, and sometimes retirement needs as well. If the health problem is severe, there may also be implications on estate planning.

Monitoring Investment Portfolios

In order to effectively monitor a portfolio's performance and make timely changes to the asset allocation mix, financial planners must establish a simple but useful portfolio evaluation system. Normally, there are two types of portfolio monitoring tools. The first helps to track the portfolio changes by recording the transactions and corresponding profits and losses. Most people use spreadsheets to handle this task. The macro-functions of Excel can handle a few portfolios with 20–30-

million dollars worth of investment products. For a financial planner with more clients, a commercial grade portfolio tracking software will be needed.

The second tool is a portfolio optimization program. The most basic and commonly used routine involves a mean-variance optimization algorithm based on Harry Markowitz's portfolio theory and efficient frontier. The optimization program helps us to compute the optimal mix of asset classes. Based on the risk-return trade-offs and correlations among these asset classes, the portfolio frontier consisting of the most efficient (highest return at a given risk level) investment choices can be identified. In wealth management, unless substantial changes occur in macroeconomic and financial market conditions, major adjustment to the portfolio mix should not be needed. Nevertheless, wealth managers should monitor the market closely and make sure that the most updated forecasts of risk-return data are used in estimating the portfolio choices. In Chapter 14, we will learn about some advanced asset allocation strategies and portfolio performance evaluation. It is quite difficult for an individual to keep track of investment products, market conditions, and portfolio performances all by himself. Consequently, wealth managers should consider forming teams and make use of existing research support from the companies to handle these tasks collaboratively.

Maintaining a Long-term Relationship with Clients

Once the financial plan is developed and presented by the financial planners, is accepted by the clients, and is implemented by the financial planners, it seems that both the objectives of the clients and the financial planners for financial planning services are fulfilled. Does that imply the end of the relationship? The answer, of course, is "no."

Although the acceptance of the financial plan by clients may imply that the financial planners have successfully sold the financial planning services to the clients, the acceptance of the financial plan is not a termination of the relationship between the financial planners and the clients. Besides providing financial planning services for clients, which may be the objective of financial planners in the short term, their long-term objective should be to maintain the client-planner relationship. To maintain a long-term relationship, it is essential to keep in touch with the clients. Financial planners should not give clients the impression that they are no longer important to the financial planners once the financial plan is accepted.

Financial planners can keep in touch with their clients by phone, fax, and e-mail. If clients find the financial planners to be reliable and good, they may introduce more potential clients (friends, relatives, and colleagues) who are also interested in financial planning services. Long-term clients can contribute to a stable and profitable business for the financial planners this way. In addition, a long-term client-planner relationship strengthens the reputation and professional image of the financial planners and the financial planning profession.

Solving Disputes with Clients

According to the Code of Ethics and Professional Responsibility, financial planners should always act in the best interests of their clients. However, disputes and disagreements between people are inevitable, so it is unrealistic to assume that there will never be any dispute or misunderstanding between financial planners and clients. So besides monitoring the implementation of the financial plan, it is also important for financial planners to monitor their relationship with their clients.

First, financial planners need to be aware of the sources of potential disputes in the client-planner relationship. Clients may have misconceptions about the role of financial planners (some of which have been discussed in Chapter 1). They may wrongfully think that the financial planners can fulfill all their financial objectives. Disputes may arise when the performance of the financial planners does not meet the expectation of clients. If there is financial loss in investments, clients may also hold the financial planners responsible.

Disputes and conflicts may arise at any time and may be due to different reasons. We are not able to forecast all types of disputes and problems and recommend solutions to handle them. However, we can suggest some basic rules to deal with disputes. Financial planners should:

- Respect their clients.
- Follow the principle of objectivity and fairness of the Code of Ethics and Professional Responsibility.
- Fully understand the viewpoints and needs of their clients.
- Follow the procedures, professional codes, and legal guidelines in dealing with any disputes.
- Keep records of all conversations, documents, and e-mail with the clients as evidence throughout the financial planning process.

Recent Emphasis on Periodic Review and Plan Monitoring

In the early days, after the implementation stage of the financial plan, financial planners (both fee-based and commission-based) would conduct periodic reviews for their clients as a necessary task of providing comprehensive financial planning services. Recently, there has been an industry-wide awareness of the importance of constantly monitoring the plan (step 6). Through an informal interview, Elizabeth W. Jetton, Chair of the Financial Planning Association (US) 2005, and Principal of Financial Vision Advisors, Inc., has suggested to the author that monitoring activities are needed to measure the progress of reaching the client's financial goals. In addition to the performance of investment portfolios, there are other aspects of the financial plan including the appropriateness of the recommended consumption behavior, initial performance benchmarks, and savings targets, that are important in determining if the original financial goals are still optimal and can be reached as expected.

Elizabeth also points out that while financial planners can help their clients to manage the financial aspects of their lives, learning to control one's own financial affairs cannot be done in a few meetings. It takes time and it may be necessary for clients to discover what they want by a trial-and-error process. Thus a periodical review of the plan and meetings with clients play an important role in fine-tuning the financial and even life goals of clients.

The idea of putting more emphasis on step 6 is also embraced by Ameriprise Financial Services. Ameriprise understands the importance of maintaining a long-term planner-client relationship. In the financial planning business, repeat customers and brand loyalty are two major elements for success. Plan monitoring provides a channel for the financial planners to strengthen these two elements in their services. In short, both large and small financial planning firms are trying to do a better job in monitoring the plans for their clients, which is certainly a win-win situation for the financial planning industry and the consumers.

Key Terms

incomplete client   *329*   micro-level factors   *329*
macro-level factors   *329*

Questions &Problems

Multiple-choice Questions

1. Which of the following are the main responsibilities of a financial planner in implementing the financial plan?
    I.   Conducting a strategic review
    II. Selecting and identifying personal financial investment products or services
    III. Coordinating with other professionals

    A. II only
    B. I and II
    C. II and III
    D. I, II, and III

2. Which of the following statements regarding maintaining client records are correct?
    I.   It is an internal procedure of some general financial planning companies.
    II. The documents are required to be kept continuously in the whole process of business operation.
    III. Only the documents and records of those clients who have accepted the financial plan and suggestions provided by the financial planner should be kept.
    IV. The documents and records can be used as evidence when there are legal disputes against the financial planner or company.

    A. I and III
    B. II and IV
    C. I, II, and III
    D. I, II, and IV

3. Which of the following is the correct sequence of steps in a strategic review?
   1. Review the client's objectives and needs.
   2. Review the financial and investment strategies.
   3. Review the financial plan with the client on time.
   4. Check that the plan is being followed.
   5. Adjust the investment portfolio.
   6. Assess the current value and performance of the investment portfolio.
   7. Assess the advantages and disadvantages of the current investment portfolio.

   A. 1, 2, 6, 7, 5, 3, 4
   B. 1, 6, 7, 5, 2, 3, 4
   C. 2, 1, 7, 6, 3, 5, 4
   D. 3, 1, 2, 7, 6, 5, 4

4. Micro-level factors include _____.
   I. GDP
   II. getting married
   III. having children
   IV. interest rate
   V. business cycle

   A. I only
   B. II and III
   C. II and IV
   D. I, II, III, and V

5. The reasons for maintaining the records of an incomplete client are _____.
   I. in case the client returns and wants to have a financial plan again
   II. to impress the regulatory authority that you keep a record of everything
   III. in case the incomplete client comes and wants a copy of the data
   IV. to serve as evidence when there is a dispute

   A. I only
   B. I and IV
   C. I, III, and IV
   D. II and III

Problems

1. Describe two of the three important issues for plan implementation.

PART III

Wealth Management

Investment Techniques (Part I)

Learning Objectives

After studying this chapter you should be able to:

1 Define risk and return.
2 Understand the portfolio theory.
3 Understand the capital asset pricing model.
4 Understand fundamental analysis.
5 Understand technical analysis.
6 Describe the stock valuation model.

Before we begin our discussion on investments, we would like to state the objective of the investment-related chapters in the book and set the boundary of our coverage. As a wealth manager, understanding the risk-return trade-off of the investment choices available to your clients is a very important task. In addition, knowing how to combine these investment choices into a portfolio in order to pursue the financial goals for your clients is the key to success for wealth management. Unfortunately, to be able to do a good job in these two tasks, the wealth manager has to master all kinds of investment concepts including both basic principles and to advanced theories in investment. The whole area of investment planning for wealth management is so comprehensive that it covers almost all the topics (all three levels) of the Chartered Financial Analyst (CFA®) examinations. Thus, it is really a challenge for us to explain these concepts in a few chapters. After careful consideration, we have decided to take a pragmatic approach: we focus on the techniques and concepts needed to construct a portfolio for the client for long-term goals without explaining in detail the mathematical and conceptual framework. In other words, while we will mention the concepts and techniques of investment, this book will not teach you all the quantitative techniques from scratch. We understand that some readers may have a hard time understanding the big picture (portfolio construction) without having the pieces of the puzzle. In this case, please remember that the purpose of this book is to give you an overview on financial planning and wealth management. Additional training and reading in advanced investment and areas of financial planning are needed before you can become a professional in this field.

12.1   Investments in the Context of Financial Planning

In Chapters 4 and 5, we discussed the different components of the financial planning process. One of the components is investment planning. In this chapter we hope to give you a basic understanding of investment planning, especially the concepts to understand risk profiling techniques and the construction of an investment portfolio to meet the predetermined life goals of clients.

So far, we have talked about investments many times. But what is a formal definition of *investments*? Investments can be viewed as a process involving the current commitment of financial resources with the goal of earning an acceptable return while taking the investment period and risk involved into consideration. The term *investments* in the context of personal financial planning is somewhat different from the traditional meaning of investments mentioned in regular textbooks focusing on institutions. In personal financial planning, the investment for a client should be goal-oriented. As life goals are highly correlated with an individual's lifestyle and life cycles, maximizing return is not necessarily a proper objective in investment strategies for financial planning. In addition, the client's risk tolerance, personal profile, and limitation of income and wealth may not always allow him or her to select the portfolio and the necessary trading strategies which can maximize return. In fact, the key motto for investment strategies in financial planning is to adopt long-term investment strategies in order to achieve the life goals of the client instead of just maximizing return.

There is a close relationship between life goals and investment planning. For a young couple with no savings but needs an education fund for a child in 15 years, a 10-year insurance plan with a savings element plus a 15-year investment plan focusing on a medium-risk equity mutual fund should be a good strategy. The key to selecting a good strategy is to first provide some basic insurance protection and then sufficient funds for the basic college education of the child instead of maximizing return by taking high risks, which may result in losses and insufficient money for education.

For a couple planning for retirement in 20 years, the investment strategy should be more aggressive and a higher percentage of equity in the portfolio can be employed. However, if the couple is retiring in 3 years, then the asset allocation mix of the retirement portfolio should be gradually shifted to a fixed income and no more than 20% of the portfolio should be in equity when they reach the retirement age as the fund is needed for daily expenses. Once again, such an investment strategy should focus on the needs of the clients and the goals of the investment rather than maximizing the investment return. Consequently, the choices of the investment vehicle for financial planning can be somewhat limited. All high-risk investment products and strategies such as options, futures, penny stocks, margin trading, high-risk hedge funds, and junk bonds would not be appropriate for financial planning clients.

Let us emphasize that it does not mean that our clients cannot trade aggressively or even speculate in the stock market with risky investment vehicles. As long as the clients have a clear understanding of setting aside enough money for investment planning in order to achieve their life goals, using some of the money for risky investment is not a concern to the financial planners. In fact, speculating in the stock market is a popular hobby for professionals and wealthy individuals. In some ways, investment speculation is no different from gambling on horses and soccer games, or buying fancy cars. But the clients have to have financial discipline not to mix up the "play money" for investment speculation with the money for meeting financial goals.

Finally, it is important for wealthy clients to understand that there is room for them to use alternative investments and high-risk strategies as long as they have professional managers to execute those strategies for them in the framework of a diversified portfolio. As reported in the Merrill Lynch Capgemini World Wealth Report 2004, alternative investments such as hedged funds have become a common asset class used by the ultra-high-net-worth clients. It is not uncommon that these large client portfolios have up to 20% of their money in alternative investments. In addition, these wealthy clients may be able to hire professional money managers who practice active asset allocation strategies with sophisticated quantitative financial modeling for investments. However, the details of these advanced strategies are beyond the scope of this book.

Since this book is targeted at financial planners and wealth managers dealing with middle-income clients, mass-affluent clients, and wealthy clients with a maximum investable asset of about US$1 million, we will focus our discussion on investment strategies with mainstream products. Advanced readers can read the interview with Dr. Wai Lee on tactical asset allocation strategies in the Application Corner in Chapter 14.

12.2   Risk and Return

return The gain or loss from the investment.

risk Refers to the uncertainty of future returns on an investment.

In finance and investment, there are two terms that we have to get familiar with. They are **return** and **risk**.

Return

The return on an investment is the gain or loss from the investment. For instance, the return on an investment in stocks may take two forms. Firstly, the shareholders are entitled to the distribution of the issuing firms, the dividend. Secondly, the shareholders may have capital gain due to the price appreciation of the shares purchased.

There are various ways to measure return. Return can be measured in dollar terms and in percentage terms. Total dollar return is the sum of all cash flows and capital gain (loss) from the investment minus the initial outlays of the investment. If the investment is in stocks, the total dollar return is the sum of dividends and capital gain (loss). If the investment is in fixed-income securities, the total dollar return is the sum of all coupon payments and the difference between par value and selling price of the securities. The percentage return expresses the dollar return as a percentage of the cost (initial outlay) of investment. Since the return of a stock investment is in the form of dividend and capital gain (loss), the percentage return is the sum of dividend yield and capital gain yield.

Dividend yield is defined as follows:

$$\text{Dividend yield} = \frac{\text{Dividend}_{t+1}}{\text{Price}_t}$$

and capital gain yield is defined as:

$$\text{Capital gain yield} = \frac{\text{Price}_{t+1} - \text{Price}_t}{\text{Price}_t}$$

Example

$$\begin{aligned}
\text{Stock price at time } t &= \$100 \\
\text{Stock price at time } t + 1 &= \$110 \\
\text{Dividend at time } t + 1 &= \$5 \\
\text{Dollar return} &= \$5 + (\$110 - \$100) \\
&= \$15 \\
\text{Percentage return} &= \frac{\$5 + (\$110 - \$100)}{\$100} \\
&= 15\%
\end{aligned}$$

Risk

The market is full of uncertainty. Uncertainty may be related to firm-specific characteristics or related to macroeconomic factors such as business cycle, inflation rate, and exchange rate (see Chapter 3). When we consider making an investment, we would like to estimate the expected return of the investment. However, all investments involve some uncertainty of return. In finance, we usually use the term "risk" to refer to uncertainty of future incomes. Risk always exists when the outcome of a set of circumstances or an event is uncertain and so, investment risk is the possible extent to which the future price of an investment may deviate from the expected or forecasted price.

Let us illustrate how risk and expected return are closely related and why we need to consider both risk and expected return together. When we make investment decisions, we should consider the probability of the different states (good or bad) of the market in the future. These different market conditions cause the actual rate of return to deviate from the expected rate of return. The expected return of the investment (expected return$_I$) is the weighted average of returns of all possible scenarios of the investment (rate of return$_{Is}$), with the weight being the probability of occurrence of the scenario (probability$_{Is}$):

$$\text{Expected return}_I = \sum_{s=1}^{n} \text{Probability}_{Is} \times \text{Rate of return}_{Is}$$

In a scenarios analysis, the three commonly used scenarios are: good state, average state, and bad state. Let us say that the probabilities of good, average, and bad states are 0.25, 0.50, and 0.25, respectively. In this example, the $10,000 capital is to be invested in an index fund. When the stock market is in a boom (good state), you will expect to earn $5,000. The rate of return is 50%. However, when the stock market is in a recession (bad state), the rate of return is −10%, losing a dollar value of $1,000. When the stock market is in an average state, the rate of return is 20%. Table 12.1 shows the probability distribution of the scenarios analysis of the example.

In this example, the expected return of the investment is 20%. This rate of return is called "expected" because this 20% may not necessarily be realized all the time. In reality, there is risk (uncertainty) in the market. When the market is in a good state, the investor earns 30% more than the expected return. However, when the market is in an average or bad state, the investor earns 0% or 30% less than the expected return. Therefore, there is always a difference between

Table 12.1 Scenarios analysis

Scenario	State of market	Probability of state	Dollar return	Actual rate of return	Weighted return (WR)	Deviation of actual and expected return
1	Good	0.25	5,000	50%	12.5%	30%
2	Average	0.50	2,000	20%	10%	0%
3	Bad	0.25	−1,000	−10%	−2.5%	−30%
		Σ Prob = 1			Expected return (ΣWR) = 20%	

actual return and expected return. A very simple measure of investment risk is the assessment of the deviation of the actual return from the expected return. Other commonly used measures of dispersion of returns are variance and standard deviation of the distribution of expected returns. Standard deviation for a sample is defined as the squared root of the variance, which is measured as the sum of the squared deviations of the observations from the mean divided by (sample size −1). The larger the values of variance and standard deviation of the distribution (all other things being equal), the wider the dispersion of the distribution and hence the greater the uncertainty or risk for the investment would be.

While standard deviation is a commonly used measure of risk in the academic and professional world, it may not be the best measure of investment risk for most people because standard deviation does not differentiate up-side potential from down-side risk. The calculation procedure of standard deviation treats a deviation of 2% above or below the mean return to be the same. But in real life, making a 2% return is certainly much better than losing 2%. Investors have a very different feeling toward the uncertainty of earning money and losing it. Thus financial planners should consider using other risk measures such as maximum loss or frequency of losses to supplement standard deviation when communicating investment risk to clients.

Risk-Return Trade-off

All rational investors who are reluctant to accept risk are risk averse. Since investors can still earn returns from risk-free assets (default risk-free such as treasury bonds), most are not willing to invest in risky assets if there is no extra reward to compensate for the risk involved. The extra reward for bearing risk or the difference between the expected return of a risk-free asset and a risky asset is called the risk premium. For example, if the coupon rate paid on a 1-year treasury bill is 5%, the risk premium on the investment in the index fund is 8% (the expected return of the index fund is 13%). Therefore, in order to entice the investors to consider investments in risky assets such as stocks and bonds, the issuers of stocks and bonds have to offer a positive risk premium to compensate for the risk in excess of that on risk-free assets. Rational investors would take on a risky investment only if there is a favorable risk-return trade-off or a prospect of a risk premium in the risky asset. The risk-return trade-off is the balance between the desire for the lowest possible risk and for the highest possible returns which an investor must decide. That is why there is a maxim in the market: "High risk, high returns."

As the market is full of investment opportunities of various levels of risk and return, it is rare that the rational investors would make an all-or-nothing investment choice. Therefore, the basic investment decision is how to allocate the capital to different asset classes. This decision is called the choice of asset allocation. Depending on the preference of the investors on the risk-return trade-off, the asset allocation choice is usually the choice among the broad investment classes of varying degrees of risk and return.

Diversification and Portfolio Theory

We have mentioned that the market is full of investment choices. It is extremely unusual that one would invest in a single class of assets. The investment practice of a well-diversified asset allocation is based on the concept of portfolio diversification (Markowitz 1952). In layman's terms, "Do not put all your eggs in one basket." Although diversification is effective in reducing firm-specific risk (unique risk, nonsystematic risk, or diversifiable risk), there are certain risks such as market risk (systematic risk or nondiversifiable risk) that cannot be diversified away.

portfolio theory Gives a formal way to establish the risk-return relation in the portfolio context: as long as the stocks in the portfolio are not perfectly correlated among each other, each additional stock would exert a risk-reducing impact on the aggregate risk of the portfolio.

Based on the mean-variance criterion in **portfolio theory**, as long as the stocks are not perfectly correlated among each other, each additional stock would exert a risk-reducing impact on the aggregate risk of the portfolio. Repeating the step of adding one stock at a time to the portfolio calculation, eventually all stocks will be analyzed and form the space called the feasible set. The feasible set covers the area of which the portfolios can be formed from a given set of stocks. Among all these feasible choices, the best risk-return combination (i.e., mean-variance efficient) is the efficient set. By dropping the lower-tail portion of the efficient set, which consists of inferior choices compared with the upper portion, the remaining portion is called an "efficient frontier" which includes the best possible return at any given point of risk.

An efficient portfolio is characterized by the highest level of return for a given amount of risk. Therefore, the efficient portfolio set (or frontier), which is the border line of the area covered by the feasible set, is a collection of all the efficient portfolios. The investors have to make decision based on the risk-return trade-off governed by the efficient frontier. That is, the investors must choose between how much return they expect and how much risk they can handle. Based on the decision of the efficient frontier, the investors can allocate the appropriate proportion between risk-free and risky assets in their portfolios.

Figure 12.1 shows the formation of the optimal portfolio. We use two indifference curves (A and B) to represent the attitudes of the investors toward risk and return (the risk-return trade-off). Without a risk-free asset, the optimal portfolio for the investor should be the tangency point between the efficient frontier and the indifference curve of the investor. When a risk-free asset is added to the investment choice, the investors can create portfolios with the combination of risky and risk-free assets. In such a case, a new efficient frontier called the

Figure 12.1 Formation of the optimal portfolio

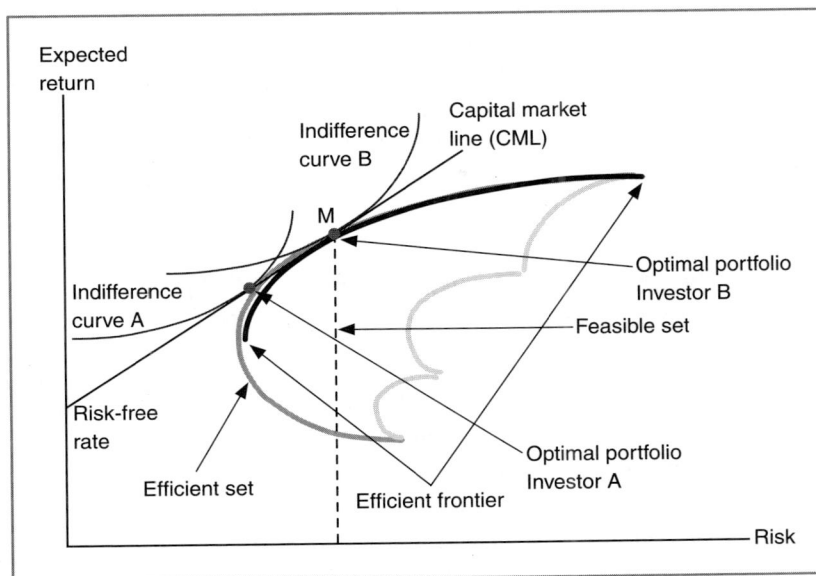

capital market line (CML), which is the line connecting the risk-free rate and point M (the tangency point), is created. As the CML becomes the new efficient frontier, it implies that all portfolios below the CML are inferior to the portfolios on the CML. "Inferior" means that a lower level of return is earned for a given amount of risk or a higher level of risk is borne for a given amount of return. Hence, rational investors should choose a portfolio on the CML.

For a well-diversified portfolio, the risk of an individual stock which is relevant to a portfolio is represented by the beta coefficient of the stock. Beta measures the risk contribution of a stock to the aggregate riskiness of the portfolio. Therefore, a well-diversified portfolio enables the investors to do away with a substantial portion of the total risk of holding stocks. However, as an increasing number of stocks are added to the portfolio, each new stock has a smaller risk-reducing impact on the portfolio. Usually, the portfolio risk decreases slowly after about 40 stocks are added to the portfolio.

In real life, it is important for us to understand the concept of using 40 stocks to form a diversified portfolio, which is based on statistics using over a thousand simulations for each portfolio with a given number of stocks. In other words, the conclusion that 40 stocks can diversify almost all unsystematic risk is based on the average risk of 1,000 portfolios consisting of 40 stocks. However, if a client invests in one portfolio, the actual risk of that particular portfolio can be much higher or lower than the mean risk. Consequently, we cannot practice the textbook conclusion that 40 stocks are sufficient to form a diversified portfolio. It is a conclusion for an average situation with enough observations in a sample but not for a client with only one portfolio. Newbould and Poon (1993) indicate that to minimize the risk of not getting the mean portfolio risk, it will take about 80 stocks in the US to diversify if using only one portfolio. For more details, see Challenge 4 in the section on "Key Issues in Forming the Portfolio" in Chapter 14.

Diversification mixes a wide variety of investments within a portfolio in order to minimize the impact that any one stock has on the overall performance of the portfolio and hence lowers the risk. Investors can achieve diversification by spreading the portfolio among multiple asset classes such as cash, stocks, bonds, mutual funds, and real estate. Then, the investors can select different investments within each asset class. An easy way to choose stocks for diversification is to select securities of different industries, as stocks within the same industry normally have similar risk.

Capital Asset Pricing Model (CAPM) and Arbitrage Pricing Theory (APT)

capital asset pricing model Measures the risk-return relation for each financial asset and provides a standard rate of return or a benchmark for evaluating various potential investment projects.

The portfolio theory developed by Markowitz (1952) provides us with an effective way to diversify unsystematic risk by using a portfolio of financial assets. Portfolio theory also gives us a formal way to establish the risk-return relation in the portfolio context. However, in order to use this concept in calculating portfolio risk and return, we have to know the risk and return for individual assets first. The **capital asset pricing model** (CAPM) built by Sharpe (1963) enables us to measure the risk-return relation for each financial asset. The CAPM has been widely used in financial economics to provide a standard rate of return or a benchmark for evaluating various potential investment projects and an estimate of expected return for an asset not yet traded in the market.

There are several assumptions of the CAPM. In the prediction of the risk and expected return relation, the CAPM assumes a single holding period. All assets are perfectly divisible. For simplicity, there are no tax and transaction costs. The investors are assumed to have identical expectations of risk and return, to be able to borrow and lend unlimited amount at the risk-free rate, and to be price-takers. This implies that no buying and selling activities from anyone can influence the market prices.

The CAPM depicts the risk-return relation of efficient portfolios on the CML. The security market line (SML), which is part of the CAPM and an extension of the CML, describes the risk-return relation for individual stocks. The measure of risk in the SML is the beta coefficient. By the security market line (SML), the return of a stock is defined as follows:

$$\text{Return of stock } i = \text{Risk-free rate} + \text{Beta coefficient of stock } i \times (\text{Market return} - \text{Risk-free rate})$$

The equation mentioned above shows the mathematical relation of asset pricing. Conceptually, we can explain the model by a three-step approach. Step 1 focuses on the market premium (market return − risk-free rate). When the market is at equilibrium, the risky stock market should provide a higher return than the risk-free debt market. Thus, we expect a positive market premium. At a time when the market is at disequilibrium and the risk-free rate is higher than the market return, investors should not put money in the stock market at all.

Most of the time, the market premium is positive and we should go to step 2: calculate the risk premium (beta × market premium) for the stock. A higher beta indicates a higher undiversifiable risk and the investors should demand a higher return for the risk taken. A simple way to estimate such a risk premium is to assume a linear relation between beta and compensation demanded. Thus, the risk premium gives us a good measure of an appropriate return expected by investors to take on the systematic risk inherited by a particular stock.

Finally, step 3 combines risk-free return and risky return to invest in a stock. Without taking risks, the market is willing to pay any investors a risk-free rate to compensate for their opportunity cost of not using the money. By adding a risk-free rate to the risk premium, we can find out the total expected return for investing in any risky assets. By using the three-step approach, we rationally build the logic to calculate the required return for an individual stock. That is also the conceptual framework of the CAPM.

After the proposal of the CAPM, a lot of researchers examined its practicality and validity in real life. One common criticism is that CAPM uses the market risk as the only risk measure. However, many people believe that there is more than one risk factor used by investment professionals to price the stock. Consequently, a multifactor model called the arbitrage pricing theory (APT) was developed by Ross (1976) to better capture different risk factors in pricing a stock. Unfortunately, the APT employs a statistical method called factor analysis, which is a great multivariate mathematical technique, but interpreting the factors created economically is relatively difficult. This is because each factor created in the model can be a combination of different financial and economic variables used in the input process. In addition, in order to generate an accurate APT analysis for each stock, different variables may be selected in the final form. Compared with the CAPM, the APT is definitely more comprehensive and accurate in pricing stocks. However, it is more difficult to conceptualize economically by beginners in the investment arena. In short, we believe that the details of APT are beyond the scope of this book. Sophisticated investment professionals should read other advanced investment books to better understand this concept.

12.3   Valuation Process

As we mentioned in the beginning of this chapter, the whole area of investment planning for wealth management is so comprehensive that it covers almost all the topics (all three levels) of the Chartered Financial Analyst (CFA®) examinations. Among all these topics, valuation is one of the most fundamental and critical areas. Here we will provide only an overview of the basic concepts while explaining the implications and practical ways to integrate these concepts in the portfolio construction process.

In the previous section, we defined investment as the current commitment of financial resources in order to earn profits in the future. Therefore, we need to know some valuation methods or processes to measure or to determine the values of the investment as well as how to compute the risks and returns of various commonly found financial instruments. How these various financial instruments are traded in the markets and the characteristics of the financial instruments have been discussed in Chapter 3.

The valuation process can be constructed as a three-step process. The first step is an analysis of the aggregate economies and overall securities markets.

Since these economic and financial variables exert a significant impact on the industries and firms in the economy, it is important that we first consider the general economic influences before we move on to the second and third steps of the valuation process. In the second step, the valuation process is narrowed down to an industry level. Following the industry analysis, the final step involves the valuation of the securities issued by the individual firms within the industries. However, the universal trend of globalization of investment may make it necessary to start the valuation analysis from a global perspective. Perhaps in future this conventional three-step valuation process may have to be modified to a four-step process to accommodate an analysis of the world economy at the very beginning.

Is it really important to have the three-step process include an analysis of the aggregate economies and overall securities markets, an industry analysis, and an analysis of individual investment? The answer is yes, as numerous research studies in economics and finance (e.g., King 1966; Brown and Ball 1967) have shown that there is a relation between the returns of the aggregate economy, aggregate market, industries, and individual investments. Since the economic and financial variables which may affect the aggregate economy and financial market have been discussed in Chapter 3, we will discuss the analyses of industry and individual securities here.

Industry Analysis

Although it is difficult to define and classify an industry, in practice we group firms into different industry sectors. All markets usually employ a coding system to group the firms with similar industrial characteristics together. In the United States, the firms are classified into industry groups using numerical codes called the Standard Industry Classification codes (SIC codes). All firms in the US are labeled primarily with a four-digit SIC code to identify industries. The first two digits and last two digits of the SIC code define the firms into industries broadly and narrowly, respectively.

In China, there are two sets of industry codes, code A and code B. Code A denotes broad industry groupings into six sectors: finance (0001), utilities (0002), properties (0003), conglomerates (0004), industrials (0005), and commerce (0006). Code B defines the industry classification more narrowly. As at October 2003, Code B classifies the firms listed on the Shanghai Stock Exchange and on the Shenzhen Stock Exchange into more than 100 and 74 narrowly-defined industry sectors, respectively. In Hong Kong, since the number and types of firms are less, the industry classification code (from 1 to 7) is much simpler. The firms in Hong Kong are grouped into seven sectors: finance (1), utilities (2), properties (3), consolidated enterprises (4), industrial (5), hotels (6), and miscellaneous (7).

In order to analyze an industry, we need to understand the industrial cycle. There are four distinct stages in the life cycle of an industry. They are start-up stage, consolidation stage, maturity stage and stage of relative decline. The start-up of an industry is usually led by the invention of a new technology or product. When the industry is at the start-up stage, there is rapid growth in investment opportunities and profits. As compared to the start-up stage, the growth rate of the industry in the consolidation stage is less rapid, although it still exceeds that of the market average. The profitable investment and high return attract new firms to enter the industry, making the competition more intense and the profits lower. The maturity stage is a phase in which the growth rate of the industry no longer exceeds that of the market average. The firms in the mature industry, labeled "cash cows," enjoy the stable growth in earnings and the low risk in investment. The last stage of the life cycle of an industry, the stage of relative decline, is the time when the previously new technology or product becomes obsolete and hence causes the industry to shrink.

Fundamental Analysis

fundamental analysis
Focuses on the selection of mispriced securities.

technical analysis
Focuses on the timing of entering the market.

The objective of the investors trading in the market is to earn profits. One of the ways to earn profits is to search for mispriced securities and arbitrage trading opportunities. There are two traditional schools of thought among market analysts: fundamental analysis and technical analysis. **Fundamental analysis** focuses on the selection of securities while **technical analysis** focuses on the timing of entering the market.

Fundamental analysis employs information (including financial, economic, accounting, management, and product information) about the current and future performance of the firms to evaluate the market and economic value of stocks. That is, the price of the securities is determined by the underlying market and economic factors. The reason why such securities analysis is called fundamental analysis is that the data usually used for analysis such as sales, earnings per share, shareholders' equity, and cash flow are termed fundamental factors.

One of the sources of information for fundamental analysis is financial statements which record the past performance of firms. The three commonly reported financial statements are balance sheet (statement of financial position), income statement (profit and loss statement) and cash flow statement. The balance sheet depicts the financial position of the firm at a specific date. The income statement describes the revenue, expenses, and net income for a specific period of time. The cash flow statement reports the way cash has changed during a specific period of time. These financial statements provide information about the assets, liabilities, equity, revenue, expenses, and cash movement. Since fundamental analysts believe that there exists an intrinsic value for stocks, the financial data and other company information should be used in estimating the value of the firm.

Financial Ratios

Financial accounting data reported on the balance sheet, income statement, and cash flow statement are readily available in financial reports issued by listed firms at least annually, and can be used for making valuation analysis. Table 12.2 reports some of the commonly used ratios used in evaluating the value of a firm.

There are two approaches used in fundamental analysis. The first is a top-down approach to construct a portfolio using the valuation process just mentioned

Table 12.2 Financial ratios

Ratio	Formulae	Explanation
Price-earnings ratio	$\dfrac{\text{Price}}{\text{Earnings per share}}$	Measures how much the investors are willing to pay for the potential earning power of the equity and the reasonableness of the stock price
Earnings yield	$\dfrac{\text{Earning per share}}{\text{Price}}$	Measures the profitability and the earning power for the period
Price-cash flow ratio	$\dfrac{\text{Price}}{\text{Cash flow per share}}$	Works as the supplement to price-earnings ratio as cash flow is argued to be less subject to accounting manipulation than earnings.
Price-sales ratio	$\dfrac{\text{Price}}{\text{Sales per share}}$	Measures the ability to generate sales growth
Market-book ratio	$\dfrac{\text{Market value of equity}}{\text{Book value of equity}}$	Measures the market value of equity relative to the historical value of equity
Return on equity	$\dfrac{\text{Net profit}}{\text{Common stockholders' equity}}$	Measures the return on investment to the common stockholders
Return on asset	$\dfrac{\text{Earnings before interest and tax}}{\text{Total assets}}$	Measures the efficiency with which the financial resources (assets) are employed

(macroeconomic analysis, industrial analysis and firm analysis). In this case, the analysts first pick a desirable economy to invest in, then they pick the appropriate industry, and finally they pick the right stock within that industry. The second is a bottom-up approach. In this case, the analysts pick all the undervalued stocks using fundamental analysis to form the portfolio. The securities market practitioners usually employ several valuation methods to estimate the investment value of the securities. These methods include price-earnings ratio, price-to-net book ratio, and dividend discount model.

Technical Analysis

Unlike fundamental analysis which proposes that economic fundamentals are significant determinants of the price of securities, technical analysis argues that prices move in recognizable patterns and there is no need to understand the economic forces molding these patterns to profit from the market. There are three basic assumptions for technical analysis: (1) market behavior reflects all information available, (2) price tends to change in a pattern, and (3) history always repeats itself. The share price is expected to move following a trend and to persist for some time. Technical analysis is popular among practitioners because it provides an easy way to identify price levels for trading.

Dow theory provides the basis for technical analysis, which aims to detect the trend of share prices. There are three distinct types of trends proposed by Dow theory. The long-term record of past movement (e.g., from months to years) is depicted in the primary trend. The secondary (or intermediate) trend portrays the temporary and short-term share price movement away from the trend. Lastly, the tertiary trend records the daily fluctuation. Dow theory suggests that only long-term and medium trends are useful for prediction. Daily fluctuations are not useful as they are mainly noise and do not contain price patterns. Recently, with the help of powerful computer and transaction data, technical analysts and quantitative financial researchers have been able to predict intra-day price trends. For more details of basic technical analysis, refer to the appendix at the end of this chapter.

Implications of the Efficient Market Hypothesis (EMH) to Fundamental and Technical Analysis

efficient market hypothesis A concept which argues that if markets are efficient, market prices always reflect all information, and so it is not possible to buy a stock at a bargain price.

According to the **efficient market hypothesis** (EMH), it is impossible to beat the market because the market prices already incorporate and reflect all relevant information. Supporters of the efficient market believe that it is not rewarding for average investors to search for undervalued stocks or to predict trends in the market through any technique (e.g., fundamental or technical analysis). If markets are efficient, market prices always reflect all information; it is not possible to buy a stock at a bargain price by using these techniques except when luck is on your side.

There are three forms of efficient market hypothesis. In the weak form (WF) efficiency, the securities prices reflect all historical price and volume data. If the market is WF efficient, then no one can make abnormal profit consistently by using historical price and volume data in the long run. In the semi-strong form (SSF) efficiency, the securities prices reflect all historical and public information. If the market is SSF efficient, no one can make abnormal returns consistently by using historical and public price and volume data in the long run. In the strong form (SF) efficiency, the securities prices reflect all information (both public and private). If the market is SF efficient, no one can make abnormal returns consistently by using any data in the long run.

Technical analysts believe in using historical data and charts to predict stock price movement. Thus, technical analysts who want to make abnormal profits consistently do not believe in weak form efficiency. Fundamental analysts believe in using historical and public data to predict stock price movements. Thus, fundamental analysts who want to make abnormal profits consistently do not believe in semi-strong form efficiency. Finally, it is important to point out that if the market is semi-strong form and/or weak form efficient, we expect no one to make abnormal profit by using historical data and public data.

However, it does not mean that fundamental and technical analysts are wasting their time. We need professionals to keep monitoring the market and analyzing the data to make sure that the market is efficient. At any given point in time, if the market is not efficient for some reason, the analysts will be able to identify the inefficiency and conduct trading to make the profit. By doing so, the supply and demand forces will be in equilibrium and the market becomes efficient again. Thus from a practical perspective, if the wealth manager believes that the market is efficient, and he is not prepared to be a full-time financial analyst, then there is no strong reason for him to engage in active trading strategies in managing the client's portfolio. On the other hand, if the wealth manager truly believes that the market is inefficient, then it may be worth his while to explore various active investment strategies in managing the client's assets.

Bridging the Gap between the Fundamental and Technical Approaches

Although it seems that the approaches used by fundamental and technical analysts are different, it does not mean that they cannot be used at the same time. Practitioners often employ these two techniques to trade in the market. Firstly, fundamental analysis is used to select the appropriate or mispriced stock. When the stock is selected, practitioners can use technical analysis to search for the best time to enter the market. When the trading is conducted, practitioners usually continue to use technical analysis to monitor the market movement to check whether the market trend has changed and whether a correction of the trading strategy is required for the selected stock. Lastly, practitioners also apply technical analysis to determine the best exit time. So far, we have discussed the various analysis techniques of these two different approaches. There is no best technique. It is better to use more than one tool to reaffirm investment decisions.

12.4 Stock Valuation Models

There are two major methods to measure the economic value of stocks: using the dividend discount model and the price ratio method.

Dividend Discount Model

The discounted cash flow model is a commonly used valuation method of securities market practitioners. The discounted cash flow model assumes that the present "fair" price of an investment is the sum of the discounted values of the future cash flows for risk and time value of money. For a stock investment, future cash flow is in the form of future dividend payments. Therefore, by the **dividend discount model**, the value of a share is the sum of the present value of the expected future dividend payments. In mathematical expression, the present value of a stock is:

dividend discount model A stock valuation method which assumes that the value of a share is the sum of the present value of the expected future dividend payments.

Present value of stock

$$= \frac{\text{Dividend}_t}{(1 + \text{Discount rate})^t} + \frac{\text{Dividend}_{t+1}}{(1 + \text{Discount rate})^{t+1}} + \ldots + \frac{\text{Dividend}_{t+n}}{(1 + \text{Discount rate})^{t+n}}$$

We illustrate the calculation of the present value of a stock by the dividend discount model with the following example:

Dividend for year 1   = $100
Dividend for year 2   = $150
Dividend for year 3   = $200
Discount rate   = 10%

$$\text{Present value of stock} = \frac{\$100}{(1.1)^1} + \frac{\$150}{(1.1)^2} + \frac{\$200}{(1.1)^3}$$

$$= \$365.14$$

The dividend discount model is the simplest method to estimate the value of a stock. There are different variations of the dividend discount model. The constant dividend growth rate model assumes that there is a constant growth rate for dividend payments to increase through the years. Therefore, the dividend payment in $t + 1$ is estimated as:

$$D_{t+1} = D_t \times (1 + \text{Dividend growth rate})$$

Dividend for year 1   = $100
Dividend growth rate = 8%
Discount rate   = 10%

$$\text{Present value of stock} = \frac{\$100}{(1.1)^1} + \frac{\$100 \times (1.08)}{(1.1)^2} + \frac{\$100 \times (1.08^2)}{(1.1)^3}$$
$$= 267.80$$

Or simply, by the constant dividend growth rate model, the present value of a stock is defined as:

Present value of stock

$$= \frac{\text{Dividend in current year} \times (1 + \text{growth rate})}{\text{Discount rate} - \text{Growth rate}} \left[1 - \left(\frac{1 + \text{growth rate}}{1 + \text{discount rate}}\right)^{\text{number of annual dividends}}\right]$$

This formula works as long as the discount rate is not equal to the growth rate. Therefore, we can use this formula to calculate the present value of the stock in the previous example.

$$\text{Present value of stock} = \frac{\$100}{0.1 - 0.08}\left[1 - \left(\frac{1 + 0.08}{1 + 0.1}\right)^3\right]$$
$$= \$267.80$$

Since the constant dividend growth rate model assumes that the dividend payment increases at a constant growth rate, then an extension of the constant dividend growth rate model can be a model assuming an everlasting constant growth rate for dividend payments. This extended model is called the constant perpetual growth model. The formula to estimate the present value of a stock is no more complicated than the one for the constant dividend growth rate model:

$$\text{Present value of stock} = \frac{\text{Dividend in current year} \times (1 + \text{growth rate})}{\text{Discount rate} - \text{Growth rate}}$$

This formula works as long as the discount rate is greater than the growth rate. We use the same data as in the previous example but assume that the dividends grow forever.

$$\text{Present value of stock} = \frac{\$100}{0.1 - 0.08}$$
$$= \$5,000$$

A more advanced approach is the variable growth model. It utilizes several growth rates by dividing the company's life into several growth stages. The concept is similar to combining several constant growth models into one. However, the calculation is a little more complicated due to the requirement of discounting the sum of the present values of the dividends for each stage. For the purpose of financial planning, the understanding of the mathematics of the variable growth model is not that important. Thus, we will not cover the details of this model here.

Price Ratio Method

Two price ratios are commonly used: the price-earnings ratio and the price-to-net-book ratio.

The price-earnings (P/E) ratio divides the share price by the earnings of the securities. The P/E ratio is commonly used because it is a simple method to demonstrate the relative value of a firm. There are three different views to interpret P/E ratio. First, from a mathematical point of view, it indicates how much an investor is willing to pay for each dollar of earnings that the company generates. The higher the P/E ratio, the greater the payment the investor is willing to give to buy one dollar earnings. Second, from the payback perspective, the P/E ratio can be regarded as the time (in years) it takes to get your money back. Third, from an investment perspective, a high P/E ratio implies that the company has a high growth opportunity, and is commonly regarded as a growth stock. On the other hand, a low P/E ratio implies that the stock is cheap in terms of the cost to buy one dollar earnings. A low P/E listed firm is normally regarded as a value stock.

Figure 12.2 shows the P/E ratio band of a sample stock. The darker line with an upward trend on the top represents the last price (the daily closing price) of the stock. The lighter line with up and down fluctuations near the bottom shows the P/E ratios. The left-hand side y-axis is the scale for the P/E ratio and the

Figure 12.2 Price-earnings ratio

right-hand side y-axis is the scale for the stock price. The upper and lower dotted straight lines around the P/E ratios represent the boundary with two standard deviations away from the mean P/E ratio on each side. The existence of the boundary helps to identify the P/E ratios exceeding the upper and lower bounds for selling and buying signals, respectively.

The price-to-net book (P/B) ratio shows the price premium trading above the net book value of a stock. The P/B ratio is commonly used for evaluating financial institutions. The P/B ratio is measured by dividing the share price by the net book value. A high P/B ratio also indicates a high growth opportunity, leading to a higher price premium paid by the investors for the asset value. A small P/B ratio is preferable as it means that the investor can pay a lower price to buy the assets of the company.

Figure 12.3 shows the P/B ratio band of a sample stock. The darker line with an upward trend on the top represents the last price (the daily closing price) of the stock. The lighter line with up and down fluctuations near the bottom shows the P/B ratios. The left-hand side y-axis is the scale for the P/B ratio and the right-hand side y-axis is the scale for the stock price. The upper and lower dotted straight lines around the P/B ratios represent the boundary with two standard deviations away from the mean P/B ratio on each side. The existence of the boundary helps to identify the P/B ratios exceeding the upper and lower bounds for selling and buying signals, respectively.

Figure 12.3 Price-to-net book ratio

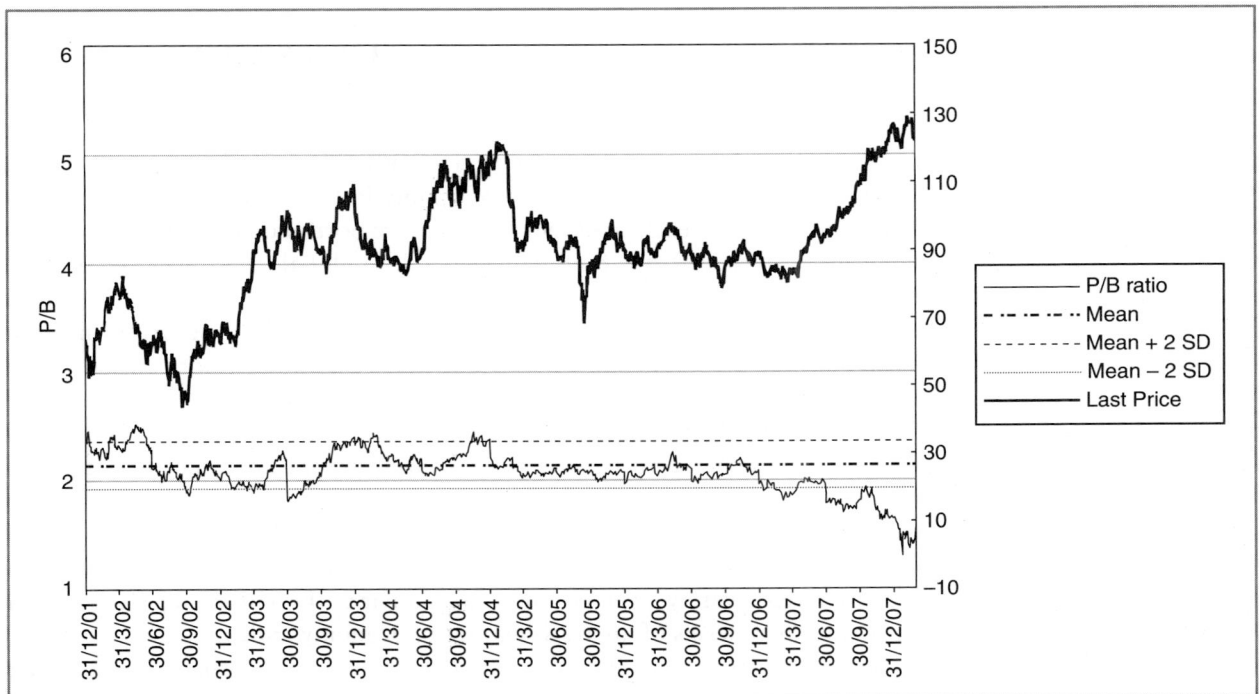

12.5   Investment Strategies for Equity Investment

Investment strategy can be broadly categorized into two types: active and passive. An active strategy aims to achieve a higher level of return by identifying mispriced securities and predicting market movements. The investors who take on an active strategy may trade actively to earn excess profit due to market inefficiency. An active strategy usually identifies undervalued securities and employs market timing strategies. In a sense, active investors believe that the market is not efficient and that there are a lot of opportunities and conditions of market inefficiency. They make use of fundamental and/or technical analyses to identify mispricing and undervalued stocks. Some institutional investors may employ program trading and advanced risk-arbitrage strategies using derivatives to enhance returns.

The second type of investment strategy is a passive strategy. Investors adopting the passive strategy tend to sustain the preferred risk-return balance at a given market opportunity setting instead of trading aggressively to outperform the market. A passive strategy is based on the belief that the market is in general efficient, making the active trading activities cost-inefficient. In order to reduce transaction cost, "buy and hold" is a passive investment strategy with no active buying and selling of stocks. Passive investors invest in market indices or a well-diversified portfolio to avoid unsystematic risk. However, even passive investors employ asset allocation strategies in order to bet on the movements of different regions and stock markets. Passive investors buy index funds such as MSCI, i-shares or ETFs (exchange traded funds) for each market and allocate their money among different regional markets accordingly.

Active and Passive Strategies for Equity Investment

Active Strategy: Stock Selection

In order to beat the market, investors need to know which stock and which market to trade in. Fund managers who invest mainly in the domestic market have to decide the weight of each stock within the entire portfolio. The weight is termed the securities weight. If the fund managers take a global investment perspective, there are two portfolio weights, the weight of each market (or country) within the entire portfolio (country weight) and the weight of the securities in each market within the entire portfolio (securities weight). Therefore, whether the fund managers are able to earn excess return depends on their skills in market (country) picking and/or securities picking. The excess return of mutual fund managers is attributed to the market allocation return and securities selection return.

Performance attribution analysis is about the whole portfolio selection process, which breaks down the overall performance of the portfolio into different levels layer by layer. For instance, similar to the valuation process which consists of three levels of analysis (market or economy, industry, and securities), performance attribution analysis also has three levels (broad asset market allocation, industry, and securities).

Active Strategy: Market Timing

Besides possessing the ability to pick the "right" securities in order to outperform the market, investors also need to have market timing ability to trade in the selected stock at the "right" time. Market timing means shifting funds between a safe asset and a market index portfolio. One common example of a safe asset is the treasury bill. If the market is expected to outperform (underperform) the safe asset, the funds are to be invested into a market index portfolio (safe asset). Although in theory, the funds should be shifted totally between a safe asset and a market index portfolio, a total shift is seldom applied.

Passive Strategies

Recently, owing to the increasing popularity of efficient market hypothesis, some major mutual funds and wealth managers have adopted a passive approach to investment. By investing in a basket of securities tracking a market index, these passive portfolios can take advantage of the capital appreciation experienced in the markets while minimizing transaction costs involved in active strategies. Of course, some investment firms take a dual approach, and divide their money into two portions: the first portion using active strategies and the second portion using passive strategies. By late 2006, the exchange-traded funds (ETFs) in the United States have become the fastest growing product. The variety of ETFs helps smaller investors to adopt indexing strategies with more flexibility. For the past few decades, academics and practitioners have been debating about the pros and cons of passive strategies. From the financial planning perspective, which normally takes a longer term view of investment, passive strategies through indexing or a diversified portfolio with less frequent trading can be rewarding and cost-efficient. Wealth managers should understand their investment ability and limitations before adopting active strategies for their clients. For junior financial planners practicing limited investment wealth management, using passive strategies to achieve a diversified portfolio with ETFs focusing on major market indices is a practical and easier way to achieve the investment goals for the clients.

Mutual Funds

We have briefly described mutual funds in Chapter 3. Mutual funds investment is popular because it allows the individual investors to invest in a wide variety of financial products. Through mutual funds investment, small investors can enjoy the benefits of large-scale investment, international diversification, liquidity, and risk positioning which otherwise cannot be achieved. In addition, the investors also benefit from the investment management of professional mutual fund managers.

Mutual funds investment is broadly divided into open-end and closed-end funds. Open-end funds offer to buy and sell shares to existing or new investors at any time and do not have a limit on the number of outstanding shares. The total number of fund units can be changed at any time and hence an advantage of mutual funds investment is liquidity. The fund-holders of open-end funds can redeem the shares and get cash at net asset value from the fund investment company. The selling price of the fund is based on the net asset value of the fund. However, fund-holders can only sell the mutual funds back to the fund investment company but not to other parties. In contrast, closed-end funds do not buy or sell shares. In addition, closed-end funds are not redeemable. Unlike open-end funds, there is a fixed amount of shares to be issued (bought and sold) for closed-end funds. Since closed-end funds are not redeemable, the fund-holders have to buy the funds from and sell the funds to other parties.

There are two major types of open-end funds: short-term funds and long-term funds. Short-term funds can be called money market mutual funds as the short-term funds focus on investments in interest-bearing, short-term, and low-risk money market financial instruments. In contrast, the long-term funds specialize in investments of relatively longer term. There are three types of long-term funds and one type of short-term fund. The three types of long-term funds are equity (stock) funds, bond funds, and hybrid funds (a combination of stocks, bonds, and other securities). The short-term funds are the money market funds which usually have a shorter investment term of less than a year.

If the mutual funds companies operate their business by pooling the funds of the investors to make diversified investment portfolios in the financial market, how does one quantify the investment return for mutual funds? The value of mutual funds is measured in terms of the net asset value (NAV), also known as fund share price. Net asset value is defined as:

$$\frac{\text{Market value of asset} - \text{Market value of liabilities}}{\text{Number of outstanding shares}}$$

The fund holders can buy and redeem the mutual fund shares at the net asset value on a daily basis. Therefore, mutual funds investment is highly liquid. For open-end funds, the price to buy and to sell shares is the net asset value. Closed-end funds, similar to common stocks, can be traded over-the-counter or on the stock market at market-determined prices (a price which may be different from the net asset value of the fund).

The dollar return for mutual funds investment is determined by the change in the net asset value as well as the income and capital gains from diversified investment. In mathematical terms, the rate of return is expressed as:

$$\frac{\text{Net asset value}_{t+1} - \text{Net asset value}_t + \text{Income}_{t+1} + \text{Capital gain}_{t+1}}{\text{Net asset value}_t}$$

Before the funds are sold, the fund investment companies usually distribute a fund prospectus which states clearly all the necessary information such as the investment objective and composition of the funds for potential investors to evaluate and make informed decisions. The information in the prospectus about the composition of funds may include whether the funds are capital appreciation and growth funds; conservative income funds; well-balanced funds; money market funds or cash funds; property funds; tax-free funds; and exchange-traded funds (ETF).

Mutual fund investment companies may also have to publish annual reports for their shareholders. In the prospectus and annual reports, the financial statements provide information on the fees, expenses, assets, fund goals, and management policy of the companies. Financial planners can make use of the information on the fund prospectus to recommend the most appropriate mutual funds for their clients. Since the various types of mutual funds provide different investment choices for clients with different investment preferences, financial planners should carefully evaluate the financial circumstances and investment preferences of their clients so as to recommend the most appropriate mutual funds for investment.

In addition to the various types of mutual funds, financial planners have to consider whether the fund carries a load and charges other expenses for managing the funds. A load is a sales charge attached to the fund, to be paid to the seller of funds for the professional services provided. The funds which have such charges are called load funds. There are two types of loads: front-end loads and back-end loads (or contingent deferred sales charge). Front-end loads are charged when the shares are purchased while back-end loads levy the sales charge when the shares are sold. Fund managers usually charge a redemption fee to cover the administrative expense, other than the sales charge, in the event of redemption by fund-holders. In addition, if fund-holders have to shift investments between funds within the same fund family, fund managers would charge fund holders an exchange fee.

For instance, when you invest $100,000 in a load fund with 5% sales charge, the net amount to be invested in the mutual fund is actually $95,000 rather than $100,000 because $5,000 is deducted as the sales charge. Or you may have to pay a price, called the offering price, in excess of the net asset value, to purchase the shares. Therefore, in this example, you may have to pay $105,000 to purchase the shares in a load fund with the net asset value of $100,000 and 5% sales charge. The percentage charge of front-end loads varies from fund to fund. Low-load funds are used to describe funds with loads which are charged at a relatively low percentage of around 2–3%. No-load funds are traded at net asset value because there are no sales charges attached to no-load funds. Since load funds and no-load funds are both popular in the United States, financial magazines and articles differentiate load funds and no-load funds for the investors by adding an "NAV/Offer" column in the "Mutual Fund" section. "NAV" indicates that there is a no sales charge attached to the fund and "Offer" indicates that the fund carries a load.

Besides the sales charge levied by the seller of funds, there are other expenses (including management fee, transaction cost, and brokerage fee) associated with the investment in mutual funds. As the amount of fees varies from fund to fund, it is important that investors and financial planners consider the fee structure in addition to the profit potential of mutual funds when making decisions on mutual fund investment. The fund managers who are responsible for the purchase and sales transactions of the fund may charge a percentage of fund assets as their management, administrative, or advisory fee (usually lower than 1% of the total funds assets). In addition, when the fund managers conduct trading on the market, trading costs are incurred. Therefore, fund-holders have to pay the brokerage expenses incurred in securities trading depending on the trading activity of the fund managers. In the United States, the Securities and Exchange

Commission (SEC) requires that mutual fund managers pay a distribution fee called 12b-1 which is used for marketing and selling fund shares; advertising, printing and mailing the prospectus; and compensating brokers and others who sell the fund shares

Since its introduction in the United States in the 1920s, mutual funds have grown in market share and variety. Table 12.3 shows the statistics from the *Investment Company Fact Book 2007* for the number of mutual funds by type of fund in 1984 and in 2006 in the United States. The statistics show that the number of mutual funds available in the market has increased enormously and points to the growing demand of investors for mutual funds. Mutual funds have not only grown in the United States but also worldwide.

According to the statistics of the *Investment Company Fact Book 2007*, the value of mutual fund assets in the global market as at 2006 is US$21.8 trillion. The US market is the largest mutual fund market, which makes up 48% of the global value of mutual fund assets. The value of total assets of mutual funds in the United States as at 2006 is US$10.4 trillion, comprising 23% of assets (approximately US$2.39 trillion) in money market funds, 14% of assets (approximately US$1.45 trillion) in bond funds, 6% of assets (approximately US$624 billion in hybrid funds), and 57% of assets (approximately US$5.92 trillion) in equity funds.[1]

Table 12.3 Statistics for growth of mutual funds investment

Type of funds		Number of funds	
		1984	2006
Equity funds		459	4,770
	Capital appreciation	306	3,070
	World	29	915
	Total return	124	785
Hybrid funds		89	508
Bond funds		270	1,993
	Corporate	30	289
	High-yield	36	207
	World	1	113
	Government	45	309
	Strategic income	47	364
	State municipal	37	481
	National municipal	74	230
Money market funds		425	849
	Taxable	329	576
	Tax-exempt	96	273
Total		1,243	8,120

Source: *Investment Company Fact Book 2007* (www.icifactbook.org).

---

[1] Note that the dollar amounts of the mutual fund asset components may not add up to US$10.4 trillion because of rounding.

The value of mutual fund assets in other markets besides the US is US$11.4 trillion. While the market in the Americas (consisting of the United States, Canada, Brazil, Argentina, Chile, Mexico, and Costa Rica) remains the largest mutual funds market in the world (53%), the European market and the Asia/Pacific/Africa market occupy 36% and 11% of the worldwide mutual fund assets, respectively.

Academic research on mutual fund performance became popular in the 1960s. These studies on mutual fund performance yielded mixed results. Shawky (1982), Rahman, Fabozzi, and Lee (1991) and Christopherson and Turner (1991) report index-like or below-index performance of mutual fund managers. Ippolito (1993) observed that the risk-adjusted performance of mutual fund managers was no different from that of the index funds, on a net of expenses basis. However, there were also other studies, such as those by Friend, Blume, and Crockett (1970), Mains (1977), and Grinblatt and Titman (1993), which found mutual fund managers to possess superior ability.

Exchange-traded Funds (ETFs)[2]

exchange-traded fund (ETF) An extension of closed-end funds which are listed and traded like stocks on an exchange.

Other types of investment companies which are very similar to mutual funds are **exchange-traded funds** (ETFs). ETFs are traded on the market in a similar way to other marketable securities. The shares of ETFs are listed on the stock exchanges and can be purchased and sold through securities dealers at market prices. These different types of investment companies which are managed by professional portfolio managers provide various investment options for investors to achieve diversification.

ETFs are an extension of closed-end funds which pool the money of the investors and invest it in securities. The shares of ETFs are listed and traded like normal shares on an exchange. Compared with an investment in a single stock, an investment in an ETF index product provides diversified exposure to a market or a market segment.

Investment in ETFs is becoming popular. ETFs allow investors to diversify globally. ETFs provide an easy way for investors seeking to establish and increase exposure to international markets. For instance, in the United States, investors can invest in the Dow Jones basket via the Diamonds Trust Series (Ticker: DIA), the NASDAQ basket via NASDAQ 100 shares (Ticker: QQQQ), the China market via iShares MSCI China Tracker, the UK market via iShares MSCI UTD KINGDM (Ticker: EWU), and the European market via iShares S&P Euro 350 IDX (Ticker: IEV).

ETFs also offer intra-day trading opportunities for investors. As ETFs trade continuously throughout the day, investors can buy and sell ETFs all day at market prices on the exchange, not just at market close. In addition, the ETF is a transparent investment option at a relatively low cost. The ETF is designed in

---

[2] Most of the material in this section is extracted from the education article "Exchange Traded Funds as an Investment/Hedging Tool," Cheng, L. and Cheng, K., published by the Hong Kong Exchange, issue no. 14, June 2002.

such a way that its price closely reflects that of the underlying index being tracked. If investors trade in ETFs, the only costs for the investors are the brokerage fee, and commission and transaction costs. The ETF is a type of passively managed fund, and the cost involved for a passively managed fund is lower than that for an actively managed fund as passive management usually results in lower overall expenses associated with indexing. Owing to the unique feature of the low trading cost of ETFs, ETFs allow investors to gain access to the domestic market very efficiently. In addition, ETFs also enable investors to gain diversified access to foreign markets.

ETFs provide a means for investors to construct efficient asset allocation strategies, to improve cash flow management, and to exploit arbitrage opportunities. Investors, particularly fund managers, can make use of ETFs to quickly and easily reduce or increase exposure to a particular sector or economy. In addition, ETFs can be used to gain exposure to the market speedily and effectively, thus reducing the possibility of a cash drag. On the other hand, when there is a need for investment managers to raise cash, ETFs offer a more cost-effective alternative to having to sell a large number of stocks on the market. ETFs may allow investors to exploit arbitrage opportunities if they trade between ETFs, the underlying index, and futures. Furthermore, in view of an upcoming market decline, investors may establish a short position on the ETFs. The ETFs can be short-sold against long stock holdings in a portfolio as a hedge against a market decline.

Key Terms

capital asset pricing model *346*
dividend discount model *352*
efficient market hypothesis *351*
exchange-traded funds *361*
fundamental analysis *349*

portfolio theory *344*
return *341*
risk *341*
technical analysis *349*

References

Brown, P. and Ball, R., "Some Preliminary findings on the Association between the Earnings of a Firm, Its Industry, and the Economy," *Empirical Research in Accounting: Selected Studies*, supplement to *Journal of Accounting Research*, vol. 5 (1967): 55–77.

Christopherson, J. A. and Turner, A. L., "Volatility and Predictability of Manager Alpha," *Journal of Portfolio Management*, vol. 17 (1991): 5–12.

Friend, I., Blume, M., and Crockett, J., *Mutual Funds and Other Institutional Investors* (New York: McGraw-Hill, 1970).

Grinblattt, M. and Titman, S., "Performance Measurement without Benchmarks: An Examination of Mutual Fund Returns," *Journal of Business*, vol. 66 (1993): 47–68.

Ippolito, R. A., "On Studies of Mutual Fund Performance, 1962–1991," *Financial Analysts Journal*, vol. 6 (1993): 42–50.

King, B., "Market and Industry Factors in Stock Price Behavior," *Journal of Business*, vol. 39 (1966): 139–190.

Mains, N., "Risk, the Pricing of Capital Assets and Evaluation of Investment Portfolios: Comment on Jensen," *Journal of Business*, vol. 50, no. 3 (1977): 371–384.

Markowitz, H. M., "Portfolio Selection," *Journal of Finance*, vol. 7, no. 1 (1952): 77–91.

Merrill Lynch Capgemini World Wealth Report 2004 (www.us.capgemini.com/worldwealthreport04).

Newbould, G. D. and Poon, P. S., "The Minimum Number of Stocks Needed for Diversification," *Financial Practice and Education*, vol. 3, no. 2 (Fall 1993): 85–87.

Rahman, S., Fabozzi, F. J., and Lee, C. F., "Errors in Variables, Functional Form, and Mutual Fund Returns," *Quarterly Review of Economics and Business*, vol. 31 (1991): 25–35.

Ross, S. A., "Return, Risk and Arbitrage," in *Risk and Return in Finance*, Friend, I. and Bicksler, J., eds. (Cambridge, MA: Ballinger, 1976).

Sharpe, W. S., "A Simplified Model for Portfolio Analysis," *Management Science*, vol. 9 (1963): 227–293.

Shawky, H., "An Update on Mutual Funds: Better Grades," Journal of Portfolio Management, vol. 8 (1982): 29–34.

Questions & Problems

Multiple-choice Questions

1. The concept of investments in the context of personal financial planning is somewhat different from the concept of traditional investments. In personal financial planning, the investment for a client should be _____.
   A. focused on return maximization
   B. for asset protection only
   C. focused on making the client's dreams come true
   D. goal-oriented

2. As reported in the Merrill Lynch Capgemini World Wealth Report 2004, alternative investments such as _____ have become a common asset class used by the ultra-high-net-worth clients.
   A. hedged funds
   B. high yield junk bonds
   C. real estate investment in Africa
   D. private equity and foreign currencies

3. Based on the mean-variance criterion in portfolio theory, as long as the stocks are _____ among each other, each additional stock would exert _____ impact on the aggregate risk of the portfolio.
   A. perfectly correlated; a risk-reducing
   B. not perfectly correlated; a risk-reducing
   C. not perfectly correlated; a risk-increasing
   D. not perfectly correlated; no

4. A major difference between the CAPM and APT is that CAPM has _____ risk factor while APT uses _____ risk factor.
   A. multiple; one
   B. two; three
   C. no; one
   D. one; multiple

5. The three-step valuation process involves the sequence of the following three factors:
    A. Step 1 - overall economy; Step 2 - industry involved; Step 3 - a particular stock
    B. Step 1 - a particular stock; Step 2 - another stock; Step 3 - an industry
    C. Step 1 - an industry; Step 2 - overall economy; Step 3 - a particular stock
    D. Step 1 - the bond factor; Step 2 - stock factor; Step 3 - hedged funds

6. One of the three views to interpret P/E ratio is that P/E ratio can be regarded as _____ it takes to _____.
    A. the time; get 10% return
    B. the time; allocate your money into different asset classes
    C. the time; get your money back
    D. the risk; get your money back

Problems

1. Explain the implication of EMH on technical analysis.

appendix **12.1**

Charting Techniques
and Technical Indicators

Here we discuss some of the basic charting concepts and indicators used in technical analysis. This is only an introduction of the existing literature, which is a lot more comprehensive and complicated than the review we provide here. Technical analysts employ charts or line movements to depict the movement of past data. In general, past data used include mainly price and volume figures. Traditional Dow theory suggests that short-term daily price fluctuation should be ignored as trends can normally be detected in medium- and long-term price movements. However, more recently, technical analysts have been exploring daily trends using charting techniques.

The actual time horizon used for technical analysis depends on the purpose of the chart. For instance, to predict a short-term price movement (i.e., one week), a 5-day or 10-day moving average can be used to plot the price line. A long-term prediction may require a 200-day or 250-day moving average to plot the graph. To provide more information in the chart, technical analysts develop symbols to indicate the high, low, open, and closed positions in the chart so that the investors can better visualize the intra-day price movement while considering the price trends over a period of time. Table 12.4 describes some basic charting techniques used.

Since the candlestick chart is more complicated, we illustrate it in greater detail in Figure 12.4 and Figure 12.5. If the market close is higher than the market open, the real body which represents the high-low range is in white. If the market close is lower than the market open, the real high-low range is represented by black.

In addition, it is a common practice for technical analysts to connect certain critical points such as minimum, maximum, and turning points. These techniques of using supplementary lines to better identify trend directions are called trend-line analysis. There are three common trend lines: up trend line, down trend line, and sideways trend line. The up trend line is drawn by joining the low point with another low point with a straight line. Therefore, an up trend line is recognized when the next new low point is persistently higher than the previous low point. In contrast, the down trend line is drawn by joining the different high points with a straight line. The down trend line is found when the next new high point is persistently lower than the previous high point. Unlike the up trend or down trend lines, the sideways trend line is found when there is no obvious up or down trend line. The sideways trend line can be drawn by joining the high point or low point with another high point or low point with a straight line.

Table 12.4 Charting Techniques

Type of chart	Description	Advantages	Disadvantages
Line chart	• X-axis represents time • Y-axis represents price level; • The closing prices are joined by a line	• Easy to understand • Easy to show long-term trends • Saves time	• Only records the closing price • More difficult to show short-term trends
Bar chart	• X-axis represents time • Y-axis represents price level • Price range is represented by a bar	• Shows some daily information about the market	• Cannot show the difference between market open and market close if they are too close; • Cannot demonstrate the trend clearly if the market is too volatile
Candle-stick chart	• X-axis represents time • Y-axis represents price level • Real body represents high-low range • Upper shadow represents the highest price • Lower shadow represents the lowest price • Hollow-body means market close > market open • Solid-body means market close < market open	• Shows market trend and intra-day price movement in one graph	• Quite complicated; more difficult to manage the charting technique

Figure 12.4 Candlestick structure: Hollow body means market close > market open; solid body means market close < market open

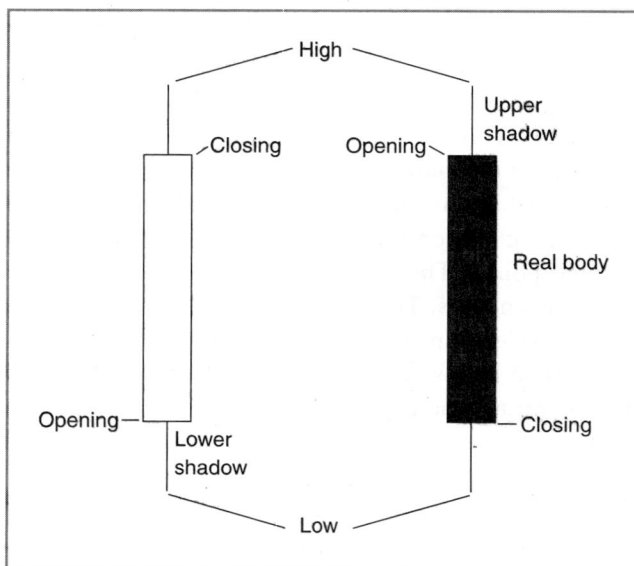

Figure 12.5 Candlestick chart: Hollow body means market close > market open; solid body means market close < market open

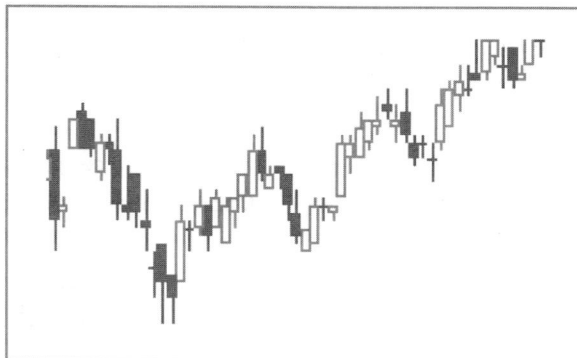

While it is not the focus of technical analysis to explore the reasons behind these trends, it is a common practice to relate these trends to certain economic and financial factors such as changes in interest rates, corporate profits or major corporate announcements. For a trend-line analysis, more price points and a longer time period are required to confirm the trend movement and the slope of the trend. The trend-line analysis can be more reliable and valid if the closing price information is complemented with trading volume data. The main objective of trend-line analysis is to identify and confirm the price patterns in trends. *Psychological barrier, support level, resistance level, breakout, bottom out,* and *top out* are technical terms used to label the different positions of patterns in price movements.

The support level is the point below which a stock or the market is not likely to go while the resistance level is the point above which a stock or the market is not likely to reach. Support and resistance levels are often used to describe the psychological barriers of the investors and market. When the price is able to pass through the psychological barrier, the support level, or the resistance level, it is a *breakout. Bottom out* and *top out* are the respective terms used to portray the points at which the prices fall and rise no further.

In the securities market, practitioners usually employ different indicators to identify the psychological barriers of investors and to predict the turning points of the market. Table 12.5 provides some of these turning point indicators.

In addition to the commonly used charting and trend-line techniques, technical analysis also employs certain key indicators to summarize and predict future market trends. The three major types of technical indicators mentioned in this section are sentimental indicator, flow of fund indicator and market structure indicator. Table 12.6 describes these indicators one by one.

Among the various technical indicators, moving average is the most popular tool in the market as it is the easiest indicator. The time horizon for measuring the moving average is divided into short-term (5 days and 10 days), medium-term (20 days, 40 days, and 50 days) and long-term (100 days, 200 days, and 250 days). Practitioners usually have some trading principles when using the moving average. It is time to buy if:

- The price crosses above the moving average from below.
- The price hits the moving average from above.
- The price crosses below the moving average from above and is followed by pull back (resistance line becoming support line).
- The price crosses below the moving average from above, drops sharply, and is followed by a rebound.

Table 12.5 Indicators of turning points

Possible turning point indicator from bull to bear market	Possible turning point indicator from bear to bull market
Price-earning ratio climbs to historical high	Price-earnings ratio drops to historical low
Money supply falls	Money supply increases
Interest rate starts to rise	Interest rate starts to fall
Number of new companies increases	Number of new companies drops
Major shareholders start to reduce shareholdings	Major shareholders start to increase shareholdings
Market index does not react to good news positively	Market index does not react to bad news negatively
Professional investors start to increase shareholdings in utilities	Professional investors start to reduce shareholdings in utilities
Head and shoulder pattern	Reverse head and shoulder pattern

It is a time to sell if:

- The price crosses the moving average from above.
- The price deviates from the moving average and the accumulated advance is large enough.
- The slope of the moving average turns flat.
- The price hits the moving average from below without a breakout.
- The price crosses above the moving average from below and is followed by pull back (support line becoming resistance line).

A closely related indicator to moving average is a Bollinger's band—the upper band (moving average + (2 × standard deviation of the price for the given period)) and the lower band (moving average − (2 × standard deviation of the price for the given period). The width of the band changes according to the fluctuations of the market. The stock price is assumed to swing inside the band. Usually a too wide or too narrow Bollinger's band is followed by a price correction.

Table 12.6 Technical indicators

Technical indicator	Numerical formula	Explanation
1. Sentimental indicator		Measures market expectation.
a. Trin statistic	$$\dfrac{\dfrac{\text{Volume declining}}{\text{Number declining}}}{\dfrac{\text{Volume advancing}}{\text{Number advancing}}}$$	The strength of the share price movement can be reinforced by trading activity. Share price increase (decrease) together with increased buying (selling) activity can be a signal of continued upward (downward) trend of share price. A trin statistic higher than 1 is an indicator of an unfavorable market.
b. Odd-lot ratio	$$\dfrac{\text{Odd-lot purchase}}{\text{Odd-lot sale}}$$	Odd-lot transaction usually refers to trading of less than 100 shares. Odd-lot theory suggests that if the value of the odd-lot ratio is higher (less) than 1, it means that there is pervasive buying (selling) activity by the odd-lot traders or small traders, which is a signal of an unfavorable (a favorable) market.
c. Confidence index	$$\dfrac{\text{Average yield of 10 top-rated corporate bonds}}{\text{Average yield of 10 intermediate-grade corporate bonds}}$$	If bond traders have confidence in the economy and bond market, a smaller default premium is expected, thus making the yield spread between bonds of different ratings to be narrower. Therefore, a value of confidence index closer to 1 is a signal of a favorable market.
d. Put/call ratio	$$\dfrac{\text{Number of put options outstanding on shares}}{\text{Number of call options outstanding on shares}}$$	Call (put) is a hedge against market growth (decline), thus indicating a bullish (bearish) view. The number of outstanding call (put) can be a signal for future share price increase (decrease). A high put/call ratio is an indicator of an unfavorable market.
d. Mutual fund cash position	$$\dfrac{\text{Cash in mutual fund portfolio}}{\text{Total assets in mutual fund portfolio}}$$	Mutual fund cash position is an indicator of potential buying and selling power. A high (low) cash position is a signal of high (low) level of potential buying power and a forthcoming favorable (unfavorable) market.
2. Flow of funds indicator		Measures the propensity of buying and selling activities.
a. Short interest	Number of short-sold shares in the market	As short-sellers have to reverse their previous short-sale transactions by making purchase transactions in the future, short interest is an indicator of a latent future demand for shares.
3. Market structure indicator		Measures price trends.
a. Moving average	Average level of stock price over a given period of time	When the current market price is lower (higher) than the moving average, it is a signal of an unfavorable (a favorable) market.
b. Relative strength	$$\dfrac{\text{Price of securities}}{\text{Price index of industry/market}}$$	Relative strength is an indicator of the performance of an investment as compared to that of the industry or market. A high (low) value of relative strength is a signal that the stock outperforms (underperforms) the industry average or market index.

chapter 13

Investment Techniques (Part II)

> **Learning Objectives**
>
> *After studying this chapter you should be able to:*
>
> 1 Understand bond valuation models.
> 2 Understand the valuation of derivatives.
> 3 Know investment strategies for equity investment.
> 4 Grasp investment strategies for fixed-income securities.

13.1 Bond Valuation Models

Fixed-income securities are financial instruments that promise to pay a specified stream of cash flows over a specified period according to a predetermined schedule. This type of securities is preferred by those investors who favor less risk and a more stable stream of income over the investment period. The most common forms of fixed-income securities are bonds and preferred stocks.

Finance Theories for Fixed-income Securities

In Chapter 3 we learnt that there are different types of fixed-income securities. These various types of fixed-income securities differ in the following ways: the kind of issuer (government or private organization), yield to maturity, length to maturity (1 month, 1 year, or 10 years), and level of coupon rate (5%, 10%, or 20%). All these factors are determinants of the price and return of the fixed-income securities. Since price and rate of return are the factors that financial planners and their clients should consider when making investment decisions, we need to understand the term structure of interest rates and the yield curve which relates interest rate, yield to maturity, and term to maturity of fixed income securities.

The term structure of interest rates describes the relation between time to maturity and the interest rate of default-free debt instruments. The yield curve plots the yield and maturity of coupon bonds. Before we learn how to value fixed-income securities, we need to distinguish the spot interest rate and future interest rate and to know the finance theories about term structures of interest rates and yield curves. Spot interest rate is the interest rate fixed today on a loan which is made today. Future interest rate is the interest rate fixed today on a loan to be made at some future date. Basically, there are three traditional theories. They are expectations (also known as non-deviated expectations) theory, liquidity preference theory, and market segmentation theory.

According to the expectations theory, the most important determinant of yield to maturity is the expectation of future interest rates. The expectations theory holds that each forward rate equals the expected future interest rate for the relevant period. The future interest rate represents the expectation of the whole market of the average level of the spot interest rate in the future. At equilibrium, the expected spot interest rate is the future interest rate. An upward sloping yield curve means that there will be an increase in interest rate while a downward sloping yield curve indicates that there will be a decrease in interest rate. No change in the expected interest rate is depicted by a flat yield curve.

The liquidity preference theory holds that the market is controlled by short-term investors who have an investment preference for short-term investments with high liquidity. The liquidity premium, which is the difference between the future interest rate and the expected spot interest rate, should be provided to encourage investors to invest in long-term investment with a longer time to maturity and a higher risk. By the liquidity preference theory, lenders have a preference for short-term lending in order to avoid funds being tied up for too long while borrowers' first choice is long-term borrowing in order to secure financing. Therefore, in order to entice the lenders to provide funds for longer-term loans, the borrowers have to offer a higher rate to get loans for a longer term. Hence, the difference in interest rates between a long-term loan and a short-term loan is the maturity or liquidity premium.

The market segmentation theory argues that the debt market is divided into various distinct segments by different maturities of debt instruments in the market and the interest rates of different debt instruments with different maturities which are shaped separately in the respective segments. Therefore, the shape of the yield curve is determined by the demand and supply for securities within each maturity. Long-term and short-term bonds are traded on separate markets. Each type of bond has its own equilibrium status. While long-term financing activities decide the interest rate for long-term bonds, short-term financing activities decide the short-term interest rate which is different from the rate on the long-term bonds. Therefore, the interest rate for a loan with the maturity term of three years is determined by the supply and demand of the funds in the segment for three years.

For a given term structure, we assume that all the securities (normally treasury issues) are of the same liquidity and default risk level. Of course, when we evaluate the interest rate for other financial assets, such as corporate bonds, then these two types of risk will vary. A liquidity premium should be added to compensate for the risk of the fixed-income securities being less liquid. Similarly, a default premium should supplement paying off the risk due to the possibility of non-payment. In addition, an interest rate (maturity) risk premium should be added to the longer-term fixed-income securities as their prices are more volatile and more sensitive to interest rate fluctuation than those of shorter-term fixed-income securities. In conclusion, three types of risk premium—interest rate risk premium, liquidity premium, and default premium—should be considered in determining the interest rate for assets of different risk levels. Based on the concept mentioned above, the interest rate for any asset should comprise two major components with five elements: Component I: risk-free return (two elements: real rate and inflation premium) and component II: risk premium (three elements: maturity premium, liquidity premium, and default premium).

Bond Price

The value of a financial instrument is estimated by discounting the expected future cash flows using an appropriate discount rate. For a bond investment, future cash flows include the periodic coupon payments over the bond holding period until maturity and the final payment of par value upon maturity:

$$\text{Bond value} = \sum_{t=1}^{T} \frac{\text{Coupon}}{(1 + \text{discount rate})^t} + \frac{\text{Par value}}{(1 + \text{discount rate})^T}$$

where t is the time period and T is the maturity date.

Example

Par value of bond	: $100
Coupon rate (interest rate on bond)	: 5%
Maturity	: 3 years
Discount rate	: 10%

$$\text{Bond value} = \frac{\$5}{1.1} + \frac{\$5}{1.1^2} + \frac{\$5}{1.1^3} + \frac{\$100}{1.1^3}$$
$$= \$87.57$$

The formula shows that the value of a bond is affected by the coupon rate (coupon yield or nominal yield), par value, and discount rate. The higher (lower) the coupon rate, the higher (lower) the value of the periodic coupon payment and hence the higher (lower) the value of the bond. The higher (lower) the final payment to the bondholder upon maturity (par value), the higher (lower) the current price of the bond.

Discounting the expected future cash flow means finding the present value of the cash flow. The market interest rate is often employed as the discount rate to estimate the present value. Therefore, the value of the bond is affected by the level of market interest rate. The higher (lower) the market interest rate, the lower (higher) the discounted present value of the sum of the periodic coupon payments and the final payment of par value and hence the lower (higher) the bond value is. Put simply, the value of a bond is inversely related to the level of the market interest rate (discount rate). Therefore, bonds are subject to risk due to the interest rate fluctuation.

Bond Yield

bond yield a measure of the rate of return for a bond.

Bond yield is a measure of the rate of return for a bond. Besides using the coupon yield (coupon rate) as a measure to analyze the returns on bonds, there are two other indicators of yield: current yield and yield to maturity (YTM). The current yield shows the return earned per annum.

$$\text{Current yield (\%)} = \frac{\text{Interest payment per annum}}{\text{Bond price}} \times 100\%$$

In other words, current yield is computed by dividing the annual coupon payment by the bond price.

Example

Par value of bond	: $100
Coupon rate (interest rate on bond)	: 5%
Maturity	: 3 years
Market price of bond	: $110

$$\text{Current yield (\%)} = \frac{\$5}{\$110} \times 100\%$$
$$= 4.55\%$$

The relation between bond price and current yield is negative. When the bond price increases, the current yield decreases. Current yield is a simple way to measure the rate of return of a bond. However, the current yield just takes into account the current income of the bond (coupon payment) as a measure of bond return without considering the potential capital gains (increase in bond value) or losses (decrease in bond value) of the bond over the life of the bond.

Yield to maturity is another indicator of return on bond investment over the life of the bond. As compared to current yield, yield to maturity is a better measure of bond return because it takes into account the current interest income and the change in bond value until maturity.

$$\text{Bond price} = \frac{\text{Annual interest}}{(1 + \text{YTM})^t} + \frac{\text{Annual interest}}{(1 + \text{YTM})^{t+1}} + \cdots$$
$$+ \frac{\text{Annual interest} + \text{Bond face value}}{(1 + \text{YTM})^n}$$

where t is the time period and n is the total number of time periods until the bond matures.

This formula shows that the yield to maturity is the discount rate which equates the sum of the present value of future cash flows of the bond to the current bond price. Therefore, the yield to maturity is also called the promised yield or the internal rate of return and is widely used as a measure of average return.

We use the same data to calculate current yield to measure yield to maturity:

Example

Par value of bond	: $100
Coupon rate (interest rate on bond)	: 5%
Maturity	: 3 years
Market price of bond	: $110

$$\$110 = \frac{\$5}{(1 + \text{YTM})^1} + \frac{\$5}{(1 + \text{YTM})^2} + \frac{\$5 + \$100}{(1 + \text{YTM})^3}$$
$$\text{YTM} = 1.562\%$$

When the market price of the bond is the same as the face value of the bond, the current yield is equal to the yield to maturity. The price of the bond and the yield are inversely related. The calculation is easy if the number of time periods until the bond matures is small. However, the calculation of bond price and yield to maturity becomes more complicated if the life of the bond is long.

$$\text{Bond price} = \frac{\text{Annual coupon}}{\text{Yield to maturity}} \left[1 - \frac{1}{\left(1 + \dfrac{\text{Yield to maturity}}{2}\right)^{2 \times \text{Number of coupon periods}}} \right]$$

$$+ \frac{\text{Par value}}{\left(1 + \dfrac{\text{Yield to maturity}}{2}\right)^{2 \times \text{Number of coupon periods}}}$$

We use this formula to calculate the bond price of the previous example given a yield to maturity of 1.562%.

Example

Par value of bond   : $100
Coupon rate (interest rate on bond) : 5%
Maturity   : 3 years
Yield to maturity   : 1.562%

$$\text{Bond price} = \frac{\$5}{0.01562} \left[1 - \frac{1}{\left(1 + \dfrac{0.01562}{2}\right)^{2 \times 3}} \right] + \frac{\$100}{\left(1 + \dfrac{0.01562}{2}\right)^{2 \times 3}}$$

$$= \$110.04$$

The answer shows that, for a three-year 5% coupon bond with par value of $100, given that the yield to maturity is 1.562%, the market price is approximately $110.

So far, we have learnt the formula to compute bond value, coupon yield, current yield, and yield to maturity. Bond value may not necessarily equal par value. Coupon yield, current yield, and yield to maturity are unlikely to be the same. What are the relations between bond value and yield? The relations between coupon yield, current yield, and yield to maturity are different for different types of bonds. For par bonds where the bond price is the same as the par value, the coupon yield, current yield, and yield to maturity are the same. For premium bonds where the bond price is greater than the par value, the coupon yield is greater than the current yield which is greater than the yield to maturity. For discount bonds where the bond price is less than the par value, the coupon yield is less than the current yield which is less than the yield to maturity.

In our examples to compute bond yield, we assume that the bonds are held until maturity. However, in Chapter 3, we learnt that there are different types of bonds such as callable bonds. The issuers of callable bonds can redeem the callable bonds at the call price until the end of the call protection (call deferment) period (a period in which the callable bonds cannot be called) before the bonds mature. Then what would be the yield of callable bonds if they are not held until maturity?

Bond price is inversely related to market interest rate. When the market interest rate decreases, the present value of the sum of the promised payments (coupon payment and payment of par value) increases. If the call price under the call provision is less than the present value of the sum of the promised payments, the issuer of the callable bonds would redeem the bonds before maturity. Therefore, the values (prices) of a straight bond (a bond without a call provision or callability) and a callable bond are different depending on the level of the market interest rate. The difference in values between a straight bond and a callable bond becomes wider (narrower), i.e., they diverge (converge) if the level of market interest rate decreases (increases). The value disparity is due to the value of the call option (explained in greater detail in a later section).

Therefore, if the bond is callable, there is a possibility that the issuer would redeem the bond before maturity, particularly when the market interest rate decreases. In such a case, yield to maturity may not be the appropriate measure of the rate of return for a callable bond as callable bonds may not always be held until maturity. We need to compute the yield to call rather than the yield to maturity. Although yield to call is different from yield to maturity, there is no extra complication. Using the same formula used to compute yield to maturity, we just need to substitute n by the total number of time periods until the bond is called rather than until the bond matures and to replace par value by call price (Table 13.1).

> *Example*
> Par value of bond price : $100
> Coupon rate (interest rate on bond) : 5%
> Maturity : 3 years
> Market price of bond : $110
> Additional information : Interest is paid semi-annually
> Call price is $105
> Bond is callable in 2 years

In this example, the yield to call or the return of the callable bond at the earliest possible call date is 1.16%. Since the call provision gives the bond issuers the right to redeem the bond before the expiration date, the issuers should offer other compensatory advantages for the potential buyers. The compensatory advantages for the investors of callable bonds may be in the form of a discount or higher coupon rate.

Risk for Fixed-income Securities

Before we discuss the investment strategies to manage the fixed-income securities, we need to first understand their risk exposures. They are interest rate risk, call risk, default risk, and liquidity risk.

Table 13.1 Comparison of calculations for yield to maturity and yield to call

	Yield to maturity	Yield to call
Coupon payment	2.5	2.5
Number of years	3	2
Number of semi-annual periods	6	4
Final payment	100	105
Market price	110	110
Yield	0.79%	1.16%

Interest Rate Risk

interest rate risk
Refers to the possibility of the loss in the value of a bond due to interest rate movement.

The fundamental risk of fixed-income securities is due to interest rate fluctuation. The possibility of loss in the value of a bond due to interest rate movement is called **interest rate risk**. There are two types of interest rate risk: price risk and reinvestment risk. As the value of fixed-income securities is inversely related to the interest rate, price risk means that the accumulated value of the fixed-income securities is affected adversely by interest rate change. When interest rate fluctuates, the price of a bond also varies. If interest rate increases (decreases), the price of a bond rises (falls).

When the fixed-income securities mature, the proceeds may be reinvested. The additional income from the reinvestment is called the "interest-on-interest." The interest rate fluctuation may affect the rate of return for the reinvestment of the matured fund. This is reinvestment risk which refers to the uncertainty about the future value of the matured fund reinvested at a rate not known in advance. Reinvestment risk is greater for fixed-income securities with a long-term period to maturity and a high coupon rate. It is also important to note that price risk and reinvestment risk exert offsetting effects.

Call Risk

As the call option attached to the bond (callable bond) allows the bond issuer the right to redeem the bond before the maturity date, the issuer can exercise this right if the market interest rate falls below the coupon rate. This callability feature creates call risk for the bondholders. Firstly, future interest payments from the callable bonds cannot be known with certainty. Secondly, if the bond issuers usually exercise the call option when the market interest rate falls below the coupon rate, the bondholders are exposed to reinvestment risk as they have to reinvest the redeemed funds at a lower interest rate. Thirdly, since it is not common for the price of callable bonds to exceed the callable price, the potential for capital appreciation of a callable bond is greatly reduced. These disadvantages are the call risks for the bondholders holding callable bonds.

Default/Credit Risk

Although fixed-income securities investment promises the investors a periodic coupon payment and final payment of par value, there is a chance that the issuers of fixed-income securities, particularly the corporate issuers, may default on the promised payments. This risk is called default or credit risk.

Liquidity/Marketability Risk

The liquidity or marketability risk refers to the uncertainty of whether the fixed-income securities can be traded at a price close to their value. Liquidity risk is measured by the size of the bid-ask spread; the wider the spread, the higher the liquidity risk.

Interest Rate Risk and Duration

We learn that the value of fixed-income securities is affected mainly by the fluctuations of the market interest rate. Therefore, most of the strategies are related to the ways of dealing with interest rate risk. Before we introduce the strategies, we need to understand interest rate risk and the concept of duration because duration is the key element in investment strategy for fixed income securities to manage interest rate risk. If interest rates rise and fall a lot, the return of fixed-income securities can vary substantially, hence making the fixed-income securities investment risky. So how risky is the fixed-income securities investment? It depends on how sensitive the value of the fixed-income securities is to interest rate fluctuations.

duration A measure of the effective maturity of a bond, it assesses the sensitivity of the bond value to the changes in bond yield and interest rate.

Term to maturity, coupon rate, and yield to maturity are crucial factors of interest rate risk and interest rate sensitivity (i.e., the sensitivity of bond price to interest rate fluctuation). Therefore, we need a better measure of maturity, perhaps an average of the maturities of all promised payments, in order to manage interest rate risk. **Duration**, which is a measure of the effective maturity of a bond, assesses the sensitivity of the bond value to the changes in bond yield and interest rate (Macaulay 1938). Bond duration is the weighted average of all the times until the receipt of each payment (coupon payments and final payment of par value), with the weight for each payment time as the present value of the payment divided by the price of bond $\left(\frac{\text{Payment}_t\ /\ (1 + \text{Yield to maturity})^t}{\text{Bond price}}\right)$. Therefore, the formula of duration is defined as:

$$\text{Duration} = \sum_{t=1}^{T} \text{time until payment (in years)} \times \text{Weight}_t$$

Example
Par value of bond price   : $100
Coupon rate (interest rate on bond) : 5%
Maturity   : 3 years
Yield to maturity   : 15%

Time until payment (in years)	Payment	Present value of payment	Weight	Time until payment × Weight
1	5	4.35	0.06	0.06
2	5	3.78	0.05	0.10
3	105	69.04	0.89	2.68
		77.17	1	2.84

In this example, the duration of a three-year 5% coupon bond is 2.84, which is shorter than the term to maturity. It means that the effective maturity of all the cash flows paid out by a coupon bond is less than the time to maturity of a bond because duration gives weight to the interim payments of a coupon. You may then wonder about the duration of a zero-coupon rate bond. No calculation is required. Since there is only one cash flow payment of a zero-coupon bond (i.e., the final payment of par value when the bond matures), the duration of a zero-coupon bond must equal its time to maturity as the weighted average until the only one payment of par value is the maturity. Therefore, for two bonds with an equal term to maturity, the duration of a zero-coupon bond must be greater than that of a non-zero coupon bond because early coupon payments exert less impact (less weight) on the weighted average time of all payments. This concept of duration is important in risk management.

13.2 Investment Strategies for Fixed-income Securities

There are two main types of active strategies in fixed-income securities management. In order to handle the interest rate risk, the active managers may predict the future movement of interest rates or make an intra-market analysis to spot the mispriced fixed income securities. You may observe that many of the strategies involve swaps of bonds. Bond swap is a useful technique to change the current yield and yield to maturity to improve the quality of the bond portfolio. Bond swap is a relatively more sophisticated strategy in bond portfolio management, which is beyond the scope of this book.

For passive strategy managers, the main task is to control the interest rate risk in order to shield the current and future values of the fixed-income securities from financial loss due to interest rate fluctuation. Immunization strategy is one of the most common techniques used by the passive strategy manager (Redington 1952). The objective of the immunization strategy is to shield the return of the fixed income securities from interest rate risk. One form of immunization strategy is the duration-matching strategy. Duration matching means making use of the relation between duration and maturity to adjust the maturity structure of the assets and liabilities in the investment portfolio. Consequently, the effects of the price risk and reinvestment risk can offset each other to minimize the uncertainty of the values of the matured portfolio and reinvestment portfolio.

For instance, financial planners may have to manage the pension fund for their clients. There are both assets and liabilities in the pension fund. The assets of the pension fund are used to generate income to pay out the periodic payments (liabilities) to the retired clients. One of the risks faced by financial planners and the pension fund managers is the mismatch of the maturities between assets and liabilities. In addition, the return of the assets and the value of the liabilities are subject to changes in the market interest rate. The duration-matching strategy helps to match the maturities of assets and liabilities and protect the value of the pension fund against interest rate volatility.

Fixed-income securities are subject to two types of interest rate risks: price risk and reinvestment risk. There is a negative relation between price risk and reinvestment risk. When the interest rate increases (decreases), price risk gets higher (lower) and reinvestment risk gets lower (higher). As the value of fixed-income securities is inversely related to interest rate, when interest rate increases, the value of the accumulated fund of the investment decreases. On the contrary, when the fixed-income securities mature, the proceeds of the matured fund can be reinvested at a higher rate when interest rate increases. Consequently, the capital loss and capital gain may offset each other. Therefore, using the same logic, when interest rate falls, the value of the accumulated fund and the reinvested fund increases and decreases, respectively.

If the portfolio duration of the fixed-income securities equals the investment horizon, the capital gain and loss from price risk and reinvestment risk can offset each other, thus immunizing the total portfolio return from interest rate risk. Therefore, through duration matching, the financial planners and the pension fund managers can cause the values of the assets and liabilities to react similarly to the change in interest rate. Consequently, the return of the assets can be sufficient to meet the obligation of the liabilities in case there is interest rate fluctuation.

13.3   Valuation of Derivatives

Financial assets can be broadly classified into primary assets and derivative assets. Equities and fixed-income securities, which we have discussed in the previous sections, are examples of primary financial assets. Primary assets are issued for the purpose of raising capital. Derivative assets are called "derivatives" because their values are "derived" from the prices of other securities. Therefore, another name for derivatives is *contingent claims* as the payoffs of these derivatives are conditional, and depend on the prices of other securities. Derivatives are mainly used for hedging and speculation. Hedging means that the investors use the derivatives to protect against price volatility while speculation means that the investors trade in the derivatives to make profits from their price movements. There are two types of derivatives: options and futures. Examples of underlying assets for options and futures include stocks, stock indices, market indices, industry indices, foreign currency, future prices of agricultural commodities, precious metals (gold, silver), fixed-income securities, and interest rate options.

The commonly used derivative instruments in the market are options, futures contracts, and forward contracts. Other derivatives include swaps (which entitle the participating sides to exchange current flows at a prescribed date or several dates in the future), futures rate agreement (FRA), and note issue facilitation (NIF). Options, futures contracts, and forward contracts are similar in the way that there may be a transaction (purchase or sale) of underlying assets at a specified date in the future. However, options are different from futures or forward contracts in that the holders of options may decline exercising the options if they are not profitable. On the contrary, the holders of futures or forward contracts have to fulfill their obligations to buy and sell at the specified date and price as agreed upon in the contract.

A futures contract is different from a forward contract as the futures contract is the formalized forward contract with the gains and losses on the futures contract settled daily in a marking to market process rather than upon the delivery of the underlying asset. The transaction of a futures contract is a zero-sum game between the two parties of the contract as the gain earned by the buyer equals the loss made by the seller and vice versa. Table 13.2 shows the terminology commonly used in the derivatives market. (As Derivatives is a topic that comes under advanced financial management and risk management, we do not discuss derivatives in depth in this book. We briefly introduce the derivatives instruments here because they are closely related to equity, bonds, and risk management.)

Table 13.2 Terminology of derivatives

Term	Definition
Option	The right but not an obligation to buy or sell an underlying asset at a specific price on or before a certain date.
Call option	The right but not the obligation to purchase an asset at a specified price (exercise price/strike price) on or before a specified expiration date.
Put option	The right but not the obligation to sell an asset at a specified price (exercise price /strike price) on or before a specified expiration date.
Exercise/Strike price	The specified price on the options contract at which the underlying asset can be purchased for a call or sold for a put, or simply the specified price at which the options can be exercised.
Premium	The purchase price of options.
Expiration date	The last day specified on the option contract on which the options can be exercised.
Options writer	The seller of call (put) options who receives premium as compensation against the possibility on or before the specified expiration date and is obligated to sell (buy) the asset in return for an exercise price lower (higher) than the market value of asset if it is a call (put).
In the money option	An option, when exercised, which would produce positive payoff for the holder.
Out of the money option	An option, when exercised, which would be unprofitable.
At the money option	An option with an exercise price equal to asset price.
American option	The right to purchase the underlying asset if it is a call and to sell the underlying asset if it is a put, and to exercise options on or before the expiration date.
European option	The right to exercise options only on the expiration date (note that American options provide more flexibility than European options; American options are more valuable than European options).
Margin requirement of option	The option writer is required to post margin to guarantee their contract obligations are fulfilled. Factors that determine the amount of margin requirement: a. The amount by which the options are in the money—the value of moneyness is an indication of the potential obligation of the options writer whether the options would be exercised. b. The amount by which the options are out of the money—options which are out of the money require less margin. c. The possession of the underlying asset by the options writer—if the call options writers own the underlying asset, the call options writers can satisfy the margin requirement by making the asset readily available when the options are exercised.
Forward contract	A contract made today between buyer and seller who commit to a transaction for a future delivery of underlying asset at a specified date and price agreed upon now so as to avoid future price fluctuations of the underlying asset.
Futures contract	A formalized forward contract between buyer and seller who specify a price today for future delivery of an underlying asset upon contract maturity A standardized contract with respect to the types of contract, contract size, futures price, precise requirements of underlying asset, allowable grade of underlying asset, maturity date, and delivery procedure managed through an organized futures exchange.
Futures price	The price agreed between buyer and seller to be paid to fulfill the contract obligation upon contract maturity.
Long position	The futures contract buyer buying the underlying asset upon contract maturity and profiting from the increase in futures price.
Short position	The contract seller selling the underlying asset upon contract maturity and profiting from the decrease in futures price.
Spot price	Actual market price of the underlying asset on the delivery date.

Table 13.2 continued

Term	Definition
Margin account of futures	Deposit of funds in a futures trading account as a security account to guarantee that futures traders are able to fulfill the obligations of the futures contract and to cover potential loss due to outstanding futures position.
Marking to market	Daily settlement of gains and losses on futures contract in the margin account of futures traders due to the futures price fluctuation.
Maintenance/variation margin	A predetermined level in the margin account which activates a margin call (a notification) to the futures traders to replenish the loss in the margin account.

In general, the purchase of derivative instruments is regarded as a substitute for the direct investment in the underlying asset. Then you may wonder why it is more attractive to invest in derivatives rather than in the underlying asset. Table 13.3 shows the payoff of the traders of derivatives under different scenarios.

Derivatives are attractive because they provide leverage for the traders. Options can be viewed as a levered investment in the underlying asset since the values of the options vary more than proportionately to the changes in the values of the underlying asset, however, with a lesser investment outlay requirement. In addition, options are an attractive investment because the downside risk is limited. No matter how much the market price of the underlying asset falls below (rises above) the call (put) exercise price, the net loss to the call (put) purchaser is limited to the premium amount paid to purchase the options. Similarly, the initial outlay for the purchase of the actual asset is much larger than the cost for setting up a margin account of futures contract. Consequently, greater leverage can be achieved through futures trading than through direct investment in the underlying asset.

Table 13.3 Payoff table of derivatives traders

Scenario	Strategy	Value of derivatives	Net profit/Loss for holder	Net profit/loss for seller
Market price of asset > Call exercise price	Exercise options	Asset price – Exercise price	[Asset price – Exercise price] – Premium	Premium – [Value of asset – Exercise price]
Market price of asset ≤ Call exercise price	Not exercise options	0	– Premium	Premium
Market price of asset < Put exercise price	Exercise options	Exercise price – Market price	[Exercise price – Market price] – Premium	Premium – [Exercise price – Value of asset]
Market price of asset ≥ Put exercise price	Not exercise options	0	– Premium	Premium
Expected spot price > Futures price	Long position	Spot price – Futures price	Spot price – Futures price	– [Spot price – Futures price]
Expected spot price < Futures price	Short position	Futures price – Spot price	Futures price – Spot price	– [Futures price – Spot price]

Another reason why traders may prefer to invest in options and futures contracts rather than the actual underlying assets is that the transaction cost for trading in the options and futures market is much less. Besides, as we have mentioned, the main purpose of derivatives investment is to control risk. This function of risk management can be attained by making different combinations of call and put options investments with the underlying assets.

In addition to the usefulness of derivative instruments in risk management, we need to understand derivatives because there are many option-linked investment securities. One example of option-linked securities that we have mentioned is the callable bond. Other more common examples are convertible bonds (the right to exchange bonds for shares), convertible preferred stocks (the right to exchange preferred stocks for common stocks), and traditional warrants (call options delivered by listed firms for the holders to buy shares issued).

In Hong Kong and Germany equity warrants issued by investment banks (like a stock option) are very popular among investors for investment and hedging. More recently, equity-linked notes (ELNs) offered by investment banks and brokerage houses through their retail networks and commercial banks have become important vehicles in the investment arena for both small and large players. ELNs, existing in different forms, can be used as a hedging device for both financial and commercial institutions. The most popular format is the Bull ELN, which imbeds a put option to purchase some underlying assets (normally some blue chip stocks) and a fixed-term note in one product, and allows small investors to participate in writing options at the retail level. These instruments provide a new platform for investments and risk management for institutions in a more competitive and efficient manner. Wealth managers must fully understand the benefits and risk of these new instruments and the financial implications to their clients in order to ensure proper risk control for the portfolios under their management.

Key Terms

bond yield   *373*
duration   *378*

interest rate risk   *377*

References

Investment Company Fact Book 2006 (www.icifactbook.org).

Macaulay, F., *Some Theoretical Problems Suggested by the Movements of Interest Rates, Bond Yields and Stock Prices in the United States Since 1856* (New York: National Bureau of Economic Research, 1938).

Redington, F. M., "Review of the Principle of Life-Office Valuations," *Journal of the Institute of Actuaries,* vol. 78 (1952): 286–340.

Multiple-choice Questions

1. The term structure of interest rates describes the relation between _____ and _____ of default-free debt instruments.
    A. risk; return
    B. time to maturity; interest rate
    C. risk; interest rate
    D. discount rate; coupon rate

2. The following illustrates the calculation of bond value:

    Par value of bond   : $100
    Coupon rate (interest rate on bond) : 8%
    Maturity   : 3 years
    Discount rate   : 10%

    What is the bond value?
    A. $87
    B. $95
    C. $99
    D. $103

3. A callability feature in a bond creates risk for the _____.
    A. government
    B. issuers
    C. bondholders
    D. option holders

4. Bull ELN, which imbeds a _____ option to purchase some underlying assets and a fixed-term note in one product, allows small investors to participate in writing options at the retail level.
    A. call
    B. futures
    C. currency
    D. put

chapter **14**

Asset Allocation Strategies

After studying this chapter you should be able to:

1 Explain asset allocation strategies.
2 Understand the complementary portfolio concept.
3 Know about portfolio performance measurements.
4 Understand strategic asset allocation.
5 Understand tactical asset allocation.

14.1 An Overview of Investment Planning and Asset Allocation

Investment planning here refers to investment for medium-term goals such as education funds and home purchase. Determining the client's financial states (step 3) normally involves assessing the appropriateness of existing investment products and portfolio composition of the clients. With the understanding that most clients, especially those in Asia, will not tell the planners about all their wealth and financial assets, the planner has to be careful about the potential effects of his recommendation on investment strategies and products used. One solution to the problem of giving advice on the partial wealth of clients is to ask the client or his investment advisor for the remaining wealth or to at least tell you the riskiness of the unknown portfolio and the value of that portfolio relative to the known portion that you are aware of. In this case, you can try to come up with a complementary portfolio to serve the overall goals of the client.

Another way to deal with the existence of unknown financial assets of clients is to design a portfolio to focus on your portion of the wealth/income to achieve a special life goal, such as education funds for children. In this case, you have a very specific goal with known investment horizon and risk level. Of course, dividing the money up into different portfolios based on the investment goals appears to be inefficient from the administrative and cost perspectives. However, there are some advantages of doing so for the client in terms of managing his or her expectations and giving a proper evaluation of your performance. By directly relating the investment portfolio with a specific goal, it is much easier to educate the clients about the appropriate risk-return trade-off, the reason for the asset mix, and the optimal duration of the investment. This is especially true when the planner handles only part of the wealth. This goal-specific portfolio approach will give the client a clear linkage between your advice and the performance of your suggested portfolio.

As we mentioned above, the information on existing investments is important for the planner to decide how the investment goals of the client should be achieved. In most cases, some changes in the investment vehicles and asset allocation would be necessary. In the case of using savings per month for investment, the planner should consider investment plans that have minimum cost. As the execution of new investment plans may involve selling existing securities, timing of the implementation can be tricky and the planner should consider the impact of timing uncertainty on implementation when forming the new investment portfolio strategies.

14.2 Investment Strategy Recommendations

Investment strategy in the context of financial planning is very different from investment to maximize returns. For financial planners and their clients, investment planning has several distinctive features. These features include relating investment to life goals, taking a long-term perspective in most cases, and staying away from high-risk products and strategies such as options, futures, warrants, and high-yield securities. Of course, we are not saying that clients should never participate in short-term investment activities. However, their speculative behavior should have nothing to do with the investment portfolios managed by their financial planners. Before we move on to the actual asset allocation strategies, let us briefly discuss three topics related to investment planning for clients.

Investment for Goals

Not everybody believes that investment for goals and partitioning the portfolio by goals are good ideas. Traditional wealth management practice would simply take all the money of clients and form one portfolio. Of course, there would be some matching between risk tolerance levels and the portfolio choices. However, this practice assumes that the clients are relatively wealthy and that they do not need to withdraw money from the investment portfolio for medium-term goals such as education needs for children. Middle-income clients, for whom education funding may be a significant financial obligation, would appreciate the setting up of a separate investment portfolio for education needs.

Most middle-income clients cannot afford to have private banking services that offer proprietary investment funds or individual securities. For clients with very limited wealth with a clear goal, a more efficient method to construct the portfolio is to use mutual funds. For example, there are managed funds available for education purposes in the United States such as Fidelity's College Savings Plan accounts (which are also tax-deferred when the money is used for education purposes). Using a managed portfolio format, the predetermined portfolios are established based on the age of the children. The longer the duration before college, the riskier the portfolio would be. The risk of the managed portfolio declines through time. The managed portfolios automatically and systematically switch money from equity to fixed income when the children approach college-entering age.

Such a goal-specific investment portfolio is easy to understand and to be evaluated for performance by clients. Of course, for any given client, there should be no more than two to three goal-specific portfolios; otherwise, it will be too tedious to follow. There is also another academic problem of such a practice: the suitability of risk-return trade-off for the combined portfolio. As each portfolio is formed based on a specific goal, there is no guarantee that the combined portfolio is the best one in terms of risk tolerance level and return for the clients. However, if the emphasis of financial planning is on prudence and meeting financial goals instead of finding the most efficient portfolio, then a goal-specific strategy would be acceptable as the criteria using risk tolerance level, investment horizon, and return expectation are imposed on each segmented portfolio to come up with the appropriate asset allocation. In this case, the risk of the combined portfolio should not be higher than the individual ones.

Of course, by doing so, the overall return may be suboptimal and transaction costs may be more than necessary. However, given the fact that mutual funds would most likely not be used, and turnover and switching are minimal due to the relatively long-term nature of these goals, the potential drawbacks are limited. Finally, due to the different investment horizons of different goals (e.g., 5 to 10 years for education, but 15 to 20 years for retirement), it can be challenging to use one portfolio which is required to incorporate the earlier liquidation of partial portfolio in the initial analysis. The bottom line is that there are pros and cons of using goal-specific portfolios. For a middle-income client with two or three major goals, a goal-specific strategy appears to have more merits than drawbacks.

Complementary Portfolio Concept

To gain trust from clients is not an easy task. It would take years for most clients to totally trust a planner. Thus, it is very common that a brand new client would not disclose all his or her wealth to a financial planner for investment purposes. Even if the client may trust the planner, due to different specialties of investment expertise, it is not uncommon for a wealthy client to divide his wealth and apportion the money to different investment advisors based on their expertise (e.g., fixed-income, high growth, international). Consequently, many financial planners would not control or manage all the investable assets of a client. The concept of a **complementary portfolio** is useful here. It simply means that the purpose of the partial or supplementary portfolio managed by the financial planners have to take into consideration the overall financial wealth of the clients.

complementary portfolio The partial portfolio that aims to complement the client's existing financial assets to achieve an optimal risk and return combination.

For example, if for some reason the client has 70% of his money locked into a fixed-income portfolio with a maturity of 5 to 10 years in staggered terms, which is out of the control of the planner, then the remaining 30% managed by the planner have to complement the other 70% in a way that will achieve an optimal risk-return benchmark for the client. Of course, this is not easy and sometimes the final portfolio may still be suboptimal. For financial planning that focuses on long-term life goals, the precision and efficiency of the portfolio strategy are not the only things that matter. As long as the financial planners pay attention to this issue and try their best to reduce the effect of the problem, the clients should be satisfied. As we all know, return maximization is not the right goal for the client and not the right strength of a financial planner. Once clients and financial planners have a mutually agreed portfolio and recognize the limitations of the investment strategies, the planners should move on and tie all the pieces together to develop a balanced plan without spending too much time to worry about the investment side.

Investment Objectives

We discussed the benefits and content of an investment policy statement in Chapter 5. Investment goals and objectives are the very first element of the policy statement. The goals and objectives serve as the foundation to benchmark the performance expectations of the investment portfolio, and are very important for evaluating future performance of the portfolio and the financial planner. An example of an investment objective is "to earn an average return exceeding the 5-year and the 10-year benchmarks." Of course, there can be more details like how the returns should be earned, the rationale and calculation of the benchmarks, and the boundary of the asset allocation, in order to spell out how the objectives can be implemented. For individual clients, the investment objectives should be related to their life goals. As making money is only a means, not an end, for most people, there should be a clear connection between qualitative life goals and quantitative investment objectives, so that the clients can understand why certain risks and returns are used as benchmarks.

14.3   Asset Allocation Strategies

In order to come up with recommendations on asset allocation for an investment portfolio, there are several necessary steps involved.

1. Financial planners should have an appropriate risk tolerance assessment tool to evaluate the risk profiles of their clients.
2. Financial planners should have access to all the required return and risk data for all asset classes and individual mutual funds and securities to be used to construct the portfolio. In addition, they should have some idea of preferred investment vehicles in each asset class for current market conditions. As different time horizons, risk tolerance levels, and investment sizes may result in different optimal investment vehicles, financial planners should also have some preferred choices for each of these different client profiles.
3. Upon matching the risk tolerance level with the efficient frontier proxied by a range of five to seven portfolio choices, a specific portfolio mix suitable for the client's risk preference can be identified.
4. Upon identification of the asset allocation mix, specific mutual funds or securities should be identified within each asset class. In addition, alternatives must be provided as much as possible for all recommended investment vehicles so that the clients can have some freedom in choosing their own investments. Also remember that in case of any rebate in commission and potential conflict of interest for some of the recommended vehicles, full disclosure must be provided for clients.
5. A forecast of returns using the recommended portfolio mix should be provided for clients from the near future all the way to the expected liquidation year so that the clients can have a sense of overall wealth

accumulation. If possible, different scenarios of returns based on various economic and market conditions should be simulated so that the clients will know the possible range of returns instead of believing that they can earn the mean returns reported in the single-scenario forecast.

Asset allocation strategies can be relatively straightforward or extremely complicated. For an active investment fund, the fund manager can adopt quantitative-oriented strategies such as strategic asset allocation, tactical asset allocation, and dynamic asset allocation. Some of these advanced strategies emphasize computer modeling with high turnovers. For financial planning purposes, we do not encourage planners to focus on these approaches as their clients do not have the investment size to justify the cost of using these approaches. Unless their clients are ultra-high net-worth clients or clients of a private banking division which pools different clients' money into in-house investment funds, financial planners should focus on more passive asset allocation strategies with occasional but less frequent switching activity to minimize transaction costs. Research indicates that unless the portfolio managers are exceptionally smart and successful, most active portfolios do not earn enough to justify the high transaction costs due to the high turnover.

Risk Tolerance Assessment

We have discussed the concept of risk profiling and the use of risk tolerance questionnaires in evaluating a client's risk preference in Chapter 6. Remember that most risk tolerance questionnaires are not very accurate. Thus, we should not count on the risk tolerance score too much in helping us to form the optimal portfolio. Other quantitative assessments on family background, life values, human capital, and even health condition should be considered in making the decision on the riskiness of the chosen portfolio. It is more important to make sure that the clients are comfortable with the riskiness of the portfolio so that when the performance is bad, they do not insist on liquidating some of the assets and jeopardize the long-term performance of the portfolio.

When the portfolio is targeted for retirement purposes, the power of money through compounded returns is much more important than speculating on the ups and downs of the market. As long as the chosen securities and mutual funds are financially sound, given a long enough time period, the gain from the portfolios will be close to the forecast and the clients will be able to enjoy the profit from the investment at retirement. In short, the risk tolerance assessment exercise should not be viewed as the key indicator in choosing the optimal portfolio. Instead, the financial planner should view the risk tolerance assessment exercise as a safety check in order to eliminate inappropriate investments.

14.4   Key Issues in Forming the Portfolio

Understanding the Return Calculation Procedures and their Limitations

In any given portfolio, many asset classes are involved. Thus it is a common practice for planners to use secondary data (i.e., financial data generated by another services provider) to generate the weighted average return for their home-made portfolios for clients. Owing to computational convenience, the returns or prices provided are in the form of monthly figures, so that the users/planners can form their own return for a given time period through mathematical aggregation. Two commonly used methods for aggregation are arithmetic return (based on the sum of returns in each period) and geometric return (based on the product of return in each period). Of course, the best way to compute returns for most clients is to use the holding period return, which reflects the actual profit for the investment period:

$$HPR = \frac{(\text{Ending price} - \text{Beginning price} + \text{Cash dividend})}{\text{Beginning price}}$$

The following example illustrates a potential problem in using the arithmetic return method to compute the overall return for two periods.

Example for Return Aggregation

Year	Price (end)	Holding period return (HPR)
1996	$50	$(P_t - P_{t-1})/P_t$
1997	$70	$(70 - 50)/50 = 40.0\%$
1998	$90	$(90 - 70)/70 = 28.6\%$

2-year HPR: ($90 − $50)/$50 = 80%
2-year arithmetic return: (40% + 28.6%) = 68.8%
2-year geometric return: [(1 + 0.40) × (1 + 0.286)] − 1 = 80%

The above example demonstrates the fact that using the arithmetic return approach to aggregate single-period returns to form a longer-period performance measure can lead to a wrong conclusion. In this case, the 2-year return based on the arithmetic approach understates the actual return by more than 11%. The reason is that the arithmetic method implicitly assumes periodical (in this case, annual) liquidation and immediate reinvestment in the same asset. However, this is an inappropriate assumption if the client intends to hold the asset for 2 years. Then there is no reason to count money at the end of each year and restart the clock the next year for the purpose of calculating return. In fact, there are other price patterns for which the arithmetic method can lead to a nontrivial error. The conclusion is that the geometric method is always accurate. Unfortunately, the arithmetic method is simple to use and some planners would be tempted to use it to generate returns for different clients.

Understanding the Risk Calculation Procedures and their Limitations

Most textbooks and publicly available performance fact sheets use standard deviation to measure risk. Standard deviation reflects the deviation from the mean return, which shows the uncertainty of receiving a return other than the mean value. However, standard deviation does not differentiate upside potential from the downside risk of investment. For most clients, their main concern is the probability of losing money. Thus the chance of suffering loss and the magnitude of maximum loss are more practical measures of risk than standard deviation. Of course, one may suggest that we can replace the standard deviation with semi-variance focusing on the negative aspect. By doing so, we can use a better measure for measuring risk for clients. Unfortunately, the derivation of key investment theories such as portfolio theory and CAPM requires the use of financial parameters coming from a normal distribution. As mean and standard deviation are the two parameters describing normal distribution, we have no choice but to use standard deviation to measure risk when using asset allocation strategy based on portfolio theory. In short, there are limitations of using different risk measures. Therefore, we have to be aware of the potential effects of these limitations when making asset allocation recommendations.

Forming Asset Classes

Many planners may wonder how to decide the number of asset classes used in a portfolio. Too few classes may lead the client to have an impression that they are not getting a sophisticated asset allocation strategy. However, too many classes would definitely create too much work in the subsequent steps on choosing investment vehicles and performance tracking. From a practical perspective, by excluding cash (for simplicity, mandating 10% cash for emergency reserve and liquidity and using the remaining 90% to form the portfolio for asset allocation purpose) from the asset classes, as few as two asset classes (equity and bonds) can be sufficient for a small-size portfolio for retirement or education. For a high risk tolerance client with a sizable portfolio, possible asset classes can include investment grade bonds, high-yield bonds, local equity (blue chips), local equity (small firm/high growth), international equity (region 1), international equity (region 2), foreign currencies, alternative investments (not likely but possible), and even real estate investment (popular among clients in Asia-Pacific areas). Of course, the clients may already have existing assets for some classes such as real estate and currencies. Thus the planners are expected to estimate the optimal percentage of these classes but are not required to give advice on specific investment choices for them. Table 14.1 shows an example of risk and return inputs for four asset classes and the process to generate the efficient frontier.

In addition, whether the planners would use mutual funds or individual securities within each asset class also has some bearing on the number of asset classes used. As mutual funds can help clients to invest in a diversified basket of securities with limited capital, it is possible to use mutual funds to invest in more asset classes under a limited budget. However, it may not be possible to do so if individual securities are used within asset classes. Based on market practice among independent financial planners in the United States, it is believed that it is more common, more time-efficient and more cost-efficient to use mutual funds than to use individual securities to form portfolios.

Based on the concept of portfolio theory, it is not difficult to employ a portfolio optimization software to produce a series of three to seven portfolios with different risk-return combinations along the efficient frontier. The software can also provide the details of percentages of each asset class that comprise

Table 14.1 Generating the efficient frontier using four asset classes

| | **(Annual return 1989–2001)** | | | |
	Bond	**Global stock**	**HK stock**	**Cash**
Return	9.54%	10.99%	17.96%	6.56%
STD	13.71%	16.58%	41.00%	1.81%

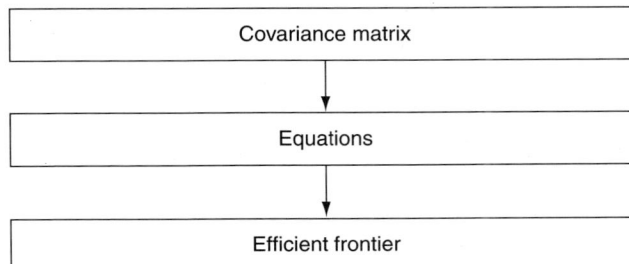

```
┌─────────────────────────────────┐
│       Covariance matrix         │
└─────────────────────────────────┘
                │
                ▼
┌─────────────────────────────────┐
│          Equations              │
└─────────────────────────────────┘
                │
                ▼
┌─────────────────────────────────┐
│        Efficient frontier       │
└─────────────────────────────────┘
```

Note: The bond return is based on Lehman Brothers' Aggregate Bond Index. The global stock return is based on MSCI World Index. The Hong Kong stock return is based on Hang Seng Index. Cash return is proxied by 1-month HIBOR rate.

the portfolios. Table 14.2 shows an example of allocation mixes for three portfolios with different risk levels. Of course, the choice of input data as asset class benchmarks would affect the final weights and the combination of asset classes. The planners should make sure that the return inputs used reflect the forecast return of the investment vehicles available for the clients. Otherwise, the portfolio returns used to demonstrate the future performance of the client's investment would not be a fair return estimate for the invested portfolio. Finally, the planners should check with the local regulations on the boundary of providing investment advice to clients under certain investment-related licenses. To avoid the problem of violating regulations on giving home-made forecast return and investment advice, the financial services firms can produce these analyses and recommendations on behalf of the planners.

Table 14.2 An example of asset allocation mix for a three-portfolio approach

	Conservative	**Moderate**	**Aggressive**
Return	9.50%	10.50%	11.50%
Standard deviation	8.32%	11.15%	14.01%
	Allocation percentage		
Global stock	7.06%	10.29%	13.52%
Hong Kong stock	14.03%	18.66%	23.29%
Bond	32.85%	45.86%	58.70%
Cash	46.07%	25.19%	4.50%

Note: The results in this table are based on data from 1989 to 2001 of the four asset classes listed in Table 14.1.

Understanding the Challenges Related to Asset Allocation Strategies and Performance

Challenge 1

There exists a difference between what the traditional portfolio theory implies and what most investment professionals and financial planners practice in terms of asset allocation. Assuming that the market is perfectly efficient and there exists an equity market index which can accurately reflect the risk-return combination depicted at the tangency point "M" (the true market portfolio) on the efficient frontier (Figure 14.1), all investors should follow the principle of two-fund separation. In other words, all clients should have a portfolio (along the capital market line, CML, which is the capital allocation line passing through M) consisting of a risk-free bond portfolio and a market portfolio, which is normally proxied by index funds or ETFs (exchange-traded funds with underlying stocks mimicking indices). Figure 14.1 shows the CML and the efficient frontier.

In reality, the concept of market efficiency is a matter of degree instead of choosing between the two extreme cases: perfectly efficient or totally inefficient. For investment professionals who believe that the existing market indices are not a good proxy of the true market portfolio, or that they possess superior stock selection and timing skills in the world of inefficient markets, active investment strategies selecting undervalued securities or funds are a better deal than passive strategies through indexing. Following this logic, many investment professionals would not promote the usage of index funds but invest in objective-specific mutual funds or individual securities in the hope of beating the market by identifying undervalued assets and by active timing. In other words, few planners would actually practice two-fund separation and recommend their clients to buy equity index funds only. Thus the majority of the investment industry promotes the idea of using active funds (nonindexed portfolios) for investment.

Figure 14.2 shows the practice of matching clients' risk tolerance level directly to the efficient frontier for risky portfolios. The approach in Figure 14.2

Figure 14.1 Two-fund separation and efficient frontier

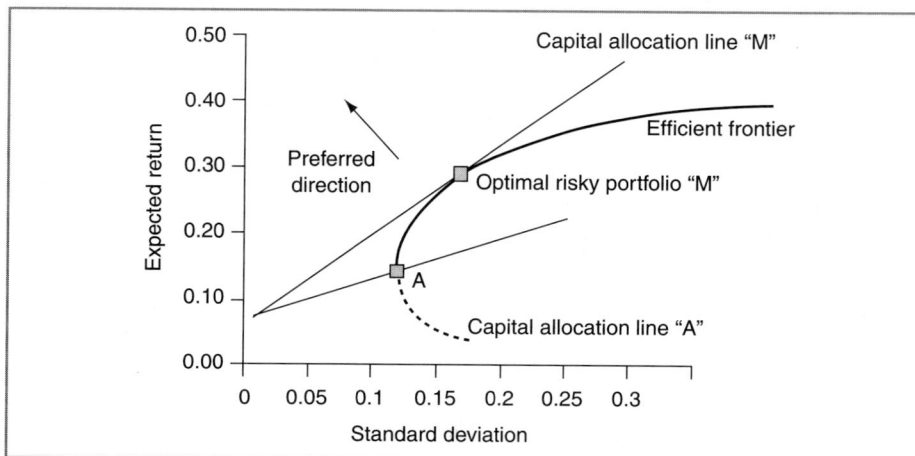

Figure 14.2 Identifying five-benchmark portfolio on efficient frontier

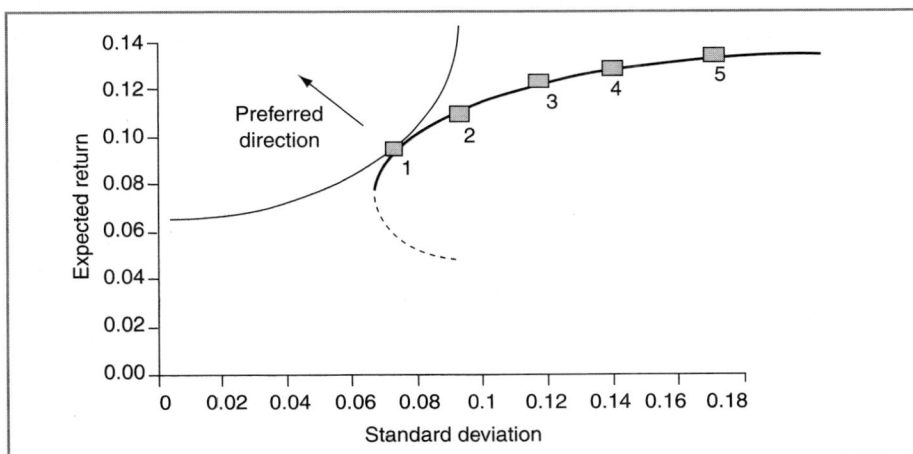

does not include risk-free assets in the analysis. Risk-free rates exist as long as the investment horizon is a certainty. In practice, there is always a chance that the default risk-free bond portfolio may be liquidated earlier than expected. Owing to interest rate risk, the overall risk of the bond portfolio can still be non-zero. In addition, the efficient frontiers for risk portfolios constructed from recent data are relatively flat and closed to the Y-axis. Thus the shape and position of the real-life risky efficient frontier is not much different from the CAL based on two-fund separation.

Of course, there are some others who prefer to use index funds for each asset class but pursue an asset allocation strategy based on regional market movements. In this case, a mix of passive and active strategies is employed. Within the asset class, a passive strategy (indexing) is followed. However, active timing and selection strategies are used to decide the weightings of the asset classes.

Challenge 2

Another challenge related to practicing asset allocation strategies is the occasional flat efficient frontier (for risky assets). Table 14.2 illustrates this problem. The differential return for aggressive and conservative portfolios is 2%, but the risk differential is about 6%, indicating a pretty flat efficient frontier. Such a risk-return trade-off makes it difficult to justify investing in high-risk portfolios, as the small increase in return does not nearly compensate for the much higher risk involved. There is no easy solution to this challenge. The financial planner should examine carefully if the same risk-return combinations would persist in the future and advise their clients about the small risk premium accordingly.

Challenge 3

So far we have discussed the financial capital which can be invested to generate income. However, there is one source of capital which is equally important but often neglected in asset allocation and investment by the financial planners and the clients themselves. The third challenge to be discussed here is the human capital of the clients. Human capital is related to the investment choice of the clients. Human capital is the discounted present value of future labor income, which is analogous to the price of financial assets. There are two major functions, hedging effect and cushion effect, of human capital in asset allocation.

The hedging function of human capital means that the clients can use the labor income to hedge against the risk in financial investment and vice versa. For instance, if there is a high income risk (high uncertainty about future income due to high unemployment rate or high corporate bankruptcy rate) in the labor market, financial planners should suggest that clients hold a smaller proportion of risky assets in the portfolio.

Human capital can provide a cushion effect for investment income. If there is a high variability in the financial market, the investments are subject to market volatility. Sometimes, the investments may result in a loss. Then the cushion effect of human capital may come to play a role by allowing the labor supply flexibility to be used to offset the shock to financial investments. Financial planners may suggest that clients work more to make up for the losses in the financial market. Therefore, financial planners have to take the nature of the job and the labor supply flexibility of clients into consideration when making investment suggestions.

Challenge 4

The fourth challenge that financial planners need to realize is related to the misunderstanding of expecting a declining risk when the portfolio consists of more independent stocks. The research evidence of declining portfolio risk when the number of independent stocks increases is based on a large-scale simulation and the curve reflects the mean value of risk for many portfolios containing the same number of stocks. However, if we look at the curve with a three-dimensional perspective (see Figure 14.2), we should realize that at each point on the curve, there exists a whole distribution. In reality, all clients invest in one portfolio, not a thousand. Thus there is a high chance that the actual risk of the client's portfolio would be higher or lower than the mean value. In this case, a lucky client with 30 independent stocks may have a lower portfolio risk than another unlucky client with a 40-stock portfolio. Of course, when the planners aggregate all the clients' portfolio risks through a long period of time, the mean value declining curve would be an accurate reflection between risk and number of independent stocks in a portfolio. The planners have to understand this when looking at the statistics of portfolio risks for their clients. Newbould and Poon (1993) concluded that, in the US market, investing in 80 stocks can minimize the risk of not getting the mean portfolio risk to an acceptable level (as Figure 14.3 shows that the cross-sectional distribution is getting more narrow when the number of stocks increases). Therefore, the connotation is that, for a client investing in one portfolio, the planner has to use at least 80 independent stocks to achieve traditional risk diversification as predicted in the mean curve. If capital is limited, then using mutual funds would be a good choice in achieving this effect.

Figure 14.3 The minimum number of stocks needed for diversification

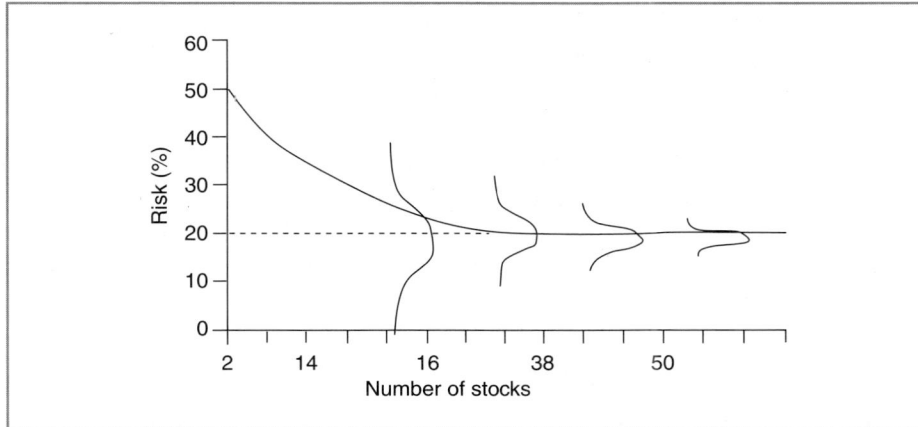

Source: "The Minimum Number of Stocks Needed for Diversification," Newbould, G. D. and Poon, P. S., *Financial Practice and Education*, vol. 3, no. 2 (Fall 1993): 85–87.

Challenge 5

The final challenge is related to the investment product selection within each asset class. The planners should understand that, in making an appropriate choice of investment, they should consider capital growth of the investment, cash income, risk level, liquidity of the investment, transaction cost, and tax implications related to the investment. Depending on the degree of sophistication required of the investment strategies and the manageability skills of the financial planners on different types of investment, the financial planners and clients may choose to make direct investment and indirect investment. Indirect investment means investment through fund management companies or financial institutions. Those investments which are not through the fund management house or financial institutions are direct investments. Direct investments can be made on fixed deposits, equities, and real estate.

14.5 Portfolio Performance Measurement

There are three commonly used portfolio performance measurements. They are the Treynor measure, the Sharpe measure and the Jensen measure. All these performance measures are risk-adjusted.

Treynor Measure

Treynor measure The ratio of the portfolio excess return (portfolio return minus risk-free rate) to the systematic risk (beta) over the sample period.

The **Treynor measure** is the ratio of the portfolio excess return (portfolio return minus risk-free rate) to the systematic risk (beta) over the sample period. The Treynor measure is defined as:

$$\frac{\text{Sample period portfolio return} - \text{Sample period risk} - \text{Free rate}}{\text{Portfolio beta}}$$

The numerator, the difference between sample period portfolio return and sample period risk-free rate, is the risk premium. The portfolio beta is a measure of the volatility of the portfolio. Therefore, the Treynor measure is an indicator of the portfolio return per unit of risk; the higher the value of the Treynor measure, the better the performance. Now you may be concerned about the sign of the Treynor measure. If the risk premium is negative (positive) and the beta is positive (negative), the Treynor measure will be negative, indicating poor (good) management performance. In such a case, it is difficult to distinguish the performance of the portfolio manager if the Treynor measure is negative. Fortunately, the case of negative beta and positive risk premium seldom occurs. If beta is negative, the portfolio can hardly earn a rate of return higher than the risk-free rate, causing the risk premium to be negative and hence the Treynor measure to be positive.

Sharpe Measure

Sharpe measure The ratio of portfolio excess return to standard deviation of portfolio return over the sample period.

Similar to the Treynor measure, the **Sharpe measure** also makes use of the portfolio excess return and volatility as performance indicators. The Sharpe measure is the ratio of portfolio excess return to standard deviation of portfolio return over the sample period. Unlike the Treynor measure, the Sharpe measure employs the total risk (variability) rather than the systematic risk (beta) as the Sharpe measure considers the well-diversified nature of the portfolio. The Sharpe measure is an indicator of the reward to total volatility trade-off. The Sharpe measure is defined as:

$$\frac{\text{Sample period portfolio return} - \text{Sample period risk} - \text{Free rate}}{\text{Standard deviation of portfolio returns}}$$

It appears that the Sharpe measure and the Treynor measure are very similar. The only difference between the Sharpe measure and the Treynor measure is the measure of risk. The Sharpe measure takes into account the total risk (systematic and nonsystematic) of the portfolio while the Treynor measure allows for only the systematic risk. There is a chance that the Sharpe measure and the Treynor measure yield the same value. When the portfolio is well-diversified, the nonsystematic risk can be fully diversified away. Therefore, only the systematic risk is left in the measurement of total risk, causing the values of the Sharpe measure and the Treynor measure to be the same.

Jensen Measure

Jensen measure Estimates the alpha of the portfolio investment, which is the difference of the portfolio return and the expected return calculated by the capital asset pricing model for the sample period.

The **Jensen measure** estimates the alpha of the portfolio investment, which is the difference of the portfolio return and the expected return calculated by the capital asset pricing model for the sample period. The alpha value or the Jensen measure is defined as:

$$\text{Portfolio return} = [\text{Risk-free rate} + \text{Portfolio beta (Average market return}} - \text{Risk-free rate})]$$

The Jensen measure as a performance index assumes stationarity in systematic risk. Similar to the Treynor measure, the Jensen measure allows for only the systematic risk. The alpha value may be interpreted as the average incremental rate of return of the portfolio. A high value of alpha indicates that there is a high risk-adjusted return for the investment in the examination period. If the investment performance is evaluated using the Jensen measure, there are two ways to achieve a high value of alpha. The portfolio managers may have the stock selection ability to pick underpriced securities and/or the forecasting ability of market turns. Some academic studies (Jensen 1968; Admati and Ross 1985; Dybvig and Ross 1985) find that if there are market timers in the market, the Jensen measure tends to induce negative alpha estimates.

14.6   Morningstar Ratings[1]

Mutual funds do not only attract the attention of the academics; they also arouse the interest of some commercial institutions to set up a rating system to assist practitioners and investors in evaluating fund performance. Morningstar Inc. (Morningstar hereafter) is a well-known rating agency and a trusted source of insightful information on stocks, mutual funds, closed-end funds, exchange-traded funds, variable annuities, and separate accounts. With its headquarters in Chicago, Morningstar has business operations in 16 countries and tracks more than 100,000 investment offerings worldwide.

The rating system of Morningstar, Morningstar Rating™, which was set up in 1985, has been useful in helping investors spot the funds and the fund managers with superior risk-adjusted performance. Through the years, this star rating system has exerted an immense influence in directing the flows of fund assets. The star rating scale provides a summary of the historical risk-adjusted performance of funds. The rating system helps investors build better portfolios by providing more focused comparison groups. Using the star rating results, investors are able to quickly and easily identify the funds that are worthy of trading. To distinguish itself from other rating agencies, Morningstar Rating™ uses stars to grade the relative performance of the funds within different groups which have similar investment objectives on a curve. The ranking system is a five-star scale rating assigned with refined categories. Figure 14.4 shows the bell-shaped distribution of ratings between 1 and 5 stars.

Among the funds in a given category, the funds are ranked based on the level of returns. The fund with the highest score (top 10% of funds) gets 5 stars. The next 22.5%, 35%, 22.5%, and the bottom 10% receive 4 stars, 3 stars, 2 stars, and 1 star, respectively. Morningstar computes the total return of a fund for a given month as:

$$\left\{ \frac{\text{NAV per share at end of month}}{\text{NAV per share at beginning of month}} \prod_{i}^{\text{Number of distribution in the month}} \left(1 + \frac{\text{Distribution per share at time } i}{\text{Reinvestment NAV per share at time } i}\right) \right\} - 1$$

The distributions in the return model take into account the dividends, capital gains, and return of capital. However, the model does not incorporate taxes and transaction costs into the computation. In addition, all the distributions are assumed to be reinvested in the next period. For instance, to incorporate the state

---

[1] The information on the Morningstar Ratings is extracted from the Morningstar Research Report, October 1, 2003, and the New Morningstar Rating™ Report with the permission of Morningstar Asia Limited.

Figure 14.4 Bell-shaped distribution of Morningstar Rating™ System

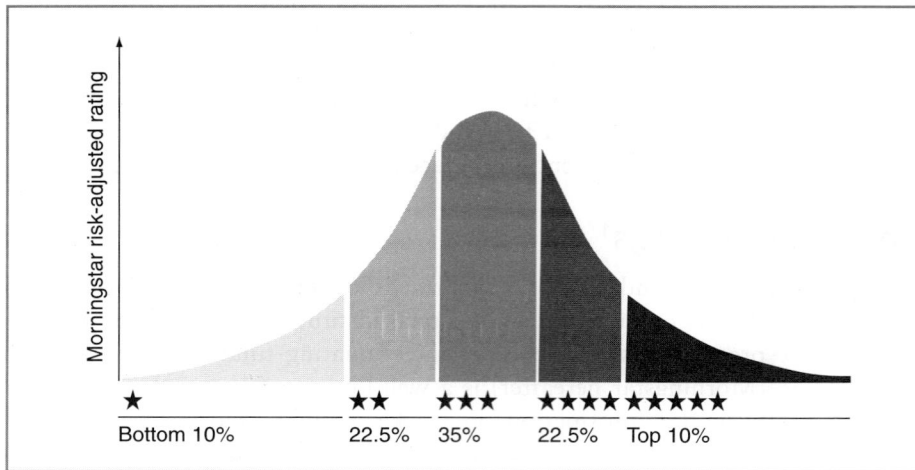

Source: Morningstar Asia Limited.

tax and federal tax levied on dividend income in the United States, Morningstar recomputes the tax-adjusted dividend per share at time *i* by

$$\frac{\text{Dividend per share at time } i}{(1 - \text{maximum state tax rate at time } i)(1 - \text{maximum federal tax rate at time } i)}$$

If there are no loads (front-load (FL) or deferred-load (DL)) and/or redemption fees (RF) on the mutual funds, the cumulative value of the mutual fund is:

$$\prod_{t=1}^{T} (1 + \text{Total return for month } t)$$

If there are loads and redemption fees for the funds, the cumulative value adjusted for loads and redemption fees is

$$(1 - \text{FL})(1 - \text{RF})(\text{Cumulative value}) - (\text{DL})(1 - \text{FL})\frac{\text{minimum (NAV per share at time 0, NAV per share at time T)}}{\text{NAV per share at time 0}}$$

Since the establishment of the rating system, Morningstar has been working to improve its rating system to better facilitate investors to streamline the fund research and selection process. The original Morningstar Rating™ evaluates all funds in a broadly defined asset class. In view of the wide variety of the types of mutual funds, Morningstar has modified its rating system as a category-based system, Morningstar Category™, to rank fund managers with different levels of skills in managing different categories of portfolios in June 2002.

There are two levels of categorization: categorization by asset type and categorization by investment focus. Under the categorization by asset type, there are five asset baskets: equity, fixed income, blend, money-market, and derivatives and warrants; and three baskets of structured products: guaranteed, capital-protected, and hedge. Table 14.3 describes the fund categories by asset type used by Morningstar Asia Limited. Once the funds are categorized into one of the eight asset types, they are assigned on the basis of sector or geographic area under

Table 14.3 Fund categorization by asset type of Morningstar Asia Limited, 2003

Categorization by asset type	Definition
Equity	Fund that aims for capital growth by investing primarily in stocks.
Fixed-income	Fund whose assets, usually bonds and preferred stocks, pay investors a fixed amount.
Blend	Fund that aims to provide some combination of growth, income, and conservation of capital by investing in a mix of stocks, bonds, and/or money market instruments.
Money-market	Fund that invests in short-term debts and "money-like" securities such as US treasury bills, commercial paper, repurchase agreements, certificates of deposit, and bankers' acceptances.
Derivatives and warrants	Fund that aims to achieve exceptional high return by investing primarily in derivative instruments. A warrant fund invests mainly in warrants, or the entitlement to purchase a certain amount of common stocks at a set price over a period of time.
Guaranteed	Principal-protected fund that is designed to offer investors potential gains with limited downside risk. These portfolios invest mainly in fixed-income securities to meet capital and return guarantee obligations while the remaining assets may be invested in stocks and options for the purpose of enhancing ultimate returns. These funds are typically run for a term of years and the minimum capital and returns guaranteed at maturity vary from one fund to another.
Capital-protected	Fund that offers investors principal protection and capital gains at the end of an investment period, which usually covers a few years. In contrast to capital-guaranteed funds, the principal protection offered by capital-protected funds is not guaranteed, for the protection is not backed by an eligible guarantor of a licensed bank or an authorized insurance company, and is subject to specific risks related to the financial instruments employed.
Hedge	Fund that blends different investment strategies and makes extensive use of unconventional investment tools such as derivatives.

Source: Morningstar Asia Limited.

categorization by investment focus. Table 14.4 describes the fund categories by investment focus for an equity basket employed by Morningstar Asia Limited. As at 2003, there were 62 fund categories defined by Morningstar Inc. in the United States.

In order to further enhance the effectiveness of the rating system, Morningstar has implemented several improvements. The improvements include incorporating all variations of the month-to-month performance in a fund, particularly the downward variations, and modeling a new performance measurement formula. In this way, Morningstar risk-adjusted return metric (MRAR) reduces the rating susceptibility to market drifts. This new return measure, which is motivated by the expected utility theory, aims to reward consistent performance and penalize risks acted upon by the mutual fund managers at all times.

The MRAR is a very sophisticated metric of portfolio return measurement which assumes no particular distribution of excess return; fits into the concept of utility function, and takes into account the different degrees of risk aversion of investors (denoted by γ). Investors rank the various alternative portfolios using the mathematical expectations of a function (called the utility) of the ending values of the portfolios. Morningstar uses the MRAR_γ to measure the annualized value of the certainty equivalent geometric excess return for a given value of risk aversion (γ). The geometric excess return in month t (r_{Gt}) is defined as

Table 14.4 Fund categorization by investment focus of Morningstar Asia Limited, 2003

By sector	By geography and capital size				
	Global	**The Americas**	**Greater Europe**	**Greater Asia**	**Special**
Financial	Global Equity Aggregate	Canada Equity	Continental Europe Equity Aggregate	ASEAN Equity Aggregate	Convertible
Gold and precious metal	Global Small/Mid Cap Equity Aggregate	Latin America Equity Aggregate	Core Continental Europe Single Country Equity	Asia Equity Aggregate	
Health	Emerging Markets Equity Aggregate	North America Equity Aggregate	Emerging Europe Equity Aggregate	Asia ex-Japan Equity Aggregate	
Natural resources		North America Small/Mid Cap Equity Aggregate	Europe Equity Aggregate	Australia, New Zealand Equity Aggregate	
Technology, media and telecommunications		US Equity	Europe Small/Mid Cap Equity Aggregate	China Equity	
			Non-core Continental Europe Single Country Equity	Emerging Asia Single Country Equity	
			UK Equity	Greater China Equity Aggregate	
				India Subcontinent Equity Aggregate	
				Hong Kong Equity	
				Japan Equity	
				Japan Small/Mid Cap Equity	
				Korea Equity	
				Singapore Equity	
				Taiwan Equity	

Source: Morningstar Asia Limited.

$$\frac{1 + \text{Total return for month } t}{1 + \text{Return on risk} - \text{Free asset in month } t} - 1$$

The certainty equivalent geometric excess return of a risky investment is the guaranteed excess return which can be used as the surrogate for the uncertain geometric excess return. In mathematical terms, MRAR_γ is defined as (where γ is non-zero)

$$\left[\frac{1}{T}\sum_{t=1}^{T}(1+r_{Gt})^{-\gamma}\right]^{-\frac{12}{\gamma}} - 1$$

If γ is assumed to be zero, $MRAR_0$ is the annualized geometric mean of geometric excess return which is calculated as:

$$\left[\prod_{t=1}^{T}(1+r_{Gt})\right]^{-\frac{12}{T}} - 1$$

The fund analysts of Morningstar in the United States suggest that a degree of risk aversion (γ) equals 2 is most consistent with the risk tolerance level of typical retail investors. Therefore, the rating system of Morningstar employs 2 as the degree of risk aversion in the calculation of the MRAR.

The MRAR metric described here has not been adjusted for loads and redemption fees yet. An even better measure of geometric excess return is to use monthly adjusted total return (adjusted for loads and redemption fees) rather than the monthly total return. To fine-tune the total return, Morningstar makes use of an adjustment factor:

$$\left(\frac{\text{Cumulative value adjusted for loads and redemption fees}}{\text{Cumulative value not adjusted for loads and redemption fees}}\right)^{\frac{1}{T}}$$

Then, the monthly adjusted total return is defined as

$$\text{Adjustment factor} \times (1 + \text{Total return for month } t) - 1$$

Therefore, if Morningstar has to rank the performance of the mutual funds net of loads and redemption fees, the adjusted total return would have to be used to calculate the load and redemption fee adjusted MRAR.

14.7 Advanced Investment Strategies

Asset Allocation

asset allocation The distribution of investment funds across different classes of assets.

Asset allocation is the distribution of investment funds across different classes of assets. After deciding on asset allocation, the next decision to be made is securities selection which involves the selection of specific securities within a particular class of assets for investment. Establishing an appropriate asset mix in the portfolio is a dynamic process which can be active or passive. There are several different strategies of asset allocation. Table 14.5 summarizes the characteristics of the management approaches of asset allocation strategies.

Although asset allocation is a popular investment management approach, its implementation is not easy. Campbell (2002) suggests some rules of thumb for the financial planners: aggressive investors hold stocks while conservative investors hold bonds; and long-term investors can afford to take more stock market risk than short-term investors.

As there are many types of asset allocation strategies, how does one decide on the most appropriate asset allocation? The choice of these different management approaches of asset allocation strategies is determined by the investors' financial goals, tax code (tax brackets and tax shelters), investment horizon (short-term,

Table 14.5 Asset allocation strategies

Asset allocation	Management approach
Strategic asset allocation	An asset allocation strategy employing a constant weight mix of assets based on some long-term predicted risk-return relation, risk tolerance of the investors, and limitations and mandates of the investors assuming that the market is somewhat efficient.
Advanced asset allocation strategies	
Tactical asset allocation	An active strategy which attempts to deliver a positive information ratio by systematic asset allocation shifts (Lee 2000).
Dynamic asset allocation	A strategy which emphasizes the dynamic approach of capturing market inefficiencies and market timing through high frequency adjustment of asset weights (Bergen 2004).
Insured asset allocation	A strategy which emphasizes risk protection by providing certain minimum base portfolio value through some predetermined formula or portfolio insurance. When the value of the portfolio exceeds the predetermined base value, the fund managers of insured asset allocation employ active management to achieve higher value. When the value falls and reaches the base value, the assets would be protected from further price decline (Bergen 2004).
Integrated asset allocation	A strategy which considers both economic expectation of future market returns and client preference for risk tolerance level (Bergen 2004).

medium-term and long-term), age (young and old), return expectation (aggressive and conservative), and risk tolerance (risk-averse and risk-taking) (Campbell 2002). Sharpe (1987) argues that, depending on the investors' preference and attitude toward risk, there would be different responses to asset allocation decision.

Canner, Mankiw, and Weil (1997) present the asset allocation puzzle by summarizing the model portfolios recommended by four well-known US investment advisors, Jane Bryant Quinn (a financial journalist), Fidelity, Merrill Lynch, and the *New York Times*. They recommend that aggressive investors hold more stocks and conservative investors hold more bonds relative to stocks. This recommendation is similar to the suggested rules of thumb for financial planners by Campbell (2002).

Strategic Asset Allocation

strategic asset allocation Employs a constant weight mix of assets based on some long-term predicted risk-return relation, risk tolerance of the investors, and limitations and mandates of the investors, assuming that the market is somewhat efficient.

Strategic asset allocation (SAA) strategy employs a longer-term (usually at least a 5-year investment horizon) investment philosophy on asset allocation based on some predicted risk-return relations at equilibrium, risk tolerance of the investors, and limitations and mandates of the investors. Thus, the primitive form of SAA anchors a relatively constant mix of weightings for various asset classes. In addition, the base mix must be driven by policies and strategies with the assumption that the market is somewhat efficient. Such an asset allocation strategy results in a set of constant weights. When the individual asset classes or securities appreciate or depreciate, the weighting of these assets will deviate from the original benchmark weighting. Consequently, portfolio rebalancing by selling overweighted assets and buying underweighted assets will be necessary to maintain the original policy mix. While there is no concrete rule on how much deviation from the original benchmark weighting should trigger a portfolio rebalancing, a commonly used guideline is that any deviation of more than 5% from its benchmark should call for some action.

While the definition of SAA is quite straightforward, it is not clear theoretically and practically how the guideline for investors should be established, one that is based on their unique circumstances and characteristics in order to establish an optimal policy for making strategic asset allocation decisions. In addition, the term SAA is being used by various financial institutions and investment professionals to represent different things. As you can see, SAA is the very first step of any advanced asset allocation strategy which exploits market timing and pricing inefficiencies in a much shorter investment horizon using a more dynamic asset allocation approach.

UBS AG in its website describes strategic asset allocation as the first step in helping investors meet financial goals. The process of strategic asset allocation comprises four components: (1) disciplined team approach which develops an individual allocation based on risk profile and goals, (2) securities selection from a range of global equity and fixed-income products, (3) active management of assets by shifting allocations according to market and personal goals, and (4) ongoing global review of industry trends and currency activities (http://www.ubs.com/1/e/wealth_mgmt_ww/u_s/growng_wealth/total_wealth.html). Strategic asset allocation is a relatively more rigid strategy as this allocation approach holds on to a constant weighting of assets based on the predicted rates of return for each asset class.

Advanced Asset Allocation Strategies: Tactical Asset Allocation

tactical asset allocation Refers to active strategies which seek to enhance performance by opportunistically shifting the asset mix of a portfolio in response to the changing patterns of reward available in the capital markets.

Before we go into the details of some advanced asset allocation strategies, we have to point out that there is no clear definition of some of the terms used. Also, the labeling of these strategies is not mutually exclusive. For instance, any active asset allocation strategy must employ certain time-varying strategies, which lead to a nonconstant portfolio mix over time. Consequently, the portfolio insurance and the **tactical asset allocation** (TAA) approaches can both be labeled as dynamic asset allocation (DAA) in theory. Of course, if a portfolio manager advertises that he is taking a dynamic asset allocation approach, we may expect the adjustments to asset mix to be very frequent. On the other hand, a portfolio manager who classifies himself as a tactical asset allocator capturing exceptional short-term profit opportunities and market timing advantages would have a lower frequency of asset mix adjustments than the DAA manager. Unfortunately, the lack of consensus on how high the frequency of adjustments should be in order to be classified as DAA leaves the labeling of approaches mainly subjective with room for potential abuse in using the terminology. For our purpose, we only focus on tactical asset allocation. (For readers who are interested in more information on dynamic asset allocation, insured asset allocation and integrated asset allocation, refer to Bergen (2004) at the website http://www.investopedia.com.)

We introduce TAA in this chapter because it has become an important investment management tool. During the 1973–1974 stock market decline, many investment companies were determined to explore enhanced asset allocation strategy as an investment management tool. TAA as an investment management tool was developed by Wells Fargo Investment Advisors in the United States. Between 1973 and 1976, when there was a harsh economic downturn, Wells Fargo Investment Advisors implemented the TAA system to earn profits in the market. Since then, the TAA products have become popular and widely used among investment companies. Although the TAA products were first developed in the United States in the 1970s, global TAA only started to grow in the late 1980s and early 1990s. The rapid expansion of global TAA is consistent with the trend of globalization of investment.

What then is TAA? There are several definitions of TAA. Arnott and Fabozzi (1988) provide a broad definition of TAA:

> Tactical asset allocation broadly refers to active strategies which seek to enhance performance by opportunistically shifting the asset mix of a portfolio in response to the changing patterns of reward available in the capital markets. Notably, tactical asset allocation tends to refer to disciplined processes for evaluating prospective rates of return on various asset classes and establishing an asset allocation response intended to capture higher rewards.

Later, Philips, Rogers and Capaldi (1996) propose a more applied meaning of TAA by explaining that the objective of TAA investment is to forecast returns for more than two classes of assets in a systematic manner in order to obtain better-than-benchmark returns with (possibly) lower-than-benchmark volatility.

More recently, Lee (2000) defines tactical asset allocation strategy as "strategy which attempts to deliver a positive information ratio by systematic asset allocation shifts." Information ratio is the ratio of alpha to tracking error (alpha and tracking error will be defined in the next section). Information ratio is a performance indicator which takes into account both the return and risk of making portfolio investments. The higher the information ratio, the better the tactical asset allocation managers perform.

According to Jacowski (2003), tactical asset allocation strategies are different from systematic asset allocation shifts as the aim of implementing TAA strategies is to enhance performance and to add extra value to the investment portfolio. The value may be in terms of higher return and/or lower risk. The approaches of TAA strategies can be qualitative and quantitative. The strategies of qualitative approach focus on how global themes such as disinflation, deflation, political and economic stability, terrorism, and wars affect the asset allocation in different geographic areas. In contrast, the strategies of quantitative approach mainly employ the techniques of econometric and statistical modeling to forecast asset returns which are used as inputs in the optimization process to construct portfolios. Lee (1998; 2000) suggests that TAA strategy is more popular among global fund managers than domestic fund managers.

Measuring Asset Allocation Strategies

Before we explain the measures to evaluate the performance of asset allocation managers, we need to be familiar with some terms. Firstly, we need to construct two portfolios to make the comparison. The portfolio which provides the point of reference is called the benchmark portfolio. The skills of the asset allocation managers are reflected in the performance of the asset allocation portfolio. Therefore, the performance of the asset allocation portfolio, and hence the managers, is evaluated against the performance of the passive benchmark portfolios. There are several indicators—alpha, tracking error, information ratio, and hit ratio—to evaluate the performance of asset allocation managers (Lee 2000). Aggressiveness in making bets is incorporated into measures such as alpha and tracking error, in which the frequency of trading affects the performance measures.

Alpha

In the investment market, the term *alpha* is used to refer to the excess return due to active asset allocation bet or decision. In mathematical terms, alpha is expressed as:

$$\text{Alpha}_t = \text{Return of asset allocation portfolio}_t - \text{Return of benchmark portfolio}_t$$

The common use of alpha in the investment field is derived from Jensen's alpha in finance literature, which is the intercept in the regression model for measuring performance. For easier comparison of performance among the asset allocation managers, the usual practice in the investment industry is to compute alpha over a certain horizon. The most frequently used alpha measure is the annualized alpha.

There is a common misunderstanding that annualized alpha is similar to annual alpha. However, annualized alpha and annual alpha are different. If alpha is annualized by monthly data, the annualized alpha for each rolling 12 months is estimated by using the monthly alphas in the earlier 12 months. Annualized measure is preferred because annualization avoids the inter-month volatility of alpha and reflects the true performance of the managers. A positive alpha is used to denote that the portfolio managers earn higher returns than the benchmark portfolio. There are two methods to annualize the alpha:, geometric alpha and arithmetic alpha.

The main difference between geometric alpha and arithmetic alpha is that the geometric method takes into account the effect of compounding in each period. Therefore, the geometric alpha is a relatively better indicator of investment return and accumulation of wealth than the arithmetic alpha, although the arithmetic alpha is easier to measure. While the arithmetic alpha is a simple linear function of the degree of aggressiveness, the geometric alpha is not. The annualized geometric alpha does not change at the same rate as the degree of aggressiveness. Therefore, when using the arithmetic method to estimate alpha, the annualized alpha can be a simple multiple of the aggressive factor, making the arithmetic alpha more analytically tractable. This feature makes the arithmetic alpha an easier performance indicator and profitability measure to be analyzed.

We will learn to measure the easier way first, i.e., to estimate the annualized alpha. The arithmetic alpha is defined as:

$$\frac{12}{T} \sum_{t=1}^{T} \text{Return of asset allocation portfolio}_t - \text{Return of benchmark portfolio}_t$$

There are two ways to estimate the geometric alpha. The first method of geometric alpha is defined as:

$$\left\{12 \times \left[\prod_{t=1}^{T}(1 + \text{Return of asset allocation portfolio}_t\right]^{\frac{1}{T}} - 1\right\} -$$

$$\left\{12 \times \left[\prod_{t=1}^{T}(1 + \text{Return of asset benchmark portfolio}_t\right]^{\frac{1}{T}} - 1\right\}$$

The second method of geometric alpha (Goodwin 1998) is defined as:

$$\left[\prod_{t=1}^{T} \frac{1 + \text{Return of asset allocation portfolio}_t}{1 + \text{Return of benchmark portfolio}_t}\right]^{\frac{12}{T}} - 1$$

$\prod$ is the multiplication operator. Although the geometric alpha takes into account the effect of compounding, the geometric alpha is benchmark dependent. The same data of return for active portfolio and holding period may yield different annualized measures of geometric alpha if different benchmark portfolios are used. Without knowing the benchmark portfolios, comparisons of performance based on the geometric alpha may become unfair and difficult.

Tracking Error

Besides using the level of returns as a performance indicator, the performance of the asset allocation managers can also be measured by the consistency of outperformance in each period of time, which is quantified by the volatility or dispersion of alpha, more commonly known as the tracking error. Tracking error is a more advanced performance indicator.

In practice, to ensure that the portfolio managers have adequate tracking and to limit active portfolio risk, tactical ranges are imposed. Tactical ranges are the constraints on tactical deviations from benchmark weights, which set the maximum percentage deviation of weight differentials between the actual portfolio and the benchmark portfolio. Therefore, we need to provide measures for tracking error. There are different statistical indicators of tracking error. The easiest measure of tracking error or degree of dispersion is standard deviation:

$$\sqrt{\frac{1}{T-1}\sum_{t=1}^{T}\left(\text{Alpha}_t - \frac{1}{T}\sum_{t=1}^{T}(\text{Alpha}_t)\right)^2}$$

Similar to alpha, which is reported in annualized form, we may quantify tracking error in annualized form too. The tracking error is annualized by:

$$\sqrt{\text{Number of time periods in a year} \times \text{Tracking error}_t}$$

If the alphas are estimated on a monthly basis, the tracking error is the standard deviation of the monthly alphas. Hence, the number of time periods in a year is 12. Using the annualization formula, annualized tracking error is the product of the square root of 12 and monthly tracking error. Similarly, if the alphas are estimated on a weekly basis, the annualized tracking error is the product of the square root of 52 and weekly tracking error.

Other examples of the more commonly used measures are the correlation coefficient between the tracking portfolio and benchmark, the first or second moment of deviations between returns of portfolio and benchmark. Ammann and Zimmermann (2001) describe two more. The first tracking error measure is the square root of the noncentral second moment of return deviations. Mathematically, it is defined as:

$$\sqrt{\frac{\sum\limits_{\text{Period } k}^{\text{Sample size}} (\text{Return of tracking portfolio in period } k - \text{Return of predetermined benchmark portfolio in period } k)^2}{\text{Sample size} - 1}}$$

This measure is a noncentral measure because this tracking error is affected not only by random positive and negative deviations but also by the constant outperformance or underperformance relative to the benchmark.

The second measure is the residual volatility of the tracking portfolio relative to the benchmark (Treynor and Black 1973). In mathematical terms, it is defined as:

$$\text{Volatility of tracking portfolio} \times \sqrt{1 - (\text{Return correlation of portfolio and benchmark})^2}$$

Ammann and Zimmermann (2001) examined the effects on the tracking error measures of three types of changing allocation strategies: random rebalancing, rebalancing based on trend following, and tracking error maximization. They found that theoretically, high correlation coefficients and low tracking errors relative to a passive benchmark can be achieved by selecting typical tactical allocation ranges. However, in practice, the portfolio managers usually employ active strategies within individual asset classes. Empirically, when passive returns are replaced by fairly active returns, the correlation of returns between the portfolio and the benchmark becomes lower. In simpler terms, the correlation coefficient between the tactical portfolio and the benchmark is very sensitive to the tracking accuracy of the individual asset classes.

There are several practical implications from the findings of Ammann and Zimmermann (2001). This result provides a useful application for portfolio managers in that the constraints for asset allocation are not confined to the weight ranges of the individual asset classes only, but also to the tracking of the individual asset classes. Therefore, there is no need to push the portfolio managers to adopt an active management process to manage the asset classes. Rather, the portfolio managers can use a mixture of actively and passively managed asset classes to scale the tracking error.

In addition, the measurement of the tracking error can be used to determine the implied value of performance fees. A portfolio manager earning a fixed fee for participating in the positive excess performance of a portfolio is like owning an exchange option with the right to exchange the benchmark portfolio for the active portfolio being managed (Kritzman 1987). Using the model of Margrabe (1978), the value of the exchange option is related to tracking error (Ammann and Zimmermann 2001). Ammann and Zimmermann find that the performance fee or the value of the exchange option is approximately proportional to the tactical portfolio range.

Information Ratio

When alpha and tracking error are used to measure the performance of the asset allocation managers, the investment and profitability returns may be the result of skills and the degree of aggressiveness of the managers. The degree of aggressiveness depends on how much risk the managers are willing to take in making bets and the form in which the asset allocation strategy is implemented. Aggressiveness is measured by the aggressiveness factor which is the multiple of the signal in order to scale the signal into a bet. The more aggressive managers are more willing to make tactical shifts. Therefore, higher values for alpha and tracking error may be due to the managers being highly aggressive rather than having the best skills in making bets.

Consequently, using the alpha or tracking error as a performance indicator may not necessarily reflect the true ability of the managers in managing the portfolio. While alpha and tracking error are aggressiveness dependent, information ratio is preferred as information ratio reflects the skill rather than the aggressiveness of the managers in making bets. Information ratio is defined as the ratio of alpha to tracking error. Annualized information ratio is therefore the ratio of annualized alpha to annualized tracking error. For instance, if alphas and tracking errors are estimated using weekly data, the annualized information ratio is computed as:

$$\sqrt{52} \times \frac{\text{Average weekly alpha}}{\text{Weekly tracking error}}$$

Hit Ratio

Hit ratio, which is the proportion of times that the managers add value to the portfolio, is another aggressiveness independent performance indicator besides information ratio. Unlike the other performance indicators, the hit ratio measures the frequency rather than the degree of success. For a 3-year period with 36 months, if the manager is able to have positive alpha for 27 months and negative alpha for 9 months, the hit ratio is 75%. Note that a high percentage of hit ratio (more than 50%) does not mean that the asset allocation manager is able to add value to the portfolio managed as the magnitude of the positive alphas may not exceed that of the negative alphas although the number of positive alphas is larger than that of negative alphas. Therefore, only 100% hit ratio indicates that there is positive value added to the portfolio. Although the hit ratio is aggressiveness independent, the hit ratio is not a good signal of profitability.

Henriksson-Merton Test

While alpha, tracking error, information ratio, and hit ratio are measures of the profitability of the asset allocation strategy, the Henriksson-Merton test is an indicator of the market-timing ability of the asset allocation managers (Weigel 1991; Philips, Rogers, and Capaldi 1996; Lee 2000). The Black-Merton-Scholes option pricing model regards the market-timing strategy as an option (Merton 1981). Following Henriksson and Merton (1981), Chang and Lewellen (1984) employ a two-beta parametric model to evaluate the performance, both the macro market-timing and micro stock selection abilities, of mutual fund managers:

$$Z_{pt} - RF_t = \alpha_{pt} + \beta_1 X_1(t) + \beta_2 X_2(t) + \varepsilon_{pt}$$

where Z_{pt} is the actual rate of return of portfolio at time t; RF_t is the rate of return of risk-free asset at time t; α_{pt} is the average residual or abnormal component on the return of the portfolio due to the selection ability of portfolio manager; β_1 is the average down-market beta of the portfolio; X_1 is the excess market return during down market which is expected to be lower than the risk-free rate; β_2 is the average up-market beta of the portfolio; and X_2 is the excess market return during up market which is expected to be higher than the risk-free rate; and ε_{pt} is the random error term.

The value of α_{pt} is used to measure the micro-stock selection ability of the mutual fund managers. The statistically positive and significant α_{pt} indicates that the fund managers are able to select mispriced stocks. The difference between β_1 and β_2 measures the change of portfolio beta in the test period, which is used to evaluate the macro-market timing ability of the mutual fund managers.

14.8 Empirical Evidence of Portfolio Performance

Profitability of Mutual Funds

McDonald (1974) examines the objectives and performance of mutual funds between 1960 and 1969. Over the 10 years of study it was found that the aggressiveness of fund objective is positively related to risk (beta of Treynor measure and total variability of Sharpe measure) and return measures. Therefore, aggressive funds should have higher return and risk level than conservative funds. Martin, Keown, and Farrell (1982) study the impact of fund objectives on the diversification policies using 72 mutual funds. The result shows that fund objective explains only a small portion of the extra-market variation of the fund.

Stock Selection and Market-timing Abilities of Mutual Funds

Many academic studies have been done to evaluate the stock selection and market-timing abilities of mutual funds to react to stock mispricing and market cycles. The results on the stock selection and market-timing abilities of the mutual fund managers are mixed. Treynor and Mazury (1966) and Veit and Cheney (1982) hypothesize that the mutual fund managers should increase the portfolio beta and decrease the portfolio beta before the bull and bear market, respectively. The results of these studies show that the managers of the US funds have poor timing ability and overall performance. Moreover, there is no evidence that the mutual fund managers are able to shift the portfolio beta in anticipation of future market movement. In contrast, Kon and Jen (1979) reported significant changes in the risk measures in line with the market movement and superior market-timing ability of the mutual fund managers to time market changes.

Merton (1981) and Henriksson and Merton (1981) employ an alternative performance evaluation model (two-beta parametric model) by breaking down the overall performance of the fund managers into "macro" market-timing ability and "mirco" stock selection ability. Their results report no evidence of market-timing and stock selection abilities. Later, Henriksson (1984) uses a heteroscedasticity adjusted parametric model and a nonparametric model to measure the performance of 116 open-end mutual funds. Similar to the results of most of the earlier studies, the mutual fund managers under examination do not exhibit superior ability in market timing and stock selection.

Cumby and Glen (1990) also find that the fund managers of a sample of 15 US-based international funds are poor market timers. From a sample of 19 international funds, Eun, Kolodny, and Resnick (1991) suggest that, from the perspective of the US investors, although including the international funds helps enhance the efficiency of the fund portfolios, there is weak evidence of good timing ability. Chan and Chen (1992) show evidence of poor timing ability and overall performance of the managers of 19 asset allocation funds.

Droms and Walker (1994), using the Jensen's one-beta model, report no superior risk-adjusted performance for international fund managers. Using the ordinary least square and autoregressive conditional heteroscedasticity (ARCH) models to study market-timing and stock selectivity ability of 97 international mutual funds managers, Kao, Cheng, and Chan (1998) find the international mutual funds managers possess good selectivity and poor market-timing ability. In addition, there is a negative relation between selectivity ability and market-timing ability of the fund managers. In short, the results of these studies show that the managers of the US funds have poor timing ability and overall performance.

Performance of Asset Allocation Strategies

Because of the popularity of the asset allocation strategies, a number of research studies have been conducted on the performance of asset allocation managers. Dahlquist and Harvey (2001) describe that there are three distinct levels of asset allocation strategy. The first level is benchmark asset allocation or indexing which replicates the benchmark index of some well-known market indices such as the MSCI world portfolio. In the second level, the strategic asset allocation, which has a longer-term perspective (conventionally a 5-year investment horizon), employs a tracking error strategy. The third level of asset allocation strategy is the tactical asset allocation which has a shorter-term perspective (conventionally a 30-day to 4-months investment horizon) to deviate from the strategic weights to induce tracking error. Some research studies have been conducted to evaluate the profitability of the tactical asset allocation strategy. Brinson, Hood, and Beebower (1986) and Brinson, Singer, and Beebower (1991) find that the asset allocation strategy explains more than 90% of the portfolio returns of the pension plans. Using a sample of 300 UK pension funds, Blake, Lehmann, and Timmermann (1999) report a slow mean reversion in the portfolio weights toward a common time varying strategic asset allocation. In addition, the strategic asset allocation explains most of the variation in the portfolio returns.

FINANCIAL PLANNING IN PRACTICE

An Interview with Dr. Wai Lee on Tactical Asset Allocation (TAA)

By Louis Cheng

Background of Dr. Wai Lee

Wai has had a fascinating career path since he graduated from the PhD program. From being a postdoctoral research fellow at Harvard Business School, he became an assistant vice president at JP Morgan Investment Management responsible for the improvement of asset allocation strategies. Later on, he was in charge of quantitative research and risk management of the global balanced group. Then, in 2000, Wai joined Credit Suisse Asset Management. He served as the director and head of Quantitative Engineering Group of the firm and led the firm's quantitative research activities. At the same time, he was also responsible for building a global TAA model as well as for expanding the business in this area. In 2004, Wai joined Lehman Brothers Asset Management where he started as the director of Quantitative Investments. Currently, Wai is a managing director at Lehman's New York office and continues his responsibility for the quantitative investment function. At the same time, he is leading the Quantitative Investments Group which manages hedge funds for the firm.

Judging from Wai's various roles in his career in investment research, we can see that his strength is definitely in quantitative finance, especially in TAA. His book *Theory and Methodology of Tactical Asset Allocation* has become the most important textbook used by the industry and academia. His frequent publications in the *Journal of Portfolio Management* and his being a member of its advisory board also prove that his investment research is well recognized by the industry as well as the academic world. The following interview focuses on his views on the development of TAA and the challenges involved in using it.

Can you explain the meaning of TAA and why it is useful?

Generally speaking, I can say that TAA strategies aim to add value to a portfolio in terms of higher return, lower risk, or a combination of the two, by making systemic asset allocation shifts. When I say "add value," it means that it must be benchmarked to some standard, which is normally based on a predetermined static portfolio, normally a policy portfolio that the client prefers over a long investment horizon. From another perspective, TAA can be used as an absolute return strategy (e.g., in the form of a global macro hedge fund). While this general definition covers most asset allocation strategies under the TAA categories, even market timing (which I personally believe is an ineffective form of TAA) can be regarded as a special form of TAA. In this case, the fund manager trades aggressively and makes frequent shifts in asset allocation. The traditional wisdom on static asset allocation argues that, based on a long-term investment policy, we should maintain a fixed weighting for various asset classes in a portfolio. Of course, through time, owing to different performance of asset classes, the value of some asset classes would increase more and the asset weighting would change. One may argue that automatic rebalancing should be done to maintain the original allocation mix. However, under a dynamic capital market and the condition of new incoming information, adjustments to the weighting of the asset mix may be necessary. Thus, implementing TAA does make sense to me.

Can you briefly discuss the major forms of TAA being used currently?

In my view, there are two major types of TAA: discretionary (or qualitative) and quantitative. Discretionary approaches normally involve a global theme such as macroeconomic events, political events, and so forth. Discretionary strategies attempt to predict how these factors may affect the return and risk trade-off of various asset classes in different parts of the world. Since asset returns are affected by the economic cycle, some regions may be more reactive to certain events and economic stimulants, leading to potential investment opportunities and profits through proper trading strategies. For quantitative approaches, most TAA strategies are based on some econometric or statistical models. After using these models to generate the expected returns, these forecasts would be used as inputs in an optimization process. We will then construct the final portfolio with the designated and appropriate characteristics. In general, qualitative approaches tend to have fewer positions and more concentration in risks, and are less diversified than the quantitative approaches.

No matter what approach we use, TAA should begin with some basic inputs in terms of data, experience, and knowledge. Next, an investment view should be established. Traditionally, the investment view includes three main ingredients: direction, magnitude, and confidence. Then, these views should be quantified and converted into a risk-return space, which is in turn used to form the portfolio under the framework and constraints such as limits on transaction costs and client requirements. This process should be repeated until an optimal portfolio is formed. Finally, by comparing the optimal portfolio with the initial portfolio, a trade list consisting of buys and sells would be generated to achieve the tactical adjustments.

Can you name some major challenges faced by TAA practitioners?

Challenge 1: Skepticism and Misunderstanding

One of the most difficult challenges faced by TAA specialists is the general skepticism and misunderstanding of fund managers using TAA. For instance, many people think that TAA and market timing are the same thing, which is not true; or that one has to make a perfect economic forecast to implement TAA and make money, which is also not true. Another common and unjustified criticism is that many would conclude that TAA is not trustworthy if the user cannot explain fundamentally why he implements certain trades concerning some particular securities. Actually, depending on the type of investment process used by the manager, it is possible that the trades made in these particular securities are a net result of a large-scale modeling which considers many securities with a certain investment view. In fact, the TAA specialist may not even have a particular view on the fundamental value of some of these securities. Thus, requiring an explanation based on fundamental and economic factors from every TAA manager on all traded securities is truly not necessary.

Challenge 2: Trap of Using False Statistical Relationships

Another main challenge TAA managers face is the pursuit of a logical explanation for every price movement, and falling into the trap of misinterpreting some false statistical relationships among variables – datamining. My personal view is that most price volatility cannot be explained. Thus, spending tremendous effort in predicting minor fluctuations based on seemingly high R-square and t-statistics in regression models can be a dangerous game.

Challenge 3: Market Globalization

A final noteworthy challenge is the increasing globalization and market integration. Owing to the integration of capital markets, asset prices tend to move together and the duration for arbitrage trading has become shorter and shorter. Such a high correlation of asset prices make relative long-short trades less risky, and therefore, potentially less profitable. Nowadays, in order to make the same profit, TAA specialists would need to make bigger trades. This may present a problem to some TAA managers if they lack experience and confidence. In other words, market integration presents a real test to differentiate a successful TAA manager from the less competent one.

What do you think about the future of TAA?

I strongly believe that TAA is here to stay. Judging from the rapid expansion of hedge funds and alternative investments, I can conclude that TAA would become more popular and be employed by more investment specialists. For a TAA manager to be successful, both experience and training are very important. TAA is both an art and a science. Sound judgment and well-designed models are both important in building the TAA process. Clearly, more communication and education are needed to help the investment community and investors better understand the role and benefits of TAA. Finally, I believe that proper due diligence must be imposed on fund managers using TAA in order to gain the confidence of investors who are still skeptical about this strategy.

Key Terms		
asset allocation	*403*	strategic asset allocation *404*
complementary portfolio	*388*	tactical asset allocation *405*
Jensen measure	*398*	Treynor measure *397*
Sharpe measure	*398*	

References

Admati, A. R. and Ross, S. A., "Measuring Investment Performance in a Rational Expectations Equilibrium Model, *Journal of Business,* vol. 58 (1985): 1–26.

Ammann M. and Zimmermann, H., "Tracking Error and Tactical Asset Allocation," *Financial Analyst Journal,* vol. 57 (2001): 32–43.

Arnott, R. and Fabozzi, F. J., *Asset Allocation: A Handbook of Portfolio Policies, Strategies and Tactics* (Chicago, Illinois: Probus, 1988).

Bergen, J. V., *Asset Allocation Strategies*, Investopedia.com Article (March 17, 2004).

Blake, D., Lehmann B. N., and Timmermann, A., Asset Allocation Dynamics and Pension Fund Performance, *Journal of Business,* vol. 72, no. 4 (1999): 429–461.

Brinson, G. P., Hood, L. R, and Beebower, G. L., "Determinants of Portfolio Performance," *Financial Analysts Journal,* vol. 42, no. 4 (1986): 39–44.

Brinson, G. P., Singer, B. D., and Beebower, G. L., Determinants of Portfolio Performance II: An Update, *Financial Analysts Journal,* vol. 47, no. 3 (1991): 40–48.

Campbell, J. Y., *Strategic Asset Allocation*, Invited address to the American Economic Association and American Finance Association, Atlanta, Georgia, January 4, 2002

Canner, N., Mankiw, N. G., and Weil, D. N., "An Asset Allocation Puzzle," *The American Economic Review*, vol. 87, no. 1 (1997): 181–191.

Chan, A. and Chen, C. R., "How Well Do Asset Allocation Mutual Fund Managers Allocate Assets?," *Journal of Portfolio Management,* vol. 18 (1992): 81–91.

Chang, E. C. and Lewellen, W. G., "Market Timing and Mutual Fund Investment Performance," *Journal of Business,* vol. 57, no. 1, (1984): 57–72.

Cumby, R. E. and Glen, J. D., "Evaluating the Performance of the International Mutual Funds," *Journal of Finance,* vol. 45 (1990): 497–521.

Dahlquist, M. and Harvey, C. R., "Global Tactical Asset Allocation," *Emerging Markets Quarterly* (Spring 2001): 6–14.

Droms, W. G. and Walker, D. A., Investment Performance of International Mutual Funds," *Journal of Financial Research*, vol. 17 (1994): 1–14.

Dybvig, P. H. and Ross, S. A., "Performance Measurement Using Differential Information and a Security Market Line," *Journal of Finance*, vol. 40 (1985): 383–399.

Eun, C. S., Kolodny, R., and Resnick, B. G., "US-based International Mutual Funds: A Performance Evaluation," *Journal of Portfolio Management*, vol. 17 (1991): 88–94.

Goodwin, T. H., "The Information Ratio," *Financial Analysts Journal*, vol. 54 (1998): 34–43.

Henriksson, R. D. and Merton, R. C., "On the Market Timing and Investment Performance: II. Statistical Procedures for Evaluation Forecasting Skill," *Journal of Business*, vol. 54 (1981): 513–533.

Henriksson, R. D., "Market Timing and Mutual Fund Performance: An Empirical Investigation," *Journal of Business*, vol. 57 (1984): 73–96.

Jacowski, M. J., "Recent Advances in Tactical Asset Allocation: A Conversation with Dr. Wai Lee," *The Monitor*, vol. 18, no. 3 (May–June 2003): 34–40.

Jensen, M. C., "The performance of Mutual Funds in the Period 1945–1964," *Journal of Finance,* vol. 23 (1968): 289–416.

Kao, G. W., Cheng, L. T. W., and Chan, K. C., "The International Mutual Fund Selectivity and Market Timing During Up and Down Market Conditions," *The Financial Review*, vol. 33 (1998): 127–144.

Kon, S. J. and Jen, F. C., "The Investment Performance of Mutual Funds: An Empirical Investigation of Timing, Selectivity and Market Efficiency," *Journal of Business*, vol. 52 (1979): 263–289.

Kritzman, M., "Incentive Fees: Some Problems and Some Solutions," *Financial Analyst Journal*, vol. 43 (1987): 21–26.

Lee, W., "Risk and Return Characteristics of TAA under Imperfect Information," *Journal of Portfolio Management*, vol. 25, no. 1 (1998): 61–70.

Lee, W., *Theory and Methodology of Tactical Asset Allocation* (Hoboken, N. J.: Wiley, 2000).

Margrabe, W., "The Value of an Option to Exchange One Asset for Another, *Journal of Finance,* vol. 33 (1978): 177–186.

Martin, J. D., Keown, A. J., and Farrell, J. L., "Do Fund Objectives Affect Diversification Policies?" *The Journal of Portfolio Management*, vol. 8, no. 2. (1982): 19–28.

McDonald, J. G., "Objectives and Performance of Mutual Funds, 1960–1969," *Journal of Financial and Quantitative Analysis*, vol. 9 (1974): 311–333.

Merton, R. C., "On Market Timing and Investment Performance I: An Equilibrium Theory of Value for Market Forecasts," *Journal of Business,* vol. 54 (1981): 363–406.

Morningstar Research Report (October 1, 2003).

New Morningstar Rating™ Report (October 1, 2003).

Newbould, G. D. and Poon, P. S., "The Minimum Number of Stocks Needed for Diversification," *Financial Practice and Education*, vol. 3, no. 2 (Fall 1993): 85–87.

Philips, T. K., Rogers, G. T., and Capaldi, R. E., "Tactical Asset Allocation: 1977–1994," *Journal of Portfolio Management*, vol. 23, no. 1 (1996): 57–64.

Sharpe, W. F., "Integrated Asset Allocation," *Financial Analysts Journal*, vol. 43 (1987): 25–32.

Treynor, J. L. and Black, F., "How to Use Security Analysis to Improve Portfolio Selection," *Journal of Business,* vol. 46 (1973): 66–86.

Treynor, J. L. and Mazury, K. K., "Can Mutual Funds Outguess the Market?" *Harvard Business Review,* vol. 44 (1966): 131–136.

Veit, E. T. and Cheney, J. M., "Are Mutual Funds Market Timers?" *Journal of Portfolio Management*, vol. 8 (1982): 35–42.

Weigel, E., "The Performance of Tactical Asset Allocation," *Financial Analysts Journal* (September/October 1991): 63–70.

Questions & Problems

Multiple-choice Questions

1. The steps involved in asset allocation strategies include the following:
    I.   Determining the risk tolerance of the client
    II. Having some idea about preferred investment vehicles in each asset class
    III. Matching the risk tolerance level with the efficient frontier to identify the right portfolio mix
    IV. Selling all the existing investments of the client to preserve capital
    V.   Advising the client to set up a trust to avoid capital gains tax

    A. I, II, and III
    I, III, and IV
    I, II, IV, and V
    II, III, IV, and V

2. Which of the following factors should be considered in choosing types of investment?
    I.   Liquidity
    II. Tax consequence
    III. Capital growth
    IV. Risk level
    V.   Manager's expertise

    A. I, III, and V
    B. II, III, and IV
    C. I, II, III, and IV
    D. I, II, III, IV, and V

3. The typical types of asset allocation portfolio in retirement planning include _____.
    I.   High-yield
    II. Moderate
    III. Aggressive
    IV. Conservative

    A. I and IV
    B. II and III
    C. I, II, and III
    D. II, III, and IV

Problems

1. Describe the return calculation procedures and their limitations.

PART IV

Advanced Topics

chapter 15

The Concept of Total Life Planning

Learning Objectives

After studying this chapter you should be able to:

1 Define total life planning.
2 Understand the importance of physical well-being.
3 Understand the importance of psychological well-being.
4 Understand the importance of financial well-being.

In this chapter, we will introduce total life planning, a new concept which consists of three important aspects of well-being: physical, psychological well-being, and financial well-being. Traditionally, financial planners have only taken care of their clients' financial aspect. However, total life planning suggests that financial planners should pay attention to all three aspects of well-being. Achieving an optimal balance in these three aspects is a challenging job.

15.1   Relating Financial Planning with Total Life Planning

Is There Life Beyond Financial Planning?[1]

One of the major reasons for the popularity and recognition of the CFP® mark throughout the world is the rapid accumulation of personal wealth. Personal financial services have increasingly become a profitable business. In the name of wealth management, banks attempt to capture middle-income clients by providing services and products that used to be available only to high net-worth clients in their private banking business. On the other hand, securities and brokerage firms also try to capture a share of the business by setting up their own wealth management division. As for life insurance companies, most of them have established a financial planning division and are in the process of converting some of their suitable agents into financial planners providing more comprehensive services to their clients.

Thus, it is clear that financial services companies from the banking, investment, and insurance sectors are trying to provide better services and product mix for their clients by conducting financial planning. Judging from the steady increase in CFP® certificants in the US and the rest of the world, the concept of comprehensive personal financial planning should be well known among financial services professionals. However, for those practitioners who have obtained the CFP® mark, does it mean that they have learnt everything in financial planning and will be successful ever after? Of course, the answer is *no*.

---

[1] Based on "Is There Life beyond Financial Planning?" *HK Financial Planner*, no. 5 (Summer 2004): 38–41. Used with permission.

The Trend: From Quantitative to Qualitative Approach

Research in social science shows that in general, the success in one's professional career is based on two major factors. Professional knowledge and technical expertise only constitute 15% of the success. The remaining 85% is due to the individual's interpersonal and leadership skills and personal characteristics. This finding reinforces the importance of establishing client-planner relationship and determining goals and expectations; the first two steps of the financial planning process. In other words, successful financial planners have to possess excellent communication and interpersonal skills. In addition, they have to commit themselves to developing a long-term relationship with their clients. In doing so, professional ethics and putting the clients' needs first become critical factors to secure a prosperous and long-term relationship with clients.

While all these concepts are being preached everywhere, both in study materials and by speakers in financial planning seminars, we all know that it is easier said than done. Very often, when we face a client, and try to establish an initial friendship, we learn quickly that, while the clients expect the planners to help them in financial matters, the real problems of the clients go well beyond money or investments. In fact, it is possible that what it takes to establish the client-planner relationship is not the ability of the planners in conducting quantitative financial planning. In many cases, a client decides to choose a planner simply because the client perceives that the planner is trustworthy and genuinely cares for his or her best interest.

We are not trying to trivialize the importance of quantitative financial skills in financial planning. A child cannot learn to run well if he does not know how to walk well and balance himself first. Similarly, financial planners should have a solid foundation in the basic principles of finance before they have the ability to put together a sound financial plan that will meet the needs of their clients. Unfortunately, having a good grasp of quantitative skills is a necessary but not sufficient condition to conduct proper financial planning.

Based on our experience in interacting with financial services professionals in various countries, we realize that many well-educated planners and customer managers put too much emphasis on their ability in estimating returns, and in formulating asset allocation strategies, but overlook the psychological and emotional needs of their clients.

What is Life Planning?

In the Success Forum 2003 held in Philadelphia in November 2003 organized by the Financial Planners Association in the United States, one of the themes of the forum was the concept of life planning. The term "life planning" has been around for many years and so it is not new. In fact, the traditional and narrower meaning of life planning refers to estate planning, transference planning, or so called legacy planning. Recently, owing to the popularity of a healthy diet, body fitness, and emotional quotient among more sophisticated consumers, the concept of a better lifestyle or how to enjoy life is gaining momentum all over the world, particularly in Asia where personal wealth is being accumulated at an alarming speed. Consequently, the idea of financial planners engaging in a full spectrum of client advisory to promote a better lifestyle has become a credible idea.

What is Total Life Planning (TLP)?

Total life planning (TLP) emphasizes a balanced approach toward life. TLP assumes that an individual's well-being will be better in the long run when he achieves an optimal balance in his physical, psychological, and financial well-being. Financial planners should be equipped with a basic understanding of how to accommodate their clients' desire to pursue a balanced lifestyle.

Knowing the Boundaries

First, we want to make it clear that not all clients prefer their planners to know in detail about the condition of their physical and psychological well-being, let alone give them advice on a balanced lifestyle. Thus, we are not suggesting that a planner should insist on accessing private information in this area in order to conduct financial planning. Instead, the planners should possess some training and ability in evaluating the psychological and physical well-being of the clients so that these important factors would be considered during the financial planning process.

For instance, owing to a bad experience in childhood, a client may have a very pessimistic view on the financial burden of raising a child. Thus, the individual may tend to overinsure his own life and purchase too many whole life insurance policies (with no investment-link element), leading to insufficient funds for retirement coverage using equity mutual funds. Using traditional risk profiling techniques, one may draw the conclusion that the client is simply an extremely risk-averse person. However, if a planner is able to draw inference from his client's social and personal behavior through casual conversations and careful observations during their meetings, the planner should realize that the emotional and psychological burden of the client concerning his children is unusually heavy. If the client has no objection, it may not be a bad idea to remind him about the potential psychological effect of this burden on his retirement plan. By doing so, the financial needs of the client can be better served. We understand that the case mentioned above does not fully address all the challenges and problems the client faces, and there is no guarantee that the planner can do a good job in evaluating the physical and psychological well-being of the client. Nevertheless, there is no doubt of the importance of having a balanced lifestyle in order to achieve happiness. Thus a financial planner should at least consider all three aspects of their clients' well-being when giving financial planning advice.

Second, financial planners practicing total life planning should understand that they have no proper training in medicine, counselling, or even nutrition science. Thus, financial planners should know their boundaries and limitations as giving bad advice (in the areas that the planners are not professionally trained) may lead to potential legal disputes and result in serious financial and personal consequences. Nevertheless, some basic knowledge of physical fitness and proper diet, and basic counseling skills can increase the planners' awareness of their clients' needs and contribute toward understanding their physical and psychological well-being. Such an understanding will greatly improve the ability of the planners in formulating an appropriate financial plan for their clients.

The focus of financial planners is still on financial planning, not on the physical and psychological well-being of the clients. However, in order to do a good job in financial planning, financial planners need to understand the physical and psychological condition of the clients as these two conditions will affect the clients' ability to understand and to implement the recommended decisions in financial planning. TLP can help the planners to consider all aspects of the clients' needs when conducting the financial planning analysis, leading to a more feasible and optimal plan for them.

In short, this interdisciplinary concept of total life planning is an attempt to formalize the importance of physical and psychological well-being into a better structured, scientific planning approach which has been adopted by successful financial services professionals. While the idea is not new, a systematic approach to practicing and implementing such a concept is not yet available. We strongly encourage financial planning and wealth management professionals who believe in total life planning to work together in researching and documenting this concept so that the industry and the consumers can mutually benefit.

The Framework of Total Life Planning

In this book, we emphasize that total well-being is a function of physical, psychological, and financial well-being. The relationship among physical well-being, psychological well-being and financial well-being in total life planning is illustrated in Figure 15.1. Some examples are used to demonstrate how these three elements are closely related for overall well-being: individuals who are well-off financially tend to have less emotional and physical problems compared to those who are poorer. We are not proposing the materialistic idea that "money is omnipotent" or "money can buy everything." However, financial difficulties due to loss of job and economic recession create a financial burden, which can

Figure 15.1 Framework of total life planning

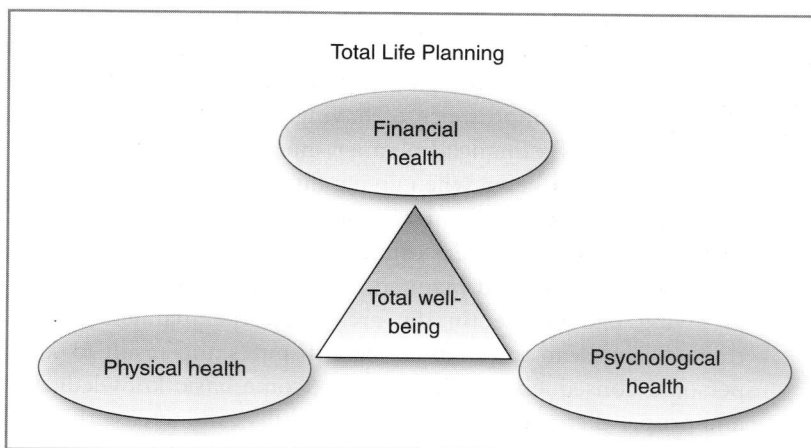

be a major cause of psychological stress and can result in lower living standards. Lower living standards may make one more susceptible to physical illness. Psychological and physical problems in turn can be causes for the loss of earning ability, thus jeopardizing one's financial well-being.

Physical Well-being

physical well-being
Refers to an individual's capability to perform everyday tasks with adequate energy while also having the energy to enjoy leisure activities.

Physical well-being does not mean an absence of disease and illness. Generally speaking, physical well-being may simply mean that a person is capable of performing everyday tasks with adequate energy, and also has the energy left for enjoying leisure activities. Also, a physically fit person tends to have more endurance and better ability to cope with problems.

Some financial planners, particularly insurance agents, emphasize the importance of the physical well-being of their clients in insurance planning. Its importance is reflected in the request of a compulsory medical check-up before the finalization of the medical insurance plan.

As one of the key objectives of financial planners in establishing a strong client relationship is to show their care and concern for their clients, they need to know the physical conditions of their clients. In addition, data about physical well-being is particularly important for planners to market the appropriate medical insurance policy. If their clients are not that healthy, they will need to spend a larger premium on their medical insurance policy. And if their clients do not take care of their health (e.g., they have unhealthy eating habits or are heavy smokers), there is a higher likelihood for them to become ill in the future, leading to increasing health costs.

Ideally, the health condition of the clients' family members is a useful indicator of the clients' medical needs. This information may be harder to gather. Some medical studies show that the likelihood of having cancer is higher for those whose family members have a history of cancer. Familial disease is another concern. Therefore, it is important for financial planners to know as much as possible about the physical well-being of their clients and their family members.

Recent medical research studies emphasize the importance of a healthy lifestyle on physical health (Shikany and White 2000; Weisburger 2000; Kim et al., 2004). Kim, Popkin, Siega-Eiz, Haines, and Lenore (2004) suggest that there are four lifestyle factors in the composite lifestyle index (LI). LI is an integrated approach to summarizing the total healthiness of lifestyles. It incorporates diet, physical activity, smoking, and alcohol to provide a comprehensive measure on healthiness.

Both psychological well-being and physical well-being are equally important. Many people complain about having headaches or abdominal pain from time to time. The cause of these problems may be related to stress and psychological issues. Psychological problems can manifest themselves as physical problems. On the other hand, being physically unfit can also cause psychological problems. For example, patients suffering from chronic illnesses are more likely to be frustrated, and individuals suffering from obesity are more likely to lose self-confidence. Physical well-being can also affect our social relationships.

In general, we would like to be financially, psychologically, and physically well for as long as possible. When we are financially and psychologically well, we would like to live longer to enjoy our lives.

Psychological Well-being

psychological well-being Reflected by a person's needs at different levels, ranging from the basic need to sustain life to the desire for self-actualization.

Professionals and academics use words like "mental health," "mental hygiene," and "psychological wellness" to denote **psychological well-being**. The term "psychological" is preferable to "mental" as the former implies a less severe problem; financial planners want to avoid presenting the idea of psychiatric or professional counseling services to clients.

In psychology literature, there are many theories about psychological well-being that are relevant to financial planning. All of us have different needs, from the basic need to sustain life to the desire for more extravagant spending. The gratification of needs can lead to a psychologically healthy status while the nonfulfillment of needs may lead to psychological problems. If we are able to understand and help fulfill the needs of our clients, it is easier to establish and maintain a relationship of mutual trust with our clients. One of the ways to understand clients' psychological well-being is by observation.

Behavioral Observation

The psychological well-being of an individual can be observed through intentional communication such as through written, verbal, and nonverbal channels, and unintentional communication such as through body language, gestures, and sometimes physical health symptoms (see Figure 15.2).

Figure 15.2 Observable behavior

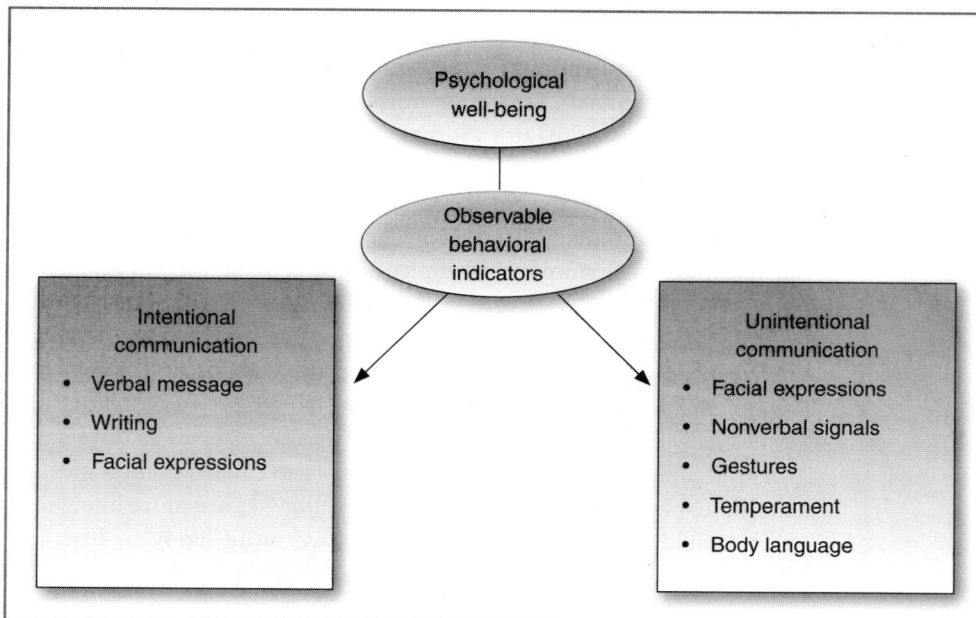

For instance, parents with a deprived childhood would tend to have a higher than necessary level of consumption spending on themselves and their own children when they have the money. In order to compensate for their past underprivileged experiences, they may prefer a materialistic and extravagant lifestyle. Such nonfinancial information is important for personal profiling to understand a client's preferences and allocation of wealth. If a financial planner wants to achieve a higher level of psychological well-being for his clients, he needs to have a basic understanding of different psychological theories.

Psychological Perspectives

Some theories in psychology focus on inputs, processes, and channels and what it takes to achieve psychological well-being (e.g., self-actualization). Another group of theories focuses on the outcomes or characteristics of a psychologically healthy person such as self-regard and creativeness. Some of the methods prescribed by the theories require active participation and effort. However, the level of psychological well-being can also be affected by environmental factors, cultural behaviors, society well-being, peer and family behavior, and even macroeconomic and political conditions. Social learning theory emphasizes these environmental and social factors and their effects on psychological well-being. Figure 15.3 shows some major psychological theories.

Psychodynamic Theory and Financial Planning

According to Freud (1900), everything humans do is to satisfy their internal sexual and aggressive drives. He came up with psychoanalysis, which focuses on the unconscious conflicts everybody experiences which are rooted in childhood. The theory suggests that what you desire in your heart would escape and appear in your dreams, your speeches (in a slip of the tongue) or your "careless" mistakes (parapraxes). To be well in psychoanalytical terms, we need to have a harmonious balance among the three personality subsystems – the id (your internal pleasure

Figure 15.3 Major psychological theories

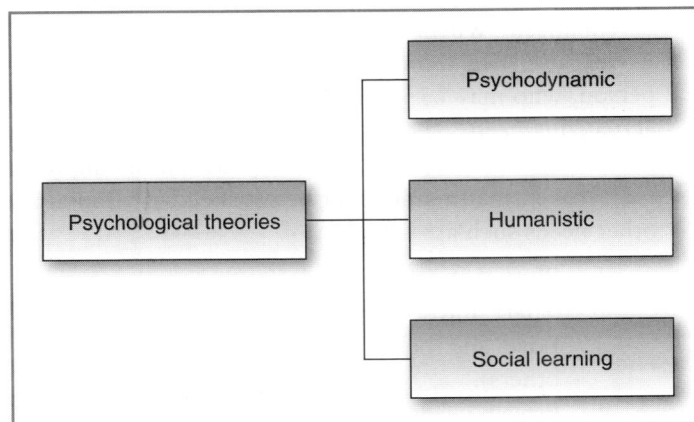

seeker), the ego (the one that warns you of the reality) and the superego (the one that reminds you of morality).

The conflicts among the three happen all the time inside us. They might be suppressed or denied for a moment through defense mechanisms, yet can never be ruled out. Individuals are always in a state of ambivalence. The ego is responsible for being the "middleman" of the id and the superego, making appropriate responses to satisfy the needs after perceiving the external environment, learning from past experience, following morals, and rejecting taboos. Anxiety and other psychological problems result when the id, ego, and superego are not in harmony.

Financial planners need to pay attention to these psychological problems when they are designing financial plans as their client's ego is affected by both the id and the superego at the same time.

Jung (1926) proposes that human experiences consist of qualities that are opposites and tend to balance each other (polarities). People are dominated by either introversion or extraversion traits. Introverts preoccupy themselves with inner experiences and are less outgoing. On the other hand, extraverts are more outgoing, concentrate on external experiences, and spend most of their time interacting with the world around them. Both qualities facilitate adaptation. Note that even if you think you belong to one personality type, the other quality lies within you, opposing and balancing what you are more inclined to. The issue of introversion versus extraversion traits of a client is an important topic for financial planners in establishing a proper relationship with their clients.

Humanistic Theory and Financial Planning

The main focus of the humanistic theory is on the perception of reality through the process of self-actualization. Rogers (1959) was among the first to suggest the idea of self-actualization. He believed in that "every person is to be prized." His ideas give us the concept of how potential is realized and what can keep it from being realized. According to him, the potential for healthy growth will express itself naturally if there are no other strong opposing forces. This growth process is called actualization. It is assumed to exist in every living organism, and has a natural tendency to develop capabilities so that the organism is maintained or enhanced. When it has its effect on the self, it is called self-actualization. Rogers used the term "fully functioning person" to describe a self-actualizing person, who may be willing to work with a financial planner with a higher self-actualizing need.

Later, Maslow (1970) also emphasized the importance of self-actualization. He believed that man cannot be satisfied by bread alone, and that there are still other needs such as:

1. Physiological needs (air, food, water).
2. Safety and security needs (shelter, protection from predators).
3. Love and belonging needs (companionship, affection, acceptance by others).
4. Esteem needs (sense of mastery, power, appreciation from others) (Leary and Baumeister, 2000).

5. Self-actualization needs (need for ongoing actualization of potential, capacities, and talents; as fulfillment of a mission; as a fuller knowledge and acceptance of intrinsic nature; as an unceasing trend toward unity, integration, or synergy within the person).

The satisfaction of these five needs is in a hierarchical sequence, from the lowest to the highest. The first four are called the deficiency needs, while self-actualization is a growth need. We achieve psychological health if we are able to fulfill these needs. The higher the level of needs we can satisfy, the healthier we are.

Most clients would have earned enough money to take care of their basic needs (i.e., first two levels). Planners can help their clients to achieve the top three levels of needs by proper financial planning.

Applying Social Learning Theories to Financial Planning

We are not usually satisfied with what nature has given us. We gain experience throughout our lifetime. We learn. Based on our prewired repertory, the process continues, rewiring the consequences of our experiences. The simplest form of learning is habituation, which is a decline in the response to certain stimuli that are familiar as a result of repeated exposure. Suppose a fire alarm goes off suddenly. You get frightened. A few minutes later it goes off again. You respond less to it. Later it goes off a third time. You may just ignore it altogether.

Behaviorists think that everything is learnt and what you input leads to what you get as the output. One famous example is how Ivan Pavlov (1927) trained his dog. When the dog heard a bell ring (input), it salivated straightaway (output), even when there was actually no food to eat. This is called classical conditioning. Later, psychologists developed the instrumental conditioning theories, which suggest that it is the reinforcements or punishments for doing something that motivate people. For example, you get money (output) after you have done a certain amount of work (input). This is now part of your experience and you learn from it. So next time, in order to get money, you will work. For example, a financial planner can use classical conditioning to link a good referral (input) with his proposed financial plan (output) in order to reinforce his client's belief.

The social learning theory is more "out-of-the-lab." An example of a famous social learning theorist is Albert Bandura (1963), who demonstrated that children treated a doll differently after viewing video clips of other children beating up the doll followed by reinforcements or punishments. While the behavioristic theory emphasizes the reinforcement and punishment system for learning, the social learning theory proposes "observational learning." That is, people learn by observing and imitating others. There are social reinforcers, like acceptance, praises, smiles, hugs and so on. Therefore, a referral by your client's good friend is very important as social networking may help your client to have a better image of you as the clients tend to generalize the feeling of this friendship upon you.

However, by observation and imitation, it does not mean that the behavior of everyone would be the same. There is no duplicate as individuals have different levels of competence, encoding systems, expectancies, plans, and values; and are subject to different environmental factors. How a person perceives a certain event is crucial. So even if two people experience the same thing, they may have different thoughts and emotions, and thus learn different things at the end of it. Also, acquiring certain qualities does not necessarily mean exhibiting them.

In summary, the above theories are important and relevant for financial planning professionals to understand the psychological elements behind the well-being of their clients.

How Stress Affects Our Psychological Well-being

Psychological well-being is the emotional well-being of an individual which can be observed. One of the major emotional and affective dimensions of psychological well-being is stress.

Stress refers to the "worn out" signs that take their toll on our bodies when we attempt to adapt to the ever-changing environment. Stress affects us both physically and emotionally, and results in positive or negative feelings. When stress is positive, it is known as eustress, which can help motivate us and fill our lives with anticipation and excitement. On the other hand, when stress is negative, it is called distress, which can make us feel angry, depressed, and rejected, and can thus lead to a lot of health problems like insomnia, headache, upset stomach, high blood pressure, or even stroke. Both happy and unhappy events can bring us stress, like the arrival of a new family member, a job promotion, a move to another city, or a loved one's death. Stress affects an individual's ability to make rational decisions.

The reason why we focus on stress is that it could lead to emotional instability resulting in suboptimal financial decisions and the inability to execute recommended decisions by the clients. However, stress is not only an element in the onset of poor psychological and physical well-being, but also part of the progression and outcome. Therefore, our objective is to help the financial planners have a better understanding of how to maintain the psychological well-being of the clients through stress management. Our goal is to help the clients understand and control their own emotions when making and executing financial planning decisions.

It is very important that financial planning professionals should not show any sign of stress symptoms when interacting with the clients. A financial planner will not be able to gain the trust of his clients if they find that he is also under great stress. Therefore, a financial planner should also know how to maintain his own acceptable level of psychological well-being and to relieve stress. If a financial planner is unable to deal with his own stress, how can he convince others that he is able to handle their stress?

Positive Stress (Eustress)

As mentioned before, positive stress (eustress) brings us excitement and anticipation, and most of us thrive when there is some amount of positive stress. Deadlines, competitions, and even frustrations deepen and enrich our lives. The goal is not to "kill" all the stress, but to learn how to manage and use stress to help us. When there is insufficient stress, we feel bored and dejected; on the contrary, excessive stress makes us feel desperate and ready to explode. We need to find the optimal level of stress that will motivate but not overwhelm us.

There is no determined level of stress that is optimal for everybody. Every one of us is unique. What makes one person feel unhappy might make another person feel just a little stressed. The responses and tolerance to stress change with our age too. Most illnesses tend to have some relation to unrelieved stress. If you are experiencing some stress symptoms, it is likely that stress has gone beyond your optimal level. You will need to reduce the stress or improve your ability in managing it. The Application Corner on page 437 gives some tips on stress management.

Mutual self-disclosure is a useful way to start, maintain, and preserve a relationship. Since everyone faces stress, "stress" may be a common topic to start your conversation and relationship with your clients. You can show your concern about the stress experienced by your clients, and, remember to present your recommendations for stress reducers.

Implications to Financial Planning Practice

Although there are different assumptions and proposed arguments in the different psychological theories, they all share some points in common. All of us have needs. These needs are of different levels. Some basic needs such as food and water are essential to sustain life, and have to be satisfied. Otherwise, we cannot live. However, the satisfaction of these essentials is not sufficient for us to be happy. All of us have higher levels of "want." We would like to achieve our higher self (psychosynthesis theory), self-realization (analytical psychology theory), self-actualization (humanistic theory), self-sufficiency, independence, and security (independent security argument). The gratification of these needs can make us happier and feel more secure.

However, we seldom convey our desire to satisfy our needs to others because of the fear of disclosure and insecurity. Mutual self-disclosure is extremely unusual, particularly among Asians. Although we have freedom of speech, we seldom exercise our freedom. Instead, we have the fear of disclosure. We choose the topics we would like to disclose and select our listeners.

We also know that past experience is an important factor influencing future decisions. That is the reason why financial planning professionals need to gather personal data about the background of the clients. The only way for us to get to know one another is through mutual self-disclosure (social exchange theory). Although it is hard to accomplish, mutual self-disclosure may be a good technique to adopt so that there can be open communication and better understanding between financial planners and their clients. In the communication process, financial planners may be able to know their clients' unfulfilled needs and extravagant wants.

Furthermore, a financial planner can convey the message to his clients that, although self-reliance is the most desirable for achievement, some of the needs or wants may be extremely difficult, if not impossible, to be fulfilled independently without seeking help. Sometimes, "mature dependence" may be a better choice. Security and happiness can be obtained through mature dependence such as mutual help and mutual relationship. The financial planners should signal to their clients that they are willing and able to establish a mutual trust relationship so that the both parties can benefit from the satisfaction of needs and wants of different levels.

As we emphasize that psychological well-being is one of the three components of our concept of total life planning, we suggest here some factors that may affect our psychological well-being:

1. Culture
2. Social class
3. Gender
4. Age level
5. Strengths
6. Weaknesses
7. Religion
8. Education level
9. Occupation
10. Marital status
11. Number of dependants
12. Background of parents

These are the usual data that we need to gather in the second step of the financial planning process, "Gathering Client Data."

Financial Well-being

financial well-being refers to the satisfaction of one's consumption, insurance, and investment (short/medium-term/long-term) needs.

Financial well-being refers to the satisfaction of one's consumption, insurance, and investment (short/medium-term/long-term) needs. Every client has his or her own financial needs and objectives. Clients sometimes have unrealistic financial objectives. When financial planners meet this kind of clients, they should let them know what the reality is. Otherwise, the clients' disappointment may affect their trust level toward financial planners. Therefore, financial planners should fine-tune the clients' expectations to make them more realistic.

Importance of Financial Well-being

Although we state that money cannot buy everything, we do need money to survive. Obviously money is crucial in our daily lives. According to Maslow (1968), before we can satisfy our higher needs of self-esteem, love, and self-actualization, we need to gratify our basic needs of food, water, and sense of security. Although the higher needs may not necessarily be fulfilled by having money, we can use money to meet our lower basic needs. After all, to maintain our physical well-being, we need to have a quality diet. Nutritious food is not necessarily expensive, but we do need to pay for it. Therefore, we have to maintain and improve our financial well-being.

To be financially healthy, we need to set our financial goals and to devise plans to achieve them. Some financial goals are:

1. Optimize income for consumption and leisure
2. Minimize expense
3. Maximize asset worth
4. Minimize liability
5. Maximize investment return
6. Minimize tax liability
7. Have adequate insurance coverage
8. Maximize net worth
9. Have adequate retirement funds
10. Maximize estate worth

The list is not exhaustive. Gratification of these financial goals gives us financial security and comfort. How then do we achieve it? One of the ways is through financial planning and wealth management, and this is what the rest of the book is about. Figure 15.4 illustrates how the different subject areas of financial planning help achieve the short-term and long-term financial goals.

Combining Physical, Psychological, and Financial Well-being

Here we would like to introduce the conceptual framework of identifying the optimal mix of physical, psychological and financial well-being. Before going into the concept of optimal weighting for the three aspects of well-being, we first make an assumption that different people have different lifestyles. Kim, Popkin, Siega-Eiz, Haines, and Lenore (2004) suggest that there are four factors affecting lifestyle, namely diet quality, physical activity/exercise, smoking consumption, and alcohol consumption. However, studies such as this one define lifestyle from the perspective of activities and behaviors related to physical well-being. In our framework, lifestyle can also incorporate the psychological and spiritual needs of an individual.

Figure 15.4 Financial goals and financial plans

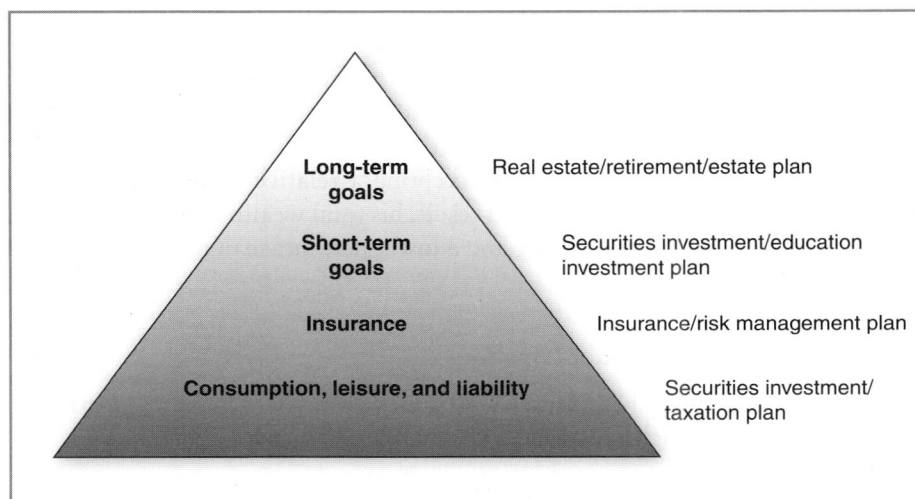

Work and Lifestyle

An individual's lifestyle is strongly affected by how he or she views work and career. For example, a person who chooses to work most of the time will probably bring in more money compared to others in the same profession who prefer to work less. Of course, while a workaholic can make more money for consumption, he also has less time for leisure to maintain his psychological and physical well-being. So we have another way of defining lifestyle: it is how individuals spend their time and money.

Financial Well-being and Lifestyle

Since lifestyle can be defined by how people spend their money and time, it is obvious that the attitude toward money is a major factor determining lifestyle. The degree and the optimal level of financial well-being in turn are related to the choice of preferred lifestyle. In order to achieve satisfaction, a person has to achieve a balance and face the trade-off between consumption (through work or labor) and leisure (not working or engaging in activities not related to making money). It is not difficult to see that achieving psychological and physical well-being is closely related to leisure. As we have only 24 hours a day, the trade-off between consumption and leisure is also a trade-off between time spent on making money and time spent on leisure.

In other words, if lifestyle is related to how people spend their money and time, then lifestyle is related to activities concerning financial well-being (i.e., through making money), and psychological and physical well-being (i.e., through leisure). Consequently, we can argue that we can redefine the lifestyle of an individual through their preference for their optimal level of physical, psychological, and financial well-being. For instance, a client with a so-called "fortune-builder" lifestyle will prefer to spend most of his effort and time in achieving a higher level of financial well-being.

Fortune-builder Lifestyle

As long as the purpose of making money is for consumption, then the argument for the fortune-builder lifestyle that represents people focused on working and laboring to make money will hold. Every person has a "pie" representing 100% of resources and effort, and this type of client is willing to pursue financial well-being at the expense of accepting a relatively lower level of psychological and physical well-being. As a result, his total wealth will comprise a higher percentage of financial well-being and a lower percentage of psychological and physical well-being.

Spiritual Leader Lifestyle

A client with a spiritual leader lifestyle favors a higher percentage in psychological well-being in his pie of total happiness.

Body-builder lifestyle

A client with a so-called "body-builder" lifestyle is keen to spend most of his effort in keeping to a proper diet and exercising regime, and is willing to accept a lower level of financial and psychological well-being.

We want to make it clear that accepting a lower level of wellness or well-being in any of these three aspects does not mean that the individuals will ruin their lives in that category. Accepting a lower level of well-being still requires achieving a minimum level of healthiness in order to constitute an acceptable lifestyle in our framework. Our lifestyle approach of the total well-being index (covered in Chapter 16) recognizes the fact that different people have their own preferred lifestyle. As long as an acceptable or minimum level of healthiness is maintained in each aspect, the individuals should have their own freedom to focus on one or two aspects if they believe that such an approach will result in a happy life for them.

We do not encourage financial planners to take a predetermined optimal lifestyle and to judge their clients using such a moral standard. As long as the preferred mix of the three aspects of well-being by the clients does not lead to obvious deficiency in their physical, psychological, and financial conditions, the planners should respect the clients' decisions and conduct financial planning within this boundary.

Applying Total Life Planning to the Financial Planning Process

Total life planning (TLP) is more an art than a science. Used properly, TLP can be very useful in personal profiling, life-cycle analysis, establishing client-planner relationship (step 1), establishing goals for clients (step 2), and monitoring the financial plan (step 6).

In order to develop and maintain a good understanding of physical, psychological, and financial well-being, it is important that the planners know about the backgrounds of their clients, such as personality, family values, cultural values, and lifestyle preferences. These non-financial data are essential for the first step of the financial planning process as well as total life planning.

Gathering client data and determining goals is the second step of the financial planning process. In this step, the financial planners have to determine both the personal and financial goals of the clients and then set priorities for their achievement. Therefore, financial planners should not only care about the financial well-being of the clients but also pay attention to their personal desires. When the financial planners help to fulfill the personal goals of the clients, they are helping the clients to achieve their total life plan through financial planning.

The last step of the financial planning process is monitoring the financial planning recommendations. As we have mentioned before, we undergo different life-cycle stages throughout our lives. At different stages, we have different goals. For instance, as a young adult, we do not care much about retirement but pay more attention to current consumption. Then when we have plans to get married and have children, we start to think about savings. When we are in middle age, we worry about retirement. While we are retired, we think about estate planning. Therefore, a financial planner has to note the expected and unexpected changes throughout the different stages of their clients' lifecycle. These changes may alter the physical, psychological, and financial status of the clients. Therefore, the financial planners may have to modify the current financial planning recommendations if necessary.

15.2 Conclusion

A financial planner presenting a financial plan to the clients is like a chef preparing a dish for the customers. The financial planner has to be familiar with every basic financial analysis skill and topic, e.g., time value of money, asset management strategies and tax planning technique. The chef has to be competent in every kind of culinary skill, e.g., baking, steaming, and stewing. However, these skills may not be sufficient.

If the chef does not understand the needs and tastes of a customer, e.g., a vegetarian, or one who is allergic to certain ingredients, the customer cannot enjoy the chef's food, no matter how skilled the chef is in preparing the dishes. Similarly, although financial planners are capable of devising the best financial plan to improve the financial well-being of their clients, if the financial planners have no concern for their psychological needs and physical well-being, the financial plan recommended cannot satisfy the client comprehensively.

Understanding psychological and physical well-being helps financial planners know more about their clients which can improve the ability of financial planners to devise financial plans for their clients, which in turn would help to fulfill all their clients' financial needs. However, the more desirable goal of financial planners may be, at their very best, to enhance their clients' psychological happiness and physical health as well, in addition to their financial well-being. Eventually, what matters is how financial planners can improve the total well-being of their prestigious clients. The financial plan is not the end-product, but a means to achieving total life planning.

Total life planning is an art rather than a science. It takes time and effort for the planners to learn how to incorporate other techniques, such as personal profiling and life-cycle analysis, which use clients' nonfinancial data in their financial planning process. Therefore, it is easy to hold the entry ticket to this profession by grasping basic financial skills to satisfy the financial needs of your clients. However, it is hard to excel in this profession to help enhance the psychological and physical well-being of your clients as it requires professional judgment and experience to quantify the nonfinancial data in order to design a total life plan. The Application Corner provides some tips on improving one's overall well-being.

APPLICATION CORNER

Tips for Improving Physical and Psychological Well-being

1. Practicing a healthy diet

There is an ongoing debate among medical and health science professionals on what the key factors of a healthy diet are. Obviously, there is no one magic formula for everyone. However, everyone needs to have a well-balanced diet because nutrition deficiency can be a risk factor for chronic diseases. A well-balanced diet is one that incorporates grain, vegetables and fruits, some dairy products, meat, beans and nuts, and of course less oil and fat.

2. The importance of exercise

Blair, Kohl, Gordon, and Paffenbarger (1992) report that habitual physical activity enhances health while an inactive lifestyle increases the likelihood of chronic illnesses. Habitual physical activity gives rise to a number of benefits: it improves the functions of the heart and lung, enhances the immune system, drains off excess fat, reduces the chance of being overweight, and releases endorphins. By making us less susceptible to illnesses and helping us to lessen the stress level, it means that exercising improves both our physical and psychological well-being. Therefore, persistent and habitual physical activity not only helps to train our body physically, but it also helps to develop our mind, self-control, and patience.

Physical activity is measured by the level, frequency, and duration of doing exercises. The physical activity index (PAI) of Kim, Popkin, Siega-Eiz, Haines, and Lenore (2004) identifies five activity level groups: very active; active, moderate, light, and sedentary.

3. Managing stress

In this section, some stress management techniques are suggested. The list provided here is not exhaustive; you can obtain a fuller and more comprehensive discussion of stress management from many books relating to psychological well-being and stress. Most the suggestions listed here aim to handle stressful situations and to minimize the level of unnecessary stress (Posen 1995).

  (a) Avoid stressful situations and seek stress reducers.
    i. Minimize the chance of losing something (a job, a relationship) that may cause stress.
    ii. Improve time management techniques.
    iii. Have a break and time-out to stop stress level from increasing.
    iv. Find a listener. We all like to express our feelings and experiences, both good and bad, to others. They may not be able to solve our problems, but psychologically, we feel better after sharing. That is the reason why there is an increasing number of "complaint columns" in newspapers and phone-in sessions on radio shows. However, it is easier to find someone to share good things with rather than bad things. It is more difficult to find a listener for one's problems. Financial planners should be their clients' listeners. Here are some tips for being a listener: listen attentively and patiently; do not interrupt; show concern and support; offer willingness to listen

anytime; and give advice only if necessary. Remember this is a way to establish a long-term relationship with your clients by making yourself their friend and offering support.

(b) Change your habits.

i.   Ensure sufficient rest to regain energy.

ii. Exercise regularly to relieve stress and tension, and to facilitate a good night's sleep.

iii. Practice relaxation and meditation techniques to neutralize stress. Examples include sitting quietly; deep breathing; self-hypnosis; yoga relaxation; Zen meditation; progressive muscular relaxation; and relaxation imagery.

iv. Have a balanced diet, and consume less food containing caffeine (coffee, tea, chocolate, cola).

v.   Pace yourself at work. As we have mentioned, there are two types of stress: good stress and bad stress. We can use good stress to motivate our performance. However, when the stress level becomes too much (distress), our performance deteriorates. Fatigue is a warning signal of distress. When we are tired, we become inefficient. Therefore, we need a break from time to time. That is the reason why there are always morning breaks and afternoon breaks during seminars.

vi. Practice appropriate time allocation between work and leisure, i.e., make yourself less busy and more relaxed. There is a negative relation between stress and leisure. Many psychological theories suggest that we need to know and understand ourselves, as well as the people and the nature around us. If we engage ourselves too much in our work, we have less time to know ourselves, and the people and things around us. Therefore, we need to allocate time for leisure. The word "leisure" originates from the Latin word *licere*, which means "permission." Sometimes, it is absolutely your own choice to place yourself under stress. Do permit yourself and others to have some leisure time.

(c) Change your way of thinking.

i.   Learn to be more realistic. Some unhappiness and stress are due to unrealistic desires. Have a clearer understanding of your own roles and responsibilities; plan to achieve something that is reasonable and manageable; and set sensible priorities for your tasks. Do not push yourself too hard to be the top performer of your firm or to get the largest number of head count for policies sold.

ii. Learn to be more patient. Things take time to be done. Be patient with yourself and your clients. Do not show your impatience and frustration when you find your clients to be unreasonable.

iii. Learn to change risks to opportunities. One of the most powerful stress management techniques is "reframing." Reframing means changing our original perception about things so that we can feel better about them. We can look at things from different angles. The Chinese translation of the word "risk" is composed of two Chinese words with opposite meanings: "crisis" and "opportunity." We can perceive a situation as a disaster (negative perception) or as a prospect (positive perception). Therefore, financial planners should try to reduce their negative and pessimistic thinking. A critical boss may make your life miserable. However, you can use this situation as an encouragement to motivate you to perform better. A stubborn client may create difficulties for financial planners in selling their proposal. However, financial planners can use the situation as a challenge to assess their ability. These are valuable experiences to improve themselves. If financial planners are able to pass the test of dealing with their critical bosses and stubborn clients successfully, they will be able to handle many more challenges in the future. This is how financial planners can remove the "crisis" element from "risk" to make it a priceless "opportunity," an overture of your forward movement.

iv. Learn to have a sense of humor. Fun and laughter can help release stress.

These stress management techniques are suggestions for financial planners to not only minimize stress and lessen its harmful impact, but also to prepare them in confronting stress. Lastly, if the stress is too serious to be self-managed, do not hesitate to seek professional help. It is better to solve the problem as soon as possible before it gets out of control.

Key Terms

financial well-being *432*

physical well-being *425*

psychological well-being *426*

References

Bandura, A. and Walters, R., *Social Learning and Personality Development* (New York: Holt, Rinehart, & Winston, 1963).

Blair, S. N., Kohl, H. W., Gordon, N. F., and Paffenbarger Jr., R. S., "How Much Physical Activity Is Good for Health?," *Annual Review of Public Health,* vol. 13 (1992): 99–126.

Freud, S., "The Interpretation of Dreams," in Strachey, J., trans. (ed.), *The Complete Psychological Works*, 4–5, (1900). (New York: Norton, 1976).

Jung, C. G.., "The Structure and Dynamics of the Psyche," *Collected Works*, 8. (Princeton, NJ: Princeton University Press, 1960) (Originally published in German, 1926).

Kim, S., Popkin, B. M., Siega-Riz, A. M., Haines, P. S., and Arab, L., "A Cross-national Comparison of Lifestyle between China and the United States, Using a Comprehensive Cross-national Measurement Tool of the Healthfulness of Lifestyles: The Lifestyle Index," *Preventive Medicine*, vol. 38 (2004): 160–171.

Leary, M. R., and Baumeister, R. F., "The Nature and Function of Self-esteem: Sociometer Theory. In Zanna, M. P., ed., *Advances in Experimental Social Psychology*, vol. 32 (San Diego, CA: Academic Press, 2000): 1–62.

Maslow, A. H., *Motivation and Personality*, Revised Edition. (New York: Harper & Row, 1970).

Maslow A. H., Toward a Psychology of Being, Second Edition. (New York: Van Nostrand Reinhold, 1968).

Pavlov, I. P., *Conditioned Reflexes* (Oxford, England: Oxford University Press, 1927).

Posen D. B., "Stress Management for Patient and Physician," *Canadian Journal of Continuing Medical Education* (1995).

Rogers, C. R., "A Theory of Therapy, Personality and Interpersonal Relationships, as Developed in the Client-centered Framework." In Koch, S., ed., *Psychology: A Study of a Science*, vol. 3. (New York: McGraw-Hill, 1959).

Shikany J. M., and White Jr., G. L., "Dietary Guidelines for Chronic Disease Prevention," *South Medical Journal*, vol. 93, no. 12 (2000): 1138–1151.

Weisburger J. H., "Prevention of Cancer and other Chronic Diseases Worldwide Based on Sound Mechanisms," *BioFactors*, vol. 12, nos. 1–4 (2000): 73–81.

Questions & Problems

Problems

1. Why is physical well-being important to both the client and financial planner?

2. How can psychological well-being be observed? Suggest some tips for improving psychological well-being.

3. What are the major elements of financial well-being?

Managing Client Expectations in Financial Planning[2]

Financial products are diverse, ranging from a simple product such as a savings account to a more complex product such as a structured product. Nowadays customers are confronted with a variety of financial products and they encounter difficulties in choosing the right financial products to suit their needs. These financial products are intangible in nature, and some are highly complex, making it difficult for customers to evaluate and compare them prior to their purchase. This will heighten prepurchase uncertainty and perceived risk (Harrison 2000). Thus, customers might devote greater effort and time to prepurchase activities, and rely on other informative cues or credible sources (Murray 1991). Some might defer their purchase decision until they feel that there is a strong need for the service. Those who have purchased a complex financial product may feel uneasy and disappointed with their choices because of a lack of knowledge and ability to appreciate the values of these products before purchasing them.

Financial planners are crucial to helping their clients understand their financial situations, and developing a tailor-made financial plan that best suits their needs. McKechnie (1992) suggests two characteristics which are ascribed to financial services, namely fiduciary responsibility and two-way information flow between customer and provider. Fiduciary responsibility refers to the implicit responsibility of a financial provider in managing customers' funds and the nature of financial advice given to them. Two-way communication flow refers to the regular interactive communication between the provider and customer over an extended period of time. Unlike most physical products which are one-off purchases, financial products and services are consumed continuously over an extended time period. As clients mature, their financial needs and service expectations may change. Financial planners need to review their clients' financial situations periodically, and understand and manage client expectations in order to make their clients feel comfortable and confident about the financial plan.

---

[2] An in-depth discussion on managing client expectations in financial planning by Dr. Jackie Tam, Assistant Professor in the Department of Management and Marketing, Hong Kong Polytechnic University. Professor Tam wants to express her thanks to Palgrave Macmillan for granting permission to use some of the material in an article she wrote entitled "Managing Customer Expectations in Financial Services: Opportunities and Challenges" published in *Journal of Financial Services Marketing*, 2007. Reproduced with permission of Palgrave Macmillan.

Client Decision-making Process and Expectations

The client decision-making process can be broadly divided into three stages: prepurchase, encounter and postencounter (Lovelock and Wirtz, 2007). In the prepurchase stage, it is assumed that consumers are aware of a need, which may compel them to search for more information, and to evaluate the alternatives. After selecting a financial provider, consumers are assumed to move on to the encounter stage which involves a series of interactions with the chosen provider. During the encounter stage, consumers start evaluating the quality of the interaction with the provider, and the performance of the products. This evaluation process can continue to the postencounter stage.

Predictive expectations are clients' anticipation of the level of performance of a product or a service (Churchill and Surprenant 1982). They play a major role in the client decision-making process (van Raaij 1991; Spreng et al. 1993). In the prepurchase stage, they guide clients' purchase decision. When clients recognize a need for financial planning, it is assumed that they will select a financial planner who can meet or perform better than their expectations. During the encounter stage, the initial expectations can serve as standards against which a service performance is evaluated (Zeithaml et al. 1993; Walker and Baker 2000). If clients perceive service performance that matches or is better than their expectations, their relationship with the planner is expected to continue, otherwise it will be very likely terminated. Effective management of client expectations is vital for long-term success (Clow and Vorhies 1993). From the standpoint of the financial planner, setting adequate expectations can attract the right clients and get them to acquire the financial service, and meeting these expectations will reinforce the clients' beliefs that they have made the right choice, which increases the likelihood that they will use more of the service and recommend other people to use it as well. Success in developing relationships with clients may depend on how well the financial planner understands and manages customer expectations.

This section discusses the challenges of managing client expectations in the context of financial planning services, and examines how financial planners can manage their client expectations to their advantage. The notion that clients can form realistic expectations about financial planning may be too idealistic (O'Neill and Palmer 2003). Financial planning is a long-term oriented service and its benefits may take time to realize. As there is no immediate perceivable benefits, prospects may not be able to recognize the need for it. Some might find it difficult to anticipate what they will receive from a financial planner. In order to arouse prospects' need for the services, there should be more communication and promotion programs with strong emphasis on the benefits offered by the financial planners. Helping clients formulate clear and realistic expectations of the services, and managing clients' expectations during the encounter are crucial to satisfactory outcomes and a long-term relationship.

Oliver and Winer (1987) proposed an expectations framework consisting of arousal, knowability of the outcome, uncertainty, and ambiguity. These components are said to influence the accuracy, predictive ability, and stability of expectations. Arousal is associated with the degree of activity needed for retrieval of expectations, and is classified as active and passive expectations (van Raaij 1991). Active expectations are those which the client has consciously thought of, and they may be instrumental in the purchase of a service. For example, the interest rate paid on a savings account is identifiable and comparable. The client is aware of it and may actively process this information to determine the expected return. Passive expectations are those which the client is not consciously aware of. They exist as "true beliefs" and reside passively and permanently in the memory. They are probably not processed until disconfirmed (van Raaij 1991). For example, the security of a savings account in a bank is taken for granted, and clients generally assume that the bank will safeguard their funds.

When clients are confronted with a purchase decision, active expectations are very likely to be generated to guide their decision. But if the information relevant to the purchase is highly abstract, which is often the case with financial services, clients would have difficulty in forming clear expectations. Obviously, to help clients form clear and realistic expectations, the service and any related information should be made explicit and presented in a manner that is easy to understand. Passive expectations are common in continuously provided services (Bolton and Drew 1991). Clients are accustomed to a particular service performance so they might not devote cognitive resources to evaluating the actual performance of a service against their expectations. When service performance is improved, clients may not easily discern any intangible differences. Financial planners may need to communicate the improvement clearly to clients, and highlight any specific enhancement.

Knowability refers to the immediacy of the knowledge that generates expectations (Oliver and Winer 1987). "Present" knowledge is developed based on historical events or information at hand; for example, search attributes such as color and size can be classified as knowable data. "Anticipatory" knowledge consists of data which cannot be known until some future point in time. Anticipatory knowledge includes knowledge about services that offer experiential attributes. The level of these attributes cannot be determined until the service is in use. Services that possess credence attributes, where customers may not have the knowledge and skills to evaluate a service adequately, can be classified as unknown outcomes.

Financial services are low in search attributes and high in experiential and credence attributes (Howcroft et al. 2003). Acquiring these services involves some risks, particularly services that are high in credence attributes, such as investment products. The lack of knowledge in appreciating these services is likely to diminish customers' interest and confidence in making a decision. Financial planners can attempt to increase customers' interest and confidence by providing the tools and programs that can facilitate their learning more about financial products. When clients become more financially literate, they can assess the value of the service, distinguish the differences between competitive offerings, and feel more at ease in making their financial decisions.

For some financial services, the final outcome is influenced by factors that are beyond the control of a financial planner (Harrison 2000). Clients should be informed and aware of potential risks and returns on any purchase. When there is a high degree of uncertainty, clients' estimations will be less precise, and their expected performance of a given service is likely to be a range rather than a specific value. Financial planners need to understand clients' financial situations, risk attitudes, and financial objectives so as to develop a plan that meets their clients' needs. Although there is a high uncertainty of the outcome, financial planners can help clients reduce relative uncertainty by portraying the performance outcome with both a worst-case scenario and a best-case scenario.

Ambiguity arises where the probability distribution of the occurrence of future events is unknown (van Raaij 1991). It is regarded as a "second order" uncertainty with the extreme case of ambiguity being called "ignorance" (Oliver and Winer 1987). When the probability distribution of outcomes cannot be ascertained, high levels of uncertainty and ambiguity result, hindering clients from forming expectations. For example, the outcomes of a novel service cannot be easily anticipated because there is no historical precedent (Oliver 1997). It might be useful to present the performance of a similar service as a reference for clients to predict the likelihood of the outcomes.

Other Expectation Standards

There are other types of expectation standards, which are referred to as "comparison standards" (Miller 1977; Iacobucci et al., 1994). These standards include "ideal standards," which reflect the level of performance a client would ideally hope to receive; "deserved standards," which reflect what a client feels the performance "should be" in the light of the costs of the service; and "minimum tolerance standards," which reflect the lowest level of performance that is acceptable to a consumer. Another type of standards is known as experience-based norms, which are derived from a client's breadth of experience of the focal brand, similar brands, or a product class (Woodruff et al., 1983). These expectation standards can coincide with one another, and with predictive expectations.

When clients evaluate the quality of a service, they use a point of reference to judge whether a service is good or bad. Hence, there can be many different levels of quality depending on which comparison standards clients use to make their judgment. Financial planners need to understand which expectation standards their clients will use for making a purchase decision, assessing service quality, determining customer satisfaction, and influencing word-of-mouth recommendation (Kopalle and Lehmann 2001). Zeithaml et al. (1993) introduced a "zone of tolerance" which is bound by a desirable level and a minimum acceptable level, and suggests that providers should not deliver services below minimum acceptable levels, and at times they should strive to exceed desired levels. The size of "zone of tolerance" may be influenced by many factors (Zeithaml and Bitner 2003). Financial planners need to understand the extent of the influence of these factors on the size of the "zone of tolerance", and develop effective strategies to influence these factors.

Dynamics of Expectations

Expectations are dynamic, and they will be revised based on experience and new information. There is some evidence to suggest that customers revise their expectation following an experience (Tam 2005). Because of the intangibility of the services, clients' initial expectations toward the financial planner may be shaped by informative cues such as qualifications, educational background, years of experience, and quality awards and certificates. In subsequent interactions with the financial planner, clients will be able to determine whether they have made the right choice or not. Financial planners should carefully plan every interaction with the client in order to cultivate their clients' trust and confidence. Carlson (1989) described "moments of truth" as the quality of the interaction between a service provider and a client. The "moments of truth" provide opportunities for the financial planner to not only update and exchange information with the client, but also to reinforce client trust and strengthen the relationship.

Clients' expectations of financial products/services tend to be more vulnerable to change. The performance of a financial product is very sensitive to economic factors. Hence, it is important that timely, accurate, and complete information should be provided so as to help clients adjust their expectations. The information should be presented in a manner that is easy to understand and comprehend. Financial planners may also need to revise the financial plan because of the changing market environment.

Client Involvement and Expertise

Client involvement   Involvement is an observable state reflecting a consumer's regard for a product category, in terms of degree of personal relevance, importance, interest, and perceived risk (Richins and Bloch, 1986). Clients who are highly involved in financial products and services may have a greater desire to learn and understand the products and services than those who are not so involved. Swinyard (1993) suggests that highly involved customers are more likely to attend to information about a financial product and service, and to elaborate more meanings and inferences in connection with it. These clients are curious to know about the available investment options, the structure of these investment products, and the potential returns. They are also eager to participate in the financial planning process and co-produce the financial plan. Because of the high level of participation, clients may feel a greater sense of control, and thus feel more responsible for, and greater satisfaction with, the outcomes (Van Raaij and Pruyn 1998).

Clients who have a low involvement in financial products and services are not as active as the high involvement clients in the financial planning process. They may trust the financial planners for their advice and suggestions, and delegate the responsibility to them. They may even blame the financial planners when the plan does not work out as expected. Hence, it is imperative that financial planners clarify and educate their clients about their respective roles and responsibilities. Helping clients to understand their roles and responsibilities, and getting them to be involved in the financial planning process can lead to a highly satisfactory outcome.

Client expertise   Clients who are financially illiterate will find it difficult to decode a complex financial product and service because of a lack of relevant knowledge structure (Sujan 1985). These clients will find it difficult to develop clear and realistic expectations about financial planning services. Effective communication, and programs and tools that aim at facilitating customer learning of financial products and services seem to be a viable strategy. As clients become more knowledgeable, they can recognize the value of these products and services, are able to anticipate outcomes, and have greater confidence in making purchase decisions. This may lead to less disappointment with the purchase, greater satisfaction, and a long-lasting relationship. On the other hand, clients with a high level of expertise have greater ability to decode new information, thus timely, complete, and accurate information are important to forming realistic expectations. These clients also possess greater ability to discern the differences between competitive offerings, thus highlighting the distinct advantage of an offer or making a comparison easier would be a desirable strategy. Such clients may also serve as opinion leaders who exert powerful influence on potential prospects.

Conclusion

This discussion has explored the challenges financial planners face when managing client expectations of financial planning services. We have looked at the nature, types and dynamics of expectations, and the different levels of client involvement and expertise. Uncertainty and ambiguity surrounding financial planning reduce clients' ability to form clear expectations, which may lead them to withdraw from making a purchase decision. Thus, presenting the service components in a transparent and easy-to-understand manner can help clients develop clear expectations about what they will receive. There are multitype expectation standards, and financial planners should understand how these are used in the purchase and evaluation process. Clients with different levels of expertise and involvement may have different expectations toward financial planning. Designing separate strategies for clients with different levels of expertise and involvement would be desirable.

Client expectations should be continuously monitored as there is evidence to suggest that they might change over the course of the consumption period. Financial planners not only need to contact clients on a regular basis, but also to carefully manage every interaction in a way that can instill customer trust and build a relationship. As a client relationship evolves, it would be more efficient for the financial planner to shape client expectations and preferences, and this might result in a wider zone of acceptable standards, higher client satisfaction, and long-lasting relationships.

References

Bolton, R. and Drew, J., "A Longitudinal Analysis of the Impact of Service Charges on Customer Attitude," *Journal of Marketing*, vol. 55 (January 1991): 1–9.

Carlson, J., *Moments of Truth* (New York: Harper Collins, 1989)

Clow, K. and Vorhies, D, "Building a Competitive Advantage for Service Firms," *Journal of Services Marketing*, vol. 7 (1993): 22–32.

Churchill, G. and Surprenant, C, "An Investigation into the Determinants of Customer Satisfaction," *Journal of Marketing Research*, vol. 19 (November 1982): 491–504.

Harrison, T., *Financial Services Marketing* (UK: Pearson Education Limited, 2000).

Howcroft, B., Hewer, P., and Hamilton, R., "Consumer Decision-making Styles and the Purchases of Financial Services," *The Services Industries Journal*, vol. 23, no. 3 (2003): 63–81.

Iacobucci, D., Grayson, K., and Ostrom, A., "The Calculus of Service Quality and Customer Satisfaction: Theoretical and Empirical Differentiation and Integration," in Swartz, T., Bowen, D., and Brown, S., eds., *Advances in Services Marketing and Management*, vol. 3 (Greenwich: JAI Press Inc., 1994): 1–67.

Kopalle, P. and Lehmann, D., "Strategic Management of Expectations: The Role of Disconfirmation Sensitivity and Perfectionism," *Journal of Marketing Research*, vol. 38, (August 2001): 386–394.

Lovelock, C. and Wirtz, J., "Services Marketing: People, Technology, Strategy," 6th edn., (US: Pearson, 2007).

McKechnie, S., "Consumer Buying Behaviour in Financial Services: An Overview," *International Journal of Banking Marketing*, vol. 10, no. 5 (1992): 4–12.

Miller, J., "Studying Satisfaction Modifying Models, Eliciting Expectations, Posing Problems, and Making Meaningful Measurement," in Hunt, K., ed., *Conceptualization and Measurement of Consumer Satisfaction and Dissatisfaction* (US: Marketing Science Institute, 1977): 72–91.

Murray, K., "A Test of Services Marketing Theory: Consumer Information Acquisition Activities," *Journal of Marketing*, vol. 55 (January 1991): 10–25.

Oliver, R. and Winer, R., "A Framework for the Formation and Structure of Consumer Expectations: Review and Propositions," *Journal of Economic Psychology*, vol. 8, (1987): 469–499.

Oliver, R., "Consumer Satisfaction," (US: McGraw Hill, 1997).

O'Neill, M. and Palmer, A., "An Exploratory Study of the Effects of Experience on Consumer Perceptions of the Service Quality Construct," *Managing Service Quality*, vol. 13, no. 3, (2003): 187–196.

Richins M. and Bloch, P., "After the New Wears Off: The Temporal Context of Product Involvement," *Journal of Consumer Research*, vol. 13 (September 1986): 280–285.

Spreng R., Dixon, A. and Olshavsky R., "The Impact of Perceived Value on Consumer Satisfaction," *Journal of Consumer Satisfaction, Dissatisfaction and Complaining Behavior*, vol. 6 (1993): 50–55.

Sujan, M., "Consumer Knowledge: Effects on Evaluation Strategies Mediating Consumer Judgment," *Journal of Consumer Research*, vol. 12 (June 1985): 31–46.

Swinyard, W., "The Effects of Mood, Involvement, and Quality of Store Experience on Shopping Intentions," *Journal of Consumer Research*, vol. 20 (September 1993): 271–280.

Tam, J. L. M., "Examining the Dynamics of Consumer Expectations in a Chinese Context," *Journal of Business Research*, vol. 58 (2005): 777–786.

van Raaij, F. W., "The Formation and Use of Expectations in Consumer Decision Making," in Robertson, T. and Kassarjian, H., eds., *Handbook of Consumer Behaviour*, (US: Prentice-Hall, 1991): 401–418.

Van Raaij, F. W. and Pruyn, H., "Customer Control and Evaluation of Service Validity and Reliability," *Psychology and Marketing*, vol. 15, no. 8 (1998): 811–832.

Walker, J. and Baker, J., "An Exploratory Study of a Multi-expectation Framework for Services," *The Journal of Services Marketing*, vol. 14, no. 5 (2000): 411–431.

Woodruff, R., Cadotte, E., and Jenkins, R., "Modeling Consumer Satisfaction Processes Using Experience-based Norms," *Journal of Marketing Research*, vol. 20 (August 1983): 296–304.

Zeithaml, V. and Bitner, M., *Services Marketing*, 3rd edn., (New York: McGraw Hill, 2003).

Zeithaml, V., Berry, L., and Parasuraman, A., "The Nature and Determinants of Customer Expectations of Service," *Journal of the Academy of Marketing Science*, vol. 21 (1993): 1–12.

chapter 16

Total Well-being Index

The previous chapter introduced the concept of total life planning (TLP), which consists of three important aspects of well-being: physical, psychological, and financial well-being. Used properly, TLP can be very useful in personal profiling, life-cycle analysis, establishing client-planner relationship (step 1 of the financial planning process), establishing goals for clients (step 2 of the financial planning process), and monitoring the financial plan (step 6 of the financial planning process). In this chapter we introduce a tool for financial planners to determine the level of total life balance: the total well-being index.

In order to develop and maintain a good understanding of the physical, psychological, and financial well-being of their clients, it is important that the planners know about their clients' personalities, family values, cultural values, and lifestyle preferences. Unfortunately, it is not easy for a financial planner to scientifically integrate all these personal data into a single indicator for financial planning analysis needed in the steps mentioned above. In order to facilitate the development of TLP, an overall indicator such as a total well-being index is extremely useful. A total well-being index will measure and integrate the financial health, physical health, and psychological health of a person into a single indicator. Planners can use this index in two ways. First, comparing the client's index with some benchmark, the planner can evaluate the overall health condition of the client and pay attention to the areas of deficiency. Second, by monitoring the index level through time, the planner can keep track of the total wealth condition of the client. This monitoring exercise can help to identify areas of improvement and deterioration easily.

Experienced planners can conduct TLP properly for clients without using a formal index. However, for young planners and wealth management firms that employ a lot of planners and wealth managers, a formal index can serve as a scientific tool for inexperienced planners and as a scalable TLP service which can be expanded more easily.

16.1   Measurement Design

If you want to solve a mathematical problem, you need a formula. In the same way, if you want to obtain your physical, psychological, and financial well-being status, you need a tool to assist you. In this section, we are going to provide a guideline to help financial planners create an effective tool to measure their clients' total well-being index, which includes their physical, psychological, and financial well-being. The first step of designing a proper foundation to construct the total well-being index is to understand the basic meaning of each dimension of total well-being. Basically, each well-being status is indicated by different dimensions. For example, the measurement indicators of physical well-being include drinking and smoking habits, diet, and so on.

Framework of the Total Well-being Index

total well-being index Includes and combines financial well-being, physical well-being, and psychological well-being into a simple index to provide a tool to understand the total well-being status of an individual.

The **total well-being index** includes physical well-being, psychological well-being, and financial well-being combined into a simple index (Figure 16.1).

Measurement of Physical Well-being Status

Physical well-being does not simply mean the absence of disease and illness. Basically, we can say that a person is physically fit when he has the energy to perform daily tasks including work and leisure. Several research studies have revealed that a healthy lifestyle leads to physical fitness (Kim et al., 2004). Other physical lifestyle indicators include diet quality, physical activity, smoking, and drug consumption (Kim et al., 2004). In order to measure the physical well-being status comprehensively, we should consider all these different lifestyle aspects when designing the questionnaire.

Figure 16.1 Framework of the total well-being index

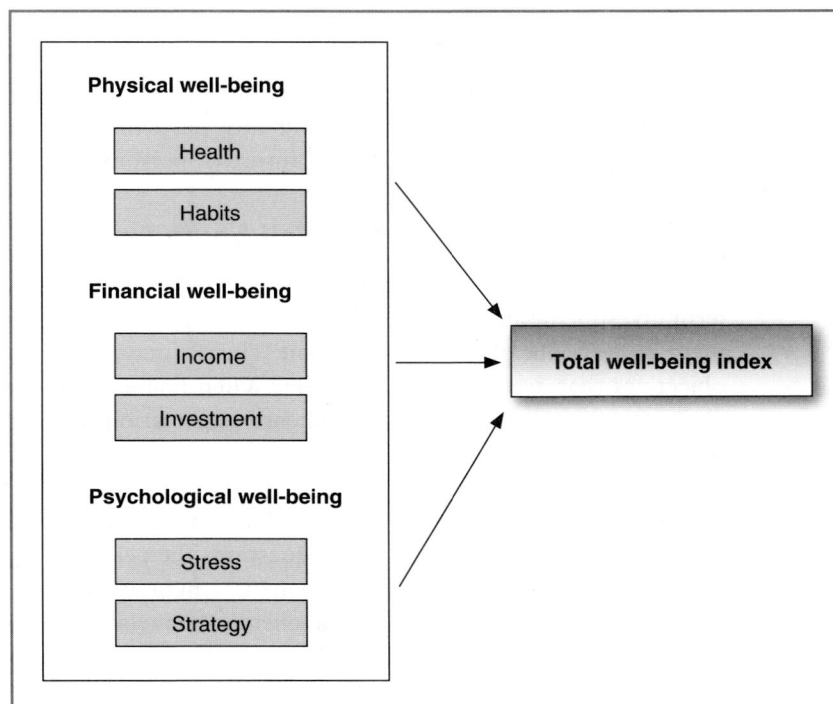

The measurement indicators of physical well-being employed to determine the construct of physical well-being include habits (smoking and drinking), exercise, and diet. In fact, physical well-being is related to the different life stages. The physical well-being status varies with age. As a result, financial planners should interpret the information about the physical well-being of the clients together with the appropriate characteristics of different life stages.

Examples of questions relating to physical well-being
1.   How would you describe your diet habits listed below?
     (a)   Daily fruit and vegetable intake (ideally three pieces of fruit/servings of vegetables a day).
     (b)   Daily water intake (ideally eight glasses).
     (c)   Overall daily diet (ideally a balanced meal).
2.   Overall, how would you describe your health condition?

Measurement of Psychological Well-being Status

Different psychologists have different definitions of psychological well-being. Maslow's hierarchy of needs (1970) is used as one indicator of our blueprint to design our questions. Maslow classified human needs into five levels: physiological needs, safety needs, belonging needs, esteem needs, and self-actualization needs. The higher the level of needs we satisfy, the "healthier" we are psychologically.

Stress is another important element to determine our psychological well-being. However, the stress level of psychological status varies at different life stages. For example, some young adults may have stress due to their social needs, such as stress arising from a romantic relationship. Middle-aged adults may have a higher stress level due to their financial burden of raising a family.

Example of a question relating to psychological well-being
Do the following statements describe you?
(a)   I am forgetful about a lot of minor things (e.g., my friend's birthday).
(b)   I always feel scared without any particular reason (e.g., I'm overly worried about my financial future or personal safety).

Measurement of Financial Well-being Status

Financial well-being includes consumption needs, insurance needs, short/medium-term investment, and long-term investment (Figure 16.2). Clients need to realize their own financial objectives. Some clients may have unrealistic financial objectives that are difficult to achieve. When financial planners meet this kind of clients, they should manage the clients' expectations and let them know what the reality is.

The questions determining consumption needs include expenditure and tax elements, whereas insurance needs include life and asset protection. Financial planners need to state clearly in the questions the period of investment, whether it is short-, medium- or long-term, to avoid ambiguity.

A questionnaire to measure a client's financial well-being status should cover the major areas of financial planning including consumption planning, tax planning, insurance planning, investment planning, retirement planning,

Figure 16.2 Principles in formulating financial objectives

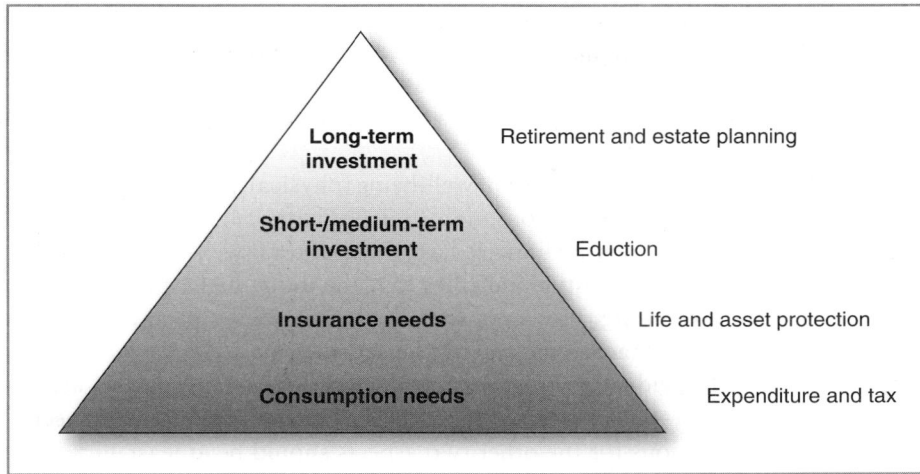

and estate planning. Here, we suggest a way to design the questions such that the result will be inclusive and explanatory. For example, financial planners can design some questions asking about their clients' consumption planning. Figure 16.3 shows a sample of questions designed to measure financial well-being.

Figure 16.3 A sample of financial well-being questions

1. Savings

<u>Subjective question:</u>

How important is savings in your personal financial management?

| 1 | 2 | 3 | 4 | 5 | 6 | 7 |

Very unimportant   Neutral   Very important

<u>Objective question:</u>

Apart from major expenses such as wedding preparations and home purchase, what percentage of your income do you save per month?

In debt   Less than 3%   3–5.9%   6–8.9%   9–11.9%   12–14.9%   15% or more

2. Investment

<u>Subjective question:</u>

Specify your satisfaction level of meeting your intermediate goals through investment.

	Highly dissatisfied			Neutral		Highly satisfied	
Education	1	2	3	4	5	6	7
Home purchase	1	2	3	4	5	6	7

Determining the Lifestyle Category of Clients

As the total well-being index consists of physical well-being, psychological well-being, and financial well-being, we roughly classify clients into four lifestyle categories: physical focus lifestyle (Figure 16.4), psychological focus lifestyle (Figure 16.5), financial focus lifestyle (Figure 16.6), and finally, balanced lifestyle (Figure 16.7).

Ideally, each aspect of well-being (physical, psychological and financial) should be of equal proportions, i.e., 33.3%. Figure 16.4 illustrates that individuals with a physical focused lifestyle have 50% of total well-being focusing on the physical aspect. This lifestyle indicates that the individuals spend a lot of time on sports and exercising. However, the allocation of 25% each for the psychological and financial dimensions may not be satisfactory.

Individuals who are classified as having a specific aspect focus should have 44–67% of their total well-being focused on that aspect. The remaining proportions for the other two aspects should be at least 17%.

How these figures are derived

Minimum = $\frac{1}{3}$ more than average (33.3% × 1.3 = 44%)

Maximum = double the average (33.3% × 2 = 67%)

Minimum = $\frac{1}{2}$ less than average (33.3% × 0.5 = 17%)

Financial planners and clients need to work together in order to decide on the specific weight of each aspect of total well-being that would best describe the lifestyle of the clients. The above are examples that illustrate the different lifestyle categories that clients belong to. We can get the total score of each well-being aspect (physical, psychological, and financial) from the questionnaire to make the correct classification.

Figure 16.4 Physical focus lifestyle

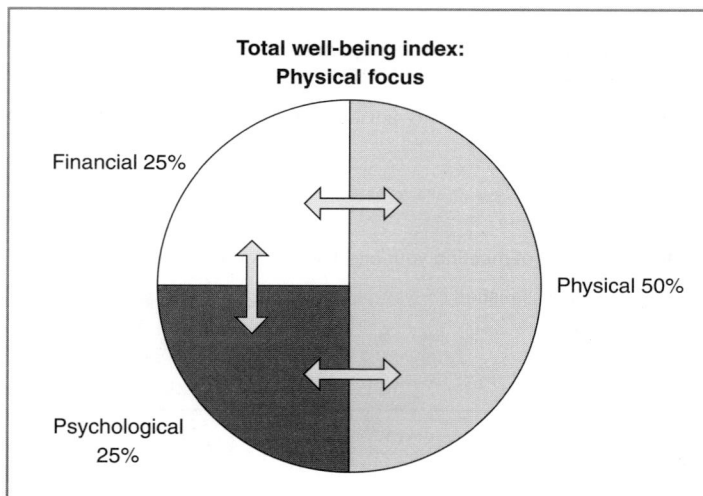

Range: Physical focus varies from 44% to 67%.

Figure 16.5 Psychological focus lifestyle

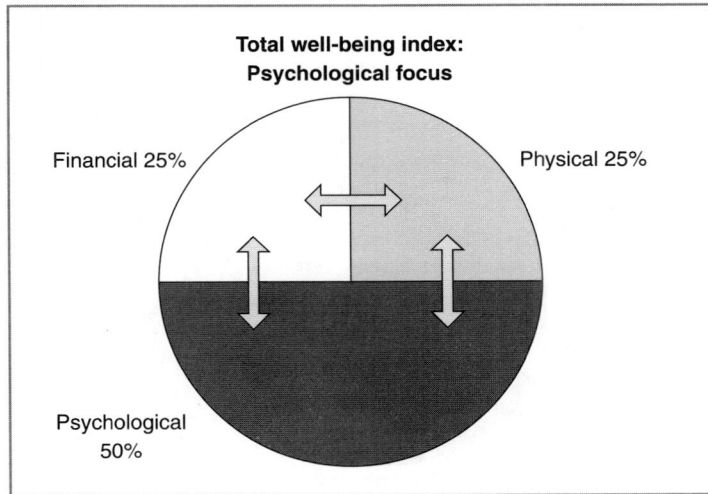

**Total well-being index:
Psychological focus**

Financial 25%

Physical 25%

Psychological
50%

Range: Psychological focus varies from 44% to 67%.

Figure 16.6 Financial focus lifestyle

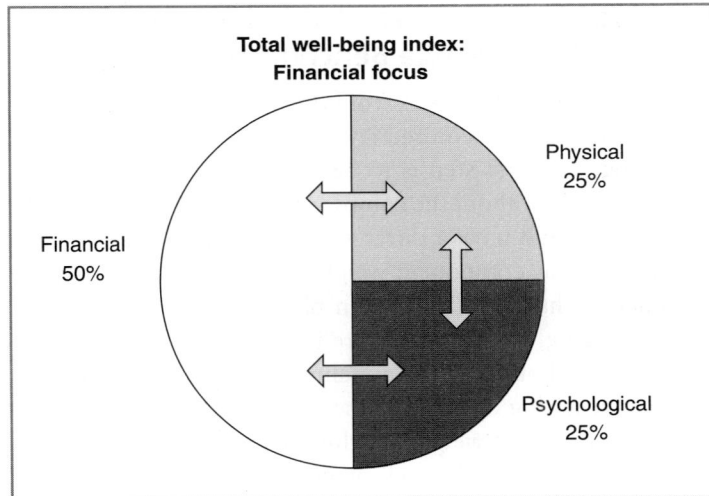

**Total well-being index:
Financial focus**

Physical
25%

Financial
50%

Psychological
25%

Range: Financial focus varies from 44% to 67%.

Figure 16.7 Balanced lifestyle

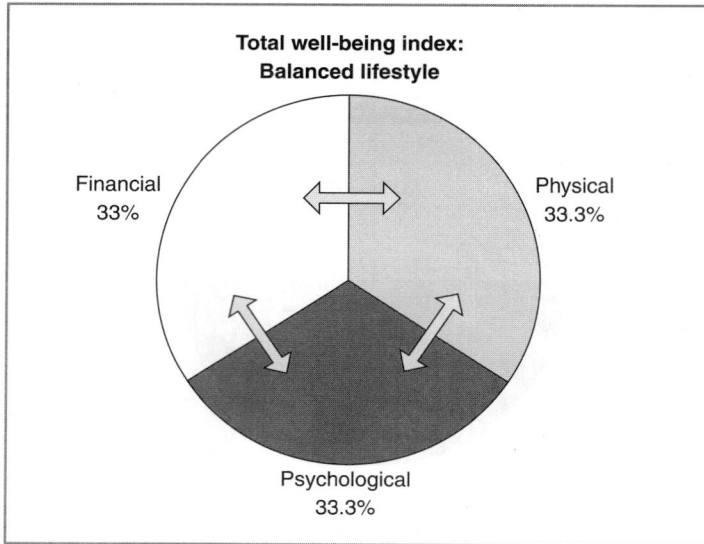

Range: Each aspect should not be greater than 44%.

Matching the Total Well-being Index with the Lifestyle Benchmark

After getting the scores from the questionnaires, the financial planners can figure out the clients' required level of well-being for each of the aspects in total well-being. The first step is to determine the component weight. We can obtain the information about the component weight from the answers of the clients. As every client would have a different perception of the degree of the various well-being aspects, the component weights should be different for each client. For instance, client A has a 40% score in physical well-being, a 42% score in psychological well-being, and a 68% score in financial well-being (Table 16.1). The perceived lifestyle should be more inclined to a financial focus. Assuming this client has the weighting of 56% in one aspect and 22% for each of the other two aspects, the component weights of this client for physical well-being, psychological well-being, and financial well-being are 0.22, 0.22, and 0.56, respectively. The total

Table 16.1 Total weighted well-being index of a financial focus client

	Component weight (a)	Component score (b)	Total (a × b)	Comment
Physical	0.22/1	40%	8.8%	Not satisfactory
Psychological	0.22/1	42%	9.2%	Not satisfactory
Financial	0.56/1	68%	38%	Satisfactory
Total weighted well-being index			55.8%	

weighted well-being index can be calculated by summing up the products of the component weight and the component score for each of the well-being aspects.

We use another example to illustrate the calculation. Assuming that client B has a balanced lifestyle. Client B has 56% score in physical well-being, 48% score in psychological well-being and 60% score in financial well-being (Table 16.2). Hence, the component weights of client B for physical well-being, psychological well-being, and financial well-being are 0.33, 0.33, and 0.33 respectively. The total well-being index for client B is 54%.

Results of US Survey

A survey was conducted in the US (see Appendices 16.1–16.3) to illustrate how the total well-being index is measured. The questionnaires were given to part-time students with full-time jobs at the University of Missouri, St. Louis and at St. John University in New York in 2005. While the respondents came from only two universities, they were all full-time employees and studying part-time in major US cities (St. Louis and New York City). Many of these respondents actually came from other cities in the US for work. We believe that the survey results can serve as a good example of how we can measure the total well-being of a typical financial planning client in the United States.

The sample size of the survey is 70. 1.4% of the respondents have their focus on the physical aspect, 5.7% on the psychological aspect, 1.4% on the financial aspect, and 91.4% on the well-balanced lifestyle. Once the financial planners know the total well-being index of their clients, the next step is to determine how to help them to achieve an optimal score in the total well-being index. The total well-being index score can be used as a point of reference for the clients and the financial planners to understand their physical, psychological, and financial well-being status.

Based on our survey results, five respondents are selected as examples to illustrate the measurement of the total well-being index (Table 16.3). The details of the survey questionnaires and the design of the questions are explained in Appendices 16.1 and 16.2. Appendix 16.3 discusses the research methodology, the scoring method, and the worksheet used to compute the score, and the analysis of the survey. Finally, Appendix 16.4 reports some key findings of the survey.

Respondent 1 is a *physical-focused* client who engages in the physical aspect (68.1% compared to 46% of the benchmark). However, the scores

Table 16.2 Total weighted well-being index of a balanced lifestyle client

	Component weight (a)	Component score (b)	Total (a × b)	Comment
Physical	0.33/1	56%	18.5%	Slightly satisfactory
Psychological	0.33/1	48%	15.8%	Average
Financial	0.33/1	60%	19.8%	Satisfactory
Total weighted well-being index			54%	

Part IV Advanced Topics

for psychological well-being and financial well-being (40.5% and 51.4%, respectively) are not satisfactory as compared to the benchmark of 50% and 60%, respectively. This result reveals that Respondent 1 should improve in the deficient areas of psychological well-being and financial well-being.

Respondent 2 is a *psychological-focused* client with a high score for psychological well-being (67.9%) as compared to the average benchmark of a similar age group (54%). Besides, the score for financial well-being is 66.2% (as compared to 57% of the benchmark). This high score reflects that Respondent 2 has sufficient money for monthly expenditure. Moreover, the score for physical well-being is good (58%), as compared to 52% of the benchmark.

Respondent 3 is a *financial-focused* client. The scores for financial well-being (59%) and psychological well-being (58%) are high as compared to the benchmark of 57% and 54%, respectively. The score for physical well-being is 45.2%, which is bad compared to the benchmark of 52%. The low physical well-being score for Respondent 3 may be attributed to smoking and drinking behaviors. The financial planner should consider this aspect in insurance planning.

Respondent 4 has a *well-balanced lifestyle* with comparatively high scores in physical (67.1%) and psychological (65.5%) aspects; both scores are 10–15% higher than those of the benchmark. The total well-being index is 64.2%. The reason for the high scores may be attributed to the fact that Respondent 4 has a healthy life and knows how to relax.

Respondent 5 is a *financial-focused* client with a very high score in the financial aspect (78.6%) as compared to the average benchmark of a similar age group (57%). The total well-being index is 52.1%. For Respondent 5, the score for physical well-being (31.4% only) is not satisfactory. Respondent 5 should try to have more healthy eating habits.

These are the suggestions on how to use the total well-being index to pinpoint the deficient area(s) in the different aspects of total well-being. Therefore, the total well-being index not only provides a point of reference for clients to understand their well-being status but also facilitates financial planning by the financial planners accordingly. Table 16.3 is the summary of the results of the five respondents based on the survey done in the United States. Table 16.4 is the benchmark summary of the survey showing the total well-being index per different age group and is useful as reference only.

Table 16.3 Total well-being index of selected respondents

	Age	Physical well-being	Psychological well-being	Financial well-being	Perceived lifestyle	Total well-being index (weighted)
1	21–25	68.1%	40.5%	52.4%	Physical-focused	53.7%
2	26–30	58.1%	67.9%	66.2%	Psychological- focused	64.1%
3	26–30	45.2%	58%	59%	Financial-focused	54.1%
4	41–45	67.1%	65.5%	60%	Well-balanced	64.2%
5	46–50	31.4%	46.4%	78.6%	Financial-focused	52.1%

Table 16.4 The benchmark of the total well-being index

	(1) Physical health			(2) Psychological health			(3) Financial health			
Age	Habit	Healthy lifestyle	Subtotal	Stress	Strategy	Subtotal	Income	Investment	Subtotal	Total
20 or below	33%	59%	46%	46%	53%	50%	60%	59%	60%	52%
−25	n = 48	n = 48		n = 48	n = 48		n = 48	n = 48		
26–50	41%	63%	52%	42%	65%	54%	56%	58%	57%	54%
	n = 22	n = 22		n = 22	n = 22		n = 22	n = 22		
Total	37%	61%	49%	44%	59%	52%	58%	59%	59%	53%

Area of deficiency and health risk

What is the next step when the financial planners have the information about the total well-being index of the client? The answer is to determine which area(s) of total well-being the client needs to improve. We use client A as an example. Client A has a high score in the financial aspect (68%). However, the scores in the physical (40%) and psychological (40%) aspects are not that satisfactory. The results reveal that client A needs to improve in the deficient areas of physical and psychological well-being. When the financial planner looks at Client A's answers to the questions relating to physical and psychological well-being, the financial planner would be able to observe that client A has a bad drinking habit. Consequently, the financial planner should be able to identify that physical health is a high-risk area for client A, and may have to consider a better insurance coverage plan for client A.

Questionnaire sample

Figure 16.8 shows a sample questionnaire. Some selected questions are listed so as to indicate how we can make use of the questions to measure the client's physical, psychological, and financial well-being status. The full questionnaire is shown in Appendix 16.1.

Symbolic Framework of the Total Well-being Index

Life consists of so many unknown and unpredictable areas that make it difficult to plan and control. However, the introduction of the total life concept can help us to plan our life in a more organized manner. The total life concept is represented in Figure 16.9. The concept is useful in helping us understand our personal lifestyle by showing the level of physical, psychological, and financial well-being in a symbolic way.

The sky represents psychological well-being. The mountain represents physical well-being, and the river represents financial well-being. The measurement of physical well-being includes a healthy lifestyle and healthy habits. A healthy lifestyle is indicated by the level of exercise and fruit, vegetables, and water intake

Figure 16.8 Questionnaire Sample

Physical well-being aspect

How would you describe your habits and health?

1. Overall daily diet habit (ideally a balanced meal).

Very poor	Poor	Bad	Fair	Good	Very good	Excellent
1	2	3	4	5	6	7

2. Daily exercise habit (ideally 30 minutes of daily physical activity).

Very poor	Poor	Bad	Fair	Good	Very good	Excellent
1	2	3	4	5	6	7

3. Overall, how would you describe your health condition?

Very poor	Poor	Bad	Fair	Good	Very good	Excellent
1	2	3	4	5	6	7

Psychological well-being aspect

How often do you feel or do what is described in the activities or situations below?

1. I am worried about a lot of *minor* things (e.g. forgetting my friend's birthday).

Never	Rarely	Occasionally	Often	Sometimes	Always	Very often
1	2	3	4	5	6	7

2. Striving to fulfill what others want me to be (e.g., the best employee) makes me feel pressured.

Never	Rarely	Occasionally	Often	Sometimes	Always	Very often
1	2	3	4	5	6	7

3. I find myself getting very tense even during leisure time.

Never	Rarely	Occasionally	Often	Sometimes	Always	Very often
1	2	3	4	5	6	7

Financial well-being aspect

To what extent do you agree or disagree with the statements below?

1. Having enough money to spend does not worry me too much.

Strongly disagree	Disagree	Slightly disagree	Neutral	Slightly agree	Agree	Strongly agree
1	2	3	4	5	6	7

To what extent are you satisfied or dissatisfied with the statements below?

2. Enough money to pay my credit card bill on time.

Strongly dissatisfied	Dissatisfied	Slightly dissatisfied	Neutral	Slightly satisfied	Satisfied	Strongly satisfied
1	2	3	4	5	6	7

3. My insurance coverage against death and accidents.

Strongly dissatisfied	Dissatisfied	Slightly dissatisfied	Neutral	Slightly satisfied	Satisfied	Strongly satisfied
1	2	3	4	5	6	7

Figure 16.9 Life picture and key index of client 1

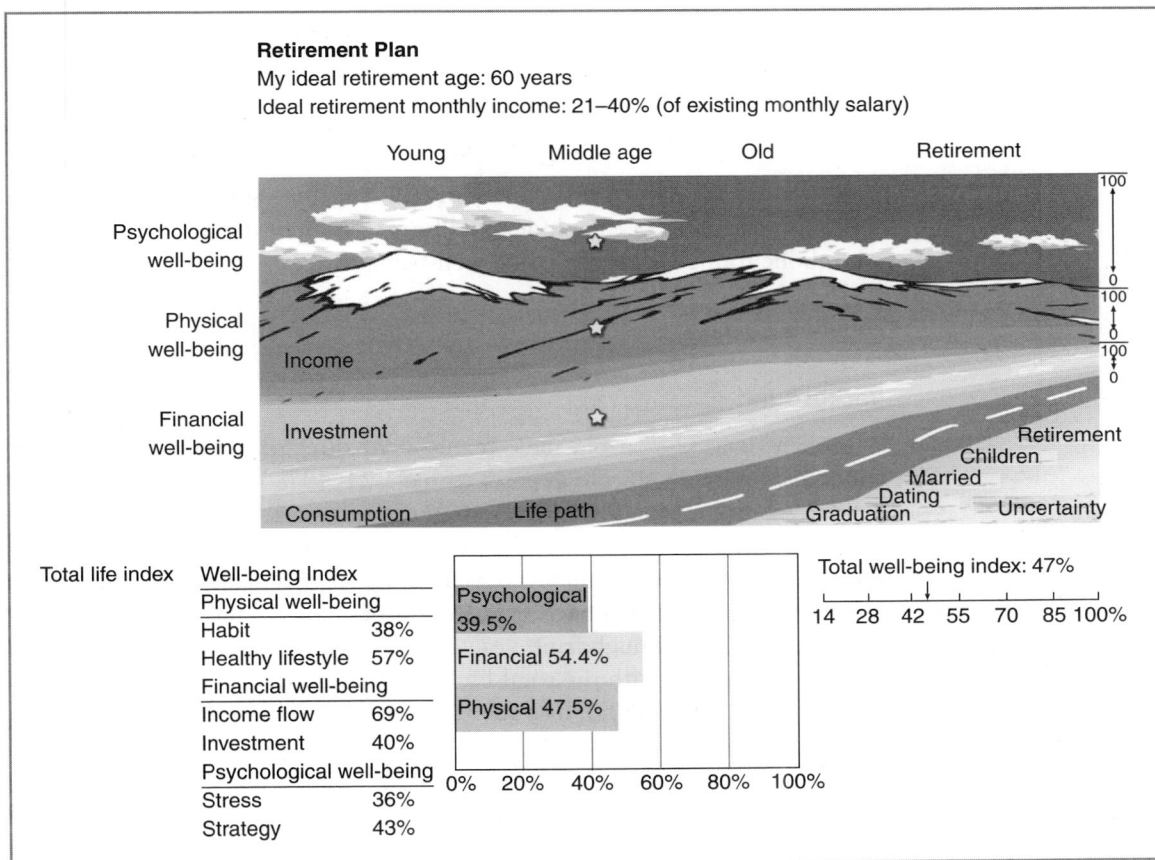

Retirement Plan
My ideal retirement age: 60 years
Ideal retirement monthly income: 21–40% (of existing monthly salary)

Total life index	Well-being Index	
	Physical well-being	
	Habit	38%
	Healthy lifestyle	57%
	Financial well-being	
	Income flow	69%
	Investment	40%
	Psychological well-being	
	Stress	36%
	Strategy	43%

Psychological 39.5%
Financial 54.4%
Physical 47.5%

Total well-being index: 47%

while habits can be measured by smoking and drinking behaviours. We use stress and strategy as our measures of psychological well-being. Stress refers to the level of tension while strategy measures the life goal to achieve. For example, an individual with a high score in strategy means that the individual has a clear life goal to achieve.

The life path includes the different stages of graduation, dating, married with children, and retirement. By looking at this picture, financial planners can find out how well the physical well-being, psychological well-being, and financial well-being of their clients are. Total life balance is a function of physical, psychological, and financial well-being. One of the most important aspects of overall well-being is to achieve a total life balance that reflects an "optimal" balance among physical, psychological, and financial well-being.

Physical well-being The characteristics of a healthy lifestyle and healthy habits (e.g., having enough exercise and a proper diet, abstinence from smoking and alcohol consumption) provide useful indicators of physical well-being.

Financial well-being Financial well-being can be achieved by adopting a good financial plan with different financial strategies and planning.

Psychological well-being   Environmental factors, cultural behaviors, societal well-being, peers, family behavior, and macroeconomic and political conditions can affect the level of psychological well-being.

Key Indices of Total Well-being Survey (Client Analysis)—For Reference Only

This subsection provides a summary of two case analyses to demonstrate how to calculate the scores of each index and how to present the results to clients using a symbolic framework of the total well-being index.

Client 1

Background

Our client is a 32-year-old male manager or director, who is married with no children (Figure 16.9). He expects to have 21–40% of his monthly income as his retirement income. His target retirement age is 60. This client has a balanced lifestyle with scores of 39.5% in psychological well-being, 47.5% in physical well-being, and 54.5% in financial well-being. His physical well-being score is not good as he smokes half a pack of cigarettes per day and has a drinking habit. He also does not take enough fruit, vegetables, and water. His total well-being index is 47%. Compared with the total life index benchmark of the respondents aged between 31 and 35 (58%), his index score is relatively low. The score analysis is summarized on page 462.

Client 2

Background

The client is a 32-year-old female executive, who is married with one child (Figure 16.10). She expects to have 21–40% of her monthly income as her retirement income. Her target retirement age is 52. She has a balanced lifestyle with fair scores in psychological well-being (61.5%) as well as physical well-being (59.5%), but a relatively low score in financial well-being (46%). Her physical well-being is good as she always takes plenty of fruit, vegetables, and water. Her total well-being index is 56%, which is slightly higher than the benchmark score of 54% of other respondents who is aged between 31 and 35. The score analysis is summarized on page 463.

Figure 16.10 Life picture and key index of client 2

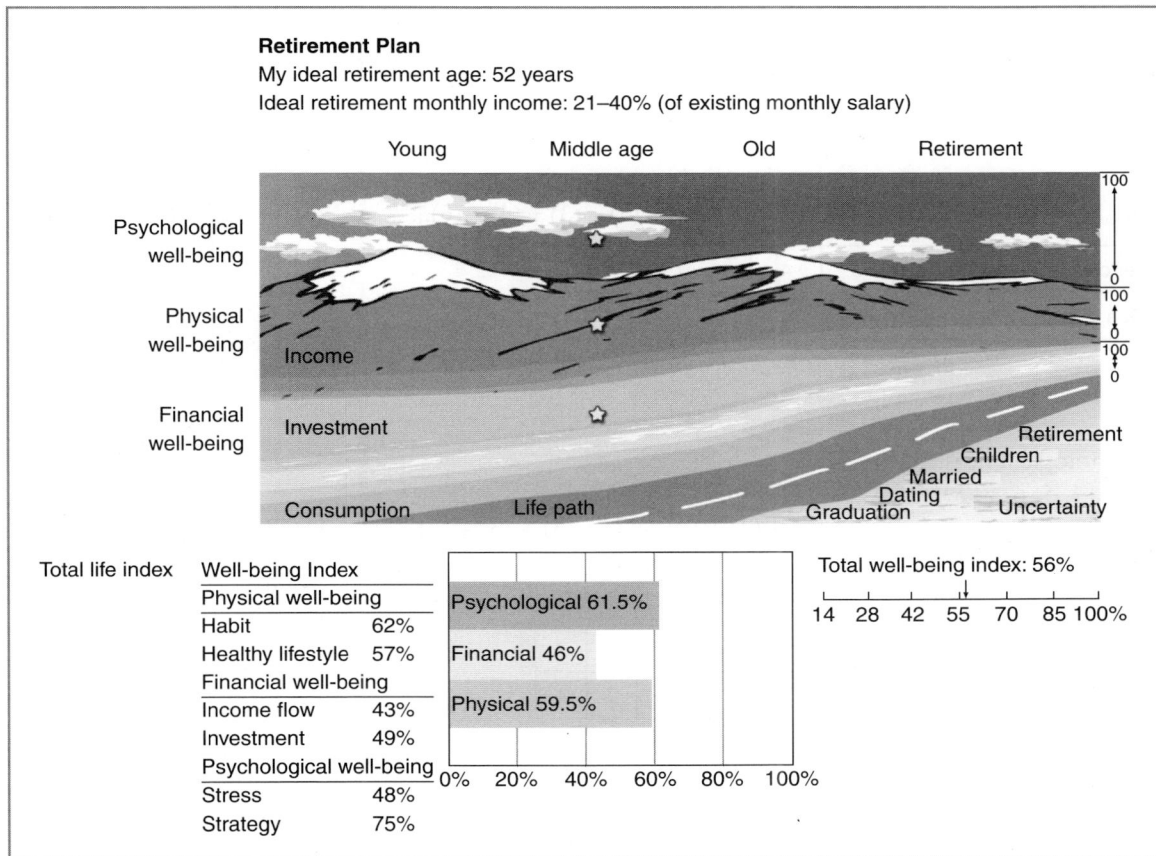

Retirement Plan
My ideal retirement age: 52 years
Ideal retirement monthly income: 21–40% (of existing monthly salary)

Well-being Index		Psychological 61.5%
Physical well-being		Financial 46%
Habit	62%	Physical 59.5%
Healthy lifestyle	57%	
Financial well-being		
Income flow	43%	
Investment	49%	
Psychological well-being		
Stress	48%	
Strategy	75%	

Total well-being index: 56%

14 28 42 55 70 85 100%

0% 20% 40% 60% 80% 100%

References

Kim, S., Popkin, B. M., Siega-Riz, A., M., Haines, P. S., and Arab, L., "A Cross-national Comparison of Lifestyle between China and the United States, Using a Comprehensive Cross-national Measurement Tool of the Healthfulness of Lifestyles: the Lifestyle Index," *Preventive Medicine*, vol. 38 (2004): 160–71.

Maslow, A. H., *Motivation and Personality*, revised ed. (New York: Harper & Row, 1970).

Client 1: Score Analysis

A. Total well-being index

(1) Physical health

		Subtotal	Benchmark (for males)

Habit: *1, 2a, 2b**.........................Ans [7] [6] [3]

Scores (1) + (2) + (5).. 8/21   38% (i)   (34%)

Healthy lifestyle: 11a, 11b, 11c, 12, 13.....Ans (3) + (4) + (3) + (4) + (6)............ 20/35   57% (ii)   (56%)

Answer choice	1	2	3	4	5	6	7
Q1, Q2a, Q2b	7	6	5	4	3	2	1

Physical well-being total [i + ii/2] (a)   <u>47.5</u> (%)   <u>(45%)</u>

(2) Psychological health

Stress: *3, 4, 5, 6, 7, 8,*............. Ans [6] [6] [5] [5] [5] [6]

Scores (2) + (2) + (3) + (3) + (3) + (2)......... 15/42   36% (iii)   (72%)

Strategy: *9, 10, 15, 16*...... ....Ans [6] [6] [6] [6]

Scores (2) + (2) + (2) + (6)...................... 12/28   43% (iv)   (64%)

Answer choice		1	2	3	4	5	6	7
Q3–Q10, Q15, 18a–b,19–20		7	6	5	4	3	2	1

Psychological well-being total [iii + iv]/2 (b)   <u>39.5</u> (%)   <u>(68%)</u>

(3) Financial health

Income: 14, 17a, 17b, 17c, 17d..........Ans (5) + (5) + (7) + (5) + (2) .... 24/35   69% (v)   (69%)

Investment: *18a, 18bi, 18bii, 19, 20* Ans [7] [6] [3] [5] [5]

Scores (1) + (2) + (5) + (3) + (3)................ 14/35   40% (vi)   (51%)

Financial well-being total [v + vi]/2 (c)   <u>54.5 (%)</u>   <u>(60%)</u>

Total well-being index [a% + b% + c%] / 3   <u>47</u> (%)   <u>(58%)</u>

---

* For those question numbers in italic, please refer to the question-answer table, otherwise follow the rule (Ans 1 = 1, Ans 2 = 2 ..., etc.).

Client 2: Score Analysis

A. Total well-being index

(1) Physical health

	Subtotal	Benchmark (for females)

Habit: *1, 2a, 2b** ....Ans [2] [4] [5]

Scores (6) + (4) + (3)... 13/21   62% (i)   (33%)

Healthy lifestyle: 11a, 11b, 11c, 12, 13.....(3) + (4) + (4) + (5) + (4)................... 20/35   57% (ii)   (52%)

Answer choice	1	2	3	4	5	6	7
Q1, Q2a, Q2b	7	6	5	4	3	2	1

Physical well-being total [i + ii/2] (a)   <u>59.5</u> (%)   <u>(43%)</u>

(2) Psychological health

Stress: *3, 4, 5, 6, 7, 8,*............. Ans [5] [6] [5] [4] [6] [2]

Scores (3) + (2) + (3) + (4) + (2) + (6)......... 20/42   48% (iii)   (52%)

Strategy: *9, 10, 15,* 16...... ....Ans [2] [4] [2] [5]

Scores (6) + (4) + (6) + (5)....................... 21/28   75% (iv)   (51%)

Answer choice	1	2	3	4	5	6	7
Q3–Q10, Q15, 18a–b,19–20	7	6	5	4	3	2	1

Psychological well-being total [iii + iv]/2 (b)   <u>61.5</u> (%)   <u>(52%)</u>

(3) Financial health

Income: 14, 17a, 17b, 17c, 17d..........Ans (3) + (2) + (3) + (3) + (4) .... 15/35   43% (v)   (65%)

Investment: *18a, 18bi, 18bii, 19, 20* Ans [7] [4] [3] [4] [5]

Scores (1) + (4) + (5) + (4) + (3)................ 17/35   49% (vi)   (66%)

Financial well-being total [v + vi]/2 (c)   <u>46</u> (%)   <u>(66%)</u>

Total well-being index [a% + b% + c%] / 3   <u>56</u> (%)   <u>(54%)</u>

---

* For those question numbers in italic, please refer to the question-answer table, otherwise follow the rule (Ans 1 = 1, Ans 2 = 2 ..., etc.).

Questionnaire

Please circle <u>one</u> answer.

Lifestyle

How often do you feel or do what is described in the activities or situations listed below?

1	2	3	4	5	6	7
Never			Sometimes			Very often

1. My smoking habit (e.g., half a pack of cigarettes per day).	1 2 3 4 5 6 7
2. My daily intake of: a. Alcoholic drinks (e.g., three alcoholic drinks per day).	1 2 3 4 5 6 7
b. Caffeine drinks (e.g., three cups of coffee or tea per day).	1 2 3 4 5 6 7
3. I am worried about a lot of *minor* things (e.g., forgetting my friend's birthday).	1 2 3 4 5 6 7
4. I always feel scared without any particular reason (e.g., overly worried about the future of our earth).	1 2 3 4 5 6 7
5. I am tense and alert every day (e.g., feeling frustrated, angry, restless, or irritable).	1 2 3 4 5 6 7
6. Striving to fulfill what others want me to be (e.g., the best employee) makes me feel pressured.	1 2 3 4 5 6 7
7. I find myself getting very tense even during leisure time.	1 2 3 4 5 6 7
8. It is hard to calm myself down once I am irritated by a minor thing (e.g., noise).	1 2 3 4 5 6 7
9. I find it hard to have the initiative to make a major decision (e.g., change to a new job).	1 2 3 4 5 6 7
10. I find myself *not* feeling enthusiastic about important decisions (e.g., change my career).	1 2 3 4 5 6 7

Daily habits

	1	2	3	4	5	6	7
	Very poor	Poor	Bad	Fair	Good	Very good	Excellent

11. How would you describe your habits and health?	
(a) Daily fruit and vegetables intake (ideally three pieces of fruit/servings of vegetables a day).	1 2 3 4 5 6 7
(b) Daily water intake (ideally eight glasses).	1 2 3 4 5 6 7
(c) Overall daily diet habit (ideally a balanced meal).	1 2 3 4 5 6 7
12. Daily exercise habit (ideally 30 minutes of daily physical activity).	1 2 3 4 5 6 7
13. Overall, how would you describe your health condition?	1 2 . 3 4 5 6 7

	1	2	3	4	5	6	7
To what extent do you agree or disagree with the statements below?	Strong disagree	Disagree	Slightly disagree	Neutral	Slightly agree	Agree	Strongly agree

14. Having enough money to spend does not worry me too much.	1 2 3 4 5 6 7
15. I do not know my whole life goals (e.g., to enjoy life).	1 2 3 4 5 6 7
16. I know clearly what my goals are (e.g., to be financially independent).	1 2 3 4 5 6 7

Financial aspect

	1	2	3	4	5	6	7
	Totally dissatisfied	Dissatisfied	Slightly dissatisfied	Neutral	Slightly satisfied	Satisfied	Strongly satisfied

17. To what extent are you satisfied or dissatisfied with the statements below?	
(a) Enough money for my normal monthly expenditure.	1 2 3 4 5 6 7
(b) Enough money to pay my credit card bill on time.	1 2 3 4 5 6 7
(c) My insurance coverage against death and accidents.	1 2 3 4 5 6 7
(d) My insurance coverage against disability and illness.	1 2 3 4 5 6 7

Please put an "x" into the box for each question to show your preference.

18a. Assuming that you have HK$20,000 to invest or save and you have only one choice, which one would you select?

☐ Savings account ☐ Time deposit ☐ Government bonds ☐ Corporate bonds

☐ Bond mutual funds ☐ Stocks mutual funds ☐ Stocks

b. Assuming that you invest all $20,000 in the stock market only:

(i) To what extent are you comfortable with this single investment?

☐ Totally uncomfortable ☐ Uncomfortable ☐ Slightly uncomfortable ☐ Indifferent

☐ Slightly comfortable ☐ Comfortable ☐ Totally comfortable

(ii) Which one of the returns of the above investment would you prefer?

☐ $2,000 ☐ $6,000 gain ☐ $10,000 gain ☐ $14,000 gain ☐ $18,000 gain ☐ $22,000 gain ☐ $26,000 gain
sure gain   or $3,000 loss   or $5,000 loss   or $7,000 loss   or $9,000 loss   or $11,000 loss   or $13,000 loss

19. When you think of the word *risk*, which one of the following words comes to your mind first?

☐ Disaster ☐ Accident ☐ Bad Luck ☐ Indifference ☐ Luck ☐ Good chance ☐ Golden opportunity

20. In general, how would your best friend describe your investment behavior?

☐ Real risk avoider ☐ Highly cautious ☐ Conservative ☐ Indifferent ☐ Risk taker ☐ High risk taker ☐ Real gambler

Personal profile

Please put an "x" into the box for each question.

1. **Sex:** ☐ Male   ☐ Female

2. **Age:** ☐ 20 or below ☐ 21–25 ☐ 26–30 ☐ 31–35 ☐ 36–40 ☐ 41–45
☐ 46–50 ☐ 51–55 ☐ 56–60 ☐ 61–65 ☐ 66–70 ☐ above 71

3. **Education:** ☐ Primary or below ☐ Secondary ☐ Post-Secondary ☐ Others (please specify) _____

4. **Occupation/Employment status:**
☐ Clerk/Worker ☐ Salesperson ☐ Executive ☐ Engineer ☐ Professional (e.g., doctor)
☐ Manager/Director ☐ Teacher ☐ Student ☐ Housewife ☐ Self-employed
☐ Unemployed ☐ Social worker ☐ Owner ☐ Others (please specify) _____

5. **Industry of occupation:**
☐ Import-export and trading ☐ Transport, communication ☐ Business services: Nonfinancial
☐ Personal services ☐ Manufacturing ☐ Building and construction
☐ Financial institutions ☐ Social services ☐ Education and civil service/Government
☐ Tourism, Hotel, Retail, and Wholesale ☐ Others (please specify) _____

6. **Total monthly household income in HK$** (e.g., your salary *plus* your wife/husband's salary):
☐ < $10,000 ☐ $10,000–19,999 ☐ $20,000–29,999 ☐ $30,000–39,999 ☐ $40,000–49,999
☐ $50,000–69,999 ☐ $70,000–99,999 ☐ $100,000–149,999 ☐ $150,000–199,999 ☐ > $200,000

7. **Marital status:** ☐ Single ☐ Married ☐ Divorced ☐ Others

8. **No. of children:** ☐ 0   ☐ 1   ☐ 2   ☐ 3   ☐ 4   ☐ 5 or above

9. **Residential type:** ☐ Private ☐ Public ☐ Quarters ☐ Others (please specify) _____

10. **Area (sq. ft):** ☐ Below 200 ☐ 201–500 ☐ 501–1,000 ☐ 1,001–1,500
☐ 1,501–2,000 ☐ 2,001–3,000 ☐ 3,001 or above

References of Questions

Question	Content	Source/Modified from
1	Habit	*How to Beat Depression: Middle Age Manual*, The Hong Kong Jockey Club Centre for Suicide Research and Prevention, The University of Hong Kong.
		Miller-Smith Lifestyle assessment inventory, http://csrp.hku.hk/WEB/eng/pageHandler.asp?id=70
2a	Habit	*How to Beat Depression: Middle Age Manual*, The Hong Kong Jockey Club Centre for Suicide Research and Prevention, The University of Hong Kong.
		Miller-Smith Lifestyle assessment inventory, http://csrp.hku.hk/WEB/eng/pageHandler.asp?id=70
2b	Habit	*How to Beat Depression: Middle Age Manual*, The Hong Kong Jockey Club Centre for Suicide Research and Prevention, The University of Hong Kong.
		Miller-Smith Lifestyle assessment inventory, http://csrp.hku.hk/WEB/eng/pageHandler.asp?id=70
3	Safety needs	University Health Service, http://wellness.uwsp.edu/medinfo/handouts
4	Safety needs	University Health Service, http://wellness.uwsp.edu/medinfo/handouts
5	Stress	University Health Service, http://wellness.uwsp.edu/medinfo/handouts
6	Stress	Quality of Life Profile for Adults, http://www.utoronto.ca/qol/profile/adultVersion.html
7	Stress	University Health Service, http://wellness.uwsp.edu/medinfo/handouts
8	Stress	University Health Service, http://wellness.uwsp.edu/medinfo/handouts
9	Esteem	Quality of Life Profile for Adults, http://www.utoronto.ca/qol/profile/adultVersion.html
10	Esteem	University Health Service, http://wellness.uwsp.edu/medinfo/handouts
11a	Diet	Satin Well-being health questionnaire, http://www.satinwell-being .com/SATFITASSESSMENT.pdf
11b	Diet	Satin Well-being health questionnaire, http://www.satinwell-being .com/SATFITASSESSMENT.pdf
11c	Diet	Satin Well-being health questionnaire, http://www.satinwell-being .com/SATFITASSESSMENT.pdf
12	Exercise	Satin Well-being health questionnaire, http://www.satinwell-being .com/SATFITASSESSMENT.pdf
13	Exercise	Satin Well-being health questionnaire, http://www.satinwell-being .com/SATFITASSESSMENT.pdf
14	Safety needs	Quality of Life Profile for Adults, http://www.utoronto.ca/qol/profile/adultVersion.html

Question	Content	Source/Modified from
15	Self actualization	Quality of Life Profile for Adults, http://www.utoronto.ca/qol/profile/adultVersion.html
16	Self actualization	Quality of Life Profile for Adults, http://www.utoronto.ca/qol/profile/adultVersion.html
17a	Consumption	Ross Levin, *The Wealth Management Index: The Financial Advisor's System for Assessing and Managing Your Client's Plans and Goals.*
17b	Consumption	Ross Levin, *The Wealth Management Index: The Financial Advisor's System for Assessing and Managing Your Client's Plans and Goals.*
17c	Insurance	Ross Levin, *The Wealth Management Index: The Financial Advisor's System for Assessing and Managing Your Client's Plans and Goals.*
17d	Insurance	Ross Levin, *The Wealth Management Index: The Financial Advisor's System for Assessing and Managing Your Client's Plans and Goals.*
18a	Risk tolerance	John Grable and Ruth H. Lytton, "Financial Risk Tolerance Revisited: The Development of a Risk Assessment Instrument," *Financial Services Review*, vol. 8 (1999): 163–81.
18bi	Risk tolerance	John Grable and Ruth H. Lytton, "Financial Risk Tolerance Revisited: The Development of a Risk Assessment Instrument," *Financial Services Review*, vol. 8 (1999): 163–81.
18bii	Risk tolerance	John Grable and Ruth H. Lytton, "Financial Risk Tolerance Revisited: The Development of a Risk Assessment Instrument," *Financial Services Review*, vol. 8 (1999): 163–81.
19	Risk tolerance	John Grable and Ruth H. Lytton, "Financial Risk Tolerance Revisited: The Development of a Risk Assessment Instrument," *Financial Services Review*, vol. 8 (1999): 163–81.
20	Risk tolerance	John Grable and Ruth H. Lytton, "Financial Risk Tolerance Revisited: The Development of a Risk Assessment Instrument," *Financial Services Review*, vol. 8 (1999): 163–81.

Results of Survey

Research Methodology

Before we conducted the survey in the US, we did a pretest of the survey using the same set of questions to first test the validity of the instrument. The research was conducted in Hong Kong through face-to-face interviews. A total of 207 questionnaires were collected.

When financial planners start to explore the total well-being index of their clients, they should decide what kind of tools to use. A questionnaire-based survey would be more appropriate. The financial planners can design the related questions from different sources such as journal papers in the academic field, surveys done by some research institutes, and so on. The advantage of designing/modifying questions based on secondary sources is the reduction of errors such as inappropriate wording and ambiguous meaning during the questionnaire design stage.

Scoring Method

Based on the results of the factor analysis, the major factors affecting physical, psychological, and financial well-being can be identified for the financial planners to do simple analysis. If the financial planners are not familiar with this sophisticated analysis, they can just take the average of the scores to analyze the performance of the clients. For example, the financial planners may obtain an average score of the questions measuring the physical, psychological, and financial well-being of the clients. Based on these average scores, they may interpret the well-being of the clients. A sample score sheet is provided on page 470 as an example to analyze the total well-being index of clients.

Questionnaire Analysis: Working Sheet

A. Total well-being index

<u>(1) Physical health</u>   Subtotal

Habit: *1, 2a, 2b** ....Ans [ ] [ ] [ ]

Scores ( ) + ( ) + ( )....................................... ____/21   ____% (i)

Healthy lifestyle: 11a, 11b, 11c, 12, 13.....( ) + ( ) + ( ) + ( ) + ( )................... ____/35   ____% (ii)

Answer choice	1	2	3	4	5	6	7
Q1, Q2a, Q2b	7	6	5	4	3	2	1

Physical well-being total [i + ii/2] (a)   ____ (%)

<u>(2) Psychological health</u>   Subtotal

Stress: *3, 4, 5, 6, 7, 8,*.............. Ans [ ] [ ] [ ] [ ] [ ] [ ] [ ]

Scores ( ) + ( ) + ( ) + ( ) + ( ) + ( )......... ____/42   ____% (iii)

Strategy: *9, 10, 15, 16*...... ....Ans [ ] [ ] [ ] [ ]

Scores ( ) + ( ) + ( ) + ( )....................... ____/28   ____% (iv)

Answer choice	1	2	3	4	5	6	7
Q3–Q10, Q15, 18a–b,19–20	7	6	5	4	3	2	1

Psychological well-being total [iii + iv]/2 (b)   ____ (%)

<u>(3) Financial health</u>   Subtotal

Income: 14, 17a, 17b, 17c, 17d..........Ans ( ) + ( ) + ( ) + ( ) + ( ) .... ____/35   ____% (v)

Investment: *18a, 18bi, 18bii, 19, 20* Ans [ ] [ ] [ ] [ ] [ ] [ ]

Scores ( ) + ( ) + ( ) + ( ) + ( )................ ____/35   ____% (vi)

Financial well-being total [v + vi]/2 (c)   ____(%)

Total well-being index [a% + b% + c%] / 3 = ____ (%)

---

* For those question numbers in italic, please refer to the question-answer table, otherwise follow the rule (Ans 1 = 1, Ans 2 = 2, etc.).

16.4

Analysis of Sample

Profile of Sample

The demographic profile of the 207 respondents has an even spread from ages 21 to 40 although some respondents fall into the age groups of 20 and below and 41 to 60. The limitation of this research is that only one-third of the respondents earn a monthly household income of more than HK$30,000. We recommend that future research should have a greater sample of higher income individuals.

Measures

Most of the questions used in the questionnaire are quoted or modified from other literature. We use a seven-point Likert type scale to assess the well-being level. We use different forms of the seven-point scale: (1) 7 = Strongly agree and 1 = Strongly disagree; (2) 7 = Very often and 1 = Never; (3) 7 = Excellent and 1 = Poor; (4) 7 = Totally satisfied and 1 = Totally dissatisfied. The remaining questions provide seven choices on a continuous scale for respondents.

Data Analysis and Results

Factor analysis is used to determine the underlying dimensions of the total well-being index – physical, psychological, and financial well-being. In each area, we fine-tune the questionnaire by using factor analysis to eliminate some question items that have low correlations with another variable and low loading on each factor. We extract factors based on the eigenvalues of the factors which are greater than one. In order to make the correct interpretation, we reverse the coding for negative statements. The Varimax method is used to run the factor analysis. After conducting the factor analysis with rotation, the first two highest factors in each area are selected. Health and habits (Table 16.6) are the constructs to measure the level of physical well-being. Stress and strategy are the constructs to measure the level of psychological well-being. Income and investment are the constructs to measure the level of financial well-being. In the physical well-being construct, five statements under the Well-being factor are extracted with 21.602% of the variance. Three statements under the Habits factor are extracted with 15.943% variance. In the psychological well-being area, six statements under the Stress factor are extracted with 18.253% variance. Four statements under the

Table 16.6 Results of factor analysis of independent variables for the Hong Kong sample

Independent items	Factor loadings
Physical well-being	
Factor 1—*Health* ($\alpha = 0.791$, variance = 21.602%)	
Daily fruit and vegetables intake (ideally three servings of fruit or vegetables per day).	.763
Daily water intake (ideally eight glasses of water).	.706
Overall daily diet habit (ideally balanced meal).	.836
Daily exercise habit (ideally 30 minutes of daily physical activity).	.736
Overall, how would you describe your health condition?	.606
Factor 2—*Habits* ($\alpha = 0.716$, variance = 15.943%)	
My smoking habit (e.g., half a pack of cigarettes per day) is:	.728
Alcoholic drinks (e.g., three alcoholic drinks per day) is:	.867
Caffeine drinks (e.g., three cups of coffee or tea per day) is:	.708
Psycho-social well-being	
Factor 3—*Stress* ($\alpha = 0.800$, variance = 18.253%)	
I am worried about a lot of minor things (e.g., forgetting my friend's birthday).	.629
I always feel scared without any particular reason (e.g., overly worried about the future of our earth).	.721
I am tense and alert every day (e.g., feeling frustrated, angry, restless, or irritable).	.797
Striving to fulfill what others want me to be (e.g., the best employee) makes me feel pressured.	.607
I find myself getting very tense even during leisure time.	.681
It is hard to calm myself down once I am irritated by minor things (e.g., noise).	.699
Factor 4—*Strategy* ($\alpha = 0.711$, variance = 12.707%)	
I find it hard to have the initiative to make a major decision (e.g., change to a new job).	.540
I find myself not feeling enthusiastic about important decisions (e.g., change my career).	.633
I do not know my whole life goals (e.g., to enjoy life).	.791
I know clearly what my goals are (e.g., to be financially independent).	.749
Financial well-being	
Factor 5—*Income* ($\alpha = 0.821$, variance = 13.618%)	
Having enough money to spend does not worry me too much.	.595
To what extent are you satisfied or dissatisfied with the following:	.735
Enough money for my normal monthly expenditure.	
Enough money for paying my credit card bill on time.	.599
My insurance coverage against death and accidents.	.885
My insurance coverage against disability and illness.	.852
Factor 6—*Investment* ($\alpha = 0.68$, variance = 12.556%)	
Assuming that you have HK$20,000 to invest or save and you have only one choice, which one would you select?	.780
Assuming that you invest all $20,000 in the stock market only, to what extent are you comfortable with this single investment?	.638
Which one of the returns of above investment would you prefer?	.610
When you think of the word "risk", which one of following words comes to your mind first?	.521
In general, how would your best friend describe your investment behavior?	.762

Strategy factor are extracted with 12.707% variance. Lastly, in the financial well-being area, five statements under the Income factor are extracted with 13.618% variance and five statements under the Investment factor are extracted with 12.556% variance.

We use Cronbach's coefficient alpha (α) to check the degree of internal consistency and the reliability inside each construct. If the Cronbach's alpha coefficient (α) is greater than or equal to 0.6, the internal consistency and reliability of the questions within a construct is acceptable (Churchill 1979). The value of Cronbach's alpha coefficient (α) of these six factors is greater than 0.7 except for factor six (Investment α = 0.68) and satisfies the exploratory research norm (Nunnally 1978).

After conducting the factor analysis with rotation, the first two highest factors in each area are selected. Health is the construct to measure the level of physical well-being. Stress is the construct to measure the level of psychological well-being. Investment, Income, and Insurance are the constructs to measure the level of financial well-being. In Table 16.7, for the physical well-being construct, five statements under the Health factor are extracted with 35.38% of the variance. In the psychological well-being area, six statements under the Stress factor are extracted with 31.624% variance. Lastly, in the financial well-being area, eight statements under the Investment factor are extracted with 31.688% variance, six statements under the Income factor are extracted with 26.478% variance, and four statements under the Insurance factor are extracted with 17.196% variance.

Again, we use Cronbach's coefficient alpha (α) to check the degree of internal consistency and the reliability inside each construct. The value of Cronbach's alpha coefficient (α) of these five factors is greater than 0.7, which satisfies the exploratory research norm.

Table 16.7 Results of factor analysis of independent variables for the US sample

Independent items	Factor loadings
Physical well-being	
Factor 1—*Health* (α = 0.78, variance = 35.38%)	
Daily exercise habit (ideally 30 minutes of daily physical activity).	.672
Daily fruit and vegetables intake (ideally three servings of fruit or vegetables per day).	.710
Daily water intake (ideally eight glasses of water).	.703
Overall daily diet habit (ideally balanced meal).	.876
Overall, how would you describe your health condition?	.724
Psychological well-being	
Factor 2—*Stress* (α = 0.83, variance = 31.624%)	
I am worried about a lot of minor things (e.g., forgetting my friend's birthday).	.775
I always feel scared without any particular reason (e.g., overly worried about the future of our earth).	.727
I am tense and alert every day (e.g., feeling frustrated, angry, restless, or irritable).	.724
Striving to fulfill what others want me to be (e.g., the best employee) makes me feel pressured.	.630
I find myself getting very tense even during leisure time.	.832
I worry about my finance and money matters.	.546
Financial well-being	
Factor 3—*Investment* (α = 0.94, variance = 31.688%)	
Estate planning (e.g., enough money for the next generation).	.876
Saving for retirement.	.775
Saving for emergency cash purpose.	.578
Saving for investment of various life goals.	.762
Investment for various life goals.	.799
Investment for education.	.639
Basic estate planning.	.895
Money for retirement.	.885
Factor 4—*Income* (α = 0.93, variance = 26.478%)	
Money available for normal monthly expenditure	.799
Money for paying credit card bill on time	.807
Money available for paying tax on time	.736
Cash available for regular expenses	.834
Cash flow to cover nonroutine major purchases and expenses	.811
Money to pay taxes	.765
Factor 5—*Insurance* (α = 0.88, variance = 17.196%)	
Insurance coverage against death and accidents.	.937
Insurance coverage against disability and illness.	.925
Insurance coverage for life.	.686
Insurance coverage for other items (e.g., car, house).	.611

References

Churchill, G. A., Jr., "A Paradigm for Developing Better Measures of Marketing Constructs," *Journal of Marketing Research*, vol. 16 (1979): 64–73.

Nunnally, J. C., *Psychometric Theory*, Second ed. (New York, NY: McGraw-Hill, Inc., 1978).

Physical well-being

Age	Male			Female			Total
	Habit	Healthy lifestyle	Subtotal	Habit	Healthy lifestyle	Subtotal	
21–25	40%	58%	49%	26%	56%	41%	45%
26–30	35%	58%	47%	24%	60%	44%	44%
31–35	34%	56%	45%	33%	52%	43%	44%
36–40	33%	55%	44%	24%	59%	42%	43%
41–45	41%	51%	46%	20%	49%	35%	40%
46–50	35%	63%	49%	21%	54%	38%	43%
51–55	39%	70%	55%	22%	58%	40%	47%

Psychological well-being

Age	Male			Female			Total
	Stress	Strategy	Subtotal	Stress	Strategy	Subtotal	
21–25	45%	57%	51%	49%	54%	52%	51%
26–30	43%	55%	49%	43%	54%	49%	49%
31–35	72%	64%	68%	52%	51%	52%	60%
36–40	44%	53%	49%	45%	60%	53%	51%
41–45	42%	54%	48%	44%	51%	48%	48%
46–50	36%	49%	43%	47%	60%	54%	48%
51–55	41%	48%	45%	49%	56%	53%	49%

Financial well-being

Age	Male			Female			Total
	Income	Investment	Subtotal	Income	Investment	Subtotal	
21–25	60%	54%	57%	55%	70%	63%	60%
26–30	65%	51%	58%	67%	68%	68%	63%
31–35	69%	51%	60%	65%	66%	66%	63%
36–40	68%	56%	62%	64%	63%	64%	63%
41–45	69%	57%	63%	72%	52%	62%	63%
46–50	83%	55%	69%	64%	64%	64%	67%
51–55	82%	62%	72%	63%	78%	71%	71%

Total well-being index

Age	Male	Female	Total
21–25	52%	52%	52%
26–30	51%	53%	52%
31–35	56%	53%	56%
36–40	51%	53%	52%
41–45	52%	48%	50%
46–50	54%	52%	53%
51–55	57%	54%	56%

CHAPTER 17

Conclusion

By now you should know how to conduct financial planning. Throughout the book, practical examples from the financial planning industry and interviews with successful financial planners have been included in order to bring some perspectives from the real world. We will now summarize the whole process and remind you of the key concepts and techniques in financial planning.

Before you start, you have to make sure that you have the basic knowledge and skills in all the financial planning areas. Then you should check if you know the six-step financial planning processes.

Checklist 1: Planning Areas

1. Consumption planning
   - Financial statement analysis
   - Ratio analysis
   - Estimating optimal consumption and savings
   - Preparing cash budgets
2. Tax planning
   - Local tax regulations
   - Tax reduction strategies
3. Insurance planning
   - Estimating insurance needs through various life stages
   - Term-life products
   - Cash value products (e.g., whole life)
   - Investment-linked products
   - General insurance products
4. Investment planning
   - Time value of money
   - Macroeconomic variables
   - Financial market operation
   - Investment products
   - Investment analysis
   - Asset allocation strategies
5. Retirement planning
   - Investment portfolio for retirement
   - Other retirement goals
6. Estate planning
   - Will preparation
   - Establishing a trust
7. Financial planning techniques
   - Personal profiling
   - Risk profiling
   - Life-cycle analysis
8. Local regulations

Checklist 2: Six-step Financial Planning Process

1. Establishing client-planner relationship
   - Practice Standards 100 Series

- Communication techniques
- Conducting interviews

2. Determining client goals and expectations and gathering client data
   - Practice Standards 200 Series
   - Managing client's expectations
   - Goals prioritization
   - Data collection

3. Determining client's current financial status
   - Practice Standards 300 Series
   - Financial data analysis
   - Relating financial status analysis to financial needs
   - Financial forecasts

4. Developing and presenting the financial plan
   - Practice Standards 400 Series
   - Developing recommendations for each planning area
   - Conducting asset allocation analysis
   - Knowing the core content and other content of a written plan
   - Presenting the financial plan

5. Implementing the financial plan
   - Practice Standards 500 Series
   - Scheduling for implementation
   - Coordinating with other professionals
   - Maintaining client's records

6. Monitoring the financial plan
   - Practice Standards 600 Series
   - Monitoring the macro-level and micro-level factors
   - Solving disputes

Checklist 3: Wealth Management

1. Investment techniques
   - Risk-return trade-off
   - Diversification and portfolio theory
   - Capital asset pricing model (CAPM) and arbitrage pricing theory (APT)
   - Valuation process
   - Industry analysis
   - Fundamental analysis
   - Financial ratios
   - Technical analysis
   - Implication of efficient market hypothesis (EMH)
   - Dividend discount model
   - Price ratio method
   - Bond valuation models
   - Finance theories for fixed-income securities
   - Bond price
   - Bond yield
   - Interest rate risk and duration

- Valuation of derivatives
- Investment strategies for equity investment
- Active and passive strategies for equity investment
- Mutual funds
- Exchange-traded funds (ETFs)
- Investment strategies for fixed-income securities
2. Determining asset allocation strategies
   - Investment strategy recommendations
   - Investment for goals
   - Complementary portfolio concept
   - Investment objectives
   - Asset allocation strategies
   - Risk tolerance assessment
   - Key issues in forming the portfolio
   - Understanding the return calculation procedures and their limitations
   - Understanding the risk calculation procedures and their limitations
   - Forming asset classes
   - Understanding the challenges related to asset allocation strategies
   - Portfolio performance measurement
   - Advanced investment strategy
   - Asset allocation
   - Strategic asset allocation
   - Advanced asset allocation strategies: Tactical asset allocation
   - Measuring asset allocation strategies
   - Empirical evidence of portfolio performance
3. Advanced topics
   - Total life planning
   - Total well-being index

Three Ingredients for Successful Financial Planning

1. Strong financial planning knowledge
2. Excellent communication skills
3. High ethical and professional standards

First, financial knowledge, regulations, and computer technology are constantly changing, and financial planners need to keep on learning and improving their skills to be able to do a good job. Second, good communication skills and building relationships are major components of any service industry. Listening to clients and communicating with clients are as important as having all the knowledge and skills. Finally, you have to have a long-term perspective as a financial planner. It takes at least 5 to 10 years for financial planners to build a successful practice. Establishing a good reputation by maintaining high ethical and professional standards is the key to retaining long-term clients. Combining all three factors together will allow you to establish a trusting relationship with clients, which will enable you to enjoy a stable and fruitful practice in financial planning for years to come.

Key Issues in Wealth Management

Contemporary wealth management deals with investment management for clients in the context of financial planning. Understanding investment techniques and the latest products is important. However, successful wealth management contains two additional critical elements:

1. Well-defined investment goals
2. Effective asset allocation

Finally, advanced wealth managers can consider practicing total life planning and employ scientific measures such as the total well-being index to identify and monitor the total well-being of their clients.

APPLICATION CORNER

In order to provide an opportunity for you to work with a financial planning case, the following student case study is reprinted here. The intention is to give you a glimpse of a typical case. It is not to teach you the analysis of resolving a comprehensive financial planning case, so no solution or analysis is provided. However, some guidelines for handling the case are listed at the end to provide some directions.

MPFA and IFPHK Student Case Study[1]

You are a financial planner and a registered MPF intermediary working with a major bank in Hong Kong. Mr. and Mrs. Chan are your customers whom you see regularly in the bank. Recently they have come to you for some advice on their investment portfolio. During the discussion, you found that in order for you to provide sound and meaningful advice, you needed to understand more of their needs and goals. Mr. and Mrs. Chan were glad that you could offer a six-step financial planning process to them and agreed to do a thorough interview. During the interview, you collected the following information from them.

Mr. and Mrs. Chan are in their early forties. They have been married for more than 10 years and have a son, Johnny, aged 8. Both Mr. and Mrs. Chan's parents are deceased. Mr. Chan is a marketing manager in a multinational company. His monthly income is about HK$40,000, which includes basic salary and commissions. He has been with the company for 10 years. He expects to have an estimated annual salary increase of 2% till 60 and he will retire at 65. Mrs. Chan is a housewife and mainly takes care of the family.

Their son, Johnny, is currently a Primary 3 student at an elite school. His school grades are very good and his parents would like to send him to a good university in the United States after his secondary schooling in Hong Kong. The total tuition fees and other expenses for attending a US university are estimated to be HK$400,000.

Because Mr. Chan is the sole source of income for the family, he is very concerned about financial protection for his family. He bought a 26-year term life insurance policy when Johnny was born. He thinks that he should have enough savings for the family's needs when he turns 60 so there is much less need for insurance protection after that. The face amount of the policy is HK$2.5 million and the monthly premium is HK$3,000. He did not buy any whole life insurance policy because he thinks it makes more sense to "buy term, invest the rest."

Mr. Chan has some basic knowledge in investments and is interested in following the financial and economic news. He considers himself a modest risk-taker as he enjoys day-trading in small company stocks for the high potential returns. However, he does not have the time or skills to perform any investment analysis himself. His colleagues will share some investment "tips" with him from time to time. Sometimes he will act on the tips if he thinks they are reliable, but so far the investment returns have not been very good. On several occasions when the market dropped significantly very suddenly, like during the financial crisis in 1997, he had been worried and suffered many sleepless nights.

Mrs. Chan, on the other hand, has no interest in investments at all. She is tied up with the household chores, so all investment decisions are made by Mr. Chan alone. The couple has a joint account with the bank and all their investments are held in the bank account for convenience.

They bought their residence flat for HK$2 million 10 years ago in 1995 with some financial help then from their parents. The mortgage loan has been paid up. The estimated current value is HK$2.5 million. They are considering buying a newer flat in the range of HK$3 million, but have not decided whether to keep the current flat for rental income or sell it for cash.

Mr. Chan's company provides good employee benefits. Mr. Chan and his family members are entitled to health insurance. When the MPF Scheme was implemented on December 1, 2000, Mr. Chan switched from the company's ORSO scheme to the MPF Scheme, because he had the right to choose the investment product under the MPF Scheme. The company offers an MPF voluntary contribution based on 5% of the individual employee's income. Currently Mr. Chan makes a mandatory contribution of HK$1,000 to his MPF account each month. The MPF Scheme chosen by his company has the choice of five funds, namely a Capital Preservation Fund, a Guaranteed Fund, a Bond Fund, a Balanced Fund, and a North American Equity Fund. Their fund expenses ratios reported on the fund fact sheets range from 0.5% to 3.0%. Mr. Chan plans to manage his MPF portfolio more actively. He wants to rebalance the portfolio monthly, based on the funds' performance in the previous month.

The couple does not have a solid investment plan. They consider their current living style quite comfortable and affordable. Therefore they would like to maintain a similar standard in the future and possibly after Mr. Chan's retirement. However, the couple does not expect their son's financial support in the future.

A.   Information Provided by Mr. Chan

Family and Background Information

	Mr. Chan	Mrs. Chan	Johnny
Relationship	Husband	Wife	Son
Age	42	42	8
Education level	MBA	F7	Primary 3
Health condition	Good	Good	Good
Life expectancy	85	85	85
Occupation	Marketing manager	Housewife	Student
Annual income	$480,000	n.a.	n.a.

Estimated Annual Family Consumption/Expenses

Items	HK$
Rate/management fee and utilities	24,000
Food	60,000
Transportation	24,000
Tuition	60,000
Clothing	12,000
Entertainment and vacation	48,000
Income tax*	64,800
Miscellaneous	12,000
Johnny's pocket money	6,000
Mr. Chan's work-related expenses	60,000
Medical expenses**	25,000

* Flat tax rate: 13.5%.
** Medical expenses are covered by Mr. Chan's employee benefit before his retirement.

Death-related Expenses

	HK$
Funeral and burial expenses	80,000
Probate costs	20,000
Emergency fund	30,000

Current MPF Allocation

Fund	% of total contribution
Capital Preservation Fund	40%
Guaranteed Fund	40%
International Balanced Fund	10%
North American Equity Fund	10%

MPF Account Balance

Fund	% of total holdings
Capital Preservation Fund	40%
Guaranteed Fund	40%
International Balanced Fund	10%
North American Equity Fund	10%
Total	$91,000(100%)

Investment Portfolio of Mr. Chan

	Market value (HK$) in 1,000s
Common stocks	
MELCO International Development (HK0200)	80
A-MAX (HK0959)	50
SHUN TAK Holding (HK0242)	40
SG-HSI European Call Warrant (HK3963)	30
Cash	
HK dollar	10
US Dollar (USD)	10
Australian Dollar (AUD)	10

B. Fact Sheet of Mr. Chan's MPF Scheme

Conservative, low-risk fund

Capital Preservation Fund — **Objective**   To achieve a rate of return higher than the average bank savings rate with minimum exposure to market fluctuations.
Strategy   Mainly invests in Hong Kong dollar-denominated monetary instruments. Average remaining maturity of investments in the portfolio is 90 days or less.

Guaranteed Fund — **Objective**   To achieve long-term capital growth with low volatility while preserving underlying capital.
Strategy   Mainly invests in cash, short-term bank deposits, or international bonds and equities, with a guaranteed interest rate of not less than 0%.

Moderate, low- to medium-risk fund

Bond Fund — **Objective**   To achieve a modest but stable level of income with low volatility.
Strategy   Invests in international bonds issued by governments and different commercial organizations. Terms of maturity range from 3 to 30 years.

Moderate, medium- to high-risk fund

International Balanced Fund — **Objective**   To achieve medium-high capital growth with medium volatility.
Strategy   Invests in international equities, bonds, and deposits with emphasis on equities.

Aggressive, high-risk fund

North American Equity Fund — **Objective**   To achieve long-term capital growth.
Strategy   Invests in a portfolio of selected shares traded on the US stock exchanges such as NYSE and NASDAQ.

1. Voluntary Contributions
   - The immediate vesting, portability, and preservation requirements of the MPF system do not apply to voluntary contributions.
   - The initial subscription fee is waived for voluntary contributions into funds under the MPF scheme.
2. Performance and management fees of funds in the MPF scheme are similar to their retail peers.

C. Independent Research Results Provided by the Bank

Economic Forecast

Short-term interest rate	0%
Long-term interest rate	5%
Long-term unemployment rate	6%
Inflation rate	8%5%
Growth rate of education expenses	7%
Growth rate of medical expenses	5%

Mortgage Rates

Fixed rate for loan amount $2,700,000

Repayment period	Fixed rate
20 years	10.0%
15 years	8.0%
10 years	7.0%
5 years	6.5%

Domestic Financial Markets Outlook

Investment	Expected return	Beta
Small cap stocks	15.0%	2.0
Large cap stocks	10.0%	1.0
Bonds	6.0%	0.5
Bank deposit	5.0%	0.0
Residential property*	6.0%	0.5
Net rental income	6.0%	0.5

* In addition to the appreciation of the overall property market, the value of residential property older than 25 years depreciates 5% a year.

Past Performance of Mr. Chan's MPF Scheme

Fund	Average real return	Initial subscription fee of similar retail funds
Capital Preservation Fund	5.0%	2.5%
Guaranteed Fund	5.0%	2.5%
Bond Fund	6.0%	5.0%
International Balanced Fund	10.0%	5.0%
North American Equity Fund	12.0%	5.0%

Assumptions

- All the amounts are in today's value.
- Long-term interest rate is a reasonable return for steady asset growth.

Guidelines in Answering the Case

You are required to prepare a comprehensive retirement plan with some considerations for the major financial planning needs of the client. When preparing the detailed plan, you should make use of the case material in providing a thorough analysis and comprehensive solutions following the perspectives listed below:

1. Compile the personal financial statements and evaluate the current financial situation of the client.
   Tips
   - Some financial data are more important than others. Focus the analysis on the major items and financial variables that would cause substantial financial concern.
   - Identify inappropriate consumption and investment behavior from the financial status analysis. Consider qualitative factors and personal background when making conclusions on possible solutions and alternatives.
2. Examine insurance needs of the client if there are any.
   Tips
   - Employ the life-cycle framework in evaluating the insurance needs.
   - For life insurance, there always exist different alternatives and combinations of insurance products to protect the clients. Provide alternatives for the clients for consideration whenever possible.
3. Point out common mistakes made by the couple in managing investments for retirement.
   Tips
   - Asian clients have a tendency to use short-term trading or even speculative strategies for investments. Constant reminders are necessary to gradually change the mindset of the clients. The planner must make it clear to the clients that investment for retirement should have a long-term perspective.
4. Recommend proper investment strategies for retirement purpose.
   Tips
   - The problem of investing in inappropriate high-risk securities for retirement is severe in Hong Kong. Emphasize the importance of risk diversification and asset allocation.
5. Reflect the proper perspective of retirement planning and the role of MPF as a retirement planning vehicle.
   Tips
   - Conduct risk profiling for an optimal asset mix.
   - Consider voluntary MPF contributions. Such a buy-and-hold strategy with a dollar-cost-averaging effect allows the client to practice the financial discipline of a passive investment strategy.

6. Provide quantitative analysis on how MPF contributions can help to achieve the retirement goal of the client.

   Tips

   - Hand calculations can easily contain human errors. Learn to use Excel or basic software to do the calculations for accuracy and efficiency.
   - Use graphs and figures to enhance the understanding of the results.

7. Provide quantitative analysis for the accumulation of wealth and assets for the purpose of retirement throughout the years.

   Tips

   - Hand calculations can easily contain human errors. Learn to use Excel or basic software to do the calculations for accuracy and efficiency.
   - Use graphs and figures to enhance the understanding of the results.
   - Provide different scenarios of outcomes based on various assumptions.

FINANCIAL PLANNING IN PRACTICE

An Interview with Guy Cumbie, Chair of Financial Planning Association 2002

Can you provide a synoptic overview of the development/emergence of the personal financial planning profession in the United States?

Roughly 30 years ago, life insurance agents who were smarter and more visionary than average and were dealing with generational wealth transfer issues and business uses of life insurance began to become known as "estate planners." When these same, rather sophisticated insurance-types grew much more versatile by becoming cross-licensed to sell securities as well, they became known as "financial planners." During this same period, there was a special individual, an unusually insightful, energetic, and visionary marketing expert named Loren Dunton. Mr. Dunton organized these early pioneers and began to seed the emergence of the profession by founding the first nonprofit, educational, and public benefit institutions that were the forerunners of most of the financial planning profession's organizations that exist today. The CFP Board of Standards, the College for Financial Planning, and the Financial Planning Association can all trace their roots back to the efforts of Loren Dunton and his band of pioneers.

The earliest planners were perceived by the public basically as being insurance people who also sold mutual funds. Then the development and studying of financial planning curriculums fairly quickly led to the creation of the CFP marks which were conferred on the first graduating class of the College for Financial Planning in 1972. Obviously the marks have grown in acceptance and their ownership was later transferred from the College to what is now the CFP Board. The first graduating class of the College immediately spun off an alumni group-based professional organization they named the Institute of Certified Financial Planners or ICFP out of the existing membership organization for financial planners which was the International Association for Financial Planning, or IAFP. In the year 2000, these two organizations, the IAFP and the ICFP, recombined to form the FPA.

During the 1980s the concept of personal financial planning began to take off, partially with assistance of the US Internal Revenue Code. The tax laws of the day were such that a genre of tax-deduction-generating financial products (primarily securitized real properties) sprung up and were sold to clients seeking shelter from high marginal federal income tax rates. During this time, financial planners were largely viewed by the public as being "tax-shelter peddlers." The tax code was changed radically in the mid-80s. The big tax "write-offs" were instantly rendered a thing of the past and that sad, tax-driven era of planning's history came to a rather bloody close with lots of client money lost in noneconomic tax-savings-dependent real estate, oil and gas, and equipment leasing deals, many, if not most, of which financially imploded.

It took a while for the profession's image to recover from the tax shelter era and many CFP™ practitioners, including me, didn't even put the words "financial planner" on their business cards for a number of years to follow. In the early 1990s as the US stock market continued to boom, planners resurfaced again as huge sellers of mutual funds and, as the decade progressed, more sophisticated "asset management programs." The profession still remains in its "asset management" phase even today. However, during all these years there has been a small but erratically growing core of serious, committed, generalist personal financial planners that actually does real six-step process-based personal financial planning.

Public acceptance in the United States has grown to the point that more and more (I certainly don't say "most") individuals, especially and primarily, of the high income and/or high net-worth variety, are willing to pay for planning per se and directly—in some instances even without any accompanying implementation work (insurance business, tax preparation, asset management, etc.) being done and charged for by the planner. I believe it's fair to say that personal financial planning is now in the very early stages of beginning to come into its own as a distinct profession—somewhat discernable from the subset specialties from which it was born. However, the vast majority of those who hold out in the United States as being personal financial planners remain uncertified, and the vast majority of what's held out to the public as being "financial planning" in the United States today remains primarily little more than a financial product distribution channel for financial institutions. The emergence of a new, real, and distinct profession is indeed discernable though, and the FPA is doing all it can to lead the way.

It's important to interject into the story here that a US political and philosophical tilt toward economic self-reliance in retirement has served and still is serving as a major undercurrent driving the demand for retail financial services in general and personal financial planning specifically. In the early 1980s, defined benefit pension plans slowly started to give way to defined contribution plans as the norm. Today, employee salary deferral 401(k) plans dominate the US retirement plan scene. This shifted a lot of the responsibility for assuring adequate retirement funding from the employer to the individual. Also, the US social security system, an unfunded scheme, began to break down actuarially under the weight of the postwar baby boom generated demographic surge. The primary way the government has managed the default of the system to date has been by pushing out the benefits eligibility age, or "normal retirement age" as it's called. Americans generally feel less and less sure about their ability to rely on this fundamentally flawed government program.

In general, Americans are heavily inclined toward do-it-yourselfism anytime they believe that they can. Interestingly, planning looks "smarter" and more readily carries "perceivable value" during times of economic difficulty and turmoil when the uncertainty of the world is more apparent to everyone. Due to both the bursting of our stock market bubble and the 9/11 tragedy, the US market for real, professionally supported, strategic personal financial planning has suddenly ripened. Americans are probably as interested in seeking professional personal financial planning support right now as they have ever been. Somehow it just no longer looks like an easy layperson's hobby. The stars are truly aligned for the profession's emergence.

An Interview with David Diesslin on Running a Successful Wealth Management Firm*

David H. Diesslin founded Diesslin & Associates, Inc., a private financial advisory firm, in 1983. David has been consistently honored as one of the "Nations' 100 Most Exclusive Wealth Advisors" by *Worth*. "We do not control the future but we build options for our clients" is his philosophy of financial planning. By putting his clients' interests first and building long-term relationships with them, his firm has become a top wealth management and comprehensive financial planning advisory firm with over US$400 million assets under its management.

Can you share with us some ingredients for success in running your wealth management firm?

A unique feature of our firm is the team approach in providing financial planning services. Clients are served by a coordinated group of in-house experts, each with an area of specialization. At a fee ranging from US$8,000

---

* We would like to thank David and Deena Diesslin for the valuable opportunity to visit the firm and interview the staff at the Fort Worth, US, office for two full days in June 2006.

to $25,000, a client can receive comprehensive financial planning and wealth management services including a complete financial plan covering insurance, investments, education, retirement, and estate planning as well as implementation of the plan.

In our view, the success of Diesslin & Associates is based on three elements: (1) a business model that allows the investment management division and the financial planning division to complement each other in providing services and generating revenues; (2) an efficient use of information technology to help advisors and planners in collecting data, performing financial analysis, and sharing information; and (3) a corporate culture that supports the advisors to work together for the best interest of clients.

Index